2009-2010

EVANGELICAL SUNDAY SCHOOL LESSON COMMENTARY

FIFTY-EIGHTH ANNUAL VOLUME
Based on the
Pentecostal-Charismatic Bible Lesson Series

Editorial Staff
Lance Colkmire—Editor
Tammy Hatfield—Editorial Assistant
James E. Cossey—Editor in Chief
Joseph A. Mirkovich—General Director of Publications

Lesson Exposition Writers

J. Ayodeji Adewuya	Jerald Daffe
Lance Colkmire	Joshua F. Rice
Dale Coulter	Richard Keith Whitt

Published by

PATHWAY PRESS   Cleveland, Tennessee

*To place an order, call 1-800-553-8506.
*To contact the editor, call 423-478-7597
or email at *Lance_Colkmire@pathwaypress.org*.

Lesson treatments in the *Evangelical Sunday School Lesson Commentary* for 2009-2010 are based upon the outlines of the Pentecostal-Charismatic Bible Lesson Series prepared by the Pentecostal-Charismatic Curriculum Commission.

Copyright 2009

PATHWAY PRESS, Cleveland, Tennessee

ISBN: 978-1-59684-430-8

ISSN: 1555-5801

TABLE OF CONTENTS

INTRODUCTION TO THE 2009-2010 COMMENTARY

The *Evangelical Sunday School Lesson Commentary* contains in a single volume a full study of the Sunday school lessons for the months beginning with September 2009 and running through August 2010. The twelve months of lessons draw from both the Old Testament and the New Testament in an effort to provide balance and establish relationship between these distinct but inspired writings. The lessons in this 2009-2010 volume are drawn from the fourth year of a seven-year series, which will be completed in August 2013. (The series is printed in full on page 15 of this volume.)

The lessons for the *Evangelical Commentary* are based on the Pentecostal-Charismatic Bible Lesson Series Outlines, prepared by the Pentecostal-Charismatic Curriculum Commission. (The Pentecostal-Charismatic Curriculum Commission is a member of the National Association of Evangelicals.) The lessons in this volume, taken together with the other annual volumes of lessons in the cycle, provide a valuable commentary on a wide range of biblical subjects. Each quarter is divided into two or more units of study.

The 2009-2010 commentary is the work of a team of Christian scholars and writers who have developed the volume under the supervision of Pathway Press. All the major writers, introduced on the following pages, represent a team of ministers committed to a strictly Evangelical interpretation of the Scriptures. The guiding theological principles of this commentary are expressed in the following statement of faith:

1. WE BELIEVE the Bible to be the inspired, the only infallible, authoritative Word of God.

2. WE BELIEVE that there is one God, eternally existing in three persons: Father, Son, and Holy Spirit.

3. WE BELIEVE in the deity of our Lord Jesus Christ, in His virgin birth, in His sinless life, in His miracles, in His vicarious and atoning death through His shed blood, in His bodily resurrection, in His ascension to the right hand of the Father, and in His personal return in power and glory.

4. WE BELIEVE that for the salvation of lost and sinful men, personal reception of the Lord Jesus Christ and regeneration by the Holy Spirit are absolutely essential.

5. WE BELIEVE in the present ministry of the Holy Spirit by whose cleansing and indwelling the Christian is enabled to live a godly life.

6. WE BELIEVE in the personal return of the Lord Jesus Christ.

7. WE BELIEVE in the resurrection of both the saved and the lost—they that are saved, unto the resurrection of life; and they that are lost, unto the resurrection of damnation.

8. WE BELIEVE in the spiritual unity of believers in our Lord Jesus Christ.

USING THE 2009-2010 COMMENTARY

The *Evangelical Sunday School Lesson Commentary* for 2009-2010 is presented to the reader with the hope that it will become his or her weekly companion through the months ahead.

Quarterly unit themes for the 2009-2010 volume are as follows:
• Fall Quarter—Unit One: "The Expanding Church (Acts, Part 2)"; Unit Two: "The Gospel Fulfills the Law (Lev.-Deut.)"
• Winter Quarter—Unit One: "Major Prophets"; Unit Two: "Bible Answers to Crucial Questions"
• Spring Quarter—Unit One: "Ephesians: Understanding God's Eternal Purposes"; Unit Two: "Commended by Christ"
• Summer Quarter—Unit One: "Books of Samuel"; Unit Two: "Sin and Holiness"

The lesson sequence used in this volume is prepared by the Pentecostal-Charismatic Curriculum Commission. The specific material used in developing each lesson is written and edited under the guidance of the editorial staff of Pathway Press.

INTRODUCTION: The opening of each week's lesson features a one-page introduction. It provides background information that sets the stage for the lesson.

CONTEXT: A time and place is given for most lessons. Where there is a wide range of ideas regarding the exact time or place, we favor the majority opinion of conservative scholars.

PRINTED TEXT: The printed text is the body of Scripture designated each week for verse-by-verse study in the classroom. Drawing on the study text the teacher delves into this printed text, exploring its content with the students.

CENTRAL TRUTH and FOCUS: The central truth states the single unifying principle that the expositors attempted to clarify in each lesson. The focus describes the overall lesson goal.

DICTIONARY: A dictionary, which attempts to bring pronunciation and clarification to difficult words or phrases, is included with many lessons. Pronunciations are based on the phonetic system used by *Nelson's Illustrated Bible Dictionary* (Thomas Nelson Publishers) and by *Pronouncing Bible Names* (W. Murray Severance, Broadman & Holman Publishers). Definitions are based on various sources.

EXPOSITION and LESSON OUTLINE: The heart of this commentary—and probably the heart of the teacher's instruction each week—is the exposition of the printed text. This exposition material is organized in outline form, which indicates how the material is to be divided for study.

QUOTATIONS and ILLUSTRATIONS: Each section of every lesson contains illustrations and sayings the teacher can use in connecting the lesson to daily living.

TALK ABOUT IT: Questions are printed throughout the lesson to help students explore the Scripture text and how it speaks to believers today.

CONCLUSION: Each lesson ends with a brief conclusion that makes a summarizing statement.

GOLDEN TEXT CHALLENGE: The golden text challenge for each week is a brief reflection on that single verse. The word *challenge* is used because its purpose is to help students apply this key verse to their life.

DAILY BIBLE READINGS: The daily Bible readings are included for the teacher to use in his or her own devotions throughout the week, as well as to share with members of their class.

SCRIPTURE TEXTS USED IN LESSON EXPOSITION

Genesis

1:1-2, 24-26	February 7
1:27-31	February14
2:16-17	August 1
2:17	February 14
2:18-25	February 28
3:8	August 8
3:9-12	August 1
3:16-19	August 8
3:22-24	August 8

Leviticus

4:1-7	October 25
16:29-34	October 25
18:1-5	November 8
18:4-6, 19-23, 30	February 21
19:15-18	November 29
20:1-10	November 1

Deuteronomy

5:1-15	November 15
5:16-22, 33	November 22
6:4-5	November 29
6:13-18, 25	November 8
7:6-11	November 1

1 Samuel

1:19-20, 24-28	June 6
3:1-4, 10, 19-21	June 6
7:5-17	June 6
8:4-7, 19-22	June 13
9:1-2, 15-19, 27	June 13
10:1, 9-11, 17-27	June 13
13:1-14	June 20
15:1-23, 34-35	June 20
16:1-3, 6-7, 11-13	June 27
19:1-2, 9-10, 18-20	June 27
20:1-2, 30-33	June 27
22:1-2	June 27
27:1-4	June 27

2 Samuel

2:1-11	July 4
3:1	July 4
5:1-12	July 4
6:12-23	July 4

2 Samuel (cont.)

7:1-25	July 11
11:1-5, 14-17, 25-27	July 18
12:1-16, 22-23	July 18
22:1-3, 17-22, 29-37 50-51	July 25
23:1-5	July 25

Psalms

8:3-9	February 14
14:1-3	February 7
19:1-4	February 7
139:13-16	February 14

Ecclesiastes

12:13-14	August 8

Isaiah

6:1-13	December 6
11:1-10	December 13
35:1-10	December 13
65:1-12, 17-25	December 27
66:12-14, 18-23	December 27

Jeremiah

1:4-19	January 3
3:1-10, 12-25	January 10
31:31-37	January 17

Ezekiel

2:1-10	January 24
3:1-14	January 24
18:1-4, 10-14, 19-32	January 31

Malachi

2:14-16	February 28

Matthew

1:18-25	December 20
2:1-11	December 20
5:21-22, 27-30	November 22
5:34, 37	November 15
15:3-6	November 22
16:13-19	May 9
19:3-9	February 28
22:34-40	November 29
25:34, 41	August 8

Mark		
5:25-34	May 9	
7:20-23	August 1	
10:13-27	April 18	

Luke		
7:1-10	May 2	
7:36-50	April 25	
8:4-15	April 18	
8:26-39	May 16	
10:25-37	November 29	
10:30-37	May 30	
10:38-42	May 9	
16:22-23	August 8	
17:11-19	May 16	
18:9-14	May 9	
18:35-43	May 16	
21:1-4	May 30	
23:39-43	May 2	
24:13-18, 26-35	April 4	

John		
14:15-18, 26	May 23	
14:23-24	November 8	
15:1-8, 15-17	August 29	
15:26-27	May 23	
16:7-14	May 23	
17:15-23	August 29	
20:1, 11-18	April 4	
21:1-2, 15-19	April 4	

Acts		
2:1-4	May 23	
13:1-16, 32-33, 38, 42-49	September 6	
15:1-35	September 13	
16:6-18, 25-34	September 20	
17:10-34	September 27	
17:24-28	February 14	
18:1-11	September 27	
20:17-38	October 4	
26:4-29	October 11	
27:1, 13-26, 40-44	October 18	
28:1-10, 16-24, 29:31	October 18	

Romans		
1:18-25	February 7	
1:21, 24	August 1	
1:26-28	February 21	
1:28-32	August 1	
5:1, 6-12, 15, 17-21	August 15	
5:12, 19	August 1	
6:1-7, 11-13, 22-23	August 15	
6:23	August 8	
7:18-21	August 1	
8:5-8	August 1	
8:26-27	May 23	

1 Corinthians		
6:18-20	February 21	
7:1-5	February 28	
8:4-6	November 15	
10:14, 21	November 15	

Galatians		
3:10-14, 19, 22, 24	November 8	
5:13-14	November 8	

Ephesians		
1:3-23	March 7	
2:1-3, 12	August 8	
2:1-22	March 14	
3:1-21	March 21	
4:1-6, 17-24	March 28	
4:18-19	August 8	
4:25, 28	November 22	
5:1-2	March 28	
5:3-5	February 21	
5:8-11, 21-33	March 28	
6:1-9	March 28	
6:10-20	April 11	

Philippians		
2:5-11	May 30	

Colossians		
1:16-18	February 7	
3:5-11	November 1	

Titus		
2:11-12	November 1	

Hebrews		1 Peter	
4:9-11	November 15	1:15-16	November 1
8:1-9, 13	January 17		
9:11-22, 28	October 25	**1 John**	
10:22-25	October 25	1:5-10	August 22
12:14, 18, 22, 28	November 1	2:1-11, 15-17	August 22
		4:10-21	August 29
13:4	February 28		
		Revelation	
James		4:11	February 7
4:1-3	November 22	21:8	August 8

SCRIPTURE TEXTS USED IN GOLDEN TEXT CHALLENGE

Genesis		Ezekiel	
1:1	February 7	3:11	January 24
2:24	February 28	18:20	January 31
Deuteronomy		**Micah**	
5:1	November 15	6:8	June 20
5:33	November 22		
		Mark	
2 Samuel		10:15	April 18
5:12	July 4		
		Luke	
1 Chronicles		10:27	November 29
29:11	December 13	18:13	May 9
Psalms		**John**	
29:2	July 11	14:15	November 8
34:1	July 25	15:5	August 29
34:18	April 25	15:26	May 23
46:1	May 2		
75:7	June 27	**Acts**	
103:1-2	May 16	13:2	September 6
106:15	June 13	16:9	September 20
139:14	February 14	17:11	September 27
		20:28	October 4
Proverbs		26:22	October 11
28:13	July 18		
		Romans	
Isaiah		1:16	September 13
6:8	December 6	5:19	August 1
7:14	December 20	6:22	August 15
30:18	December 27	6:23	August 8
Jeremiah		**1 Corinthians**	
1:5	January 3	6:20	February 21
3:12	January 10		
31:33	January 17		

2 Corinthians		Philippians (cont.)	
4:1	October 18	3:10	April 4
Ephesians		**Hebrews**	
1:3	March 7	9:26	October 25
2:1	March 14		
3:3, 6	March 21	**1 Peter**	
5:1-2	March 28	1:15	November 1
6:10	April 11	4:10	June 6
Philippians		**1 John**	
2:5, 8	May 30	1:7	August 22

ACKNOWLEDGMENTS

Many books, magazines and Web sites have been used in the research that has gone into the 2009-2010 *Evangelical Commentary*. The major books that have been used are listed below.

Bibles
English Standard Version (ESV), Good News Publishers, Wheaton, Illinois
King James Version, Oxford University Press, Oxford, England
Life Application Study Bible, Zondervan Publishing House, Grand Rapids
New American Standard Bible (NASB), The Lockman Foundation, La Habra, CA
New International Version (NIV), Zondervan Publishing House, Grand Rapids
New King James Version (NKJV), Thomas Nelson Publishers, Nashville
The Message (TM), NavPress, Colorado Springs
The Nelson Study Bible, Thomas Nelson Publishers, Nashville
Word in Life Study Bible, Thomas Nelson Publishers, Nashville

Commentaries
Adam Clarke's Commentary, Abingdon-Cokesbury, Nashville
Barnes' Notes, BibleSoft.com
Commentaries on the Old Testament (Keil & Delitzsch), Eerdmans Publishing Co.,
    Grand Rapids
Ellicott's Bible Commentary, Zondervan Publishing House, Grand Rapids
Expositions of Holy Scriptures, Alexander MacLaren, Eerdmans Publishing Co.,
    Grand Rapids
Expository Thoughts on the Gospels, J.C. Ryle, Baker Books, Grand Rapids
Jamieson, Fausset and Brown Commentary, BibleSoft.com
Life Application Commentary, Tyndale House, Carol Stream, IL
Matthew Henry's Commentary, BibleSoft.com
The Bible Exposition Commentary: New Testament, Warren Wiersbe, Victor Books,
    Colorado Springs
The Expositor's Greek Testament, Eerdmans Publishing Co., Grand Rapids
The Interpreter's Bible, Abingdon Press, Nashville
The Pulpit Commentary, Eerdmans Publishing Co., Grand Rapids
The Wesleyan Commentary, Eerdmans Publishing Co., Grand Rapids
The Wycliffe Bible Commentary, Moody Press, Chicago
Zondervan NIV Bible Commentary, Zondervan Publishing House, Grand Rapids

Illustrations
Choice Contemporary Stories and Illustrations, Baker Books, Grand Rapids
Fresh Illustrations for Preaching and Teaching, Baker Books, Grand Rapids
Illustrations for Preaching and Teaching, Baker Books, Grand Rapids
Knight's Master Book of New Illustrations, Eerdmans Publishing Co., Grand Rapids
1,000 New Illustrations, Al Bryant, Zondervan Publishing Co., Grand Rapids
Quotable Quotations, Scripture Press Publications, Wheaton
The Encyclopedia of Religious Quotations, Fleming H. Revell Co., Old Tappan, NJ
The Face of God, The Hands of God, and *The Heart of God*, Woodrow Kroll, Elm
    Hill Books, Nashville
The Speaker's Sourcebook, Zondervan Publishing House, Grand Rapids
Who Said That?, George Sweeting, Moody Press, Chicago

Reference Books

Biblical Characters From the Old and New Testament, Alexander Whyte, Kregel Publications, Grand Rapids

Harper's Bible Dictionary, Harper and Brothers Publishers, New York

Pictorial Dictionary of the Bible, Zondervan Publishing House, Grand Rapids

Pronouncing Bible Names, Broadman & Holman Publishers, Nashville

The Interpreter's Dictionary of the Bible, Abingdon Press, Nashville

Pentecostal-Charismatic Bible Lesson Series (2006-2013)**

Fall Quarter September, October, November	Winter Quarter December, January, February	Spring Quarter March, April, May	Summer Quarter June, July, August
Fall 2006 1 • Old Testament Survey 2 • New Testament Survey	**Winter 2006-07** 1 • Beginnings (Gen. 1—11) 2 • Basic Christian Doctrine	**Spring 2007** 1 • Teachings of Jesus in Matthew 2 • The Christian Family	**Summer 2007** 1 • Prayers in the Psalms 2 • God's Providence
Fall 2007 1 • Abraham (Gen. 12—25) 2 • Great Women of the Bible	**Winter 2007-08** 1 • Isaac, Jacob, & Joseph 2 • Christian Discipleship	**Spring 2008** 1 • Romans & Galatians 2 • Ecclesiastes	**Summer 2008** 1 • God Delivers His People (Ex.) 2 • Great Hymns of the Bible
Fall 2008 1 • The Early Church (Acts, Part 1) 2 • Wisdom From Proverbs 3 • Job (Faithfulness)	**Winter 2008-09** 1 • 1 & 2 Corinthians 2 • Profiles of Faith in Christ	**Spring 2009** 1 • Mark* (The Servant Messiah) 2 • Practical Christian Living (James)	**Summer 2009** 1 • Joshua and Judges 2 • Prayers in the Psalms
Fall 2009 1 • The Expanding Church (Acts, Part 2) 2 • The Gospel Fulfills the Law (Lev.—Deut.)	**Winter 2009-10** 1 • Major Prophets (Isa., Jer., & Ezek.) 2 • Bible Answers to Crucial Questions	**Spring 2010** 1 • Ephesians 2 • Commended by Christ	**Summer 2010** 1 • Books of Samuel 2 • Sin and Holiness
Fall 2010 1 • Counsel for Christlike Living (1 & 2 Peter) 2 • The Person and Work of the Holy Spirit	**Winter 2010-11** 1 • Learning From Spiritual Leaders (1 & 2 Kings; 1 & 2 Chron.) 2 • Christian Ethics	**Spring 2011** 1 • Jesus' Life and Teachings (Luke*) 2 • Ruth and Esther	**Summer 2011** 1 • Maturing in Christ (Phil.) 2 • Wholeness in Christ (Col.) 3 • Friends of Jesus
Fall 2011 1 • Justice and Mercy (Minor Prophets) 2 • Priorities and Values	**Winter 2011-12** 1 • 1, 2, 3 John & Jude 2 • Growing Spiritually	**Spring 2012** 1 • Return From Exile (Ezra and Neh.) 2 • Gifts of the Spirit	**Summer 2012** 1 • 1 & 2 Thessalonians (The Second Coming) 2 • Redemption and Spiritual Renewal
Fall 2012 1 • Hebrews 2 • Who Is God? (The Nature of God)	**Winter 2012-13** 1 • Pastoral Epistles (1 & 2 Tim., Titus, Philem.) 2 • Prayer	**Spring 2013** 1 • John* (The Son of God) 2 • The Church	**Summer 2013** 1 • Daniel and Revelation (Triumph of Christ's Kingdom) 2 • Help for Life's Journey

*Emphasizes the uniqueness of each Gospel.

15

Introduction to Fall Quarter

"The Expanding Church (Acts, Part 2)" is the theme of the first seven lessons, which begin with the calling of Paul and Barnabas as missionaries (ch. 13) and concludes with Paul's ministry in Rome (ch. 28).

Expositions were compiled by Lance Colkmire (B.A., M.A.), editor of the *Evangelical Commentary* and *Real Life* young adult curriculum for Pathway Press. He also serves the South Cleveland (TN) Church of God as children's pastor.

The second unit is "The Gospel Fulfills the Law." Each of these lessons begins with the study of specific passages in Leviticus and/or Deuteronomy, and then explores their fulfillment in the New Testament.

Expositions were written by the Reverend Joshua F. Rice (B.A., M.A., Th.M.), director of student ministries and Christian education at Mount Paran Church of God, Atlanta, Georgia. He is currently writing his doctoral dissertation toward a Ph.D. in New Testament Studies from the Lutheran School of Theology at Chicago.

September 6, 2009 (Lesson 1)
Sent by the Holy Spirit

Acts 13:1-52

INTRODUCTION

The events of this lesson occurred approximately twelve years after the conversion of Saul of Tarsus. Presumably he spent most of those twelve years in his home city of Tarsus. Tradition accords him the responsibility of having founded the church in that city. It is highly unlikely that he would have spent a long period of time in Tarsus without working for Christ.

In Galatians 1:17 Paul related that he spent some time in Arabia and even returned to Damascus. Then he went into Jerusalem, where he met with some of the apostles, and finally returned to Cilicia, of which Tarsus is the capital city.

It is clear that Paul did not launch immediately into his large-scale ministry following his conversion. The twelve years of preparation and limited ministry were necessary for his full development as a minister of Christ. God did not forget His servant during this period. All the time His eye was on Saul of Tarsus. From the beginning it had been known that he would be used to carry the Gospel to the Gentiles as well as to the children of Israel (see Acts 9:15).

This lesson tells how God moved the apostles out into full-time missionary work. From this point on in the Book of Acts, the attention of recorded apostolic history follows the life of Paul.

Unit Theme:
The Expanding Church (Acts, Part 2)

Central Truth:
God calls and empowers believers in Christ to proclaim the Gospel.

Focus:
Investigate how the Holy Spirit sends and empowers people to do His work and cooperate with the Spirit.

Context:
Around AD 45 in Antioch of Syria, Cyprus, Paphos, Perga, and Antioch of Pisidia

Golden Text:
"As they ministered to the Lord, and fasted, the Holy Ghost said, Separate me Barnabas and Saul for the work whereunto I have called them" (Acts 13:2).

Study Outline:
I. The Spirit Calls (Acts 13:1-4)
II. The Spirit Empowers (Acts 13:5-12)
III. Many Believe (Acts 13:13-16, 32-49)

Simeon . . . Niger (NIE-jur), Lucius (LOU-see-us) of Cyrene (sie-REE-nuh), Manaen (MAN-ah-en)—v. 1—spiritual leaders of the church in Antioch

Talk About It:
1. Why does the church need "prophets and teachers" (v. 1)?
2. What role did fasting and prayer play in this event?

I. THE SPIRIT CALLS (Acts 13:1-4)
A. Separation (vv. 1-2)

1. Now there were in the church that was at Antioch certain prophets and teachers; as Barnabas, and Simeon that was called Niger, and Lucius of Cyrene, and Manaen, which had been brought up with Herod the tetrarch, and Saul.

2. As they ministered to the Lord, and fasted, the Holy Ghost said, Separate me Barnabas and Saul for the work whereunto I have called them.

Antioch was the capital of Syria and was situated on the Mediterranean Sea. The church in Antioch consisted of a group of notable men, most of whom were from Cyprus or Cyrene. Barnabas, it seems, was a leader of the group (11:20-22).

As the work of the Lord prospered, Barnabas went to Tarsus in Cilicia and brought Saul with him to Antioch. Saul assisted in the Antioch church for about a year. During this time he and Barnabas went into Jerusalem to take contributions to the Judean churches (v. 30).

Another fact of interest during this period is that the disciples first began to be called Christians in Antioch (v. 26). Until this time they had been called simply disciples. The word *Christian* means "a follower of Christ." Their worship of Christ kept believers together.

In Antioch there was an illustrious group of prophets and teachers. Acts 11:27 says "prophets from Jerusalem [came] unto Antioch." In this way Antioch became a central point of spiritual activity for the young church. Barnabas came from the isle of Cyprus and Saul from Tarsus in Cilicia. "Simeon that was called Niger" (13:1) probably came from North Africa. A man named Lucius definitely came from Cyrene in North Africa. Nothing more is known of him. Last of the Antiochene prophets mentioned here is Manaen, who "had been brought up with Herod the tetrarch." Manaen was a foster brother of Herod Antipas, son of Herod the Great. The meaning of this relationship is that Manaen had been reared in the royal court with Herod Antipas. It implies intimate friendship between the two.

As Barnabas, Simeon, Lucius, and Saul were worshiping God and fasting, the Holy Spirit revealed His will to them regarding the ministry of Barnabas and Saul. Precisely how the Holy Spirit spoke is not stated, but it was probably through a prophetic utterance by one of the prophets. Barnabas was gifted in the prophetic ministry, which consisted of edification, exhortation, and comfort (1 Cor. 14:3). Saul, a young minister, would profit much from such an association.

It is interesting that "separate" (Acts 13:2) is the verbal form of the noun "Pharisee." Saul had been a Jewish Pharisee. But he says in Romans 1:1 that he was "separated unto the gospel." Thus the Spirit worked to make Saul, the Pharisee of the Jews, into Paul, the Pharisee for Jesus!

"The power of God is given to enable us to do a spiritual thing in a spiritual way in an unspiritual world."
—Malcolm Cronk

B. Consecration and Obedience (vv. 3-4) *Blessing & with them*
    3. And when they had fasted and prayed, and laid their hands on them, they sent them away.
    4. So they, being sent forth by the Holy Ghost, departed unto Seleucia; and from thence they sailed to Cyprus.

The company of prophets and teachers fasted and prayed before sending Barnabas and Saul out as missionaries. They laid hands on the two as a token of apostolic blessing and human acceptance of the divine will. The laying on of hands indicated the bonds of brotherhood and fellowship that would remain even when the anointed ones departed from their home company.

The word translated "sent them away" (v. 3) conveys the sense of being "let go" into the world. Yes, the missionaries had a mission and a message, but they were called to live by faith in a world which would not always receive the message they carried. Yet how beautiful the message in verse 52: Believers thrown into the world are able to have joy in the Holy Spirit.

Barnabas and Saul departed from Antioch and went to Seleucia, the seaport of Antioch, about sixteen miles away. From Seleucia they sailed to the island of Cyprus, which was the home of Barnabas. This was a sea voyage of about 130 miles.

II. THE SPIRIT EMPOWERS (Acts 13:5-12)
A. The Word Is Preached (v. 5)
    5. And when they were at Salamis, they preached the word of God in the synagogues of the Jews: and they had also John to their minister.

Barnabas and Saul landed at Salamis, the chief harbor of Cyprus. Being Jews, they went into the synagogues and there preached that the Jewish Messiah had come. For many years all Christian missionary work was done in this fashion. It was only when the Jews refused to receive the message of their Messiah that the Gospel was turned to the Gentiles.

John Mark, a cousin of Barnabas, accompanied the two men on their missionary journey. The expression "to their minister" indicates that Mark's role was to serve the needs of Barnabas and Saul. This could mean he was responsible for looking after manuscripts; or it could mean he knew, as F. F. Bruce suggests, "certain important phrases of the story of Jesus, in particular the passion narrative." Perhaps Mark gave instruction to new converts.

B. The Word Is Resisted (vv. 6-8)
    6. And when they had gone through the isle unto Paphos, they found a certain sorcerer, a false prophet, a Jew, whose name was Bar-jesus:
    7. Which was with the deputy of the country, Sergius Paulus, a prudent man; who called for Barnabas and Saul, and desired to hear the word of God.

Seleucia (see-LOU-see-uh)—v. 4—the port of the city of Antioch

Talk About It:
1. Explain the laying on of hands (v. 3).
2. How were they "sent forth" (v. 4)?

Salamis (SAL-uh-mis)—v. 5—a city on the east side of the island of Cyprus

Paphos (PAY-foss)—v. 6—a city on the west side of Cyprus

Bar-jesus (v. 6)—means "the son of Jesus," but not Jesus Christ

8. But Elymas the sorcerer (for so is his name by interpretation) withstood them, seeking to turn away the deputy from the faith.

At the completion of their ministry in Salamis, Barnabas and Paul traveled about ninety miles across the island of Cyprus to Paphos, the capital city. The governor of the island was named Sergius Paulus, who was the representative of the Roman government. Sergius Paulus was apparently a deeply religious man, for he had attached to his court a Jewish prophet named Bar-jesus. This man, also called Elymas, was a false prophet, a sorcerer, one who mixed elements of true faith with elements of superstition, magic, and heresy.

Unfortunately this kind of false religion was worse than no religion at all. It kept people from ever learning about the true faith, for they took comfort in the sorcery of the false prophet. In the Book of Acts we encounter three of these Jewish false prophets: Simon Magus in Samaria (8:9), the seven sons of Sceva (19:14), and Elymas (Bar-jesus) in Cyprus.

Sergius Paulus had, no doubt, heard of the work of Barnabas and Saul on the island of Cyprus, so he desired to meet with them when they arrived in Paphos. Paulus was either converted to the Christian faith or was giving it earnest consideration, for Elymas attempted to "turn away the deputy from the faith." The sorcerer, no doubt, saw his position of influence over Paulus slipping away from him. The position as spiritual adviser to the ruler would have given him certain distinctions, privileges, and other benefits. He certainly did not want to lose these, so he became angry at the activities of Barnabas and Saul.

C. The Word Is Vindicated (vv. 9-12)

9. Then Saul, (who also is called Paul,) filled with the Holy Ghost, set his eyes on him,

10. And said, O full of all subtilty and all mischief, thou child of the devil, thou enemy of all righteousness, wilt thou not cease to pervert the right ways of the Lord?

11. And now, behold, the hand of the Lord is upon thee, and thou shalt be blind, not seeing the sun for a season. And immediately there fell on him a mist and a darkness; and he went about seeking some to lead him by the hand.

12. Then the deputy, when he saw what was done, believed, being astonished at the doctrine of the Lord.

The scene was probably before the seat of Sergius Paulus. Like the astrologers, soothsayers, sorcerers, advisers, prophets, and magicians that were frequently attached to the court of a ruler, Bar-jesus no doubt stood near the seat of Sergius Paulus. Saul was filled with righteous fury at the sorcerer. As he looked at Bar-jesus, with his attempts to pervert the truth, Saul was filled with divine wrath.

The observation is made here that Saul was also called Paul. There is no spiritual significance to this. Paul, a Hellenistic Jew, had a Hebrew name, *Shaul* (Greek/Latin: *Saulos*), and also a Greek/Latin name, *Paulos*. From this time on, however, the Roman name *Paul* was to be used exclusively by the apostle. Furthermore, from this time on, Paul was clearly to be the leader of the Christian faith. Up until the time of this episode we read of "Barnabas and Saul." Hereafter, Paul is named first.

So this encounter represented a turning point in the history of the church and in the history of Paul. From this point on, the ministry to which Paul had been called and for which his earlier life had been a preparation was to begin to be realized. He was to become the leader, he was to get a new name, and his ministry to the Gentiles was clearly to be indicated.

Paul's words to Elymas are some of the angriest words in the New Testament. He called the sorcerer a "child of the devil" and an "enemy of all righteousness." Bar-jesus deserved this barrage of anger, for he who should have built up the faith of others actually worked toward tearing it down.

Paul pronounced judgment upon Bar-jesus by the power of the Holy Spirit (v. 9). Bar-jesus would be stricken blind for a judgment upon him because of his evil deeds. It would not be permanent, however, but would last only for a season.

God's judgment was immediate. Quickly the man's sight became dim and misty, and then disappeared altogether. He who had so arrogantly stood beside the Roman ruler became a blind beggar, seeking someone to lead him wherever he would go. The Venerable Bede said, "The apostle, remembering his own case, knew that by the darkening of the eyes the mind's darkness might be restored to light."

The work of faith that had been begun in Sergius Paulus' heart was made complete. When he saw the sure and immediate judgment of God upon his former spiritual adviser, he recognized the truth as Paul and Barnabas had preached it. Quite likely he was already impressed with their arguments, and the blindness of Elymas confirmed the truth of what they said.

Ernst Haenchen points out three significant aspects of this story: (1) At the beginning of the Pauline mission, a high authority in the government believes in the message of Jesus; (2) Paul, hitherto a small actor in the story, rises to prominence and becomes the spokesman for Christianity; (3) there is a gulf between Christianity and magic that can be crossed only by the blood of Jesus.

"All that is necessary for the triumph of evil over good is that good men do nothing."
—Edmund Burke

III. MANY BELIEVE (Acts 13:13-16, 32-49)
A. Invited to Speak (vv. 13-16)
13. Now when Paul and his company loosed from Paphos, they came to Perga in Pamphylia: and John departing from them returned to Jerusalem.

Perga in Pamphylia (pam-FILL-ee-uh)— v. 13—a city

14. But when they departed from Perga, they came to Antioch in Pisidia, and went into the synagogue on the sabbath day, and sat down.

15. And after the reading of the law and the prophets the rulers of the synagogue sent unto them, saying, Ye men and brethren, if ye have any word of exhortation for the people, say on.

16. Then Paul stood up, and beckoning with his hand said, Men of Israel, and ye that fear God, give audience.

To emphasize the prominent role which Paul assumed in the mission, Luke indicates that "Paul and his company" set sail from Paphos and came to Perga (v. 13). But John Mark left the tour and returned to Jerusalem. Why he left cannot be answered. But the fact that his leaving created some problems is evidenced in 15:37-39.

Acts 13:14 moves the duo quickly from Perga to Antioch in Pisidia. That is a journey of nearly 100 miles, and there is no record of any missionary work. Either Luke had no record of their work in Perga or very little success was evident. Antioch of Pisidia was in the area known as southern Galatia. The city was about 3,600 feet above sea level. It was probably to the churches in southern Galatia that Paul wrote the Book of Galatians (about AD 50).

Luke tells us that Paul went into the synagogue on the Sabbath. The usual order of service was conducted with the reading from the Pentateuch and the Prophets. Paul was then invited to speak a "word of exhortation" to the people gathered.

Paul addressed two groups of people in the service. "Men of Israel" refers to Jews and Gentiles who proselyted to Judaism, and "ye that fear God" to Gentiles who were attracted to the monotheism and moral life of the Jews. Note that Paul used his hand to get their attention (v. 16).

B. The Gospel Presented (vv. 32-41)
(Acts 13:34-37, 39-41 is not included in the printed text.)

32. And we declare unto you glad tidings, how that the promise which was made unto the fathers,

33. God hath fulfilled the same unto us their children, in that he hath raised up Jesus again; as it is also written in the second psalm, Thou art my Son, this day have I begotten thee.

38. Be it known unto you therefore, men and brethren, that through this man is preached unto you the forgiveness of sins.

Paul's sermon treats the role of the Jews in the death of Jesus the same as Peter did in Acts 3:17. The Jews acted ignorantly "because they knew him not, nor yet the voices of the prophets" (13:27). Thus, if the Jews listening in Antioch would allow the

Spirit to open their eyes to faith, they would understand exactly who Jesus is. Here the essential contrast is set up between the Gentile proconsul Sergius Paulus, who had understanding, and the Jews who had access to the Scriptures yet refused to understand!

Verse 23 provides the key theological fact around which the argument of verses 26-41 hinge. Paul affirmed that it was through David's line that God brought the promised Savior, Jesus. Verse 32 mentions the "glad tidings," or Gospel, referring to the "promise" in verse 23. Paul then, in verses 33-35, quotes from three Old Testament passages to clarify what has happened to Jesus through the power of God to raise Him (Pss. 2:7; 16:10; Isa. 55:3).

Acts 13:38 introduces the powerful conclusion to the sermon with a call to "know." Now that the message that Jesus had been raised from the dead could be preached, there was no excuse for not receiving the Word! "Through this man [Jesus] is preached unto you the forgiveness of sins."

Verse 39 functions to indicate how comprehensive the reality of forgiveness of sins is: it means one is "justified," set free from everything the Law could not set free. Paul is making the Gospel message practical. Freedom is the result of believing in Jesus— new life that comes through His resurrection (see Rom. 6–8).

The sermon concludes with a warning taken from Habakkuk 1:5, a call for the people to respond to the work which God was doing in their day (Acts 13:40-41).

C. The People Respond (vv. 42-49)

42. And when the Jews were gone out of the synagogue, the Gentiles besought that these words might be preached to them the next sabbath.

43. Now when the congregation was broken up, many of the Jews and religious proselytes followed Paul and Barnabas: who, speaking to them, persuaded them to continue in the grace of God.

44. And the next sabbath day came almost the whole city together to hear the word of God.

45. But when the Jews saw the multitudes, they were filled with envy, and spake against those things which were spoken by Paul, contradicting and blaspheming.

46. Then Paul and Barnabas waxed bold, and said, It was necessary that the word of God should first have been spoken to you: but seeing ye put it from you, and judge yourselves unworthy of everlasting life, lo, we turn to the Gentiles.

47. For so hath the Lord commanded us, saying, I have set thee to be a light of the Gentiles, that thou shouldest be for salvation unto the ends of the earth.

2. How did Paul compare Jesus to David (vv. 36-37)?
3. What did Jesus provide (vv. 38-39)?
4. What warning did Paul present (vv. 40-41)?

"Jesus whom I know as my Redeemer cannot be less than God."
—**Athanasius**

48. And when the Gentiles heard this, they were glad, and glorified the word of the Lord: and as many as were ordained to eternal life believed.

49. And the word of the Lord was published throughout all the region.

Talk About It:
1. What do the Gentiles of Antioch request (v. 42)?
2. Explain the opposition that Paul faced (vv. 44-45).
3. Describe the change in Paul's ministry (vv. 46-47).
4. Describe the results (v. 48).

Verses 42 and 43 describe the response of the people in the synagogue to Paul's sermon. The people desired to hear "these words" the next Sabbath—Friday evening at sundown to Saturday evening at sundown. Since Christian communities had not been established in these areas, Paul and Barnabas did not speak on the Christian day of the Resurrection.

Verse 43, which states "the congregation was broken up," does not mean that discord was among them; rather, it means the congregation was dismissed. Serious conflict did not emerge until the next Sabbath. The "religious proselytes" refers both to the Gentiles who had become Jews and to the Gentiles who were God-fearers.

The story follows logically the events of the previous Sabbath. Paul and Barnabas spent the week urging the new converts to "continue in the grace of God" (v. 43).

Verse 44 indicates that most of the local Gentile population turned out for the service. Luke makes it clear they did not come to hear Paul; rather, they came to hear the faithful and powerful Word of God.

The multitude of Gentiles responding to the salvation of God brought jealousy to the Jews. This incident reminds us of Romans 11:11-16 and the jealousy of the Jews that Paul discusses there. Certainly his theology in Romans was greatly influenced by events such as this in his mission work.

The blaspheming by the Jews (Acts 13:45) has as its object Jesus. Both Paul and Barnabas boldly responded to the charges of the Jews, giving the impression of an open debate with few rules of order. The reference to "everlasting life" in verse 46 is a Jewish phrase which meant "life belonging to the age to come"— that is, the messianic age which the Jews themselves looked to with hope. Thus, Paul indicates they were denying their own hope!

Paul quoted Isaiah 49:6 in referring to his mission as "a light to the Gentiles." Verse 48 of the text describes the response of the Gentiles as one of great rejoicing in the Word of God. Those who believed in the Gospel helped to spread the good news throughout southern Galatia (v. 49).

"When the Spirit of God comes into a man, He gives him a worldwide view."
—Oswald Chambers

CONCLUSION

The titles of the three sections of today's lesson show us how the Holy Spirit operated in the Book of Acts and how He still ministers today.

• *The Spirit Calls*—He selects and sets apart individuals for specific ministries.

- *The Spirit Empowers*—He equips individuals to accomplish the tasks He calls them to do.
- *Many Believe*—When Spirit-called people do God's work through the Spirit's enablement, things happen.

GOLDEN TEXT CHALLENGE
"AS THEY MINISTERED TO THE LORD, AND FASTED, THE HOLY GHOST SAID, SEPARATE ME BARNABAS AND SAUL FOR THE WORK WHEREUNTO I HAVE CALLED THEM" (Acts 13:2).

The most outstanding thing in this verse is the fact that the Holy Spirit communicated directly to the church. Observe the spiritual state of the church at the time the Lord made known His will. They were engaged in a season of worship and fasting. Fasting is sometimes used by Christians when they desire to seek God earnestly in order to know His will.

Individuals are not to enter the ministry, or any other phase of Christian service, as they would enter a secular profession. These positions are for those whom the Lord shall call. What a high privilege it is to be called by God to perform some definite task. Preaching and teaching the Word of God, either at home or abroad, is never to be looked upon as just a job, but rather as a high calling.

William Carey had high hopes that his son Felix would follow his footsteps by becoming a missionary. Official honors in Burma, however, caused the young man's soul to shrivel toward divine things. The disappointed father requested prayer for his son, saying, "Pray for Felix. He has degenerated into an ambassador of the British government!"

Daily Devotions:
M. Joshua Set Apart for Service
Numbers 27:12-23
T. Naaman Believes in God
2 Kings 5:4-15
W. Spirit-Empowered Prophetic Ministry
Micah 3:5-8
T. Jesus Sends the Twelve
Luke 9:1-6
F. Power to Be Witnesses
Acts 1:1-8
S. Faith Based on God's Power
1 Corinthians 2:1-5

The Church Becomes More Inclusive

Acts 15:1-35

Unit Theme:
The Expanding
Church (Acts, Part 2)

Central Truth:
Through Christ, God
makes salvation
available to all people.

Focus:
Examine how God
taught the Church to
be more inclusive and
accept all whom Christ
accepts.

Context:
The Jerusalem
Council on Christian
freedom took place
around AD 50.

Golden Text:
"I am not ashamed of
the gospel of Christ: for
it is the power of God
unto salvation to every
one that believeth"
(Rom. 1:16).

Study Outline:
 I. Dissension in the
    Church
    (Acts 15:1-12)
 II. Wise Counsel
    Brings Resolution
    (Acts 15:13-21)
III. Affirming
    Acceptance in
    Christ
    (Acts 15:22-35)

INTRODUCTION

The Council of Jerusalem, as recorded in Acts 15, was occasioned by the progress of the Gospel among the Gentiles. This success and the Christian freedom they emphasized aroused the religious prejudice of the Pharisees in Jerusalem. To admit Gentiles into the Christian church without observing the Mosaic rite of circumcision was a serious infraction of the ceremonial law, according to this Jewish segment of the church. When this question became a problem of contention in the Antioch church, Jerusalem was consulted and the great council on Christian freedom was called.

Philip Schaff wrote, "It was the first and in some respects the most important council or synod held in the history of Christendom, though differing widely from the councils of later times. It is placed in the middle of the Book of Acts as the connecting link between two sections of the apostolic church and the two epochs of its history."

Paul recognized how crucial this issue was. His letters are full of references to the fact that the act of salvation in Jesus Christ is dependent upon faithful obedience to the lordship of Jesus, and not the demands of Moses' law. Romans 2:25-29 contains Paul's classic defense for the priority of faith and obedience over circumcision.

It is easy for even good things to take the place of a vibrant, personal faith in the lordship of Jesus Christ. But salvation can be obtained only through power of the blood of Jesus.

I. DISSENSION IN THE CHURCH (Acts 15:1-12)

A. The Problem (v. 1)

1. And certain men which came down from Judaea taught the brethren, and said, Except ye be circumcised after the manner of Moses, ye cannot be saved.

Our text moves immediately into the crisis faced by the early community: "Some men came down from Judea" (NIV). (Note the Jewish custom of always referring to movement away from Jerusalem as "coming down." Regardless of geographical location, the Israelite always "went up" to Jerusalem. Thus Luke retained a Jewish outlook upon the world.)

We are not given the identities of these men. They were Judeans who preached that salvation could not be obtained apart from the circumcision of Moses. It is likely these men represented a conservative Jewish-Christian group. They might have been some of the priests and Pharisees who had joined the church (6:7; 15:5). Their theology showed an understanding of the mission of Jesus and His call to salvation, which includes the acceptance of Moses' law as authoritative upon all who believe.

The issue posed by the teachers from Judea was crucial to the Gentile mission of Paul and Barnabas. Gentiles had received the message of salvation throughout Asia Minor; yet, these men were claiming that the reception of the Gospel in faith was not enough to bring salvation.

B. The Delegation (vv. 2-5)

2. When therefore Paul and Barnabas had no small dissension and disputation with them, they determined that Paul and Barnabas, and certain other of them, should go up to Jerusalem unto the apostles and elders about this question.

3. And being brought on their way by the church, they passed through Phenice and Samaria, declaring the conversion of the Gentiles: and they caused great joy unto all the brethren.

4. And when they were come to Jerusalem, they were received of the church, and of the apostles and elders, and they declared all things that God had done with them.

5. But there rose up certain of the sect of the Pharisees which believed, saying, That it was needful to circumcise them, and to command them to keep the law of Moses.

A serious debate took place in the Antioch church regarding the salvation issue. Paul and Barnabas did not sit idle while this breach of faith was preached. Recognizing just how much the circumcision controversy endangered the Gentile mission, the church at Antioch determined to send Paul, Barnabas, and certain others to Jerusalem to consult with the apostolic leaders there.

Talk About It:
What were "certain men" teaching?

"When a prejudiced man thinks, he just rearranges his thoughts."
—Speaker's Sourcebook

Talk About It:
1. Why were Paul and Barnabas sent to Jerusalem (v. 2)?
2. What caused "great joy" (v. 3)?

3. Why did some Jewish Christians believe circumcision was necessary?

Jerusalem was considered to be the center of the church. Those who had been with Jesus during His ministry were still located there, and their authority was still taken seriously. It was not until the destruction of Jerusalem (AD 70) that the focus of the church shifted from the east (Jerusalem) to the west (Rome).

The group led by Paul and Barnabas went by land through Phoenicia and Samaria. There were churches in these areas, and the group from Antioch took time to tell them of the mighty acts of God in the Gentile world. The Greek word for "declaring" (v. 3) means "to tell in detail." Thus, events of the first missionary journey were related to these churches to ground them in the doctrine of salvation through faith.

This message of salvation caused great joy for the churches in this area. These believers were probably also being forced under the yoke of the Law. Thus their great joy came from the freedom found in Christ Jesus.

The Antioch delegation was received by the Council at Jerusalem, where the church had apostles and elders. The elders were probably laypeople who served in spiritual leadership. In Acts 6, deacons in the Jerusalem church are mentioned. They took care of the administrative needs of the community. The apostles were spiritual leaders who provided care for all the churches.

When Paul and Barnabas came before this group, the missionaries "declared" to them the works which God had accomplished among them (15:4). Here the word *declare* means to "give a report."

No sooner had Paul and Barnabas declared God's saving work among the Gentiles through these two missionaries than certain of the Pharisaic party in Jerusalem stood forth from the church body and lodged their protest against the methods of the Gospel missionaries. To preach Christ to the Gentiles was apparently not criticized, for these were Pharisees who had accepted Jesus as the Messiah, but they insisted that circumcision be an additional "must" for every believer.

"The spread of the Gospel must not be limited by the prejudices and traditions of people."
—*Evangelical Commentary*

C. The Debate (vv. 6-12)

6. And the apostles and elders came together for to consider of this matter.

7. And when there had been much disputing, Peter rose up, and said unto them, Men and brethren, ye know how that a good while ago God made choice among us, that the Gentiles by my mouth should hear the word of the gospel, and believe.

8. And God, which knoweth the hearts, bare them witness, giving them the Holy Ghost, even as he did unto us;

9. And put no difference between us and them, purifying their hearts by faith.

The Church Becomes More Inclusive

10. Now therefore why tempt ye God, to put a yoke upon the neck of the disciples, which neither our fathers nor we were able to bear?

11. But we believe that through the grace of the Lord Jesus Christ we shall be saved, even as they.

12. Then all the multitude kept silence, and gave audience to Barnabas and Paul, declaring what miracles and wonders God had wrought among the Gentiles by them.

Verse 6 indicates a formal gathering of the church with the apostles and presbyters to discuss the difficult question now before them. If Paul's visit described in Galatians 2:1-10 is identical with his presence at the Jerusalem Council, then there seems to have been a space between the first gathering of the church leaders and the assembly now described. Paul says that he had explained his position "privately to them which were of reputation" (v. 2). These private conferences were a necessary preparation for the more public debate which alone is noted by the historian.

As in the days of our Lord upon the earth, so now in the early church, the apostle Peter takes the floor as the foremost of the apostles to defend the cause of Christian freedom. There had been lengthy discussion, but Peter now rose to remind the gathering that the fundamental principle which they were discussing had already been decided, when nearly ten years earlier he had been led by the Lord to the house of Cornelius to bring the Gospel of grace to the Gentiles. Not only were they to hear the Gospel, but believe and be saved.

God alone really knows "the hearts" (Acts 15:8)—the inner thoughts, motives, and intentions of people—whether sincere or not. With His testimony of the believers' sincerity of heart, one can be sure that there had been a genuine experience of salvation. God had put the uncircumcised on the same level with the circumcised in giving them the Holy Spirit. God had made no distinction. What was given to the new Gentile converts was the same which had been given at the first outpouring of the Holy Spirit on the Day of Pentecost. Faith in Jesus Christ had purified the hearts of Cornelius and his friends apart from circumcision, and even before evident and oral confession, the Holy Spirit had come upon them. Why then should further conditions be imposed upon them which God himself plainly did not require?

Peter's illustration from his preaching mission in the house of Cornelius is undeniable historical fact. A logical deduction and application must follow. They must not "tempt God" (v. 10). People are said to tempt God when they distrust His guidance and, in consequence, disobey His revealed will (Ps. 95:8-11; Heb. 3:9; 1 Cor. 10:9).

Peter concluded that to enforce the Law of Moses on the Gentiles would be to "test" God (Acts 15:10 NIV). It is a test in

Talk About It:
1. What convinced Peter there was "no difference between us and them" (v. 9)?
2. Compare the "yoke" (v. 10) with "grace" (v. 11).
3. What did Paul and Barnabas testify about (v. 12)?

the sense that one says by his actions of legalism that he cannot trust God to save by faith. Thus the test focuses on the validity of God's Word.

The Greek conjunction translated *but* (v. 11) implies an exhortation for which the remainder of the verse states the reason. That is, do not continue to demand circumcision for salvation in view of the above facts, for salvation is by grace through faith alone for Jews as well as Gentiles. Due to the free kindness of the Lord Jesus, salvation is for us all.

"Said Peter, here is the fact: God has already given the Gentiles all grace without ceremony, ritual, rite and observance. Here is the deduction: Do not be afraid to follow God, even though He seems to be breaking through things dear to our heart; do not tempt God by refusing His guidance" (G. C. Morgan).

Peter's speech brought the crowd to silence. His sermon had touched the hearts of even the Pharisees. Then Paul and Barnabas were given an opportunity to relate more of what God had done among the Gentiles. The Greek word translated *declaring* in verse 12 means "narrating" or "interpreting events."

The "miracles and wonders" related were probably the acts of God during the first missionary journey. The word translated *miracles* is the Greek word for "signs." It is the word used in the Gospel of John to describe the miracles of Jesus.

These miracles were meant to point beyond themselves. The multitude was to understand that God had approved the Gentile mission by allowing these signs to take place.

II. WISE COUNSEL BRINGS RESOLUTION (Acts 15:13-21)
A. Prophecy Fulfilled (vv. 13-18)

13. And after they had held their peace, James answered, saying, Men and brethren, hearken unto me:

14. Simeon hath declared how God at the first did visit the Gentiles, to take out of them a people for his name.

15. And to this agree the words of the prophets; as it is written,

16. After this I will return, and will build again the tabernacle of David, which is fallen down; and I will build again the ruins thereof, and I will set it up:

17. That the residue of men might seek after the Lord, and all the Gentiles, upon whom my name is called, saith the Lord, who doeth all these things.

18. Known unto God are all his works from the beginning of the world.

We now move to the third major speaker in the drama: James, the brother of Jesus. James was the leader of the Palestinian church. He spoke with authority, commanding the council to listen to him. He began by affirming the message of "Simeon"

Crisis Repeated
The crisis at Antioch is often repeated in the church. Sometimes the crisis is that the church has few who are willing to go into the world and carry out the evangelism call. At other times the crisis occurs as a result of that evangelism.

The church must be willing to live with the fruit of the seed of evangelism. It may not produce what we have always expected, but is certainly fruit which God desires and calls us to reap.
—A. D. Beacham Jr.

residue (v. 17)—
remnant

Talk About It:
1. What did God do "at the first" (v. 14)?

The Church Becomes More Inclusive

(Peter) regarding the conversion and acceptance of Cornelius. He tied this event to Amos 9:11-12 to affirm for the community that the Gospel includes all.

The first part of the Amos passage, as interpreted by James, refers to the death and resurrection of Jesus. Verse 16 of the text relates Christ's death to the phrases "the tabernacle of David, which is fallen down" and "the ruins thereof." The resurrection of Christ is depicted in the phrases "I will build again" and "I will set it up."

The death and resurrection of Jesus was the turning point in the history of humanity; Christ was lifted up to draw all people unto Himself (John 3:14; 12:32). James spoke of the "residue of men," meaning all people could seek after the Lord. This includes the Gentiles, specifically mentioned in the last part of Acts 15:17. The phrase "upon whom my name is called" is better translated "who are called by my name."

Verse 18 says God planned to include the Gentiles in His blessings since the beginning of the world. In whatever manner the Jews might have responded to the presence of Christ, the Gentiles were included in the plan of blessing for the world. If the Jews had accepted Jesus as the Messiah, then the Gentiles would have received the blessings as promised to Abraham and would have been blessed through Israel. But since the Jews rejected the message and person of the Messiah, the Gentiles were included through the preaching of the Word.

The Word functions to bring the message of life and liberty to those who are confused and uncertain. We need more men and women who will hear God's Word and act upon it.

B. Agreement Reached (vv. 19-21)

19. Wherefore my sentence is, that we trouble not them, which from among the Gentiles are turned to God:

20. But that we write unto them, that they abstain from pollutions of idols, and from fornication, and from things strangled, and from blood.

21. For Moses of old time hath in every city them that preach him, being read in the synagogues every sabbath day.

In view of the foregoing evidence from events and prophecy, James authoritatively announces his decision. All attempts to impose circumcision and its attendant legal obligations on Gentile converts must be refused. They had turned to God in faith, and God had received them, as evidenced by Spirit baptism. Such evidence permits no interference.

A further recommendation from James is to send a formal memorandum from the church in Jerusalem to the Gentile Christians exhorting them on practical matters of Christian conduct.

2. In verses 16 and 17, why did James quote from Amos 9:11-12?

"The inclusive Gospel cannot be shared by an exclusive people."
—George Sweeting

Talk About It:
1. Explain the phrase "trouble not them" (v. 19).
2. What guidelines did James suggest (v. 20)?

Without compromising the Gentiles' Christian liberty, they were to be asked to respect the scruples of their Jewish brethren by following four guidelines. Each of these commandments is rooted in the Old Testament and serves an important function.
1. *Abstain from pollutions of idols*. This refers to eating food that has been sacrificed to pagan idols. This is based on Numbers 25:1-2: The children of Israel worshiped the pagan gods as they ate of the meat sacrificed to those gods. For many Gentile Christians, to continue eating of the meat offered to idols could constitute a form of belief that those idols still had power.
2. *Abstain from fornication*. Most commentators take this to mean abstaining from marriages that are unclean for believers, such as marrying a person who is not a believer. Certainly this should also include sexual activity outside of God-ordained marriage. In 1 Corinthians 6:14-20, Paul relates that fornication was practiced by the Gentiles who went to the pagan temples and engaged with the male and female prostitutes in those temples.
3. *Abstain from things strangled*. There were meats considered a delicacy in the pagan world which were strangled. Therefore blood would be mixed with the food. Thus, the prohibition on food strangled is related to the fourth prohibition.
4. *Abstain from blood*. This is a major theme of the Old Testament. In Genesis 9:4 this demand was put upon all people through Noah, and not just upon the Jews (see Lev. 3:17; 17:10-14). The Jews considered blood to be the lifeforce; it was therefore illegal to eat or drink.

Acts 15:21 reflects James' knowledge that the Law of Moses was known in every city, and that the Gentiles should be willing to make these concessions to their brothers in Christ. This would help to foster true Christian unity and fellowship between the Jewish and Gentile believers.

III. AFFIRMING ACCEPTANCE IN CHRIST (Acts 15:22-35)
A. A Letter of Reconciliation (vv. 22-29)
22. Then pleased it the apostles and elders with the whole church, to send chosen men of their own company to Antioch with Paul and Barnabas; namely, Judas surnamed Barsabas and Silas, chief men among the brethren:
23. And they wrote letters by them after this manner; The apostles and elders and brethren send greeting unto the brethren which are of the Gentiles in Antioch and Syria and Cilicia:
24. Forasmuch as we have heard, that certain which went out from us have troubled you with words, subverting your souls, saying, Ye must be circumcised, and keep the law: to whom we gave no such commandment:
25. It seemed good unto us, being assembled with one accord, to send chosen men unto you with our beloved Barnabas and Paul,

26. Men that have hazarded their lives for the name of our Lord Jesus Christ.

27. We have sent therefore Judas and Silas, who shall also tell you the same things by mouth.

28. For it seemed good to the Holy Ghost, and to us, to lay upon you no greater burden than these necessary things;

29. That ye abstain from meats offered to idols, and from blood, and from things strangled, and from fornication: from which if ye keep yourselves, ye shall do well. Fare ye well.

After hearing the speeches of Paul, Peter, and James, the council decided to send a delegation to the Antioch church. The Greek for the phrase "then pleased it" (v. 22) was a word used regularly to describe the decision-making process of an assembly. (It is the same word translated "it seemed good" in verses 25 and 28.) They voted to send the delegation, which was tantamount to accepting James' decision.

The men chosen to return to Antioch with Paul and Barnabas were Judas Barsabas and Silas, who was a Roman citizen. Silas becomes more prominent in the lessons ahead.

A letter was sent to the churches at Antioch, Syria (probably Damascus), and Cilicia. The city of Antioch was part of the province of Syria-Cilicia. Thus we get the impression there were several churches in the area of Antioch, where Gentiles formed the major part of the congregation. The letter was written by the apostles and elders in the Jerusalem church and carried by Silas and Judas.

The contents of the letter are seen in verses 24-29. The letter describes the beginning of the crisis, and clearly indicates that the Judaizers were not acting on orders from the Jerusalem church. The actual debate of the issue was omitted from the letter. But the most important things were mentioned: The sending of the letter by Silas and Judas, who would verify the letter verbally (v. 27); the courageous testimony of Paul and Barnabas (vv. 25-26) was emphasized to make it clear to the Antioch church that it was not considered a second-class church; the fact that the Holy Spirit had been present in the workings of the council (v. 28); and the list of prohibitions (v. 29).

This was a letter of reconciliation. James and the members of the Jerusalem church recognized the validity of the Gentile mission and showed an appreciation for the struggle encountered at Antioch.

Talk About It:
1. What "pleased . . . the apostles and elders" (v. 22)?
2. How had the teaching on circumcision affected the Gentiles (v. 24)?
3. Explain the phrase "good to the Holy Spirit and to us" (v. 28 NIV).

"The Gospel is neither a discussion nor a debate. It is an announcement."
—Paul Rees

B. The Joy of Unity (vv. 30-35)

30. So when they were dismissed, they came to Antioch: and when they had gathered the multitude together, they delivered the epistle:

31. Which when they had read, they rejoiced for the consolation.

consolation (v. 31)— "encouraging message" (NIV)

Talk About It:
1. How did the Antioch church respond to the decision (v. 31)?
2. Describe the ministry of Judas and Silas (v. 32).
3. How did "many others" minister with Paul and Barnabas (v. 35)?

Teachers Needed
New issues and challenges are facing the Church. The world is constantly changing, and there are new human ideas and religious teachings that are contrary to the clear teaching of Scripture. The situation calls for godly teachers who accept the Spirit-inspired Word of God as the standard for faith and practice and are gifted by the Holy Spirit to teach and guide the Church.
—French Arrington

32. And Judas and Silas, being prophets also themselves, exhorted the brethren with many words, and confirmed them.

33. And after they had tarried there a space, they were let go in peace from the brethren unto the apostles.

34. Notwithstanding it pleased Silas to abide there still.

35. Paul also and Barnabas continued in Antioch, teaching and preaching the word of the Lord, with many others also.

The entire church community of Antioch, and probably those churches in the outlying regions, gathered together to hear the letter read. The scene was one of great rejoicing and ministry. The church understood this as a vindication of its efforts to evangelize the pagan world. Thus, by the efforts of God-fearing men, the call given the Antioch church in Acts 13 was authenticated.

Silas and Judas, as prophets, preached to the people and confirmed through the Word the validity of their effort.

Note the low-key role Silas played in the story. There was no hint of conflict between Paul and Barnabas that included Silas as an accomplice. Luke diligently shows that Silas was well qualified to take over the work started by Barnabas, for Silas was a faithful worker for the Lord.

Judas and Silas had completed their work in Antioch and were allowed to return to Jerusalem. But only Judas returned, as Silas would soon join with the missionary efforts of Paul.

The story concludes with Paul and Barnabas in Antioch, carrying on the work of teaching and preaching.

CONCLUSION

It is said that all of us have prejudices; some conscious, many unconscious. Our lifestyle is expressed in our speech, which is sometimes marred by careless remarks or slurs toward other racial or ethnic groups. Charles Lamb, in offering a frank statement of his own prejudices, stated, "For myself, earthbound and fettered to the scene of my activities, I'm a bundle of prejudices made up of likings and dislikings."

A prejudice is a judgment formed before due examination, or an attitude which is the result of a narrow or closed mind.

Prejudices develop out of a lack of strong and biblically sound moral principles. An elimination or hindrance from Christian fellowship and involvement, regardless of the circumstances or reason, is fundamentally not a social but a moral issue. The only cure for prejudice is love—love which takes seriously the words and actions of Christ. Prejudices keep us from our brothers. Love breaks down man-made barriers and teaches us that all God's children are worthy of His and our fellowship.

GOLDEN TEXT CHALLENGE

"I AM NOT ASHAMED OF THE GOSPEL OF CHRIST: FOR IT IS THE POWER OF GOD UNTO SALVATION TO EVERY ONE THAT BELIEVETH" (Rom. 1:16).

Why did Paul, the great spokesman for Christianity and apostle to the Gentiles, state his belief in the Gospel in a negative way? Why did he not write, "I am proud of the Gospel"? Or, "I glory in the Gospel"? Why did he speak of the Gospel in terms of what he was *not*?

Paul stated that the Gospel was "unto the Jews a stumbling-block, and unto the Greeks foolishness" (1 Cor. 1:23). In the early days of Christianity it could not be otherwise. Chrysostom said he was about to preach of One who "passed for the son of a carpenter, [was] brought up in Judea, in the house of a poor woman—and who died like a criminal in the company of robbers." Rome, on the other hand, was the citadel of all worldly authority and power. Rome was the center of the might of the empire and the pagan religions; but even in Rome, Paul was willing to proclaim the Gospel boldly, and was not ashamed of it.

Paul was not ashamed of the Gospel, for it is powerful! Although the Gospel may appear to some to be weak and ineffectual, its power is greater than any force on earth because it is the power to change lives. It changed Paul from persecutor to apostle. It has changed the captain of slave ships (John Newton) into a hymn writer ("Amazing Grace"), and criminals into model citizens. The Gospel continues to change lives because it operates on a vast and constantly enlarging scale, taking effect in a countless number of individuals. Christianity is not primarily a system for the intellect, although it does present a reasoned system. It is not primarily an appeal to the emotions, although it does appeal to one's feelings. The Gospel is first and foremost a source of power.

The power of the Gospel produces salvation, or deliverance from the perils menacing to life. Through the Gospel we are justified, or freed from guilt and punishment for our sins. We are given power to live victoriously in the present. We are assured of eternal life in heaven. Paul was not ashamed of the Gospel, for it is universal in scope. The Gospel was "to the Jew first," as the latter part of the Golden Text says, but not to the Jew exclusively. It is available to everyone who will believe and accept life-giving power.

The Gospel goes forth universally; but it must be appropriated individually. The Gospel is proclaimed for everyone to hear; but to benefit from its power, an individual must believe and accept the message.

Daily Devotions:
M. Blessing Promised to All Nations
Genesis 12:1-3
T. Wise Counsel Is Beneficial
Proverbs 24:3-6
W. Salvation Promised
Isaiah 49:1-7
T. A Divisive Situation Resolved
Acts 6:1-7
F. Unity of the Spirit
Ephesians 4:1-6
S. Lamb Slain for All People
Revelation 5:1-10

Moving Into New Territory

Acts 16:6-40

Unit Theme:
The Expanding
Church (Acts, Part 2)

Central Truth:
The Spirit will lead
Christians to present
the Gospel to unbe-
lievers.

Focus:
Recognize that God
guides the mission of
His church and trust
Him to transform lives.

Context:
Ministry from Phrygia
to Macedonia in AD
53-54

Golden Text:
"A vision appeared to
Paul in the night;
There stood a man
of Macedonia, and
prayed him, saying,
Come over into
Macedonia, and help
us" (Acts 16:9).

Study Outline:
  I. The Spirit Guides
     (Acts 16:6-10)
 II. The Lord Opens
     Hearts
     (Acts 16:11-15)
III. The Gospel
     Changes Lives
     (Acts 16:16-34)

INTRODUCTION

After Paul and Barnabas' successful ministry in Asia Minor (Acts 13 and 14), two important things happened. First, there was a conference in Jerusalem to consider Paul and Barnabas' ministry to the Gentiles (ch. 15). There was strong opposition to their ministry by some of the Jewish Christian leaders. These leaders felt it was inappropriate for Gentiles to come directly to Christ without first becoming adherents of the Jewish law and ritual. The decision of the council was that Gentiles who come to Christ did not need to submit themselves to the Jewish ritual (vv. 19-21). The decision of this council was a turning point in the growth of Christianity. It paved the way for Paul and others after him to preach the Gospel freely to the Gentiles.

A second incident that would have great effect on the growth of the Christian message was the separation of Paul and Barnabas (vv. 36-41). The two apostles felt they should return to the churches they had established in Asia Minor during their missionary tour. John Mark, a cousin of Barnabas, had accompanied the two men on their first journey, but he deserted them in Pamphylia.

As the two men planned this second journey, Barnabas wished to take John Mark with them again. Paul felt that the young man should not go, inasmuch as he had failed them the first time. "The contention was so sharp between them, that they departed asunder one from the other" (v. 39). In the end Barnabas took Mark with him into Cyprus, and Paul took Silas with him into Syria and Cilicia.

It was sad that the old missionary group should break up, but the result was good. There were now two missionary groups instead of one. Barnabas was able to strengthen and encourage Mark so that the young man became a great Christian leader, and Paul was able to develop the potential that was in Silas.

As this lesson begins, we find Paul and Silas working together in Asia Minor.

I. THE SPIRIT GUIDES (Acts 16:6-10)

Verses 1-5 describe the addition of Timothy to Paul's ministry team. From the second letter Paul wrote to him, we learn that his mother was Eunice (2 Tim. 1:5). She was a Jewish woman who had married a Greek man. Some Bible scholars believe that Timothy's father was dead. His grandmother was Lois, and both these women were Christians from Paul's first missionary journey. The church in Lystra had been instrumental in laying hands on Timothy for God's anointing to help him fulfill God's call in his life (see 1 Tim. 1:18; 4:14; and 2 Tim. 1:6).

Thus, Timothy was probably a young man when the Gospel was first preached and the church was established in Lystra. About two years had passed since Paul had seen any of the Christians in Lystra. When he returned he enjoyed their fellowship again and noted the spiritual growth that had happened in Timothy's life (Acts 16:2). Paul, who had just argued decisively against circumcision as a necessity for salvation, took the young man and had him circumcised. This in no way reflected a change in Paul's theological thinking. Rather, it reflected his understanding of the Gospel and the necessity to be "all things to all men" in order that he "might by all means save some" (1 Cor. 9:22). Timothy lived in no-man's-land in terms of Jews and Gentiles. Although his mother was Jewish, he may have been regarded by some as a Gentile. There was only one solution: have him circumcised so as to find acceptance among the Jewish communities they would visit and to whom they would initially bring the Gospel.

Thus, when we come to our lesson, we have the beginnings of a mission team consisting of Paul, Silas, and Timothy.

A. Blocked by the Spirit (vv. 6-7)

6. Now when they had gone throughout Phrygia and the region of Galatia, and were forbidden of the Holy Ghost to preach the word in Asia,

7. After they were come to Mysia, they assayed to go into Bithynia: but the Spirit suffered them not.

The region of Phrygia and Galatia was the area where the churches established on the first journey were located. Paul, Silas, and Timothy moved throughout this region sharing the good news of Jesus to whoever would hear. No doubt they made plans as to what cities they should go to next. The likely city in Asia Minor (modern Turkey) was Ephesus. It was the main city of the entire region and was the most reasonable destination. Yet, we discover that the men were sensitive to the voice of God regarding their destination. They were ambassadors of Christ, and it was His agenda they were to follow.

The Holy Spirit *forbade* them to preach the Gospel as they went throughout that part of Asia. The Greek word for *forbid* means "to hinder, restrain, withhold" (Vine). That did not mean

Phrygia (FRIG-ih-uh)—v. 6—a large province of the mountainous region of Asia Minor

Mysia (MISS-ee-uh)—v. 7—a province in northwestern Asia Minor

Bithynia (bi-THIN-ih-uh)—v. 7—a coastal province in northwestern Asia Minor

Talk About It:
Describe the ministry of the Holy Spirit seen in these verses.

they were not to travel in that area, but they were not to preach the Word in that area. In ministry, it is often just as important to know what *not* to do as it is to know what to do. It is so easy to get caught up in a pattern of things in the church and not remain sensitive to the voice of the Holy Spirit.

Since the Spirit had refused to allow them to speak in Asia, they turned northward toward the area of Bithynia (near the Black Sea). But again the Spirit would not allow them to move northward. On a map one can see the purposes of God. The men were led in a northwesterly direction that put them at the seaport of Troas awaiting further direction from God. They were at the gates of Western society, the Greek world. At that point they did not know what to do. All they could do was wait and trust God to reveal His will. Here were men on no timetable other than God's. They were prepared to wait as long as it took to hear God speak clearly.

"As you walk through the valley of the unknown, you will find the footprints of Jesus both in front of you and beside you."
—**Charles Stanley**

B. Guided in a Vision (vv. 8-10)

8. And they passing by Mysia came down to Troas.

9. And a vision appeared to Paul in the night; There stood a man of Macedonia, and prayed him, saying, Come over into Macedonia, and help us.

10. And after he had seen the vision, immediately we endeavoured to go into Macedonia, assuredly gathering that the Lord had called us for to preach the gospel unto them.

Talk About It:
1. Describe the vision Paul saw.
2. Explain the significance of the words "immediately" and "assuredly" (v. 10).

The delays and hindrances, all of which came through the Holy Spirit, had the express purpose of getting Paul to the place where he could clearly hear God speak. In the previous section, it was noted that the Holy Spirit himself hindered their work. How this was done is not known. It could have been through prophetic utterances (Silas was called a prophet in 15:32). It could have been through opposition of city officials or through illness.

In 16:10 we encounter the first of the "we" sections of Acts. This is clearly a "diary" section of firsthand reports from Luke himself. At Troas, Luke, a physician and a Christian, was united with Paul, Silas, and Timothy. Was he contacted as a physician due to illness among the original three? There is no clear answer. But it is sufficient to say that the Holy Spirit is capable of using a variety of means to accomplish His will and get us going in the direction He desires for a given time. It is our responsibility to be receptive to His voice regardless of the avenue He chooses to reveal His will.

While waiting in Troas for God's will, Paul had a vision at night. The implication here is that the vision occurred in a dream. The word for *vision* is used frequently in Acts to describe God's revealing power: 9:10, 12; 10:3, 17, 19; 11:5; 16:9, 10; 18:9. In the mind of the Greek, seeing was more important than hearing; thus, a Greek like Luke (the only Gentile writer in the New

Testament) would naturally be drawn to that which reflected his cultural background. In the vision, a man of Macedonia stood before him "praying." The word for *praying* is better translated "begging" (NIV) or "beseeching" (RSV). There is a desperate plea for help implied in the word.

Macedonia was an area that stretched about 250 miles east to west from the Aegean Sea to the Adriatic Sea. In 168 BC it came under Roman control and, though declared free, was divided into four districts. In 148 BC it was made an official Roman province. The major seat of administration was Thessalonica.

As mentioned above, in 16:10 the narrative shifted to Luke's "we" journal that indicated he was already part of the ministry team at the time of the vision. The vision was taken by the other men as God's clear sign they were to proceed to Europe with the Gospel.

> "Teach me thy way, O Lord, and lead me in a plain path."
> —Psalm 27:11

II. THE LORD OPENS HEARTS (Acts 16:11-15)
A. Arrival in Macedonia (vv. 11-12)

11. Therefore loosing from Troas, we came with a straight course to Samothracia, and the next day to Neapolis;

12. And from thence to Philippi, which is the chief city of that part of Macedonia, and a colony: and we were in that city abiding certain days.

The journey across the Aegean Sea from Troas to the coast of Europe was but a few days. The men arrived in Philippi and looked for a way to share the message of Christ.

Philippi was a city about 10 miles inland from the sea. Founded about 360 BC, it was located near the river Gangites and had a mixed population of Thracians, Greeks, and Romans. With such a mixed population it also had a multiplicity of gods: the Thracian god Liber Pater; the Greek Athena; the Roman Jupiter, Mars, and the emperor cult; the Anatolian Cybele; and the Egyptian Isis and Seraphis (*Interpreter's Dictionary of the Bible*).

Paul was able to have an effective ministry there, and his letter to the Philippians bears witness to the joy he experienced in their commitment to Christ.

Samothracia (SAM-oh-thray-shuh)—v. 11—a small Greek island in the Aegean Sea

Neapolis (ne-AP-oh-lis)—v. 11—a seaport serving the city of Philippi

B. Lydia's Conversion (vv. 13-15)

13. And on the sabbath we went out of the city by a river side, where prayer was wont to be made; and we sat down, and spake unto the women which resorted thither.

14. And a certain woman named Lydia, a seller of purple, of the city of Thyatira, which worshipped God, heard us: whose heart the Lord opened, that she attended unto the things which were spoken of Paul.

15. And when she was baptized, and her household, she besought us, saying, If ye have judged me to be faithful to the Lord, come into my house, and abide there. And she constrained us.

Thyatira (thy-uh-TIE-ruh)—v. 14—the small but wealthy hometown of Lydia

Talk About It:
1. What do verses 14 and 15 reveal about Lydia?
2. How did Lydia respond to the Gospel?

These verses describe the conversion of the first Christian on European soil, a woman named Lydia. Paul and companions went to the banks of the river Gangites and found women who had gathered for spiritual reasons. Apparently there was no synagogue in Philippi, indicating an extremely small Jewish population. Paul's normal procedure was to use the synagogue as a forum for declaring Jesus. But where a synagogue could not be found, he had to discover the place where religious people might gather.

As the men spoke of the Lord Jesus Christ, Lydia responded to the move of the Holy Spirit in her heart and accepted the Lord Jesus as Savior. She was a seller of purple cloth (v. 14) and was originally from the Asian city of Thyatira (see Rev. 2:18-28). She was likely a financially secure woman and had a strong business. Although women generally were treated poorly in the ancient world, Macedonia was noted for its liberal attitudes toward women. She invited Paul and the other men to stay in her home, and there the first church in Europe was established.

"The Holy Spirit can't save saints or seats. If we don't know any non-Christians, how can we introduce them to the Savior?"
—**Paul Little**

Consider how the Holy Spirit continued to guide Paul once he arrived in Macedonia. An important lesson for us concerning obedience comes from this reality: If God has called us to a particular task, He will continue to provide the power to accomplish that task and give wisdom and guidance every step of the way. Phillips Brooks expressed this reality in these words: "Do not pray for easy lives. Pray to be stronger men! Do not pray for tasks equal to your powers. Pray for powers equal to your tasks."

III. THE GOSPEL CHANGES LIVES (Acts 16:16-34)
A. Demonic Witnessing (vv. 16-18)

16. And it came to pass, as we went to prayer, a certain damsel possessed with a spirit of divination met us, which brought her masters much gain by soothsaying:

17. The same followed Paul and us, and cried, saying, These men are the servants of the most high God, which shew unto us the way of salvation.

18. And this did she many days. But Paul, being grieved, turned and said to the spirit, I command thee in the name of Jesus Christ to come out of her. And he came out the same hour.

Talk About It:
1. Describe this "certain damsel" (v. 16).
2. What "grieved" or "troubled" (v. 18 NIV) Paul?

James 2:19 shows that demons believe in God's power and live in fear of His presence. The ministry of Jesus is filled with examples of demonic spirits recognizing the presence of Christ and crying out (Mark 1:23-25, 34; 3:11-12; 5:6-13; 9:20-27). Jesus commanded the unclean spirits to be quiet, as they told who He was; and then He cast them out. Jesus forbade the unclean spirits to speak because their form of proclamation was meant to create confusion and chaos. It also meant that Jesus was being announced to the world by the spirits of demons rather than the

cleansed lives of anointed men and women who preached from the Holy Spirit.

In this, Paul did not encounter anything different from what Jesus experienced in His ministry. The woman in Acts 16 was under the control of two masters: a spirit of divination and men who manipulated her for economic gain. The spirit of divination is a form of witchcraft and sorcery. In fact, the word for *soothsaying* in verse 16 is used only here in the New Testament. W. E. Vine remarks, "The word is allied to *mainomai*, 'to rave,' and *mania*, fully displayed by those who were possessed by the evil spirit while delivering their oracular messages." It is also important to note that this radically differs from the New Testament form of messages characterized by the word *prophesy*.

The woman's message was correct: Paul and the men were servants of the Most High God who revealed the way of salvation. Yet Paul knew that her testimony did not originate from the Holy Spirit and thus would only create confusion by identifying the Gospel with magic and fortune-telling. This says something about proclaiming Christ in our generation. There are many forms of modern religion that are using Christian terms but are not anointed by the Holy Spirit. These religions are generating destructive confusion in the lives of many.

Paul was "grieved" by the girl's constant efforts to discredit the Christian mission. The same word is used in Acts 4:2 to describe how the Jewish officials felt about the preaching of Peter and John. There was an annoying, disturbing quality about her speech. The Jews could do nothing to stop the preaching of the Gospel; the truth would be proclaimed regardless of the cost. But Paul was determined that spiritual darkness would not undermine the effectiveness of the Gospel in Philippi, and he took action, spiritually, against the spirit.

B. Accusation and Imprisonment (vv. 19-24)

(Acts 16:19-24 is not included in the printed text.)

The woman apparently remained with her owners for a period of time following the exorcism. But it did not take them long to realize her powers were broken. Now that she was a free woman, they were suffering financial loss. We discover from this assessment of their loss that she likely filled the role of what we call today a fortune-teller. Christians should, without reservation, reject all horoscopes, fortune-tellers, and anything that comes close to such. These things are far more than unfortunate nonsense; they are demonic avenues Satan uses to gain control and influence in our lives.

Note that Paul and Silas were not attacked because of Christian preaching or even their acts of spiritual ministry. They were attacked because the Gospel affected the finances of the woman's masters. However, these men hoped to disguise the

"The gift of discernment is the God-given power to distinguish what comes from the Spirit of Truth and what comes from other possible sources."
—French Arrington

Talk About It:
1. Why were Paul and Silas taken captive (v. 19)?
2. What false charges were filed (vv. 20-21)?
3. What was the jailer ordered to do (vv. 22-23)?

real cause for their anxiety—the loss of their revenue—and appear to be civic-minded by complaining that their city was being troubled (v. 20).

The emperor Claudius had just recently expelled the Jews from Rome. By this official act, it seems very likely that anti-Semitism swept over the empire with varying degrees of intensity. Here at Philippi these slave owners refer to religious "customs" of Paul and Silas, such as circumcision and other strictly Jewish practices, which are "unlawful for us Romans to accept or practice" (v. 21 NIV). Never mind that the missionaries were not advocating such practices!

The Philippian mob was incensed to violence and called for the apostles to be punished, whereupon the rulers ordered the apostles stripped and beaten. Under Roman law, corporal beatings were done with rods. In 2 Corinthians 11:25 Paul related that he was beaten with rods on three occasions. The Scriptures do not tell us about the other two.

The Jewish law limited the beating of a prisoner to forty stripes. In order not to exceed the limit of the law, the Jews only gave thirty-nine stripes. Among the Romans, however, there was no such limit. Hence, the record says that Paul received "many stripes" (Acts 16:23). This seems to be what he had in mind when he wrote to the Corinthians that he had received "stripes above measure" (2 Cor. 11:23).

The jailer threw the prisoners into the inner prison where less light and air were available, and where the possibility of escape was much less. They were further restricted by having their feet fastened in stocks. The stocks had two holes so positioned that the prisoner's legs were spread far apart. This caused great discomfort and made it impossible for one to walk, or to move more than the slightest bit. The missionaries were placed in the custody of a jailer who was instructed to watch them carefully.

> "Here I stand; I can do no other. God help me. Amen."
> —Martin Luther

C. Midnight Praises (vv. 25-27)

25. And at midnight Paul and Silas prayed, and sang praises unto God: and the prisoners heard them.

26. And suddenly there was a great earthquake, so that the foundations of the prison were shaken: and immediately all the doors were opened, and every one's bands were loosed.

27. And the keeper of the prison awaking out of his sleep, and seeing the prison doors open, he drew out his sword, and would have killed himself, supposing that the prisoners had been fled.

Talk About It:
1. Why did Paul and Silas pray and sing at midnight?

The severe treatment Paul and Silas had received could not repress the joy they felt in their spirits. They sang praises to God at midnight. This is exactly what Jesus intended when He said, "Blessed are ye, when men shall revile you, and persecute you,

Moving Into New Territory

and shall say all manner of evil against you falsely, for my sake. Rejoice, and be exceeding glad: for great is your reward in heaven" (Matt. 5:11-12).

The other prisoners listened to the singing of Paul and Silas. They must have thought the missionaries were the strangest of prisoners. They were in prison on trumped-up charges and had been treated exceedingly badly, and yet they sang. Their singing was probably one of the psalms, possibly one of deliverance.

The other prisoners were not alone in hearing the songs of Paul and Silas. God also heard and responded to their praise in a miraculous way. An earthquake jarred the foundations of the prison and pulled loose the sockets that held the bonds and chains on the prisoners. Not only were Paul and Silas set free, but all the other prisoners were freed as well. This was a blessing that fell upon the unbelievers merely because they were in prison at the time the missionaries were. With their bonds broken off and the doors of the prison open, every prisoner could have escaped if he had wanted to.

The prison guard had been asleep before the earthquake. It was customary in those days for the jailer to have living quarters in the jail. It is apparent from what happened later that this was true in this case. The jailer and his family seemed to have been asleep in quarters of the jail, separate from the cells that held the prisoners.

After having been sternly instructed to keep the prisoners with care, the jailer knew that his own life would be forfeited when it was realized they had escaped. Rather than face the dishonor of having allowed his prisoners to escape, which could possibly have been punished by death, the jailer intended to kill himself with a sword. In the darkness he was not able to see that the prisoners were still there.

2. What damage did the earthquake *not* do?

3. What did the jailer decide to do (v. 27), and why?

"Praise God even when you don't understand what He is doing."
—Henry Jacobsen

D. A Jailer's Conversion (vv. 28-34)

28. But Paul cried with a loud voice, saying, Do thyself no harm: for we are all here.

29. Then he called for a light, and sprang in, and came trembling, and fell down before Paul and Silas,

30. And brought them out, and said, Sirs, what must I do to be saved?

31. And they said, Believe on the Lord Jesus Christ, and thou shalt be saved, and thy house.

32. And they spake unto him the word of the Lord, and to all that were in his house.

33. And he took them the same hour of the night, and washed their stripes; and was baptized, he and all his, straightway.

34. And when he had brought them into his house, he set meat before them, and rejoiced, believing in God with all his house.

Talk About It:
1. Why did Paul say, "We are all here" (v. 28)?
2. What does it mean to "believe on the Lord Jesus Christ" (v. 31)?
3. How did the jailer's decision affect his family (v. 33)?

By this time Paul was the obvious spokesman for all the prisoners. He assured the guard that all of them were there. It is noteworthy that none of the prisoners took advantage of the situation to escape. They were no doubt impressed by the singing of Paul and Silas, and their indomitable optimism, and then were awestruck by the earthquake. They likely realized that their greatest safety lay in remaining with the missionaries.

The jailer was totally confused. In spite of the unexpected stroke of deliverance, all of his prisoners were still there. None had made a move to escape. He could not help realizing that there was something different about Paul and Silas. The circumstances of their imprisonment, their singing at midnight, the earthquake that coincided with their singing, and finally their making no move to escape amazed the jailer. With a mixture of awe and fear, he fell at the feet of Paul and Silas.

The question the jailer asked perhaps refers to his spiritual salvation rather than to his personal safety; he no longer feared for physical life since all the prisoners were still there. He had suddenly lost all concern for himself and the captives; conviction had arrested him, and held him prisoner; he now could see that the freest men are those whose spirits cannot be chained.

"Believe on the Lord" (v. 31) is a comprehensive statement of the truth that encompasses trusting in Christ's atonement. It involves accepting His blood sacrifice for the personal sins one has committed.

It is not implied, as it may seem at first reading, that the jailer's faith was sufficient for both him and his household. Rather, while the same door of salvation was open to him and to them, no one can be saved against their will.

Verse 32 says Paul and Silas then expounded the Gospel more thoroughly to him and his household. The fact that they were able to do this is indication that the jailer and his family lived in quarters of the jail. Otherwise his family would not have come with him to investigate the effects of the earthquake.

Even though the hour would have been very late, the jailer and his family desired to be baptized. First, however, the jailer washed the stripes of the missionaries and cared for them in a humane way. His acceptance of the Gospel bore immediate fruit of kindness and gentleness. Unable to wait until the coming of dawn, the jailer and his household were baptized in the middle of the night.

The jailer and the missionaries returned to the jailer's quarters and spent the rest of the night in rejoicing. The scene was quite different from what it had been earlier in the night. The missionaries were washed, fed, and comforted; the jailer and his family were converted and happy; and instead of their relationship being that of guard and prisoners, they were now Christian brethren.

"Example is not the main thing in influencing others. It is the only thing."
—Albert Schweitzer

CONCLUSION

Paul and Silas, upon their arrest at Philippi, were subjected to the utmost physical restrictions, thrust into the inner prison, then made doubly secure with their feet fastened in stocks. But their spirits soared on wings of praise.

Of course, an earthquake came and shook the prison; but that was not the source of their freedom. It was the other way around. The liberties they took jarred the jailhouse.

If we lead lives empowered and guided by God's Spirit, we can expect to experience Him to do amazing things in our world.

GOLDEN TEXT CHALLENGE

"A VISION APPEARED TO PAUL IN THE NIGHT; THERE STOOD A MAN OF MACEDONIA, AND PRAYED HIM, SAYING, COME OVER INTO MACEDONIA, AND HELP US" (Acts 16:9).

There is a lot of interesting speculation about the "man of Macedonia" who appeared to Paul in this vision. Some think Paul saw a vision of Luke, since he immediately became part of this missionary endeavor (v. 10). Others think this mysterious man was obviously a Macedonian by the way he dressed. Another thought is that a guardian angel from Macedonia made the plea.

The certain and significant truth is that divine guidance was given to Paul for his missionary journey. He was directed to Macedonia, a mountainous country north of Greece. At once Paul and his companions sailed to Philippi, the leading city of Macedonia, and began witnessing there.

If we, like Paul, are willing to obey the guidance of God's Spirit, we can expect to receive it. His direction may come through a vision, a sermon, a scripture, a prophetic word, or through some other means, but it will come.

Daily Devotions:

M. Spirit-Inspired Wisdom
Genesis 41:28-38

T. Spirit-Guided Support
1 Chronicles 12:16-18

W. Spirit-Filled in Tragic Circumstances
2 Chronicles 24:17-22

T. Hearts and Eyes Opened
Luke 24:25-32

F. Transformed Lives
1 Corinthians 6:9-11

S. Receptive Hearers
1 Thessalonians 1:2-10

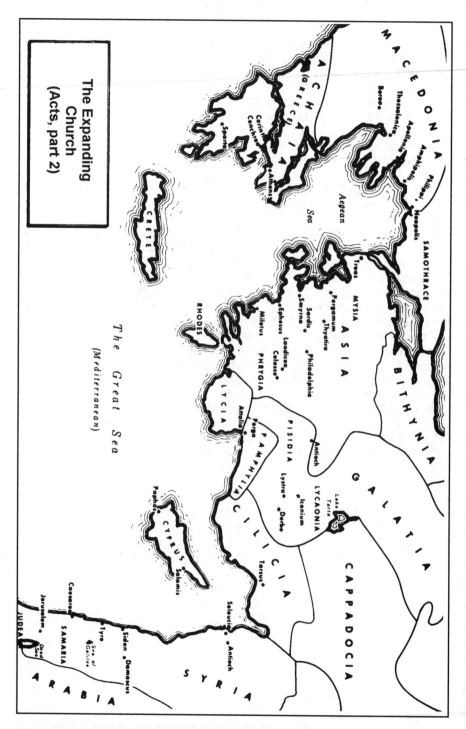

The Expanding
Church
(Acts, part 2)

MACEDONIA

ACHAIA / GREECE

Berea
Thessalonica
Apollonia · Amphipolis
Philippi · Neapolis
Corinth · Cenchrea
Athens
Sparta

Aegean Sea

SAMOTHRACE

BITHYNIA

CRETE

Troas

MYSIA

ASIA

Pergamum
Sardis · Thyatira
Smyrna
Ephesus · Laodicea
Miletus · Colosse
· Philadelphia

PHRYGIA

GALATIA

RHODES

LYCIA

Attalia
Perga
PAMPHYLIA

PISIDIA
Antioch

CAPPADOCIA

LYCAONIA
Lystra · Iconium
· Derbe

Lake Tatta

The Great Sea
(Mediterranean)

CILICIA

Tarsus

CYPRUS
Paphos · Salamis

Seleucia
· Antioch

SYRIA

Caesarea
Tyre
Sidon · Damascus
Sea of Galilee
Jerusalem
SAMARIA
JUDEA
Dead Sea

ARABIA

Responding to the Gospel

Acts 17:10 through 18:11

INTRODUCTION

In his travels, Paul had established the practice of going to the Jewish synagogue to preach the Gospel. This custom was both practical and ideal. Jesus was the Jewish Messiah, and it was therefore fitting that His message be preached first to the Jews. It was appropriate for the Christian missionaries to announce first to the Jews that their Messiah had come.

It was also a practical procedure, because Paul was a rabbi of the Jews and any qualified rabbi had a right to be heard when he visited any local synagogue. The traveling rabbi would introduce himself to the resident rabbi, whereupon the visitor would be invited to address the congregation and share with them any doctrine or word of exhortation he might have. Following such a formal statement, the visitor then could attend the synagogue as frequently as he wished. Paul used this privilege to great advantage. He would visit the synagogue and there declare that the Messiah had come. In Thessalonica (Acts 17:1-9), Paul went to the synagogue three straight weeks. This in no way suggests that he stayed in the city only three weeks, but the events of this lesson occurred after he had visited the synagogue for that period.

The burden of Paul's message was always the necessity of Christ's suffering and death. He began his exhortation with a statement of the Jewish belief in the Messiah. This was an accepted fact wherever Jews were found. From this fact he proceeded to say that the Messiah had already come, in the person of Jesus of Nazareth. This was a positive declaration, and would typically meet with some opposition.

The way Jesus had come and lived on earth did not fit with the Jewish notion of how their Messiah would come. Furthermore, the fact that He had died on a Roman cross proved especially difficult for the Jews who expected an all-conquering Messiah. Paul therefore needed to exhort from the Scriptures that it was necessary for Christ to die. It was because of His death that people can live. The proof of Christ's messianic claims was the fact that He rose from the dead. Jesus was not merely executed on the cross; He willingly gave Himself to be a sacrifice for humanity. Even His death was a matter of His will and acceptance. His resurrection from the dead was full and final proof that He was the Son of God, the Messiah of the Jews.

Unit Theme:
The Expanding Church (Acts, Part 2)

Central Truth:
Christians are to confidently proclaim the Gospel, regardless of how people respond.

Focus:
Realize that people react and respond to the Gospel in various ways and fearlessly proclaim the Gospel.

Context:
Paul takes the Gospel to Berea, Athens, and Corinth (AD 55-56).

Golden Text:
"These were more noble than those in Thessalonica, in that they received the word with all readiness of mind, and searched the Scriptures daily, whether those things were so" (Acts 17:11).

Study Outline:
I. Honest Inquiry (Acts 17:10-15)
II. Intellectual Curiosity (Acts 17:16-34)
III. Informed Belief (Acts 18:1-11)

I. HONEST INQUIRY (Acts 17:10-15)

In Thessalonica, a few of the Jews were persuaded by Paul's preaching and accepted the fact that their Messiah had come. A far greater number of Greek proselytes accepted the Gospel and professed their faith in Christ, as did a large number of prominent women (vv. 1-4).

The unbelieving Jews were jealous of Paul's success and agitated real trouble for the apostle. The Jews incited a riot, and even drew "lewd fellows of the baser sort" (v. 5) into the uproar. The meaning of these words is that they went into the marketplace and recruited a group of rowdy men to lead in the disorder.

Unable to find Paul and Silas, the mob attacked the house of Jason, where the missionaries were lodged. The mob dragged Jason to the city authorities and brought charges against Paul and Silas. The mob accused the missionaries of "turning the world upside down" (see v. 6). This was similar to the charge brought against them in Philippi, where they were called men who "exceedingly trouble our city" (16:20). This accusation was an unintentional compliment to the missionaries, for the servants of Christ are called to upset the world in order to set it right again.

A. Ministry in Berea (vv. 10-12)

10. And the brethren immediately sent away Paul and Silas by night unto Berea: who coming thither went into the synagogue of the Jews.

11. These were more noble than those in Thessalonica, in that they received the word with all readiness of mind, and searched the scriptures daily, whether those things were so.

12. Therefore many of them believed; also of honourable women which were Greeks, and of men, not a few.

The Christian converts in Thessalonica spirited Paul and Silas out of the city at night. Once the rabble had been roused, they might have done harm to the missionaries if they had been located. The two missionaries went to Berea, a town about fifty miles west of Thessalonica. Berea was not a metropolitan area such as Philippi and Thessalonica. It was a small, out-of-the-way town by comparison to those cities. Nevertheless, there was a synagogue of the Jews there, which made it a likely place for the preaching of the Gospel.

The Jews of Berea are paid a high compliment in Scripture. It is noted that they were more noble than the Jews in Thessalonica. When Paul spoke in their synagogue, the Bereans listened eagerly to his words and searched the Scriptures to see if he spoke truly. They did not listen to the apostle with such deep-seated prejudice that they gave no heed to what he said. The open-mindedness of the Bereans has forever made the word *Berean* a synonym for learning and eagerness to know. Many Christian colleges and universities have been given the name *Berea* in honor of those noble people. The Scriptures that the Bereans searched were the scrolls of the Law and the Prophets.

Talk About It:
1. How did the Bereans show their noble character (v. 11)?
2. How did many Jews and Greeks respond to the Gospel (v. 12)?

Many Jews in Berea were convinced by Paul's preaching that Christ was the Messiah. In addition to the Jews who accepted the Gospel, a number of prominent Greek women, proselytes to the Jewish faith, were converted. The Berean revival was one of Paul's most successful missionary efforts in Macedonia.

B. Trouble in Berea (vv. 13-15)

13. But when the Jews of Thessalonica had knowledge that the word of God was preached of Paul at Berea, they came thither also, and stirred up the people.

14. And then immediately the brethren sent away Paul to go as it were to the sea: but Silas and Timotheus abode there still.

15. And they that conducted Paul brought him unto Athens: and receiving a commandment unto Silas and Timotheus for to come to him with all speed, they departed.

The spiteful Jews in Thessalonica heard of Paul's great success in Berea. They went to the city and treated Paul in Berea the same as they had done in Thessalonica. They were not content to stop his work in their own city but hounded him to the other. This indicated the degree of hatred that people sometimes have for the gospel of Christ. No mention is made of a riot in Berea, but it is intimated that there may have been one. The Thessalonian Jews incited the crowd and leveled their baseless accusations against them.

To avoid further trouble, the Berean Christians took Paul away to the sea. Silas and Timothy remained in Berea and probably continued the work there. There is no specific mention that a church was established in Berea. There is no evidence of a letter ever being written to the Berean Christians, and no Berean church is mentioned in Scripture. This indicates that the Thessalonian Jews may have had some success in thwarting the work of God in Berea.

The Christians of Berea who escorted Paul out of the city continued with him to Athens. After having been repeatedly mistreated in Macedonia, Paul's life was in peril in that region. This would be compounded by the fact that he was traveling alone. The Berean Christians provided both encouragement and protection to him.

Once Paul arrived safely in Athens, the Berean Christians returned to their home city. They carried a message for Silas and Timothy to join Paul as quickly as they could. But apparently his two companions were unable to join him during the short period he was in Athens. Thus, Paul's Athenian experience was a lonely one, with no one to strengthen or encourage him.

II. INTELLECTUAL CURIOSITY (Acts 17:16-34)
A. Idolatrous City (vv. 16-18)

"During my eighty-seven years I have witnessed a whole succession of technological revolutions. But none of them has done away with the need for character in the individual or the ability to think."
—Bernard Baruch

Talk About It:
1. Who "stirred up" the people, and why (v. 13)?
2. Why was Paul separated from Timothy and Silas for a while (v. 14)?

16. Now while Paul waited for them at Athens, his spirit was stirred in him, when he saw the city wholly given to idolatry.

17. Therefore disputed he in the synagogue with the Jews, and with the devout persons, and in the market daily with them that met with him.

18. Then certain philosophers of the Epicureans, and of the Stoicks, encountered him. And some said, What will this babbler say? other some, He seemeth to be a setter forth of strange gods: because he preached unto them Jesus, and the resurrection.

In the marketplace in Athens, along an avenue where a multitude of idols were displayed, Paul reasoned ("disputed," v. 17) with the Athenians about the one true God. Meanwhile, Paul also reasoned with the Jews and God-fearing Greeks in the synagogue. This was the common manner of teaching in Athens. The philosophers of Athens generally taught by conversation in such settings.

When the Stoic and Epicurean teachers heard the things Paul taught, they compared him to a crow hopping about picking up random seed. (The word *babbler* can be translated "seed picker.") This indicates that the Athenian philosophers did not take Paul seriously. To them he seemed to be a strange Jew with a stranger doctrine.

B. Paul on Mars Hill (vv. 19-21)

19. And they took him, and brought him unto Areopagus, saying, May we know what this new doctrine, whereof thou speakest, is?

20. For thou bringest certain strange things to our ears: we would know therefore what these things mean.

21. (For all the Athenians and strangers which were there spent their time in nothing else, but either to tell, or to hear some new thing.)

Paul was invited by the Athenians to speak publicly at a place called the Areopagus, or Mars Hill. The Areopagus was a prominent mound of stone that overlooked the marketplace. Towering above it was a great height called the Acropolis, where there were gleaming temples to Athena, the goddess for whom Athens was named, and numerous other gods. Its situation made Mars Hill one of the most conspicuous and prominent features of the city. It was the regular meeting place for teachers and philosophers and their students. The people sat on the craggy rocks of the mound and listened with interest to any new doctrine that might be expounded there. The Athenians were too sophisticated to persecute those who seemed strange to them, so they gave them a hearing at Areopagus and then decided upon the validity of their doctrine.

The Athenians were so fussy about the precision of their beautiful Greek language that they insisted upon its purity by anyone who spoke on the Areopagus. It is said that they would hiss and jeer so loudly that if a hapless orator mispronounced even a single syllable, he could not continue to speak. The only language permitted there was the pure Attic, or classical, Greek. There was a common language of the Greeks known as Koine, which was the language used by Paul in His epistles. The fact that he spoke on Mars Hill indicates that he also spoke the Attic Greek, and did so very well. Paul's educational credentials were such that he was invited to speak to the Athenians, so now they would judge the validity of what he taught.

C. The Unknown God (vv. 22-25)

22. Then Paul stood in the midst of Mars' hill, and said, Ye men of Athens, I perceive that in all things ye are too superstitious.

23. For as I passed by, and beheld your devotions, I found an altar with this inscription, TO THE UNKNOWN GOD. Whom therefore ye ignorantly worship, him declare I unto you.

24. God that made the world and all things therein, seeing that he is Lord of heaven and earth, dwelleth not in temples made with hands;

25. Neither is worshipped with men's hands, as though he needed any thing, seeing he giveth to all life, and breath, and all things.

too superstitious (v. 22)—very religious

Paul stood on the rocky crest of Mars Hill, while the listeners sat on the rocks around him. Far below him sprawled the marketplace; towering behind him was the Acropolis with its gleaming temples. This was a strange and different setting for the apostle. He was now ready to give one of the most important discourses of his life. In his opening statement he referred to the religious nature of the Athenians. The word *superstitious* has reference to their religious nature. It is better translated "religious." Paul was referring to the Athenians' dedication to the great number of deities in evidence through the city.

Even as Paul spoke, he was surrounded by the material devotion of the Athenians to their gods. The mighty temples of the Acropolis were behind him. Below and around him were smaller temples, chapels, and idols of the gods.

In Athens there was one prominent avenue where, it is said, all of the gods and goddesses were represented. The Athenians believed in many gods and gave reverence to them all. For fear that they might be unaware of some deity, and unwittingly offend him, they had erected an altar with the inscription "TO THE UNKNOWN GOD." Their purpose was to show any god they had omitted from their pantheon that they had not intended to ignore him. The Athenians were too broad-minded and sophisticated to exclude any god from their city.

Talk About It:
1. Explain the phrase "ignorantly worship" (v. 23).
2. According to verses 24 and 25, how does God differ from the gods of Athens?
3. What does God *not* need (v. 25)?

It is also likely that deep in the Greek heart there was an awareness that neither Athena nor all the host of other gods fully represented their god-consciousness. It may have been that they knew there must be something more. Paul seized upon this opportunity to expound the message of the one true God. He declared, "Now what you worship as something unknown I am going to proclaim to you" (v. 23 NIV). Paul did not begin by denouncing the false gods the people worshiped, but he positively proclaimed to them the true God.

In presenting God as the one Creator of the universe, Paul revealed that all other gods were both false and unnecessary. The God of creation could certainly not be contained in any shrine or temple. Not even the splendid temples atop the Acropolis were worthy of Him. Even the great Temple that Solomon had built in Jerusalem had been insufficient for God (1 Kings 8:27; Acts 7:47-50).

In 17:25, Paul denied the idea that God is dependent upon man for anything. He is the Creator, and man is the creature—and there is nothing that the creature can give to the Creator. In pagan religions the people presented material gifts and offerings to their deities, often loading their idols with such gifts. But the true God does not require anything of His creatures. His only desire is that they know and worship Him. Human skill and art in fashioning ornate temples and exquisite idols are not sufficient for the worship of God. God gives man everything, including the breath he breathes.

There were times when even the Jews had believed that God was dependent upon them. This idea was repudiated in Psalm 50:9-15, where God declared that He would accept no offering other than thanksgiving and glory.

D. Lord of All (vv. 26-31)

26. And hath made of one blood all nations of men for to dwell on all the face of the earth, and hath determined the times before appointed, and the bounds of their habitation;

27. That they should seek the Lord, if haply they might feel after him, and find him, though he be not far from every one of us:

28. For in him we live, and move, and have our being; as certain also of your own poets have said, For we are also his offspring.

29. Forasmuch then as we are the offspring of God, we ought not to think that the Godhead is like unto gold or silver, or stone, graven by art and man's device.

30. And the times of this ignorance God winked at; but now commandeth all men every where to repent:

Responding to the Gospel

31. Because he hath appointed a day, in the which he will judge the world in righteousness by that man whom he hath ordained; whereof he hath given assurance unto all men, in that he hath raised him from the dead.

A general belief in ancient times was that each nation had its own god or gods. Paul set forth the idea that there was one God, and this God made all nations. He was therefore the God of the universe. He created and allotted the earth to people, setting bounds for their habitation. He created the heavens and the earth, even before He created humanity, and made this earth the dwelling place for His creatures.

At one time it was believed that the different races had different blood. Nothing less than divine inspiration pointed out here that God "made of one blood all nations of men" (v. 26). The blood of man is the same whether the man is black, white, brown, or yellow; whether he is educated or uneducated; whether he is a city-dweller or a backward cave-dweller.

People were created to enjoy fellowship with God. The search for God is our greatest responsibility as well as our greatest drive. All of the temples in Athens were testimony to how the Athenians sought after God. God is found by means of a sincere heart and faith that accepts Him.

To illustrate his argument, Paul quoted from a Greek poet, "For we are also his offspring" (v. 28). Similar expressions are found in the writings of both Aratus and Epimenides. In the Greek literature Zeus was represented as the father god. Certainly Paul did not accept this identification. He merely made this point in the same way he had made the point regarding the unknown God: the Greeks recognized certain truths about God even though they did not recognize Him. Paul was able to tell them who that God is—the Father of all, in whom all men live and move and have their being.

Paul's argument was pointed. If people are the offspring of God, then most assuredly the likeness of God cannot be gold or silver. God cannot be devised by man's art. Just as man is alive, so God is alive. Man lives, moves, and has being; so does God. By the institution of images, philosophers may be aware that images are mere representations of invisible divinity, but the people almost universally worship the images and idols themselves.

There was a time when God looked at such ignorance with mercy. Now the time has come when God will no longer excuse ignorance. The truth is made available to humanity, and everyone must accept or reject that truth. The dividing line was the coming of the Lord Jesus Christ. Since His coming, people everywhere are without excuse. He represents a new start for all the earth, and everyone will at last be accountable to Him. God will no longer overlook ignorance and lack of understanding. By repentance all people must forsake their sins and by faith accept God in Christ.

Talk About It:
1. What does God want people to do (v. 27)?
2. How dependent are people on God (v. 28)?
3. What does God no longer overlook (vv. 29-30)?
4. Describe the "day" Paul mentions in verse 31.

"It isn't easy to prove that there is a God. In fact, nowhere in the Bible does God attempt to prove His existence. But have you ever considered how much more difficult it is to disprove God's existence?"
—C. Neil Strait

Paul reached the heart of his message in verse 31: the revelation of God on earth is Jesus Christ. All the world will be judged by Him, by the standard of His person, His life, His words, and His commandments. Although Christ lived and died in Palestine, He was raised from the dead and now sits forever to redeem or judge all people.

E. A Crucial Decision (vv. 32-34)

32. And when they heard of the resurrection of the dead, some mocked: and others said, We will hear thee again of this matter.

33. So Paul departed from among them.

34. Howbeit certain men clave unto him, and believed: among the which was Dionysius the Areopagite, and a woman named Damaris, and others with them.

The resurrection of the man Jesus, and the general resurrection of all people, was the strange doctrine that had aroused the curiosity of the Athenians (vv. 18-20). Now, when they heard Paul plainly declare such a resurrection, the listeners interrupted him with mocking and derision. However, some of the people were sufficiently moved by the doctrine and wanted to hear more about it at a later time. Despite the interest of some, this represented one of Paul's least successful missionary efforts. In some places the people had reacted angrily when he preached; they had stoned him, imprisoned him, and abused him. In Athens, however, they merely laughed at him.

It has been suggested that Paul departed from Athens with the laughter of the Athenians ringing in his ears. Silas and Timothy, for whom he had sent, had not arrived yet; and so he faced the scorn and the mockery alone. Possibly he never felt more alone in all his life than he did at that moment. Nevertheless, the apostle had sowed good seed, and in a future day that seed would bear fruit.

A few persons were converted by Paul's words. Two were mentioned by name: a man named Dionysius and a woman named Damaris. Dionysius was a member of the Areopagus; that is, those who heard and judged the doctrines set forth on Areopagus. According to tradition, Dionysius later became the leader of the church in Athens. Nothing is known of the woman Damaris, except her name as it is mentioned here. The fact that her name is mentioned, however, indicates she was a prominent woman. This is further indicated by the fact that it was uncommon for women to be present at such meetings.

III. INFORMED BELIEF (Acts 18:1-11)

A. Partnership (vv. 1-3)

1. After these things Paul departed from Athens, and came to Corinth;

Dionysius (die-o-NISH-e-us)—v. 34— a member of Athens' high court who became a Christian

Talk About It:
What were the responses to the doctrine of resurrection (v. 32)?

"Reality, in fact, is always something you couldn't have guessed. That's one of the reasons I believe Christianity. It's a religion you couldn't have guessed."
—C. S. Lewis

2. And found a certain Jew named Aquila, born in Pontus, lately come from Italy, with his wife Priscilla; (because that Claudius had commanded all Jews to depart from Rome:) and came unto them.

3. And because he was of the same craft, he abode with them, and wrought: for by their occupation they were tent-makers.

After his disappointing experience in Athens, Paul went into Corinth, a city even more unlikely for the Gospel. Although northern Greece and southern Greece were joined by a small neck of the land called the Isthmus of Corinth, it is likely that Paul made the journey by land, not by sea.

Corinth was a city of such commercial emphasis and sexual license that even the Christians would have difficulty in resisting its influence. Even in that pre-Christian day, Corinth was noted for its low degree of culture and morality.

God immediately strengthened Paul and lifted up his spirits by providing him with two splendid associates and friends. A husband and wife team, named Aquila and Priscilla, lived in Corinth. They had only recently come to Corinth from Italy, refugees from the persecution of Emperor Claudius. Evidently Aquila and Priscilla had already accepted Christ when Paul met them. Paul first became associated with them because they, as he, were tent-makers. They worked with leather and wove cloth with which ship sails and tents were made.

Frequently in God's work He encourages His servants by giving them companions in their labor. This is how it happened with Paul. Silas and Timothy were not with him, but God gave him Priscilla and Aquila. This man and his wife supplied Paul with encouragement and fellowship, and increased his ability and effectiveness.

Most of the time when the two are mentioned, Priscilla's name precedes her husband's. This indicates that she may have come from a higher social background than Aquila. It may also indicate that she was the more conspicuous of the two. In his later ministry, Paul referred to the admirable couple with the greatest of confidence and appreciation. In Romans 16:3-4, he called them "my fellow workers in Christ Jesus" and spoke of them as having "risked their own necks for my life" (NKJV). He stated that not only did he thank them for this, but all the Gentile churches thanked them as well. They entered the apostle's life at a time when he needed their companionship and strength. They did not fail him, and in assisting him, they assisted the work of the Lord.

Talk About It:
1. Why were Aquila and Priscilla living in Corinth (vv. 1-2)?
2. What did this couple have in common with Paul (v. 3)?

"It's when you rub elbows with a man that you find out what he has up his sleeve."
—Quotable Quotations

B. Preaching (vv. 4-5)

4. And he reasoned in the synagogue every sabbath, and persuaded the Jews and the Greeks.

Talk About It:
Explain the phrase "pressed in the spirit" (v. 5).

5. And when Silas and Timotheus were come from Macedonia, Paul was pressed in the spirit, and testified to the Jews that Jesus was Christ.

Sometime after the arrival of Paul in Corinth, he was joined by his old friends, Silas and Timothy. These joined him from Macedonia, where they had remained when he left for Athens (17:14). From Philippians 4:15 we gather that the Philippian church sent a gift of money to Paul by Silas and Timothy. This probably relieved him of some work and enabled him to preach the Gospel more exclusively. At any rate, there was an intensification of his proclamation that Jesus was the Christ.

C. Persistence (vv. 6-8)

6. And when they opposed themselves, and blasphemed, he shook his raiment, and said unto them, Your blood be upon your own heads; I am clean; from henceforth I will go unto the Gentiles.

7. And he departed thence, and entered into a certain man's house, named Justus, one that worshipped God, whose house joined hard to the synagogue.

8. And Crispus, the chief ruler of the synagogue, believed on the Lord with all his house; and many of the Corinthians hearing believed, and were baptized.

Talk About It:
1. How did the Jews respond to Paul's preaching (v. 6)?
2. Explain Paul's statement, "I am clean" (v. 6).
3. What is the significance of Crispus' conversion (v. 8)?

Since all of Paul's Corinthian ministry up to this point had been in the Jewish synagogue, he had preached only to the Jews and converts to the Jewish faith. When he pressed upon them the fact that the Messiah had already come, the Jews rejected his message. The opposition to his presence in the synagogue became so intense that Paul had to find another place to preach. He dramatically shook the dust from his cloak so as to be rid of even the dust of the synagogue. He had made a similar, dramatic gesture in Pisidian Antioch (13:51). Paul declared to the Corinthian Jews that he was clean of their blood and of their blasphemy. Their guilt would rest upon their own heads. He had delivered the Gospel to them, and they had rejected it.

Paul's announcement that he would now turn to the Gentiles represented a major break between Christianity and Judaism. Virtually all of Christianity at that time was associated with the Jewish faith. The Christians were simply Jews who believed that Jesus of Nazareth was the Messiah. There was no break between Jew and Christian. The Christians were regarded by the pagans as being simply a sect of the Jews. With Paul's announced intention of turning to the Gentiles, he was declaring that, at least in Corinth, there would hereafter be a sharp distinction between the Jews and the Christians. Even at the time of Paul's conversion the Lord had revealed to Ananias that Paul would "bear my name before the Gentiles" (9:15).

Paul departed from the synagogue and began to conduct meetings in the home of Justus, who had been converted to Christ. The expression that his "house joined hard to the synagogue" (18:7) means that it was next door to it. Likely only a single wall separated the two.

Among the Jews who accepted Christ was a man named Crispus, called the chief ruler of the synagogue. His entire family accepted Christ. This naturally deepened the breach between the nonbelieving Jews and the new Christians. In addition, many of the Corinthian people now heard the Gospel and were baptized. Much of Paul's preaching was now directly to the Corinthian people, that is, Gentiles—and this further angered the unbelieving Jews. Despite the deepening tensions between the Christians and the Jews, the Word of God was being preached with marvelous results. Many Gentiles were coming to Christ, as had some of the choice people of the synagogue.

D. Progress (vv. 9-11)

9. Then spake the Lord to Paul in the night by a vision, Be not afraid, but speak, and hold not thy peace:

10. For I am with thee, and no man shall set on thee to hurt thee: for I have much people in this city.

11. And he continued there a year and six months, teaching the word of God among them.

While it is not specifically stated here, the danger to Paul's safety must have been considerable. The Lord encouraged His servant by a vision at night. As Paul lay sleeping, the Lord appeared to him and admonished him to have courage. Corinth was a fertile ground for the Gospel, and the Lord assured Paul that there were many God-fearing people in the city. Although Paul's life was in some jeopardy, he would be safe in the protection of the Lord. Paul was encouraged to speak even more boldly. The house of Justus became a preaching center for the Christian faith.

Encouraged by the vision, and motivated by the great number who came to Christ, Paul remained in Corinth for eighteen months. During that time there was a considerable missionary party at work: Paul, Silas, Timothy, Priscilla, and Aquila.

CONCLUSION

The Lord told Paul, "Be not afraid, but speak, and hold not thy peace" (Acts 18:9). This verse tells us that Christ is always with us. He may not always be felt, but He is always present. He is never failing in His interest and His concern for His witnesses. He is always ready to reveal Himself and His will in exact proportion to our needs. He may reveal Himself in unique and unusual ways. So we are encouraged to speak up.

"God is on the lookout for a man whose heart is perfect toward Him. Will you be quiet enough to hear Him, brave enough to proclaim Him, and honest enough to obey Him?"
—**Vance Havner**

Talk About It:
1. What promise did God make to Paul (vv. 9-10)?
2. How did Paul show his confidence in God's promise (v. 11)?

Silence is golden, but a silent witness will not suffice when the command of the Lord is to speak. To speak in the midst of total corruption requires a special kind of courage and boldness. This is our imperative today as we view a world of total rebellion, yet in the midst of this seemingly hopeless cause, God is at work. His sovereign grace is being bestowed upon those who will hear.

GOLDEN TEXT CHALLENGE
"THESE WERE MORE NOBLE THAN THOSE IN THESSA-LONICA, IN THAT THEY RECEIVED THE WORD WITH ALL READINESS OF MIND, AND SEARCHED THE SCRIPTURES DAILY, WHETHER THOSE THINGS WERE SO" (Acts 17:11).

Alexander Maclaren states: "The Berean Jews did exactly what their compatriots elsewhere would not do—they looked into the subject with their own eyes, and tested Paul's assertions by Scripture. 'Therefore,' says Luke, with grand confidence in the impregnable foundations of the faith, 'many of them believed' (v. 12).

"True nobility of soul consists in willingness to receive the Word, combined with diligent testing of it. Christ asks for no blind adhesion. The true Christian teacher wishes for no renunciation, on the part of his hearers, of their own judgment. 'Open your mouth and shut your eyes, and swallow what I give you' is not the language of Christianity, though it has sometimes been the demand of its professed missionaries; and not the teacher only, but the taught also, have been but too ready to exercise credulity instead of intelligent examination and clear-eyed faith. If professing Christians today were better acquainted with the Scriptures, and more in the habit of bringing every new doctrine to them as its touchstone, there would be less currency of errors and firmer grip of truth" (*Expositions of Holy Scripture*).

It is a positive sign when people check what they hear taught or preached by the Word of God. They should be encouraged to do so. When they see what the Bible has to say on any matter, they are generally more inclined to accept it. Teaching is not truly Christian unless it can be supported by the Word of God. The apostle Paul said, "Study to shew thyself approved unto God, a workman that needeth not to be ashamed, rightly dividing the word of truth" (2 Tim. 2:15).

Daily Devotions:
M. Decision to Follow God
   Ruth 1:11-18
T. Failure to Inquire of God
   2 Kings 1:2-8
W. Change of Mind
   Daniel 3:13-15, 24-29
T. We Would See Jesus
   John 12:20-26
F. Fruitfulness of the Gospel
   Colossians 1:3-8
S. Be Ready With an Answer
   1 Peter 3:8-16

Responding to the Gospel

Encouraging Godly Leaders

Acts 20:13-38

INTRODUCTION

Paul's great ministry in Ephesus was fruitful for the Christian faith, but it caused a great uproar among the pagan worshipers (Acts 19). The worshipers of Diana were particularly upset and endeavored to do Paul great harm. Diana was the most important deity in Ephesus, and a statue to her in Ephesus was world-famous.

After leaving Ephesus, Paul went back into Macedonia, where he visited and strengthened the churches in Philippi and Thessalonica (20:1-6). Paul came to Troas, where he met with the Christians as they came together to worship on Sunday (v. 7). Because Paul was leaving the next day, he kept teaching until midnight. The people were crowded together in an upstairs room, and a young man named Eutychus, who was sitting in a window, fell asleep. "He fell to the ground from the third story and was picked up dead" (v. 9 NIV). Rushing downstairs, Paul threw himself upon Eutychus and put his arms around him, and the young man came back to life. Paul then resumed his message, speaking until daybreak.

Now the apostle turned his thoughts and purposes toward Jerusalem. He set his schedule to be in Jerusalem by Pentecost. In those days of uncertain travel, he had to leave early and travel by boat. The apostle left Macedonia and traveled into Asia Minor, stopping at seaport towns all along the way. He stopped only briefly at most of the places, yet long enough to communicate with the Christians there (vv. 13-16).

This lesson concerns Paul's brief stop near Ephesus and his communication with the Ephesian elders. Paul realized he was facing danger in Jerusalem. This would likely be his last meeting with the Ephesians, and there were many things he wanted to tell them about problems they would face. Paul wanted to leave counsel and instructions that would guide his followers if for any reason he should not return to them. Paul's communication with the Ephesian elders reflects this type of care and concern.

Unit Theme:
The Expanding Church (Acts, Part 2)

Central Truth:
Christians can best encourage godly leaders by following their example.

Focus:
Examine principles of godly leadership and make them priorities in living for Christ.

Context:
Around AD 59 in Miletus

Golden Text:
"Take heed therefore unto yourselves, and to all the flock, over the which the Holy Ghost hath made you overseers, to feed the church of God, which he hath purchased with his own blood" (Acts 20:28).

Study Outline:
I. Serve God Wholeheartedly (Acts 20:17-24)
II. Care for God's People (Acts 20:25-31)
III. Love Sacrificially (Acts 20:32-38)

I. SERVE GOD WHOLEHEARTEDLY (Acts 20:17-24)

A. Faithful Service (vv. 17-21)

17. And from Miletus he sent to Ephesus, and called the elders of the church.

18. And when they were come to him, he said unto them, Ye know, from the first day that I came into Asia, after what manner I have been with you at all seasons,

19. Serving the Lord with all humility of mind, and with many tears, and temptations, which befell me by the lying in wait of the Jews:

20. And how I kept back nothing that was profitable unto you, but have shewed you, and have taught you publicly, and from house to house,

21. Testifying both to the Jews, and also to the Greeks, repentance toward God, and faith toward our Lord Jesus Christ.

The ship on which Paul was a passenger made a landing at the important seaport of Miletus. From Troas, where he had made his last landing, the apostle could have taken a ship directly to Ephesus. This would have hindered his voyage to Jerusalem, however, and he was determined to be in the Holy City for the approaching Easter season. He therefore took the faster ship to Miletus.

Paul's ship was harbored in Miletus for about three days. This gave him time to send for the Ephesian elders to come to him. Ephesus was about thirty miles north of Miletus, so it is likely that the elders arrived in Miletus on the third day of his three-day anchorage.

Luke recorded in considerable detail the discourse that Paul gave to the Ephesians. In the introductory part of his speech, Paul reviewed his manner of conduct while in Ephesus. During his three years of ministry there, the apostle endured a great deal of personal hardship and particular trials at the hands of the unbelieving Jews. In verse 19 Paul mentioned "the lying in wait of the Jews," which he did not further explain. These words seem to hint of a particular peril he faced, but we are not told exactly what happened.

In the face of this peril, Paul preached the Gospel in Ephesus both publicly and privately. He held back nothing, but declared to the Ephesians the full counsel of God. He preached Christ to both the Jews and the Greeks, at first in the synagogue, then in the school of Tyrannus, and in various private residences (see 19:8-10). The elders were well aware of Paul's ministry in Ephesus, but he reviewed it to establish the basis of further things he had to say.

B. A Secure Future (vv. 22-24)

22. And now, behold, I go bound in the spirit unto Jerusalem, not knowing the things that shall befall me there:

Talk About It:
1. How did Paul describe the nature of his ministry in Ephesus (vv. 19-20)?
2. What message did Paul preach in Ephesus (v. 21)?

"It takes a very short time to lose a good reputation but a long, long time to get another one."
—*Muncie Evening Press*

Encouraging Godly Leaders

23. Save that the Holy Ghost witnesseth in every city, saying that bonds and afflictions abide me.

24. But none of these things move me, neither count I my life dear unto myself, so that I might finish my course with joy, and the ministry, which I have received of the Lord Jesus, to testify the gospel of the grace of God.

Paul proceeded to tell the Ephesians about his present determination to go to Jerusalem. He felt a spiritual compulsion to go there, not knowing exactly what awaited him. Clearly Paul had misgivings about his trip to Jerusalem.

The apostle had continuing affection for the Jews. The course of his recent ministry had led him away from the Jews to the Gentiles, so he probably had a great longing to visit once again in the greatest of all Jewish cities.

Another way of saying "I go bound in the spirit unto Jerusalem" is "I have my heart set on going to Jerusalem." This is reminiscent of the similar occasion in the life of Christ, recorded in Luke 9:51, "And it came to pass, when the time was come that he should be received up, he stedfastly set his face to go to Jerusalem."

Paul's apprehension about going to Jerusalem was increased by frequent warnings by the Holy Spirit. There had been prophetic utterances that bonds and afflictions awaited Paul there. There were to be other warnings of the Spirit before Paul reached Jerusalem (Acts 21:4, 11). The Holy Spirit did not forbid Paul to go to that city, but only gave him warning of what would happen to him there.

So great was Paul's determination to go to Jerusalem that none of his anxieties or apprehensions could dissuade him from doing so. He recognized that this visit to the city would be a closing chapter in his long ministry. He was determined to fulfill it with joy and victory.

Paul did not regard his life as his own, but as belonging to Christ. And his ministry was Christ's also. As Christ saw fit to bring His own ministry to a close after a mere three years, Paul was willing to have his own ministry cut short. Whatever the will of God was, that was most important. Paul had preached the good news of the grace of God faithfully, and now he would lean on that same grace for his own future life and ministry.

II. CARE FOR GOD'S PEOPLE (Acts 20:25-31)
A. Clean Record (vv. 25-27)

25. And now, behold, I know that ye all, among whom I have gone preaching the kingdom of God, shall see my face no more.

26. Wherefore I take you to record this day, that I am pure from the blood of all men.

27. For I have not shunned to declare unto you all the counsel of God.

Talk About It:
1. Explain the phrase "bound in the spirit" (v. 22).
2. Describe Paul's determination and focus (vv. 23-24).

"Lord, give me the determination and tenacity of a weed."
—**Mrs. Leon Walters**

Talk About It:
1. What did Paul "know" (v. 25)?
2. Explain Paul's declaration of innocence (vv. 26-27).

Paul's message to the Ephesian elders assumed a note of finality. He told them they would never see him again. This was his way of saying farewell both to Ephesus and to the Asian field. Even if he should manage to enter and leave Jerusalem without losing his life there, the labors of the apostle would hereafter be directed westward to Rome and beyond.

At about this same time Paul wrote his letter to the Romans, in which he said: "But now having no more place in these parts, and having a great desire these many years to come unto you; whensoever I take my journey into Spain, I will come to you: for I trust to see you in my journey, and to be brought on my way thitherward by you, if first I be somewhat filled with your company. But now I go unto Jerusalem to minister unto the saints. For it hath pleased them of Macedonia and Achaia to make a certain contribution for the poor saints which are at Jerusalem" (Rom. 15:23-26).

In verse 26 of our text, Paul asserted himself to be without guilt toward other men. This meant that he had discharged his responsibility toward them. If people should be lost, it would not be because of negligence or guilt on his part.

Both in Ephesus and all of Asia Minor, Paul had faithfully declared the gospel of God. He had in no way neglected to tell people of the blessings of God available through Christ. Neither had he neglected to warn them of the penalties for rejecting Christ. He had been as the faithful shepherd who leads the flock to good pasture and warns them where there is danger. Having fulfilled his calling to preach the Gospel, Paul had a good conscience concerning wherever he had preached in Asia.

"Some wish to live within the sound of church and chapel bells. I want to run a rescue shop within a yard of hell."
—C. T. Studd

B. A Parting Charge (vv. 28-31)

28. Take heed therefore unto yourselves, and to all the flock, over the which the Holy Ghost hath made you overseers, to feed the church of God, which he hath purchased with his own blood.

29. For I know this, that after my departing shall grievous wolves enter in among you, not sparing the flock.

30. Also of your own selves shall men arise, speaking perverse things, to draw away disciples after them.

31. Therefore watch, and remember, that by the space of three years I ceased not to warn every one night and day with tears.

Leaders in the church should be persons whom the Holy Spirit definitely is using and whom He has appointed. Such persons should give evidence of being inspired by God. Such inspiration will be evidenced by their holy lives, wise decisions, gracious attitudes, and by their eagerness to help and to participate when the Kingdom needs them.

Talk About It:
1. How should church leaders view their ministry (v. 28)?
2. Describe Paul's warning (vv. 29-30).

Paul places upon these "overseers" a tremendous responsibility to "feed the Church" through the faithful preaching and teaching of the doctrines and practices of Christ so that those young in the faith should grow mature in it. That which cost Christ the loss of His life and the shedding of His blood to obtain should not be administered lightly but seriously and wisely.

In verse 29 there is no indication that Paul is concerned with external persecutions, such as that of Nero. He knew there would be persons who would "enter in" after his departure, exploit his absence of leadership, and try to take over the work. These would be in contrast to those leaders mentioned in verse 28, who were appointed by the Holy Spirit. There would be those who were ambitious position-seekers and politicians, having as the least of their goals the spiritual life and growth of the church.

These "wolves" might enter the flock like "wolves in sheep's clothing" (see Matt. 7:15), but their intent would be to destroy the flock of God. There would be some who would actually attach themselves to the church as if they were a part of it with the malicious purpose of doing it harm. There would always be wolves that would stand on the outside of the flock to devour weak Christians living on the fringe of the fold, but there would be other wolves who would actually enter the group to slaughter and devour.

Of great peril to the church would be onetime believers who would degenerate into apostasy (Acts 20:30). This meant that some within the church would become enemies of the cause of Christ. The word *perverse* means they would teach things contrary to the truth. These persons would be a danger to the faith because of their erroneous and perverted teaching. The church could survive the attack of wolves from without better than it could the crooked teaching of those within. These perverse teachers would win disciples to themselves rather than to Christ.

The greatest danger to the Church today comes from those who call themselves Christian but who are twisted and perverted in their thinking and doctrine.

Once again the apostle reminded the Ephesian elders of how he had worked among them for a period of three years (v. 31). In this verse we see something of the emotional nature of Paul. In Romans 9:1-3 Paul mentioned the great heaviness he felt for his own people, the Jews. Here he spoke of his compassion for the Gentiles.

The picture is a solemn and impressive one. The apostle Paul worked to support himself, taught publicly in the hall of Tyrannus, and went from door to door (sometimes during the day and sometimes during the night), teaching the people about Christ. The fact that he warned the people with tears indicated that he dwelt much on the judgment and punishment that would be meted out to those who reject Christ.

3. What did Paul do for three years (v. 31)?

"The one thing no church can stand is a pastor who really wants to be something else. The men who really want out ought to be helped out, for the Christian ministry is no place for a man who wants to be something else."
—**Duke McCall**

III. LOVE SACRIFICIALLY (Acts 20:32-38)

A. Holy Inheritance (v. 32)

32. And now, brethren, I commend you to God, and to the word of his grace, which is able to build you up, and to give you an inheritance among all them which are sanctified.

Talk About It:
Explain the blessing Paul pronounces.

In his farewell remarks to the Ephesians, Paul could do no better than to commend them to the keeping grace of the Lord. Only the word of His grace would be able to build them up in the faith and secure to them an inheritance of eternal life. The word *sanctified* here means "those who are set apart." Those who have been separated to the Lord Jesus Christ should be strengthened by the grace of the Lord and gain eternal life through Him. The Ephesians could no longer depend on Paul's preaching, for he would be gone. They would be called on to gather their own strength and assurance.

B. Material Matters (vv. 33-35)

33. I have coveted no man's silver, or gold, or apparel.

34. Yea, ye yourselves know, that these hands have ministered unto my necessities, and to them that were with me.

35. I have shewed you all things, how that so labouring ye ought to support the weak, and to remember the words of the Lord Jesus, how he said, It is more blessed to give than to receive.

Talk About It:
1. How had Paul approached the financial aspect of his ministry (vv. 33-34)?
2. Why is it "more blessed to give than to receive" (v. 35)?

It is from these verses that we know Paul worked for his own support during the years he was in Ephesus. He did not preach for material benefits, but only in an effort to win the souls of those who were lost. This does not mean Paul declined the assistance he might have received from the people, for he did receive assistance from other churches; but that was not the primary purpose of his ministry among them. The thought of material gain was not a matter of consequence to him.

Paul tried consistently to illustrate the teachings of Christ with his own life. We would do well to follow his example. He plainly teaches the responsibility of strong Christians to help "support the weak" (v. 35), and, undoubtedly, this includes material support.

Paul's support of himself was intended to be an example to others who were to follow him. In 1 Corinthians 9:7-18 Paul clearly established the fact that the minister is to be supported by those to whom he ministers. Yet he did not personally avail himself of this right. This was for a purpose: he wanted to establish the example of unselfishness and prohibit any accusation that his ministry was motivated by selfish purposes.

During the course of his ministry and writing, Paul seldom quoted directly from the words of Jesus. Acts 20:35 is one of the times that he did so. The apostle must have felt that this statement of Jesus about the blessedness of giving was of great importance.

"Money is a means, not an end—a tool to provide people with opportunities to hear and accept the gospel of Christ."
—Charles Stanley

Encouraging Godly Leaders

C. A Final Prayer (vv. 36-38)

36. And when he had thus spoken, he kneeled down, and prayed with them all.

37. And they all wept sore, and fell on Paul's neck, and kissed him,

38. Sorrowing most of all for the words which he spake, that they should see his face no more. And they accompanied him unto the ship.

Paul concluded his discourse to the Ephesians and then knelt down to pray with them. In the event that this should be the last time he would ever see his friends, he wanted his last act to be one of prayer and devotion. This is a fitting way for any human association to terminate.

The Ephesians responded by weeping, embracing Paul, and kissing him. They were like children bidding sorrowful farewell to a parent they know they are seeing for the last time. The tearful scene was caused by Paul's prediction that the Ephesians would see him no more. They were grieved at the thought that they were seeing him for the last time.

The Ephesians then accompanied Paul to the ship on which he would sail from Miletus. Apparently the meeting had been somewhere in the city, possibly in a private home. Since Ephesus was thirty miles away from Miletus, and the ship stayed in port only three days, the Ephesian elders probably saw Paul only part of one day. It was a brief but meaningful encounter in which the apostle looked soberly into the future and warned the Ephesians of things to come.

Talk About It:
What kind of relationship did Paul have with the Ephesian elders?

"There are not many things in life as beautiful as true friendship, and there are not many things more uncommon."
—*Megiddo Message*

CONCLUSION

On his way through Macedonia and Achaia toward Jerusalem, and ultimately to Rome, Paul stopped in Miletus. There he summoned the elders of the Ephesian church and gave his final charge to them. He was keenly sensitive to the perils that threatened the church; therefore he reminded the elders of the resources at their disposal.

Paul entrusted the Ephesian church to the protection and care of God. His call constrained him to be absent from the church, but he confidently left the congregation in the Lord's hands. He believed that God would take care of the Ephesian church, supply all her needs, sustain her amid all difficulties, and bring her to the ultimate condition of glory in her final inheritance.

This building up of this church—bringing her to her final glory—would be accomplished through God's gracious Word. The Word is no weak instrument. It is the power of God unto salvation. It originates in grace, reveals grace, and produces grace. It is by this Word that God is building up His church today and preparing her for the inheritance that belongs to all those who have been set apart for God.

GOLDEN TEXT CHALLENGE

"TAKE HEED THEREFORE UNTO YOURSELVES, AND TO ALL THE FLOCK, OVER THE WHICH THE HOLY GHOST HATH MADE YOU OVERSEERS, TO FEED THE CHURCH OF GOD, WHICH HE HATH PURCHASED WITH HIS OWN BLOOD" (Acts 20:28).

Paul told the Ephesian elders that they were now responsible for feeding the flock of God. They had been charged with this responsibility by the Holy Ghost, and now they were responsible for the welfare of God's heritage.

The flock of God had been purchased at great price—the blood of the Lord Jesus Christ. It was now the responsibility of the Ephesian leaders to keep themselves guiltless of the blood of that flock.

Observe that Paul called upon the Ephesians to take heed to themselves first of all; that is, they were to keep their lives spotless and pure. All that he had previously said about himself, they were thereafter by faithfulness and good conscience to manifest in their own ministry. They were to give heed to their own responsibility as they took note of the need of the flock of God. Paul would no longer be with them, so the responsibility would thereafter be theirs.

Testifying About Christ

Acts 26:1-32

INTRODUCTION

The apostle Paul willingly experienced persecution and being held unjustly under arrest because he sensed he was in the will of God and that the Lord was accomplishing something through him in spite of the circumstances. In Acts 25 and 26, Paul is a prisoner in Caesarea, the headquarters of the Roman government over Judea, for about two years.

Just days after Festus became governor of Caesarea, the Jewish officials in Jerusalem tried to get him to send Paul to Jerusalem for another trial. They had in mind a plot of ambushing Paul along the way to kill him. Instead, Festus invited the Jewish leaders to come to Caesarea and accuse him there. They did so, and the same old charges were brought, without evidence or witnesses, and Paul's innocence stood out clearly. Festus, however, was anxious to please the Jews and tried to persuade Paul to go to Jerusalem to be tried on the religious charges leveled against him.

Instead, being a Roman citizen, Paul made an appeal to stand trial before Caesar. This would do two things: (1) give Paul a final decision concerning his case and (2) get him to Rome, where God had revealed that He wanted Paul to testify for Him. "After Festus had conferred with his council, he declared: 'You have appealed to Caesar. To Caesar you will go!'" (25:12 NIV).

A few days later, while Paul was waiting to be shipped to Rome, King Agrippa II and his wife, Bernice, came to Caesarea to welcome Festus into his new role as governor. Soon the subject of the prisoner Paul came up. Agrippa's curiosity was aroused, and he asked to have a hearing with Paul, which was arranged for the next day.

Unit Theme:
The Expanding Church (Acts, Part 2)

Central Truth:
Christians are to witness about Christ.

Focus:
Review Paul's testimony before Agrippa and use it as a model for witnessing of Christ.

Context:
The apostle Paul witnesses to King Agrippa in Caesarea, about AD 59.

Golden Text:
"Having therefore obtained help of God, I continue unto this day, witnessing both to small and great, saying none other things than those which the prophets and Moses did say should come" (Acts 26:22).

Study Outline:
I. Life Before Conversion (Acts 26:1-11)
II. Encounter With the Living Christ (Acts 26:12-18)
III. Obedience to Christ's Call (Acts 26:19-29)

I. LIFE BEFORE CONVERSION (Acts 26:1-11)

It was an occasion of great pomp and ceremony as King Agrippa and Bernice entered the audience hall in Caesarea wearing their royal robes. With them came military and civil dignitaries. Then Paul was brought in, and Festus introduced him to Agrippa (25:23-24).

It must have been a remarkable scene: Paul, the humble prisoner in his chains, face-to-face before the leaders of both Roman and Jewish authority in the province. The opportunity to witness to Christ was uppermost in Paul's mind.

A. Nothing to Hide (vv. 1-5)

(Acts 26:1-3 is not included in the printed text.)

4. My manner of life from my youth, which was at the first among mine own nation at Jerusalem, know all the Jews;

5. Which knew me from the beginning, if they would testify, that after the most straitest sect of our religion I lived a Pharisee.

Festus introduced Paul by saying, "I found he had done nothing deserving of death, but because he made his appeal to the Emperor I decided to send him to Rome. But I have nothing definite to write to His Majesty [Caesar] about him. Therefore I have brought him before all of you, and especially before you, King Agrippa, so that as a result of this investigation I may have something to write" (25:25-26 NIV).

Realizing that the hearing was going to be unhurried, and feeling the need of filling in Agrippa with his background, Paul began by greeting the king respectfully and telling of his childhood and youth, emphasizing how he had been raised strictly in the Jewish faith.

By calling Agrippa an "expert in all customs and questions which are among the Jews" (26:3), Paul was not using flattery. Instead, he knew that, although Agrippa was pro-Roman and had been appointed to his position by the Roman government, he also was a student of the Old Testament and therefore could understand Paul's arguments.

Paul said his life was an open book to the Jews. He had been reared as a Pharisee—a member of the strictest group in the Jewish religion. Paul said that if his Jewish opponents were honest, they would have to admit that he had lived in accordance with their strictest laws.

B. Once a Persecutor (vv. 6-11)

6. And now I stand and am judged for the hope of the promise made of God unto our fathers:

7. Unto which promise our twelve tribes, instantly serving God day and night, hope to come. For which hope's sake, king Agrippa, I am accused of the Jews.

8. Why should it be thought a thing incredible with you, that God should raise the dead?

Talk About It:
1. What was King Agrippa knowledgeable about (vv. 2-3)?
2. How was Paul brought up (vv. 4-5)?

"You cannot change the past, and you can't always control the present, but you can push the past into its proper perspective and you can face the present realistically."
—Hugh Fellows

Testifying About Christ

9. I verily thought with myself, that I ought to do many things contrary to the name of Jesus of Nazareth.

10. Which thing I also did in Jerusalem: and many of the saints did I shut up in prison, having received authority from the chief priests; and when they were put to death, I gave my voice against them.

11. And I punished them oft in every synagogue, and compelled them to blaspheme; and being exceedingly mad against them, I persecuted them even unto strange cities.

Paul said he was being persecuted for the very hope the Jews were holding onto—the coming of the Messiah. God had made this promise to the "fathers" (v. 6) of the faith (Abraham, Isaac, and Jacob), and the 12 tribes of Israel were still anticipating its fulfillment. Through his studies, Agrippa would know that the Jewish faith was focused on the prophesied Messiah.

Paul pinpoints the source of the conflict by asking, "Why should any of you consider it incredible that God raises the dead?" (v. 8 NIV). The Jews did not believe that Jesus Christ was the Messiah, so they certainly did not believe God had resurrected Him after His crucifixion.

Paul had once been like the other Pharisees in his stand against Christians. He was so certain that Jesus was a blasphemous impostor that he did everything he could to stop the spread of the Christian faith. Through the authority of the chief priests, he arrested every Christian he could find.

The phrase "gave my voice" (v. 10) means that Paul cast his vote against arrested believers, sentencing them to death. This may indicate that he gave his consent to their death, or that he literally had a part in deciding their fate. However, as seen in John 18:31, the Jews were not normally authorized to exercise the death penalty.

Paul was not satisfied with arresting only the Christians living in Jerusalem. In his misguided zeal, he also went to foreign cities to persecute Christ's followers.

II. ENCOUNTER WITH THE LIVING CHRIST (Acts 26:12-18)
A. Christ Reveals Himself (vv. 12-15)

12. Whereupon as I went to Damascus with authority and commission from the chief priests,

13. At midday, O king, I saw in the way a light from heaven, above the brightness of the sun, shining round about me and them which journeyed with me.

14. And when we were all fallen to the earth, I heard a voice speaking unto me, and saying in the Hebrew tongue, Saul, Saul, why persecutest thou me? it is hard for thee to kick against the pricks.

15. And I said, Who art thou, Lord? And he said, I am Jesus whom thou persecutest.

Talk About It:
1. Why did Paul say he was being judged (vv. 6-8)?
2. Describe Paul's former life (vv. 9-10).
3. How far did Paul go in persecuting believers (v. 11)?

"Mr. Lely, I desire you would use all your skill to paint my picture truly like me, and not flatter me at all; but remark [re-create] all these roughness, pimples, warts, and everything as you see me, otherwise I will never pay a farthing for it."
—Oliver Cromwell

Talk About It:
1. What "authority" had Paul been given (v. 12)?
2. What did Jesus say is difficult to do (v. 14)?

Paul related how he was on his way to Damascus of Syria, located 140 miles north of Jerusalem, when a blinding light shone on him. It came from heaven, but it was not the sun—it was brighter than the sun. This was a supernatural light.

Paul and his traveling companions were knocked to the ground, and then a voice spoke to him in the Hebrew language, asking, "Why do you persecute me? It hurts you to kick against the goads" (v. 14 RSV). *Goads* were pointed rods used to keep oxen in line when plowing a field. Paul had been kicking against much more than a farmer's efforts—he had been opposing the divine will.

When Paul asked for the speaker to identify Himself, it is obvious that he knew the speaker was divine, for Paul called Him "Lord" (v. 15). The answer came, "I am Jesus whom thou persecutest." Jesus took Paul's attacks against Christians personally. They represented Christ, so it was as if Paul were persecuting Christ, whom Paul had thought was dead.

This is the third time in the Book of Acts that the story of Paul's conversion is recorded. First is the narrative describing his coming to Christ (ch. 9). The second time, Paul is in Jerusalem testifying to a crowd who is angry when Paul is charged with blaspheming the Temple (ch. 22). Now Paul is speaking to civil and religious officials, with his focus on one man—Agrippa.

"During a long life I have had to eat my words many times, and I have found it a very nourishing diet."
—**Winston Churchill**

B. Christ Commissions Paul (vv. 16-18)

16. But rise, and stand upon thy feet: for I have appeared unto thee for this purpose, to make thee a minister and a witness both of these things which thou hast seen, and of those things in the which I will appear unto thee;

17. Delivering thee from the people, and from the Gentiles, unto whom now I send thee,

18. To open their eyes, and to turn them from darkness to light, and from the power of Satan unto God, that they may receive forgiveness of sins, and inheritance among them which are sanctified by faith that is in me.

As does the original account in Acts 9, we see Jesus telling Paul to get on his feet. However, in this abbreviated version, Paul does not tell how he was literally blinded for three days by the heavenly light. Instead, Paul details the mission Jesus gave him to carry out: he was to be both a servant and a witness of what was being revealed to him and what would be shown to him. Paul later wrote, "The gospel I preached is not something that man made up. I did not receive it from any man, nor was I taught it; rather, I received it by revelation from Jesus Christ" (Gal. 1:11-12 NIV).

At his calling, Jesus warned Paul that he would face opposition from both Jews and Gentiles, as was happening now: Paul was standing before his Jewish accusers while in the custody of the

Talk About It:
1. Why did Jesus appear to Paul (v. 16)?
2. How would Jesus help Paul (v. 17)?
3. What would Jesus accomplish through Paul (v. 18)?

Roman government. Yet Christ would be with Paul, and deliver him. And God would use him to open the spiritually blinded eyes of Gentiles, bringing them out of darkness into light, and leading them into sanctification and eternal life through faith in Christ.

That was Paul's mission right now: to lead this one man, Agrippa, into a relationship with the living Christ.

III. OBEDIENCE TO CHRIST'S CALL (Acts 26:19-29)
A. Following the Vision (vv. 19-23)

19. Whereupon, O king Agrippa, I was not disobedient unto the heavenly vision:

20. But shewed first unto them of Damascus, and at Jerusalem, and throughout all the coasts of Judaea, and then to the Gentiles, that they should repent and turn to God, and do works meet for repentance.

21. For these causes the Jews caught me in the temple, and went about to kill me.

22. Having therefore obtained help of God, I continue unto this day, witnessing both to small and great, saying none other things than those which the prophets and Moses did say should come:

23. That Christ should suffer, and that he should be the first that should rise from the dead, and should shew light unto the people, and to the Gentiles.

Paul advised Agrippa that he had accepted the challenge and call of Christ and had become devoted to serving Him faithfully, in every way striving to obey the will of Christ in evangelizing the Gentiles. He reviewed how the Lord had led him to witness, first at home and then abroad to the Gentiles, to accomplish the three-fold effect in their lives: repentance, conversion, and good works.

Verse 21 is not just narrative; it is also an accusation against the Jews for opposing the very things they claimed to stand for. They were so prejudiced against the Gentiles, and so proudly exclusive, that they could not bear the thought of sharing God with others. For all practical purposes, a lot of professing Christians today exhibit this same attitude toward non-Christians around them.

Paul gave the Lord the credit for helping him to have such a wide ministry, and for being with him, even at this very moment (v. 22)! His statement was made in such a way that his hearers would understand that, at that very moment, he was obeying God in witnessing to them.

Paul claimed to base his teachings squarely upon the Bible and Jewish orthodoxy. Nothing that he preached was contrary to the Scriptures. It would be wonderful today if all the preachers in our land could truthfully make this claim of preaching the pure Word of God.

Talk About It:
1. How did Paul respond to Christ's call (vv. 19-20)?
2. How did the Jews respond to Paul (v. 21)?
3. Describe the scope and the message of Paul's ministry (vv. 22-23).

Christ crucified and Christ resurrected were the two central themes of Paul's preaching wherever he went. Any effective preaching today should emphasize these themes also. It was Christ's suffering and death that was such a stumbling block to the Jews, for they had a strong, preconceived idea that He would be to them like an earthly king, and that He would be theirs exclusively, elevating them to superiority over the Gentiles.

B. Reprimanding Paul (vv. 24-26)

24. And as he thus spake for himself, Festus said with a loud voice, Paul, thou art beside thyself; much learning doth make thee mad.

25. But he said, I am not mad, most noble Festus; but speak forth the words of truth and soberness.

26. For the king knoweth of these things, before whom also I speak freely: for I am persuaded that none of these things are hidden from him; for this thing was not done in a corner.

Festus probably thought that Paul's strong statements were offensive to his guest, King Agrippa, and that he had better step in and halt Paul's words. He stated that he thought Paul was a bit out of his mind and confused by being overeducated.

Answering Festus with respect, Paul insisted on the correctness and truthfulness of what he was saying, and that he understood perfectly what he was talking about. In verse 26, Paul spoke very frankly, directing his words mainly to Agrippa. He knew that Agrippa would not deny accepted Jewish doctrine concerning the prophecies of the Messiah. He knew also that Agrippa would be well aware of the growth of Christianity in his kingdom, and what its beginnings were, tracing back to Golgotha. Paul expected his testimony to receive every consideration and implied, by his words, that his present circumstances did not permit any frivolous presentation of fanaticism.

Talk About It:
1. How did Festus respond (v. 24)?
2. What two things were on Paul's side (v. 25)?

C. Challenging Agrippa (vv. 27-29)

27. King Agrippa, believest thou the prophets? I know that thou believest.

28. Then Agrippa said unto Paul, Almost thou persuadest me to be a Christian.

29. And Paul said, I would to God, that not only thou, but also all that hear me this day, were both almost, and altogether such as I am, except these bonds.

Agrippa could not deny belief in "the prophets" (v. 22). His rule over his people depended on his manifesting a certain amount of orthodoxy in order to have their allegiance. Again, out of sheer fear of the Almighty, he probably believed. There are many people today like Agrippa, who are intellectually orthodox, but who have never let the doctrines change them in any way.

Talk About It:
1. What "almost" happened (v. 28)?
2. What was Paul's desire for those who heard him (v. 29)?

Testifying About Christ

Paul's question implied belief in the Messiah, and hence belief in the Christ whom Paul preached. Agrippa properly understood it as an invitation to express his acceptance of Paul's testimony and interpretation of Scripture, which, in turn, would lead to Agrippa's becoming a Christian.

Whether spoken in sincerity or in sarcasm, Agrippa's words in verse 28 indicate that he had no way of countering Paul's argument. However, Paul's question had called for a decision, and Agrippa, seemingly reluctantly, decided against becoming a Christian.

One cannot become a half-Christian, or a part-Christian. In the words of Christ, one "cannot serve God and mammon" (Matt. 6:24).

Verse 29 of the text contains Paul's last dramatic words, spoken as he held up his arms draped with chains, looking into Agrippa's eyes and speaking with gripping sincerity. Here is Paul's desire, not only for Agrippa, but for you and me! His overwhelming concern, even as a prisoner, was not his personal freedom from physical bondage, but everyone's freedom from spiritual bondage.

Concluding the hearing, the king arose and remarked to Festus that Paul certainly was innocent and could have been set free if he had not appealed to Caesar (vv. 30-32).

"Man is lost because he is separated from God, his true reference point, by true moral guilt. But he never will be nothing. Therein lies the horror of his lostness. For man to be lost, in all his uniqueness and wonder, is tragic."
—**Francis Schaeffer**

CONCLUSION

Paul took advantage of this unusual opportunity to witness for Christ. Our opportunities come daily, and we are not restricted as Paul was. Do we make the most of these opportunities to testify about our relationship with Christ?

GOLDEN TEXT CHALLENGE

"HAVING THEREFORE OBTAINED HELP OF GOD, I CONTINUE UNTO THIS DAY, WITNESSING BOTH TO SMALL AND GREAT, SAYING NONE OTHER THINGS THAN THOSE WHICH THE PROPHETS AND MOSES DID SAY SHOULD COME" (Acts 26:22).

It was now above 20 years since Paul was converted, and all that time he had been very busy preaching the Gospel in the midst of hazards. And what was it that bore him up? Not any strength of his own resolutions, but having obtained help of God; for therefore, because the work was so great and he had so much opposition, he could not otherwise have gone on in it, but by help obtained of God. . . .

Paul mentions it as an evidence that he had his commission from God and that from Him he had ability to execute it. The preachers of the Gospel could never have done, and suffered, and prospered, as they did, if they had not had immediate help from heaven, which they would not have had if it had not been the cause of God that they were now pleading.

Paul preached no doctrine but what agreed with the scriptures of the Old Testament: He witnessed both to small and great, to young and old, rich and poor, learned and unlearned, obscure and illustrious, all being concerned in it. It was an evidence of the condescending grace of the Gospel that it was witnessed to the meanest, and the poor were welcome to the knowledge of it; and of the incontestable truth and power of it that it was neither afraid nor ashamed to show itself to the greatest.

The enemies of Paul objected against him that he preached something more than that men should repent, and turn to God, and do works meet for repentance. These indeed were but what the prophets of the Old Testament had preached; but, besides these, he had preached Christ, and His death, and His resurrection, and this was what they quarreled with him for.—*Matthew Henry's Commentary*

Ministering in Adversity

Acts 27:1 through 28:31

INTRODUCTION

When the hearing before Festus and Agrippa was over, it was agreed that Paul could properly have been set at liberty if he had not appealed to Caesar (Acts 26:32). However, he would never have had this hearing with such a verdict if he had not appealed his case from the hands of the malicious Jews who would have killed him. But now the issue was settled. He must go to Rome.

For a number of years Paul had set his eyes on Rome, where he longed to preach. It had always been his policy to select strategic centers that had not been worked by the apostles. From these major cities the natural intercourse of life would carry the Gospel out as converts became faithful witnesses.

Rome, as capital of the empire, was especially desired as a location. Paul had written perhaps his greatest epistle to the body of believers that had sprung up there. And he continued to pray and hope for the day he would visit Rome in person. His prayers were answered in a strange way, but wonderfully in spite of everything.

It is the same with servants of Christ today. The Lord may place a burden upon our heart for a particular place or a specific ministry, and we may envision ourselves in that certain place or performing that certain task. However, the way God eventually moves us into that place of service is often not the way we expected it to happen, and the ministry itself may be more challenging than we had imagined. Yet, through the grace of God, we are enabled to minister effectively, joyfully, and persistently.

Unit Theme:
The Expanding Church (Acts, Part 2)

Central Truth:
God gives Christians the strength and courage to minister in all circumstances.

Focus:
Acknowledge that Christians often face adversity when ministering for Christ and serve the Lord courageously.

Context:
About AD 60, Paul survives a shipwreck, ministers in Malta, and goes to Rome.

Golden Text:
"Therefore, seeing we have this ministry, as we have received mercy, we faint not" (2 Cor. 4:1).

Study Outline:
I. Adverse Circumstances (Acts 27:1, 13-26, 40-44)
II. Miraculous Ministry (Acts 28:1-10)
III. Amazing Opportunity (Acts 28:16-31)

I. ADVERSE CIRCUMSTANCES (Acts 27:1, 13-26, 40-44)

A. Support for Paul (v. 1)

1. And when it was determined that we should sail into Italy, they delivered Paul and certain other prisoners unto one named Julius, a centurion of Augustus' band.

The "we," of course, indicates that Luke, a physician and the author of the book, was in the party. It has been suggested that Luke may have been permitted as a medical man. Or since the vessel was engaged in private enterprise, it is possible that Paul's companions may have been allowed as independent passengers. In any case, Paul's position was as a prisoner among many others, though he did have preferential treatment. They were all under the charge of a Roman centurion named Julius, who was responsible for their safe delivery at Rome.

While this was not the way Paul had dreamed of visiting Rome, it was an answer to his prayers. And it may have been the best way to go.

B. Peril at Sea (vv. 13-20)

13. And when the south wind blew softly, supposing that they had obtained their purpose, loosing thence, they sailed close by Crete.

14. But not long after there arose against it a tempestuous wind, called Euroclydon.

15. And when the ship was caught, and could not bear up into the wind, we let her drive.

16. And running under a certain island which is called Clauda, we had much work to come by the boat:

17. Which when they had taken up, they used helps, undergirding the ship; and, fearing lest they should fall into the quicksands, strake sail, and so were driven.

18. And we being exceedingly tossed with a tempest, the next day they lightened the ship;

19. And the third day we cast out with our own hands the tackling of the ship.

20. And when neither sun nor stars in many days appeared, and no small tempest lay on us, all hope that we should be saved was then taken away.

Paul had warned the men not to leave port at this time of year because of the storm hazards (v. 10). But a day of fair weather encouraged them to seek a more comfortable port to spend the winter. It was not long until all Paul's fears were realized and they were at the mercy of the storm. Since the wind was so strong that they couldn't steer in the face of it, they could only go with it and hope to outlast it before shipwreck (v. 15).

Some temporary relief was found as they passed on the leeward side of a small island. This shelter gave them opportunity to bring on deck the lifeboat that was towed behind the ship.

Euroclydon (you-ROCK-lie-dun)—v. 14—meaning "east wind," a typhoon-like gale that would blow from the northeast across the Mediterranean Sea

quicksands (v. 17)—sandbars

Talk About It:
1. What wrong assumption did the sailors make (v. 13)?
2. What desperate measures did the sailors take (vv. 17-19)?
3. When did the sailors give up hope (v. 20)?

Some suggest that Luke is remembering the blisters from tugging on the rope when he mentions the "much work" in verse 16.

They apparently used cables to undergird the ship so it would not be broken by the violence of wind and wave. The "quicksands" that frightened them (v. 17) were the sandbars along the coast to northern Africa, which were some thirty-five miles away. So they "lowered the sea anchor and let the ship be driven along" (NIV).

As in the case of Jonah's storm on the Mediterranean Sea, they began to throw the cargo overboard to allow the ship to ride higher above the waves lest water fill the ship. Yet they kept some food and perhaps some other cargo for ballast (see v. 38).

The "tackling" (v. 19) probably refers to the furnishings and equipment of the ship. Anything that the passengers could lift from the deck was thrown into the sea as the fury of the storm increased.

The continued bad weather not only tossed them mercilessly through the darkness, but it also deprived them of any means of knowing their course. Conditions continued to grow worse until all natural hope had faded.

> "Sometimes we have to come to the end of ourselves before we get to the bottom of things."
> —Gary Gulbranson

C. Word of Encouragement (vv. 21-26)

21. But after long abstinence Paul stood forth in the midst of them, and said, Sirs, ye should have hearkened unto me, and not have loosed from Crete, and to have gained this harm and loss.

22. And now I exhort you to be of good cheer: for there shall be no loss of any man's life among you, but of the ship.

23. For there stood by me this night the angel of God, whose I am, and whom I serve,

24. Saying, Fear not, Paul; thou must be brought before Caesar: and, lo, God hath given thee all them that sail with thee.

25. Wherefore, sirs, be of good cheer: for I believe God, that it shall be even as it was told me.

26. Howbeit we must be cast upon a certain island.

The abstinence from food (v. 21) could be for various reasons, such as difficulty of cooking, spoiling of food by seawater, seasickness, and so on. It also may refer to Paul's intentional abstinence in order to devote himself to prayer.

Paul probably had held back from giving his advice until the others had given up hope. Maybe now they would listen to him. He reminded them of his warnings when they were back on Crete.

In the midst of the turmoil, and while the pagan passengers were calling on their gods and losing their hope, Paul had received a message from the Lord. No one's life would be lost! Some of the people aboard probably sneered at what seemed to be an impossibility, but Paul's calm and authoritative assurance must have comforted many of them.

Talk About It:
1. What does "long abstinence" mean (v. 21)?
2. What did Paul remind the sailors about (v. 22)?
3. Why should they be cheerful (vv. 22, 25)?
4. What was God's will for Paul (v. 24)?

The same angel who appeared unto Paul in Acts 23:11 to assure him that he would some day witness for God in Rome now came to remind and reassure Paul that the promise would be kept.

When God makes a promise, it will be kept. We must not lose our faith nor feel that He has forgotten us, just because we have been plunged into adverse circumstances. These very circumstances may eventually be recognized as having been very much related to the keeping of the promise. God stands by those who stand by Him. We overcome through Him; but, as someone once said, "If we're going to overcome, we'll have to be willing to undergo, also."

The angel reaffirmed the promise made more than two years before back in Jerusalem. He was still working it out.

Why did Paul have to undergo these circumstances? One reason, plainly, is that he might have the opportunity to witness to his shipmates. The Lord clearly stated that it was because of Paul's being aboard the ship that the others were saved from drowning.

Paul's utter confidence in God and the specific information that he had were the only bright spots in their situation. But these were indeed the key to the rescue. The apostle concluded his message to the sailors by saying, "Nevertheless, we must run aground on some island" (v. 26 NIV).

D. All Safe (vv. 40-44)

40. And when they had taken up the anchors, they committed themselves unto the sea, and loosed the rudder bands, and hoised up the mainsail to the wind, and made toward shore.

41. And falling into a place where two seas met, they ran the ship aground; and the forepart stuck fast, and remained unmoveable, but the hinder part was broken with the violence of the waves.

42. And the soldiers' counsel was to kill the prisoners, lest any of them should swim out, and escape.

43. But the centurion, willing to save Paul, kept them from their purpose; and commanded that they which could swim should cast themselves first into the sea, and get to land:

44. And the rest, some on boards, and some on broken pieces of the ship. And so it came to pass, that they escaped all safe to land.

As the morning light revealed their situation, the sailors saw they were near the shore. They did not recognize exactly where they were, but they knew they had to attempt to get the boat out of the ocean. They saw on the shoreline a place where a creek

Talk About It:
1. Describe the shipwreck (vv. 40-41).

Ministering in Adversity

or river entered the ocean (v. 39). If they could reach that inlet, it would provide safety from the rocks and stormy sea.

Verse 40 describes their efforts to safely beach the ship. They brought in the anchors, which had held them from the rocks, and loosed the rudders. On ancient vessels, the rudders were two large steering oars on each side of the boat. They placed the oars in the water in an effort to steer the ship into the inlet.

Verse 41 describes what happened when the ship moved into the inlet. The sailors could not see that where the sea and the river met, there was a serious undercurrent, or crosscurrent, that caught the ship. The ship was apparently caught in the clay bottom of the river in the front, and the stern was caught in the raging crosscurrents of the sea and river. The stern was battered, and because the boat could not move, the timbers were cracked and soon gave way to the constant battering of the strong currents.

In the confusion of 276 men jumping overboard to escape the breaking up of the ship, some of the soldiers thought they could best serve the empire by killing the prisoners rather than having to account for any of them escaping. But again, the centurion was used by God to save Paul and the other prisoners. Psalm 37:23 reminds us that "the steps of a good man are ordered by the Lord." That precept of Scripture was fulfilled in both Paul's and the centurion's lives because no steps (actions) were taken foolishly. It was divine wisdom (whether recognized by the centurion or not).

The men rushing to escape the sinking ship are vividly described in the final verses. Some grabbed pieces of the breaking ship and used them as flotation devices to reach the shore safely. Remember that although they ate that morning, they probably had not eaten in two weeks. They were physically and emotionally exhausted. Yet everyone arrived safely.

II. MIRACULOUS MINISTRY (Acts 28:1-10)
A. Hospitality (vv. 1-2)

1. And when they were escaped, then they knew that the island was called Melita.

2. And the barbarous people shewed us no little kindness: for they kindled a fire, and received us every one, because of the present rain, and because of the cold.

Melita is now the modern island of Malta. It is located about sixty miles south of Sicily and contains only about ninety-five square miles of land. Its name means "refuge." Paul's ship was wrecked here, and he and his shipmates found it inhabited by people who proved themselves to be peaceful and hospitable. The natives built fires to warm and dry out the shivering, water-soaked refugees. How differently these natives treated Paul than did the people of Jerusalem!

2. How did the centurion make a difference (vv. 42-43)?
3. What miracle took place (v. 44)?

"In His will is our peace."
—**Dante Alighieri**

barbarous people (v. 2)—natives

Talk About It:
How did the people of Malta help the shipwreck victims?

B. Protection (vv. 3-6)

3. And when Paul had gathered a bundle of sticks, and laid them on the fire, there came a viper out of the heat, and fastened on his hand.

4. And when the barbarians saw the venomous beast hang on his hand, they said among themselves, No doubt this man is a murderer, whom, though he hath escaped the sea, yet vengeance suffereth not to live.

5. And he shook off the beast into the fire, and felt no harm.

6. Howbeit they looked when he should have swollen, or fallen down dead suddenly: but after they had looked a great while, and saw no harm come to him, they changed their minds, and said that he was a god.

Helping with the fires, Paul had gathered a bundle of sticks from which a snake came out and bit him. The natives recognized it as a well-known poisonous kind and expected Paul to swell up and die. They looked upon it as an act of God in judging a man who was worthy of death for committing a crime; but when Paul showed no signs of weakness, after being observed for a long period of time, the natives rightly changed their minds and decided Paul had the miraculous help of God. In fact, they believed Paul to be a god himself. We can see how their minds were prepared to receive the Gospel message and the witness of Paul soon after this miracle.

C. Healings (vv. 7-10)

7. In the same quarters were possessions of the chief man of the island, whose name was Publius; who received us, and lodged us three days courteously.

8. And it came to pass, that the father of Publius lay sick of a fever and of a bloody flux: to whom Paul entered in, and prayed, and laid his hands on him, and healed him.

9. So when this was done, others also, which had diseases in the island, came, and were healed:

10. Who also honoured us with many honours; and when we departed, they laded us with such things as were necessary.

The chief man of the island of Melita was named Publius, who invited Paul and his party to stay with him three days. At this same time, Publius' father was sick. Paul went to see him, prayed, put his hands upon him, and he was healed.

After this, many others from all over the island came with their sick people, and they were healed. As a result, Paul and his party were greatly honored by the islanders, and many gifts were given them. The gifts probably consisted of things which the refugees needed since they had lost all their possessions in the shipwreck.

Talk About It:
1. What did the natives assume (vv. 3-4)?
2. How did the people's attitude change (v. 6)?

"God has marvelous ways of taking our worst tragedies and turning them into His most glorious triumphs."
—Joseph Stowell

bloody flux (v. 8)— dysentery

Talk About It:
1. Describe Paul's ministry on Malta (vv. 8-9).
2. How were Paul and his companions served (v. 10)?

Ministering in Adversity

III. AMAZING OPPORTUNITY (Acts 28:16-31)

Due to the weather, Paul and his shipwrecked associates were forced to spend the better part of the winter on Malta, probably leaving in February, after three months there. The Acts account says they left on a ship whose sign was Castor and Pollux (v. 11), probably another Alexandrian grain ship which had weathered the winter at Malta.

A. Arrival in Rome (v. 16)

16. And when we came to Rome, the centurion delivered the prisoners to the captain of the guard: but Paul was suffered to dwell by himself with a soldier that kept him.

Arriving at Rome, the centurion delivered the prisoners to the captain of the guard, but Paul was given preferential treatment and was allowed to rent a house for himself and simply be guarded by a soldier assigned to watch him and report on his movements. Thus, God, in a roundabout and miraculous way, had kept His promise and had brought Paul to Rome.

Talk About It:
What privilege was Paul given?

B. Meeting With the Jews (vv. 17-20)

17. And it came to pass, that after three days Paul called the chief of the Jews together: and when they were come together, he said unto them, Men and brethren, though I have committed nothing against the people, or customs of our fathers, yet was I delivered prisoner from Jerusalem into the hands of the Romans.

18. Who, when they had examined me, would have let me go, because there was no cause of death in me.

19. But when the Jews spake against it, I was constrained to appeal unto Caesar; not that I had ought to accuse my nation of.

20. For this cause therefore have I called for you, to see you, and to speak with you: because that for the hope of Israel I am bound with this chain.

After getting settled in his new residence, Paul invited the Jewish leaders to a conference at his house. He could not go to the synagogue because of being confined as a prisoner, but he was allowed to have guests.

Paul explained why he was there as a prisoner and began to relate the circumstances. He declared his innocence of the charges which had been trumped up against him. He did his best to establish confidence and good relationships between himself and the Jewish brethren in Rome.

Paul made it clear that the charges were those of the Jews and not of the Romans, for the Romans had acknowledged his innocence of having committed any crimes against their laws or government. Paul was leading up to a defense and explanation of the specific beliefs that he held in Christ. The charges for which he was imprisoned were to be the very basis for his witnessing for Christ in Rome.

Talk About It:
1. What did Paul tell the Jews in Rome he had *not* done?
2. What is the "hope of Israel" Paul mentions (v. 20)?

The Jews had insisted on Paul's being punished in spite of his innocence. Paul was kept under arrest because of political pressure. His only way out seemed to be an appeal to a higher court—one that was not located in the land of Judea, where he could no longer get a fair hearing. This is called, in legal language today, "a change of venue," as well as an appeal. The next higher court was that of Caesar himself. Paul made it plain that he had no accusations of his own to level against his nation. This must have relieved the Jews at Rome to know that Paul was not going to stir up any trouble for them in this regard.

Paul now appealed to the local leaders for a hearing of his religious belief. His "chain" (v. 20) testified strongly to the strength of what Paul believed, for he was willing to put up with this persecution rather than give up his faith in Christ.

C. Testimony for Christ (vv. 21-23)

21. And they said unto him, We neither received letters out of Judaea concerning thee, neither any of the brethren that came shewed or spake any harm of thee.

22. But we desire to hear of thee what thou thinkest: for as concerning this sect, we know that every where it is spoken against.

23. And when they had appointed him a day, there came many to him into his lodging; to whom he expounded and testified the kingdom of God, persuading them concerning Jesus, both out of the law of Moses, and out of the prophets, from morning till evening.

No one among Paul's accusers in Jerusalem had taken the trouble to send any official communication to the Jews at Rome to tell them what to expect when Paul arrived. They evidently were happy to have him out of their way and were content to cause him the tremendous inconvenience of the trip to Rome and his trial there. Paul's reputation for righteousness could not be denied by honest people. His testimony of innocence was borne out by his life.

Although the Jews at Rome claimed not to have any knowledge of Paul's case or background, they did say that they had heard of Christianity, and that it had a bad reputation, from all they had heard (v. 22).

A time was set for Paul to explain all the details of his case, his beliefs, Christianity, and the Bible prophecies and teachings about the Messiah. He "expounded and testified" (v. 23). That is, he read from the Bible, explaining the text as he went, and then applied what he had read to his own life by way of a personal testimony. He who would win souls must know well the Scriptures, and he must have a vital, firsthand experience of salvation.

Ministering in Adversity

Paul was untiring in his teaching, continuing "from morning till evening." It was a full day's work for him; but, undoubtedly it was extremely satisfying, for he knew that he was in God's will. His house was his church and school, and every day was a day of teaching and worship.

D. Response to Paul's Ministry (vv. 24-29)
(Acts 28:25-28 is not included in the printed text.)
24. And some believed the things which were spoken, and some believed not.
29. And when he had said these words, the Jews departed, and had great reasoning among themselves.

Paul did not have 100 percent success in his ministry, but a number of people did believe his teaching and his testimony. The Jewish community in Rome began to be split, as was inevitable.

No doubt many arguments and discussions resulted from Paul's teachings. Disagreements over interpretations of Scripture and further research into biblical passages were a daily occurrence. Paul quoted a passage from Isaiah 6:9 which says, "Go unto this people, and say, Hearing ye shall hear, and shall not understand; and seeing ye shall see, and not perceive" (Acts 28:26). From long experience, Paul knew that not all people would accept the news of Christ, especially among the Jews.

When it became apparent that most of the Jews had made up their minds whether to accept Paul's teachings, Paul announced that he would be preaching to the Gentiles as well. This caused great consternation among the Jews. They had lived lives of spiritual isolation from the other peoples of the world for so long that they were deeply prejudiced.

E. Freedom to Preach (vv. 30-31)
30. And Paul dwelt two whole years in his own hired house, and received all that came in unto him,
31. Preaching the kingdom of God, and teaching those things which concern the Lord Jesus Christ, with all confidence, no man forbidding him.

Paul continued to preach two entire years as he waited in his rented house for his trial to come up. During this time he was free to preach to all comers about the kingdom of God and the Lord Jesus Christ. He also wrote many letters, among them being Ephesians, Colossians, Philippians, and Philemon. In Philippians 4:22 we learn that Paul even won to Christ some of the emperor's servants. "The doors of the church were opened to the Gentiles by the Holy Spirit, and the Gospel continued to triumph over all barriers when the greatest missionary and preacher was in chains in Rome" (French Arrington, *The Acts of the Apostles*).

"The world has more winnable people than ever before . . . but it is possible to come out of a ripe field empty-handed."
—Donald McGavran

Talk About It:
1. How did the Roman Jews respond to the Gospel (v. 24)?
2. What did Paul say about their response (vv. 26-27)?
3. What did Paul say he would do (v. 28)?

Talk About It:
Describe these two years of Paul's Roman imprisonment (vv. 30-31).

"The Spirit of Christ is the spirit of missions, and the nearer we get to Him the more intensely missionary we must become."
—Henry Martyn

CONCLUSION

Paul's faith in God continued strong during his persecution, and he made the best of it by being a witness for Christ. His circumstances seemed to help him, in fact, for his devotion to the cause for which he could be seen to be suffering strengthened his verbal witness. Christians should determine to be faithful to God through all the circumstances of life and to witness, as Paul did, to all who will listen.

"When Pompeii was destroyed by the eruption of Mount Vesuvius, there were many persons buried in the ruins who were afterward found in very different positions. There were some found in deep vaults, as if they had gone there for security. There were some found in lofty chambers. But where did they find the Roman sentinel?

"They found him standing at the city gate where he had been placed by the captain, with his hands still grasping his weapon. There, while the earth shook beneath him; there, while the floods of ashes and cinders overwhelmed him, he had stood at his post; and there, after a thousand years, he was found.

"So let Christians stand by their duty in the post where their Captain places them" (*Gospel Trumpet*).

GOLDEN TEXT CHALLENGE

"THEREFORE, SEEING WE HAVE THIS MINISTRY, AS WE HAVE RECEIVED MERCY, WE FAINT NOT" (2 Cor. 4:1).

Ministering the gospel of the Lord Jesus Christ through words and actions during good times is enjoyable. But then there are those difficult times. The Gospel continues to be glorious, but human limitations and discouragement can take its toll.

So how can believers continue in the face of varied forms of opposition?

Paul addressed this matter here, saying we can persevere since it is God who has called us and through His mercy given us the Gospel. As partakers of this glorious truth, we can continue without succumbing to weaknesses or discouragement.

Daily Devotions:
M. Courageous
   Ministry
   1 Kings 18:1-4
T. Wait on the Lord
   Psalm 27:7-14
W. Faith in Adverse
   Circumstances
   Habakkuk 3:16-19
T. Minister Despite
   Complaints
   Mark 14:3-9
F. Minister Despite
   Troubles
   2 Corinthians
   4:7-15
S. God Testifies
   With Miracles
   Hebrews 2:1-4

God's Ultimate Solution for Sin

Leviticus 4:1-12; 16:29-34; Hebrews 9:11-28; 10:19-25

INTRODUCTION

If the problems of our world could be boiled down to one concept alone, it is sin. We cannot make sense of widespread violence, greed, divorce, and abortion outside the moral realm of good and evil. Mass murder, millions of homeless people, a massive industry of pornography, and ongoing warfare choke the life from our world. In an interview, Evangelist Billy Graham summed up the crisis this way:

> I don't see much improvement in man's heart. The whole thing is in man's heart: his desire, his greed, his lust, his pride, his ego. All of these things meshed together bring about some-times a world war and sometimes a small war, but wars are going on everywhere, even in families. It's a personal thing with each of us (*Newsweek*, March 20, 2006).

Both personally and globally, man's heart is laced with a destructive agent that the biblical story addresses head-on.

Western society has devised many sophisticated methods in the attempt to "fix" the problem of the human heart. America has used imprisonment as an answer, since we imprison more people per capita than any other industrialized nation. Walk into any bookstore and you will notice that the self-help movement is also a strategy to handle the heart, with popular books announcing that believing in yourself will solve any need you might have. Finally, the field of medicine has jumped full force into this arena, inventing new medications and counseling therapies each year to help people deal with the pressures of life. Each of these strategies has some value, but if they are the ultimate answer, why does Western society not appear to be morally improving?

Turning to Scripture, we find the true answer to the problem of the human heart. From the moment Eve bit into the forbidden fruit, God has been on a mission to rid creation from the consequences of sin. This solution culminated in the death and resurrection of Jesus, whereby sin was judicially atoned for and victoriously defeated. The Christian life is a life of freedom from sin, not by our own ability, but by the accomplishments of Jesus Christ alone. This is foreshadowed even in the Old Testament Law, which takes the crisis of sin deadly serious.

Unit Theme:
The Gospel Fulfills the Law (Leviticus-Deuteronomy)

Central Truth:
The death of Jesus Christ fulfilled the sacrificial system and brought us complete salvation.

Focus:
Discover how Old Testament sacrifices foreshadowed Christ's sacrifice for sin and receive His salvation.

Context:
Scripture passages in Leviticus point to the final solution for sin which is seen in Hebrews.

Golden Text:
"Now once in the end of the world hath he [Christ] appeared to put away sin by the sacrifice of himself" (Heb. 9:26).

Study Outline:
I. Sacrifices for Sin (Lev. 4:1-12; 16:29-34)
II. Christ's Complete and Final Sacrifice (Heb. 9:11-28)
III. Living in Christ (Heb. 10:19-25)

I. SACRIFICES FOR SIN (Lev. 4:1-12; 16:29-34)

The Book of Leviticus represents the most extensive instructions regarding animal sacrifice in the Old Testament. It stands as the third book in the Pentateuch, also called the Torah ("law"), which consists of the first five books of the Old Testament. These books continue to be the most sacred in Judaism today. Any reader will easily see that Leviticus is concerned with a priestly point of view. This point of view is principally expressed in chapter upon chapter of instructions regarding the proper rationale and methods of sacrifices.

The Book of Leviticus is not considered "pleasure reading" by most Christians. A quick reading of this priestly document seems wildly irrelevant to modern life. Also, it appears to get bogged down in an astonishing amount of detail regarding sacrifices: How precisely should animals be killed and eaten? Which animals should be sacrificed for which sins? How is the community to understand the sacrificial system in the light of faith in their loving and compassionate God? The texts methodically work through these questions, but do not miss the forest for the trees. Instead, the act of sacrifice calls to mind the individual's and the community's commitment to living a life of profound openness before God. Leviticus takes the fallen nature of the human heart seriously, and points to a God who lovingly corrects and transforms the sinner.

A. Unintentional Sins (4:1-12)

(Leviticus 4:8-12 is not included in the printed text.)

1. And the Lord spake unto Moses, saying,

2. Speak unto the children of Israel, saying, If a soul shall sin through ignorance against any of the commandments of the Lord concerning things which ought not to be done, and shall do against any of them:

3. If the priest that is anointed do sin according to the sin of the people; then let him bring for his sin, which he hath sinned, a young bullock without blemish unto the Lord for a sin-offering.

4. And he shall bring the bullock unto the door of the tabernacle of the congregation before the Lord; and shall lay his hand upon the bullock's head, and kill the bullock before the Lord.

5. And the priest that is anointed shall take of the bullock's blood, and bring it to the tabernacle of the congregation:

6. And the priest shall dip his finger in the blood, and sprinkle of the blood seven times before the Lord, before the vail of the sanctuary.

7. And the priest shall put some of the blood upon the horns of the altar of sweet incense before the Lord, which is

in the tabernacle of the congregation; and shall pour all the blood of the bullock at the bottom of the altar of the burnt-offering, which is at the door of the tabernacle of the congregation.

Verse 2 sets up the commandment by showing it was originally *spoken* to the people of Israel. That is, they lived in an oral culture, and the written word largely served the oral tradition. The nation literally stood together and learned the commandments of Leviticus by hearing them read aloud. Perhaps the most incredible thing about this particular bit of instruction is its *attention to intention*. Israel's God is not concerned principally with an abstract system of sacrifices; the human heart takes precedence over the system. Therefore, God makes a distinction between sins committed purposefully and those committed without intention. This foreshadows the teaching ministry of Jesus, who constantly appeals to the human heart's intention as the root of good and evil, particularly in the Sermon on the Mount (Matt. 5—7). A famous historian noted this very point, stating that "in all questions of morality He goes straight to the root; that is, to the disposition and the intention" (Adolf von Harnack, *What Is Christianity?*). Leviticus shows us that Jesus inherited this distinction from the Torah.

Also notable in this segment of Scripture is the acknowledgment of the sins of the "anointed priest" (v. 3 NKJV). Although the priests have been set apart for exclusive service to God in the Tabernacle, this does not elevate them above the status of routine sinners. Leviticus is clear that God will not show favoritism or allow priests to spiritually dominate the people. They are commanded to "practice what they preach" through making sacrifices.

These sacrifices took place in a large tent that could be torn down and erected as Israel made its journey to and through the Promised Land. The Tent of Meeting, or Tabernacle, was considered the community's sacred space.

In this passage we read of two of the sacrificial instruments stationed later in the Temple: the altar and the curtain of the sanctuary. Everything was laid out in precise specifications so the people would view the space as a place where heaven intersected with earth.

Talk About It:
1. What does it mean to "sin through ignorance" (v. 2)?
2. Why is "before the Lord" repeatedly stated (vv. 4, 6-7)?
3. Why were the instructions for making sacrifices so specific?

"It does not matter how small the sins are, provided that their cumulative effect is to edge the man away from the Light and out into the Nothing."
—C. S. Lewis

B. The Day of Atonement (16:29-34)

29. And this shall be a statute for ever unto you: that in the seventh month, on the tenth day of the month, ye shall afflict your souls, and do no work at all, whether it be one of your own country, or a stranger that sojourneth among you:

30. For on that day shall the priest make an atonement for you, to cleanse you, that ye may be clean from all your sins before the Lord.

31. It shall be a sabbath of rest unto you, and ye shall afflict your souls, by a statute for ever.

32. And the priest, whom he shall anoint, and whom he shall consecrate to minister in the priest's office in his father's stead, shall make the atonement, and shall put on the linen clothes, even the holy garments:

33. And he shall make an atonement for the holy sanctuary, and he shall make an atonement for the tabernacle of the congregation, and for the altar, and he shall make an atonement for the priests, and for all the people of the congregation.

34. And this shall be an everlasting statute unto you, to make an atonement for the children of Israel for all their sins once a year. And he did as the Lord commanded Moses.

Although the majority of Leviticus is concerned with the proper methods of routine sacrifices for everyday people and priests, one day per year on the Jewish calendar was set apart for the most significant sacrifice in their culture. The Day of Atonement, or *Yom Kippur* in Hebrew, remains an important holiday in contemporary Israel. It is something the entire community of Israel continues to participate in, and it stems from Leviticus 16. The writer provides a summary paragraph at the end of the chapter.

The commandment is a "lasting ordinance" (v. 29 NIV), not just something for that generation, but also something to last into Israel's perpetuity. It calls for a different kind of Sabbath, one that would not necessarily fall on the traditional time of Saturday, but just as important. Therefore, no one can work in the land, whether Jew or Gentile, and everyone must fast. This is because a single priest will perform a solitary sacrifice that will call the community to walk before God without sin. All members of Israel, and even the physical instruments of worship, will be purified in this act. It is a solemn day for the entire nation.

We know from Leviticus and from later tradition that the Jews continued to practice the sacrifice of Yom Kippur through the time of Jesus and beyond. The innermost room of the Temple, the Most Holy Place, was set aside exclusively for this annual sacrifice. The priests approached it with such reverence that they later tied bells onto the high priest's clothing and a rope around his ankle. Should they cease to hear the sound of the bells, they would have a means of removing his dead body without entering the holy area through the great curtain. This is the context of Mark 15:38, in which Jesus' final breath results in the rending of the Temple's curtain. At Jesus' death, the sacrificial system was fulfilled. Good Friday is the final "day of atonement" for the entire world.

II. CHRIST'S COMPLETE AND FINAL SACRIFICE
(Heb. 9:11-28)

No New Testament book is as emphatic about the connection between the Old Testament system of animal sacrifice and the

---

Talk About It:
1. What instructions were the Israelites given regarding the Day of Atonement (v. 29)?
2. What was the role of the Old Testament priest (v. 30)?
3. Name everything for which atonement was made on this day (v. 33).

"Any cloth may cover our sores, but the finest silk will not cover our sins."
—Henry Smith

God's Ultimate Solution for Sin

death of Jesus as the Book of Hebrews. This is interesting given the fact that we know so little about the origins of this book. Its author, for instance, is unknown. Although several early church fathers assumed that Paul wrote Hebrews, this is unlikely, since the language is not similar to the other Pauline letters, and it would be quite unlike Paul to be anonymous in his writings.

Whoever the author is, he or she knows of Timothy, and probably writes from Rome (see 13:23-24). However, the trail stops there. What is more, the author calls the work a "short letter" (v. 22 NIV), which is strange because it is far from short and doesn't fit the structure of a letter. There are no introductory remarks or personal details. Instead, the book reads like a sermon, or collection of sermons, mailed off to unknown recipients. Perhaps the other designation in verse 22 best describes Hebrews: a "word of exhortation." The author's exhortation appears to concern Jewish Christians who are being tempted or even threatened to rejoin the sacrificial system of the Temple. Hebrews offers no quarter for such a decision. To backpedal on the efficacy of Christ's sacrifice is tantamount to denying Christ himself.

A. The Inaugurator of a New Covenant (vv. 11-15)

11. But Christ being come an high priest of good things to come, by a greater and more perfect tabernacle, not made with hands, that is to say, not of this building;

12. Neither by the blood of goats and calves, but by his own blood he entered in once into the holy place, having obtained eternal redemption for us.

13. For if the blood of bulls and of goats, and the ashes of an heifer sprinkling the unclean, sanctifieth to the purifying of the flesh:

14. How much more shall the blood of Christ, who through the eternal Spirit offered himself without spot to God, purge your conscience from dead works to serve the living God?

15. And for this cause he is the mediator of the new testament, that by means of death, for the redemption of the transgressions that were under the first testament, they which are called might receive the promise of eternal inheritance.

Hebrews 7—10 puts the reader on especially sacred ground, since these chapters explain the way that the death of Jesus perfectly reflects and fulfills the previous covenant God has formed with Israel. Jesus himself originally announced this fulfillment in the Sermon on the Mount in Matthew 5:17, and the writer of Hebrews explores the implications of this in great detail. Yet here we are on tricky ground, for some have read what is called "dispensationalist theology" into texts such as Hebrews 9. Dispensationalist theology arose in the latter half of the 19th century, culminating in the publication of the *Scofield Reference*

Talk About It:
1. How did Jesus enter into the Holy of Holies, and for what purpose (v. 12)?
2. Explain the phrase "without spot" (v. 14).
3. What did Christ's sacrifice accomplish (vv. 14-15)?

Bible just after the turn of the 20th century. This mode of thinking claims that God has worked throughout biblical history in a series of "dispensations." In each of these, God mediated His salvation through differing means. The writer of Hebrews, however, says nothing of this sort. In fact, Hebrews declares that the sacrifice of Christ has mediated salvation to all believers, even those before Christ who participated in the sacrificial system of the Temple! This is because those animal sacrifices functioned as signposts, marking the way to a time when they would be rendered unnecessary. As the writer says in Hebrews 9:13-14, these sacrifices effected an external cleansing, but the sacrifice of Christ works on the inner heart of man.

Whereas animal sacrifices forgave one from the penalties of sin on a judicial basis (that is, the penalty of the sin was transferred to the animal), the sacrifice of Christ works directly on the human conscience, which then directly affects human action. It works not from the outside in, but from the inside out. This is the direction that the singular story of God has been moving toward since the fall of man in Eden, so that despite two distinct covenants in the biblical story, the story itself is one story.

The concept of Jesus Christ as a mediator is not common in the New Testament, although it is preeminent in Hebrews. Outside of Hebrews, it appears in only two passages, both written by Paul (Gal. 3:19-20; 1 Tim. 2:5). Neither of these references convey Christ as the mediator of a new covenant. In fact, without the Book of Hebrews, later theologians may not have come up with the title "New Testament" for the Christian Bible. They may, instead, have referred to a "Hebrew Bible" and a "Christian Bible." Yet by referring to Christ as the mediator of a new covenant/testament/contract, the Book of Hebrews portrays the way Jesus reflects the righteousness of all previous commandments.

Verse 15 of our text indicates the sacrificial system of the old covenant left something lacking. Forgiveness was meted out, but the human heart was not transformed. Jesus' new covenant allows both external and internal freedom from sins.

B. The Centrality of Blood (vv. 16-22)

16. For where a testament is, there must also of necessity be the death of the testator.

17. For a testament is of force after men are dead: otherwise it is of no strength at all while the testator liveth.

18. Whereupon neither the first testament was dedicated without blood.

19. For when Moses had spoken every precept to all the people according to the law, he took the blood of calves and of goats, with water, and scarlet wool, and hyssop, and sprinkled both the book, and all the people,

God's Ultimate Solution for Sin

20. Saying, This is the blood of the testament which God hath enjoined unto you.

21. Moreover he sprinkled with blood both the tabernacle, and all the vessels of the ministry.

22. And almost all things are by the law purged with blood; and without shedding of blood is no remission.

The term "New Testament" does not appear in the actual New Testament in the sense of a body of Christian literature. In fact, anytime the New Testament refers to "scripture," it speaks exclusively of the Old Testament. Before the New Testament, the Old Testament was the only Scripture that the early church possessed.

Hebrews 9 displays the varying meanings Scripture gives to the term *testament*. In verse 16, the same word is used for a will, which can only come into effect after the death of the one it names. Both the old and new covenants worked in this way. In the former, animal sacrifice effected the terms of God's forgiveness. In the latter, the death of Jesus takes its place. The common link is the necessity of the shedding of blood. But why?

Blood denoted the essential life force of creation itself; it was something the Jews were forbidden to ingest under any circumstances. The necessity of bloodshed points to our need to remember that we are created beings, that we do not make the rules, that God and His law are the ultimate realities for appropriate human life. Whenever blood was shed, these things were to be remembered, especially in the light of Jesus' death.

C. The End of Animal Sacrifices (vv. 23-28)

(Hebrews 9:23-27 is not included in the printed text.)

28. So Christ was once offered to bear the sins of many; and unto them that look for him shall he appear the second time without sin unto salvation.

The primary difference between the sacrifices in the Old Testament and the sacrifice of Christ concerns the scope of each. The Old Testament sacrifices required a physical temple; Jesus' sacrifice allowed entrance into the heavenly, or spiritual throne room of God. Equally important, the Old Testament sacrifices were virtually never-ending. In contrast, Jesus' sacrifice was total and complete, inaugurating a new age in which freedom from sin is truly possible.

It seems strange to our ears that the writer would have to make this truth so explicit, but we must keep in mind the context of the audience. They had been steeped in the rituals of sacrificing at the Temple, and it was remarkably radical that Jesus would only have to make one sacrifice that was effective forever. Verse 28 declares that salvation was further reaching than simply the forgiveness of the saved and their entrance into heaven. He will come again to rule and reign on the earth—to bring salvation to those who wait patiently.

Talk About It:
What are the similarities between the Old Testament sacrifices and Christ's sacrifice?

"It is a destructive addition to add anything to Christ."
—**Richard Sibbes**

Talk About It:
1. Where has Christ entered, and what is He doing there (v. 24)?
2. How is Christ's sacrifice superior to the Old Testament sacrifices (vv. 25-26)?
3. Who benefits from Christ's sacrifice (v. 28)?

"Christ is the most tender-hearted Physician. He has ended His passion but not His compassion. He is not fuller of skill than sympathy. . . . Every wound of the patient goes to the heart of the Physician."
—**Thomas Watson**

III. LIVING IN CHRIST (Heb. 10:19-25)

In Hebrews 10, the writer reaches a turning point in the sermonic letter. Since chapter 1, Hebrews has expounded the accomplishments of God in Christ Jesus. Christ is greater than angels (ch. 1) and Moses (ch. 3). He is a great High Priest (chs. 4-5) like Melchizedek (ch. 7). He has initiated a new and glorious covenant (ch. 8) through His sacrifice (chs. 9-10). Finally, in 10:19, the author moves in a new and vital direction toward our response to this great story of God.

A. Christ's Completed Work (vv. 19-21)

(Hebrews 10:19-21 is not included in the printed text.)

The author predicates this new direction with a pithy summary of all that has been said about the accomplishments of Jesus. His death has provided a renewed confidence for the believer, and a pathway to God through the curtain of His broken body. However, it is not just His death but also His resurrected life that continues to profoundly affect the Christian. This is because Christ was resurrected to a new role—that of Great High Priest, the One who presides over the whole house of God.

Talk About It:
1. Why should Christians be bold (v. 19)?
2. Describe "the new and living way" (vv. 20-21).

B. Human Response to Christ's Work (vv. 22-25)

22. Let us draw near with a true heart in full assurance of faith, having our hearts sprinkled from an evil conscience, and our bodies washed with pure water.

23. Let us hold fast the profession of our faith without wavering; (for he is faithful that promised;)

24. And let us consider one another to provoke unto love and to good works:

25. Not forsaking the assembling of ourselves together, as the manner of some is; but exhorting one another: and so much the more, as ye see the day approaching.

Talk About It:
1. In what ways do we need cleansing (v. 22)?
2. What must we "hold unswervingly" (v. 23 NIV)?
3. Why is corporate worship so important (vv. 24-25)?

The writer of Hebrews is not expounding theology for theology's sake. No, the completion of God's story in Christ is vitally relevant to the human situation. In verse 22, the writer begins to explain this human element in the terms of the appropriate response to all that God has done in Christ, saying we should "draw near to God with a sincere heart in full assurance of faith" (NIV). Faith that springs from sincerity of heart brings us close to God. Such a faith will affect both the internal guilty heart and the external body in baptism.

Faith is founded upon hope, and hope takes some aggressiveness on the part of its holder "Let us hold unswervingly to the hope we profess" (v. 23 NIV). We do not only look backward to the death of Christ, but forward to the promise of future salvation for the entire created order. Such a hope calls for an advancing profession of faith.

God's Ultimate Solution for Sin

Love completes the triad of the human response to Christ's death and resurrection (v. 24). This verse is reminiscent of Paul's beautiful treatise on love in 1 Corinthians 13, which he concludes by stating, "And now these three remain: faith, hope and love. But the greatest of these is love" (v. 13 NIV). This love is not individualistic but is formed in the garden of community.

None of Christ's accomplishments can be applied to the heart of the believer apart from the larger community of faith, as verse 25 of the text states. Following Christ is always personal, but never individual. The encouragement of the body of Christ is all the more vital as we await the day of His return. Without that encouragement, we may become sullen and bored. But with the promise of that great day, we are freed to live out the sacrifice of Christ.

"If the true travelers are men of broken heart, poor in spirit, who mourn for sin, who know the music of the Shepherd's voice, who follow the Lamb, who delight in the throne of grace, and who love the place of the cross, then there are but few . . . [who] journey to heaven in fellowship and communion."
—Octavius Winslow

CONCLUSION

The great epochs of the story of God in Scripture center on the cross of Christ. It is the point at which the story of the old age of Israel and the story of the new age of the Church converge. It works backward to restore humanity's fall in Eden and forward to look toward the restoration of all things, in which "God [will] be all in all" (1 Cor. 15:28). The Book of Hebrews connects straightaway to the sacrificial system laid out in Leviticus, in order to prove this vital connection between the new covenant in Christ and the old covenant in the Law. This connection allows us to read the Torah through the lens of Christ, the One who fulfills its every requirement.

GOLDEN TEXT CHALLENGE

"NOW ONCE IN THE END OF THE WORLD HATH HE [CHRIST] APPEARED TO PUT AWAY SIN BY THE SACRIFICE OF HIMSELF" (Heb. 9:26).

One of the first high school students to come to faith in my ministry quickly became a student of Scripture. One Sunday school class we were discussing the return of Christ, and Nate asked a simple question: "When Jesus returns, will He have to die again?" I hadn't been around many new believers, so the question startled me. The answer, however, was easy. Because the Book of Hebrews announces Christ's death once and for all, we can be sure that the guilt of our sin has been wiped clean forever. His return will be one of power and glory!

Daily Devotions:
M. Substitutionary Sacrifice
   Leviticus 1:1-4
T. Sacrifice Is Costly
   2 Samuel 24:18-25
W. The Sacrifice of Christ
   Isaiah 53:4-12
T. A Sacrificial Life
   Mark 10:35-45
F. Sacrifice for Redemption
   1 Peter 1:17-21
S. Sacrifice for Sin
   1 John 1:8—2:2

Be Holy

Leviticus 20:1-10; Deuteronomy 7:6-11; Colossians 3:5-11;
Titus 2:11-12; Hebrews 12:14-28; 1 Peter 1:15-16

Unit Theme:
The Gospel Fulfills the Law (Leviticus-Deuteronomy)

Central Truth:
God commands every Christian to live a holy life.

Focus:
Recognize the need for holiness and live a holy life.

Context:
Old and New Testament passages highlighting the necessity of holiness

Golden Text:
"As he which hath called you is holy, so be ye holy in all manner of conversation" (1 Peter 1:15).

Study Outline:
I. Commanded to Live Holy (Lev. 20:7-8; 1 Peter 1:15-16)
II. Instructions for Holy Living (Lev. 20:1-6, 9-10; Col. 3:5-11; Titus 2:11-12)
III. Motivation for Holy Living (Deut. 7:6-11; Heb. 12:14, 18, 22-28)

INTRODUCTION

When it comes to basic morality, Western culture, especially America, has become quite a mixed bag. There was a time, of course, when America deemed itself a Christian nation, leading many to presently describe it as a "post-Christian nation." Of course, the days of our "Christian" nation were also the days of slavery, Civil War, racism, and sexism. It hardly seems that those days were any more Christian than today. The difference most people are pointing to in this distinction between America as Christian versus post-Christian, however, typically concerns the bedrock of our moral character as a culture. Even though we were often blinded to following our moral codes, the nation largely agreed on what those codes were or should be. But we can say this no longer.

Even though a *USA Today* poll found that 70 percent of Americans actually approve of the public display of the Ten Commandments on monuments and in courtrooms, our nation's media outlets tell a different story. The rise of abortion, divorce, materialism, and the homosexual agenda have largely polarized our nation into liberals and conservatives who maintain completely separate camps. Perhaps pop singer Madonna best characterized our nation's moral temperature in 2003, when she ended a song on national television with the lyrics, "I'm bored with the concept of right and wrong."

Amid such moral relativity, the Bible elevates a concept called *holiness*, which includes a godly call to the highest morality. However, holiness is more than simply living according to the right moral code. Instead, it is the primary attribute of God himself. We know that God is not perfect because He consistently adheres to moral principles; He is perfect because it is His nature to be perfect. By His own nature, God simply cannot act imperfectly or immorally. To the skeptic who asks whether God can do anything immoral, the answer is an emphatic *no*. It is impossible for God to go against His own nature and act immorally. God's holiness means that His being is perfectly integrated, perfectly *whole*.

This is the Biblical definition of *holiness*—"wholeness." The promise of Scripture is that people can live a life that is the integrated sum of each of its parts—that we do not have to be fragmented in our motives and compartmentalized in our morality. Instead, the continuity of God's own character can come to dominate the fabric of our lives. Seen this way, the command to holiness becomes a gracious invitation to share in the person of God and the abundant life that He intended for each of us.

I. COMMANDED TO LIVE HOLY (Lev. 20:7-8; 1 Peter 1:15-16)

It is easy to miss the forest for the trees in studying the Book of Leviticus. A book handed down from a priestly point of view, it comes to us in a series of meticulous, detailed, minute laws, the great majority of which do not appear to apply to our culture today. Most contemporary Christians don't worry about eating shrimp or steak. We don't celebrate many of the Jewish festivals in our tradition. Modern medicine has largely eradicated the infectious skin diseases like leprosy that dominate so much of Leviticus. So what is the over-arching theme that *does* have poignant relevance to our culture and our lives? It is the command of holiness, which is the overall goal of every segment of the book.

A. The Command With a Promise (Lev. 20:7-8)

7. Sanctify yourselves therefore, and be ye holy: for I am the Lord your God.

8. And ye shall keep my statutes, and do them: I am the Lord which sanctify you.

The command to be holy takes the shape of a particular formula that occurs at three crucial junctures of the Book of Leviticus. In chapter 12, the content shifts from laws governing clean and unclean food (ch. 11) to regulations concerning childbirth and contagious diseases. We are prone to viewing such laws as unnecessary and "religious," but we must remember they were matters of physical life and death. Because poor sanitation was so common in the ancient world, and could lead to death, the way people approached certain foods and diseases could prevent the spread of terrorizing plagues. For example, recent research has shown that circumcision decreases the spread of sexually transmitted diseases. Although there is always a spiritual component to these commandments, they are not spiritual alone. God gave them for the good, and the survival, of the Israelite people.

In 18:2, the Levitical laws shift toward interpersonal relationships and, in chapter 19, especially the proper observance of the Ten Commandments. There, the holiness formula is injected as a motivator for worshiping God alone, for doing justice to all people, and for honoring the elderly and the alien. This flows naturally into chapter 20, which deals with the necessary punishments for those members of the community that thumb their noses at such injunctions. This often took the form of the worst sin possible in the eyes of God—human sacrifice of children to the neighboring Canaanite god, Molech (vv. 2-5). In light of such a tragedy, God reminds the people why He will not tolerate such behavior—because of His holiness (v. 7).

Because holiness is God's very identity, it should also be the nature of His people. God does not offer a laundry list of the benefits of holiness. He does not cajole or bribe. "Be holy because I am" is all that needs to be said. "Be holy because I can be nothing

Talk About It:
1. What does the Lord tell His people to do in verse 7?
2. What does the Lord promise to do in verse 8?

---

other, therefore you can be nothing other if you are to be My people." And far from being the stringent dictates of a divine tyrant, this command is set in juxtaposition to Molech—the god who demands human sacrifice! In such a context, we should not be afraid of this commandment which has often been interpreted so harshly in some churches. In lieu of all other options in ancient Israel and our society, it is a gracious gift, which verse 8 explicitly expresses.

Not only does Yahweh offer a path of life that is so much more beneficial than other neighboring gods; He then takes the initiative in seeing to it that His people can follow through. God did not hand over the Torah to the people of Israel and then expectantly wait on them to get it all right. Instead, the promise of His empowerment is built into the commandment of holiness itself. The standard is set high; the decrees should be followed to the letter. But no one is alone in this endeavor, because *no one can actually make themselves holy*. Remember, holiness is primarily an attribute of God. Only He can choose to share it with humanity. The beautiful message of Leviticus is that God has made such a decision, and we need simply reap the benefits of the gift of God's gracious holiness.

conversation (v. 15)—conduct

Talk About It:
What does it mean to be holy?

B. The Hallmark of the Early Church (1 Peter 1:15-16)

15. But as he which hath called you is holy, so be ye holy in all manner of conversation;

16. Because it is written, Be ye holy; for I am holy.

Some believers struggle with reconciling the ministry and message of Jesus with the legal codes of Leviticus. After all, isn't it the Pharisees who are concerned with issues over ceremonial washing, the observance of the Sabbath, and food regulations? We know that Jesus is a scandalous personality just for challenging the conventional interpretation of some of the Levitical commands by touching a leper, by eating with Gentiles, by doing good on the Sabbath. However, this is simply because Jesus fulfilled the Torah. That is, He radically lived out the heart of God as expressed in the Old Testament, so that this heart came to have a personal expression in the very person of Christ. Therefore, in His Sermon on the Mount, which offers a sweeping interpretation of the Torah, Jesus restates the holiness formula in even more radical terms: "Be perfect, therefore, as your heavenly Father is perfect" (Matt. 5:48 NIV). Jesus did not break from the holiness tradition of the Old Testament by any means at all. Instead, He reflected that tradition to the utmost.

It is no surprise, then, that His foremost disciple is the only New Testament writer to specifically quote the Levitical formula toward holiness. Only just like Jesus, Peter increases the commandment's impact, as we see in our lesson text: "But just as he who called you is holy, so be holy in all you do; for it is written: 'Be holy, because I am holy'" (vv. 15-16 NIV).

Be Holy

Peter does not have just Temple regulations, disease laws, or food norms in view. Because of the message of the Gospel, the Church can incorporate the lifestyle of holiness into "all" that they do. The Levitical command, then, becomes fulfilled not only in the life, death, and resurrection of Christ, but also in the ongoing life of the early church. Holiness is its hallmark, being mentioned over a hundred times throughout the New Testament. It is the promise and the property of the New Testament church, both then and now.

II. INSTRUCTIONS FOR HOLY LIVING (Lev. 20:1-6, 9-10; Col. 3:5-11; Titus 2:11-12)

Biblical holiness is never an abstract concept. Although a primary attribute of God, it is not a theological category alone. Instead, it is lived out in ordinary, practical terms by ordinary people. As 1 Peter says, it affects everything about the believer's everyday life. It is no surprise, then, that the commandments to live a holy lifestyle found in Scripture tend to cover even what appear to be some of the most mundane aspects of life. That is the point of holiness! It is wholeness of every component of life, both extraordinary and ordinary.

A. Punishment for Immorality (Lev. 20:1-6, 9-10)

1. And the Lord spake unto Moses, saying,

2. Again, thou shalt say to the children of Israel, Whosoever he be of the children of Israel, or of the strangers that sojourn in Israel, that giveth any of his seed unto Molech; he shall surely be put to death: the people of the land shall stone him with stones.

3. And I will set my face against that man, and will cut him off from among his people; because he hath given of his seed unto Molech, to defile my sanctuary, and to profane my holy name.

4. And if the people of the land do any ways hide their eyes from the man, when he giveth of his seed unto Molech, and kill him not:

5. Then I will set my face against that man, and against his family, and will cut him off, and all that go a whoring after him, to commit whoredom with Molech, from among their people.

6. And the soul that turneth after such as have familiar spirits, and after wizards, to go a whoring after them, I will even set my face against that soul, and will cut him off from among his people.

9. For every one that curseth his father or his mother shall be surely put to death: he hath cursed his father or his mother; his blood shall be upon him.

10. And the man that committeth adultery with another man's wife, even he that committeth adultery with his neighbour's wife, the adulterer and the adulteress shall surely be put to death.

Molech (MO-lek)— v. 2—a god worshiped by the Ammonites whose worship included the sacrifice of children

Talk About It:
1. What did God say was the penalty for worshiping the god Molech (v. 2)?
2. What impact would the worship of Molech have (v. 3)?
3. What is prohibited in verse 6?
4. How does God seek to protect the family in verses 9 and 10?

Because the holiness of God is His primary gift to humanity for the most fruitful life on earth, it is never something to be taken lightly. God is not simply throwing around His nature to whoever might want to try it on for size. Those who are flippant about the standards of God need not apply for holiness. It is a free gift, of course, but one that requires an open and committed heart. Again, we turn to Leviticus 20 to soberly reflect on the consequences of rejecting this gift.

First, and most shocking, is the punishment for those who turn against Yahweh for a quick fix from Molech. Although Baal was probably the most popular rival god in Canaan at the time, Molech was the most feared. In this religious tradition, children were offered up by their own parents as appeasing sacrifices, so that the land might produce rich crops. God decrees that any such parent in Israel, be it mother or father, should be immediately stoned to death by that parent's community. God's infinite value of children comes to us in the most graphic terms imaginable.

God uses a four-pronged attack on the accused follower of Molech. He will be ignored by God and disconnected from the community of faith because he has not only defiled the Tabernacle but has blasphemed against the very name of God. The name of God was nothing to toy with in Israel. In synagogues still today it is never pronounced out loud due to the reverence of the community of faith. The ultimate slap in the face to the holy God of the universe is to defy His holiness by turning to a bloodthirsty rival god who is nothing but an idol. This offense to God's holiness is so great that should any community have mercy on one who offers child sacrifice to Molech, the offender's punishment will transfer to every member of the community. What is more, this standard applies to anyone who turns to false gods, including magicians and sorcerers.

In verses 9 and 10, we see that holiness is centered practically in the family. Should the family unit break down, God knows there is no chance for His great dream of a holy people to become a reality. Therefore, He enforces strict requirements concerning honoring one's parents as a child, then one's spouse as an adult. Simply put, children should speak honorably of and to their parents, and parents should be completely faithful to one another in marriage. Note that women do not have a worse lot than men when it comes to adultery—they both are to receive the same penalty for the sin of adultery. God is serious about the family, because it is the primary vehicle of His great gift of holiness.

> "Even with God's help, pursuing holiness is difficult. Anyone who thinks differently either is foolish or has never tried to live a holy life."
> —Dale Coulter

members which are upon the earth (v. 5)—"earthly nature" (NIV)

B. The New Nature of Holiness (Col. 3:5-11)

5. Mortify therefore your members which are upon the earth; fornication, uncleanness, inordinate affection, evil concupiscence, and covetousness, which is idolatry:

6. For which things' sake the wrath of God cometh on the children of disobedience:

7. In the which ye also walked some time, when ye lived in them.

8. But now ye also put off all these; anger, wrath, malice, blasphemy, filthy communication out of your mouth.

9. Lie not one to another, seeing that ye have put off the old man with his deeds;

10. And have put on the new man, which is renewed in knowledge after the image of him that created him:

11. Where there is neither Greek nor Jew, circumcision nor uncircumcision, Barbarian, Scythian, bond nor free: but Christ is all, and in all.

Some of the most practical teachings about a holy lifestyle fall into the Book of Colossians, even though it is an epistle of cosmic scope. Nowhere is the majesty of Jesus depicted so universally, the One in whom "all things hold together" (1:17 NIV). Yet in chapter 3, Paul gets into the nitty-gritty of what the cosmic authority of Christ means for the daily life of the believer. The plan he lays out could not be clearer.

First, there are things believers must "put to death" (v. 5 NIV) and "put off" (v. 8). These include the sins of sexual immorality, lust, and idolatry, which are also mentioned in Leviticus 20. Yet the worship of a rival god is no longer in view here in Colossians. Instead, a holy lifestyle cuts across the lines of the individual's "earthly nature" (v. 5 NIV). This nature was once the heart's driving force before coming to faith in Christ, but it is no longer relevant. Yet these evils are not only individual issues. They work themselves out in community.

The list of vices in verse 5 deals with individual errors, but the list in verses 8 and 9 concerns how to live in holy relationships with other church members. These prohibitions are centered on the tongue, culminating in the Old Testament commandment to renounce lying, since to distort the truth is property of the old self. The new self, however, though far from perfect, is in the divine process of reaching the goal of Genesis 1:27, the very image of God. This happens through the transformation of the mind and heart, as one learns and applies the knowledge about God found in Scripture.

C. The Life of Salvation (Titus 2:11-12)

11. For the grace of God that bringeth salvation hath appeared to all men,

12. Teaching us that, denying ungodliness and worldly lusts, we should live soberly, righteously, and godly, in this present world.

uncleanness (v. 5)—immorality

inordinate affection (v. 5)—lust

concupiscence (v. 5)—desire

Scythian (SITH-ee-un)—v. 11—The Scythians were "a tribe of raiders notorious for their cruelty and barbarism" (Nelson).

Talk About It:
1. What brings about the wrath of God (v. 6)?
2. What must we "put off" and "put on" (vv. 8-10)?
3. Explain the unity described in verse 11.

1. What does God's grace offer (v. 11)?
2. What does God's grace teach (v. 12)?

"Nothing whatever pertaining to godliness and real holiness can be accomplished without grace."
—Augustine

The short letter of Titus also reiterates the Gospel's instructions of practical holiness. The implications of this passage are clear. First, God desires that all people receive salvation. Second, salvation is not something that is only otherworldly, although it certainly includes a secure afterlife. But practically it is focused on "this present age" (NIV) through empowering believers to condemn the same things God condemns, and to take on God's own righteousness. Believers are to "say 'No' to ungodliness and worldly passions, and to live self-controlled, upright and godly lives" (v. 12 NIV). Verse 13 says God's holy people should live in anticipation of the "blessed hope" of Christ's return, when their salvation will reach its completion.

III. MOTIVATION FOR HOLY LIVING (Deut. 7:6-11; Heb. 12:14, 18, 22-28)

The Biblical necessity of holiness is not something that can be disconnected from God's relationship with humanity. In fact, none of God's gifts or promises can exist outside of that same relationship that God has formed. God is omnipresent, or present everywhere all at one time, and this presence is not just in physical space. Indeed, God's presence somehow is one with His commandments, especially the command to holiness. As such, the command and the motivation to holiness always go hand in hand, because God himself intersects with the heart of man in the biblical commands.

A. God's Love Motivates the Believer (Deut. 7:6-11)

6. For thou art an holy people unto the Lord thy God: the Lord thy God hath chosen thee to be a special people unto himself, above all people that are upon the face of the earth.

7. The Lord did not set his love upon you, nor choose you, because ye were more in number than any people; for ye were the fewest of all people:

8. But because the Lord loved you, and because he would keep the oath which he had sworn unto your fathers, hath the Lord brought you out with a mighty hand, and redeemed you out of the house of bondmen, from the hand of Pharaoh king of Egypt.

9. Know therefore that the Lord thy God, he is God, the faithful God, which keepeth covenant and mercy with them that love him and keep his commandments to a thousand generations;

10. And repayeth them that hate him to their face, to destroy them: he will not be slack to him that hateth him, he will repay him to his face.

11. Thou shalt therefore keep the commandments, and the statutes, and the judgments, which I command thee this day, to do them.

We especially see this vital relational connection within God's commandment to holiness in the Book of Deuteronomy. The final book of the Torah, Deuteronomy stands as a motivating summary of the relationship between God and His people, and the expectations of each in the relationship. Nowhere in Scripture are the blessings of following God and the curses of rejecting Him laid out so systematically. Interestingly, when Jesus is tempted by Satan in the wilderness, He quotes exclusively from Deuteronomy in order to defeat him. Even for Jesus himself, we see the centrality of this book in the way it describes the relationship between God and humanity.

The book also contains the final instructions of Moses before his death. Therefore it should be read as the passionate cry of an aging leader who has invested the last 40 years in getting Israel to the entrance of the Promised Land. In chapter 7, Moses describes the comprehensive manner in which the Israelites are to destroy the pagan religions of Canaan when they enter the Promised Land. He predicts that if they do not act vehemently against idolatrous cults, they will sway future generations. We know from the books of Kings and Chronicles that Israel easily fell into such compromise when they disregarded this commandment. However, at the end of these commandments, Moses explains why the people must be set apart so exclusively, and why religious pluralism would not be an option in the new land of Israel. They are God's "treasured possession . . . a people holy to the Lord" (see v. 6 NIV).

The Israelites do not have the luxury of looking at the plethora of Canaanite gods and choosing the one that suits them best. In fact, they did not even choose Yahweh, but Yahweh chose them on His own initiative. What is more, Yahweh does not relate to Israel the way Molech or Baal related to the Canaanites. He does not need appeasement; He treats Israel as His personal treasure. It is this tender relationship that gives impetus to the many commandments of the Torah.

"Therefore" (v. 11) stems from a Hebrew particle that here means "In the light of what has just been said." And it is the great love of God that has just been expounded. The Israelites were to always be careful not to mistake their own qualities as the rationale for God's choice. That choice was only because God loved them and chose to enter into covenant with them. The Lord never breaks His covenant, and it is the responsibility of His people to love Him in return. They show their love to God by keeping His commands.

B. God's Command Motivates the Believer (Heb. 12:14)

14. Follow peace with all men, and holiness, without which no man shall see the Lord.

Talk About It:
1. It wasn't because of their _____ that Israel was chosen by God (v. 7).
2. Why did God choose Israel (v. 8)?
3. How is God described in verse 9?
4. What is Israel's part in their covenant with God (v. 11)?

"Salvation is from our side a choice, from the divine side it is a seizing upon, an apprehending, a conquest by the Most High God. Our 'accepting' and 'willing' are reactions rather than actions."
—A. W. Tozer

Talk About It:
1. What does it mean to "follow peace"?
2. Why is holiness demanded?

The anonymous author of Hebrews draws a remarkable comparison between two kingdoms—ancient Israel and the present kingdom of God as unlocked by Jesus—in this chapter. The common strand of holiness ties the two together.

In verse 14, to "follow" connotes an earnest and diligent pursuit. If we are following peace with all people, we are doing nothing contrary to the Word of God. We are obeying the injunction to love our neighbor as ourselves to the extent that consideration for others has become for us a way of life. Likewise, we are pursuing the way of holiness, knowing that without it no one will see the Lord. To live and die in an unholy condition is paramount to eternal exclusion from God, for God is holy.

This is not to say, however, that we earn the right to see God by living a holy life, for only the blood of Christ entitles us to heaven. Yet, that blood is able to wash us clean from all our sin and "to keep [us] from falling, and to present [us] faultless before the presence of his glory with exceeding joy" (Jude 24).

Peace and holiness are two objectives the believer should actively seek to cultivate. The practical living out of a life of peace toward people and holiness toward God will attract others to the way of Christ.

C. God's Kingdom Motivates the Believer (vv. 18, 22-28)
(Hebrews 12:23-27 is not included in the printed text.)
18. For ye are not come unto the mount that might be touched, and that burned with fire, nor unto blackness, and darkness, and tempest,

22. But ye are come unto mount Sion, and unto the city of the living God, the heavenly Jerusalem, and to an innumerable company of angels,

28. Wherefore we receiving a kingdom which cannot be moved, let us have grace, whereby we may serve God acceptably with reverence and godly fear.

Talk About It:
1. What privileges does the Christian have (vv. 22-24)?
2. Describe the kingdom Christians have joined (vv. 27-28).

At Mount Sinai there were fearful manifestations of God's power. The people were reminded of His awesome holiness, a God not to be trifled with. When you think of Sinai, you think of something tangible; you see a mountain that is ablaze with fire, and you envision darkness and gloom and a raging storm. It is vividly described in Deuteronomy 4:11: "And ye came near and stood under the mountain; and the mountain burned with fire unto the midst of heaven, with darkness, clouds, and thick darkness."

William Barclay observed: "In the giving of the Law at Mount Sinai, three things are stressed: (1) *The sheer majesty of God.* The whole story stresses the shattering might of God, and in it there is no love at all. (2) *The absolute unapproachability of God.* So far from the way being opened to God, it is barred; and he who tried to approach God met death. (3) *The sheer terror of God.* Here there is nothing but the awe-stricken fear which is afraid to look and even afraid to listen."

The kingdom of God is no longer a setting of fear and trembling, but one of jubilant rejoicing both in heaven and earth. In heaven (Mount Zion), the angels sing of God's glory (Heb. 12:22), and on earth, the Church celebrates the work of perfection that God renders in the hearts of its members (v. 23). This does not make the ancient community of Mount Sinai irrelevant to the later church. It is the same God who presides over both, and He is deserving of reverence. Nonetheless, through the work of Christ the world has been shaken apart so that God's kingdom alone has been left standing. The realization of the kingdom of God is an essential motivator toward worshiping and living before God in reverence and awe, which together equal holiness.

> "He has rescued us out of the darkness and gloom of Satan's kingdom and brought us into the Kingdom of His dear Son."
> —Col. 1:13 LB

CONCLUSION
Holiness is far from an option in the believer's life, according to both the Old and New Testaments. We see the principles of holiness expounded first in the Pentateuch. From there they run throughout the proclamations of the prophets, the worship of the Psalms, the wisdom of Israel, the teachings of Jesus, and the life of the early church. These principles take the form of moral commandments, practical instructions, and divine motivations. When these three arenas are placed together, the holy lifestyle is difficult to resist. It is both a promise and a gift of God.

GOLDEN TEXT CHALLENGE
"AS HE WHICH HATH CALLED YOU IS HOLY, SO BE YE HOLY IN ALL MANNER OF CONVERSATION" (1 Peter 1:15).

At first, it seems impossible to fulfill this command. How could we be as holy as God? But would God allow it to be placed in His Word if it were not attainable?

The clue to defining *holiness* is the phrase "all manner of conversation." In this verse, "conversation" means more than talking; it means walking—our actions, our conduct, the way we live.

Holiness simply means living like Jesus, who lived like the Father. That's why He could say, "He that hath seen me hath seen the Father" (John 14:9). After Jesus came and lived on earth, no one ever again had to ask, "What is God like?" Jesus was God in the flesh. He lived in such a way that people of His time could learn about the love of God as it was demonstrated in Jesus' everyday actions.

Jesus' miracles were demonstrations of love, not just power— loving actions, concern for the hungry, a helping hand for the distressed, forgiveness to the sinner, kindness to those despised by others, hope for those in despair, liberty for those bound by the power of Satan—that's how Jesus expressed the holiness of God.

Can we really be holy as God is holy? Yes, for on any given occasion, we can act as Jesus would.

Daily Devotions:
M. A Nation Set Apart
   Exodus 19:1-8
T. A Holy Priesthood
   Leviticus 21:1-8
W. The Nazarite Vow
   Numbers 6:1-8
T. Transformed by Mercy
   Romans 11:25-32; 12:1-2
F. Chosen to Be Holy
   Ephesians 1:3-10
S. Holy and Useful for God
   2 Timothy 2:19-26

Obedience to God's Commands

Leviticus 18:1-5; Deuteronomy 6:13-25;
John 14:23-24; Galatians 3:10-25; 5:1-14

Unit Theme:
The Gospel Fulfills the Law (Leviticus-Deuteronomy)

Central Truth:
Salvation through Christ must be followed by a life of obedience to Him.

Focus:
Realize that saving faith in Christ results in obedience to God and His Word.

Context:
Selected Scripture passages concerning obedience to God

Golden Text:
"[Jesus said,] If ye love me, keep my commandments" (John 14:15).

Study Outline:
I. Obedience to God Demanded (Lev. 18:1-5; Deut. 6:13-25)
II. Justified by Faith, Not Law (Gal. 3:10-25)
III. Freedom to Love and Obey (John 14:23-24; Gal. 5:1-6, 13-14)

INTRODUCTION

The Bible has the ability to be, at the same time, both wonderfully complex and painfully simple. Its major principles are understandable from even a child's point of view. Yet it also comes to us in multiple languages, from dozens of authors, in many differing cultural settings caused by thousands of factors. It is impossible to read the hundreds of injunctions in the Torah or the stringent teachings of Jesus without being struck by how far-reaching and comprehensive the commands of Scripture truly are. Given the sheer volume of the directives found in the Bible, what could possibly make them uncomplicated at their core? Simply this: Each commandment of Scripture offers a fork in the road—a choice that even a child can make. That choice is between obedience and disobedience.

When Adam and Eve were faced with the Tree of Knowledge of Good and Evil, they had that choice. When Noah was challenged with a ridiculous building project, he had that choice. When David unexpectedly met Saul in a cave, he had that choice. When Jeremiah was given a grave responsibility, he had that choice. When Jesus was tempted by the devil in the wilderness, and then on the Mount of Olives, even He had that choice. Scripture presents the story of God as consistently boiling down to human choice in the face of God's choice. God has chosen to present humanity with a particular path of life. But God will never force us to go His way. The substance of what it means to be human is wrapped up in the freedom to choose.

John Calvin, the great Protestant Reformer and founder of the Presbyterian Church, said, "True knowledge of God is born out of obedience." Without consistent obedience, God cannot be known. With consistent obedience, He cannot be unknown. Such consistency comes about when we have thoroughly internalized the script of the Bible—the stories of those who have learned the same obedience we must learn. As author Eugene H. Peterson states, "With a biblical memory we have two thousand years of experience from which to make the off-the-cuff responses that are required each day in the life of faith. If we are going to live adequately and maturely as the people of God, we need more data to work from than our own experience can give us" (*A Long Obedience in the Same Direction: Discipleship in an Instant Society*). When we understand the command to obedience given in Scripture, we draw from this biblical well of memory and empowerment.

I. OBEDIENCE TO GOD DEMANDED (Lev. 18:1-5; Deut. 6:13-25)

Obedience to God's commands is not a static process. A theological system called *Deism* teaches that God, like a great clockmaker, created the universe, set it in motion, and then left it alone for man to deal with. Whether or not one follows God's law makes no impression on God himself. Of course, this is not the scriptural view of God. When it comes to following His commandments, God is intimately involved in giving us every possible chance to succeed.

A. Unique Obedience (Lev. 18:1-5)

1. And the Lord spake unto Moses, saying,

2. Speak unto the children of Israel, and say unto them, I am the Lord your God.

3. After the doings of the land of Egypt, wherein ye dwelt, shall ye not do: and after the doings of the land of Canaan, whither I bring you, shall ye not do: neither shall ye walk in their ordinances.

4. Ye shall do my judgments, and keep mine ordinances, to walk therein: I am the Lord your God.

5. Ye shall therefore keep my statutes, and my judgments: which if a man do, he shall live in them: I am the Lord.

In Leviticus 16 and 17, Moses has announced important laws concerning how to properly conduct sacrifices, including the requirements for the Day of Atonement. These laws were no doubt given in a sober tone, since they explained God's manner of solving the problem of sin until the coming of Christ.

In chapter 18, before introducing new codes that will govern the nation's sexual activity, the Word of God pauses in order to once again remind the Israelites of the context for these laws. They are not given to be a burden on the people or to ruin anyone's fun. God is no arbitrary judge designing complex laws simply to prove His authority. Instead, verse 2 indicates that God offers these commandments because He has made the choice to become Israel's God. As a result, they have been called to a unique obedience. This obedience has already been challenged by way of their connection to a former way of life in Egypt (v. 3). In fact, the Book of Leviticus is given during their wilderness wanderings, which were a consequence for failing to completely disconnect from that former way of life. An entire generation had to die in the wilderness so the bonds of Egypt could be fully broken.

However, Egypt is not the only threat to obeying God as individuals and as a nation. The new threat is forthcoming: the people in and around Canaan are all too eager to gain converts to their gods and to their ways of life. Israel must not follow such paganism. They are called to a unique obedience under Yahweh.

Talk About It:
1. Restate verse 3 as God might speak it to Christians today.
2. How do God's people live (vv. 4-5)?

In 2003, Alabama Chief Justice Roy Moore was removed from his judgeship after refusing to follow a federal court ruling that ordered him to take down a monument of the Ten Commandments erected outside his courtroom. His response to the media was direct: "To do my duty, I must obey God." Obeying the commands of God must always remain the believer's priority, no matter the consequences.

After warning the people of these threats, God gives them an overarching injunction: "You must obey my laws and be careful to follow my decrees. I am the Lord your God" (v. 4 NIV). In this case, the first "you" is plural, directed at the entire nation. Again, the rationale for obeying the laws and decrees of God is the relationship that God has forged with the nation. It is a relationship that simply *is*, in the same way that God is the great "I Am."

Next, God moves this collective relationship to the realm of the personal, saying, "Keep my decrees and laws, for the man who obeys them will live by them. I am the Lord" (v. 5 NIV). God is not only forging a national pact or constitution. His concern is equally with the individual. The person who obeys God's commands can and will form his or her entire life around the path God has constructed and intended. Why? Because God is God! God's very identity has shaped these laws, so they are a perfect fit for each person whom He has created.

B. God's Gracious Response (Deut. 6:13-25)

(Deuteronomy 6:19-24 is not included in the printed text.)

13. Thou shalt fear the Lord thy God, and serve him, and shalt swear by his name.

14. Ye shall not go after other gods, of the gods of the people which are round about you;

15. (For the Lord thy God is a jealous God among you) lest the anger of the Lord thy God be kindled against thee, and destroy thee from off the face of the earth.

16. Ye shall not tempt the Lord your God, as ye tempted him in Massah.

17. Ye shall diligently keep the commandments of the Lord your God, and his testimonies, and his statutes, which he hath commanded thee.

18. And thou shalt do that which is right and good in the sight of the Lord: that it may be well with thee, and that thou mayest go in and possess the good land which the Lord sware unto thy fathers.

25. And it shall be our righteousness, if we observe to do all these commandments before the Lord our God, as he hath commanded us.

The Ten Commandments having just been recited, Deuteronomy 6 is a poetic call to the nation to keep God's commandments in love. However, this love flows both ways. God has acted first, by delivering Israel from all her enemies and settling her in a rich land. Israel now has the chance to respond to God by obedience to His commands, thereby further securing their future. They are to fear God, serve Him, and take oaths in His name (v. 13).

Talk About It:
1. Why does God call Himself "jealous" (v. 15)?
2. What does it mean to tempt God (v. 16)?
3. What does righteousness look like (v. 25)?

The Lord declares that He is a jealous God (v. 15). He warns Israel not to "tempt," or test, Him as they did at Massah (v. 16). Early in their wilderness wanderings, the Israelites had murmured against Moses there because of lack of water, asking, "Is the Lord among us, or not?" (Ex. 17:7).

The call of Moses is sobering. Again and again he reminds the Israelites to not reject God's commands. If they follow through with their end of the relationship, good things will come to them in life, particularly in the land God is about to give them. For an agrarian population of farmers and livestock raisers, their future was intertwined with that of the land. God's blessing upon the land meant a secure future (Deut. 6:17-18).

Not only will the land be blessed, but the people will be blessed spiritually when they obey (vv. 24-25). In verses 20-23, Moses has commanded the people to recite Israel's history to each generation as they grow up. This is to remind the people that they are never blessed based on their own righteousness, but only on the grace and mercy of Yahweh. In fact, if they will simply obey His decrees, He will declare them righteous (v. 25).

"The Lord, whose name is Jealous, is a jealous God."
—Exodus 34:14

II. JUSTIFIED BY FAITH, NOT LAW (Gal. 3:10-25)

It can be jarring to shift from reading the Torah itself to the discussions on the Torah in Paul's epistles. After all, we just finished a passage in which Moses declared that the nation would gain righteousness through following the Ten Commandments. But the nation often does not follow through. We must remember that by the time of Israel's judges and then kings, the pagan religions of the Canaanites have wreaked havoc. Finally, God gives Israel over to her enemies, leading to the Roman domination in the New Testament world. Now Israel is no longer a powerful nation, but an oppressed and scattered colony. Such a situation has called for a new negotiation of God's relationship with Israel, most importantly in the light of the advent of the Messiah.

A. Man's Curse and God's Redemption (vv. 10-14)

10. For as many as are of the works of the law are under the curse: for it is written, Cursed is every one that continueth not in all things which are written in the book of the law to do them.

11. But that no man is justified by the law in the sight of God, it is evident: for, The just shall live by faith.

12. And the law is not of faith: but, The man that doeth them shall live in them.

13. Christ hath redeemed us from the curse of the law, being made a curse for us: for it is written, Cursed is every one that hangeth on a tree:

14. That the blessing of Abraham might come on the Gentiles through Jesus Christ; that we might receive the promise of the Spirit through faith.

Talk About It:
1. Who is "cursed" (v. 10)?
2. How are we justified (v. 11)?
3. How and why did Christ become accursed (v. 13)?

The Book of Galatians provides more background data than any other single Pauline letter. From the outset, Paul lets the reader know he is embroiled in a heated controversy over the salvation of the Gentiles, which was a new phenomenon in the life of the fledgling church. New Testament scholar Charles Cousar poignantly sets the scene of this letter:

> The church in its earliest stages was largely Jewish in character, meaning that matters such as circumcision and dietary regulations were not pressing issues for its members. They simply assumed that these laws and customs would continue to be practiced. But along comes Paul, who is called to be an 'apostle to the Gentiles' and who preaches to non-Jews a gospel that essentially ignores the demands of the Mosaic law. . . . It is in the Galatian communities that these two categories of mission to non-Jews encounter one another.
> —Charles B. Cousar, *The Letters of Paul*

In chapter 3, we meet Paul facing this encounter head-on. How shocking it must have been to Paul's opponents to hear Paul combat the centrality of the Law with a verse from the Law itself, as he does in verse 10. But we must remember that Paul himself is a rabbi, schooled in the tradition of Old Testament interpretation. Therefore, he makes careful use of the text. Citing Deuteronomy 27:26, he asks if there is anyone at all who does not fall under this curse. If this were possible, the Law would not have introduced the sacrificial system to atone for sins against it. Yet even in the Old Testament there were echoes of another path of justification.

The prophet Habakkuk, in 2:4, had said something that the Jewish teachers in Galatia had been conveniently ignoring. He does not say that the righteous will live by the Law, but only by putting faith in God (Gal. 3:11). This becomes the entryway whereby Paul explains the differences between faith and the Law. Because the sacrificial system became the means by which man dealt with his own inability to follow God's law—his own cursedness—the gift of Christ took away the curse by the Cross. This reversal of the curse was effected through Christ so that the promise to Abraham that he might be a blessing to all nations of the earth might be fulfilled through the conversion of the Gentiles to Christianity.

"Behold, what manner of love is this, that Christ should be arraigned and we adorned, that the curse should be laid on His head and the crown set on ours."
—Thomas Watson

B. The Continuity of the Law (vv. 15-25)
(Galatians 3:15-18, 20-21, 23, 25 is not included in the printed text.)

19. Wherefore then serveth the law? It was added because of transgressions, till the seed should come to whom the promise was made; and it was ordained by angels in the hand of a mediator.

22. But the scripture hath concluded all under sin, that the promise by faith of Jesus Christ might be given to them that believe.

24. Wherefore the law was our schoolmaster to bring us unto Christ, that we might be justified by faith.

Paul realizes that the danger of his teaching here could be the complete devaluation of the Law, as if the Old Testament were unimportant or had no present relevance. In fact, nothing could be further than the truth! Again, he focuses on the promise to Abraham, noting that the promise of a blessing to all the nations of the earth would come through his single seed (v. 16). Although Abraham assumed this meant Isaac alone, Paul explains that it also pointed to Christ. What is more, Abraham received this promise with no strings attached some four centuries before the giving of the Torah (v. 17). Although God's covenant with Abraham was made apart from any sort of law, the Torah not only sanctioned it but worked in tandem with that promise. Nonetheless, the gift of the Christ was not set into motion by the Law, but by the promise (v. 18).

The purpose of the Law is certainly the most significant question at hand, given the fact that Paul has set it in a lower light in comparison to God's promise. But until that promise could be reached in the gift of Christ, the Law had to exist to solve the problem of sin through the sacrificial system, and thus to further point the way to Christ. In the same way that Moses the mediator enacted the Law, Jesus enacted the promise (vv. 19-21). So we see that God's work in the world is ongoing. There was a plan set in place that took millennia to complete. Yet this was God's perfect plan to reveal Himself to all peoples. This revelation was founded on humanity's inability to function apart from God.

The situation is irreparable, even by obeying the commandments of the Law. Humanity has not simply lost its way; it is completely enslaved to the powers of sin. However, the promise to Abraham has been ultimately fulfilled by way of faith in Christ, who offers a freedom that the Law had been unable to provide (v. 22). This, then, depicts the vital function of the Law.

God's plan required that all of salvation history would point the way to the need for Jesus, beginning with God's promise to Abraham and moving through the time of the Law. The advent of the Messiah has not abolished the beauty of the Law, but simply set it in a new light. Paul has no problem with Jews continuing to follow the cultural aspects of the Law, but this should not be forced on Gentiles. A new law has dawned—the law of exclusive faith in Christ (vv. 23-25).

III. FREEDOM TO LOVE AND OBEY (John 14:23-24; Gal. 5:1-6, 13-14)

Freedom from the sacrificial system of the Law is not simply a judicial, or forensic, freedom. By this we mean that God is not concerned with the mathematics of sin, as if there is a scorecard or calculator in heaven for each human being. Some Christians

Talk About It:
1. Which came first—God's covenant with Abraham or the Law given through Moses—and why does this matter (vv. 15-18)?
2. What was the Law's purpose (v. 19)?
3. Why couldn't righteousness come through obeying the Law (vv. 21-22)?
4. What purpose did the Law serve (vv. 19, 24-25)?

"The essence of faith is being satisfied with all God is for us in Jesus."
—**John Piper**

today live as if the goal of faith is to simply manage one's sin successfully, as if God has simply set us free to cease from sinning. But life with God is so much richer than merely the absence of sin! Instead, God has set us free from sin through Christ in order that we might be fully obedient to Him through an ethic of love toward God and neighbor.

A. Love and Obedience Connected (John 14:23-24)

23. Jesus answered and said unto him, If a man love me, he will keep my words: and my Father will love him, and we will come unto him, and make our abode with him.

24. He that loveth me not keepeth not my sayings: and the word which ye hear is not mine, but the Father's which sent me.

Talk About It:
1. What does Jesus promise those who love Him (v. 23)?
2. How do we prove our love for Jesus (v. 24)?

The last words of a dying man are always sacred. Here in John 14, Jesus gives His final instructions to His scared disciples who remain unaware of His impending mission of the cross. His words to them are intimate, dealing with the vital relationship they have with the Father through Him. In verse 22, Judas ("not Iscariot") becomes frustrated at Jesus' tone, wondering why He refuses to speak in such terms about Himself to the entire world. After all, how else will the masses come to believe that He is the Messiah?

In response, Jesus champions the centrality of love. God is not looking for those who will follow Him based on being convinced by amazing things they have seen and heard. Instead, God longs for disciples who will learn to live according to the teachings of Jesus through simply obeying them.

Love for Christ is evidenced by obeying what He has taught. This love will be reciprocated by God, and both the Father and the Son will mystically move into the life of the believer, making a home with him or her.

For Jesus, obedience equals love, and love equals obedience. But this formula also works in the other negative direction: "He who does not love me will not obey my teaching" (v. 24 NIV). As if recognizing the graphic harshness of His words, Jesus reminds the disciples that He has not made them up out of thin air. He is communicating the heart of the Father. There is no manner of loving Jesus apart from obeying His commandments. A loving heart will always be displayed by working hands.

> "God is most glorified when we are most satisfied in Him."
> **—John Piper**

B. Love Triumphs Over Culture (Gal. 5:1-6, 13-14)

(Galatians 5:1-6 is not included in the printed text.)

13. For, brethren, ye have been called unto liberty; only use not liberty for an occasion to the flesh, but by love serve one another.

14. For all the law is fulfilled in one word, even in this; Thou shalt love thy neighbour as thyself.

Perhaps the greatest obstacle to the fulfillment of God's promise to Abraham was the institution of Israelite culture. Although culture itself is certainly a God-given gift, it can become a means of isolation, not evangelization. This appears to be precisely what occurred in Israel, so that the cultural hallmarks of circumcision and the Law were not inclusive, but exclusive. In Galatians 5, Paul claims that these hallmarks are fully secondary to faith in Christ, who has rendered such markers unnecessary for the Gentiles. Because of this preaching, Paul continues to be persecuted, but he is not dismayed. He knows that he proclaims the offense of the cross.

Yet there were no doubt some who believed Paul was preaching a gospel devoid of ethics. "If the Law is now secondary," they might have said, "what is to prevent a believer from abject sin?" Paul, however, will have none of such an argument. Believers are "called to be free," but not so they can "indulge the sinful nature" (v. 13 NIV). Perhaps the realization of such a comprehensive freedom was causing some of the Gentiles to look down on their Jewish brothers and sisters. Remember that Paul does not devalue Jewish customs, but opposes their enforcement on Gentile converts. In case these converts were then enforcing their culture on the Jewish believers, Paul reminds them that their freedom from the Law was given with the goal of a servant's lifestyle. If both sides of the Christian community would take on Christ's role as a slave, the controversy between the two parties would cease for good.

If the Torah-keeping Jews in Galatia needed a justification for Paul's ethic of servanthood, he would take one from the Book of Leviticus—"Love your neighbor as yourself" (19:18 NIV). On the flipside, if the Gentile Christians would truly learn this commandment, they would then fulfill the requirements of the Law so demanded by the Jews. Love is Paul's answer—love one another. Love triumphs over cultural differences, racial lines, and socioeconomic status. Love summarizes the mission and promise of God that began in Abraham, continued in the Law, and has reached fulfillment in Jesus Christ. Love is the only ethic for the Christian community, because to love God and neighbor sums up the entire corpus of commandments in Scripture.

CONCLUSION

Scripture is packed with the wonderful benefits of obeying God's commandments and the severe consequences of disobeying them. The tone of each passage is God's merciful hope that humans will choose rightly. When they do, God rewards them. When they don't, they must receive due punishment before God opens up another way of blessing. In Christ, however, the punishment for all sins has been concluded, and eternal blessing has

Talk About It:
1. How can we "keep standing firm" (v. 1 NASB)?
2. What does "fallen from grace" mean in verse 4?
3. How must Christians use the liberty God has given them (vv. 13-14)?

"The Christian, like a chalice without a base, cannot stand on his own nor hold what he has received any longer than God holds him in His strong hands."
—**William Gurnall**

been put into effect for all who believe. What is more, faith in Christ empowers the believer to obey each of God's commands, thus completing the story of Scripture.

GOLDEN TEXT CHALLENGE

"[JESUS SAID,] IF YE LOVE ME, KEEP MY COMMAND- MENTS" (John 14:15).

In the New Testament, love consistently appears not as an emotion but as a commitment—as the result of a mind motivated and empowered by the Holy Spirit. Love for God, then, never exists apart from commitment to the divinely mandated ethic. In other words, if we love we act consistently with that decision to love. Of course, positive emotions usually ensue. But the love which Jesus commands is not identical with or dependent on such emotion. Rather, it results from a decision to love based on the knowledge that God is love and that He requires His followers to act consistently with that love.

The Ten Commandments, Part 1

Deuteronomy 5:1-15; Matthew 5:33-37;
1 Corinthians 8:4-6; 10:14-22; Hebrews 4:6-11

INTRODUCTION

The Bible is not compartmentalized, much less polarized, into either/or categories such as religion or relationship, love or law, mercy or justice. In Scripture, the full package of who God is and how He has called His people to live is presented in a range of manners. There is the worship of the psalmists, the wisdom of the ages, the passion of the prophets, the compassion of Jesus, and the shepherding of the apostles. In addition to this list, we must not neglect the sturdiness of the commandments.

Yet even the word *commandment* is long out of fashion in our contemporary world. It sounds so harsh, so absolute. One would be hard-pressed to ever even hear this term used in the business world, in public schools, or in the household. In fact, it sounds so militant perhaps because the military is the last bastion of an organization built around commandments and those who simply follow them. There is nothing necessarily wrong with any of this, except that it can taint the way we read the Old Testament. Because our culture predisposes us to view commandments as something harsh and condescending, we can transfer that view to God. But in reality, the Ten Commandments reveal the heart of a tender, merciful, loving God who wants the best for His children and all of humanity.

Imagine a sporting event without referees or boundary lines. Imagine a nation without recognized borders. Imagine a family unit without any clear roles. Imagine a workplace with no job descriptions. In each instance, the result would be chaos, suffering, and lethargy. We have come to expect various sets of guidelines for almost every aspect of life. Through the Ten Commandments, God chooses to encircle all of these aspects with governing rules that protect His people from chaos, danger, and brokenness.

Through the Ten Commandments, God has given humanity the most wonderful script to live by. The word *scripture* refers to the most authoritative script for living. We have not been left alone to attempt to just "do our best" at living on earth and following God. We have been given a clear portrait of what it looks like to walk with Him and live an abundant life.

Unit Theme:
The Gospel Fulfills the Law (Leviticus-Deuteronomy)

Central Truth:
We are commanded to honor God above all things.

Focus:
Examine the Commandments that address our relationship with God and live to honor Him.

Context:
Old and New Testament perspectives on four of the Ten Commandments

Golden Text:
"Moses called all Israel, and said unto them, Hear, O Israel, the statutes and judgments which I speak in your ears this day, that ye may learn them, and keep, and do them" (Deut. 5:1).

Study Outline:
I. Prologue: Our Covenant-Making God (Deut. 5:1-6)
II. Worship God Only (Deut. 5:7; 1 Cor. 8:4-6)
III. Idolatry Forbidden (Deut. 5:8-10; 1 Cor. 10:14-22)
IV. Honor God's Name (Deut. 5:11; Matt. 5:33-37)
V. Keep the Sabbath (Deut. 5:12-15; Heb. 4:6-11)

I. PROLOGUE: OUR COVENANT-MAKING GOD
(Deut. 5:1-6)

The *covenant* provides the most significant context behind the relationship between God and His people throughout the scriptural story, from the Old Testament to the New. The word appears well over two hundred times throughout the Bible. Most of these references are in the Old Testament, where the people of God are established based on and through God's covenant with them. This was inaugurated between God and Abram, in which the sign of circumcision was given to mark the covenant forever. The covenant was so strong that not even a deceiver like Jacob or a tyrant like Pharaoh could nullify it. By the time of the Ten Commandments, God's covenant with Israel has only been made stronger by their deliverance from Egypt. Yet now they must keep the covenant in the Promised Land by being faithful to their divine deliverer.

A. A Vital Pact of Promise (vv. 1-3)

1. And Moses called all Israel, and said unto them, Hear, O Israel, the statutes and judgments which I speak in your ears this day, that ye may learn them, and keep, and do them.

2. The Lord our God made a covenant with us in Horeb.

3. The Lord made not this covenant with our fathers, but with us, even us, who are all of us here alive this day.

The Book of Deuteronomy represents a series of speeches from Moses to the nation of Israel at the end of the leader's life. He will not enter the Promised Land himself, but continues to prepare the people for their new home. Each speech begins with the imperative to "hear."

The first commandment to the people is not to follow or to obey. These always come after the command to hear. Moses wants the people to first listen carefully, to think on the commands he is giving them. After this, they are to learn those commands— to set them to memory. Since few had need of literacy, it was expected that every Jew should be able to recite the Ten Commandments. Only after one had internalized these commands could they then be adequately followed.

But before the commands will be heard, Moses gives the vital context of the pact God is making with Israel. This context looks back to Mount Sinai in Exodus 20. Moses reminds the people that the covenant has not changed since then. In fact, it has not even passed yet to the next generation. They have no excuses for backing out on this pact with God.

B. Covenant Born From Relationship (vv. 4-6)

4. The Lord talked with you face to face in the mount out of the midst of the fire,

5. (I stood between the Lord and you at that time, to shew you the word of the Lord: for ye were afraid by reason of the fire, and went not up into the mount;) saying,

---

Horeb (v. 2)—the place where God gave the Law to Moses

Talk About It:
What did God want His people to do with His commandments (v. 1)?

Better Living
What would a nation be like without murder, adultery, stealing, lying, and greed? What would a nation be like where people governed their speech? What would a nation be like that properly balanced work and rest? In this sense, the Ten Commandments transcend any particular religious community. Like Jesus, they represent a universal way of life that benefits all.

The Ten Commandments, Part 1

6. I am the Lord thy God, which brought thee out of the land of Egypt, from the house of bondage.

Moses then reminds the people that God had not entered into covenant with them from a distance. No, they had seen with their own eyes His very power and glory on the mountain where God had met them. Their terror was such that Moses became their mediator, but this terror was alleviated at the first words of God, declaring the Israelites to be His people.

The covenant God makes with Israel includes the Ten Commandments, but does not begin with these commandments. It begins with the relationship that God alone initiated with Israel through the patriarchs, and especially by virtue of saving them from Egyptian bondage to Pharaoh. Relationship does not stem from covenant. Covenant grows from a preexisting relationship.

Talk About It:
1. How did Moses explain his role in receiving the Law (v. 5)?
2. What had God done for Israel (v. 6)?

II. WORSHIP GOD ONLY (Deut. 5:7; 1 Cor. 8:4-6)

The uniqueness of the Old Testament and the rise of the nation of Israel is often defined in the term *monotheism*. This refers to the belief in a single deity, rather than a worldview that includes multiple gods. Most cultures today have become monotheistic, though there are many people groups, such as Hindu nations, which remain polytheistic. The people of ancient Israel were called to a commitment to monotheism in a day when this was not the rule. Other nations found such a belief system peculiar. Although each tribe or nation typically had their main god, they viewed their god as one who battled against the deities of other tribes or nations. For Israel, other gods were of no importance. Yahweh alone was the Creator and Ruler of the universe.

A. A Radical Commitment (Deut. 5:7)

7. Thou shalt have none other gods before me.

The first commandment of what scholars often call the Decalogue, but what we typically refer to as the Ten Commandments, is simple and stark. When it comes to other commandments, God often chooses to elaborate and embellish, but not on the first. He has restated who He is in relation to the Israelites. He is the God who has chosen them by His own will, not because of any good they have done, but because they were oppressed in Egypt and needed a deliverer. As God acted then in order to protect His people, He acts now in the form of commandments. But for God's plan to function, the Israelites must cut off any allegiance to other gods.

Talk About It:
Why is this commandment given first?

Although most Western cultures today have traditionally been monotheistic, this trend is changing. We see the acceptance of all religions as equally valid paths to God, and this is a form of religious pluralism, or polytheism. The Israelites also lived in an age of religious pluralism. The Canaanites, who would soon become their neighbors, followed several gods, most notably Baal and Molech. Yet even these had divine entourages around them.

The Israelites were not allowed any deviation from worshiping God alone. They should pay no attention to angels, spirits, or other mediators. Only Yahweh was worthy of their allegiance.

B. One God, Not Many (1 Cor. 8:4-6)

4. As concerning therefore the eating of those things that are offered in sacrifice unto idols, we know that an idol is nothing in the world, and that there is none other God but one.

5. For though there be that are called gods, whether in heaven or in earth, (as there be gods many, and lords many,)

6. But to us there is but one God, the Father, of whom are all things, and we in him; and one Lord Jesus Christ, by whom are all things, and we by him.

Talk About It:
How does verse 6 explain God's uniqueness?

The Roman Empire, which was in power during the writing of the New Testament, aggressively expanded the temples of dozens of gods and goddesses, which were erected alongside the traditional temples of local communities. In archaeological excavations at Corinth, for example, temples have been discovered to Asclepius, Osiris, Isis, Caesar, and others. These cults were woven into the fabric of every aspect of Roman life, including the marketplace. In fact, every piece of meat sold in the marketplace would have first been sacrificed to one of these gods in one of these temples. As a result, this situation produced a crisis for the Christian church in Corinth. Should they become vegetarians in light of these pagan rituals?

Paul is not so concerned about the meat or the idols. He restates what the Corinthians already agree on—none of the marketplace idols amount to anything but carved stone. The real issue is the Corinthians' commitment to the one true God, and therefore the choice to eat meat should be a matter of conscience in light of that commitment. The essential truth of the Decalogue is recast in the light of God's revelation of His personhood in Jesus. God is in the position to give the Ten Commandments because He is the source of all things, and of life itself.

"It makes the heart of God jealous when we make gods of anything but Him."
—**Woodrow Kroll**

III. IDOLATRY FORBIDDEN (Deut. 5:8-10; 1 Cor. 10:14-22)

The first commandment sets apart Israel's life as a nation to Yahweh alone. There will not be multiple options for their spiritual allegiance. They will have one choice only, if they are to keep God's covenant. This set them apart as peculiar throughout the ancient world, even one thousand years later in the Roman Empire. In the second commandment, however, the distinctiveness of Israel was increased.

A. Worship the Creator, Not the Creation (Deut. 5:8-10)

8. Thou shalt not make thee any graven image, or any likeness of any thing that is in heaven above, or that is in the earth beneath, or that is in the waters beneath the earth:

9. Thou shalt not bow down thyself unto them, nor serve them: for I the Lord thy God am a jealous God, visiting the iniquity of the fathers upon the children unto the third and fourth generation of them that hate me,

10. And shewing mercy unto thousands of them that love me and keep my commandments.

It is interesting that the second commandment is not lumped in with the first. After all, if the Israelites do not worship other gods, idolatry is then out of the question. However, this is not necessarily the direction of the commandment. Instead, the temptation appears to be toward casting an idol that would represent Yahweh in some form.

When Israel created a golden calf as an object of worship soon after the exodus from Egypt, they were not breaking the first commandment, but the second one. That is, they were ascribing the person of Yahweh to the idol of the calf, similar to the common practice among other religions of that time. God, however, will have none of this. As Creator, He must never be confused in any way for His creation, even if the Israelites were able to form an idol of a heavenly being. Any attempt to bring God to the level of man debases Him and His relationship with Israel.

In verses 9 and 10, God again reminds the Israelites of His relationship with them. The first two rules are serious business, because God is jealous after them, like a father over his child or a husband over his bride. God's language is thoroughly personal. Because of this relationship, God will punish Israel should she break the covenant. However, He will show love to her for an infinite number of generations.

Talk About It:
How does God characterize Himself (vv. 9-10)?

"Abandon yourself utterly for the love of God, and in this way you will truly become happy."
—Henry Suso

B. Prohibition Against Idolatrous Feasts (1 Cor. 10:14-22)
(1 Corinthians 10:15-20, 22 is not included in the printed text.)

14. Wherefore, my dearly beloved, flee from idolatry.

21. Ye cannot drink the cup of the Lord, and the cup of devils: ye cannot be partakers of the Lord's table, and of the table of devils.

With regard to the crisis in the Corinthian church over meat-eating, Paul draws a vital distinction that splits the issue into two segments. Because it was impossible to eat meat that had not been previously sacrificed in some temple, Paul allows individuals' conscience to dictate their choice. This is due to the fact that eating meat sold in the marketplace did not require actually attending the sacrificial ceremony. However, Paul explicitly prohibits attending such ceremonies, which were completely avoidable. The main issue at hand is not whether or not to eat meat. Paul is clear elsewhere that idolatrous sacrifice has no affect upon meat. However, idolatry itself is nothing to toy with.

Talk About It:
1. What is the power behind idol worship (vv. 19-20)?
2. Why does Paul ask if we are stronger than God (v. 22)?

Paul compares attending idolatrous feasts to the Lord's Supper. Communion is a holy and powerful act, and feasting at an idol temple is also powerful. The god of the temple is nonexistent, of course, but demons do exist, and Paul fears that eating in these temples results in the service of Satan. The Corinthian believers who shared in the community of the Lord's Table could not split their allegiance between other communities. For them, a single table was reserved.

IV. HONOR GOD'S NAME (Deut. 5:11; Matt. 5:33-37)

The ancient Hebrew concept of the name is difficult to reproduce in our modern context. A person's name was more than simply a designation of that person's title. Something of that person's nature was actually imparted to and through the name. For this reason, biblical characters such as Jacob and Paul take on changes in their names at key moments in their lives. It is no surprise, then, that the Ten Commandments include instructions on appropriately revering God's name.

A. The Name of God (Deut. 5:11)

11. Thou shalt not take the name of the Lord thy God in vain: for the Lord will not hold him guiltless that taketh his name in vain.

In the Old Testament tradition, the name of God was held in profound esteem. In fact, when we call God "Yahweh" we are actually guessing at how this name might truly be pronounced. This is because the Hebrew word leaves out any vowels in the name, so that it intentionally cannot be pronounced. It reads "YHWH," and to this day Jews will insert another name, such as *Adonai* ("Lord") when reading the holy name of God. With this kind of reverence for God's name, it is imperative that Moses recounts this vital commandment. The honor of God was bound up in God's name. When one identified God by any name, this invoked His character. Misusing that character did not only include pronouncing the holy name, but also included claiming God's name for purposes that were not necessarily of God. This included Israel's leadership, who might be tempted to claim the stamp of God over taxation, military campaigns, or other ventures without first seeking God's authentic approval.

B. Simple Speech (Matt. 5:33-37)

(Matthew 5:33, 35-36 is not included in the printed text.)

34. But I say unto you, Swear not at all; neither by heaven; for it is God's throne.

37. But let your communication be, Yea, yea; Nay, nay: for whatsoever is more than these cometh of evil.

By the time of Jesus, it was common in Israel to stretch the third commandment to its limits. In the Sermon on the Mount, Jesus provides a new commentary on the Decalogue, including the

---

"Whatever your heart clings to and confides in, that is really your God."
—Martin Luther

Talk About It:
What does it mean to use God's name "in vain"?

Talk About It:
1. What does Jesus teach about taking oaths (vv. 33-36)?
2. Explain verse 37.

The Ten Commandments, Part 1

injunction to respect God's name. He considered the common practice of taking elaborate oaths to be in competition with this commandment. So He says, "Swear not at all" (v. 34).

Jesus' Jewish listeners were certainly not in the habit of explicitly misusing the name of God. Anyone who stood up publicly and swore on that name might be stoned to death right on the scene. So, then, when they needed to emphasize the truth of their speech, they might go so far as to swear by heaven—the domain of God, but not God himself. Jesus has no toleration for such hairsplitting. When the honor of God is at stake, simple speech is preferred. Jesus said, "Let your 'Yes' be 'Yes,' and your 'No,' 'No'" (v. 37 NIV).

There was no advantage in the oath ritual, so Jesus offers a better way: Honor the name of God by speaking plainly and simply, unlike the Pharisees and teachers of the Law. The devil is the one who convolutes speech and communication. God, however, is always the author of peace.

> "Always tell the truth. Then you won't have to worry about what you said last."
> —**Robert Cook**

V. KEEP THE SABBATH (Deut. 5:12-15; Heb. 4:6-11)

In the ancient world, Sabbath was not ingrained into culture as it is in present life. Nowadays it is normal for work to cease for at least one day on the weekend, and normally two. We trace this concept directly to the Jewish commitment and the fourth commandment. However, when this commandment was followed during biblical times, it was yet another peculiarity of the Jews. In agrarian communities that were often fighting for survival, skipping a day of work was often considered a great sacrifice. Later, the Roman Empire had no such system of rest. Nonetheless, God wove this commandment into the culture of Israel as another hallmark of her obedience.

A. Protest Against Slavery (Deut. 5:12-15)

12. Keep the sabbath day to sanctify it, as the Lord thy God hath commanded thee.

13. Six days thou shalt labour, and do all thy work:

14. But the seventh day is the sabbath of the Lord thy God: in it thou shalt not do any work, thou, nor thy son, nor thy daughter, nor thy manservant, nor thy maidservant, nor thine ox, nor thine ass, nor any of thy cattle, nor thy stranger that is within thy gates; that thy manservant and thy maidservant may rest as well as thou.

15. And remember that thou wast a servant in the land of Egypt, and that the Lord thy God brought thee out thence through a mighty hand and by a stretched out arm: therefore the Lord thy God commanded thee to keep the sabbath day.

We have previously seen that God's commandment toward holiness is best defined as *wholeness*, and this is definitely the case with regard to the Sabbath. Certainly we know of the physical and emotional benefits of rest. The body and the mind are simply not constructed for unceasing work. There are also the spiritual

Talk About It:
Why did God establish the Sabbath Day?

benefits of Sabbath. It is a day to worship, to give thanks, to re-center one's life on God so that it does not spin out of control.

There is even another facet at work in this commandment, as verses 14 and 15 show. God is careful to ensure that the Israelites understand that Sabbath is for every living creature in Israel: slaves, animals, even the land itself. Recall that the only way of life Israel had previously known was in Egypt, where they were slaves in a vast industrial complex. The only thing that mattered to the Egyptians was the level of production, and so the Jews became dehumanized cogs in an economic machine. But God did not intend for life to function this way. God brought them out to establish a new kind of life. A weekly Sabbath exemplifies this kind of life, as every worker ceases, and hierarchies are broken down. Slaves do not serve masters on the Sabbath. Wives do not serve husbands on the Sabbath. Instead, all creation peacefully coexists as God intended.

Church Sign: "The competition is terrific, but we are still open on Sunday."

B. Resting From Spiritual Work (Heb. 4:6-11)
(Hebrews 4:6-8 is not included in the printed text.)
9. There remaineth therefore a rest to the people of God.
10. For he that is entered into his rest, he also hath ceased from his own works, as God did from his.
11. Let us labour therefore to enter into that rest, lest any man fall after the same example of unbelief.

Talk About It:
1. What did the Israelites miss because of their hard hearts (vv. 6-7)?
2. How do we enter the rest described here (vv. 9-11)?

In the New Testament, the command to cease from physical work is fulfilled in the deeper teaching on spiritual work. In the Book of Hebrews, the author painstakingly explains the relationship between the old and new covenants, noting the many ways in which the old covenant was given to guide us toward a greater truth. One such truth is the centrality of trusting in God. The author laments the fact that the Jews are not turning as a people to Jesus, and so are once again missing the opportunity to experience true rest. This opportunity is available because of God's providence. He has created a way of salvation that people simply must accept with no strings attached. Everything has been constructed perfectly so that people can receive free grace.

The Sabbath of the former covenant has by no means been eliminated. Instead, God offers a new Sabbath of rest from spiritual works. God's work has been completed in Christ Jesus, and people need only receive the benefits of this finished work.

CONCLUSION

The Ten Commandments represent a succinct summary of the priorities of God. Although the Old Testament is filled with other ethical material, other commandments are often a running commentary on the Decalogue. This is due to the fact that if the Ten Commandments are followed, other laws will not be broken. However, if one of the Ten is broken, it leads to other problems.

Because of this, the Ten Commandments remain the ethical heart of any godly organization. They are applicable to all peoples and never go out of style.

GOLDEN TEXT CHALLENGE

"MOSES CALLED ALL ISRAEL, AND SAID UNTO THEM, HEAR, O ISRAEL, THE STATUTES AND JUDGMENTS WHICH I SPEAK IN YOUR EARS THIS DAY, THAT YE MAY LEARN THEM, AND KEEP, AND DO THEM" (Deut. 5:1).

If you were ever a student in a classroom or a member of a team where the teacher or coach did not make his or her expectations and rules clear, you know how frustrating that can be. Even more frustrating is when a leader plays favorites—not treating all of the students or team members equally—especially if you are not one of the favorites.

We should be eternally grateful that God is nothing like that. When it was time for Moses to reiterate God's commands to His people, he summoned "all Israel." Every Israelite was given the same rules to live by. And God's rules had not changed from when they were first given in Exodus 20. Moses sounds like Israel's teacher-coach when he tells them to "learn . . . and do" the Ten Commandments. The expectations were clear: "Have no other gods; observe the Sabbath; you shall not steal," and so on. Israel just had to obey.

Daily Devotions:
M. Get Rid of False Gods
Genesis 35:1-5
T. Consequences of Serving False Gods
Deuteronomy 31:15-18
W. God-Given Rest
Joshua 1:10-15
T. Do Good on the Sabbath
Luke 6:6-10
F. True Worship
John 4:21-24
S. God's Name Is Glorified
John 12:27-29

The Ten Commandments, Part 2

Deuteronomy 5:16-33; Matthew 5:21-22, 27-30; 15:3-6;
Ephesians 4:25, 28; James 4:1-3

Unit Theme:
The Gospel Fulfills the Law (Leviticus-Deuteronomy)

Central Truth:
The Ten Commandments teach wholesome relationships.

Focus:
Examine and obey the Commandments addressing our relationship with others.

Context:
Old and New Testament passages concerning six of the Ten Commandments

Golden Text:
"Ye shall walk in all the ways which the Lord your God hath commanded you, that ye may live, and that it may be well with you, and that ye may prolong your days in the land which ye shall possess" (Deut. 5:33).

Study Outline:
I. Honor Your Parents (Deut. 5:16; Matt. 15:3-6)
II. Honor Life (Deut. 5:17; Matt. 5:21-22)
III. Honor Marriage (Deut. 5:18; Matt. 5:27-30)
IV. Do Not Steal (Deut. 5:19; Eph. 4:28)
V. Be a Truthful Witness (Deut. 5:20; Eph. 4:25)
VI. Do Not Covet (Deut. 5:21; James 4:1-3)
VII. Epilogue: The Life That God Blesses (Deut. 5:22-33)

INTRODUCTION

The Ten Commandments are not abstract theological platitudes or philosophical statements that are on some "higher" level above the grit and grime of real life. In fact, the majority of the Commandments deal explicitly with the ins and outs of everyday human relationships. The balance in the list is not to be overlooked. Four of the Commandments focus on how one relates to God. The final six target the relationships of family, community, property, and legality. When all ten are presented together, they comprise the complete portrait of a healthy life lived in obedience to God.

This is why the Old Testament is clear that the Commandments are a gift from God. They are not a product of the community's experience, nor the result of a committee of scholars or rabbis who convened in order to pinpoint the highest authority for the Jews. Instead, God himself inscribed the Ten Commandments, and so they became a means by which heaven intersected with the earth. Ancient Jews did not consider that keeping the Commandments satisfied the whims or desires of a distant God, but that by living according to the Commandments one somehow overlapped his life with the life of God himself. This life was not only relegated to the arena of what we have come to call "religion," but also encompassed human relationships.

In fact, the Old Testament knows no Hebrew word for "spiritual." This is not because it fails to acknowledge a spiritual component to human life, but that it views all of human life as spiritual, as coming from and returning to God. God is intricately involved in all aspects of life. Biblical scholar N. T. Wright believes that the human need for relationships indicates the very voice of God calling to us:

> How is it that we ache for each other and yet find relationships so difficult? My proposal is that the whole area of human relationships forms another "echo of a voice"—an echo which we can ignore if we choose to do so, but which is loud enough to get through the defenses of a good many people within the supposedly modern secular world. Or, if you prefer, human relationships are another signpost pointing away into a mist, telling us that there is a road ahead which leads to . . . well, which leads somewhere we might want to go (*Simply Christian: Why Christianity Makes Sense*).

The Ten Commandments provide ample evidence that this yearning in the human soul for relational connection leads directly to God himself.

I. HONOR YOUR PARENTS (Deut. 5:16; Matt. 15:3-6)

The unit of the family was central to the Old Testament community of faith. This, of course, was not a technological or bureaucratic age. There was not an elaborate system of public education to impart Israel's values to the next generation. Nor was there much written information available for children to learn. Instead, the teachings of God were imparted orally, from parents to their children. As a result, God includes a commandment to preserve the value of this relationship. Indeed, it stands in the list as the only commandment with a specific promise attached.

A. The Centering Commandment (Deut. 5:16)

16. Honour thy father and thy mother, as the Lord thy God hath commanded thee; that thy days may be prolonged, and that it may go well with thee, in the land which the Lord thy God giveth thee.

The fifth commandment represents a sudden turn in the list. The previous commandments have dealt specifically with the relationship between God and His people. They have been lofty, focusing on the priority of God, the name of God, and the day of God. Now, however, the text turns toward what we might call "mundane" matters. In fact, they are anything but ordinary.

Biblical scholars have recently championed the emphasis on honor in both the Old and New Testaments. Philip F. Esler writes, "Honor is the pivotal social value in [ancient] society. Honor means the perception someone has of his or her own worth and an appreciation of how he or she is rated by a relevant social group. It is a claim to worth and a social acknowledgment of worth" (*Social-Scientific Approaches to New Testament Interpretation*).

In the fifth commandment, children have the responsibility of ascribing this worth and appreciation to their parents. The Old Testament has no toleration for ungrateful children. The key to a long and prosperous life starts in the home, by relating appropriately to the family hierarchy.

B. Jesus' Passion for the Fifth Commandment (Matt. 15:3-6)

3. But he answered and said unto them, Why do ye also transgress the commandment of God by your tradition?

4. For God commanded, saying, Honour thy father and mother: and, He that curseth father or mother, let him die the death.

5. But ye say, Whosoever shall say to his father or his mother, It is a gift, by whatsoever thou mightest be profited by me;

6. And honour not his father or his mother, he shall be free. Thus have ye made the commandment of God of none effect by your tradition.

Talk About It:
What promises come with being obedient to one's parents?

"Obedience is the only virtue that plants the other virtues in the heart and preserves them after they have been planted."
—**Gregory the Great**

Talk About It:
How had the Pharisees twisted this commandment, and why?

Although for many Jews, the fifth commandment lost its luster, for Jesus it was nothing to toy with. He especially opposed the Pharisees' practice whereby someone could transfer the honor owed to one's parents directly to God. To Jesus, this was an affront both to the Torah and to the family unit. We know that Jesus honored His parents, and He expected nothing less from others.

For Jesus, the Ten Commandments mean what they say. There is no complicated interpretive maneuvering necessary. In fact, such thinking merely clouds the meaning of the text. Tradition is never a substitute for following God's commands.

II. HONOR LIFE (Deut. 5:17; Matt. 5:21-22)

The Israelites existed as a peculiar community of life although surrounded by a world of death. Not only was death at a young age a common reality in this time before modern medicine, but neighboring religions practiced human sacrifice, even the sacrifice of children. Archaeologists have found ancient graveyards of dozens of babies offered up as sacrifices to pagan gods. Not only would God not allow such practices in Israel, He demanded that they respect both human and animal life.

A. The Commandment of Life (Deut. 5:17)

17. Thou shalt not kill.

> "For us, murder is once for all forbidden. . . . It makes no difference whether one take away the life once born, or destroy it as it comes to birth. He is a man, who is to be a man; the fruit is always present in the seed."
> —**Tertullian**

The Commandments heretofore have dealt with God's relationship to His people, man's relationship to God, and the family bond. The rest of the Commandments from here on will focus on the relationship between man and neighbor. They begin with the fundamental starting point of that relationship—recognizing the other's right to life.

No commentary is needed for the pithy prohibition against murder. Despite one's disputes, despite one's anger, despite whether one has been legitimately wronged—physical violence is never a workable solution.

B. The Root of the Sixth Commandment (Matt. 5:21-22)

21. Ye have heard that it was said by them of old time, Thou shalt not kill; and whosoever shall kill shall be in danger of the judgment:

22. But I say unto you, That whosoever is angry with his brother without a cause shall be in danger of the judgment: and whosoever shall say to his brother, Raca, shall be in danger of the council: but whosoever shall say, Thou fool, shall be in danger of hell fire.

raca (v. 22)—an expression of contempt meaning "worthless" or "stupid"

Talk About It:
When are words deadly?

The teachings of Jesus have a way of cutting from the commandment itself to the core of the human heart. In His exposition on this sixth command, Jesus takes such an approach. The harshness of Jesus' words is jarring, for who has not lashed out in anger against another person? But we must remember Jesus'

context. By this time, the Jews are a conquered and colonized people. Not only this, they are marked by internal divisions, factions, and rivalries. Since the people despised the Romans, different parties blamed one another for the nation's fate. Jesus first restates the commandment against violence. It would not get them anywhere with the Romans. But the problem is deeper than this. Their anger was also destructive.

The potency of Jesus' teaching is that if it is followed, the sixth commandment is rendered unnecessary. Murder does not arise out of thin air. It begins with unresolved anger, as seen by the words "raca" and "fool." "*Raca* scorns a man's mind and calls him stupid; *moros* ('fool') scorns his heart and character" (Vines). The miracle of Jesus is to cure the human heart of this disposition, so that the action of murder is never approached.

> "A tongue three inches long can kill a man six feet tall."
> —*Japanese proverb*

III. HONOR MARRIAGE (Deut. 5:18; Matt. 5:27-30)

A commandment concerning the parent-child relationship would be incomplete without directives on the husband-wife connection. After all, the two aspects of family life are dependent on one another. Interestingly, however, they are not paired together in the list. Instead, the commitment to sexual boundaries is placed after the commitment to nonviolence. This indicates the priority of human life and human sexuality in the heart of God.

A. Sexual Purity in Marriage (Deut. 5:18)
18. Neither shalt thou commit adultery.

A society's sexual boundaries are always clear indicators of that society's overall ethic. If a society has no marked boundaries sexually, other boundaries of law, order, and even gender will also begin to break down. For this reason, God makes Himself quite clear in how sexual relationships are to be governed in Israel.

The starkness of the commandment against adultery speaks volumes on its own. For the household unit to function as the vehicle whereby Israel's way of life was passed down, the marital relationship had to be preserved at all costs. This commandment also reflects a shift away from polygamy in the life of Israel. Although in the nomadic communities of the patriarchs, multiple wives were common, the Ten Commandments reflect a respect for women that was uncommon in the ancient world, which typically viewed women as property. Among God's people, women were to be respected sexually as partners in the household.

> "Marriage is a record of human relationship meant to be played in high fidelity."
> —*Quotable Quotations*

B. Sexual Purity in the Mind (Matt. 5:27-30)
27. Ye have heard that it was said by them of old time, Thou shalt not commit adultery:

28. But I say unto you, That whosoever looketh on a woman to lust after her hath committed adultery with her already in his heart.

29. And if thy right eye offend thee, pluck it out, and cast it from thee: for it is profitable for thee that one of thy members should perish, and not that thy whole body should be cast into hell.

30. And if thy right hand offend thee, cut it off, and cast it from thee: for it is profitable for thee that one of thy members should perish, and not that thy whole body should be cast into hell.

Talk About It:
What does it mean to commit adultery in one's heart?

Jesus' Sermon on the Mount continues to comment on the list of commandments. His transformation of the seventh commandment is no more shocking than the sixth. This new Kingdom ethic betrays humanity's failure at living according to God's heart that lies behind the Commandments. To fantasize having a sexual relationship with a woman is to commit adultery in one's heart. While not carrying out the physical act keeps the other party out of an adulterous relationship, the man who "looks . . . to lust" (NKJV) must deal with the sin in his heart.

In verses 29 and 30, Jesus exaggerates the Pharisees' way of dealing with the sin in the human heart. In the same way that the people were failing to follow the spirit of the Ten Commandments, even if they followed them externally, they should not take an external approach to following Jesus' teachings. If they did, they might as well tear out their eyes. Instead, such purity stems from God's work on the inner soul.

IV. DO NOT STEAL (Deut. 5:19; Eph. 4:28)

As the scope of the Ten Commandments narrows to the basic, daily needs of life in a community, personal property comes into view. Radically, wives are not included in this property. Yet the concept of individual ownership is prized in the Commandments. For this reason, in the same way that one is to respect the life and family of the neighbor, the neighbor's property should also be held in esteem.

A. Commitment to Personal Ownership (Deut. 5:19)

19. Neither shalt thou steal.

The Old Testament people of Israel lived millennia before the invention of modern capitalism. Most, but not all, economies today are based on free markets, that is, businesses and resources that are not owned by governments, but individuals. Even though it is not a perfect system, it seems to be the best available, and its roots are found in the eighth commandment that champions personal ownership.

Although given in the form of a prohibition, "You shall not steal" (v. 19 NIV), this commandment also has an affirming edge. To refrain from stealing is to acknowledge that another's property is sacred. Although back in Egypt the Israelites were constantly

in competition over resources, things would be different in the Promised Land. There would be enough for everyone, preventing the need for thievery. The commandment reflects the need to trust in God during times of economic stress which Israel would later know. God would allow them to provide for their households without ruthless competition over property.

B. The Christian Emphasis on Work (Eph. 4:28)

28. Let him that stole steal no more: but rather let him labour, working with his hands the thing which is good, that he may have to give to him that needeth.

The eighth commandment also affirms God's plan that His people work for their income. This became a problem in the Ephesian church, where new converts to Christianity struggled to master a new way of life.

Paul encourages new converts to learn a trade, not only that they might provide for themselves, but even for others. This is a poignant expression of the biblical view of prosperity. There is certainly the expectation that the new believer will be able to provide above his or her own needs. However, there is absolutely no thought given to the idea that such provision would merely be used to cushion the life of the person blessed by God. Instead, the provision is given to share with others in the community. So we see that in the New Testament, the centrality of private property remains, but its ethic is transformed into service to the under-privileged and needy.

Talk About It:
What positive alternative is given?

V. BE A TRUTHFUL WITNESS (Deut. 5:20; Eph. 4:25)

The Pentateuch is filled with specific instructions regarding the resolution of legal problems. There are laws in place to mediate court proceedings over property rights, murder convictions, and all manners of crime and dispute. We must remember, however, that in this milieu there was only one form of admissible evidence—personal testimony. There were, of course, no photographs, DNA, or fingerprints. The Old Testament call to maintain a truthful witness formed the bedrock of the entire judicial process in Israel.

A. The Danger of False Testimony (Deut. 5:20)

20. Neither shalt thou bear false witness against thy neighbour.

The ancient Israelites experienced the same moral pressures that face contemporary people in all societies. One of those pressures was to gain advantage over others by way of the legal process. Rather than enforcing a modern version of our oath to truthfulness, taken by a witness before taking the stand, God built a firm commitment to truthfulness directly into the Ten Commandments.

Talk About It:
Why must we tell the truth?

There are no provisions given concerning the personal relationship between a man and his neighbor. It does not matter whether they care for one another, or even whether they are locked in a legal battle. The truth triumphs over all other claims they might have on one another. Since this commandment was embraced, cultures across the world have esteemed the law court as a place of discovering the truth. Then, as now, that discovery rests on truthful testimony. By committing to such testimony, the Israelites added yet another vital component to their core commandments.

B. The Danger of False Relationships (Eph. 4:25)

25. Wherefore putting away lying, speak every man truth with his neighbour: for we are members one of another.

Paul's letter to the Ephesian church personalizes this commandment in order to meet the needs of people in a new context. In the Roman Empire, the courts were largely instruments of the upper classes, and so well out of reach to most, but certainly not all, Christians. Yet this did not mean that truthfulness was less vital for the believer. Instead, the call of the Gospel led to the purification of relationships through a radical commitment to consistently speaking the truth.

This commitment to the truth does not stem from the value of the truth itself, although Christ himself is the Truth. In the Ephesian context, speaking the truth to one another stems from the identity of the community of faith. No longer are they caught up in the world's system of ruthless competition. They have become members of a single family.

VI. DO NOT COVET (Deut. 5:21; James 4:1-3)

We have seen that several of the Commandments form thematic pairs. The first and second commandments, for example, concern the relationship of Yahweh to neighboring gods. The fifth and seventh commandments center on the family unit. Finally, the tenth commandment pairs comfortably with the eighth, since both are concerned with property. However, the tenth goes to the root of man's heart.

A. A Broadened Commandment (Deut. 5:21)

21. Neither shalt thou desire thy neighbour's wife, neither shalt thou covet thy neighbour's house, his field, or his manservant, or his maidservant, his ox, or his ass, or any thing that is thy neighbour's.

The tenth commandment resumes a format of lengthier commentary that ceased with the giving of the sixth commandment. This break occurred when the focus of the Decalogue shifted from man's relationship to God and family, to man's relationship with neighbor. The final commandment in effect summarizes this segment concerning the latter relationship.

The tenth commandment shows us the tradition which Jesus himself takes over, whereby the Commandments move toward man's internal disposition. If the Israelites will stamp out the lust for another's wife or property, the commandments against adultery, stealing, and even murder will almost always take care of themselves. The commandment shows us that God is not concerned with external form or ritual. He desires for His people to govern their own thoughts and motivations that might be hidden from view. If that is neglected, then the Ten Commandments cannot be truly obeyed.

> "Envy is the art of counting the other fellow's blessings instead of your own."
> —Harold Coffin

B. Warnings Against Materialism (James 4:1-3)
1. From whence come wars and fightings among you? come they not hence, even of your lusts that war in your members?
2. Ye lust, and have not: ye kill, and desire to have, and cannot obtain: ye fight and war, yet ye have not, because ye ask not.
3. Ye ask, and receive not, because ye ask amiss, that ye may consume it upon your lusts.

James, the brother of Jesus, writes a scathing rebuke against pockets of early Jewish Christians that were neglecting the tenth commandment. His rebuke shows us that these commandments continued to be extremely relevant in the life of the church. James sees no break between Old and New Testaments. The New Testament community has all the more reason to follow the Ten Commandments.

James teaches that coveting causes not only dissension between people, but negatively affects one's relationship to God. Coveting is an issue of motives, and James does not see a division of motives between man's relationship with others and his relationship with God. They cannot be kept separate, and the community's failure to recognize this resulted in terrible greed. They were not using money and property for God's glory, but for their own pleasure.

Talk About It:
1. Where do fights and wars originate (v. 1)?
2. What can covetousness lead to (v. 2)?
3. What prayers should we not expect to be answered (v. 3)?

VII. EPILOGUE: THE LIFE THAT GOD BLESSES (Deut. 5:22-33)
The Ten Commandments are a singular package that represents the life that God blesses. They cannot be torn apart and obeyed haphazardly any more than one can separate God himself into compartments. They cannot be prioritized in order of importance because they stand as one body. After Moses passionately recounts each one, he moves on to summarize the history of their reception, then to issue a challenge to the people to walk in God's way of holy blessedness.

A. The Awesome Nature of God at Mount Sinai (vv. 22-27)
(Deuteronomy 5:23-27 is not included in the printed text.)

22. These words the Lord spake unto all your assembly in the mount out of the midst of the fire, of the cloud, and of the thick darkness, with a great voice: and he added no more. And he wrote them in two tables of stone, and delivered them unto me.

Talk About It:
1. What did God himself do for Israel (v. 22)?
2. What did the Israelites fear (vv. 23-25).

The impact of Moses' opening summary of the Ten Commandments reaches back to his introduction, in which he reminds Israel of the awesome nature of their God. This not only reinforces the fact that he has just delivered serious and indispensable commandments (not just suggestions) that must govern the nation's life, but also their source in God. They came from God's voice alone. God alone wrote them down and proved His presence to the people on the mountain. And Moses was chosen both by God and by the people themselves to be God's mouthpiece. Moses reminds the people that he never asked for such a position. The people are without excuse. They are responsible for their response to all that God has done.

Talk About It:
1. What did God desire for His people (v. 29)?
2. What did God promise Moses (v. 33)?

B. The Hopeful Heart of God (vv. 28-33)
(Deuteronomy 5:28-32 is not included in the printed text.)
33. Ye shall walk in all the ways which the Lord your God hath commanded you, that ye may live, and that it may be well with you, and that ye may prolong your days in the land which ye shall possess.

Moses' conclusion to the Decalogue is not a gloomy picture. Even though the Israelites shook with fear at Mount Sinai, the Lord assured Moses that He was on the side of the people—that He truly believed they could walk in His commands. God is not a harsh taskmaster, but a gentle Father.

In biblical thought, virtue is not simply its own reward. Instead, God promises physical rewards to accompany obedience to His commandments. The Israelites undoubtedly were anxious to occupy their new land. Moses reminds them that they have a covenant, a contract with God, and they must be careful to follow its requirements in Canaan.

A Godly Nation
In defending the new constitution of the United States, founding father John Adams wrote the following: "The United States of America have exhibited, perhaps, the first example of governments erected on the simple principles of nature." In reality, the Ten Commandments prove that the Old Testament nation of Israel was the first to be erected on the basic principles of God's creation. These commandments show us what a godly nation can be—a land of freedom, peace, and holiness.

CONCLUSION
The Ten Commandments are simple enough for a child to understand and follow; yet they profoundly govern the deepest desires of the human heart. They affirm that people were meant for God, for family, and for one another. They offer firm and healthy boundaries for worship, work, and marriage. Without them, the Bible would be incomplete, since much of Jesus' teaching ministry reflects on them. Because of this, they have remained in the center of Western culture for centuries, and although they continue to experience pressure in our ever-changing world, they will always remain at the center of the life of the people of God.

GOLDEN TEXT CHALLENGE

"YE SHALL WALK IN ALL THE WAYS WHICH THE LORD YOUR GOD HATH COMMANDED YOU, THAT YE MAY LIVE, AND THAT IT MAY BE WELL WITH YOU, AND THAT YE MAY PROLONG YOUR DAYS IN THE LAND WHICH YE SHALL POSSESS" (Deut. 5:33).

A long life is a great blessing, if a man live to God, because it is in life, and in life alone, that a preparation for eternal glory may be acquired. Those who wish to die soon, have never yet learned to live, and know not the value of life or time. Many have a vain hope that they shall get either in death, or in the other world, a preparation for glory. This is a fatal error. Here, alone, we may acquaint ourselves with God, and receive that holiness without which none can see Him.—Adam Clarke

Daily Devotions:

M. Murder Prohibited
   Genesis 9:1-6
T. Consequences
   of Coveting
   Joshua 7:1, 19-26
W. The Pain of
   Adultery
   Proverbs 7:24-27;
   9:17-18
T. Restitution for
   Stealing
   Luke 19:1-9
F. Truth Versus Lies
   John 8:42-47
S. A New Command
   John 13:31-34

The Greatest Commandments

Leviticus 19:15-18; Deuteronomy 6:4-5;
Matthew 22:34-40; Luke 10:25-37

Unit Theme:
The Gospel Fulfills the Law (Leviticus-Deuteronomy)

Central Truth:
Christians grow spiritually as they love God and others.

Focus:
Consider God's greatest commandments and make loving God and others the priority of your Christian walk.

Context:
Old and New Testament perspectives on the most important commandments

Golden Text:
"Thou shalt love the Lord thy God with all thy heart, and with all thy soul, and with all thy strength, and with all thy mind; and thy neighbor as thyself" (Luke 10:27).

Study Outline:
I. Love God Supremely (Deut. 6:4-5; Matt. 22:34-38)
II. Love Your Neighbor (Lev. 19:15-18; Matt. 22:39-40)
III. Everyone Is My Neighbor (Luke 10:25-37)

INTRODUCTION

The Torah is a massive book, and it only represents the first five books of the sixty-six books in the Bible. As the most sacred segment of Scripture for ancient Jews, many even committed it to memory. However, the danger always loomed of "missing the forest for the trees." That is, because the Torah deals with almost every conceivable aspect of life—work, worship, sacrifices, sexuality, family, government, law, and so on—it can be easy to overlook the larger principles and themes that lie at the heart of these commandments. When this occurs, legalism results. By "legalism" we mean the routine and external obedience to commandments without a corresponding internal orientation toward the character of their Giver. Legalism neglects the fact that the commandments have been lovingly given to humanity by a gracious God. For this reason, Scripture constantly points back to the attributes of God that are worthy of awe, love, and worship. These attributes best represent the source of the whole of Scripture.

The Book of Deuteronomy, the prophetic books, and the teachings of Jesus often offer summaries of the heart of the hundreds of commandments in the wider Old Testament. This does not denote a hierarchy of importance with regard to the commandments, but a common God behind them all. These summaries also allow the reader a broader perspective on the great themes of Scripture. They are similar to footholds on a mountain climb, in that they help the Christian to work through the Bible by brightly painting its chief priorities. We would struggle to understand the Bible without them. These summaries also find parallels throughout the wider evangelical movement today. Several years ago, "What Would Jesus Do?" bracelets were popular, since they summarized a Christian response to any situation. Other such items and slogans help Christians remember key scriptural truths as well. Still, we must always be careful that our summaries are in line with the Bible's summaries. Many troublesome movements have cropped up based on faulty interpretations of a relatively few verses or themes—movements that turn a truth into the truth. We protect ourselves from such fallacies by studying segments of Scripture that summarize other segments. Providentially, there are many of these to choose from, so that we can be certain of grasping the overall story and heart of God.

I. LOVE GOD SUPREMELY (Deut. 6:4-5; Matt. 22:34-38)

The commandments of Scripture are neither detached from the character of God nor from the everyday life of the believer. Because of this, they are undergirded with the priority of the human heart's orientation toward God. He is not satisfied with external obedience alone, because external obedience does not have the ability to transform the heart. Instead, the heart first becomes oriented toward God through a loving relationship, and external obedience follows.

A. The Ancient *Shema* (Deut. 6:4-5)

4. Hear, O Israel: The Lord our God is one Lord:
5. And thou shalt love the Lord thy God with all thine heart, and with all thy soul, and with all thy might.

Deuteronomy 6 continues Moses' concluding remarks regarding the importance of the Ten Commandments. Because the future of the nation of Israel depended on her obedience to them, Moses takes pains to ensure that the people understand the Commandments. The nation's survival is on the line, not to mention their quality of life. Moses' vivid summary of the significance of these commandments still stands in the center of Jewish worship today.

The first words of Moses' exhortation, declaring that "the Lord is one," represent the simplest distinctive in Israelite religion. They have come from Egypt—a place of polytheism, where people believe they are subject to the whims of a multiplicity of gods, where human ethics are always in question because there is no singular foundation for authority and morality. Not so with Israel. Because they serve a God who is one, they can be certain that the commandments given are completely dependable. God will not let them down. He has laid out a course of life that guarantees freedom, joy, and prosperity.

The Hebrew word for "hear" (v. 4) is *shema*, which later became the title of this entire passage, still prayed daily in Israel today. This is because the Shema passage represents a beautiful and poetic exaltation of the laws of God. Such laws evoked awe and beauty in the hearts of the Israelites. As Scot McKnight writes in *The Jesus Creed: Loving God, Loving Others*:

> The Shema expresses what is most important for spiritual formation: *YHWH* (the sacred Hebrew name for God) alone is Israel's God, Israel is chosen by God, and Israel is to love God—with heart, soul, and strength. . . . There is promise attached to living life according to the Shema: when Jews lived by the Shema they would be "blessed" beyond imagination.

This blessing principally is derived from the profound love that forms between God and the believer, when the believer recognizes the incredible grace of God.

Talk About It:
1. What is the meaning of "The Lord . . . is one" (v. 4)?
2. What does God expect from us (v. 5)?

God's Priorities
In the early Pentecostal Movement at the Azusa Street Revival, its leader William J. Seymour exhorted its attendees, "Now, do not go from this meeting and talk about tongues, but try to get people saved!" From the beginnings of this now worldwide

The commandments of God were not given as a burden by any means. In fact, the ability to follow the commandments does not begin with the commandments themselves! Instead, the community of faith was called to a supreme love for God, a love that included the whole of the individual: the heart, the soul, the strength (v. 5). The *heart* referred to the organizing center of the person. The *soul* referred to the dynamic life of the person. The *strength* referred to the will and the ability of the person. Every component of the believer's life was to be oriented in a loving posture toward the Lord.

B. The Greatest Commandment (Matt. 22:34-38)

34. But when the Pharisees had heard that he had put the Sadducees to silence, they were gathered together.

35. Then one of them, which was a lawyer, asked him a question, tempting him, and saying,

36. Master, which is the great commandment in the law?

37. Jesus said unto him, Thou shalt love the Lord thy God with all thy heart, and with all thy soul, and with all thy mind.

38. This is the first and great commandment.

A famous story from the life of Jesus illustrates the centrality of the Shema in Jewish life, about fourteen centuries after Moses' speech in Deuteronomy. In Matthew 22, the Pharisees and Sadducees are plying Christ with questions to try to catch Him with a bad answer. Recognize that this was a life-or-death matter. When the Gospels say the Pharisees "tested" Jesus with a question, they weren't playing some kind of trivia game. If they could catch Jesus saying something concretely against the Torah, they might rally the crowds to stone Him on the spot. So in verse 34, Pharisees and experts in the Law come up with a massive question to throw at Jesus, thinking this might give them the grounds to put Him on trial. The question regards the most significant commandment in the entire Pentateuch.

Jesus' answer could not be more conservative and safe, and His disciples must have been relieved that they had gotten out of a sticky situation. Those that would consider Jesus to be a complete rebel against His Jewish tradition neglect passages such as these. Here, Jesus responds to the question with the stock answer—the traditional prayer that the Pharisees and Sadducees prayed each day: "Thou shalt love the Lord thy God. . . ." He then adds emphasis to this point, to prove to them that He is not seeking to destroy the Torah, saying, "This is the first and great commandment."

Jesus does not want any mistakes to be made. He allows no gray area in His answer to this supreme question. He shows that He and the Pharisees have much in common. They agree that loving God is the most important commandment to live by. The difference, of course, lies in how one is to go about doing this.

II. LOVE YOUR NEIGHBOR (Lev. 19:15-18; Matt. 22:39-40)

In the overall biblical narrative, love toward God and toward other people can never be separated. This truth is rooted in the Shema, which proclaims that God is one. God has perfect integrity within Himself. He cannot be separated into compartments. He is the singular source of all things. Therefore, to follow God means to accept His nature, especially His love, into one's life. Because of this, it is impossible to love God without being nourished by His loving nature that then overflows to the world. This nature causes one to possess God's loving orientation toward other people.

A. The Levitical Orientation Toward Others (Lev. 19:15-18)

15. Ye shall do no unrighteousness in judgment: thou shalt not respect the person of the poor, nor honour the person of the mighty: but in righteousness shalt thou judge thy neighbour.

16. Thou shalt not go up and down as a talebearer among thy people: neither shalt thou stand against the blood of thy neighbour: I am the Lord.

17. Thou shalt not hate thy brother in thine heart: thou shalt in any wise rebuke thy neighbour, and not suffer sin upon him.

18. Thou shalt not avenge, nor bear any grudge against the children of thy people, but thou shalt love thy neighbour as thyself: I am the Lord.

Because Leviticus is a priestly document, readers often write it off as being concerned with things that have little relevance nowadays: Temple rituals, animal sacrifices, liturgical garments, and so on. In reality, some of the central laws of Leviticus are vitally concerned with the everyday lives of common people, particularly how people should get along with one another. What is more, these principles are not always set in the context of external laws, but point directly to the heart. They are profoundly personal.

Throughout Leviticus, God is concerned with how the nation's laws will be applied. There is the clear recognition that they could be unfortunately misused, especially toward those poorer people without a voice. Such favoritism represents nothing less than the perversion of justice, and the entire legal code was built upon God's justice. Because of this, love of neighbor begins with fair and correct judgment.

The commandment of verse 15 toward sound legal judgment, however, does not simply apply to the courts. Instead, it extends to sound speech when it comes to personal matters (v. 16). The Israelites are to guard their tongues by not spreading malicious talk about anyone. When this is followed, it is only natural to

Talk About It:
1. What is the justice God expects (v. 15)?
2. In what ways must we not mistreat others (v. 16)?
3. When is it right to rebuke someone (v. 17)?
4. How are the two commands in verse 18 related?

protect the life of the neighbor. God accentuates this emphasis on life by invoking His name—*Yahweh*, the "I Am." The value of the neighbor's life stems from God's own life and value system.

This orientation toward the neighbor's life does not begin and end with the prohibition toward murder, but with personal hatred (v. 17). Such hatred forms when people fail to work out differences and disputes. Therefore, God commands that neighbors practice the art of gracious rebuking. Otherwise, bitterness can set in, which is the root of murder.

God continues to attack the dangers of human bitterness in verse 18. Revenge and grudges are completely out of place among the people of God. However, if people unselfishly love one another, the laws of Leviticus will be automatically fulfilled. Again, God invokes His name as His stamp of approval on the significance of these commandments. As God has loved the Israelites, so they are called to love one another.

B. Jesus Amends the Shema (Matt. 22:39-40)

39. And the second is like unto it, Thou shalt love thy neighbour as thyself.

40. On these two commandments hang all the law and the prophets.

As we have seen, Jesus has placed Himself on safe ground in a very dangerous situation with Israel's religious leaders. He has been asked a single, simple question, and at first it appears that the altercation between Him and the Pharisees is over. However, Jesus pushes the envelope by using the tense situation as a teaching opportunity. Moving beyond the question that had been posed, He broadens the discussion at great peril to Himself, mentioning the second greatest commandment.

Talk About It:
How is the second great commandment like the first one?

Of course, no one had asked Jesus about a second commandment. Incredibly, Jesus moves past the Shema to add an important amendment: Love for neighbor is always attached to the love for God. This teaching looks both forward and backward. It is both progressive and conservative. It is conservative in that it shows the foundation of the Torah in Jesus' teaching. He was not called "Rabbi" for no reason; Jewish rabbis were given the task of interpreting the Torah. Jesus does not make up any new commandments. He simply invokes those that the Pharisees were neglecting. On the other hand, this teaching is radical in that no one had ever added to the Shema before! Scot McKnight writes, "Loving others is central to Judaism, but it is not central to the creed of Judaism, to the Shema. So, what Jesus says is Jewish. But the emphasis on loving others is not found in Judaism's creed the way it is found in the Jesus Creed."

It is not that Jesus and the Pharisees disagree about the centrality of the Torah. Their dispute lies in which portions of the Torah should be most emphasized. The Pharisees focused on the

Torah's external regulations, while Jesus focused on the passages that speak to the human character and heart. For Jesus, the entire Torah hinges on the two greatest commandments (v. 40).

What an astounding proclamation! Jesus both upholds the significance of the Torah for the life of Israel while also boiling it down to a simple creed that a child can understand: love God and love others. This is a shocking contrast to the complex interpretations of the Torah offered by the Pharisees, and shows once again that Jesus is a different kind of rabbi.

III. EVERYONE IS MY NEIGHBOR (Luke 10:25-37)

Luke writes with great detail about the life and ministry of Jesus. Traditionally he is considered a physician, which makes sense given his precise writing style. Within the subject of the greatest commandment, Jesus addresses a different situation than we see in Matthew 22. However, this does not bear any difference on the meaning of Jesus' parable here. The parable of the good Samaritan sharpens the radical edge to Jesus' teaching on loving one's neighbor, showing He is not talking about love as some kind of sentimental feeling. Instead, Jesus' commandment to love has serious and life-altering consequences.

A. A Fellow Rabbi's Question (vv. 25-29)

25. And, behold, a certain lawyer stood up, and tempted him, saying, Master, what shall I do to inherit eternal life?

26. He said unto him, What is written in the law? how readest thou?

27. And he answering said, Thou shalt love the Lord thy God with all thy heart, and with all thy soul, and with all thy strength, and with all thy mind; and thy neighbour as thyself.

28. And he said unto him, Thou hast answered right: this do, and thou shalt live.

29. But he, willing to justify himself, said unto Jesus, And who is my neighbour?

We should not be surprised that different situations in the Gospels describe similar teachings. This is simply a result of Jesus' itinerant missionary strategy. That is, Jesus does not stay stationary, but travels from place to place, and presumably teaches many of the same things time and time again. Here, however, an expert in the Law stands up to test Jesus, much like the Pharisees do in Matthew 22. He asks, "What shall I do to inherit eternal life?" (Luke 10:25). Jesus reflects the expert's question back at him. When the man replies, "Love the Lord thy God . . . and thy neighbour," Jesus appears perfectly willing to end the discussion right there. This time it is the expert who pushes the envelope, asking, "And who is my neighbour?" (v. 29).

This rabbi does what rabbis did at that time—he wants to debate about the particulars of an Old Testament text. Jesus, of course, is up to the challenge.

> "I think love is the only spiritual power that can overcome the self-centeredness that is inherent in being alive. Love is the thing that makes life possible, or, indeed, tolerable."
> —**Arnold Toynbee**

Talk About It:
1. How sincere was the lawyer in asking his question (v. 25)?
2. Why did Jesus answer the lawyer's question with a question (v. 26)?

Talk About It:
What was similar
about the response of
the priest and Levite?

B. The Robbery Victim (vv. 30-32)

30. And Jesus answering said, A certain man went down from Jerusalem to Jericho, and fell among thieves, which stripped him of his raiment, and wounded him, and departed, leaving him half dead.

31. And by chance there came down a certain priest that way: and when he saw him, he passed by on the other side.

32. And likewise a Levite, when he was at the place, came and looked on him, and passed by on the other side.

As a master teacher, Jesus was proficient at telling vivid stories that immediately captured the minds of His hearers. When asked about the intricacies of how a neighbor is defined, Jesus does not launch into a complex diatribe, but tells a compelling story.

The journey from Jerusalem to Jericho had a reputation for danger. Although the Roman Empire guarded its advanced system of roads with brutal force, crucifying road bandits with no trial, they still existed at the bottom of society. Travelers were often wealthy, so robbers prowled the rural segments of these roads. In Jesus' story, they leave the traveler with nothing but his life, and this was even questionable.

Although the notion of a minister so easily neglecting a wounded person seems extreme, the impact of this passage lies in the fact that the priest believes he is faithfully obeying the Torah by neglecting the man. The man is probably unconscious, so the priest believes he is dying or is already dead. In Numbers 19:11-13, regulations are given regarding contact with corpses. Contact with dead bodies could quickly spread disease, so such regulations were necessary. The Torah required that the person touching a dead body must purify himself and stay in isolation for seven days. A priest traveling to Jerusalem for duties at the Temple was especially liable to such regulations.

The tension in Jesus' story builds with the introduction of this second character who follows the pattern of the priest. The listener awaits the conclusion of the poor man's fate and wonders when the twist will come. Of course, the priest and the Levite largely represent Israel's response to the suffering among them. The Pharisees in particular are concerned with purity norms more than with hurting people, and for Jesus this is intolerable. Finally, the resolution of the man's fate begins, but in a way that the Jews could never have believed.

"Love is not big-headed; it is big-hearted."

—George Sweeting

C. The Unlikely Hero (vv. 33-37)

33. But a certain Samaritan, as he journeyed, came where he was: and when he saw him, he had compassion on him,

34. And went to him, and bound up his wounds, pouring in oil and wine, and set him on his own beast, and brought him to an inn, and took care of him.

35. And on the morrow when he departed, he took out two pence, and gave them to the host, and said unto him, Take care of him; and whatsoever thou spendest more, when I come again, I will repay thee.

36. Which now of these three, thinkest thou, was neighbour unto him that fell among the thieves?

37. And he said, He that shewed mercy on him. Then said Jesus unto him, Go, and do thou likewise.

In verse 33, the hatred between Jews and Samaritans takes center stage in Jesus' subversive parable. To the Jews, Samaritans were half-breed impostors who worshiped at a different temple and adhered to some different traditions. Jesus subverts this racism by portraying a Samaritan as the only one in the story who follows the heart of the Torah by loving his neighbor. In fact, New Testament scholar John Dominic Crossan notes that verses 34-35 represent the longest section of the parable on purpose, which sets up Jesus' conclusion in verse 36:

> Even in English translation, far more space (66 words) is devoted to this description than to any of the other elements in the story. Why? When the hearer is confronted with the rhetorical question in 10:36, he might negate the entire process by simply denying that any Samaritan would so act. So, before the question can be put, the hearer must see, feel, and hear the goodness of the Samaritan for himself. The function of 10:34-35 and its detailed description is so to involve the hearer in the activity that the objection is stifled at birth (*In Parables: The Challenge of the Historical Jesus*).

How, the Jews might ask, could a Samaritan do such good deeds? Jesus' answer is that loving one's neighbor is not the property of a single group or sect.

The expert in the Law had asked for the identity of one's neighbor, but Jesus responds with the challenge to *become* a neighbor—to act neighborly toward all persons, particularly the despondent. In the "Jesus Creed," there is nothing more to it. Loving God requires the love of neighbor, and loving one's neighbor requires becoming a neighbor to all. "Go and do likewise" (v. 37), Jesus says, and that ends the lesson. Mercy is the heart of God, even more than cleanliness regulations.

CONCLUSION

It is not that the commandments of the Old Testament are incomplete without a commandment to love, but that they only have meaning in the light of the commandment to love. Without love of God and neighbor, all other commandments are rendered powerless. This is because the love of the human heart toward God and His creation is the first prerequisite to becoming a part of the community of faith. We see this love expressed poignantly

Talk About It:
1. Describe the Samaritan's feelings toward the victim (v. 33).
2. How far did the Samaritan go in helping the man (vv. 34-35)?
3. How does Jesus expect us to treat others (v. 37)?

"To love the whole world
For me is no chore;
My only real problem's
My neighbor next door."
—**C. W. Vanderbergh**

in both the Torah and the teachings of Jesus. In fact, Jesus illuminates the ancient teachings of the Old Testament that vividly express God's heart of love.

GOLDEN TEXT CHALLENGE

"THOU SHALT LOVE THE LORD THY GOD WITH ALL THY HEART, AND WITH ALL THY SOUL, AND WITH ALL THY STRENGTH, AND WITH ALL THY MIND; AND THY NEIGHBOUR AS THYSELF" (Luke 10:27).

The whole Law may be summed up in one word: *love*. The requirements of the Law are fulfilled when we love God and our fellow man as we should.

In what measure are we to love God? The lawyer's answer, which Jesus commended, calls for total commitment in our love for the Lord. We are to love Him with all our *heart*. When we speak of doing something with all our heart, we think of putting everything we have into it, giving it our very best. Our love for God is to be wholehearted and truehearted. There is to be no hypocrisy about it. Also, we are to love God with all our *soul*. When we think of something having soul, we think of emotion, feeling, and warmth. Our love for God is not to be cold and distant, it is to be fervent and intimate. Then, we are to love God with all our *strength*. The thought Jesus is conveying here is intensity and energy. Every fiber of our being should be involved in our love for the Lord. Finally, we are to love the Lord with all our *mind*. Devotion is sometimes regarded as mindless. But true Christianity is intellectually honest. Our reasons for loving God are based on sound principles. An understanding of Him leads to an intensified love for Him.

As it relates to our neighbor, the Golden Rule applies here. We are to love God supremely, but we are also to show love to our neighbor in the same way we would want him to show love to us. Jesus said, "Therefore all things whatsoever ye would that men should do to you, do ye even so to them: for this is the law and the prophets" (Matt. 7:12).

Introduction to Winter Quarter

The theme for the first unit is "Major Prophets," focusing on the books of Isaiah, Jeremiah, and Ezekiel. The call of God is the subject of three of these eight lessons, while accountability to God and the new covenant are the other primary subjects.

The expositions were written by the Reverend Dr. Jerald Daffe (B.A., M.A., D.Min.), who earned his degrees from Northwest Bible College, Wheaton College Graduate School, and Western Conservative Baptist Seminary. An ordained minister in the Church of God, Dr. Daffe has served in the pastoral ministry for ten years and has been a faculty member at Northwest Bible College and Lee University for thirty years. Dr. Daffe received the Excellence in Advising Award at Lee University. His books include *Spiritual Gifts*, *Speaking in Tongues*, and *Life Challenges for Men*.

The Christmas study (lesson 3) was compiled by Lance Colkmire (see biographical information on page 16).

The second unit is "Bible Answers to Crucial Questions." The topics are intelligent design, the sanctity of life, sexual purity, and the institution of marriage as viewed from Old and New Testament perspectives.

The writer of these lessons is Richard Keith Whitt (B.A., M.Div., Ph.D. cand.). Reverend Whitt has earned degrees from Lee University and the Church of God Theological Seminary, and has done doctoral work at the University of Nottingham, England. An ordained bishop in the Church of God, Keith has served his denomination as a pastor for twenty-three years, district overseer for twelve years, and as a member of various boards and committees. He has taught courses for the Church of God Theological Seminary and Lee University External Studies.

Responding to God's Call

Isaiah 6:1-13

INTRODUCTION

The books of the prophets are rich in both theology and practical aspects of living in a manner acceptable to our heavenly Father. Frequently these aspects are overlooked by our tendency to emphasize the foretelling or futuristic content. This imbalance can rob us from seeing the prophets as real humans that we can learn from even now in the twenty-first century.

Each of the major prophets presents a dimension of God's redemptive plan through His people, the nation of Israel. Isaiah is first in chronological order. His ministry spans the second half of the eighth century BC.

Isaiah's father was Amoz, who, according to Jewish tradition, was related to the royal house of Judah. Isaiah may have been a cousin of King Uzziah. As a relative, he would have had some access to the royal court as is evident in several scriptures (7:3ff.; 38:1ff.; 39:3-8). Isaiah was married to a "prophetess" (8:3). They had two sons.

Because of Isaiah's many prophecies concerning the Messiah, he is often called the "Messianic Prophet." At Christmas and Easter we read those specific verses predicting Christ's virgin birth, deity, family lineage, and vicarious suffering. Isaiah also predicted the overthrow of both Jewish kingdoms at the hands of the Assyrians and the Babylonians. This made him less than popular among the populace.

This first lesson focuses on Isaiah's dramatic call to service in the prophetic role. Of special emphasis will be his submission without having all the details of ministry spelled out in advance. His willing commitment to service stands as an example for all believers. Not one of us is exempt from the call to service, specifically to spread the gospel of Jesus Christ.

As we study this lesson, let us evaluate how we are responding to God's call for us to be in His service.

I. AWED BY GOD'S MAJESTY (Isa. 6:1-4)

A. The Setting (vv. 1-2)

1. In the year that king Uzziah died I saw also the Lord sitting upon a throne, high and lifted up, and his train filled the temple.

2. Above it stood the seraphims: each one had six wings; with twain he covered his face, and with twain he covered his feet, and with twain he did fly.

The sixth chapter of Isaiah describes his call to the prophetic office through a dramatic vision of the Lord. It begins with a specific historical landmark, the death of King Uzziah.

The reign of Uzziah is recorded in 2 Chronicles 26. Also known as Azariah (2 Kings 14:21-22), he came to the throne at the age of sixteen after the killing of his father due to a military fiasco. Early in his reign, Uzziah successfully defeated his father's enemies as well as strengthening the kingdom of Judah. He demonstrated strong leadership.

Initially this king stayed close to the Lord through the influence of the prophet Zechariah. Later his successes resulted in tremendous self-pride to the point of his going into the Temple and burning incense to the Lord. Even though a delegation of priests attempted to discourage this action, Uzziah persisted. As a result, God struck him with leprosy. For the rest of his years Uzziah lived in a separate house from the palace while his son had charge of the palace and governed the kingdom.

A great contrast exists in Judah at the point of Isaiah's call. There is a sense of material prosperity, but spiritual corruption dominates. Isaiah 1 furthers the concept of the people's following positive outward actions but lacking the necessary inner conviction and commitment to God.

With this as the backdrop, Isaiah experiences a marvelous vision. Apparently he is sitting somewhere in the court of the Temple. Then it is as if the veil of the Temple is pulled back and he experiences the marvelous glory of God.

The veil separates the Holy Place from the Most Holy Place, which houses the ark of the covenant. This place of the presence of God is available only to the high priest on the Day of Atonement. But now Isaiah is given a glimpse of the glory of God.

Isaiah sees six-winged heavenly creatures, the seraphim. This is the only place where these celestial beings are recorded in Scripture. With two wings they fly, with two wings they cover their faces, and with two wings they cover their feet. Notice their humanlike traits: they have faces and feet, and they are able to stand.

B. The Awesomeness (vv. 3-4)

3. And one cried unto another, and said, Holy, holy, holy, is the Lord of hosts: the whole earth is full of his glory.

Uzziah (you-ZIE-uh)—v. 1—Judah's king for 52 years

seraphims (v. 2)—an order of heavenly beings

Talk About It:
1. Explain the term "high and lifted up" (v. 1).
2. Why do you suppose the seraphim covered their faces?

"Before Isaiah could see God, he had to lose sight of the earthly throne [of King Uzziah]. We might say he had to lose sight to truly see."
—Ron Owens
(Return to Worship)

---

4. And the posts of the door moved at the voice of him that cried, and the house was filled with smoke.

God allows Isaiah to see His glory and the worship which occurs within the heavenly presence. The repetition of the cry "holy" could be the threefold reiteration within Hebrew to place emphasis. Or it might be the antiphonal response in which one individual or group makes a statement, a second person or group responds in the same manner, and then all make the statement together. Regardless of which is the case, we see the emphasis on God's holiness. Yes, there are other vital divine attributes; however, this is the distinctive that separates God from sin.

The holiness chapter, Leviticus 19, begins with the holiness of God and His desire for us to follow life patterns that are in accord. Psalms 29:2 and 96:9 remind us of how holiness is to be the atmosphere in which we worship. Hebrews 12:14 states, "Without holiness no one will see the Lord" (NIV).

Even the Temple in its deepest foundations shook in awe of God's presence. This reminds us of the Israelites at Mount Sinai seeing an expression of God's awesome presence. There the whole mountain shook prior to God's speaking the Ten Commandments, and it was covered with smoke (Ex. 19:18). At the dedication of Solomon's temple, a cloud descended (1 Kings 8:10-11). Each of these occasions was defined by a visible event.

II. CLEANSED FOR SERVICE (Isa. 6:5-7)
A. The Recognition (v. 5)

5. Then said I, Woe is me! for I am undone; because I am a man of unclean lips, and I dwell in the midst of a people of unclean lips: for mine eyes have seen the King, the Lord of hosts.

It is difficult for us to comprehend the emotions and racing of the mind which Isaiah must be feeling. Without any warning he is face-to-face with the glory of God and hearing the heavenly creatures speak the holiness of God.

Compare this experience with Moses' encounter with God in Exodus 33. When he requests to see God's glory, the Lord responds with a partial agreement: "You cannot see my face, for no one may see me and live. . . . You will see my back, but my face must not be seen" (vv. 20, 23 NIV).

No wonder Isaiah believes he is ruined. Not only has he seen God, but he is well aware of his condition in comparison to the holiness of God. None of us, regardless of how good we may attempt to be, can come close to matching the righteousness of God.

How do we understand Isaiah's confession of being a person of unclean lips? First, it is a statement of his being a man of

Talk About It:
1. How is God's glory seen in "the whole earth" (v. 3)?
2. What did Isaiah smell, see, and hear in these two verses?

"In the context of worship today, many times it is not God seated on His throne that people see. Instead, they see an exhibition of human ability. They hear music, but do they hear God? They hear preaching, but do they meet God?"
—Ron Owens

Talk About It:
Why did Isaiah feel he was "undone" (v. 5), or "ruined" (NIV)?

Responding to God's Call

questionable word usage. Second, he is standing silently while the heavenly creatures exalt the holiness of God. So it is also a statement of failing to offer the proper homage to God.

This same concept applies to the nation of Judah. They are failing to exalt their God, who is the exalted King due full and continuous homage. No one can stand in the presence of Jehovah and not recognize his or her own failures.

This verse deserves some practical considerations. Without seeking unusual, dramatic spiritual experiences just for the sake of testimony, it seems logical for us to desire spiritual encounters which deeply impact us. Encounters through the Word of God and the moving of the Holy Spirit bring us out of apathy and move us to a deeper level of commitment and practical knowledge.

B. The Cleansing (vv. 6-7)

6. Then flew one of the seraphims unto me, having a live coal in his hand, which he had taken with the tongs from off the altar:

7. And he laid it upon my mouth, and said, Lo, this hath touched thy lips; and thine iniquity is taken away, and thy sin purged.

Recognition of one's sin isn't in itself sufficient. One must desire to be changed. A repentant heart always precedes spiritual transformation. This must have been the case for Isaiah; otherwise, the Lord would not have initiated the cleansing.

The seraphim taking action in God's behalf toward Isaiah reminds us of the need for divine intervention in our life. We cannot personally change our sinfulness and bring about spiritual restoration. Salvation comes through the sanctifying work of the Holy Spirit based on Christ's sacrificial death for us.

A live coal represents fire which cleanses by burning away. The altar spoken of here is the brazen altar upon which the burnt offerings for sin took place. It represents the means by which the people were freed from sin and given access to God.

In direct response to Isaiah's previous description of being a man of polluted lips, the burning coal is placed on his mouth. This direct application to the perceived source of sin brings cleansing. Now Isaiah can speak the praises of God and be the prophetic spokesperson of the Lord.

Once again we are reminded of the importance of recognizing our sin and then placing ourselves in a position for God to eradicate it. In 1 Samuel 13, King Saul demonstrated the opposite. He told the prophet Samuel about his misdeed (vv. 11-12), but did not admit it was sinful and thus never repented. Saul and the whole kingdom suffered because of it (vv. 13-14).

> "Men are never duly touched and impressed with a conviction of their own insignificance until they have contrasted themselves with the majesty of God."
> —John Calvin

Talk About It:
What is the significance of the live coal?

> "We may think God wants actions of a certain kind, but He wants people of a certain kind."
> —C. S. Lewis

III. COMMISSIONED TO SERVE (Isa. 6:8-13)

A. The Call (v. 8)

8. Also I heard the voice of the Lord, saying, Whom shall I send, and who will go for us? Then said I, Here am I; send me.

Talk About It:
What was the Lord searching for?

The Master's Call

A special memory of visiting my aunt and uncle's farm on many occasions is when it was the evening milking time. My aunt would step out in the yard, cup her mouth, and give this really loud series of calls. All she would say is, "Come, boss. Come, boss." Not a cow is in sight. About five minutes later, in single file, a dozen cows are seen coming over the hill and into the barnyard.

Cows may not be the smartest animals. But these cows knew how to be obedient to their master's call!

What an experience for Isaiah! He sees the glory of the Lord; he experiences personal cleansing; now he hears the voice of the Lord seeking a person for service. Notice how different this is from how we usually perceive a divine call. Normally we see it in a distinct, personal approach. We look for the "I want you" or "I have chosen you" for a particular office or task.

In Isaiah's situation, God has a work which needs to be done. Since Isaiah is being told of this, it speaks of a human needing to accomplish it. No member of the heavenly hosts can come down to fulfill this task. God needs someone who lives among the people to be His spokesperson.

The generality of this call stands out. There's nothing said about the type of work or location. All that's there is the need for someone, and God will send this person. This is a huge consolation. This person will not be on his own but rather will have the assurance of being divinely commissioned.

Without hesitation Isaiah volunteers. There's no series of questions intended to get a clearer picture of the task. He does not offer potential restrictions that qualify this acceptance. Instead we see a straightforward statement of being ready to take on God's task. This isn't to say anyone who offers questions isn't a willing, suitable candidate. Remember when God called Moses in the desert (Ex. 3; 4). Initially his questions were in order when you consider his background. However, Moses crossed the line, so to speak, when he continually offered roadblocks which were not legitimate.

B. The Message (vv. 9-10)

9. And he said, Go, and tell this people, Hear ye indeed, but understand not; and see ye indeed, but perceive not.

10. Make the heart of this people fat, and make their ears heavy, and shut their eyes; lest they see with their eyes, and hear with their ears, and understand with their heart, and convert, and be healed.

Talk About It:
What would be the response to Isaiah's prophetic ministry?

Initial reading of these two verses raises major questions. Does God want Isaiah's ministry to consist of moving the people *away* from God? If that were the situation, then God would be inconsistent with His own purpose of awakening and drawing them closer to Himself.

Here we see a defined contrast. Upon seeing the holiness of God, Isaiah desired cleansing. This would not be true of the people to whom he would minister. The prophet would be the

messenger of the Lord, regularly speaking His word. Their hearing and not understanding wouldn't be because of the complexity of what is being said or their lack of mental capacity. Their chosen path of spiritual insensitivity would result from hardening their heart.

Keil and Delitzsch's commentary on Isaiah shows that verse 10 includes three figurative expressions of the concept of hardened hearts. To "make fat" speaks of being without feeling for the operation of God's grace. To "make heavy" relates to being dull or hard of hearing. Finally, to "shut their eyes" refers to a thick paste spread over weak eyes which hardens and restricts or blinds.

A hardened heart is seen in Moses' confrontation with Pharaoh. On several occasions the Scriptures record Pharaoh's choosing to resist God by hardening his heart rather than letting the Israelites go (Ex. 8:32; 9:34). Knowing this would happen, God indicated that He would harden of Pharaoh's heart (4:21; 7:3). In Exodus 10 there are three statements concerning God's hardening of Pharaoh's heart (vv. 1, 20, 27). Why would God do that? Isn't this inconsistent with God's wanting deliverance for His people?

There are several items to keep in mind. First, God's intention for Egypt was for the people to know He is God, not the more than seventy different ones they worshiped (7:5). Second, God's pattern of punishment on Pharaoh followed a course which Pharaoh already followed.

Even though the people's response to Isaiah's presentation of God's message is known ahead of time, it doesn't cause His word to be withdrawn from them. They will be given an opportunity to hear, receive, and change. A refusal then provides justification for later judgment. Israel could never accuse God of failing to make His will known or warning them of judgment.

C. The Duration (vv. 11-13)

11. Then said I, Lord, how long? And he answered, Until the cities be wasted without inhabitant, and the houses without man, and the land be utterly desolate.

12. And the Lord have removed men far away, and there be a great forsaking in the midst of the land.

13. But yet in it shall be a tenth, and it shall return, and shall be eaten: as a teil tree, and as an oak, whose substance is in them, when they cast their leaves: so the holy seed shall be the substance thereof.

Can you imagine being in Isaiah's position? He volunteers for a ministry which is unspecified. Then, when some of the details are given, it appears as a monumental but unsuccessful venture. Yet, Isaiah does not complain nor ask to be relieved of the task. He asks only one question: How long will this last?

In some situations God states a specific length, such as the seventy years of the Babylonian Captivity (Jer. 25:11-12). Here the Lord responds in terms of a specific environment. The people's hearts are not going to soften. They will not change their wicked ways. Their current prosperity as evident in Amos will keep them plunging headlong toward their fate. Drastic judgment will come on them.

Verse 12 of the text speaks clearly of the Assyrian policy of deportation and transplanting. Removed from their homelands and placed in foreign lands, these captive people would have little time or strength to participate in rebellion. They would be consumed with the adjustments and necessities of trying to exist. As a result of these wholesale moves, lands and houses would be left without care and become overgrown and in disrepair. All of this takes place in 722 BC when Assyria overcomes the northern ten tribes of Israel.

Isaiah speaks to God's people as a whole in spite of the division into separate nations, including the concept of a return from exile. However, also plainly seen is a series of events that would continue to befall God's people beyond this one invasion and deportation. It would continue until God's people were as trees that have been stripped and then cut down until only the stump or roots remain. Historically this is seen in the three invasions of Judah by the Babylonians under King Nebuchadnezzar. The final one results in the destruction of Solomon's temple. Note that the two types of trees used as illustrations, a terebinth and an oak (NKJV), have the peculiar ability to spring up from the roots even after being completely cut down.

Verse 13 also speaks of a return. Those individuals taken by Assyrians who do not return are often referred to as the lost tribes. Individuals not deported but who intermarry with foreign people become the Samaritans. However, after the seventy years of Babylonian Captivity there are two returns from exile. In 536 BC, Zerubbabel leads a group of nearly 50,000 back to their homeland. In 457 BC, Ezra returns with 6,000.

"There was never a night that had no morn."
—Dinah Mulock

Though devastated by enemy nations as punishment for their sins, the people of God will continue. The messianic hope is still alive. God's promise to David will be fulfilled. Even while declaring a message of destruction, Isaiah still offers hope.

CONCLUSION

Isaiah's call to the prophetic ministry comes in a very dramatic manner. The emphasis isn't on the means but the response. He quickly recognizes his inadequacies—more specifically, his sin. Then, confronted with the need and opportunity, he responds in the affirmative. There's no resistance and only one question when presented with the difficulty of his future ministry. He provides an example for each of us to follow, regardless if we are laity or clergy.

GOLDEN TEXT CHALLENGE

"I HEARD THE VOICE OF THE LORD, SAYING, WHOM SHALL I SEND, AND WHO WILL GO FOR US? THEN SAID I, HERE AM I; SEND ME" (Isa. 6:8).

When the prophet Isaiah got a glimpse of the majesty and glory of God, his first response was, "Woe is me! for I am undone" (v. 5). A real experience with God causes one to feel unworthy of God's presence. Humility will reign, and the heart will cry out exclaiming unworthiness.

After the consciousness and confession, the seraph winged his way to the lips of Isaiah with the purifying fire in his hands. There must be a consciousness of the need of the Lord Jesus as Savior and then a confession with the mouth and a repenting to the extent that no longer will the paths of sin be followed. All of this, accompanied by faith, will bring the joys of sins forgiven.

After Isaiah's rich experience with God, he was then ready to hear the voice of God saying, "Whom shall I send, and who will go for us?" Isaiah willingly answered, "Here am I; send me."

The voice of God is still calling: "Whom shall I send, and who will go for Us?" Too few have such a spiritual depth with God that they hear His voice today. One must dethrone self and enthrone the King of kings, be submissive to the will of God, and be a vessel ready for service, listening for His voice even to the faintest whisper, in order to answer, "Here am I; send me."

Daily Devotions:
M. Called With a Promise
Genesis 12:1-8
T. God Calls Moses
Exodus 3:1-10
W. God Calls the Unlikely
Judges 6:12-16
T. Called to Follow Christ
Matthew 4:18-22
F. Called to Show God's Glory
1 Corinthians 1:26-31
S. Called to Walk Worthy
Ephesians 4:1-11

The Glory of Christ's Kingdom

Isaiah 11:1-16; 35:1-10

Unit Theme:
Major Prophets

Central Truth:
All who live for Christ now will participate in the glory of His coming Kingdom.

Focus:
Describe the glory of Christ's rule and live by Kingdom principles.

Context:
The Book of Isaiah was written between 745 and 680 BC.

Golden Text:
"Thine, O Lord, is the greatness, and the power, and the glory, and the victory, and the majesty: for all that is in the heaven and in the earth is thine; thine is the kingdom, O Lord, and thou art exalted as head above all" (1 Chron. 29:11).

Study Outline:
I. Nature of the King (Isa. 11:1-5)
II. Nature of the Kingdom (Isa. 11:6-10; 35:1-2)
III. Joy of the Kingdom (Isa. 35:3-10)

INTRODUCTION

What images come to mind when you think of a kingdom?

Most of us probably look back to some of the biblical and medieval eras when power was consolidated in a single person with the title *king*. There was the golden age of Israel with kingdoms under the rule of David and Solomon. David defeated surrounding enemies and expanded his territory. Building on his father's foundation, Solomon constructed the Temple in Jerusalem, developed a sea-going fleet, and enjoyed a reputation of splendor as well as wisdom.

In the Book of Daniel we read about various kingdoms and empires beginning with King Nebuchadnezzar in Babylon. Next the Medio-Persians come to power, and the rise of the Greek and Roman empires are predicted. History tells us about the development, influence, and demise of all these kingdoms. It is amazing how each one lost power as interior disintegration took hold.

No matter how powerful and majestic each of these kingdoms and those who followed later, none will compare to the glory and magnitude of Christ's kingdom! Nebuchadnezzar is remembered for his building splendor. His temple with the hanging gardens was considered to be one of the wonders of the ancient world. Legend states this 300-foot pyramid was for his wife, who became homesick for the mountains of her country.

Other kings built palaces that drew every eye as people entered the capital city. Various Assyrian rulers built their palaces in Nineveh. But none of them had the same status as Sennacherib's. He built his palace on a large, elevated platform in the middle of the city so it was visible from all parts of the city.

The Lord's kingdom is totally different. Its splendor is not tied to beautiful buildings or powerful armies. No, His kingdom blazes outwardly in the nature of the King and His people. The glory is seen in holy principles which bring joy and peace even in the middle of turmoil. No one is exempt from this experience due to gender or race. All may participate and enter into this Kingdom's glory through accepting Jesus as Savior and Lord.

While Christ is currently reigning in the hearts of His people, in Isaiah 11 and 35 we get a picture of Christ's coming reign on the earth.

I. NATURE OF THE KING (Isa. 11:1-5)

A. Jesse's Branch (v. 1)

1. And there shall come forth a rod out of the stem of Jesse, and a Branch shall grow out of his roots.

Christmas celebration provides us with an excellent opportunity to be reminded of the nature of our King, Jesus Christ. He is the God-man. Though divine, Jesus chooses to take on human flesh. He becomes the perfect (sinless) sacrifice for the sins of humankind. It also enables Him to identify with us as we experience the issues of being human. He knows firsthand the experiences of weariness, pain, hunger, rejection, abandonment, and temptation.

Hebrews 4:15 says, "For we do not have a High Priest who cannot sympathize with our weaknesses, but was in all points tempted as we are, yet without sin" (NKJV).

In Genesis 49 we read of Jacob's blessing his sons prior to his death. He indicates the everlasting Ruler will come from the lineage of his fourth son, Judah (vv. 8-12). Approximately 1,000 years later Isaiah prophesies in much narrower terms. He places a name in the lineage through whom the Messiah will come.

As we read this first verse of Isaiah 11, it is easy to understand. Symbolically, it speaks of a tree being cut down yet from the remaining stump a mighty fruit-bearing branch will arise. The stump of Jesse refers to the mighty kingdom of Israel, as seen in the days of David and Solomon, being destroyed. The Assyrians conquer and disperse the northern kingdom in 722 BC. Nebuchadnezzar and the Babylonians come to Jerusalem on three occasions, which results in the seventy-year captivity. Israel will be an independent nation for only about 100 years (168-66 BC) before Roman domination.

It is during the Roman period that Jesus, the descendant of King David, is born. He is the fulfillment of the Davidic covenant (2 Sam. 7) made nearly 1,000 years earlier. The fulfillment is seen in the genealogical records of Jesus in Matthew 1. A descendant of David will always remain on the throne of Israel. And, Jesse is David's father as further seen in Ruth 4:22.

B. Spiritual Empowerment (v. 2)

2. And the spirit of the Lord shall rest upon him, the spirit of wisdom and understanding, the spirit of counsel and might, the spirit of knowledge and of the fear of the Lord.

This verse indicates the spiritual empowerment which would rest on Christ. Here it is important to reflect on the two natures of Christ. Philippians 2:6-8 indicates the voluntary limitation of Christ's divinity by taking on human flesh. It's a paradox of emptying oneself by taking on. As a result of limiting His deity and taking on the limitations of humankind, the empowering of the Holy Spirit becomes a vital part of His earthly ministry.

Talk About It:
Why is the Messiah referred to as "a Branch"?

"The Old Testament and New Testament alike tell of Jesus, the great Fact of history, the great Force of history, the great Future of history."
—**Robert G. Lee**

Talk About It:
How does verse 2 characterize the Messiah?

All four Gospel accounts record Jesus being baptized by John (Matt. 3:13-17; Mark 1:9-11; Luke 3:21-22; John 1:29-34). In each account the author indicates the presence of the Holy Spirit coming upon Jesus. This is not just a moment for the Trinity to be evident. The key is the Spirit's coming on and remaining with Jesus.

Isaiah 11:2 is often referred to as the verse concerning the sevenfold spirits. This does not mean the Holy Spirit is made up of seven individual spirits. Rather, it reflects dimensions of the Holy Spirit's person. In their *Commentary on the Old Testament*, Keil and Delitzsch see the Spirit of Jehovah ("the Spirit of the Lord") as the communicative vehicle of all the divine powers. Following then are three pairs. The first one relates to our intellectual life ("wisdom and understanding"); the second, to the practical life ("counsel and might"); and the third, to our relationship to God ("knowledge and the fear of the Lord").

Looking at the six we can easily see how much we need the Spirit's empowerment. Through wisdom and understanding, we are able to discern the nature of items and know the difference between what is godly and ungodly. Counsel and might help us to come to right decisions and then energetically bring them to fruition. Finally, there is the ability to know God and hold Him in reverence.

This brief look at the ministry of the Holy Spirit should encourage believers to seek the fullness of the Spirit in their life.

> "You should point to the whole man Jesus and say, 'That is God.'"
> —Martin Luther

C. Righteous Justice (vv. 3-5)

3. And shall make him of quick understanding in the fear of the Lord: and he shall not judge after the sight of his eyes, neither reprove after the hearing of his ears:

4. But with righteousness shall he judge the poor, and reprove with equity for the meek of the earth: and he shall smite the earth with the rod of his mouth, and with the breath of his lips shall he slay the wicked.

5. And righteousness shall be the girdle of his loins, and faithfulness the girdle of his reins.

Far too frequently we read of past kings or hear of current rulers who are despotic. They rule for their personal pleasures without any regard for the welfare of the people. Such is not true of the King in God's kingdom. He rules with righteousness. No citizen is marginalized or considered of lesser value.

Unlike human leaders who make decisions based on what is seen or heard, Christ the King is not so limited. Neither will His future reign be based on human prejudices and political expediency. His knowledge and understanding go beyond the normal human methods.

Verse 4 emphasizes the righteous nature of this King and Kingdom. The poor and meek who are often marginalized will receive justice. This Kingdom will be unlike any other. There will

Talk About It:
1. What kind of judge is the Messiah *not* like (v. 3)?
2. Describe the Messiah's justice (vv. 4-5).

The Glory of Christ's Kingdom

be no taking advantage of the widows, orphans, or aliens such as occurred among the Israelites when they failed to follow God's law. When God brought judgment on them, it was not just for their idolatry; it was also for the many injustices practiced (see Amos 4:1-3; Isa. 1:16-17).

The contrast to Christ's righteousness is the wickedness which prevails on earth. Under His reign it will not be overlooked or allowed to continue without receiving justice.

In verse 5 of the text, the prophet uses a common but important piece of clothing to emphasize the zeal and passion of the King for righteous justice. In everyday life the long robes were tucked up and tightly drawn around the waist, using a "girdle" (belt), enabling the individual to move freely and with speed when necessary. Christ's kingdom will be one in which He will quickly destroy wickedness and demonstrate righteousness.

II. NATURE OF THE KINGDOM (Isaiah 11:6-10; 35:1-2)
A. Peaceful (11:6-9)

6. The wolf also shall dwell with the lamb, and the leopard shall lie down with the kid; and the calf and the young lion and the fatling together; and a little child shall lead them.

7. And the cow and the bear shall feed; their young ones shall lie down together; and the lion shall eat straw like the ox.

8. And the suckling child shall play on the hole of the asp, and the weaned child shall put his hand on the cockatrice' den.

9. They shall not hurt nor destroy in all my holy mountain: for the earth shall be full of the knowledge of the Lord, as the waters cover the sea.

The description of peace within Christ's kingdom is graphically portrayed by using examples from the animal world that are opposites. But in His kingdom the predatory nature of animals will be changed. The wolf and the leopard are natural enemies of sheep and goats. They prey easily on the young. But in Christ's kingdom they will rest and dwell together peaceably. The same will be true of the lion and the calf. And to further this peaceful description, verse 6 says "a little child shall lead them."

The powerful bear, which can break the neck of a full-grown animal, will feed with the cow. They will bring their young together in harmony. No longer will the lion be a meat eater (carnivorous). His food will be vegetation like the ox.

Enhancing this sense of peace is the safety a child will have in the presence of deadly serpents. Thinking the sparkle of the serpent's pupil to be a crystal, a precious stone of some type, a child reaches into a snake's den to retrieve it. In our sin-cursed world there would be a swift, painful, deadly strike. Death would come quickly to this small child of two to five years. But not in

Brutal Reign
Adolf Hitler's dream of returning Germany to heights of power and glory resulted in horrific violence, suffering, and death. His concentration camps murdered millions of Jews as well as millions of other nationalities including Germans. Glory for Hitler wasn't in peace and prosperity but in brutality and dominance. No wonder he told his soldiers, "Close your eyes to pity! Act brutally!"

Talk About It:
1. List three adjectives describing the natural world when Christ reigns on earth (vv. 6-8).
2. How will "the knowledge of the Lord" be like the oceans (v. 9)?

ensign (v. 10)— banner

Talk About It:
What will be "glorious"?

Christ's coming kingdom. The young child plays and moves in perfect safety in the previous environment of death.

The picture of peace provided here is beyond our comprehension. When Christ sets up His kingdom on earth, the natural world will be turned upside-down. Things will be as they should be. In Christ's future kingdom, peace will dominate.

B. Unified (v. 10)

10. And in that day there shall be a root of Jesse, which shall stand for an ensign of the people; to it shall the Gentiles seek: and his rest shall be glorious.

To gain a further understanding to this verse, consider its reading in the NIV translation: "In that day the Root of Jesse will stand as a banner for the peoples; the nations will rally to him [Christ], and his place of rest will be glorious."

In 2 Samuel 7 the Lord promised David a continuing lineage. As far as a physical throne, this ended with the Babylonians' conquering of the southern kingdom. However, from the root of this tree sprang a spiritual King, Jesus Christ. His future kingdom would not be limited to the Jewish people. Rather, the banner of His kingdom would also draw the Gentiles. No longer would there be a division. His kingdom is a unified reign, including both Jew and Gentile.

The fallen genealogical tree of Jesse through David miraculously appears. From nothing more than a simple root rises a new rod or banner of strength which becomes the center around which all peoples may rally.

C. Joyous (35:1-2)

1. The wilderness and the solitary place shall be glad for them; and the desert shall rejoice, and blossom as the rose.

2. It shall blossom abundantly, and rejoice even with joy and singing: the glory of Lebanon shall be given unto it, the excellency of Carmel and Sharon, they shall see the glory of the Lord, and the excellency of our God.

Lebanon (v. 2)— means "white," referring to this mountain range's snow-capped peaks

Carmel (v. 2)—a beautifully wooded mountain range

Sharon (v. 2)—a fertile coastal plain

Talk About It:
1. What changes in nature are described in these verses?
2. What is the spiritual significance of these changes?

In chapter 34 the Lord, through the prophet Isaiah, issued the judgment which would come on the enemies of Israel. Then, in chapter 35, we see a contrast in what will be the inheritance of God's people.

What had once been desolate and isolation will spring to life. Flowers will spring up and the colors of their petals will display a beauty like that of other places. Instead of the term *rose* for the flower as seen in the King James Version, the NIV translates it *crocus.* These bulbous plants quickly shoot out of the ground and display a wide variety of color. In some areas they are the first signs of spring in the countryside.

This blossoming of the desert speaks of Christ's kingdom. The desolation of this world by the influence of Satan and sin will be changed in the future kingdom. The beauty and glory of Christ will replace the mournful past. A joyous environment will be there.

III. JOY OF THE KINGDOM (Isa. 35:3-10)
A. Retribution (vv. 3-4)
3. Strengthen ye the weak hands, and confirm the feeble knees.

4. Say to them that are of a fearful heart, Be strong, fear not: behold, your God will come with vengeance, even God with a recompence; he will come and save you.

Will justice ever prevail? Will the situations change so the downtrodden can rise? Will the oppressed see the rise of a Victor to release them from oppression? The answer is a resounding "yes"!

Sometimes God's people become weak in their faith. Instead of strength and a spirit of victory, they become enveloped in despair. Hopelessness overwhelms like a fog, obscuring clear vision. To those who may be in this condition the prophet brings words of hope. In some cases the environment causes a timidity which, in turn, dispenses a weakness in purpose and actions. To any and all, there is the directive to "be strong" (v. 4).

Our strength is in the might of the Lord. He comes to provide salvation for His people and to bring retribution on the oppressors. This surety brings strength to the weakened hands and knees which previously were unable to move with assuredness. Evil will not always prevail. Satan and His forces are a conquered enemy just waiting for the final action of defeat.

The directive to "be strong" reminds one of the Lord's direction to Joshua as he takes over the leadership of Israel. He has "big shoes to fill" being the successor of Moses. There is a huge task ahead—entering the promised land of Canaan. The first nine verses of Joshua fit so well here. Not only does the Lord tell Joshua to be strong, but He makes specific promises: "I will give you every place where you set your foot, as I promised Moses. . . . As I was with Moses, so I will be with you" (vv. 3, 5 NIV). This is followed with special directives about God's Word. Joshua is to talk about it, meditate on it, and do it (v. 8).

We too have the solid assurance of God through Christ coming to save us. He provides the opportunity for salvation through His first advent. In the future He will return again for final salvation and the total destruction of the forces of evil.

B. Restoration (vv. 5-7)
5. Then the eyes of the blind shall be opened, and the ears of the deaf shall be unstopped.

---

confirm (v. 3)—
make firm

Talk About It:
Why should God's people "fear not" (v. 4)?

"Shall not the Judge of all the earth deal justly?" (Gen. 18:25 NASB).

---

hart (v. 6)—deer

dragons (v. 7)—
jackals

Talk About It:
1. Describe the Messiah's miraculous ministry to suffering people (vv. 5-6).
2. What is the significance of "streams in the desert" (vv. 6-7)?

6. Then shall the lame man leap as an hart, and the tongue of the dumb sing: for in the wilderness shall waters break out, and streams in the desert.

7. And the parched ground shall become a pool, and the thirsty land springs of water: in the habitation of dragons, where each lay, shall be grass with reeds and rushes.

Christ's kingdom brings restoration to the whole person, not just the spiritual. The description of bodily defects such as blindness, deafness, and lameness isn't to be seen as symbolic. When Christ came in human form as the God-man, He performed the miraculous. Each of these handicaps were overcome through the healing power of Jesus. No wonder He was surrounded by those bringing their relatives and friends to be restored to health.

Remember Bartimaeus, who was begging for his livelihood when Jesus healed his eyes (Mark 10:46-52). The healing of the man born blind created a tremendous stir among the Pharisees (John 9). Just as easily, Jesus healed the crippled woman who was bent over and an invalid at the Pool of Bethesda (Luke 13:10-17; John 5:1-9). Repeatedly throughout the Gospels we read of specific miracles of restoration as well as inclusive descriptions of Jesus' healing all who were at a certain locale (Matt. 12:15; Luke 6:17-19).

After Christ's resurrection and ascension, divine healing continued in the Church through the empowerment of the Holy Spirit. The healing of the crippled beggar at the Temple (Acts 3:1-11) is the first example. James' epistle reminds us of the availability of healing to the sick (5:14-15). Paul wrote about the operation of "the gifts of healing" (1 Cor. 12:9). In Christ's future kingdom, our mortal body with all its imperfections and problems will be replaced with an immortal body like that of the resurrected Jesus (ch. 15).

Verse 7 of the text emphasizes the restoration of the earth to beauty and productivity. Instead of desert with its inherent dryness, there will be an abundance of water. Instead of barren ground, there will be vegetation of various types. This can be seen in modern-day Israel. For a number of decades now the barren land is flourishing with all types of fruits and vegetables. How unusual to see banana palms, citrus trees, and apple trees growing in the same area. One can only attempt to imagine the specifics of the heavenly kingdom.

> "For happiness one needs security, but joy can spring like a flower even from the cliffs of despair."
> —Anne Lindbergh

C. Redemption (vv. 8-10)

8. And an highway shall be there, and a way, and it shall be called The way of holiness; the unclean shall not pass over it; but it shall be for those: the wayfaring men, though fools, shall not err therein.

　　　　　　　　The Glory of Christ's Kingdom

9. No lion shall be there, nor any ravenous beast shall go up thereon, it shall not be found there; but the redeemed shall walk there:

10. And the ransomed of the Lord shall return, and come to Zion with songs and everlasting joy upon their heads: they shall obtain joy and gladness, and sorrow and sighing shall flee away.

These final three verses of our lesson point to the time when God's people are led home to Zion. Zion initially was one of the hills on which Jerusalem was situated. Later it would be a term referring to the whole city of Jerusalem. Besides its geographical reference, Zion is also used figuratively for Christ's eternal kingdom. This seems to be the usage applied here.

Christ's kingdom is a holy domain reflective of God himself (Lev. 19:2). Only those individuals who choose to be holy through the sanctifying power of the Holy Spirit will be allowed on the path which leads to Christ's eternal kingdom. Through divine redemption peoples of all nations, Jew and Gentile, will pass through this road to Zion. The person of lesser mental capacity will not go astray. No beast of prey will be able to pounce on unsuspecting travelers.

This will be a joyous event as the spiritual pilgrims reach their heavenly reward. Gladness of successfully completing the journey and being in the presence of the King will dominate. Totally absent will be the sighing and sorrow connected to life on a sinful earth. Banished will be any forms of disappointment and pain. Death no longer will bring the pangs of separation. Completely gone are all the negatives connected with sin and life in our fleshly bodies. This will not be a short-term joy and gladness that will either be plucked from us or slowly fade with time. It will be the permanent state of the redeemed through the blood of Jesus Christ.

CONCLUSION

Throughout the history of the world a number of powerful rulers and kingdoms have arisen that have amassed huge armies and often built amazing structures. Regardless of how successful their expansion and economic success, one by one they eventually have come to an end. Most of them have been marked by violence and suffering. In marked contrast is the glory of Christ's kingdom. It is filled with joy, peace, and unity. Christ's kingdom will endure forever.

GOLDEN TEXT CHALLENGE

"THINE, O LORD, IS THE GREATNESS, AND THE POWER, AND THE GLORY, AND THE VICTORY, AND THE MAJESTY: FOR ALL THAT IS IN THE HEAVEN AND IN THE EARTH IS THINE; THINE IS THE KINGDOM, O LORD, AND THOU ART EXALTED AS HEAD ABOVE ALL" (1 Chron. 29:11).

Talk About It:
1. Who will, and will not, walk on "the Highway of Holiness" (vv. 8-9 NKJV)?
2. Describe the song of the redeemed (v. 10).

"Joy, not grit, is the hallmark of holy obedience."
—Richard Foster

King David proclaims the kingdom of God and its exaltation above all on the earth. David would never know the ancient kingdoms still to come who would tower over Israel in geographical size and population. He could never have dreamed of the powerful, modern nations with their nuclear arsenals. But his limited knowledge doesn't negatively affect the statement. Regardless of all the modern inventions, these latter nations still stand as dwarfs in comparison to the greatness of God.

In attempting to describe the Lord's kingdom, David used five words: *greatness, power, glory, victory,* and *majesty.* The kingdom of God supersedes all others in splendor, majesty, and glory. Defeat is unknown. All the honor devised by humanity pales in the sight of God and His kingdom.

To put all of this in perspective, we must remind ourselves of who is authoring these words. It is David, the second king of Israel, a man after God's own heart who was unequaled as a warrior of his time. From the leader of a group of dissidents hiding in the wilderness and fleeing from Saul, he rose to carve a nation of considerable power and respect. Yet, he knew that God's kingdom far surpasses anything humans could ever develop on this earth.

The Birth of the King (Christmas)

Matthew 1:18 through 2:23

INTRODUCTION

Our Christmas lesson is taken from the Gospel of Matthew. While this book is listed first in the New Testament order, it was probably not the earliest Gospel written. Most New Testament scholarship today assumes the priority of Mark. Yet Matthew's unique emphasis on the Jewishness of Jesus makes his account the logical one to begin the story of the new covenant.

The first device this Gospel writer uses to emphasize the Jewish quality of his work is found in the opening verse of Matthew: "The book of the generation of Jesus Christ." The word *generation* comes from the Greek *genesis*, which is the title of the first book of the Old Testament. The phrasing parallels Genesis 2:4 and 5:1. Again, in Matthew 1:18, a reference to *genesis* ("birth") occurs.

A second device is in the use of Old Testament Scripture to support and validate the fact that Jesus is the Messiah.

The genealogy of Jesus is traced back to Abraham, the father of the promise. What may appear as trivial material is actually very important. His genealogy makes it plain that Jesus was legitimate and His ancestry was perfect for Him to be the rightful heir of David's throne.

Matthew 1:1 says Jesus was "the son of David, the son of Abraham." The New Testament affirms not only those facts, but also affirms that Jesus was before both David and Abraham. Jesus described Himself in Matthew 22:43 as David's Lord; and in John 8:58 Jesus affirmed, "Before Abraham was, I am." Thus, while His lineage can be traced from these two giants of Israel's faith, our Lord, as the eternal Son, stands before them.

Finally, in Matthew 1:16, the family line comes to a close with the reference to "Joseph the husband of Mary, of whom was born Jesus." It is significant that Matthew's pattern of describing the family line (from v. 2 to v. 16) is changed here. Matthew did not write that Joseph "begat" Jesus. He is only mentioned as the husband of Mary!

Matthew carefully wrote these verses; this is no mistake on his part. The Holy Spirit led him to write in such a fashion to make it clear that Jesus' royal blood came from the eternal throne of God, and flowed through the generations of humanity's greatness and sin to fulfill God's plan.

Unit Theme:
Christmas

Central Truth:
Because He is the King, Jesus is worthy of our adoration and praise.

Focus:
Recognize Jesus as the King and worship Him.

Context:
Christ is born in Bethlehem in 4 or 5 BC.

Golden Text:
"Behold, a virgin shall conceive, and bear a son, and shall call his name Immanuel" (Isa. 7:14).

Study Outline:
I. The King Is Born (Matt. 1:18-25)
II. The King Is Sought (Matt. 2:1-8)
III. The King Is Worshiped (Matt. 2:9-11)

I. THE KING IS BORN (Matt. 1:18-25)

A. Impossible Situation (vv. 18-19)

18. Now the birth of Jesus Christ was on this wise: When as his mother Mary was espoused to Joseph, before they came together, she was found with child of the Holy Ghost.

19. Then Joseph her husband, being a just man, and not willing to make her a public example, was minded to put her away privily.

Talk About It:
1. Why was it necessary for Jesus to be born "of the Holy Ghost" (v. 18)?
2. How did Joseph show himself to be "a just man" (v. 19)?

To understand these verses, we need to understand the three steps of a Jewish marriage. The first step was the *engagement*. Usually this was made between the parents while the couple were still children. In the second step, the engaged couple was *betrothed*. Barclay observes that "once the betrothal was entered into, it was absolutely binding." The betrothal lasted for one year; then the couple was considered legally married. This one-year period was so crucial that it took a bill of divorce to end the marriage contract. The third step was the actual *marriage*. Then the sexual relationship could be consummated. Thus Joseph and Mary were in the second phase of the marriage relationship when the Lord appeared to her.

Verse 18 begins by emphasizing that the birth of Jesus is the new beginning. The word translated "birth" is the Greek *genesis*. The text goes to great lengths to point out that the child had been conceived by the Holy Spirit. It notes that Mary and Joseph were betrothed ("espoused"), not married in the fullest sense. It also points out that the birth was the direct act of the Holy Spirit.

Luke 1:26-35 records how the angel Gabriel informed Mary that she would conceive under the power of the Holy Spirit. While this is not told in Matthew's account, it is certainly part of the background to the story.

It is important to keep in mind the connections between creation and redemption in our lesson, as seen in the use of *genesis* and the corresponding first book of the Bible. Note that the Spirit of the Lord was engaged in moving over the world, bringing order out of chaos "in the beginning" (Gen. 1:1-2). The same Spirit worked in the new creation which came in the person of Jesus.

Verse 19 of the text reflects what was mentioned earlier regarding the seriousness of the betrothal period: It took a bill of divorce to conclude a legal marriage.

Joseph had two legal options in this situation: In the first he could institute a lawsuit against Mary. In theory she could be stoned as a result of the lawsuit; however, Jewish law was so complex that such extreme measures were rarely enforced. The second option was the private bill of divorce. The first option would have exposed Mary to shame and disgrace of the community. Joseph is called "a righteous man," indicating a sense of compassion and his love for her. Hence he "had in mind to divorce her quietly" (NIV).

"At the very beginning of Jesus' life as a human on earth, the creative work of the Spirit made possible His birth to a virgin."
—French Arrington

B. Divine Solution (vv. 20-23)

20. But while he thought on these things, behold, the angel of the Lord appeared unto him in a dream, saying, Joseph, thou son of David, fear not to take unto thee Mary thy wife: for that which is conceived in her is of the Holy Ghost.

21. And she shall bring forth a son, and thou shalt call his name Jesus: for he shall save his people from their sins.

22. Now all this was done, that it might be fulfilled which was spoken of the Lord by the prophet, saying,

23. Behold, a virgin shall be with child, and shall bring forth a son, and they shall call his name Emmanuel, which being interpreted is, God with us.

Verse 20 reflects that Joseph was a just man. He took the time to seriously consider his actions in this "impossible" situation. The word *behold* means "to introduce a dramatic change" in the situation as Joseph perceived it. An unidentified angel appeared to Joseph in a dream, with the divine revelation of the will of God.

There are several highlights in the message of the angel. First, it took God's revelation for Joseph to understand who Jesus is. Second, Joseph was called "son of David," reminding him of his standing in the lineage of the Messiah. Third, Joseph's fear of what others might say was replaced by the confidence that he was called to live a life that pleased God, not people. Fourth, the reason he could act without fear was that the child in Mary's womb was "conceived . . . from the Holy Spirit" (NIV).

In verse 21 the message of the angel focused on the unborn Jesus. The angel announced that the name of the son was to be *Jesus*, which means "Savior" or "the Lord is salvation." *Jesus* is the Greek form of the name *Joshua*. In Hebrew there is a play on words between *Joshua* and *save* that is impossible to bring out in English translations. The purpose of His life was made clear: "He shall save his people [Israel] from their sins."

In verse 22 Matthew introduces a favorite literary device of his: the use of Old Testament references as proof-texts for incidents in the life of Jesus. (The quote in verse 23 comes from Isaiah 7:14.)

The central term in Isaiah's prophecy is the Greek word *parthenos*, which means "virgin." Liberal commentators argue that the Hebrew word in Isaiah 7:14 can be translated "young woman." This is true; however, the word can also be used to describe a virgin. It is clear that Matthew intended his readers to understand "virgin" by his use of *parthenos*.

The name *Emmanuel* (or *Immanuel*) means "God with us," and is a constant theme of Matthew's Gospel. His record begins with the reality of "God with us," and concludes with Christ's promise, "Lo, I am with you alway" (28:20). There is no conflict between calling Him "Emmanuel" and "Jesus." All believers can confess that God is with us in the person of the Savior.

Talk About It:
1. Why could Joseph "fear not" (v. 20)?
2. Why would God's Son be named "Jesus" (v. 21)?
3. Why would He be called "Emmanuel" (v. 23)?

"It is only because God's Son became 'God with us' that we can become 'us with God.'"
—**Lance Colkmire**

C. Courageous Obedience (vv. 24-25)

24. Then Joseph being raised from sleep did as the angel of the Lord had bidden him, and took unto him his wife:

25. And knew her not till she had brought forth her first-born son: and he called his name Jesus.

Remember that verses 22 and 23 are the editorial work of Matthew, and not part of the message of the angel to Joseph. There is no reason to assume, however, that Joseph did not understand the child to be born to Mary was the fulfillment of the prophecy given through Isaiah seven hundred years earlier. Being a just man, a man knowledgeable of the Law, we can assume that the importance of this event was clear to him.

Joseph's doubts had come to an end. God had spoken to him, he had listened, and now he would obey. There can be no separating these three elements of obedience in the life of the believer.

The believer must be able to hear what God has to say. This requires an open heart and spirit. It requires a life that is just before God. It requires a commitment that places His Word above all things. How tragic is it when people follow after those things that are not of God! For us to hear God speak today means we are receptive to continual contact with His Word. It means we allow the Spirit to confirm that Word in our life and give us direction.

Listening to God requires humility and the recognition that His is the most important voice we shall ever hear. To really hear God is to obey Him.

Joseph and Mary did not have intimate sexual relations until after Jesus' birth (v. 25). Mark 3:31-35 shows Jesus had half-brothers and sisters.

II. THE KING IS SOUGHT (Matt. 2:1-8)
A. Coming From the East (v. 1)

1. Now when Jesus was born in Bethlehem of Judaea in the days of Herod the king, behold, there came wise men from the east to Jerusalem.

The coming of the wise men, also known as the Magi, differs in timing from the visitation of the shepherds. The shepherds (see Luke 2:8-20) were led to Jesus by an angelic host on the night of His birth. The wise men were led to Him by a heavenly light, arriving after His birth. It has been conjectured that they arrived in Bethlehem from six months to two years after the birth of Jesus (see Herod's activity in Matt. 2:16). One thing is certain: the traditional Nativity scene with shepherds and wise men gathered around the newborn Jesus is not what happened!

There is no doubt that Jesus was born in Bethlehem. This small village was five miles south of Jerusalem. It was the ancestral home of King David, and Luke 2:1-7 tells why Joseph and Mary

Talk About It:
How did Joseph obey the Lord's instructions?

Talk About It:
Why was Jesus born in Bethlehem instead of the capital city of Jerusalem?

left Nazareth (in Galilee) and made the nearly 70-mile trip south to Bethlehem. The name *Bethlehem* is rich in theological intent, with its meaning as "House of Bread."

Matthew 2:1 indicates the time frame in which our Lord was born. His birth marks the dividing point in human history. Most calendars even mark time by virtue of His birth into BC (before Christ) and AD (anno Domini—Latin for "in the year of the Lord"). During the time of Christ the calendar dating system was based from the establishing of Rome, usually cited as AUC. It was not until AD 533 with Dionysius Exiguus that the decision was made to reckon time from the birth of Christ rather than the establishing of Rome. However, Dionysius made a slight mistake, which explains why Jesus was actually born in 4-6 BC rather than AD 1. Jews still use their own dating system for religious purposes, as do most religions and cultures of the Far East.

The word *behold* intentionally draws our attention to the surprising visit by the Magi from the East. It was used to highlight something of special significance, an unexpected turn in the story.

The "east" is *anatole* in the Greek text. Their exact origin is disputed and cannot be ascertained. There are three locations proposed.

First, the term *magoi* (used in the Greek and translated "wise men") favors the area controlled by the Medes and Persians. Second, the reference to the star (and thus astronomy and astrology) indicates the area of Babylon. We do know that Jews had been in the territory of Babylon since the Babylonian Captivity (586 BC). Third, the gifts brought by the Magi suggest an area near Arabia or the Syrian desert.

While it is difficult to ascertain their origin, we do know more about the term *magi*. The Greek historian Herodotus wrote of a group of magi in the sixth century BC who had the special power to interpret dreams. They were known as Zoroastrian priests.

Outside of Matthew's Gospel, the New Testament refers to magi ("sorcerer") negatively (Acts 8:9-24; 13:6-11). In the New Testament era the term referred "to those engaged in occult arts and covers a wide range of astronomers, fortune-tellers, priestly augurs, and magicians of varying plausibility" (Raymond Brown, *The Birth of the Messiah*).

The popular Christmas song "We Three Kings" is based on the tradition that the wise men were kings (probably under the influence of Ps. 72:10-11). It is also interesting that they were traditionally believed to be three in number, based on the fact that three gifts were given. Yet those numbers have fluctuated throughout the centuries. The catacombs in Rome have art forms with two and four Magi, and there are lists in the Eastern churches of twelve Magi. Also, interest in naming the wise men existed in the early Christian centuries.

"If we Christians would join the wise men, we must close our eyes to all that glitters before the world and look rather on the despised and foolish things, help the poor, comfort the despised, and aid the neighbor in need."
—**Martin Luther**

B. Coming to Worship (v. 2)

2. Saying, Where is he that is born King of the Jews? for we have seen his star in the east, and are come to worship him.

Talk About It:
Why did the wise men search for Jesus?

Regardless of their origin, the Magi came to Jerusalem with one intention: to worship the King of the Jews. This verse shows that the Magi followed a star. There are prevailing views regarding the appearance of this heavenly light.

First, it has been considered a supernova. "A nova or supernova involves a faint or very distant star in which an explosion takes place so that for a few weeks or months it gives out a great deal of light, sometimes to the point of being visible even in the daytime. However, there is no record of a nova or supernova just before Jesus' birth date" (Brown).

Second, it has been suggested that they followed a comet. However, the appearance of a comet was usually considered a sign of some form of catastrophe rather than the good news of a Savior.

Third, a popular view is that there was a conjunction of Jupiter, Saturn, and Mars. The astronomer Kepler saw this happen in October 1604, and calculated that it had also happened in 7-6 BC.

What is certain is that the stars and planets were created by God and He was, and is, able to use them for His purposes. It should also be noted there is a difference between *astronomy*, which is the legitimate, scientific study of the stars and planets, and *astrology*, which seeks to use the stars and planets to describe the future. Astronomy is a science and worthy of respect.

The Magi came to Jerusalem in search of the "King of the Jews." What adds to the significance of this title is that it was also applied to Herod. Thus, the Magi presented a challenge to the current royal line. The purpose of the Magi with this new King was "to worship him." Brown comments on this: "The verb *proskynein* (worship) occurs three times in this section (vv. 2, 8, 11) and ten times in the rest of Matthew. Often involving an act of prostration (v. 11), it describes homage offered to a person of dignity or of authority, as well as adoration or worship paid to a deity."

The wise men did not offer to kneel before Herod. They were using Herod only as an avenue to get to the great King. Their journey, with the star and use of Herod's information, implies a sense of journeying to discover the truth. Their search was "global" in the sense they recognized the new King's truth outside their own nationalistic horizons. They were willing to publicly confess their dependence on a Child in the presence of a symbol of earthly power—Herod.

"Let us revel in the light of that star beneath which the ordinary becomes holy and the holy ordinary, beneath which it becomes exceedingly clear that there is nothing more we must do or be to be loved by God."
—Barbara Taylor

The Birth of the King

C. Seeking Destruction (vv. 3-8)

3. When Herod the king had heard these things, he was troubled, and all Jerusalem with him.

4. And when he had gathered all the chief priests and scribes of the people together, he demanded of them where Christ should be born.

5. And they said unto him, In Bethlehem of Judaea: for thus it is written by the prophet,

6. And thou Bethlehem, in the land of Juda, art not the least among the princes of Juda: for out of thee shall come a Governor, that shall rule my people Israel.

7. Then Herod, when he had privily called the wise men, enquired of them diligently what time the star appeared.

8. And he sent them to Bethlehem, and said, Go and search diligently for the young child; and when ye have found him, bring me word again, that I may come and worship him also.

Talk About It:
1. What "troubled" Herod (v. 3)?
2. Where did Herod send the wise men, and why (vv. 4-8)?

That Herod, as political king of the Jews, would be "troubled" (v. 3) by the news of the Magi is obvious. The Greek for *troubled* means "stirred up, disturbed, unsettled, thrown into confusion." It is used of the disciples in Matthew 14:26 and Mark 6:50 to express their fear at seeing Jesus walking on the water, in Luke 1:12 to describe Zacharias' state at the appearance of the angelic visitor, by Jesus in Luke 24:38 to describe the fear the disciples had when He appeared to them following His resurrection, and in 1 Peter 3:14 as a word from the Lord for those suffering for His sake that they not be intimidated in the face of suffering.

There are four possible sources of Herod's terror: (1) A rival king had been born that Herod knew nothing of; (2) a rival king was born within Herod's jurisdiction but outside his control; (3) a new king was an obvious threat to the future (even if He was an infant); and (4) from a human standpoint, a new king implied the existence and support of a group of people and armies.

Verse 3 of the text indicates that all Jerusalem joined in this anxiety. Any threat to the established order always creates a sense of confusion and uncertainty that affects an entire community. From verse 4 we learn that Herod, as king of the Jews, was ignorant of the Jewish Scriptures. He required the religious experts (chief priests and scribes) to do his investigative work. Jesus frequently was in conflict with scribes, Pharisees, and the officers of the priesthood during His ministry. He was not only a threat to the political order, He was also a threat to the religious order (in actuality, the two can hardly be separated in relation to Jewish life at that time.)

The verb translated "demanded" in verse 4 has a sense of inquiry. While it does mean seeking to learn, it does not mean such seeking was done for the sake of a good cause. As is

known, Herod's motives for "learning" were anything but pleasant. Note also that Herod asked where "Christ" was to be born. This is interesting because the wise men had asked about the "King of the Jews." These two Christological titles were used interchangeably in the first-century Jewish circles. The idea of Christ (or Messiah) did connote a political office to the Jews. They expected the Messiah to successfully destroy the Roman occupation and establish the kingdom of God.

It is likely that a period of time elapsed between verses 4 and 5. The chief priests and scribes did their investigation and returned with the chilling news that the infant King had been born practically in Herod's backyard (note the earlier reference that Bethlehem was about five miles south of Jerusalem). In a real sense, this was no foreign invasion; this was "sedition in the household." A rival king was born practically at the gates of Jerusalem (Ps. 24:7-10).

The quote in verse 6 is from Micah 5:2. It revealed that the One born in Bethlehem was to be a ruling prince. The reference to shepherding God's people (see Matt. 2:6 NIV) connected this leader to the figure of David.

Herod's response to this news was to operate secretly to further advance his desire to kill the Child. Herod secretly called the Magi for the purpose of determining exactly when the star appeared.

Herod held information needed by the Magi: where the child of the prophecy was located. We must understand he did not know the extent of this child's kingship. Herod acted with political expedience in terms of the Magi, which explains why no military might was used initially. Note also that Herod did not intend to kill every child in Bethlehem but only the child of the prophecy.

Herod's intent was hidden in the disguise of "worship" (v. 8). The same Greek word is used as described in verse 2. Note that acts of worship do not necessarily constitute true worship. True worship comes from spirit and truth (John 4:23-24). One cannot help but think of the themes of worship/murder that stand in Genesis 4 with the story of Cain and Abel. This has a profound warning for us today. We can carry out the outward religious acts of worship, but unless the Spirit of God is free to accomplish His purposes in our hearts, we can be filled with murderous intentions.

III. THE KING IS WORSHIPED (Matt. 2:9-11)
A. The Joy of the Lord (vv. 9-10)
9. When they had heard the king, they departed; and, lo, the star, which they saw in the east, went before them, till it came and stood over where the young child was.

10. When they saw the star, they rejoiced with exceeding great joy.

The language used to describe the joy of the Magi is intensive. In verse 10 the Greek abounds with expression to convey the unlimited, matchless joy they experienced in His presence. Their rejoicing over the star did not negate their true worship of Christ. Even as the star led them to the source of their life, Christ, so also we rejoice in the Holy Spirit as He leads us to Christ. Here is a list of references to *joy* in relation to the Lord: Nehemiah 8:10; Psalms 16:11; 30:5; 42:4; 126:5; John 15:11; 16:22, 24; 17:13; Acts 8:8; 13:52; 15:3; 20:24.

Talk About It:
What brought the wise men "great joy," and why?

B. Gifts of Adoration (v. 11)

11. And when they were come into the house, they saw the young child with Mary his mother, and fell down, and worshipped him: and when they had opened their treasures, they presented unto him gifts; gold, and frankincense, and myrrh.

Even though Jesus was born in Bethlehem's manger, it is obvious that His parents were able to find housing after the busy tax season. In the presence of Jesus, the Magi prostrated themselves in worship. Note they immediately knew who He was.

Talk About It:
How did the wise men worship Jesus?

The church father Origen suggested the three gifts brought by the Magi indicated "gold, as to a king; myrrh, as to one who was mortal; and incense [frankincense], as to God" (quoted in William Hendrikson's *The Gospel of Matthew*).

Gold is often associated with royalty in the Bible (Gen. 41:42; 1 Kings 10:14-18; Dan. 2:32, 38; 5:7, 29). Gold was used lavishly in the Tabernacle and its furniture (Ex. 25—31; 35—40) and in the Temple and its equipment (1 Kings 6—7; 2 Chron. 2—5).

Frankincense (which means "pure incense") came from a tree. "In the Old Testament, it is mentioned in connection with the service of Jehovah. It was stored in a chamber in the sanctuary (1 Chron. 9:29; Neh. 13:5), and it is frequently mentioned in connection with meal offerings, as an additive (Lev. 2:1, 15-16; 6:15). According to Exodus 30:34-35 (NIV), it entered as an ingredient into the composition of incense, with respect to which it was specifically stated that it was not for the people but *only for Jehovah* (v. 37).

Myrrh, also derived from a tree, was used as a perfume with numerous uses (Est. 2:12; Ps. 45:8; Prov. 7:17; Song 3:6). It was also used in the New Testament in relation to the death and burial of Jesus (Mark 15:23; John 19:39-40). Myrrh was used in making the anointing oil (Ex. 30:22-33) but was usually used in the normal flow of life. As Hendrickson wrote, it made life "more pleasant . . . pain less dreadful, and . . . burial less repulsive."

An interesting parallel exists between these gifts and the Christian's life. God deserves the best we can offer (gold). Frankincense symbolizes a life of genuine piety and prayer. Myrrh speaks of a life so permeated with Christ's presence that it touches every area of the human experience with His grace.

"The Magi should be a great comfort to us. They brought all that they had to the Lord, not just their expensive presents, but their very lives."
—Fleming Rutledge

CONCLUSION

"The Bible says my King is a seven-way King. He's the King of the Jews; that's a racial King. He's the King of Israel; that's a national King. He's the King of righteousness. He's the King of the ages. He's the King of heaven. He's the King of Glory. He's the King of kings, and He's the Lord of lords. That's my King. Do you know Him?

"My King is a sovereign King. No means of measure can define His limitless love. No far-seeing telescope can bring into visibility the coastline of His shoreless supply. No barrier can hinder Him from pouring out His blessings. He's enduringly strong; He's entirely sincere; He's eternally steadfast; He's immortally graceful; He's imperially powerful; He's impartially merciful. Do you know Him?"—S. M. Lockridge

GOLDEN TEXT CHALLENGE

"BEHOLD, A VIRGIN SHALL CONCEIVE, AND BEAR A SON, AND SHALL CALL HIS NAME IMMANUEL" (Isa. 7:14).

Our Lord came into this world by an extraordinary event, the Virgin Birth. The importance of His supernatural birth cannot be overstated. First, the Virgin Birth reinforces our understanding of the person and work of Jesus. The miracle of His birth fits perfectly well with what we know about His atoning work, His bodily resurrection, and His return in glory. His miracles, teachings, and claims are in accord with what we would expect of One who had such an extraordinary entrance into the world.

Second, the supernatural birth of the Savior affirms the power of the Cross to save from sin and death. Only God can do that. The wonderfulness of Jesus' birth bears witness to the union of Deity and humanity in His person. No other kind of person could have accomplished the miracle of saving grace through the Cross. The miracle of His birth makes believable the miracle of the Cross.

Third, the uniqueness of the Savior's birth indicates that He is worthy of our worship. While on the earth, He asserted that He was the Son of God. A number of people recognized His deity and worshiped Him. The birth of the babe in Bethlehem cannot be separated from the worship of Him as our Lord. The Virgin Birth is part of the history of the One who said, "I am Alpha and Omega, the beginning and the ending . . . which is, and which was, and which is to come, the Almighty" (Rev. 1:8).

Daily Devotions:

M. Prince of Peace
   Isaiah 9:2-7
T. God Is Savior
   Isaiah 43:1-7
W. Christ's Birth
   Announced
   Luke 1:26-31
T. Sought by
   Shepherds
   Luke 2:8-18
F. The Word
   Becomes Flesh
   John 1:1-14
S. Imitate Christ's
   Humility
   Philippians 2:5-11

Judgment and Hope

Isaiah 65:1-25; 66:1-24

INTRODUCTION

Negative actions bring repercussions. Breaking the law results in punishment. Since this is true from a human perspective, why should we expect it to be any different in our relationship with God?

It's amazing how many people want God to be one-dimensional. They want Him to be kind, loving, caring, and protective, but never restrictive or negative. It's as though God should disregard His own nature and principles and stoop to human expectations. If that were to happen, He would not be God.

This reminds us of the ancient Greek pantheon of gods. These mythical beings were used as explanations for the various events of nature. For example, when there was thunder and lightning, it was because Zeus was angry and clapping his hands. However, since these gods were also supposed to be subject to all the passions and problems of humans, they eventually lost their position within the people's thinking. How could they be gods and still have all the passions and problems of humans?

Today's lesson causes us to focus on the reality of God's judgment on humankind in general, and even on His disobedient children (believers). No one is exempt from God's working to correct and restore righteousness. However, God does not sit on high like a bird of prey just waiting to rush down and inflict judgment. Instead, He is a loving, kind, merciful heavenly Father. Yes, He does bring judgment. But within it there is mercy and the desire for restoration. He is exalted when we turn from sin and enter into fellowship.

The central truth for this lesson is "God's mercy gives hope in judgment." Even when we are the object of His judgment due to our sinfulness and rejection of His words, there is hope. He wants us to turn and be drawn back to Himself. His mercy stems from a desire for our transformation.

Unit Theme:
Major Prophets

Central Truth:
God's mercy gives hope in judgment.

Focus:
Recognize God's mercy in judgment and trust in His restoring love.

Context:
The last two chapters of Isaiah speak of past and future judgments and blessings.

Golden Text:
"Therefore will the Lord wait, that he may be gracious unto you, and therefore will he be exalted, that he may have mercy upon you: for the Lord is a God of judgment: blessed are all they that wait for him" (Isa. 30:18).

Study Outline:
I. God Judges the Rebellious (Isa. 65:1-12)
II. God Will Renew All Things (Isa. 65:17-25)
III. God Offers Hope (Isa. 66:12-14, 18-23)

I. GOD JUDGES THE REBELLIOUS (Isa. 65:1-12)
A. The Rejection (vv. 1-5)

1. I am sought of them that asked not for me; I am found of them that sought me not: I said, Behold me, behold me, unto a nation that was not called by my name.

2. I have spread out my hands all the day unto a rebellious people, which walketh in a way that was not good, after their own thoughts;

3. A people that provoketh me to anger continually to my face; that sacrificeth in gardens, and burneth incense upon altars of brick;

4. Which remain among the graves, and lodge in the monuments, which eat swine's flesh, and broth of abominable things is in their vessels;

5. Which say, Stand by thyself, come not near to me; for I am holier than thou. These are a smoke in my nose, a fire that burneth all the day.

Talk About It:
1. What phrase does the Lord repeat in verse 1, and why?
2. Contrast the uses of the phrase "all the day" in verses 2 and 5.

Isaiah's words in these opening verses must be seen in light of the previous chapter. There the people appeal to God's compassion in view of the desolation that is described.

Wouldn't God relent and have pity on His people? In turn, the opening verses of chapter 65 seem to balance the scene or set the story straight. Their sins provide the reasons.

The contrast begins with a difficult statement in verse 1. The Lord is revealing Himself to people who are neither asking for nor seeking Him. It appears we have here the thought of God's later adoption of the Gentiles. This is based on the apostle Paul's letter to the Romans in which these verses are quoted (10:20-21). The Gentiles do not approach the heavenly Father, but He goes to them, offering Himself for their benefit.

God's own people, who should recognize their treasured relationship with Him, obstinately go their own way (Isa. 65:2). They reject the good way to pursue their own imaginations of pleasure and self-determination. The obstinacy of Israel is seen in their blatant disobedience of God and rejection of His outstretched arms. It's not an occasional missing of the mark or slight straying. Just the opposite is true. The Israelites "continually provoke" God (v. 3 NIV).

The heathen practices adopted by Israel are despicable in the sight of God. Instead of a sweet-smelling perfume of acceptable sacrifice, they are projecting a stench in the nostrils of their God. A wide variety of priorities is briefly mentioned. Sacrificing in the gardens or groves is a practice among the Canaanites (v. 3). Prior to Israel's entering the Promised Land, Moses warned them, "Destroy completely all the places on the high mountains and on the hills and under every spreading tree where the nations you are dispossessing worship their gods" (Deut. 12:2 NIV).

In Exodus 20:25 God's people were commanded not to make sculpted altars, yet the "altars of brick" in our text could refer to altars designed with brick and mortar. Or, the bricks could refer to roof tiles on which there were idolatrous altars. This can be seen in 2 Kings 23:12 when King Josiah destroyed altars on the roofs.

Verse 4 of the text indicates the practice of holding vigils among people's graves or within hidden caverns dedicated to the various gods. Apparently, the intent is to have communion with the dead or demons for the purpose of special dreams or revelations. It reminds us of those who attend seances to try to communicate with deceased loved ones or receive direction.

Another problem in Israel was people eating the flesh of pigs, which was forbidden by the law of God (Lev. 11:7). It became a sign of rejecting God, especially since other nations gave swine as part of their offerings.

The people in Isaiah's day perceived themselves to have attained a level of holiness separate from that of a righteous God. In God's eyes, all they had accomplished was to earn His wrath—a flame which will not be extinguished (Isa. 65:5).

B. The Repayment (vv. 6-7)

6. Behold, it is written before me: I will not keep silence, but will recompense, even recompense into their bosom,

7. Your iniquities, and the iniquities of your fathers together, saith the Lord, which have burned incense upon the mountains, and blasphemed me upon the hills: therefore will I measure their former work into their bosom.

The principle of sowing and reaping stands out in these verses. No one should ever assume there will be no repercussions from his or her words and actions. Verse 6 uses the word *recompense* ("pay back," NIV) when it comes to disregarding God's laws and turning to selfish devices. Here God's people, who know His specific requirements, choose to disregard them and go in the opposite direction. They are choosing to neglect the all-powerful God of creation, who is working for their redemption, to serve man-made gods of wood and stone that can offer no hope physically, spiritually, or emotionally.

Another principle stands out clearly. It is the ripple effect. No one's actions impact only his or herself. Throwing a stone in the pond sends out ripples from the point of impact which continue and widen, even though it has already sunk to the bottom. The same holds true to the actions of family leaders. One generation influences the next. Joshua provides a positive example. As a result of his spiritual lifestyle and leadership, Israel served God for an entire generation after his death (Josh. 24:31). What a heritage!

These verses from Isaiah remind us of the reality of God's judgment. He isn't willing to disregard sin—especially blatant idolatry. Those who participate will experience His judgment.

Think Again

If you think God condones sin, think again. If you think God approves of those who engage in wizardry, horoscopes, child abuse, adultery, or any other sin, you are profoundly mistaken. God takes all sin seriously. He doesn't make any distinctions when He says in Psalm 34:16, "The face of the Lord is against those who do evil" (NKJV). . . . God's face is against all those who oppose His will and wishes.

—Woodrow Kroll

Talk About It:
1. Explain the "recompense" described here.
2. Compare these verses with Galatians 6:7.

"At the day of Doom men shall be judged according to their fruits. It will not be said then, 'Did you believe?' but, 'Were you doers, or talkers only?'"

—John Bunyan

C. The Remnant (vv. 8-12)

8. Thus saith the Lord, As the new wine is found in the cluster, and one saith, Destroy it not; for a blessing is in it: so will I do for my servants' sakes, that I may not destroy them all.

9. And I will bring forth a seed out of Jacob, and out of Judah an inheritor of my mountains: and mine elect shall inherit it, and my servants shall dwell there.

10. And Sharon shall be a fold of flocks, and the valley of Achor a place for the herds to lie down in, for my people that have sought me.

11. But ye are they that forsake the Lord, that forget my holy mountain, that prepare a table for that troop, and that furnish the drink offering unto that number.

12. Therefore will I number you to the sword, and ye shall all bow down to the slaughter: because when I called, ye did not answer; when I spake, ye did not hear; but did evil before mine eyes, and did choose that wherein I delighted not.

Sharon (v. 10)—a fertile coastal plain

Achor (A-kore)— v. 10—Located near Jericho, Achan was stoned to death in this valley for his disobedience; it means "trouble" (Josh. 7:24-26).

Talk About It:
1. What would God do for His "servants" and His "elect" (vv. 8-9)?
2. What would happen to those who "forsake" and "forget" the Lord (vv. 11-12)?

Verse 8 refers to the manner in which a farmer would be careful to preserve valuable grapes in the midst of grapes that are sour or without juice. "New wine" simply refers to the "juice in grapes."

The farmer says there is a "blessing" in the good grapes. There was within those grapes the ability to make a productive contribution to the harvest and welfare of the farmer. God says similarly, as the farmer, He sees a productive, blessed remnant within the cluster that has become profane. God will be careful to not destroy the "blessed" people while judging the profane "cluster."

Verse 9 describes the faithful possessing God's dwelling places. In the first part of the verse, the faithful remnant is called a "seed" and "inheritor." The terms refer to the posterity and continued possession of the faithful. "Elect" emphasizes that the faithful have become the chosen of God. "Servants" is an apt description of the faithful because they have served and attended unto God in faith and "blessing" (v. 8).

Verse 10 is an amplification of what the faithful possesses. The first part of the verse illustrates the prosperity of the region, "flocks" and "herds." This section also describes the peace of the region because the herds are "lying down." The latter part of the verse describes the remnant as those who have "sought" the Lord. *Sought* comes from a Hebrew word which meant "to trample or tread." It pictures the faithful as those who have faithfully trodden their way to God in worship and service.

Verses 11 and 12 describe the blasphemy of the wicked and their subsequent destruction. Verse 11 describes the manner in which they had made sacrifices for the pagan deities "Fortune" ("that troop") and "Destiny" ("that number"). They had worshiped

Judgment and Hope

and sacrificed unto other gods in an effort to secure their own future.

Verse 12 indicates that God had tried to reach these people but they rejected Him. As a result, they would now face the judgment of God. This judgment is graphically illustrated with the words *sword* and *slaughter*.

II. GOD WILL RENEW ALL THINGS (Isa. 65:17-25)
A. A New Creation (v. 17)

17. For, behold, I create new heavens and a new earth: and the former shall not be remembered, nor come to mind.

There are a number of views as to the meaning of this verse. For instance, Adam Clarke suggests this ultimately refers to the full conversion of the Jews and primarily to the Jews' deliverance from the Babylonian Captivity. Some understand it to be a point where God changes the earth's atmosphere, thus causing the earth as a whole to become more productive.

It is true Isaiah's prophecies deal with the more immediate issues of the Jews' future which would occur within the next several centuries. However, his prophetic statements also reach into the distant future. Surely this speaks of God's provision of a new earth after the destruction of evil, the last great conflict with Satan and his forces. This will be a part of God's dwelling place where peace and righteousness reign (see also 2 Peter 3:13; Rev. 21:1).

B. A Rejoicing Jerusalem (vv. 18-19)

18. But be ye glad and rejoice for ever in that which I create: for, behold, I create Jerusalem a rejoicing, and her people a joy.

19. And I will rejoice in Jerusalem, and joy in my people: and the voice of weeping shall be no more heard in her, nor the voice of crying.

The immediate future for God's people is not bright. Their sinfulness and lack of repentance will result in God's judgment being poured out on them. Not only will they be overthrown by other nations who are fulfilling God's will, there will be death, destruction, and captivity. Their capital city, Jerusalem, and Solomon's temple—the place of worship and symbol of God's presence—will be destroyed. Tremendous sorrow awaits generations to come.

But that isn't the end of the story. Rejoicing will once again occur. Later centuries will see the rebuilding of the Temple (under Zerubbabel) and the city wall (under Nehemiah). God's promises of restoration will be fulfilled exactly as prophesied. A renewal will occur.

There is a new age to come in which to exult and to rejoice. The past will be forgotten with its sorrow and destruction. Weeping will be no more. Surely this must refer to the final coming of the Messiah, Jesus Christ, when His eternal kingdom will be instituted.

Talk About It:
Why will God "create new heavens and a new earth"?

Talk About It:
How will the sounds in Jerusalem change, and why?

C. A New Lifestyle (vv. 20-25)

20. There shall be no more thence an infant of days, nor an old man that hath not filled his days: for the child shall die an hundred years old; but the sinner being an hundred years old shall be accursed.

21. And they shall build houses, and inhabit them; and they shall plant vineyards, and eat the fruit of them.

22. They shall not build, and another inhabit; they shall not plant, and another eat: for as the days of a tree are the days of my people, and mine elect shall long enjoy the work of their hands.

23. They shall not labour in vain, nor bring forth for trouble; for they are the seed of the blessed of the Lord, and their offspring with them.

24. And it shall come to pass, that before they call, I will answer; and while they are yet speaking, I will hear.

25. The wolf and the lamb shall feed together, and the lion shall eat straw like the bullock: and dust shall be the serpent's meat. They shall not hurt nor destroy in all my holy mountain, saith the Lord.

Talk About It:
1. How will human life be better on the re-created earth (vv. 20-23)?
2. Explain God's promise in verse 24.

These verses point to a new future in which the curse of the past for their sinfulness will be no more. Instead of death and destruction, life and fulfillment will be the atmosphere. This must be a reference to the coming millennial reign of Christ since this prophecy has not been realized during the past 2,700 years since it was given. Yes, there have been some times of peace; however, Palestine by its location as the crossroads of three continents has been a staging ground for the military intentions of ambitious rulers. Couple this with the religious conflict associated with the land, as seen in the Crusades, and one knows these promises have not been fulfilled.

The description begins with lifespans. Infants will grow to maturity. They will not die from birth complications, hunger, disease, or invading armies. One hundred years will be a common age attainment. This is far beyond the seventy to eighty years seen as a long lifespan in Psalm 90:10. According to the United Nations, the average life expectancy worldwide is currently sixty-seven years.

Those who build houses and plant vineyards will live to enjoy the benefits of their labors (Isa. 65:22-23). The extension of life and the atmosphere of peace provides a long period of enjoyment. What a contrast to their present time and in centuries to come! Children born face the many misfortunes of life, if they even live into adulthood. People spend days, weeks, months, and even years laboring over the soil and on building projects that can come to nothing.

Notice the difference in relationship with the heavenly Father. No gap exists between the call and the answer such as is the case when there is rebellion. In fact, God will answer requests prior to their completion (v. 24).

Peace will prevail, according to verse 25. Notice the contrasts. The wolf and the lion represent destruction, while the lamb and ox ("bullock") are naturally peaceful. No longer will there be fear and conflict. Instead there will be harmony and unity. The aggressive carnivores will become content with a new diet.

III. GOD OFFERS HOPE (Isa. 66:12-14, 18-23)
A. Future Peace (vv. 12-14)

12. For thus saith the Lord, Behold, I will extend peace to her like a river, and the glory of the Gentiles like a flowing stream: then shall ye suck, ye shall be borne upon her sides, and be dandled upon her knees.

13. As one whom his mother comforteth, so shall I comfort you; and ye shall be comforted in Jerusalem.

14. And when ye see this, your heart shall rejoice, and your bones shall flourish like an herb: and the hand of the Lord shall be known toward his servants, and his indignation toward his enemies.

This final chapter of Isaiah is a combination of judgment and hope. The initial verses speak of the greatness of the Lord and His position as the Creator of all. They also establish the qualities of the person whom the Lord esteems. Then, beginning with verse 3, there are descriptions of people's rebellious actions. These deeds are seen as not only evil but of great displeasure to God.

The day will come in which the Lord will be glorified and His enemies will receive their just reward. On that day, those who have remained true to the word of the Lord will be justified for their commitment. They will experience joy while the others experience the shame of condemnation (vv. 4-6).

Beginning in verse 7, there is the description of a woman giving birth. In an unusual delivery the child is born prior to the birth pains occurring. This image is used to predict the birth of a nation in a single day (v. 8). A Hebrew teacher of the past suggests the similarity of such an event with the birth of Moses. When Jochebed birthed her son, it signaled the freeing of 600,000 men and their families from the bondage of Egyptian slavery, but the process would be painful.

This birth imagery also anticipated the birth of the Church, which Christ fulfilled some two thousand years after Isaiah's prophecy.

"The damage done to us on this earth will never find its way into that safe city. We can relax, we can rest, and though some of us can hardly imagine it, we can prepare to feel safe and secure for all eternity."
—Bill Hybels

Talk About It:
1. How does God promise to deal with His people (vv. 12-13)?
2. How will God's servants be blessed (v. 14)?

It appears that verse 12 of the text moves ahead in time. Jerusalem now stands at the center of the nations. Peace isn't just a fleeting period of time. Instead there is the continuance of health and prosperity, along with the complete absence of conflict. The Lord comforts His people in the same way in which a mother carries her child, nurses him at her breast, and bounces him on her knee.

A totally different picture is the judgment which will come on those who have chosen to be the Lord's enemies. The fury of His anger will execute judgment on all of them. Verses 15 and 16 picture it as chariots racing throughout the area with the soldiers' swords inflicting death. The description of fire speaks of cleansing and destruction.

"Get yourself into the presence of the loving Father. Just place yourself before Him, and look up into His face; think of His love, His wonderful, tender, pitying love."
—Andrew Murray

B. Future Glory (vv. 18-23)

18. For I know their works and their thoughts: it shall come, that I will gather all nations and tongues; and they shall come, and see my glory.

19. And I will set a sign among them, and I will send those that escape of them unto the nations, to Tarshish, Pul, and Lud, that draw the bow, to Tubal, and Javan, to the isles afar off, that have not heard my fame, neither have seen my glory; and they shall declare my glory among the Gentiles.

20. And they shall bring all your brethren for an offering unto the Lord out of all nations upon horses, and in chariots, and in litters, and upon mules, and upon swift beasts, to my holy mountain Jerusalem, saith the Lord, as the children of Israel bring an offering in a clean vessel into the house of the Lord.

21. And I will also take of them for priests and for Levites, saith the Lord.

22. For as the new heavens and the new earth, which I will make, shall remain before me, saith the Lord, so shall your seed and your name remain.

23. And it shall come to pass, that from one new moon to another, and from one sabbath to another, shall all flesh come to worship before me, saith the Lord.

These verses provide some difficulty for interpretation. Do they refer to several time frames widely separated from one another? It would seem to be so.

Talk About It:
What will be the primary focus on the new earth (v. 23)?

Verse 17 describes people who futilely try to "sanctify themselves, and purify themselves" through idolatrous practices. Instead, they are defiling themselves and therefore placing themselves under the wrath of God. "Because of their actions and their imaginations" (v. 18 NIV), God will "gather all nations and tongues." Here are some of the views of what this means: (1) People will come to witness divine judgment on the rebellious and to receive

divine favor. (2) Nations will gather to fight against Jerusalem, and the ungodly Jews will perish, and then the Lord will defend His chosen people. (3) The final judgment is pictured here.

Verses 19-21 also have been given a variety of explanations. This much we can say for sure: God is sovereign over all peoples and nations, and He will receive glory everywhere—specifically in Tarshish (a distant seaport), Pul (Libya), Lud (in Africa), Tubal (in Asia Minor), and Javan (Greece). Jews dispersed to these lands will be escorted back to their homeland, and they will worship the Lord and minister to Him.

In the twentieth century there was an ongoing return of Jews to Israel, highlighted by their becoming a sovereign nation in 1948. But there is no Temple. For that reason, it appears logical to assume these latter verses refer to the end-time events which include a new heaven and a new earth. Then, and only then, will the whole earth come to worship God in the fullness of His glory. All those who rebelled are then deceased. No longer will there be any who rebel against God and lead others astray.

> "Worship is a voluntary act of gratitude by the saved to the Savior, by the healed to the Healer, and by the delivered to the Deliverer."
> **—Max Lucado**

CONCLUSION

Rebellion against God results in God's judgment. However, due to His grace and mercy, there is hope for those who will repent of their sins. Rejoicing to replace sorrow is available to anyone who will submit himself or herself to the word and will of God. This applies not only to individuals, but to the whole nation of God's people.

GOLDEN TEXT CHALLENGE

"THEREFORE WILL THE LORD WAIT, THAT HE MAY BE GRACIOUS UNTO YOU, AND THEREFORE WILL HE BE EXALTED, THAT HE MAY HAVE MERCY UPON YOU: FOR THE LORD IS A GOD OF JUDGMENT: BLESSED ARE ALL THEY THAT WAIT FOR HIM" (Isa. 30:18).

Wait is the key word in this scripture. It functions as bookends, both introducing and closing this verse.

"The Lord [will] wait" means God is withholding executing punishment on rebellious people, allowing them space to repent. He is a gracious and merciful God who wants to be exalted for His grace and mercy.

The phrase "God of judgment" does not mean the Lord delights in condemning people, but that He is the "God of justice" (NKJV). He will do what is right. Therefore, people should "wait for Him"—they should not turn to any other source to save them, but only to the Lord.

The people who wait for the waiting God will be blessed!

Daily Devotions:
M. The Merciful Judge
   1 Chronicles 16:31-36
T. Judgment and Restoration
   Isaiah 40:1-2, 27-31
W. Hope in the Lord
   Lamentations 3:21-32
T. The Righteous Judge
   2 Timothy 4:1-8
F. The Better Hope
   Hebrews 7:17-25
S. Mercy for Unrighteousness
   Hebrews 8:10-13

God's Appointed Prophet

Jeremiah 1:1-19

Unit Theme:
Major Prophets

Central Truth:
God empowers those who submit to His will.

Focus:
Consider God's appointment of Jeremiah and embrace God's plan for our lives.

Context:
The Book of Jeremiah was written between 627 and 580 BC, probably in Jerusalem.

Golden Text:
"Before I formed thee in the belly I knew thee; and before thou camest forth out of the womb I sanctified thee, and I ordained thee a prophet unto the nations" (Jer. 1:5).

Study Outline:
 I. Divine Appointment (Jer. 1:4-10)
 II. Divine Word (Jer. 1:11-16)
 III. Divine Empowerment (Jer. 1:17-19)

INTRODUCTION

Does God have a plan for my life? Is there a specific vocation or task to which I am appointed to accomplish during my lifetime?

Too frequently these questions are applied only to those who go into vocational ministry or are labeled *clergy*. It is easy to assume God's appointment applies only to those who receive formal training and become credentialed ministers. In doing so we miss the reality of all of us being the "called-out ones," the body of Christ. His desire is for all of us to effectively fulfill some form of ministry within His kingdom.

The tremendous challenge facing each of us is submission. Will we empty self of our goals and ambitions so God may work His will in us? Will we embrace His directives and operate within the scope of the Holy Spirit's empowerment?

Jeremiah presents us with a distinct example of what it means to accept God's call to service in very difficult times. His ministry takes place in the years leading up to and during the Babylonian Captivity. He experiences the three occurrences of Nebuchadnezzar and the Babylonian army coming to Jerusalem. The last time, in 586 BC, Jerusalem is destroyed, including Solomon's temple.

Besides the political circumstances, Jeremiah encounters a people who prefer their apostasy rather than repenting and following God's law. As a result, Jeremiah repeatedly delivers a message of condemnation. The people respond angrily. Seen as both a meddler and traitor, there are attempts to harm him and to put him to death. In the face of this opposition, he remains true to the divine appointment.

Jeremiah turns down an offer to go to Babylon and live in relative comfort there. Instead he stays with the people in Judah. He weeps over their rejection of God, and continually desires for them to turn away from sin and experience God's grace rather than His condemnation. This first lesson from Jeremiah projects God's divine appointments and His empowering as one submits to His will.

I. DIVINE APPOINTMENT (Jer. 1:4-10)

A. The Appointment (vv. 4-5)

4. Then the word of the Lord came unto me, saying,

5. Before I formed thee in the belly I knew thee; and before thou camest forth out of the womb I sanctified thee, and I ordained thee a prophet unto the nations.

God's call of Jeremiah to the prophetic office and ministry occurs during the thirteenth year of King Josiah's reign. He begins this new journey during the leadership years of Judah's last righteous king. These first eighteen years will be followed by approximately twenty-two years of decline including the Babylonian invasion.

The specific means of God's revelation isn't stated. However, the words of the Lord are specific. He does not offer a possibility or make a suggestion. Rather, Jeremiah is confronted with a divine appointment. God chooses him for a task with the choice predating Jeremiah's conception. This stands as more than simply knowing what Jeremiah will do. Instead, we see God's selecting and appointing this young man to a spiritual task during crucial decades of Israel's history. He is called and commissioned as a prophet before even beginning the process of life development within his mother's body.

Though a Jew and living in Judah, Jeremiah's sphere of ministry is not to be limited only to God's chosen people. He will be the spokesman of God declaring the wrath of God which is to come on them. This can be clearly seen in chapter 25. Beginning with verse 15, the cup of God's wrath is being poured out on many peoples of an expanded geographical area. Verse 32 provides a summary: "Look! Disaster is spreading from nation to nation; a mighty storm is rising from the ends of the earth" (NIV).

B. The Resistance (vv. 6-8)

6. Then said I, Ah, Lord God! behold, I cannot speak: for I am a child.

7. But the Lord said unto me, Say not, I am a child: for thou shalt go to all that I shall send thee, and whatsoever I command thee thou shalt speak.

8. Be not afraid of their faces: for I am with thee to deliver thee, saith the Lord.

There can be either a negative or a positive resistance to God's plan. Negative resistance can be seen in Jonah's going the opposite direction by boarding a ship for Tarshish, and then sleeping soundly in the hold of the ship. Positive resistance can be described as expressing great concern about the task due to personal limitations. Jeremiah fits this latter category. He's not opposed to God's plan, but does understand the reality of being young and a novice.

Talk About It:
When did God determine His plan for Jeremiah's life, and what was God's plan?

"It is not you that shapes God but God that shapes you. If you are the work of God, await the hand of the artist who does all things in due season."
—Irenaeus

Talk About It:
1. What was Jeremiah's concern (v. 6)?
2. What was God's promise (vv. 7-8)?

Jeremiah might have been around twenty years old at this point. If so, God's calling of Jeremiah is reminiscent of God's coming to Solomon and offering him the opportunity to ask for anything he wants. Solomon, a young king, responds to God with the same statement, "I am but a little child" (1 Kings 3:7).

Some Jewish writers suggest fourteen as the age to which "child" still could be considered appropriate. However, it would not be surprising for someone who had not yet reached the next age of maturity, thirty, to describe himself as a child when faced with a divine task. Jeremiah's suggesting his inability to speak does not seem to be in the same category as suggested by Moses (Ex. 4:10).

The Lord immediately dispels all thoughts of Jeremiah's not being able to accomplish his assignment. He will go to everyone to whom he is sent. He will speak everything the Lord commands. The Lord knows in advance the steadfastness which Jeremiah will exhibit in the face of hostilities from his own people.

Verse 8 of the text stands as one of the Bible's key "Be not afraid" statements. In this case, the Lord adds the addendum "of their faces." This can be understood easily when considering the anger, hostility, and rejection which will be poured out on Jeremiah by his own people. Like the other settings where the Lord tells someone not to fear, He provides a promise. In this case there are two aspects. First, Jeremiah will not be alone; the Lord's presence will continue to be with him. Second, the Lord will bring deliverance.

This two-part promise to Jeremiah should encourage us. As Hebrews 13:5 promises, God will not leave or forsake us. He also brings deliverance. Sometimes it comes by enabling us to have sustaining endurance. On other occasions, the Lord takes the problem away and sets us free.

C. The Commission (vv. 9-10)

9. Then the Lord put forth his hand, and touched my mouth. And the Lord said unto me, Behold, I have put my words in thy mouth.

10. See, I have this day set thee over the nations and over the kingdoms, to root out, and to pull down, and to destroy, and to throw down, to build, and to plant.

The description of the Lord's touching Jeremiah's mouth is similar to the Lord's placing His hand on the prophet Ezekiel (see Ezek. 3:14; 8:1). Jeremiah's description is more than a symbolic statement. Jeremiah does literally feel a touch on his mouth followed by a description of what is taking place. He now goes into ministry as God's spokesman. The words God intends for the people to hear will flow from his mouth.

> "He can accomplish anything He chooses to do. If He ever asks you to do something, He himself will enable you to do it."
> —Henry Blackaby

Talk About It:
Describe the message God gave to Jeremiah.

God's Appointed Prophet

In verse 10, Jeremiah is again told he will be a prophet to the nations. This further emphasizes the breadth of his ministry. Having made this repetition, the Lord then states the content and actions in which Jeremiah will be involved. He will be a prophet of doom. God has no choice in view of His holiness and the nation's disregard for truth and sincere worship. They are in the process of sealing their doom.

The destruction which he will predict begins with tearing up what has become rooted and tearing down what has been built. This description indicates not only a destroying of buildings, cities, and people, but the overthrow of kingdoms. As would be expected, Jeremiah's words will not be accepted. Instead, the people will both reject what is spoken and persecute the spokesperson.

Positively, Jeremiah will also be a constructive prophet offering hope in the future. He will deliver the words which will lead Judah to restoration. Once again there will be an opportunity to build homes and cities. They will be able to plant fields and vineyards.

These words were overwhelming for a young man just about to begin ministry. Yet, Jeremiah had the assurance of God's being with him.

II. DIVINE WORD (Jer. 1:11-16)
A. Symbolic Pictures (vv. 11-13)

11. Moreover the word of the Lord came unto me, saying, Jeremiah, what seest thou? And I said, I see a rod of an almond tree.

12. Then said the Lord unto me, Thou hast well seen: for I will hasten my word to perform it.

13. And the word of the Lord came unto me the second time, saying, What seest thou? And I said, I see a seething pot; and the face thereof is toward the north.

Jeremiah receives two visions. The first is an almond tree branch. Since Anathoth, Jeremiah's home city, is a center for almond growing, this vision is especially appropriate. Jeremiah correctly answers the Lord's question, "What do you see?" The Lord's response of "watching to see [His] word fulfilled" (NIV) indicates soon or rapid fulfillment. The almond tree represents this in its being the first tree to blossom in the springtime. This vision symbolically states the imminent reality of the prophecies of Judah's judgment.

The second vision provides a sinister picture of destruction and the direction from which it will come. The boiling pot represents major disaster. Its "tipping southward" (v. 13 LB) indicates trouble coming from the north.

There is no way to know if there was a time interval between the two visions. Also, the interpretation of what Jeremiah sees may not have been clearly understood. If the prophet begins his

Talk About It:
How did the Lord communicate with Jeremiah?

"When I was young I was sure of everything; in a few years, having been mistaken a thousand times, I was not half as sure of most things as I

ministry about 627 BC, it will be slightly over twenty years until Nebuchadnezzar and his forces will make their first invasion of Judah and take the first group into captivity. However, if his ministry begins at the end of King Josiah's reign (he is fatally wounded in 609 BC), then the shadow of the foe from the north may be well known.

B. The Future (vv. 14-16)

14. Then the Lord saith unto me, Out of the north an evil shall break forth upon all the inhabitants of the land.

15. For, lo, I will call all the families of the kingdoms of the north, saith the Lord; and they shall come, and they shall set every one his throne at the entering of the gates of Jerusalem, and against all the walls thereof round about, and against the cities of Judah.

16. And I will utter my judgments against them touching all their wickedness, who have forsaken me, and have burned incense unto other gods, and worshipped the works of their own hands.

If there was any doubt about the second vision's meaning, it is now completely removed. The events of the future are clearly revealed. Also, very evident to Jeremiah is why his commission included uprooting, tearing down, destroying, and overthrowing.

The wording of verse 14 indicates the extent of these coming events. The NIV states, "From the north disaster will be poured out." This will not be an isolated event marring selected parts of the kingdom. No, this will be a comprehensive disaster touching the whole nation! Besides the death and ruin associated with an invasion, some will live to see the Temple reduced to rubble and the sacred vessels become plunder.

Designating the northern kingdoms as the source of evil is not a strange reference. In previous times the Assyrians were known for their cruelty and invasions, even to the point of destroying Israel. Now a new foe will arise against Judah.

The prophesying of the establishment of thrones at Jerusalem's gates (v. 15) is a symbolic statement of enemies not only invading but also ruling over their land. One can only imagine how unthinkable this must have sounded to the populace. Very quickly Jeremiah will find himself alienated by the content of his prophecies.

There is no question as to the reason for God's pouring out His wrath. The people of Judah are blatantly breaking the covenant by their idolatry. Their following after other gods indicates no continuing commitment to the Lord God. Not only have they burned incense as a worship act, they have even stooped to making idols with their own hands. There is now no difference between them and their heathen neighbors.

God's Appointed Prophet

III. DIVINE EMPOWERMENT (Jer. 1:17-19)

A. The Preparation (v. 17)

17. Thou therefore gird up thy loins, and arise, and speak unto them all that I command thee: be not dismayed at their faces, lest I confound thee before them.

Now that the real work is about to begin, the Lord gives some personal instruction to Jeremiah. A modern translation renders this, "Get yourself ready! Stand up" (NIV). This speaks of the need for tucking one's long flowing robe into the tight waist girdle (belt) to allow freedom of movements. This then has to be followed by standing up. The task at hand cannot be accomplished by leisurely reclining in one position in one place. The believer must place himself in a setting to speak to the people and appear as God's spokesperson.

God's second directive concerns the message. Jeremiah's message comes from the Lord. He isn't to offer personal opinions and feelings. No embellishments. Just the words of the Lord as given to the prophet.

Just as Judah needed to hear from God, our greatest need is to hear the word of the Lord. It is revealed through the Bible and God's messengers. Any person who preaches and teaches needs to have the same understanding as given to Jeremiah, that they are called and empowered by God.

God's third directive in this verse is a warning to Jeremiah. There is nothing subtle about it. Jeremiah must not allow fear to influence him to retreat or to flee from his mission and message. To do so will place himself in opposition to God. Then he will be completely defenseless and have to face the wrath of God.

This verse reminds us of how God prepares His messengers for the task. Jeremiah isn't aware of all he will endure. But the prophet is well aware of his commission and how the Lord will continue to be with him.

B. The Promise (vv. 18-19)

18. For, behold, I have made thee this day a defenced city, and an iron pillar, and brazen walls against the whole land, against the kings of Judah, against the princes thereof, against the priests thereof, and against the people of the land.

19. And they shall fight against thee; but they shall not prevail against thee; for I am with thee, saith the Lord, to deliver thee.

Here is another occasion in which God offers a promise after issuing a heavy directive. Having already been informed of his prophetic task, Jeremiah surely possesses some understanding of its difficulty. If he knew the specifics, he might be shaken; but when they come, he will be able to reflect on this promise.

Talk About It:
What options was Jeremiah given?

"Make my path sure, O Lord. Establish my goings. Send me when and where You will and manifest to all that Thou art my guide."
—Jim Elliot

Talk About It:
1. How was Jeremiah like a "fortified city" (v. 18 NIV)?
2. What did God promise Jeremiah (v. 19)?

God empowers His chosen servant to fulfill the ministry to which he is called. The Lord offers some specific illustrations that assure his being able to do and to say what is necessary in the face of extreme opposition. First, He likens Jeremiah to a major stronghold, an impregnable city. Though the enemy attacks, not one will be able to overcome him. Next, the Lord states he will be like an iron pillar—perhaps a major support pillar which anchors a building. Though beaten and pushed, it does not break or tip. This would be unlike the pillars of the house of the Philistines which Samson dislodged (Judg. 16:29-30). Finally, the Lord indicates Jeremiah will be as resistant to attack as a bronze wall.

This type of strength will be needed. The opposition will not be localized mob action which erupts occasionally or in a few isolated areas. Neither will it come from only one segment of the people. Though the officials of the kingdom will be the primary source of his problems, ordinary citizens will also participate in harassing and persecuting this prophet.

Notice who is specifically pointed out as the resistance. Members of the ruling royal family and the spiritual leadership will be his opponents. It hasn't been too many years prior to this time when King Manasseh "shed innocent blood" through the city of Jerusalem (2 Kings 21:16). Opposition to Jeremiah will come in the reigns of both Jehoiakim and Zedekiah. Zedekiah will agree to others' putting Jeremiah to death by the means of their choice (Jer. 38:4-6).

The religious leadership inflicts a variety of opposition. Pashhur orders Jeremiah to be beaten and placed in stocks (20:1-2). The priests and prophets (false) bring him before the city leadership and seek the death sentence after Jeremiah announces the Lord's curse on the people of Jerusalem (26:1-11).

Ordinary citizens also participate in desiring harm for Jeremiah. They join with the priests and prophets who desire the death sentence. Even the people of his home city of Anathoth reject his prophetic words and plot his death (11:18-23).

The Lord doesn't hide the struggles and difficulties which lie ahead. Though the enemies of the Lord will attempt to destroy him, they will not be successful. Jeremiah will overcome everything they attempt against him. The Lord will bring deliverance.

We can learn a great deal from this relationship. The Lord never leaves nor forsakes the faithful. He is there standing by us. He knows the right time for our deliverance. He faithfully fulfills His promises! God allows Jeremiah to be placed in a muddy cistern with the officials' intent of his starving to death. But the same king who allows this treatment is the one who orders his removal (38:6-13).

"What is courage? It is the ability to be strong in trust, in conviction, in obedience. To be courageous is to step out in faith—to trust and obey, no matter what."
—Kay Arthur

God's Appointed Prophet

CONCLUSION

God calls some individuals to difficult tasks in order for His word to be heard among the people. Jeremiah experiences the worst treatment a prophet of the Lord could expect, short of death. His commission isn't one which leaves him alone to accomplish the task. Along with it, Jeremiah is divinely empowered to speak difficult words and to endure the opposition.

GOLDEN TEXT CHALLENGE

"BEFORE I FORMED THEE IN THE BELLY I KNEW THEE; AND BEFORE THOU CAMEST FORTH OUT OF THE WOMB I SANCTIFIED THEE, AND I ORDAINED THEE A PROPHET UNTO THE NATIONS" (Jer. 1:5).

Unlike Isaiah, Jeremiah had no vision of heaven or of the Lord. Instead, he heard the Lord speak to him. How he knew for certain it was God speaking, we cannot determine—but he knew. Four distinct points are made in this passage that clarify God's call of Jeremiah.

1. *God knew him.* God knows every individual, long before he or she is born. He has known all of us even before time began. Every person ever born had been in God's plans since before the foundations of the world (see Matt. 25:34; Rev. 17:8). No one should ever feel inadequate or discouraged. Each individual is valuable in God's sight, and each has a purpose in His kingdom. This is confirmed profoundly in Psalm 139:13-16.

2. *God's claim on his life superseded all other relationships.* Since God knew Jeremiah first, even before his parents knew him, His plans had first priority. This is a strong argument against the holocaust in America known as abortion. Abortion kills a life that the infinitely wise and eternal God planned in eternity past.

3. *God sanctified him.* He set Jeremiah apart for a divine purpose.

4. *God appointed him.* All believers in God's kingdom are sanctified, but certain ones are anointed and appointed ("ordained") to carry out very specific tasks. We are all called to ministry, and we should do the general works of the church that need to be done. However, not all of us will be pastors, evangelists, prophets, or teachers. These are appointed for special purposes.

If God has never given you an explicit calling or assignment, then continue to fulfill the mission common to all believers—to serve God and obey Him—and let Him direct your steps.

Daily Devotions:
M. God Provides the Words
   Exodus 4:10-16
T. Promise of Empowerment
   Exodus 14:13-16
W. Anointed King
   1 Samuel 16:4-13
T. Spirit-Led Words
   Matthew 10:16-20
F. Empowered to Witness
   Mark 16:15-20
S. A Chosen Vessel
   Acts 9:3-6, 10-16

God's Response to Unfaithfulness

Jeremiah 3:1-25

Unit Theme:
Major Prophets

Central Truth:
God will restore those who return to Him.

Focus:
Examine God's mercy to backsliders and be completely devoted to God.

Context:
The Book of Jeremiah was written between 627 and 580 BC, probably in Jerusalem.

Golden Text:
"Return, thou backsliding Israel, saith the Lord; and I will not cause mine anger to fall upon you: for I am merciful, saith the Lord, and I will not keep anger for ever" (Jer. 3:12).

Study Outline:
I. Israel's Unfaithfulness (Jer. 3:1-10)
II. God's Admonition (Jer. 3:12-20)
III. Repentance and Promised Restoration (Jer. 3:21-25)

INTRODUCTION

How is it possible for a righteous nation to slide deeply into sin? Why would people leave a haven of spiritual and physical security to follow lifestyle patterns with no true future? The people of Judah willingly grasped for current pleasure and personal independence with no apparent regard for the future wrath of God. The God of miracles and preservation was pushed aside to delight in gods of wood, stone, and metal fashioned by human hands. It's mind-boggling!

Before we become too self-righteous, we should do some intense personal introspection. Have we as individuals or groups gone down the same path? Oh, we more than likely haven't been guilty of bowing and praying before idols. But when we place people, jobs, and pleasure above obedience to the Word of God, a similar pattern of unfaithfulness is evident.

When God's people are guilty of backsliding into the sins of their unsaved neighbors, He mercifully calls for them to return. If they do so, He will withhold the judgment that should be unleashed. However, they shouldn't expect to delay this return and, at their own timetable, choose when and how it will be accomplished.

God desires to restore individuals, families, communities, and entire nations to Himself. In fact, He pleads with His people to return.

Today's lesson helps us to examine God's mercy to those who leave the shelter of His will and law. It also provides an opportunity to review what it means to be devoted to God.

I. ISRAEL'S UNFAITHFULNESS (Jer. 3:1-10)

A. A Picture of Unfaithfulness (vv. 1-5)

1. They say, If a man put away his wife, and she go from him, and become another man's, shall he return unto her again? shall not that land be greatly polluted? but thou hast played the harlot with many lovers; yet return again to me, saith the Lord.

2. Lift up thine eyes unto the high places, and see where thou hast not been lien with. In the ways hast thou sat for them, as the Arabian in the wilderness; and thou hast polluted the land with thy whoredoms and with thy wickedness.

3. Therefore the showers have been withholden, and there hath been no latter rain; and thou hadst a whore's forehead, thou refusedst to be ashamed.

4. Wilt thou not from this time cry unto me, My father, thou art the guide of my youth?

5. Will he reserve his anger for ever? will he keep it to the end? Behold, thou hast spoken and done evil things as thou couldest.

lien with (v. 2)— "been violated" (NASB)

a whore's forehead (v. 3)—"the brazen look of a prostitute" (NIV)

These five verses are poetic in their style within the original language of the text. In them the author shares a picture of unfaithfulness which reflects Israel's relationship with God. It begins with a marriage relationship in which a man divorces his wife. She leaves and becomes the wife of another man. By law and general practice, she could never return to her first husband. It did not matter if the second husband died or divorced her. There could be no reuniting of the original couple. To do so would be considered an act of defilement and similar to the actions of a prostitute.

Such is the situation of God's people in Jeremiah's day. Playing the part of a religious prostitute, they have turned to various gods. Formally, they are married to God in the solemn covenant. Exchanged are the vows of God's care, protection, and provision, as well as the people's commitment to worship, serve, and love God. However, the people do not remain truthful to the relationship. Can divine favor ever be granted again?

Verse 1 reminds us of the story of Gomer, wife of Hosea (Hos. 1—3). She played the prostitute, leaving her husband for many lovers. The prophet's going out, finding her, and bringing her home were at the direction of God himself. It reflects how God does the unthinkable in calling Israel back to Himself.

Why were the Jewish people so prone to disobedience? When they first left Egypt, they were negatively influenced by other people who migrated with them. In times of physical need, they seemed to forget God's previous provision and prefer grumbling and complaining (Ex. 14:10-12; 16:2-3; 17:1-7). Their desire to have a king was based on wanting to be like other nations (1 Sam. 8:19-20). And it seems their idolatry was fostered by sexual desire (Ezek. 16:36-37).

Talk About It:
1. How had Israel "lived as a prostitute" (v. 1 NIV)?
2. How had Israel's rebellion affected the weather (v. 3)?
3. How did Israel's talk not match their walk (vv. 4-5)?

Verse 2 of the text presents another picture of what has taken place. In his commentary, Adam Clarke suggests this refers to the practice of desert nomads lying "in wait to plunder the caravans. Where they have no cover to lie in ambush, they scatter themselves about, and run hither and thither, raising themselves up on their saddles to see if they can discover, by smoke, dust, or other tokens, the approach of any travelers."

In the same way, God's people have been waiting for the next foreign god to appear. They are like prostitutes awaiting the next lover. As a result of this spiritual defilement, they are already suffering by God's withholding rain from the land. There have been no fall rains, which are vital for the germination and early growth of the crops. Neither have there been the spring (latter) rains to sustain growth.

Regardless of what is taking place, the people brazenly continue in their idolatrous sinfulness. They feel neither guilt nor shame. Of course, when people lose their shame, guilt does not arise. Rather than repenting before God, the people know Him as a friend who will overlook their wrongdoings and come to their rescue. The assumption seems to be, "We have pleaded and protested our problem, so now You should mercifully come to our aid!" However, that is a grave miscalculation.

B. An Unfaithful Nation (vv. 6-10)

6. The Lord said also unto me in the days of Josiah the king, Hast thou seen that which backsliding Israel hath done? she is gone up upon every high mountain and under every green tree, and there hath played the harlot.

7. And I said after she had done all these things, Turn thou unto me. But she returned not. And her treacherous sister Judah saw it.

8. And I saw, when for all the causes whereby backsliding Israel committed adultery I had put her away, and given her a bill of divorce; yet her treacherous sister Judah feared not, but went and played the harlot also.

9. And it came to pass through the lightness of her whoredom, that she defiled the land, and committed adultery with stones and with stocks.

10. And yet for all this her treacherous sister Judah hath not turned unto me with her whole heart, but feignedly, saith the Lord.

lightness of her whoredom (v. 9)— "casual harlotry" (NKJV)

stocks (v. 9)—trees or wood

Talk About It:
1. Why is Judah called Israel's "treacherous sister" (vv. 7-8, 10)?

Here we are reminded of the splitting of the tribes of Israel after the death of Solomon about 933 BC. Two tribes, Judah and Benjamin, remained under the leadership of Rehoboam, Solomon's son. The other ten rebelled and separated under the leadership of Jeroboam. This is the fulfillment of the Lord's words to Solomon (1 Kings 11:11-13), and Ahijah's prophetic statements to Jeroboam (vv. 29-39).

Due to Jeroboam's desire to ensure further separation of the tribes, he immediately initiated religious practices so different from God's plan. This set the stage for their idolatry and acceptance of other religions. Two golden calves were erected, one at Bethel and one at Dan. No longer would the people go to Jerusalem and offer sacrifices at the Temple (see 12:25-33). Soon this type of rebellion became known as "the way of Jeroboam" (15:34; 16:2, 19; 22:52).

Sadly, the people of Judah had not learned from the example of their sister nation, Israel. The people of Israel quickly became participants in fertility cults, erring on "every high mountain and under every green tree" (Jer. 3:6). They prostituted themselves in following other religions and rejecting their covenant with the Lord God. In vain, God called for them to return. It was futile due to their deep commitment to other gods. Faced with no other choice, God separated Himself from them. They were cut off.

In 722 BC the Assyrians conquered, killed, and scattered Israel's citizens. Did it make a difference to Judah? No! Under the leadership of Manasseh, Judah fell deeper than ever into apostasy. Without fear of divine retribution, they plunged forward in their chosen path of idolatry and immorality. God's judgment on Israel seemed to be of no impact on them. Verse 9 speaks so loudly of their attitude. It was a light thing or of little matter to them to be involved in activities opposite to God's decrees.

Verse 10 implies there being a point or event when Judah made at least a small turn toward God. This may refer to the reform led by Josiah (2 Kings 22—23). He covenanted with the Lord to keep His commandments. This was followed by a national cleansing of the many despicable religious practices. In spite of everything Josiah did, the people did not fully turn themselves to God. The many years of sinful leadership was deeply entrenched in the heart and minds of the people. No wonder the Lord only *delayed* His judgment until after King Josiah's lifetime.

Notice the two references to Judah as the "treacherous," or unfaithful, sister (Jer. 3:8, 10). It emphasizes not only their disobedience to God, but they are depicted as a people who will do "their own thing" with no regard for past, present, or future consequences.

2. Explain the "divorce" that occurred (v. 8).
3. What had Judah done "feignedly" (v. 10) or "in pretense" (NKJV)?

Hypocrisy Today

I'm afraid we modern Christians are long on talk and short on conduct. We use the language of power, but our deeds are the deeds of weakness. We settle for words in religion because deeds are too costly. It is easier to pray, "Lord, help me to carry my cross daily" than to pick up the cross and carry it; but since the mere request for help to do something we do not actually intend to do has a certain degree of religious comfort, we are content with a repetition of the words.

—A. W. Tozer

II. GOD'S ADMONITION (Jer. 3:12-20)
A. Repent and Return (vv. 12-13)

12. Go and proclaim these words toward the north, and say, Return, thou backsliding Israel, saith the Lord; and I will not cause mine anger to fall upon you: for I am merciful, saith the Lord, and I will not keep anger for ever.

13. Only acknowledge thine iniquity, that thou hast transgressed against the Lord thy God, and hast scattered thy ways to the strangers under every green tree, and ye have not obeyed my voice, saith the Lord.

Though the northern kingdom, Israel, has been in exile for approximately 100 years at this point in Jeremiah's ministry, God directs a message to these exiles. The call to return and God's willingness to relinquish His anger needs to be understood within context. Their previous judgment with its severity is justified. There's no regret or suggestion of its being too severe. In His mercy, God is offering them an opportunity to return and be spiritually restored. To do so will result in the lifting of punishment.

God's offer is amazing in light of their outright rejection of Him and turning to other gods. They refused to listen and to heed previous warnings. In mercy, one more chance stands before them. There is, however, a specific requirement. They must confront the reality of their sin. Their aggressive, self-serving sinfulness needs to be not only acknowledged but also confessed. That will make the difference.

"However deep you fall, you are never out of God's reach."
—*Quotable Quotations*

Still today the only way to overcome disobedience and rejection of God's voice is repentance. The only way we can receive forgiveness of our sins and avoid God's judgment is to confess our sins.

B. Return to the Land (vv. 14-18)

14. Turn, O backsliding children, saith the Lord; for I am married unto you: and I will take you one of a city, and two of a family, and I will bring you to Zion:

15. And I will give you pastors according to mine heart, which shall feed you with knowledge and understanding.

16. And it shall come to pass, when ye be multiplied and increased in the land, in those days, saith the Lord, they shall say no more, The ark of the covenant of the Lord: neither shall it come to mind: neither shall they remember it; neither shall they visit it; neither shall that be done any more.

17. At that time they shall call Jerusalem the throne of the Lord; and all the nations shall be gathered unto it, to the name of the Lord, to Jerusalem: neither shall they walk any more after the imagination of their evil heart.

18. In those days the house of Judah shall walk with the house of Israel, and they shall come together out of the land of the north to the land that I have given for an inheritance unto your fathers.

Talk About It:
1. Explain the phrase "one of a city, and two of a family" (v. 14).
2. How does verse 15 describe a godly pastor?
3. What shall "they say no more," and why (v. 16)?

The call to return continues in this section of Scripture. They are to stop their backsliding and come to the One who is truly their husband. Though they have been faithless to Him, God still declares that He is married to Israel. They are His bride.

Israel is in exile, but God indicates He will bring them back; however, it will not be a complete restoration. Just a few will come back to Zion. The reference to Zion, which is Jerusalem, indicates a unity. A remnant of the Israelites will return to their homeland and be reunited spiritually and politically.

God's Response to Unfaithfulness

The emphasis of this section is the provision of leaders who mirror the heart of God. Instead of the corruption and sinfulness of previous centuries, godliness will prevail within those who rule. They will emphasize the truth of God's law and the need to follow Him daily. This is a picture of what every local church and denomination needs within its pastoral leadership—leaders who place Kingdom work as the priority rather than personal benefit. While never compromising doctrine, they should be striving for wholeness within the body.

In verses 16-18 there is a continuing picture of the future. The insignificance of the ark of the covenant is interesting. Does it refer to its no longer being in existence, or having been placed in a secure hiding place? More than likely, this should be interpreted rather as a point in time when Jerusalem will be the symbol of the Lord's presence. Instead of following their evil ways, nations will turn their eyes to the Lord and specifically toward the city of Jerusalem.

Instead of being brothers and sisters divided into two separate nations, the Jews of Judah and Israel will walk together in unity. Together they will take possession of the land of their inheritance. These words are in harmony with the predictions of several other prophets (see Hos. 3:5; Mic. 2:12). The final unification will come when the Messiah himself rules as King over the nations.

4. What is prophesied in verses 17 and 18?

"All praise to our redeeming Lord, who joins us by His grace and bids us, each to each restored, together seek His face."
—**Charles Wesley**

C. Reminder (vv. 19-20)

19. But I said, How shall I put thee among the children, and give thee a pleasant land, a goodly heritage of the hosts of nations? and I said, Thou shalt call me, My father; and shalt not turn away from me.

20. Surely as a wife treacherously departeth from her husband, so have ye dealt treacherously with me, O house of Israel, saith the Lord.

Though having raised the need for repentance and return, the word of the Lord continues to remind Israel of their rejection of Him. Their choosing to follow personal desires rather than remain in covenant relationship fights against God's intentions for their good. The only way for Israel to inherit the Father's blessing is to recognize Him as their heavenly Father. Only then will they be restored and recognized as loyal sons and daughters.

Talk About It:
1. Contrast verse 19 with verse 4.
2. How had Israel "dealt treacherously" with God (v. 20)?

III. REPENTANCE AND PROMISED RESTORATION
(Jer. 3:21-25)
A. The Cry (vv. 21-22)

21. A voice was heard upon the high places, weeping and supplications of the children of Israel: for they have perverted their way, and they have forgotten the Lord their God.

22. Return, ye backsliding children, and I will heal your backsliding. Behold, we come unto thee; for thou art the Lord our God.

Talk About It:
Explain the phrase "backsliding children" (v. 22).

Here we see an unusual picture. The people are seen as standing on hilltops which were the places for their cultic, heathen worship. They are guilty of perverted worship and rejection of the Lord God. He will not answer any pleading and crying in this situation. Though the gods who were previously idolized there have been destroyed (see 2 Chron. 34:3-7), the people still gravitate to these locations. God doesn't respond in this situation. Their only hope is to fully return to the Lord.

Verse 22 of the text lays a straight path. The people's only hope is to recognize their faithlessness and make a complete return. This includes a total rejection of their previous pattern of idolatry and a declaration and acceptance of the Lord God. Only then will there be spiritual healing and a restoration of the heavenly Father.

"The amazing thing about Jesus is that He doesn't just patch up our lives, He gives us a brand-new sheet, a clean slate to start over, all new."
—**Gloria Gaither**

Return to the Lord comes by way of the path of repentance. Simply feeling sorrow for one's sins and desiring help isn't sufficient. Individually and corporately there needs to be recognition of the errors of the chosen path, asking for forgiveness, and a move in the opposite direction. Weeping and wailing have no value in themselves. A change of heart and mind must accompany these expressions in order to experience forgiveness and then walk in a restored relationship with the Lord God.

B. The Recognition (vv. 23-25)

23. Truly in vain is salvation hoped for from the hills, and from the multitude of mountains: truly in the Lord our God is the salvation of Israel.

24. For shame hath devoured the labour of our fathers from our youth; their flocks and their herds, their sons and their daughters.

25. We lie down in our shame, and our confusion covereth us: for we have sinned against the Lord our God, we and our fathers, from our youth even unto this day, and have not obeyed the voice of the Lord our God.

Talk About It:
1. What is "vain" (v. 23)?
2. What do verses 24 and 25 say about "shame"?

Jeremiah now presents the words of repentance which the people should say and God wants to hear. It begins with recognition of truth. First, there is no salvation to be found in the many heathen gods and their high places of worship. Second, only the Lord God can provide salvation. It's this type of recognition and confession that will bring about a renewal of God's covenant with them.

Spiritual deception and following after other gods is found too frequently in Israel's history. Verse 24 indicates an ancestral history of shameful religious straying. It began within months of leaving Egypt. At Mount Sinai they worshiped a golden calf about

a month after hearing the voice of God audibly speak the Ten Commandments. After the thirty-eight-year death march in the wilderness, Israelite men indulged in sexual immorality and idolatry with Moabite women (Num. 25:1-3). After arriving in Canaan, they failed to destroy all the inhabitants who later became the source for worshiping other gods. This behavior throughout the centuries serves to impoverish the nation as they experienced God's judgment.

The final verse strongly emphasizes the only way to a spiritual restoration. In the same way God's people rejected and turned from Him, they must now turn from their sins. The past disobedience and deafness to the voice of God is to be replaced with repentance and commitment to Him.

CONCLUSION

God desires to extend mercy to backsliders and to have them restored to relationship. Regardless of the distance of their drifting or the specific actions committed, there is an open door. However, it is impossible without the backslider openly confessing sin. Without repentance there can be no restoration. Israel's history of unfaithfulness would appear to have provided such a gulf of separation from which there could be no reconciliation. Yet, God reaches out to them, desiring their return.

GOLDEN TEXT CHALLENGE

"RETURN, THOU BACKSLIDING ISRAEL, SAITH THE LORD; AND I WILL NOT CAUSE MINE ANGER TO FALL UPON YOU: FOR I AM MERCIFUL, SAITH THE LORD, AND I WILL NOT KEEP ANGER FOR EVER" (Jer. 3:12).

The prophet is directed to proclaim these words toward the north, for they are a call to backsliding Israel, the ten tribes that were carried captive into Assyria, which lay north from Jerusalem. That way he must look, to show that God had not forgotten them, though their brethren had, and to upbraid the men of Judah with their obstinacy in refusing to answer the calls given them. One might as well call to those who lay many hundreds of miles off in the land of the north; they would as soon hear as these unbelieving and disobedient people; backsliding Israel will sooner accept mercy, and have the benefit of it, than treacherous Judah (v. 11).

Perhaps the proclaiming of these words toward the north looks as far forward as the preaching of repentance and remission of sins unto all nations, beginning at Jerusalem (Luke 24:47). A call to Israel in the land of the north is a call to others in that land, even as many as belong to the election of grace. When it was suspected that Christ would go to the dispersed Jews among the Gentiles, it was concluded that He would teach the Gentiles (John 7:35).—Matthew Henry

Where to Stand

The opposite side to unfaithfulness to truth is well demonstrated by President Abraham Lincoln. "I am not bound to win, but I am bound to be true. I am not bound to succeed, but I am bound to live up to what light I have. I must stand with anybody that stands right, stand with him while he is right, and part with him when he goes wrong."

Daily Devotions:
M. Unfaithfulness
   Confronted
   2 Samuel 12:1-12
T. Prayer of
   Repentance
   Psalm 51:1-12
W. Faithfulness
   Rewarded
   Jeremiah 35:12-19
T. Regret for Failure
   Mark 14:66-72
F. Message of
   Repentance
   Acts 2:36-40
S. Pattern for
   Repentance
   1 John 1:5-10

Promise of a New Covenant

AGREEMENTS

Jeremiah 31:31-37; Hebrews 8:1-13

Unit Theme:
Major Prophets

Central Truth:
The new covenant is established by the blood of Christ's sacrifice.

Focus:
Compare the old and new covenants and rejoice in the provisions of the New Covenant.

Context:
The Book of Jeremiah was written between 627 and 580 BC, probably in Jerusalem.

Golden Text:
"This shall be the covenant that I will make with the house of Israel; after those days, saith the Lord, I will put my law in their inward parts, and write it in their hearts; and will be their God, and they shall be my people" (Jer. 31:33).

Study Outline:
  I. Nature of the New Covenant
      (Jer. 31:31-34)
 II. Permanence of the New Covenant
      (Jer. 31:35-37)
III. Superiority of the New Covenant
      (Heb. 8:1-13)

INTRODUCTION

It is interesting how often the "new" concept is seen in Scripture. Consider just a few of them. More than likely you will think of others not mentioned.

There's the concept of newness in spiritual matters. The Scriptures include a new heart and a new spirit (Ezek. 11:19; 36:26), a new creation (2 Cor. 5:17), and a new self (Eph. 4:24).

We find a number of references to "a new song." The psalmist states the Lord placed a new song in his mouth (Ps. 40:3). Other passages in the Psalms indicate we are to "sing to him a new song . . . and shout for joy" (33:3 NIV) and "sing . . . a new song" in response to "marvelous things" (98:1).

In the nation of Israel there was what could be considered as "new" exemptions for military service (Deut. 20:5-7). A new home not yet lived in, a new vineyard not yet enjoying its fruit, and a new betrothal all qualified for a temporary exemption.

Reviewing the word *new* in a concordance provides many other instances of something new. The Philistines transported the ark of the covenant out of their territory on a "new cart" (1 Sam. 6:7). Elisha asked for a "new bowl" with salt in it for the miraculous healing of water in a well (2 Kings 2:20). Jesus' body was placed in a "new tomb" after His crucifixion (Matt. 27:60).

New doesn't always mean something positive. Newness may mean leaving the comfortable pattern of the past. (Breaking in new shoes comes to mind.) *New* sometimes includes moving to a different place and having to make many adjustments.

New does carry with it an excitement of different sounds and smells. It also may include new advantages and benefits. Such is the case of being the recipients of God's *new covenant*. We are blessed to have been born after the Cross so we can have a personal relationship with our heavenly Father through the blood of Jesus Christ and the ministry of the Holy Spirit.

This lesson allows us to not only compare the old and new covenants, but provides the opportunity to rejoice in this special blessing.

I. NATURE OF THE NEW COVENANT (Jer. 31:31-34)

A. Future Covenant (v. 31)   HEB 10:1

31. Behold, the days come, saith the Lord, that I will make a new covenant with the house of Israel, and with the house of Judah.

Jeremiah's prophetic ministry includes more than warning the people of their sins and future judgment. While those words constitute a great portion of his writings and pronouncements, there are also positive aspects, such as the nation's future restoration after seventy years of captivity. Even more significant is the prophetic statement of God's establishing a new covenant in the future.

No timetable is attached or hinted at during this announcement. Individuals hearing or reading this prophetic announcement are simply given a statement of what will come to pass. Little could they imagine the fulfillment to be some six hundred years away. Nor did they realize it would take the death and resurrection of the Messiah to bring it about.

In the first century, confession in Jesus as Savior through His blood shed on Calvary brought believers into the new covenant. They realized the blood of bulls and goats no longer provided the means to reach God.

B. Different Covenant (v. 32)

32. Not according to the covenant that I made with their fathers in the day that I took them by the hand to bring them out of the land of Egypt; which my covenant they brake, although I was an husband unto them, saith the Lord.

So many important aspects of Israel's history are contained in this short verse. It provides a reminder of their previous enslavement in Egypt. They were workers with no hope of advancement or freedom. As their population grew, Pharaoh instituted means to minimize the growth. Through a series of miraculous plagues, God provided for their release. Through the leadership of Moses, they came to Mount Sinai, where God began to develop them into a nation.

God's care for these people and His covenant relationship goes back to Abraham. God selected him and his wife, Sarah, to be the parents of a new nation through which spiritual life would be provided (see Gen. 12; 13; 15; 17). This covenant continued and then brought to full description with the giving of the Ten Commandments, as well as the rest of the Law (Ex. 19—24). During the thirteen months at Mount Sinai the Tabernacle was constructed, the priesthood instituted, and the provision for worship and confession through sacrifices and offerings was instituted.

Talk About It:
Why did God plan to make a "new covenant"?

"The sense of newness is simply delicious. It makes new the Bible, and friends, and all mankind, and love, and spiritual things, and Sunday, and church, and God Himself. So I've found."
—*Temple Gardner*

Talk About It:
Explain the phrase "took them by the hand."

Verse 32 of the text also notes their unfaithfulness. Even at Mount Sinai, shortly after the giving of the Commandments, idolatry appeared as the people demanded of Aaron a visible representation. Complaining about the leadership, as well as the physical settings, further demonstrated their lack of commitment. The rebellion at Kadesh-barnea in refusing to enter the Promised Land epitomized this spirit of separation (Deut. 1:26-46). However, the pattern continued throughout their history, regardless of God's miraculous acts of provision and protection.

Even though Israel broke the covenant, God was a husband to her. In spite of His continuing love and care, they rejected Him and moved away from an intimate relationship.

C. Internal Covenant (vv. 33-34)

33. But this shall be the covenant that I will make with the house of Israel; After those days, saith the Lord, I will put my law in their inward parts, and write it in their hearts; and will be their God, and they shall be my people.

34. And they shall teach no more every man his neighbour, and every man his brother, saying, Know the Lord: for they shall all know me, from the least of them unto the greatest of them, saith the Lord: for I will forgive their iniquity, and I will remember their sin no more.

This new covenant will be different in many ways from the original. The most significant difference is that it will not be a covenant written on stone and focused on outward actions. Instead, it will be a covenant written within the hearts and minds of the people. The distinctive symbol of the old covenant is the tablets of stone on which God wrote the basis of the Law, the Ten Commandments. Now God will again write His law, but it will be within each person. God's new covenant will provide an intimacy of relationship previously unknown under the old covenant.

All along God's desire has been for Israel to see Him as their God. So this new covenant is first offered to His chosen people. This pattern is seen as well in the Great Commission (Matt. 28:19-20). It is to be offered first to the Jews and then to the Gentiles. The apostle Paul further demonstrates this on his missionary journeys. First, he goes to the Jews in a particular city. Second, he offers the Gospel to the other peoples living there.

Under the Mosaic covenant, access to God comes through the priesthood and the prophets. Through the priests, confession and thanksgiving are given by sacrifices and offerings. The prophets and teachers know the Lord and instruct in the way of the Lord. Under the new covenant, no longer will intermediaries be needed. Once and for all, the perfect, all-encompassing sacrifice will be made. When wickedness is forgiven, it will never be remembered again.

Talk About It:
1. What would be unique about God's new covenant with Israel (v. 33)?
2. What would be different about the people's relationship with God (v. 34)?

Surely the people hearing these words must have been over-whelmed. What a drastic change! How could this be accomplished? We look back and have 20/20 vision. Christ's coming to earth as the God-man is clearly explained. The accounts of Christ's crucifixion, death, burial, resurrection, and ascension to the heavenly Father provide a foundation for us to understand this new covenant.

This emphasis of a heart covenant is hinted in other scriptures centuries prior to Jeremiah's ministry. Consider two from Deuteronomy: "These commandments that I give you today are to be upon your hearts" (6:6 NIV). "The Lord your God will circumcise your hearts and the hearts of your descendants, so that you may love him with all your heart and with all your soul, and live" (30:6 NIV).

II. PERMANENCE OF THE NEW COVENANT (Jer. 31:35-37)
A. Permanence of the Lord (v. 35)

35. Thus saith the Lord, which giveth the sun for a light by day, and the ordinances of the moon and of the stars for a light by night, which divideth the sea when the waves thereof roar; The Lord of hosts is his name.

The unfolding of a future new covenant by no means indicates God's being inadequate or insufficient when instituting the old covenant. He did not make an error or have an oversight! God's sovereign will works according to His wisdom and timing. The old covenant serves its purpose for initiating the necessary process of salvation through blood sacrifice. He then chooses to initiate a new covenant which will much more easily incorporate all peoples.

Verse 35 provides a strong reminder of who God is and what He has done. His work as the Creator provides the foundation for sovereign authority. The description of these specific acts is first recorded in Genesis 1:16 as part of the creative actions on the fourth day.

Lights are placed in the heavens to provide illumination for both day and night. The powerful rays of the sun bring both light and warmth. Describing the moon as a source of light is not a scientific error. The moon in itself does not generate light; it is a reflector of the sun. However, in common language we speak of the moon shining, meaning it does provide light, though reflected.

The last portion of Jeremiah 31:35 speaks of the stirring up and roaring of the seas. There are other passages that also speak of the seas raging (Ps. 46:3; Isa. 17:12; 51:15). We know the Lord can cause a tempest on the sea, as is seen in Jonah 1:4. This could be the concept referred to here. At the same time, we must consider the context. The moon does exert gravitational pull on the oceans and seas, creating the rise and fall of the tides on a daily basis. This is not the same as a storm at sea, but it can create powerful waves on some shores.

"As the sun shines on all things on earth in the same way, yet as if each is separate, that is how God's love is for each of us: the same yet unique."
—**Thérèse of Lisieux**

Talk About It:
How does this verse explain the Lord's relationship to nature?

ordinances (v. 36)—"fixed order" (NASB)

The power of God and the permanence of His being and creation presents itself to us daily. We see the constant process of day and night, as well as the order of the seasons. Without the permanence of God's law and creation, travel on earth by satellite guidance and travel in space would be impossible, and daily life would be chaotic.

B. Permanence of Israel (vv. 36-37)

36. If those ordinances depart from before me, saith the Lord, then the seed of Israel also shall cease from being a nation before me for ever.

37. Thus saith the Lord; If heaven above can be measured, and the foundations of the earth searched out beneath, I will also cast off the seed of Israel for all that they have done, saith the Lord.

This prophetic promise is a phenomenal hope for God's people. Even though He needed to discipline them for their disobedience, not everyone will die in exile. A remnant will be saved. There will be a future for these people as a nation; they will not always be a subjected people. In our day, we see that Israel is a sovereign nation, having been reestablished in 1948.

Talk About It:
What is the Lord's commitment to Israel?

Initially God's promise is couched in the light of the sun, moon, and stars continuing to be heavenly bodies fulfilling their appointed purpose ("those ordinances," v. 36). As long as they exist, Israel can be assured of their continuance. In the most difficult times—when the Babylonians invade Judah on three occasions, killing, enslaving, and plundering—this promise provides hope. The power of such a statement is easily seen by us. If the sun ceases to exist, all life on earth will end.

To further emphasize the permanence of Israel, God points to their inability to measure the heavens (v. 37). No one in those days could determine the size of the earth or grasp some concept of the vastness of heaven. So what was unthinkable to them is translated to an event unthinkable by God. He will not destroy these people and thereby annul the established covenant.

Ever since bringing them out of Egypt, the Lord God exhibited extreme patience in the face of their repeated rebellion. It would have been easily justified for Him to eradicate them from the earth. But God kept His word as initially covenanted with Abraham. He knew the end prior to the beginning. He saw a Savior, His Son, coming through the lineage of this nation to provide a salvation opportunity for all humans.

III. SUPERIORITY OF THE NEW COVENANT (Heb. 8:1-13)
A. Superior High Priest (vv. 1-6)

1. Now of the things which we have spoken this is the sum: We have such an high priest, who is set on the right hand of the throne of the Majesty in the heavens;

2. A minister of the sanctuary, and of the true tabernacle, which the Lord pitched, and not man.

3. For every high priest is ordained to offer gifts and sacrifices: wherefore it is of necessity that this man have somewhat also to offer.

4. For if he were on earth, he should not be a priest, seeing that there are priests that offer gifts according to the law:

5. Who serve unto the example and shadow of heavenly things, as Moses was admonished of God when he was about to make the tabernacle: for, See, saith he, that thou make all things according to the pattern shewed to thee in the mount.

6. But now hath he obtained a more excellent ministry, by how much also he is the mediator of a better covenant, which was established upon better promises.

Talk About It:
1. Where is our High Priest (v. 1)?
2. What is "the true tabernacle" (v. 2)?
3. How is Jesus' ministry "more excellent" than that of other high priests (v. 6)?

In Hebrews 7, Jesus is presented as a high priest superior to any of His predecessors. His sacrifice does not need to be repeated as required by the others. They were imperfect, but Christ, the perfect One, offers Himself rather than animals. Having said this, the author brings it home in 8:1: "The point of what we are saying is this: We do have such a high priest, who sat down at the right hand of the throne of the Majesty in heaven" (NIV).

A significant distinction of the new covenant is the superiority of Christ as the High Priest. Besides offering a once-and-for-all sacrifice, Jesus serves as our High Priest in the heavenly counterpart to the earthly Tabernacle or Temple (v. 2).

Beginning in verse 3 we see a brief review of the ministry of the Levitical priesthood. Their service to God and to their fellow Israelites consisted of presenting sacrifices to God on their behalf. Jesus Christ was not part of the Levite tribe, so He did not serve as a priest while living on earth (v. 4).

Verse 5 directs us to the sanctuary constructed while the Israelites lived at Mount Sinai. In Exodus 25—30 we find the specific instructions concerning the construction of the Tabernacle and its furnishings. Also included are directions for making the priests' clothing as well as the content of the anointing oil and incense. Then, in chapters 36-39, Moses records their having followed the directions as given.

Hebrews 8:5 says the original Tabernacle was a copy and shadow of a heavenly image. However, this is secondary to the role of Jesus.

Verse 6 provides a foundational statement. Christ's ministry as our High Priest in heaven far exceeds the ministry of the high priests who ministered during the years in which the Tabernacle and Temple existed. In the same way, this new covenant is far beyond the original one with Abraham. This superiority rests on the person of Jesus coming to earth as the God-man. He emptied

Talk About It:
1. Why was a second covenant necessary (vv. 7-8)?
2. How had God's people treated the old covenant (v. 9)?

Himself of divinity not by giving it up, but by allowing the limitations of human flesh to become His lot while living on earth. His suffering, death, and resurrection portrayed a lamb slain for sin once and for all. He continues as our constant intercessor, and can personally identify with our temptations and hurts.

How blessed we are to be part of the new covenant! We have direct access to our heavenly Father through our Savior and Lord, Jesus Christ. We have the promised Comforter, the Holy Spirit, to empower and to guide. Our sacrifice of praise needs to be ongoing in light of Jesus' supreme sacrifice.

B. Superior Covenant (vv. 7-13)
  (Hebrews 8:10-12 is not included in the printed text.)
  7. For if that first covenant had been faultless, then should no place have been sought for the second.
  8. For finding fault with them, he saith, Behold, the days come, saith the Lord, when I will make a new covenant with the house of Israel and with the house of Judah:
  9. Not according to the covenant that I made with their fathers in the day when I took them by the hand to lead them out of the land of Egypt; because they continued not in my covenant, and I regarded them not, saith the Lord.
  13. In that he saith, A new covenant, he hath made the first old. Now that which decayeth and waxeth old is ready to vanish away.

In these verses we find a restatement of the words of Jeremiah previously covered in this lesson as well as further application. The writer to the Hebrews emphasizes the need for the new covenant. If any of these believers are considering a return to Judaism, it means a backward step. The first covenant fulfills its intended purpose for the time. Its imperfection necessitates a new, superior covenant.

The first covenant's incompleteness or imperfection is not the result of God's inadequacy and inability to know its function and the future. The first covenant stands as the beginning step for human redemption from sin. God's process determines a move from stage to stage, from imperfection to perfection. Paul wrote in Galatians 4:4, "When the fulness of the time was come"—when everything was just right—"God sent forth his Son," Jesus Christ, to institute this new covenant.

The inclusion of both the house of Israel and the house of Judah emphasizes God's care for all of His people (Heb. 8:8). The division into two separate nations after the reign of Solomon doesn't mean He cares less for one than the other. Even though the nation of Israel is defeated and torn apart many years before Jeremiah's prophecy, God still cares and offers covenant to all of His chosen people.

Israel as a whole did not have a good track record of faithful obedience to their God. Their many rebellions and deviations undermined their vow of "All that the Lord has said we will do" (Ex. 24:7 NKJV). They made this vow repeatedly (19:8; Josh. 1:16), yet their history was one of grumbling, complaining, and sinning within days of seeing miracles of deliverance and provision. As a result, it became necessary for hard punishments to be leveled against them in the hope of their returning to God wholeheartedly.

In spite of all this, God offers a covenant not dependent on human intermediaries, the priests (Heb. 8:11). He is providing a covenant in which the inner relationship guides rather than the laws of the exterior (v. 10). There is to be the establishment of a bond which reconciles and binds the people's hearts to their God.

This new covenant extends mercy which will erase the unrighteousness of the past. It covers their sins, never to be remembered anymore. In the words of an old song, their sins "are buried in the sea of God's forgetfulness." What a picture of mercy!

Verse 13 emphasizes the longevity of this new covenant. It is not temporary; it will not some day be replaced by another; it is not susceptible to the ravages of time. The previous covenant becomes old, but this new one through Jesus Christ remains new forever!

CONCLUSION

The promise of a new covenant in the writings of Jeremiah is fulfilled through Jesus Christ, as expressed by the writer of Hebrews and experienced by his audience. Not only is the covenant initiated through Israel's bloodline, but it can be their experience as well. There is unqualified forgiveness to them and to anyone else who desires to experience this new covenant. The necessary imperfection of the past becomes the present perfection.

GOLDEN TEXT CHALLENGE

"THIS SHALL BE THE COVENANT THAT I WILL MAKE WITH THE HOUSE OF ISRAEL; AFTER THOSE DAYS, SAITH THE LORD, I WILL PUT MY LAW IN THEIR INWARD PARTS, AND WRITE IT IN THEIR HEARTS; AND WILL BE THEIR GOD, AND THEY SHALL BE MY PEOPLE" (Jer. 31:33).

The sin offerings of the old covenant could be nullified if the heart of the worshiper was not deeply involved in the blood sacrifice as it was offered. The weakest point of the old covenant's sin offering was that it was performed in the physical realm and subject to all the distractions of the flesh. The text defining the sacrifice was written on scrolls of animal skin or papyrus, the actions of the priest were performed in a perfunctory manner, and

Old Versus New

With the secrecy of a military operation, the Coca-Cola Company developed a formula for a new kind of Coke. With fanfare, it was released on April 23, 1985. The company chairman proclaimed it to be "smoother, rounder, yet bolder." However, public reaction was so negative the product was pulled from store shelves on July 11, less than three months after its release. The old Coke formula returned under the name Coca-Cola Classic.

Thankfully, when God replaces the old with something new, the result is always positive.

the offering could be completed without ever truly acknowledging the righteousness or demands of the God to whom the sacrifice was made.

By design, the new covenant would not be fraught with all of the encumbrances of the flesh. The law would be written upon the heart, the means of observing the demands of the law would be conscripted through the soul, and the sacrifice that enabled the covenant would be offered once for all through the Son of God.

When the new covenant arrived, the intervention of both priest and prophet would not be necessary, "for they shall all know me, from the least of them unto the greatest" (v. 34).

God's Demanding Call

Ezekiel 2:1 through 3:14

INTRODUCTION

By their nature, some jobs are much more difficult than others. Some require great physical effort. Others produce a great amount of emotional stress due to deadlines and/or pressure to meet quotas. Most jobs sometimes stretch workers to their limits. We may thoroughly enjoy our work in spite of its demands.

The life of a prophet in the biblical era never was easy. Those whose ministry was in a period of domination by outside nations as part of God's discipline experienced extra pressure. Ezekiel falls into this category.

Ezekiel's ministry took place in the exilic period when Judah was controlled by Babylon. Ezekiel was in the second group of deportees to Babylon. His ministry began in 593 BC. Seven years later the destruction of the Temple in Jerusalem was traumatic news for the refugees, even though they were separated from the Holy City. They no longer had a place that represented the presence of God and was solely dedicated for worship.

Ezekiel's wife died on the day of the third attack or siege of Jerusalem. God instructed Ezekiel not to publicly mourn as a sign that an even greater catastrophe was occurring (Ezek. 24:15-24). Regardless of his personal pain and loss, Ezekiel was to fulfill God's directive and declare God's word in this time of crisis. This man demonstrated his commitment to God's call, regardless of the demand to his personal life.

Today's lesson examines Ezekiel's call to ministry as a prophet of God. It reminds us of the need to acknowledge and submit to God's call to perseverance. When God places His hand on our lives, it is not a temporary assignment. It is to be a lifelong commitment of service to Him. Today's Central Truth needs to remain dominant while examining Ezekiel's call.

Life as God's servant is not an easy road with crowds flocking to it. Just the opposite is true. However, there are bountiful blessings in knowing we are obedient servants speaking in truth the message of the Lord. He will empower and embolden us in our task!

Unit Theme:
Major Prophets

Central Truth:
God calls us to a lifelong commitment of service to Him.

Focus:
Acknowledge and submit to God's call to perseverance.

Context:
Ezekiel was deported to Babylon in 597 BC. He was called to be a prophet during his fifth year of captivity.

Golden Text:
"Go, get thee to them of the captivity, unto the children of thy people, and speak unto them, and tell them, Thus saith the Lord God; whether they will hear, or whether they will forbear" (Ezek. 3:11).

Study Outline:
I. Challenge of God's Call (Ezek. 2:1-7)
II. Internalizing God's Word (Ezek. 2:8—3:3)
III. Emboldened by God's Call (Ezek. 3:4-14)

I. CHALLENGE OF GOD'S CALL (Ezek. 2:1-7)

A. The Appearance (vv. 1-2)

1. And he said unto me, Son of man, stand upon thy feet, and I will speak unto thee.

2. And the spirit entered into me when he spake unto me, and set me upon my feet, that I heard him that spake unto me.

Talk About It:
When did the Holy Spirit come into Ezekiel, and why?

Ezekiel's calling to the prophetic ministry begins with the vision described in chapter 1. He sees a windstorm coming in the form of a huge storm cloud. He sees four creatures having human forms, but with faces with both human and animal characteristics. He sees a series of wheels turning and the wheel within. He also sees a figure of a man who, from the waist up, looks like glowing metal but, from waist down, looks like fire. Surrounding this figure is a radiance like that of a rainbow. As Ezekiel experiences the glory of the Lord, he falls facedown.

At this point Ezekiel hears the voice of the Lord. Notice that Ezekiel isn't called by name; instead, he is addressed as *son of man* (2:1). This is the same title Jesus uses in personal reference on various occasions (see Luke 5:24; 9:22, 26, 44). However, this description of Ezekiel isn't a messianic reference. The phrase "son of man" simply means "man." Only two prophets—Ezekiel and Daniel—are referred to in this form of address. It is found once in Daniel, but over ninety times in Ezekiel.

> "The geography and the details of His plan will be different for each one of us, of course, but the Spirit's sovereign working is far beyond what the human mind can ever imagine."
> **—Charles Swindoll**

The Lord then directs Ezekiel to stand up. There are times when we should be facedown before the Lord in reverence and submission. Other times the posture is to be one of standing so we can hear the intended message. Before this prophet-to-be can physically put forth the necessary effort to stand, the Holy Spirit sets him on his feet. This will be just the first of a number of occasions in which the Holy Spirit moves him physically. (It should be noted that some believe this action takes place in the vision but not in reality.)

B. The Mission (vv. 3-5)

3. And he said unto me, Son of man, I send thee to the children of Israel, to a rebellious nation that hath rebelled against me: they and their fathers have transgressed against me, even unto this very day.

4. For they are impudent children and stiffhearted. I do send thee unto them; and thou shalt say unto them, Thus saith the Lord God.

5. And they, whether they will hear, or whether they will forbear, (for they are a rebellious house,) yet shall know that there hath been a prophet among them.

Talk About It:
1. How did the Lord describe the people of Israel (vv. 3-4)?

God doesn't sugarcoat what Ezekiel will face. He is upfront with the challenge of this audience. It will be a tough time of

ministry. They are a rebellious nation. Notice the description isn't of a people who might be rather problematic and need extra encouragement. No way! They have a history of rebellion against God, and the current generation is of the same nature.

Ezekiel isn't ignorant of the condition of his own people. He personally has been uprooted and taken into Babylonian captivity. Now he will be placed in a different situation as the spokesperson of God to these people. His mission involves going to these obstinate and stubborn people without knowing whether or not they will listen, much less obey.

God clarifies to Ezekiel what needs to be of special importance. First and foremost is his obedience in delivering God's message. He can't *make* the people listen and change their ways. His responsibility is to do what God requires of him so the people will know a messenger of the Lord is among them.

Verse 5 provides a practical application for each of us, regardless of our particular lot in the Kingdom. We can't control people's response to the Gospel message. But we do have the ability to present the truth of Jesus Christ. That's what we are commissioned to do. The question is whether or not we are on mission.

C. The Commandment (vv. 6-7)

6. And thou, son of man, be not afraid of them, neither be afraid of their words, though briers and thorns be with thee, and thou dost dwell among scorpions: be not afraid of their words, nor be dismayed at their looks, though they be a rebellious house.

7. And thou shalt speak my words unto them, whether they will hear, or whether they will forbear: for they are most rebellious.

In these verses God gives Ezekiel two firm directives or commandments. First, he is not to be afraid. Fear can creep in and make us ineffective. One source is what we see. Many years earlier fear paralyzed the Israelites and kept them from experiencing immediate possession of the Promised Land. The thought of the giants overwhelmed them.

The description of Ezekiel living surrounded by briers and thorns with the presence of scorpions indicates a difficult environment. The punctures of thorns and the stings of scorpions reflect the struggle he will experience while being the spokesman of the Lord.

Ezekiel is also warned concerning the words which will be hurled at him. Being directed not to experience terror in the midst of the people's words seems to indicate harmful threats.

Second, Ezekiel is directed to speak God's words. He will not be judged on the basis of their effectiveness. Speaking them as told becomes the criterion by which God holds Ezekiel responsible.

2. What did the Lord say the Israelites would "know" (v. 5)?

"I am only one, but I am one. I can't do everything, but I can do something. And what I can do, I ought to do. And what I ought to do, by the grace of God, I shall do."

—Edward Hale

Talk About It:
1. What images does the Lord use in describing the challenge Ezekiel will face (v. 6)?
2. What is the Lord's command to Ezekiel (v. 7)?

Painful Message
There are times when God's servant is called upon to confront or in some way tell another the truth that the individual does not want to hear. The information may be painful to

These people are rebellious. Rejection of God's words through the prophet is expected. However, they still need to hear God's message for them. Ezekiel must fulfill the specific task as that messenger.

God's call isn't without challenges. Anyone who assumes otherwise doesn't understand the conflict between righteousness and sin. The same is true for anyone today who spreads the whole gospel of Jesus Christ.

II. INTERNALIZING GOD'S WORD (Ezek. 2:8—3:3)
A. The Acceptance (2:8-10)

8. But thou, son of man, hear what I say unto thee; Be not thou rebellious like that rebellious house: open thy mouth, and eat that I give thee.

9. And when I looked, behold, an hand was sent unto me; and, lo, a roll of a book was therein;

10. And he spread it before me; and it was written within and without: and there was written therein lamentations, and mourning, and woe.

It is not sufficient for this new prophet to simply operate as a verbal robot or herald of the message written by another. God wants this message to be personalized within the man. He is to understand, feel, and agree with the words which will be spoken.

Ezekiel is to be different from the people to whom he ministers. How can a rebellious prophet who is not in agreement with the given message ever make an impact on a rebellious audience? The task stands monumental as it is. No wonder the Lord emphasizes Ezekiel's making this a message from his own heart.

This internalizing is seen in the symbolic action of eating a scroll. Since all of these events are part of a vision, no one should assume Ezekiel is being told to eat an actual scroll. Instead, the symbolism indicates the prophet's accepting the message of his ministry.

The scrolls of Ezekiel's day were made from skins or strips of papyrus. Individuals would write on only one side. Then the reader would unroll the scroll with one hand and roll with the other hand while reading. But this scroll appears to be different since there is writing on both sides. This can represent the fullness of the message given to Ezekiel.

Verse 10 gives an overview of the prophet's message. Lacking is an emphasis on joy and hope. Instead, his message dwells on God's displeasure and judgment. He will lament the people's sins and the subsequent punishment.

A quick review of Ezekiel's prophecies shows a widespread application. He doesn't speak only to God's people but to other nations as well. Laments and prophecies will be directed toward Tyre and Egypt. A prophecy of desolation is spoken toward Edom. These demonstrate the breadth of Ezekiel's ministry.

God's Demanding Call

B. The Purpose (3:1-3)

1. Moreover he said unto me, Son of man, eat that thou findest; eat this roll, and go speak unto the house of Israel.

2. So I opened my mouth, and he caused me to eat the roll.

3. And he said unto me, Son of man, cause thy belly to eat, and fill thy bowels with this roll that I give thee. Then I did eat it; and it was in my mouth as honey for sweetness.

It is difficult to be a convincing propagator of what you do not personally believe or live by. Yes, you can be a convincing actor for a period of time, but eventually your true inner being and thoughts will become evident. Then the message becomes ineffective. If this is true in the normal activities of life, how much more important it is to internalize one's message in the spiritual domain.

The symbolism of eating the scroll isn't only for the sense of Ezekiel's being personally filled and accepting what God wants said. It is also for the purpose of his being able to speak. His eating is connected to the speaking forth.

Verse 3 emphasizes how the word of God, as symbolized by the scroll, is to become a part of Ezekiel's innermost being. Upon doing so the prophet reflects on its taste. He describes it as being sweet like honey. How do we interpret this? The words he will speak are those of lament and judgment. Surely they cannot be sweet! We must assume the sweetness refers to the honor of being the spokesperson for the Lord God Almighty. He, just a mere mortal, is being selected to speak for an omnipotent God. What an honor as well as responsibility!

III. EMBOLDENED BY GOD'S CALL (Ezek. 3:4-14)
A. The Audience (vv. 4-7)

4. And he said unto me, Son of man, go, get thee unto the house of Israel, and speak with my words unto them.

5. For thou art not sent to a people of a strange speech and of an hard language, but to the house of Israel;

6. Not to many people of a strange speech and of an hard language, whose words thou canst not understand. Surely, had I sent thee to them, they would have hearkened unto thee.

7. But the house of Israel will not hearken unto thee; for they will not hearken unto me: for all the house of Israel are impudent and hardhearted.

The clarity of Ezekiel's task is without question. He is to go to God's people, Israel. There is an immediacy to the prophet's job. He is to go now and speak only the words God gives.

On the one hand, the difficulty level of Ezekiel's task is lessened by there being no speech barrier. These are not a people who have either an obscure or difficult language. There will be no

Talk About It:
1. What is the meaning of Ezekiel eating the scroll (vv. 1-2)?
2. How did this harsh message taste, and why (v. 3)?

Sweet Taste
Wheaties, "the Breakfast of Champions," was discovered by accident in 1921 when a health clinician in Minneapolis accidently spilled some bran gruel on a hot stove. This cereal has become well known for the many athletic champions whose pictures have been displayed on the box. However, at times "truth in advertising" questions have been raised. Do these athletes really eat Wheaties for breakfast?
Ezekiel "ate" what God commanded and then spoke His message.

Talk About It:
1. What did the Lord command the prophet to do (vv. 4-5)?

need to learn another language or speak through an interpreter. On the other hand, God points out if such had been the case they would have been a receptive audience in contrast to the nation of Israel.

Once again, there is a negative description of the people who will be his audience. If they haven't listened to God himself, they will not listen to His prophet. These are tough words for Ezekiel to hear.

It is interesting to note the description of Israel. The King James Version states they are "impudent" and "hardhearted" (v. 7). The NIV uses the words *hardened* and *obstinate*. The people in exile had deafened their ears to previous prophets. Apparently the deportation isn't, up to this point, producing a positive spiritual response in their hearts and lives. This reminds us that many people do not turn their hearts and minds to God as a result of difficult times in their lives.

"Sin is the irrational in human consciousness. It is the failure of free will to act reasonably."
—Charles Davis

B. The Empowerment (vv. 8-9)

8. Behold, I have made thy face strong against their faces, and thy forehead strong against their foreheads.

9. As an adamant harder than flint have I made thy forehead: fear them not, neither be dismayed at their looks, though they be a rebellious house.

adamant (v. 9)—the hardest stone

Talk About It:
Describe the strength God gave to Ezekiel.

God doesn't send or commit anyone to a task without the necessary giftedness or empowerment. He knows in advance the challenges which will be faced and how to overcome them. In Ezekiel's case, he is an inexperienced prophet facing a monumental task. Since the prophetic ministry involves face-to-face confrontation with these difficult people, God indicates Ezekiel's face and forehead will be strengthened, enabling him to meet the opposition which is sure to come.

This empowerment is described in terms of the hardest stone. The NIV states it as follows: "I will make your forehead like the hardest stone, harder than flint" (v. 9). This indicates the Israelites will not soften and accept the rebuke of the Lord. They will remain steadfast in their sins. Ezekiel's words will be strongly resisted. In the face of such opposition, God encourages the prophet to not succumb to fear or to allow terror to grip his heart in these confrontations.

Once again, God describes the house of Israel as a group of rebellious people. They will resist. They may appear as a formidable foe. Yet, in spite of all they may say and do, God is on Ezekiel's side, and he will overcome.

C. The Ministry (vv. 10-14)

10. Moreover he said unto me, Son of man, all my words that I shall speak unto thee receive in thine heart, and hear with thine ears.

11. And go, get thee to them of the captivity, unto the children of thy people, and speak unto them, and tell them, Thus saith the Lord God; whether they will hear, or whether they will forbear.

12. Then the spirit took me up, and I heard behind me a voice of a great rushing, saying, Blessed be the glory of the Lord from his place.

13. I heard also the noise of the wings of the living creatures that touched one another, and the noise of the wheels over against them, and a noise of a great rushing.

14. So the spirit lifted me up, and took me away, and I went in bitterness, in the heat of my spirit; but the hand of the Lord was strong upon me.

heat (v. 14)—"anger" (NIV)

Talk About It:
1. What was the status of Ezekiel's audience, and how was he to speak to them (v. 11)?
2. Describe the sounds Ezekiel heard (vv. 12-13).
3. Explain Ezekiel's emotions (v. 14).

Having been called and commissioned to the prophetic office, it is now time to commence this important ministry. Ezekiel's initial vision is about to close. God's final words to him are vital. Everything spoken to Ezekiel is to be heard and internalized. Though they are God's words to His people, the prophet needs to not only understand them but also be in total accord.

Verse 10 points to further revelations. God doesn't intend to give him just one message and that there will be no further words from God. Just the opposite is true. Ezekiel will continue to be the voice of God to the house of Israel.

Knowing the difficulty of ministering to such a rebellious nation, Ezekiel isn't asked to minister in the authority of his own name. Rather, as he delivers the messages of truth, it is to always be in the authority of God. "Thus saith the Lord" (v. 11) puts the message in a distinct perspective. These aren't the ideas of a human mind reflecting personal views. Ezekiel is to plainly inform Israel these are the words of their God. It doesn't change the meaning or impact, but it should relieve some pressure. He doesn't need to explain himself. It is God who speaks to them through this human messenger.

The bottom line rests with the people. Will they listen and change? Or will they listen and continue their rebellious ways? Ezekiel's responsibility ends with his obediently sharing the word of the Lord.

In verse 12, Ezekiel receives spiritual power and direction for his mission. "Then the Spirit took me up," in the light of 2:2, means the Holy Spirit came upon the prophet with such power as to fill him with zeal and inspiration for his mission. And, in light of the experiences of Elijah (1 Kings 18:12; 2 Kings 2:16), Jesus (Mark 1:12), and Philip (Acts 8:39), the Spirit also directed Ezekiel to his specific place of ministry.

Then too, he is accompanied by the cherubim which had been manifested at Chebar (Ezek. 1:3-14), evidently to encourage him on his difficult mission.

Daily Devotions:
M. Being Prepared for the Call
   Genesis 37:19-28
T. Answer the Call
   1 Samuel 3:1-10
W. Remember God's Call
   1 Kings 19:9-18
T. Deny Yourself
   Matthew 16:24-26
F. Chosen for the Call
   John 15:12-17
S. Sacrifices for the Call
   Hebrews 11:30-40

Being called by God was sweet (3:3), but carrying out the mission is bitter (v. 14). A conflict of emotions, indignation against the sins of the people, the dread of failure, and the consciousness of his unfitness created this bitterness. But the sustaining hand of the Lord and His powerful impulse urged the prophet on.

CONCLUSION

Ezekiel's call to the prophetic ministry comes through the means of a vision. This mission of ministry is to a rebellious nation who is in Babylonian exile. Their transportation from home to a foreign land seems to have had no spiritual impact. They continue to be locked in their sinful ways. In the face of this challenge, God assures Ezekiel of his being properly prepared. He does, however, have to internalize the message.

GOLDEN TEXT CHALLENGE

"GO, GET THEE TO THEM OF THE CAPTIVITY, UNTO THE CHILDREN OF THY PEOPLE, AND SPEAK UNTO THEM, AND TELL THEM, THUS SAITH THE LORD GOD; WHETHER THEY WILL HEAR, OR WHETHER THEY WILL FORBEAR" (Ezek. 3:11).

The Lord told Ezekiel to go to "thy people." The NIV reads, "Go now to your countrymen in exile." Since the prophet was in captivity along with his fellow Jews, he knew exactly how they felt. They had lost their possessions and their homeland, and so had he. Who better to minister to them?

Ezekiel was commissioned to speak with divine authority to his nation. *Thus saith the Lord God* was more than just "preacher talk"—Ezekiel had been given the word of the Lord for the nation.

Whether or not the people would listen to the message, it was Ezekiel's calling to deliver it. The results were between the people and the Lord.

Personal Responsibility to God

Ezekiel 18:1-32

INTRODUCTION

A New Testament parallel for Ezekiel 18 is Galatians 6:7-8: "Do not be deceived: God cannot be mocked. A man reaps what he sows. The one who sows to please his sinful nature, from that nature will reap destruction; the one who sows to please the Spirit, from the Spirit will reap eternal life" (NIV).

In previous lessons the corporate sinning of a nation provides the background for God's displeasure with His people, Israel. Because of the wholeness of the covenant with Israel as a nation, even those who did not follow the false gods and wanted to live righteously still experienced the punishment. Today's lesson moves to individual responsibility and the results of sin in a person's life.

No person can live his or her life as they please in direct violation of God's will and avoid negative consequences. Since God doesn't immediately thunder down His judgment, there can be the thought of "getting away with it." But eventually God does confront us. David's sin with Bathsheba is a case in point. God is silent after the adulterous affair, the conception of a child, and the arranged death of Uriah. Only after the child's birth does God send Nathan with the precise purpose of pointing out David's sin.

As believers we are not exempt from God's will and Word. We are personally responsible for our lifestyle choices. God holds us accountable for them. Since none of us is perfect, it becomes our responsibility to live as righteously as possible. We need to put on the armor of God (Eph. 6:10-17). When we fall, we have two choices. The first choice is to continue in our sin and move away from God. This will lead to spiritual death if allowed to continue. The second choice is to conscientiously repent of our sins and be restored in righteousness.

Here is a good place for all of us to be reminded of our guidebook. The Bible, though completed in its revelation many centuries ago, provides life principles which supersede times, culture, and ethnicity. Adherence to them through accepting Jesus as Savior and Lord, with the empowering of the Holy Spirit, enables us to live a life of holiness pleasing to the Lord.

Unit Theme:
Major Prophets

Central Truth:
Christians are responsible for their choices and are held accountable to God.

Focus:
Realize we are accountable to God and obey His Word.

Context:
In Babylon between 592 and 588 BC

Golden Text:
"The soul that sinneth, it shall die. The son shall not bear the iniquity of the father, neither shall the father bear the iniquity of the son: the righteousness of the righteous shall be upon him, and the wickedness of the wicked shall be upon him" (Ezek. 18:20).

Study Outline:
I. Sin Leads to Death (Ezek. 18:1-4, 10-18)
II. Each Person Is Responsible (Ezek. 18:19-24)
III. Repentance Leads to Life (Ezek. 18:25-32)

I. SIN LEADS TO DEATH (Ezek. 18:1-4, 10-18)
A. The Death Principle (vv. 1-4)

1. The word of the Lord came unto me again, saying,

2. What mean ye, that ye use this proverb concerning the land of Israel, saying, The fathers have eaten sour grapes, and the children's teeth are set on edge?

3. As I live, saith the Lord God, ye shall not have occasion any more to use this proverb in Israel.

4. Behold, all souls are mine; as the soul of the father, so also the soul of the son is mine: the soul that sinneth, it shall die.

This lesson demonstrates the scope of Ezekiel's ministry. It goes beyond events of the past which are the reason for Israel's present situation. Here the prophet works to expand their thinking concerning accountability. It begins with a well-known proverb of the past which continues to impact their thought process. The proverb can be interpreted to mean that the sufferings of the present generation ("children's teeth are set on edge") are the results of the misdeeds of the previous generations (fathers eating sour grapes). This causes the present generation to be enveloped in a spirit of fatalism and a sense of irresponsibility.

This idea sounds so contemporary. Many individuals perceive themselves to be victims and thus not responsible for their attitude or behavior. This trend toward victimization provides no sense of accountability or need to bring about change in their lives. When a society becomes permeated with this concept, it quickly decays. No one assumes personal responsibility, regardless of their unacceptable attitudes and behaviors.

Israel's familiarity and seemingly addiction to this proverb is partially seen by Jeremiah's reference to it as well (Jer. 31:29). Now the Lord moves them from the constant view of corporate responsibility to an individual accountability. Yes, they are in exile due to the idolatry, rebellion, and willful breaking of the covenant. However, those are actions of the past. They are now responsible for the present as individuals. They must understand God looks at them as individuals as well as a corporate nation.

In verse 4 God, through Ezekiel, states how every soul belongs to Him. It means every person is of concern to Him. He doesn't just see the "big picture." He knows about each person as an individual. Having established this concept, the Lord states a death principle. Those who sin will die. Of course, this must be understood in terms of adopting a lifestyle of sin. This isn't to be interpreted as a single sin due to succumbing to temptation or making a misjudgment.

The word of the Lord doesn't just end there. To guarantee understanding, three examples will follow (vv. 5-17). These illustrations will enable the people to clearly see what God intends for them.

Talk About It:
1. What is the meaning of the proverb in verse 2?
2. How did God's truth undermine the proverb (v. 4)?

"We must all appear before the judgment seat of Christ, that each one may receive the things done in the body, according to what he has done, whether good or bad."
—2 Corinthians 5:10 NKJV

Personal Responsibility to God

B. Contrasting Behavior (vv. 10-18)
  (Ezekiel 18:15-18 is not included in the printed text.)
  10. If he beget a son that is a robber, a shedder of blood, and that doeth the like to any one of these things,
  11. And that doeth not any of those duties, but even hath eaten upon the mountains, and defiled his neighbour's wife,
  12. Hath oppressed the poor and needy, hath spoiled by violence, hath not restored the pledge, and hath lifted up his eyes to the idols, hath committed abomination,
  13. Hath given forth upon usury, and hath taken increase: shall he then live? he shall not live: he hath done all these abominations; he shall surely die; his blood shall be upon him.
  14. Now, lo, if he beget a son, that seeth all his father's sins which he hath done, and considereth, and doeth not such like.

To fully grasp the context of this section it is important to read verses 5-9, which describe a righteous man—the first example. It begins with what he does not do, and then moves to his positive actions. Since idolatry attacks the heart of serving God, this description begins with this man neither going to the idolatrous places of worship nor adopting any of them as his own. He follows God's law of moral relationships—non-oppression, and not taking another's property.

This man's righteousness is seen in terms of benevolence to those in need, following God's laws, and offering fair judgment between individuals. He is one in whom God delights. It would be hoped such a righteous example would have children living in the same manner. However, his son is completely unlike him. Though difficult to understand how this can happen, it is sometimes true in real life.

Verse 10 begins the description of the wicked son—the second example. This young man lives in opposition to the religious and moral examples of his father. He follows idolatrous gods, engages in sexual immorality, oppresses the poor and needy, commits robbery, and steals and lends money at extreme interest rates. In other words, this man openly breaks the laws of God. Nothing appears to be sacred or off limits to him.

Verses 14-17—the third example—shows this wicked man has a son who lives like his grandfather and not like his sinful father. He carefully follows God's laws, living a life of righteousness. Nothing more could be asked of him.

Now the question to be answered is, "Will a person die for the sins of a family member?" The answer is a resounding "No." Each person stands responsible for his or her own sins. A father doesn't stand in judgment for the sins of his son. Neither will a son be responsible for the sins of his father. Please remember

Talk About It:
1. Describe the man depicted in verses 10-13.
2. How will this man be judged if he has a righteous father (v. 13)?
3. How will this man's son be judged if the son lives righteously (vv. 14, 17)?

Somebody and Nobody
  In the comic strip *Family Circus*, occasionally there is an episode of the mother asking, "Who did this?" Something is broken or spilled. No one will claim personal responsibility. In those cartoon frames are imaginary little figures labeled "somebody" and "nobody." It provides a graphic picture of the difficulty we humans have in saying, "I did it. Please forgive me."

that we are dealing with a spiritual principle here. Sin has negative effects on surrounding family and friends. My sinful actions may wound other people physically, emotionally, or economically, but will not change their standing with God. They will not be condemned for my sins, though my wrongdoing may cause them pain.

II. EACH PERSON IS RESPONSIBLE (Ezek. 18:19-24)
A. Personal Responsibility (vv. 19-20)

19. Yet say ye, Why? Doth not the son bear the iniquity of the father? When the son hath done that which is lawful and right, and hath kept all my statutes, and hath done them, he shall surely live.

20. The soul that sinneth, it shall die. The son shall not bear the iniquity of the father, neither shall the father bear the iniquity of the son: the righteousness of the righteous shall be upon him, and the wickedness of the wicked shall be upon him.

Talk About It:
1. Who shall "surely live" (v. 19)?
2. Whose "soul . . . shall die" (v. 20)?

Generational responsibility is being replaced with individual responsibility. Sons will not be responsible for the sins of their fathers. Each will stand in the circle of judgment based on personal actions. A generational curse will not plague a family.

The question is raised, "Why does the son not share the guilt of his father?" (v. 19 NIV). It is because the son follows the path of righteousness. This son keeps the lifestyle prescribed in God's laws. As a result, this man will live. His spiritual life will positively influence his physical life.

In marked contrast is the person who indulges himself with utter disregard for God's law. This person will die. Rebellious actions produce spiritual death and may lead to an early physical death as well.

No child inherits spiritual punishment as the result of a father's sins, nor will a parent be judged for a child's sins. Each person reaps exactly what he or she sows, nothing more or nothing less.

The apostle Paul's words to the Galatians concerning personal responsibility need to be repeated: "Do not be deceived: God is not mocked. A man reaps what he sows. The one who sows to please his sinful nature, from that nature will reap destruction; the one who sows to please the Spirit, from the Spirit will reap eternal life" (Gal. 6:7-8 NIV).

"We are free to sin, but not to control sin's consequences."
—J. Kenneth Kimberlin

B. Righteousness Through Repentance (vv. 21-23)

21. But if the wicked will turn from all his sins that he hath committed, and keep all my statutes, and do that which is lawful and right, he shall surely live, he shall not die.

22. All his transgressions that he hath committed, they shall not be mentioned unto him: in his righteousness that he hath done he shall live.

23. Have I any pleasure at all that the wicked should die? saith the Lord God: and not that he should return from his ways, and live?

The situation of the sinner is not helpless. It can be changed with a revolution of lifestyle. We know this can occur only with a heart change. Otherwise, it is nothing more than a facade. Externally following the laws of God will not survive the testing of temptations and the common struggles of life.

Repentance is not just a slight behavior modification, nor is it a list of intended future actions. Repentance means to take a 180-degree turn. You go in the opposite direction and keep the laws of God which previously were rejected and/or disregarded. This inner and outer change brings spiritual life and restored relationship with the heavenly Father.

Repentance produces permanent results. Sins of the past are eradicated, never to be remembered or resurfaced. Repentance results in righteousness.

Verse 23 gives us an added insight to God's love and mercy. He doesn't take delight in bringing punishment on the rebellious and disobedient. His justice and holiness demand this response, but it grieves His heart. This verse is vital in the understanding of our God. Some have the wrong concept of God's being like a vulture just waiting for someone to do wrong so He can swoop down in judgment. Nothing is further from the truth! God delights in the person who repents of their sins and begins to live a righteous lifestyle in obedience to the Father's laws. He doesn't delight in bringing punishment on the sinner.

C. Sin Eradicates Righteousness (v. 24)

24. But when the righteous turneth away from his righteousness, and committeth iniquity, and doeth according to all the abominations that the wicked man doeth, shall he live? All his righteousness that he hath done shall not be mentioned: in his trespass that he hath trespassed, and in his sin that he hath sinned, in them shall die.

Righteousness is not a permanent relationship before God regardless of one's actions and attitudes. Its permanence depends on right choices. No one is "once saved always saved" who continues in a lifestyle of sinful indulgences.

When a righteous person turns toward sinful practices and begins to follow the patterns of sinners, he or she turns toward death. All the positives of the past are erased. This does not refer to a brief lapse into sin as a result of being overcome by a temptation. The description here is of the person who willfully moves away from God to follow personal preferences. Rebellion and idolatry always result in separation from the heavenly Father. When this occurs, the result is spiritual death.

Talk About It:
1. What promise did God make to Ezekiel regarding "the wicked" (vv. 21-22)?
2. What does not give God pleasure (v. 23)?

"Be killing sin or it will be killing you."
—John Owen

Talk About It:
What happens to the person who turns from righteous living to sinful living?

"Christ is the answer to all inclinations to go back. When we love Him sufficiently and place our lives completely in Him, we shall never be moved."
—Charles W. Conn

III. REPENTANCE LEADS TO LIFE (Ezek. 18:25-32)

A. Contrasting Options (vv. 25-29)

25. Yet ye say, The way of the Lord is not equal. Hear now, O house of Israel; Is not my way equal? are not your ways unequal?

26. When a righteous man turneth away from his righteousness, and committeth iniquity, and dieth in them; for his iniquity that he hath done shall he die.

27. Again, when the wicked man turneth away from his wickedness that he hath committed, and doeth that which is lawful and right, he shall save his soul alive.

28. Because he considereth, and turneth away from all his transgressions that he hath committed, he shall surely live, he shall not die.

29. Yet saith the house of Israel, The way of the Lord is not equal. O house of Israel, are not my ways equal? are not your ways unequal?

The response of Israel to this new realization of individual responsibility is one of charging "foul." Instead of appreciating it, they charge the Lord with being unjust. It almost appears as a group of children shouting, "That's not fair! You can't change the rules!" Hearing this, God turns their accusation right back at them.

Beginning with the righteous person who turns to sin, God again states the result. The sinner will die because sin always results in death. In marked contrast is the person who turns from the wickedness of sin and embraces righteousness. The previous sentence of death for sin is now reversed. In its place is the new reality of life.

How can this truth be unjust? It isn't. If it were, then God would be in opposition to His own nature. He is righteous and establishes righteousness. As the Lord says in Isaiah 45:21, "There is no God apart from me, a righteous God and a Savior" (NIV).

B. Call for Repentance (vv. 30-32)

30. Therefore I will judge you, O house of Israel, every one according to his ways, saith the Lord God. Repent, and turn yourselves from all your transgressions; so iniquity shall not be your ruin.

31. Cast away from you all your transgressions, whereby ye have transgressed; and make you a new heart and a new spirit: for why will ye die, O house of Israel?

32. For I have no pleasure in the death of him that dieth, saith the Lord God: wherefore turn yourselves, and live ye.

Having laid out the contrasting options before the people, God then reminds them of their being evaluated. This isn't an evaluation that can be taken lightly, for it has eternal consequences. It results in either life or death. Whether or not they like it, God keeps a record of a person's life and responds accordingly.

Talk About It:
What charge did Israel bring against God, and how did He respond (vv. 25, 29)?

"The Old Testament knows no such doctrine as 'once saved, always saved.' The experience of salvation does not lead to final salvation without one's continuing to believe in God and walk in obedience to Him."

—French Arrington

Talk About It:
What is the solution for backslidden people (vv. 30-31)?

Personal Responsibility to God

With so much at stake, God calls Israel to repent of the actions which will plunge them into death and destruction. It calls for them to turn away from their sins, reject them, and go in the opposite direction. However, this will not last without an inner change. Repentance includes the reception of a new heart and spirit. Rebellion is replaced with submission. Instead of disdain for God's law, there will be love for it indicated by obedience.

In a later chapter the Lord gives a special message to Israel. This "new heart" is not a human creation. It doesn't come through a process of behavior modification. We receive this inner transformation by an act of God: "I will give you a new heart and put a new spirit in you; I will remove from you your heart of stone and give you a heart of flesh" (36:26 NIV).

God asks the penetrating question, "Why will you die?" (18:31 NIV). It is not necessary. Life is an option. Availability rests on heartfelt repentance.

For a second time in this chapter God states His taking no delight in the spiritual death of the rebellious (v. 32). His desire is for them to live. No wonder He continues to call for them to repent.

> "The gospel of Jesus Christ must be the bad news of the conviction of sin before it can be the good news of redemption."
> —Charles Colson

CONCLUSION

Though God deals with nations on a corporate level and rewards or judges appropriately, He also requires personal accountability. Sinful actions of one's parent or children do not bring judgment on the righteous child or parent. Each person reaps the result of his or her chosen path. The options are rebellion that brings death, or righteousness that brings life. God calls all to repentance so each may experience life.

GOLDEN TEXT CHALLENGE

"THE SOUL THAT SINNETH, IT SHALL DIE. THE SON SHALL NOT BEAR THE INIQUITY OF THE FATHER, NEITHER SHALL THE FATHER BEAR THE INIQUITY OF THE SON: THE RIGHTEOUSNESS OF THE RIGHTEOUS SHALL BE UPON HIM, AND THE WICKEDNESS OF THE WICKED SHALL BE UPON HIM" (Ezek. 18:20).

The United States Army can be deployed as a single force to battle against the enemies of our nation. That deployment, however, takes place by smaller groupings called divisions, units, squadrons, and so forth. Ultimately, the deployment of the army reaches the individual soldier. That soldier is not the whole army but is the smallest divisible element of that army. He or she must respond to the call for deployment in a personal way.

This is the way God views the Church. Together we form a formidable force that can drive Satan backward and establish God's kingdom in the earth. This cannot be done, however, if each Christian does not fill his or her role in the battle. Each member of God's church is responsible for heeding God's call, and will be judged according to his or her way of life.

Daily Devotions:

M. Reverence and
   Obey God
   Ecclesiastes
   12:9-14
T. The Lord Is Fair
   Ezekiel 33:11-20
W. God's
   Requirements
   Micah 6:6-8
T. Responsibilities
   to God
   Romans 12:1-5
F. Accountable to
   God
   Romans 14:7-13
S. Accept
   Responsibility
   Galatians 6:1-10

There is no way out of giving a personal account to God, for He knows each individual and keeps a detailed record of every life. When God says "the soul that sinneth, it shall die," He speaks full knowledge and clear observation of the life of that soul.

Intelligent Design or Chance?

Genesis 1:1-26; Psalms 14:1-3; 19:1-4;
Romans 1:18-25; Colossians 1:16-18; Revelation 4:11

INTRODUCTION

There are few things in life more beautiful than events associated with creation, such as the sunrise or sunset on a clear day, the powerful (and calming) waves of the ocean, the beauty and fragrance of a spectacular flower, the awe of a birth of a child, or the glowing face of a sinner saved by grace. God is a creative God and still creates/re-creates beautiful things today.

The first two chapters of Genesis (a book of "beginnings") can be difficult to understand, both intellectually and theologically. These two chapters have generated volumes of writings and spawned numerous debates. Though chapter 2 is not part of this lesson, let it be clear that there is no discrepancy between the Creation accounts found in the first two chapters of Genesis. Chapter 1 records the events from God's perspective, while chapter 2 reveals the Creation event from humanity's perception.

This author is a biblical scholar, not a scientist. This lesson, therefore, is presented from that viewpoint. It is my position that the biblical record is true and does not conflict with science. Science is still in the adolescent stage and has had to reexamine previously held views, while the truth of God's Word has endured the rigorous examination of both believers and unbelievers for centuries. For example, in the two months that preceded the writing of this lesson, scientists "determined" that the Grand Canyon was not six million years old, as previously held, but was actually seventeen million years old. Within weeks, the age was redetermined to be sixty-five million years old! It is no wonder that as research into the geological, fossil, and astrophysical records continues, many scientists are casting a wary eye on evolutionary theory and looking for a prime mover behind creation (intelligent design). For more information on this debate, *www.answersingenesis.org* is a valuable resource.

When the dust finally settles from the Creation-evolution debate, God's Word will prevail. However, it must be kept in mind that the Bible was written for instruction and edification, not to prove (or disprove) scientific theories. It was not written in scientific terms or to provide every detail of how God created the cosmos *ex nihilo* (out of nothing). It is a book of faith and salvation, written to provide the "His-story" of God's desire to have fellowship with His people and the interaction involved to make that happen.

Unit Theme:
Bible Answers to Crucial Questions

Central Truth:
God is to be acknowledged and worshiped as the Creator.

Focus:
Affirm that creation is by God's design and glorify the Creator.

Context:
Selected scriptures teaching the creative work of God

Golden Text:
"In the beginning God created the heaven and the earth" (Gen. 1:1).

Study Outline:
I. Witness God's Design of Creation (Gen. 1:1-26; Ps. 19:1-4)
II. Folly of Denying God (Ps. 14:1-3; Rom. 1:18-25)
III. Worship the Creator (Col. 1:16-18; Rev. 4:11)

I. WITNESS GOD'S DESIGN OF CREATION (Gen. 1:1-26; Ps. 19:1-4)

A. The Beginning of Time (Gen. 1:1-2)

1. In the beginning God created the heaven and the earth.

2. And the earth was without form, and void; and darkness was upon the face of the deep. And the Spirit of God moved upon the face of the waters.

Talk About It:
What was the world like "in the beginning"?

Some have suggested incorrectly that the Creation record was taken from Sumerian or Akkadian legends. Those stories deal with the eternal questions: *How did I get here? Why am I here? Why did this happen to me?* However, there are vast differences that reveal the Bible is unique and divinely revealed.

The Old Testament is clear that Israel is to be monotheistic (Deut. 6:4)—not incorporating other gods, idols, images, or practices thereof (Ex. 20:3-6)—and highly moral, after the example of Yahweh (Mic. 6:8). The worship ceremonies are nonsexual (Deut. 32:17-18) and strongly God-centered (11:16). Humanity is created, not a descendant of the gods (Gen. 1:26-27). Monarchs are not deified (Deut. 17:15). The Bible differs most in the presentation of God, who does not take the form of animals/beasts (Gen. 1:26; Deut. 4:15-19), is not capricious in His actions (Isa. 59:18), nor subject to human passions and limitations (Num. 23:19); He is wholly-other (Isa. 40:18), yet accessible (Ps. 50:15), and *radically* sovereign (103:19). The Canaanite, Egyptian, and Greek (ancient Near Eastern) religious literature do not have these distinctions. Further, in the New Testament we find that God lays down His life for humanity (John 3:16), rather than the other way around. No other religion has this depth of love or uniqueness.

The Creation account begins with the simple but profound statement, "In the beginning God created the heavens and the earth" (NKJV), which does not mean in the very beginning of God, as God is eternal and has no beginning or end (Isa. 44:6). Rather, it means "in the beginning of time." Here, as in John 1:1, there is no article ("the") in the original languages, so it could be translated, "In beginning [His creative acts], God created the heavens and the earth." The author (probably Moses, Ex. 24:4) makes it clear that "God" (*Elohim*, "the mighty One") is the agent of this activity. The word for "created" is reserved in this particular form (*bara*) for God's activity (e.g., Ps. 51:10; Isa. 48:6-7; 65:17) and carries the idea of a divine fiat or decree. God spoke and it happened. The term conveys the idea of "initiating something completely new." In this case, God created the "heavens." Second Corinthians 12:2-4 shows the "third heaven" is the abiding place of God. Further, His throne is eternal (Ps. 45:6); thus Genesis 1:1 is a reference to the sky (first heaven) and the expanse of the planetary systems and stars (second heaven), not the creation of God's abiding place. He also created "the earth," and details this in the verses that follow.

Verse 2 has been misinterpreted to mean that the earth "*became* without form and void." This thinking is associated with the "gap theory," wherein there is a gap of time and history between verse 1 (the creation of everything) and verse 2 (the re-creation of everything). This theory (though there are many variations) asserts that the earth was the playground of the angels and when Lucifer rebelled, the earth was destroyed, thus necessitating a re-creation. This theory is not supported by the text. God chose to create matter first, then to fashion and form it into the heavens and the earth. He created the matter out of nothing. He saw what it could become, then He formed it into what He envisioned. This is a powerful lesson with implications for our spiritual formation. God sees what can be before it is. He starts the process and works in stages, even when the process doesn't look like much. The finished product is always what He intends. And the Spirit of God is continually "hovering" (NKJV)—"fluttering" or "tending"—over the "deep" process as an active agent to remove all "darkness."

B. Five Days of Creative Activity (vv. 3-23)
(Genesis 1:3-23 is not included in the printed text.)
The first day of Creation is marked by two significant events. First, the first recorded words of God are spoken (v. 3a). In the Hebrew (*dabar*), especially in regard to God, there is no separation between a thought that is spoken and the will to accomplish it. When God speaks, there is resultant activity. He only speaks what He has determined to do. Since He is omnipotent, He is able to accomplish anything that does not violate His character (Mark 10:27).

Second, "light" was created on the earth (Gen. 1:3). Light is a dominant theme in Scripture, associated with clarity of sight (Ps. 119:105), emotional well-being (Est. 8:16), moral judgment (Job 24:13), a guiding principle (John 11:9-10), intellectual enlightenment (Prov. 6:23), watchfulness (Matt. 25:1-13), and protection (Rom. 13:12). It is also an attribute of God (John 1:4-5), is characteristic of His favor on us (Ps. 4:6), and should be reflected in His children (Eph. 5:8). When God saw the light, He declared it "good" (Gen. 1:4) and used it as a boundary for darkness to delineate day and night (vv. 4-5). "Day" can mean a literal twenty-four hours, the entire creative act (v. 5), or an extended period of time (2 Peter 3:8).

The second day (vv. 6-8) includes the separation of the earth from the sky, or heavens, through the spoken word of God. The Hebrew word (*raqi*) was translated "firmament" ("sky") by the KJV translators. Most modern translations use "expanse" (literally, "beaten out") to convey the magnitude of creation. Some view this as a description of a canopy (cf. Job 37:18) that enveloped the earth, since it may not have rained prior to the Flood (Gen. 2:5-6).

The spacious firmament on high,
With all the blue ethereal sky,
And spangled heavens, a shining frame
Their great Original proclaim.
Th' unwearied sun, from day to day,
Does his Creator's powers display,
And publishes to every land
The work of an Almighty Hand.
—**Joseph Addison** (1712)

Talk About It:
1. What is similar about how God created everything listed in verses 3, 6, 9, 14, and 20?
2. What was God's opinion about all these creative acts (vv. 4, 10, 12, 18, 21)?
3. What blessing did God pronounce in verse 22?

In ancient languages, including Hebrew, the vocabulary was considerably smaller (roughly 1,500 words) than modern English (approximately two million, according to *www.wordempire.com*); thus words carried many different meanings that had to be determined according to context. This can make the meaning of some passages difficult to ascertain. Interestingly, the Bible declared many years before science that the earth is suspended on nothing (Job 26:7). Again, it should be noted that the Creation act is depicted and revealed progressively.

The third day of Creation (Gen. 1:9-13), a continuation of the work of the second day, reveals the separation of the earth into land and seas (vv. 9-10). It also includes the creation of vegetation and fruit and the principle that presides over their propagation (vv. 11-12). Each is governed by the type and quality of the seed planted and each seed is to reproduce itself. This is true of spiritual matters, also. This day provided for the sustenance needed by humanity and the animal kingdom. As with the first day, God saw that His creation was "good" (vv. 10, 12).

The fourth day of God's activity (vv. 14-19) provides the sun, moon, and stars. At first glance this appears to be a repetition of first day (vv. 3-5), but the emphasis here is twofold. First, the earth precedes the sun and moon in the Creation event, contrary to modern beliefs that the converse should be true. Second, these "lights" are distinct from the "light" of the first day. These lights provide the rhythm or cycles of life ("signs" and "seasons," v. 14) and provide a means of keeping time.

The fifth day (vv. 20-23) begins the creation of the animal kingdom. The life forms that populate the waters as well as those that fly came into existence by the command of God. They receive God's *blessing* (the favor of a greater extended to a lesser) and command to multiply (v. 22).

C. The Crowning Glory of Creation (vv. 24-26)

24. And God said, Let the earth bring forth the living creature after his kind, cattle, and creeping thing, and beast of the earth after his kind: and it was so.

25. And God made the beast of the earth after his kind, and cattle after their kind, and every thing that creepeth upon the earth after his kind: and God saw that it was good.

26. And God said, Let us make man in our image, after our likeness: and let them have dominion over the fish of the sea, and over the fowl of the air, and over the cattle, and over all the earth, and over every creeping thing that creepeth upon the earth.

The first part of day six (vv. 24-25) is a continuation of the work begun on the fifth day. That is, the animal kingdom continues to be expanded with the creation of domesticated ("cattle") and wild ("creeping") animals. And He pronounces everything "good" up to this point (v. 25).

Six Days
Belief in a creation period of six 24-hour days and about 6,000 years ago has been the teaching of the Church for most of its history. This belief is not essential to be a Christian . . . but it is essential for consistency in doctrine and apologetics. The denial of this belief is foundationally the result of imposing outside ideas upon the Bible.
—Jonathan Safarti
(*Refuting Compromise*)

Talk About It:
1. Why was man made in God's image?
2. What authority did God give to humanity?

Verse 26 marks the crowning glory of God's creation—humanity. Four things stand out. First, God speaks in the plural, "Let us make man in our image." The word used for "God" (*Elohim*) is plural in itself (of *El*). Here, He specifically uses a plural pronoun ("us"/"our"). This does not depict three Gods, but rather the three persons of the Godhead (Father, Son, Spirit).

Second, humanity is made in the image of God. He made us to be like Him spiritually, intellectually, and morally. He has shared with us His characteristics or attributes that can be communicated (personality, creativity, righteousness, holiness, justice, and love, to name a few). Unfortunately, sin has diminished the image of God in humanity, and will continue to do its destructive work if allowed to harbor in our lives.

Third, God made humanity after His "likeness" (a synonym of "image"). Since God is Spirit and has no form (John 4:24), this is a reference to the moralistic qualities of God that He has chosen to share with us. Some have suggested this is a reference to the image that God would have if He had a physical body. When He appears to humanity, it is in human form (e.g., Num. 12:6-8).

Finally, God has given humanity "dominion" ("authority" or "the ability to rule") over that which He has created (Gen. 1:26). This is a humbling privilege and a weighty responsibility. Note that it is after the creation of humanity that God declares His work "very good" (v. 31). This is a fitting pronouncement and an excellent challenge for us to live out every day.

> "God tells man who he is. God tells us that He created man in His image. So man is something wonderful."
> —**Francis Schaeffer**

D. A Visible Declaration of God (Ps. 19:1-4)

1. The heavens declare the glory of God; and the firmament sheweth his handywork.

2. Day unto day uttereth speech, and night unto night sheweth knowledge.

3. There is no speech nor language, where their voice is not heard.

4. Their line is gone out through all the earth, and their words to the end of the world. In them hath he set a tabernacle for the sun.

line (v. 4)—"voice" (NIV)

Talk About It:
What does creation declare about God?

Psalm 19 is composed of three parts: (1) a hymn of praise to God because of creation (vv. 1-6); (2) a hymn of praise to God because of His covenantal law (vv. 7-11); and (3) the resulting humble prayer of heart-searching, seeking forgiveness, and total abandonment to God by the psalmist (vv. 12-14). It is a beautiful blending of God's handiwork and instruction to bring glory to God and reveal His infinite wisdom and completeness in dealing with humanity. A prayerful, contrite response to God's interaction in our lives is always proper.

Creation itself reflects and thus declares the glory of God. Specifically, here in verse 1, it is the "heavens" (not the abiding place of God) and "firmament" ("expanse" or "sky") that "declare" ("make conspicuous") that which is formed by His hands. This

message is repeated day after day (v. 2) in a language that is universally understood (v. 3) and reaches where we may never visit (v. 4).

II. FOLLY OF DENYING GOD (Ps. 14:1-3; Rom. 1:18-25)
A. The Disappointment of God (Ps. 14:1-3)
1. The fool hath said in his heart, There is no God. They are corrupt, they have done abominable works, there is none that doeth good.

2. The Lord looked down from heaven upon the children of men, to see if there were any that did understand, and seek God.

3. They are all gone aside, they are all together become filthy: there is none that doeth good, no, not one.

This pointed passage speaks of a class of people ("they"), as the singular noun ("fool") is used in a collective sense (v. 1; cf. Ps. 53). Specifically, they have said, "There is no God." As we have seen, creation reflects God's activity in the world for all to see. However, some look but never see. The foolish person is one who has no appreciation of God's interaction in their lives (Deut. 32:20), has no sensitivity of godly things (v. 21), embraces wickedness (Isa. 32:5-6), has an arrogant attitude (Prov. 30:22), and thus, through his or her mind-set, character, actions, and/or speech, denies the existence of God.

God, reminiscent of the Prodigal's father (Luke 15:20), "looks down from heaven . . . to see if there are any who understand, any who seek God" (Ps. 14:2 NIV). He is looking eternally for those who are wise in their ways ("understand") and have an active heart for Him ("seek"). Unfortunately, what He sees are those who have departed or defected ("gone aside") from His destiny for them; thus, they have become morally reprehensible ("filthy"), and cannot accomplish anything beneficial ("good," v. 3). God himself then asks a question that reveals those who do evil have no discernment ("knowledge"), they abuse God's people, and they do not call out to the Lord (v. 4). It is a sad commentary that reflects not only the psalmist's society but our own, too. We can only imagine how this must break the heart of God.

B. The Wrath of God on Unrighteousness (Rom. 1:18-25)
18. For the wrath of God is revealed from heaven against all ungodliness and unrighteousness of men, who hold the truth in unrighteousness;

19. Because that which may be known of God is manifest in them; for God hath shewed it unto them.

20. For the invisible things of him from the creation of the world are clearly seen, being understood by the things that are made, even his eternal power and Godhead; so that they are without excuse:

Talk About It:
1. Describe the foolish person (v. 1).
2. What do all people have in common (vv. 2-3)?

"I don't have the evidence to prove that God doesn't exist, but I so strongly suspect He doesn't that I don't want to waste my time."
—Isaac Asimov (best-selling author of popular science and science fiction)

Intelligent Design or Chance?

21. Because that, when they knew God, they glorified him not as God, neither were thankful; but became vain in their imaginations, and their foolish heart was darkened.

22. Professing themselves to be wise, they became fools,

23. And changed the glory of the uncorruptible God into an image made like to corruptible man, and to birds, and fourfooted beasts, and creeping things.

24. Wherefore God also gave them up to uncleanness through the lusts of their own hearts, to dishonour their own bodies between themselves:

25. Who changed the truth of God into a lie, and worshipped and served the creature more than the Creator, who is blessed for ever. Amen.

In this passage, Paul moves from addressing humanity in general to focusing in particular on the Hellenistic (Gentile) society of his time. He notes that the "wrath of God" (deep, personal anger) is directed toward two all-encompassing negative attributes: "ungodliness and unrighteousness" (v. 18). *Ungodliness* is a deep disregard for the things of God and His rightful worship. It is "irreverence" and "godlessness." *Unrighteousness* is broader in its focus. It includes a disregard for a proper relationship with God but also consists of a lack of right relationship with our fellow travelers in life's journey. It is a rejection of the "truth" God has revealed through His character, creation, Son, and Word (vv. 18-20). Those who practice such "are without excuse," because they have not honored God, but given in to the darkness of "their foolish heart" (vv. 20-21). They have embraced foolishness in the name of knowledge (v. 22), and replaced the worship of the "uncorruptible" (immortal) God with idols (images) taken from creation (v. 23). Since righteousness contains a power for living (Amos 5:24), unrighteousness must rob one of power for life.

Because of the deep, illicit desires ("lusts of their own hearts") that yearn for impurity, God has removed His hand of protection and provision from them, and allowed them to treat contemptuously ("dishonour") their own bodies (v. 24). They turned their attention from the Creator and focused upon the creation—which was designed to bring our attention to the Creator (v. 25). As sin does, this places them in bondage to the thing they worship. Sometimes we get what we want, but not what we expect!

III. WORSHIP THE CREATOR (Col. 1:16-18; Rev. 4:11)
A. Creator and Sustainer (Col. 1:16-18)

16. For by him were all things created, that are in heaven, and that are in earth, visible and invisible, whether they be thrones, or dominions, or principalities, or powers: all things were created by him, and for him:

17. And he is before all things, and by him all things consist.

Talk About It:
1. What stirs the anger of God (vv. 18-19)?
2. Why are people "without excuse" regarding faith in God (v. 20)?
3. Describe the digression of people who reject God (vv. 21-24).
4. How is verse 25 descriptive of modern culture?

Dangerous Proposition

A few years ago a coworker and I were discussing God's existence. He told me he did not believe in God anymore, because of things he had seen. The next day he was rushed to a hospital with a life-threatening condition. He was off work for nearly two months. When he returned, the first thing he told me was that he had prayed and God responded by calming his fears and saving his life. Denying God is a dangerous proposition.

18. And he is the head of the body, the church: who is the beginning, the firstborn from the dead; that in all things he might have the preeminence.

Talk About It:
1. What does verse 16 reveal about the creation of "all things"?
2. What does verse 17 teach about God?
3. How does verse 18 describe Jesus Christ?

Worship is reserved for the One deserving of worship. Here Paul declares that Christ is the agent of all creation (v. 16), working with the Father and the Spirit (Gen. 1:2). The Godhead worked in perfect unison to accomplish this event. In Colossians 1:16 Paul emphasizes Christ's participation in three ways: (1) All things were "created" ("called into being") "by him" (literally, "in" or "within Him"), which denotes He is the cause of and the reason for creation (see John 3:16; Rev. 4:11); (2) creation came "by him" (or "because of Him"), which emphasizes His agency; and (3) this was done "for him" (or "into Him"), emphasizing authority and ownership. All creation is subject to Him, regardless of where it is ("heaven" or "earth"), whether it is seen or not ("visible and invisible"), and regardless of who it is or what power or position they may possess ("thrones, or dominions, or principalities, or powers").

The first phrase of verse 17—"he is before all things"—can be interpreted two different ways. First, it can mean "Christ existed prior to all things," that is, Creation. This is consistent with John 1:1-3, where we find that prior to the beginning of Creation, the Word (Christ) already was. There are some, even in Pentecostal circles, who question the preexistence of Christ prior to His birth on earth (Matt. 1:18-25). This thinking is based on faulty theology and improper exegesis (in-depth study) of Scripture. Second, it can mean "Christ has preeminence over all things." While the second option is certainly true and has been emphasized in the prior verse, grammatically the first translation is preferable. Further, Paul emphasizes that through Christ "all things hold together" (Col. 1:17 NIV). Someone has noted correctly that He is the "cosmic glue" that keeps the universe together.

Therefore, He is the "head of the body, the church" (v. 18). The Church is not a denomination, a revival movement, a fad, or a building made by hands. It is the body of Christ, which includes the first child of God in history to the last soul saved before the great Day of Judgment. It is His, for He gave His life for every soul therein. He is the "beginning," or the first in authority, power, and dominion. He is the originator of all things. His position is established not only by virtue of who He is, but also what He has accomplished. He alone is the "firstborn from the dead" (v. 18). *Firstborn* carries three connotations: (1) He existed before anything else (v. 15); (2) He is in a position of favor (Rom. 8:29); and (3) He is the first to be raised from death's power and domain. Several individuals were brought back to life prior to the resurrection of Christ (1 Kings 17:22; 2 Kings 4:35; 13:21; Matt. 9:18-26; John 11:43-44). They, however, were still subject to death. Christ conquered death once and for all (Rev. 1:18). Thus, by virtue of

"There is but one God, the Father, of whom are all things, and we in him; and one Lord Jesus Christ, by whom are all things, and we by him."
—1 Corinthians 8:6

Intelligent Design or Chance?

position (Son of God) and power (resurrection), He has "pre-eminence" over everything.

B. Collective Worship (Rev. 4:11)

11. Thou art worthy, O Lord, to receive glory and honour and power: for thou hast created all things, and for thy pleasure they are and were created.

The setting of this verse is the throne room of God. The twenty-four elders have fallen down in an act of obedience and acknowledgment of the sovereignty of the Father and cast their crowns at His feet (v. 10).

Every aspect of creation was designed to bring glory to God (see Rom. 8:19-21). Worship begins with a decision of the will (mind), moves to the emotions (heart), and is expressed in the physical (body). There are times, however, when the physical act of worship precedes the emotional aspect. Worship encompasses the entirety of our being and existence. It is praise to God for who He is and thanksgiving for what He does. It is the total abandonment of self, dedicated to an audience of One—God. It will affect and bless those around us, but it is dedicated solely to God. Our concern must be to please Him, not others.

In our text, the elders, in worship directed to Him, acknowledge these five facts: (1) God's distinctive and sacred worthiness ("Thou art worthy"); (2) His sovereignty over their lives and the intimate, redemptive relationship they have with Him ("our Lord and God," NIV); (3) His splendor and majesty ("glory and honor and power"); (4) His primacy above all creation, for it originates from Him ("created all things"); and (5) His dominion and design— we exist to bring Him glory and accomplish His will ("You called all things into being, and because of Your will, they exist and were created," author's translation).

Talk About It:
What does the Lord deserve, and why?

"God-pleasing worship is deeply emotional and deeply doctrinal. We use both our hearts and our heads."
—Rick Warren

CONCLUSION

We live in the midst of a beautiful earth, created by God for us. It should not be taken for granted or mistreated. His "fingerprints" are evident throughout all creation. There is no excuse for denying His existence and supremacy. Every day is a new day in the scheme of God's economy. He created the earth for us, and He continues to create within us a new heart if we let Him (Ps. 51:10). He alone is worthy and deserving of our praise.

GOLDEN TEXT CHALLENGE

"IN THE BEGINNING GOD CREATED THE HEAVEN AND THE EARTH" (Gen. 1:1).

This verse establishes the time in which we live. It does not establish time for God. God created time, therefore, "in the beginning" is our time. God is above and before all time. Our time begins with God. God existed before time existed, and this verse speaks

with that assumption—as if to say, "In the beginning God [who already was] created. . . . "

The Creator of all heaven and earth is identified, not justified. His place is assumed. There is no second-guessing the already present God. If God is not accepted as already existing, the Bible will forever be questioned. There is no effort here or any other place in Scripture to prove existence of God. God is simply presented.

If we try to prove God before we simply believe, we will be constantly searching. We see the handiwork of God and cry, "My God," just as Thomas cried when he felt the nail prints in the Savior's hand. The God we serve is Creator not by proof but by accepting the revelation of the Word of God.

"Heaven" and "earth" are used to describe the universe. The verse indicates that all of the universe is dependent upon God for its substance and construction. Before the creative act of God there was absolutely nothing. No matter, energy, or reality existed before the act of God in Creation. Once people accept this fundamental starting point, no scientific, physic, or chemical equation is complete without recognition of God. Nothing in the universe has ever existed by itself. All points of creation run back to God.

Intelligent Design or Chance?

Life or Death?

Genesis 1:27-31; 2:7; Psalms 8:3-9; 139:13-16;
Acts 17:24-28

INTRODUCTION

Too often in life, we are encouraged not to think for ourselves. It is expressed or implied that we should accept what is said and not think too deeply on things, especially the things of God and His Word. This is contrary to the Word, which is full of admonitions to "ponder," "think," or "reflect." The Hebrew word often translated "ponder" or "consider" is also translated as "separate." We are to mentally separate truth from lies, good from evil, even better from best, so that we might know and please God. Throughout the Psalms, we find the psalmists asking hard questions concerning their faith and circumstances. Jesus often employed questions to help His audience understand more clearly the message He was communicating and apply the truths to their lives (e.g., Matt. 18:12). God asked Job some difficult questions at the end of his ordeal to teach him deep spiritual truths. We are who God made us to be, and that includes having questions.

It is not wrong to ask questions concerning verses we do not understand or that even seem to contradict other verses in the Bible. This causes us to seek a deeper understanding of God and His Word. Bible scholars will tell you that the more they study, the more questions they have; and the more they realize, the less they know. This is by divine design. It is called "intentional tension." There are passages and circumstances that create tension in our lives. It is a sort of spiritually induced disharmony. God allows that tension and lack of harmony (the feeling of dissatisfaction deep within) to motivate us to seek Him and search for resolution in His Word and worship. It is healthy as long as it keeps us moving *toward* God and maturity.

This lesson will create questions that cannot be answered within the confines of these pages or the time allotted to the teacher. It will cause us to reflect on how insignificant—and yet significant—we are in the scope of Creation. Write down the questions that come to mind. Keep them on a paper placed in a prominent place in your Bible and allow the Holy Spirit to guide the next leg of your spiritual journey.

Unit Theme:
Bible Answers to Crucial Questions

Central Truth:
God created and requires respect for human life.

Focus:
Confess that human life is a gift of God and value its sanctity.

Context:
Selected Scripture passages concerning the sanctity of human life

Golden Text:
"I will praise thee; for I am fearfully and wonderfully made: marvellous are thy works; and that my soul knoweth right well" (Ps. 139:14).

Study Outline:
I. Life Comes From God (Gen. 1:27-31; 2:7)
II. The Wonder of God's Handiwork (Pss. 8:3-9; 139:13-16)
III. We Are God's Offspring (Acts 17:24-28)

I. LIFE COMES FROM GOD (Gen. 1:27-31; 2:7)

A. The Creative God (1:27-31)

27. So God created man in his own image, in the image of God created he him; male and female created he them.

28. And God blessed them, and God said unto them, Be fruitful, and multiply, and replenish the earth, and subdue it: and have dominion over the fish of the sea, and over the fowl of the air, and over every living thing that moveth upon the earth.

29. And God said, Behold, I have given you every herb bearing seed, which is upon the face of all the earth, and every tree, in the which is the fruit of a tree yielding seed; to you it shall be for meat.

30. And to every beast of the earth, and to every fowl of the air, and to every thing that creepeth upon the earth, wherein there is life, I have given every green herb for meat: and it was so.

31. And God saw every thing that he had made, and, behold, it was very good. And the evening and the morning were the sixth day.

Talk About It:
1. What did God tell Adam and Eve to do (v. 28)?
2. How did God provide for humanity (v. 29)?
3. How did God provide for the animal kingdom (v. 30)?

This passage continues to chronicle the sixth day of Creation, wherein God created the domesticated and wild animals (see v. 24ff.). The biblical record also reflects that God (*Elohim*, "the true" or "powerful God") "created man" (v. 27). The Hebrew word for "create" (*bara*) is used here in a distinct grammatical form that is never used of anyone but God. The word in general is used to describe the work of a carpenter who takes a raw piece of wood and, with skilled hands, "beats out" or "shapes" the wood into a new creation or product. It is used to emphasize the initiation of a process, at times an ongoing process. Further, the act of creation is one of God's free will. He did not have to create humanity. He chose to do so to fellowship with us.

The second emphasis of this passage is that God created humanity "in the image of God" (v. 27). The word used for "man" is *adam* (the same as Adam's name). It is a generic term that can refer to humanity in general, as well as the male gender. The point is we were created in His image. "Image" can refer to something "cut out," like an idol (2 Kings 11:18). It is used of something that is an "exact resemblance," like a child who resembles his parent(s). Since God is Spirit (John 4:24), this must emphasize that humanity was created in the moral image of God. The primary characteristics of God are love, life, and holiness. Everything else flows from these three attributes. God has volition (will), intellect, affections, and personality, and to us He imparts these things. Thus, humanity reflects (or should!) the divine nature, but is not divine. This speaks to the quality of fellowship we should have with Him. God created us with the ability to comprehend (albeit in a very limited fashion) who He is and what He desires from us and for us.

Life or Death?

Third, God created "male and female" (Gen. 1:27). The term for "male" is not the one used for "man." Rather, it is the specific term used for the male gender. Likewise, the term for "female" is gender-specific. Both were created by God, and both were created in His image. One of the aspects communicated in the Creation event is that of intentional harmony. God said, "Let us make man in our image" (v. 26). This verse provides proof of harmony in the Godhead. Further there is relationship, equality, and voluntary submission (which requires equality). Creator and creation should be in harmony with each other. Likewise, male and female should be in harmony with each other, and follow the example of the Trinity.

A fourth point is that "God blessed them" (v. 28). *Bless* also means "to salute" or "to kneel." It can convey a sense of "happiness," often involving prosperity and power from God. It is a highly relational term; that is, blessings are designed to enhance relationships. It is primarily used of a superior extending favor to a lesser, hence the idea of God bending down to our level and intervening in our situation. Ultimate blessing is fulfilled in Jesus Christ, who indeed came to our level, bending His knees in the Garden of Gethsemane, then "bending" them again on the cross, so that we might be blessed with all the blessings of God.

Fifth, God gave two commands to the newly created humans: (1) fill the earth with offspring ("Be fruitful, and multiply, and replenish the earth"); and (2) "subdue . . . and have dominion over" (v. 28). *Replenish* in the Hebrew does not mean "to refill," but simply "to fill." Also, God gives instructions concerning the practical parts of subduing the earth (vv. 29-30). The words used indicate that the submission will not be willing, as it carries the idea of the use of power/force to accomplish the goal. This power, however, is to be used to bring glory to God through the use of the earth's resources; it is not to be used to destroy the earth.

Finally, God looked at everything He had created, especially humanity, and saw it was "very good" (v. 31). This is more than a statement of accomplishment and pride in a job well done. It also means that humanity carried the "goodness" of God. As such, Adam and Eve were free from evil and had the moral character and righteousness of God. This completed the sixth day of Creation, which in itself is more of a revelation of who God is rather than a revealing of what He did in those six days. He is the source of all things.

B. The God of Life and Relationship (2:7)

7. And the Lord God formed man of the dust of the ground, and breathed into his nostrils the breath of life; and man became a living soul.

This is one of the most compelling verses in the Bible. "The Lord God fashioned the man out of the dust of the earth and

"Without God, man has no reference point to define himself. . . . Philosophy manifests the chaos of man seeking to understand himself as a creature with dignity while having no reference point for that dignity."
—R. C. Sproul

Talk About It:
What was unique about God's creation of man?

breathed the power of life into his nostrils, and he was made a living being" (author's translation). First, this speaks of the uniqueness of humanity, and reveals there is an intimate association between God and people. The breath of life is the life of God, the Spirit of God breathing into us and fashioning us into "a living soul."

Second, there is a special relationship between God and humanity which is not found in any other aspect of creation. It is a covenant relationship. All the Bible covenants (e.g., Abrahamic, Noahic, Davidic) are empowered by, subservient to, and premised upon the basic covenantal formula in Scripture: "I will be your God, and ye shall be my people" (Lev. 26:12; Jer. 7:23). The impartation of life is the beginning of God's self-revelation to humanity (Ezek. 37:14; Deut. 32:39) and initiation of relationship with humanity. The covenant of God is His Spirit upon those who are His; thus, His breath (or Spirit) of life is the sign of the covenant (Isa. 59:21). Therefore, the covenant is one of relationship, or, more fundamentally, life itself (Neh. 9:6-8; Mal. 2:5). It can be called a covenant of relational life. To be out of relationship with God is to be under the covenant of death (Isa. 28:17-18; Ezek. 18:4) and separated from the source of life (Gen. 3:3; Ezek. 3:20). Further, an improper relationship with God has life-altering implications in the community (Deut. 17:6, 12) and political sphere (Jer. 22:1-10). With the inception of life, Adam began a life-dependent relationship with God, in whose image he was created. He lived in perfection as long as he remained in a righteous relationship with the source of life (Gen. 2:17; 3:3; cf. Deut. 30:15).

Third, inherent in Genesis 2:7 is the establishment of faith and the promise of redemption. Humanity is dependent on God for the power of life and, thus, lives by faith. What God has begun in creation, He will complete in spite of sin's effects (Rom. 8:19-22).

II. THE WONDER OF GOD'S HANDIWORK (Pss. 8:3-9; 139:13-16)

A. The Mindful God (8:3-9)

3. When I consider thy heavens, the work of thy fingers, the moon and the stars, which thou hast ordained;

4. What is man, that thou art mindful of him? and the son of man, that thou visitest him?

5. For thou hast made him a little lower than the angels, and hast crowned him with glory and honour.

6. Thou madest him to have dominion over the works of thy hands; thou hast put all things under his feet:

7. All sheep and oxen, yea, and the beasts of the field;

8. The fowl of the air, and the fish of the sea, and whatsoever passeth through the paths of the seas.

9. O Lord our Lord, how excellent is thy name in all the earth!

Sovereign Father
Several years ago on a TV show, the father, who was a doctor played by Bill Cosby, looked at his son and said sternly, "I brought you into this world, and I can take you out!" God is still sovereign over life, and our continued life (both quantity and quality) is dependent on a right relationship with Him.

Life or Death?

One can almost see the psalmist (traditionally David) standing in awe on a hill in Judea staring into the spectacular, starlit sky on a dark night. The term rendered "consider" can mean "to look" or "to see" in a general sense (v. 3). But it is also used in the prophetic sense of "to see" or "receive" a revelation from God (Isa. 6:1). Looking intently at creation will cause one to "see God revealed." We see the work of God's "fingers" (literally, "the making of His fingers"), which reminds us of His personal touch or involvement in creating "the moon and the stars" (Ps. 8:3). These things He has "ordained"—set in place, or established. In spite of humanity's best scientific efforts, no one has seen the edge or end of the universe.

With such an expanse to consider, one is correct in asking, "What is man that You are mindful of him?" (v. 4 NKJV). Humanity is so insignificant in light of such magnitude. Yet, God *is* "mindful" of us, which carries the idea of "remembering," "thinking about," and "paying attention to." As the latter part of the verse reveals, it is a remembrance that motivates action. "Son of man" is poetic convention and synonymous with "man" (v. 4). God not only knows who we are, He knows where we are, He knows what we have done, and He still loves us. Therefore, He will take care of all our needs, as we express continued faith in Him.

Verse 5 has two possible translations that can result in very different meanings. It is without dispute that God has created humanity "a little lower" (literally, "less than" or "smaller than"). That is, humanity has need of something we cannot supply. We are dependent on God for revelation, moral guidance, fellowship, and life. The difficulty comes in determining who we were created lower than. The original manuscripts (scrolls, papyri, tablets, etc.) that the psalmist wrote on no longer exist. This is true for all the books of the Bible. We have copies of copies of copies. This does not mean that they are full of errors, as the Dead Sea Scrolls have proven. There are, however, two primary types of manuscripts that we have for the Old Testament: (1) the Hebrew text, called the Masoretic text, and (2) the Greek text, called the Septuagint, often designated as the LXX. In this case, the Hebrew text says we have been created in a subservient position to "God," while the LXX says "the angels." The Hebrew is usually the more accurate text. The emphasis is not on our rank (lower, higher, or equal, though different than angels), but on our continued dependence on God, who will crown us with "glory" (the beauty of godliness) and "honor" (the majesty of godliness), as we continually look to Him. Therefore, we have a stewardship responsibility for God's creation (vv. 6-8).

As the psalmist considers humanity's insignificance in creation and God's marvelous concern for us, he breaks forth in praise (v. 9). It is not just a recognition of the lordship of God (*Yahweh*, "O Lord"), but a personal surrender to and embracement of that lordship—"our Lord" (*Adonai*).

Talk About It:
1. What overwhelmed the psalmist (vv. 3-4)?
2. Describe the position of humanity (vv. 5-8).

Humanity's Worth

We know something wonderful about man. Among other things, we know his origin and who he is—he is made in the image of God. Man is not only wonderful when he is "born again" as a Christian, he is also wonderful as God made him in His image. Man has value because of who he was originally before the Fall.

—**Francis Schaeffer**

B. The Wonderful God (139:13-16)

13. For thou hast possessed my reins: thou hast covered me in my mother's womb.

14. I will praise thee; for I am fearfully and wonderfully made: marvellous are thy works; and that my soul knoweth right well.

15. My substance was not hid from thee, when I was made in secret, and curiously wrought in the lowest parts of the earth.

16. Thine eyes did see my substance, yet being unperfect; and in thy book all my members were written, which in continuance were fashioned, when as yet there was none of them.

The first phrase of verse 13 in the KJV is somewhat difficult to understand. "Possessed" is a possible translation of the Hebrew word, but incomplete. Different forms of the term are used for "wealth" and things "redeemed" by wealth or action (Ruth 4:8, "buy"). This is certainly an aspect of the word, but it is used in several places to mean "create" (Gen. 4:1, "gotten"; Deut. 32:6, "bought"). Thus, a clearer translation is, "For You have created my inward parts; You have formed me in my mother's womb." Therefore, it carries the idea of being obligated to the One who redeemed or created. The emphasis is on God's ability (note the emphatic "thou") *and* His intimate knowledge of us that results in continued care and our awareness of our dependency upon Him.

In verse 14 the psalmist breaks forth in praise after realizing God initiated the creative process even in the womb. He observes that "we are fearfully and wonderfully made." There are different types of fear in the Bible. This particular form emphasizes being in awe of God, though keenly aware of who He is and His power over life and death. It is a fear that draws us reverently to Him, not away from Him. Also, "wonderfully" carries the idea of something "marvelous," but also "distinct." We are unique and uniquely God's. It is difficult to comprehend such creativity, love, and power directed toward us!

Verses 15 and 16 emphasize not only the creative process of God in forming us, but also His intimate knowledge of every aspect of who and what we are. Even when we were little more than "bone" (the literal rendering of "substance," or "frame"), we were not out of God's sight. When we were formed "in secret" (the womb) and, in solidarity with Adam, created from "the lowest parts of the earth," or dust (Gen. 2:7; cf. Job 1:21), God knew us then. He had a purpose for us even when we were a developing embryo—"substance, yet being unperfect" (Ps. 139:16). Before the process even started, we were recorded in His book and the length of our lives preordained.

---

possessed my reins (v. 13)—"formed my inward parts" (NASB)

covered (v. 13)—"knit" (NIV) or "wove" (NASB)

my members (v. 16)—"the days ordained for me" (NIV)

Talk About It:
1. What was the psalmist motivated to do, and why (vv. 13-14)?
2. What does God know about the newly conceived child (vv. 15-16)?

An Ethical Question
A medical-school professor once posed this medical situation to his students: "Here's the family history: The father has syphilis. The mother has TB. They already have had four children. The first is blind. The second had died. The third is deaf. The fourth has TB. Now the mother is pregnant again. The parents come to you for advice. They are willing to have an abortion, if you decide they should. What do you say?" The students were divided into small groups for "consultation," and then each group reported that they would recommend abortion. "Congratulations," the professor said, "You just took the life of Beethoven!"
—Sermon Illustrations.com

III. WE ARE GOD'S OFFSPRING (Acts 17:24-28)
A. The Limitless God (vv. 24-25)

24. God that made the world and all things therein, seeing that he is Lord of heaven and earth, dwelleth not in temples made with hands;

25. Neither is worshipped with men's hands, as though he needed any thing, seeing he giveth to all life, and breath, and all things.

This section of the lesson is taken from Paul's speech in Athens at the Court of the Areopagus (Mars Hill, see v. 22). In mythology, this was the place of justice by the gods. Underneath the hill, it was believed that Eumenides (the Furies) lived. Approximately five hundred years earlier, Socrates defended himself there against his accusers. During Paul's day it also served as a court, usually once a month; but it was there that philosophers (especially the Epicureans and Stoics), debaters, and those who wanted to present a new thought would gather for a public forum. Some of the philosophers heard Paul's message of Jesus Christ and wanted to hear more, so he addressed the crowd concerning the God they were aware of but did not know ("the unknown God," v. 23).

Paul correctly points out that mythology is wrong, because God and God alone created the universe, for He is "Lord of heaven and earth" (v. 24). Paul then sets up a stark contrast between God and the many deities of that day (especially Roman and Greek) believed to be involved in the creation and continuance of the world. Using the language of Isaiah and other Old Testament prophets, he notes that God is not confined to a temple or place made by human hands. The universe is His temple, and it was made by and continues through Him. Over what God has created, He has the right to exercise dominion and lordship. Paul's message is strongly monotheistic (see lesson 10 for the difference between the worship of God and the ancient Near Eastern beliefs), contrary to most belief systems of that time.

In the KJV, verse 25 is translated, "Neither is worshipped with men's hands." At first, this seems to be a contradiction with the many commands to worship God with our uplifted hands (Pss. 28:2; 63:4; 134:2). However, it seems to be a reference to Isaiah 2:8, where idols are worshiped by the hands that made them; thus, Paul is pointing out that God is not the invention of people, designed to be confined to a place made by humanity. He is complete within Himself. As such, He is perfect (Matt. 5:48), eternal (Rom. 16:26), immortal (1 Tim. 1:17), and unfathomable love (1 John 4:8). God alone gives and sustains life. He has need of nothing, but desires fellowship with His creation. He can live and be complete without our fellowship; we can neither live nor be complete without His.

Talk About It:
How is the Lord God greater than idols?

"In the absence of any other proof, the thumb would convince me of God's existence."
—**Isaac Newton**

B. The God of All (vv. 26-28)

26. And hath made of one blood all nations of men for to dwell on all the face of the earth, and hath determined the times before appointed, and the bounds of their habitation;

27. That they should seek the Lord, if haply they might feel after him, and find him, though he be not far from every one of us:

28. For in him we live, and move, and have our being; as certain also of your own poets have said, For we are also his offspring.

Talk About It:
1. What is God's role concerning the nations (v. 26)?
2. What is God's will for all people (v. 27)?
3. What does verse 28 teach about the Lord's relationship to humanity?

Paul, under the inspiration of the Holy Spirit, affirms that God is the Creator of all nations and they can be traced back to His original creation of Adam and Eve. Everything is under His sovereignty (v. 26). We can look at creation and know there is One who is greater than ourselves, whom we must seek; He is waiting on us to embrace His outstretched hand (v. 27).

Verse 28 raises an interesting discussion that is relevant for today's church. To prove his point and relate to his audience, Paul quotes from two pagan poets. First, he quotes from Epimenides' (a Cretan philosopher, *ca.* 600 BC) poem *Cretica*: "In him we live, and move, and have our being" (see Titus 1:12 for another quotation from this poem). Second, he quotes from Aratus' (a Greek poet, *ca.* 310 BC) poem *Phaenomena*: "For we are indeed his offspring." Interestingly, both poems were written to or about Zeus. *Cretica* argues for the immortality of Zeus, while *Phaenomena* argues for his omnipresence. Why would an apostle use secular works by pagans to communicate a biblical message? Could he not have used Scripture or his own words to communicate the same message?

These excerpts are included in *inspired* Scripture for a reason. Nothing is in the Bible by accident. Paul could have obviously used other words to communicate his thoughts. But he used these familiar poems to point to One greater than Zeus.

First, truth is truth no matter where it is found. There is an omnipresent and immortal God, as the poets declared, but He is not Zeus. Paul said He is "Lord of heaven and earth" (Acts 17:24).

Second, Jesus often used simple stories with which His hearers could relate. Most were not "spiritual" in nature, but taught spiritual truths (see Mark 4:26-34; Matt. 13:33-35).

Third, there is no division between the sacred and the secular, only the holy and the profane. Israel was Israel, whether in the Temple or on the battlefield. They worshiped in both (see Ex. 15:1-21; 2 Sam. 1:17-27). Paul was an apostle, whether in a synagogue or the Areopagus. We have devised a false dichotomy between the secular and the sacred, where none should exist. We are to be the Church wherever we are. There is, however, a difference between the holy and the profane. That is the distinction we need to emphasize.

Fourth, we must communicate with our hearers. If it takes incorporating works (songs, media, etc.) with which they are familiar, then we must consider it prayerfully. Obviously, whatever we use must communicate a message that is consistent with the Word and character of God and bring Him glory.

Some have argued that Paul's ministry in Athens is his only recorded failure; however, Acts 17:34 reveals that he did not fail in the mission of Christ, for a number of people became Christians. They put their faith in "the God who made the world and everything in it" (v. 24 NIV).

CONCLUSION

God desires a special relationship with those whom He created. He has "given us everything we need for life and godliness" (2 Peter 1:3 NIV). We are to exercise proper stewardship over those things He has placed in our care, including, but not limited to, our souls, lives, creation, and the harvest of souls. It is His garden. How are we tending it? Are we doing so through the "breath of God"?

GOLDEN TEXT CHALLENGE

"I WILL PRAISE THEE; FOR I AM FEARFULLY AND WONDERFULLY MADE: MARVELLOUS ARE THY WORKS; AND THAT MY SOUL KNOWETH RIGHT WELL" (Ps. 139:14).

Psalm 139 is the place to begin in building a biblical foundation for dealing with traumatic events such as birth defects and miscarriages. Recognizing that God cares and is involved helps to ease the pain that accompanies these difficulties. The psalm also helps establish an ethical guideline for viewing the pre-birth issues of abortion, artificial insemination, in vitro fertilization, surrogate birth, and fetal tissue research. Knowing that God has a special interest in what takes place in the womb should make anyone hesitant to misuse this sacred place where a life is formed.

David was amazed at the complexity of the human life and expressed his awe in the words "I am fearfully and wonderfully made" (v. 14). He responded with thanksgiving and saw that God had a purpose for his life, even from the embryo stage. All his days had been prenumbered and written down in the Book of Life.

"The Lord God of heaven and earth, the Almighty Creator of all things, He who holds the universe in His hand as though it were a very little thing, He is your Shepherd, and He has charged Himself with the care and keeping of you, as a shepherd is charged with the care and keeping of his sheep."
—**Hannah Whitall Smith**

Daily Devotions:
M. Choose Life
   Deuteronomy
   30:15-20
T. God Grants Life
   Job 10:8-12
W. God's Spirit
   Breathes Life
   Job 33:1-6
T. God Values Life
   Matthew 10:29-31
F. Abundant Life
   John 10:9-18
S. Acknowledge
   God in Life
   James 4:13-17

Sexual Purity or Immorality?

Leviticus 18:1-30; Romans 1:26-32;
1 Corinthians 6:12-20; Ephesians 5:3-5

Unit Theme:
Bible Answers to
Crucial Questions

Central Truth:
Our bodies belong to
God and sexual purity
honors Him.

Focus:
Examine the biblical
understanding of moral-
ity and consecrate our
bodies as temples of
the Holy Spirit.

Context:
Selected Scripture
passages addressing
sexual holiness

Golden Text:
"Ye are bought with a
price: therefore glorify
God in your body, and
in your spirit, which are
God's" (1 Cor. 6:20).

Study Outline:
 I. Sexual Immorality
    Defined
    (Lev. 18:1-30)
 II. Immoral Behavior
     and Conversation
     Prohibited
     (Rom. 1:26-32;
     Eph. 5:3-5)
 III. Our Bodies Belong
      to God
      (1 Cor. 6:12-20)

INTRODUCTION

Each year in the United States there are approximately 18.9 million new cases of STDs (sexually transmitted diseases); nine million of those cases are among teenagers (*Perspectives on Sexual and Reproductive Health*, Vol. 36:1). There are at least twenty-five different types of STDs (The Alan Guttmacher Institute, 2004). By the time they are eighteen, 45 percent of females and 48 percent of males in the U.S. have engaged in sexual intercourse (Kaiser Family Foundation, Jan. 2005). Public sex education seems to be working, but not in a positive way.

As of 2003, there were over 260 million pornographic web-pages on the Internet (N2H2, 2003). The total revenue in 2006 for producers of pornography was $97 billion (Internet Filter Review). Approximately 20 percent of all Internet pornography involves children (National Center for Missing and Exploited Children). Approximately seventy-two million adults visit a porno-graphic website on a monthly basis; 28 percent of those are women (Internet Filter Review). *Christianity Today* reported that 51 percent of the pastors they surveyed admitted that cyberporn was a real temptation and 37 percent said it was a current struggle (*Leadership Journal* survey, Dec. 2001). Fifty-seven percent of pastors surveyed said pornography was the most sexually damaging issue to their congregation (*Leadership Journal* survey, Mar. 2005).

No one wakes up one morning and suddenly decides to be sexually immoral. There is a progression (or deterioration) that takes place (see James 1:14-15) in an illicit relationship. It begins innocently enough, but the conversation begins to move to areas that should not be discussed, such as boredom or dissatisfaction in the marriage, personal feelings and thoughts, and what-ifs. Conversation moves to quick touches. The progres-sion is hand, shoulder, face, then other sensitive areas. Thoughts of the other person begin to infiltrate the mind and take over normal activities. It is a dangerous and deadly game that has no positive outcome (Rev. 21:8).

We should not emphasize the "forbiddens" of sexuality without also emphasizing the positive aspects of God's plan. Human sexuality is a gift from God. Like any other gift, it is to be used for its intended purpose to be fully valuable.

I. SEXUAL IMMORALITY DEFINED (Lev. 18:1-30)
A. Distinctly God's People (vv. 1-5)

1. And the Lord spake unto Moses, saying,

2. Speak unto the children of Israel, and say unto them, I am the Lord your God.

3. After the doings of the land of Egypt, wherein ye dwelt, shall ye not do: and after the doings of the land of Canaan, whither I bring you, shall ye not do: neither shall ye walk in their ordinances.

4. Ye shall do my judgments, and keep mine ordinances, to walk therein: I am the Lord your God.

5. Ye shall therefore keep my statutes, and my judgments: which if a man do, he shall live in them: I am the Lord.

Talk About It:
1. How did the Lord communicate His message to the Israelites (vv. 1-2)?
2. What were the Israelites ordered *not* to do (v. 3)?
3. How were they to live, and why (vv. 4-5)?

This passage is the second chapter of what scholars often refer to as the "Holiness Code" (Lev. 17:1–26:46), the section of the Law that deals with practical issues affecting Israel's relationship with and obedience to God. In studying Scripture, we must never fail to consider context in determining the Bible's application to our time and lives. Moses was writing to a large nomadic community that was composed of large family units. Close proximity can create tempestuous and tempting situations.

God instructs Moses to "speak" to the people of Israel (v. 2). The term for "speak" is the same word used of a divine word from God (*dabar*, cf. the Ten Words, or Ten Commandments, Ex. 20:1-17). Interestingly, when the negative prefix (*lo*) is added to *dabar* (*lodabar*, literally, "no word"), it becomes the word *wilderness*. This word was from God; Moses was the instrument He used to deliver it. The message began with a focal point: "I am the Lord your God" (Lev. 18:2). It was a reminder of who He is (*Yahweh Elohim*), the mighty One who is ever present, who delivered them from Egypt, and a reinforcement that they are His.

While in Egypt, they were introduced to customs or accepted practices ("ordinances," v. 3) that were contrary to God's design for them. The ancient Near East was a promiscuous society, and often incorporated sexuality into the worship of their gods. It was thought to promote fertility of the ground, livestock, and family. As well, the code of conduct for sex and marriage was much different in Canaan than the Israelites were receiving in this word from the Lord.

In verses 4 and 5, the Israelites were to "do" (abide by, or conform to) God's "judgments" (rules) and "statutes" (prescribed ways). They were to guard their lives judiciously ("keep") and "walk" (make it a way of life) in them, because the Lord God had prescribed it. Sin is not sin because it is a hurtful thing, or because it makes sense to abstain from it. Sin is sin because God says so. Further, by adhering to God's commands, it not only improves the quality of our spiritual lives, but obedience imparts life itself (v. 5; cf. Ex. 20:12; Deut. 30:15-20).

"For the first time in our history, the weird and the stupid and the coarse are becoming our cultural norm, even our cultural ideal."
—**Carl Bernstein**

(Leviticus 18:7-18 is not included in the printed text.)

6. None of you shall approach to any that is near of kin to him, to uncover their nakedness: I am the Lord.

Talk About It:
What is prohibited in verses 7-18?

In this section, God delineates those who are considered to be "near of kin" or family and gives the prohibition concerning "uncovering their nakedness" (v. 6). This phrase is a euphemism for sexual activity, and carries a sense of shame (Isa. 47:3). Thus, it is used to describe incest (Deut. 27:20). Therefore, God is lifting up unhealthy relationships—relationships that will cause pain and problems.

Abstaining from any sexual activity with a parent is almost a universal taboo, and is clearly prohibited here by God (Lev. 18:7). In a world where polygamy was acceptable (Abraham, Jacob, and David all had multiple wives), it is possible that a stepmother could be viewed as a potential partner; yet, this is an intrusion upon the father's sexuality and forbidden in both Testaments (v. 8; see 1 Cor. 5:1-13). Likewise, a sister or half-sister, by the mother or father, and whether or not she is in the same or another household, is to be considered a blood relative (Lev. 18:9). Obviously, a granddaughter is considered a family member (v. 10). If a stepsister is raised in the same family or household, she is not a possible mate (v. 11). An aunt on either the father's or mother's side is not to be pursued (vv. 12-13). Similarly, an uncle's wife (v. 14), a daughter-in-law (v. 15), or a sister-in-law ("brother's wife," v. 16) are off-limits. This last prohibition has an exception in a specific situation (see Deut. 25:5-10). One is not permitted to have relations with a woman and then her daughter, or vice versa (Lev. 18:17). This is taken as a lifetime commandment; thus, the death of either would not change the prohibition. Further, one cannot have relations with a woman and then with a stepson's or stepdaughter's daughter, as even these are considered relatives. Finally, a wife's sister is not to be taken as a "rival wife" (v. 18 NIV).

"A colleague tells me that some of his fellow legal scholars call child molestation *intergenerational intimacy.* . . . A good-hearted editor tried to talk me out of using the word *sodomy.* . . . My students don't know the word *fornication* at all."
—**J. Budziszewski**
(*First Things*)

There are a few points that need to be emphasized in light of this passage: (1) These prohibitions include sexual relations, both within and outside of the bonds of marriage. (2) Even among very large and extended families, the family unit is considered sacred. (3) There is already a progression toward monogamy evident, as some of the patriarchal families would have violated these prohibitions (e.g., Abraham and Jacob; see Gen. 20:12; 29:25-28). (4) The marriage covenant instituted by God is not to be taken lightly.

C. Prohibited Sexual Conduct (vv. 19-23)

19. Also thou shalt not approach unto a woman to uncover her nakedness, as long as she is put apart for her uncleanness.

20. Moreover thou shalt not lie carnally with thy neighbour's wife, to defile thyself with her.

21. And thou shalt not let any of thy seed pass through the fire to Molech, neither shalt thou profane the name of thy God: I am the Lord.

22. Thou shalt not lie with mankind, as with womankind: it is abomination.

23. Neither shalt thou lie with any beast to defile thyself therewith: neither shall any woman stand before a beast to lie down thereto: it is confusion.

lie carnally (v. 20)—
"have sexual relations"
(NIV)

thy seed (v. 21)—
"your children" (NIV)

Molech (MO-lek)—
v. 21—a heathen god
whose worship in-
volved children pass-
ing through or going
into a fire

confusion (v. 23)—
"perversion" (NKJV)

Verses 19-23 address conduct that is considered abnormal, and to be resisted. The first two (menstrual uncleanness and adultery) are self-evident (vv. 19-20). Surprisingly, in the midst of sexual prohibitions, there is the command concerning offering a child to Molech (v. 21). Specifically, "You shall not offer any of your children to devote them to Molech" (author's translation). In this practice, firstborn children were offered as a burnt sacrifice to Molech (literally, "king"). Sacrificing the firstborn was thought to bring prosperity from this false deity to the remaining children. It was a practice that is referenced in several places in Scripture (incl. Jer. 7:31; 32:35). Josiah tore down the altar where this occurred (2 Kings 23:10). It is strongly condemned, and those who participate are to be put to death (Lev. 20:2-5), as it does "profane the name of thy God: I am the Lord" (18:21). This is very strong language. The root term for *profane* seems to be "to pierce" or "to wound." To profane does violence to the law of God (Zeph. 3:4), breaks the covenant (Ps. 55:20; see lesson 11 for the covenant of life), and defiles the divine statutes (89:30-32). The religious practice of child sacrifice is an affront to the very nature of God, which it pierces. He calls for living sacrifices from willing participants, not the sacrificing of children, who are a reflection of His kingdom (Matt. 19:14).

The strong language continues in the next two verses of the text, where homosexuality is called an "abomination" (v. 22) and bestiality is a "perversion" (v. 23 NIV). "Abomination" is utilized in all its forms over one hundred times in the Old Testament. It represents something that is repulsive to God and humanity on a physical (Job 9:31; 30:10) and ethical level (Deut. 7:26; Mic. 3:9). Several things are revealed in Scripture as an "abomination." Obviously, homosexuality (here and Lev. 20:13) is offensive to God, as is idolatry (Deut. 7:25), human sacrifice (12:31), occult practices (18:9-14), and ritual prostitution (prostitution practiced as part of worship, 1 Kings 14:23-24). However, there are things that are an abomination to God that we might not readily associate with that term—such as dishonest business practices (Deut. 25:13-16), giving God less than the best (17:1), devious people (Prov. 3:32), prayer without obedience (28:9), unjust judgment

Talk About It:
1. What types of sexual behavior are condemned in verses 20, 22, and 23?
2. What would "profane" the Lord's name (v. 21)?

(17:15), and dishonesty (12:22). Additionally, there are seven things listed in Proverbs 6:16-19 that God abhors: (1) arrogance; (2) lying; (3) shedding innocent blood, which would include abortion; (4) devious planning; (5) embracing evil; (6) a false witness; and (7) those who stir up strife.

Homosexuality is a sin. It is not part of God's design or order, but it is not the unpardonable sin. Given the list of other abominations above, it is no more repugnant to God than things that some Christians have allowed to slip into their lives. Some Christians, and even churches, treat those who are caught in this debilitating sin like they have the plague. Will that "love" win them to Christ? If we drive them away, what shall we say of our witness (and their cries) come Judgment Day?

Sexual activity with animals (bestiality) is repulsive and unhealthy on every level (Lev. 18:23). "Perversion" (NIV) in Hebrew is found in this form only twice in the Old Testament—here and in 20:12, where incest is involved. The root of the word appropriately means "confusion." God has a divine order, and when it is violated it produces confusion for all involved.

D. Conduct and Consequences (vv. 24-30)
(Leviticus 18:24-29 is not included in the printed text.)
30. Therefore shall ye keep mine ordinance, that ye commit not any one of these abominable customs, which were committed before you, and that ye defile not yourselves therein: I am the Lord your God.

In any conduct there are positive or negative consequences. Six helpful principles are presented: (1) Abstain from anything that hinders a right relationship with God (v. 24a). (2) The disobedient will be replaced with a new people, so do God's will or get replaced (vv. 24b-25, 27-28). (3) Do right and help others to do the same (v. 26). (4) Sin brings separation and division (v. 29). (5) Learn from the example of others (both good and bad) and do right. (6) Remember there is only one "Lord your God" (v. 30); He is the final judge of what is right and wrong.

II. IMMORAL BEHAVIOR AND CONVERSATION PROHIBITED (Rom. 1:26-32; Eph. 5:3-5)
A. Unrighteousness Detailed (Rom. 1:26-32)
26. For this cause God gave them up unto vile affections: for even their women did change the natural use into that which is against nature:
27. And likewise also the men, leaving the natural use of the woman, burned in their lust one toward another; men with men working that which is unseemly, and receiving in themselves that recompence of their error which was meet.

"Chastity is the most unpopular of the Christian virtues. There is no getting away from it; the old Christian rule is, 'Either marriage, with complete faithfulness to your partner, or else total abstinence.'"
—C. S. Lewis

Talk About It:
1. What were the Israelites to learn from other nations (vv. 24-28)?
2. What warning were the Israelites given (vv. 29-30)?

28. And even as they did not like to retain God in their knowledge, God gave them over to a reprobate mind, to do those things which are not convenient;

29. Being filled with all unrighteousness, fornication, wickedness, covetousness, maliciousness; full of envy, murder, debate, deceit, malignity; whisperers,

30. Backbiters, haters of God, despiteful, proud, boasters, inventors of evil things, disobedient to parents,

31. Without understanding, covenantbreakers, without natural affection, implacable, unmerciful:

32. Who knowing the judgment of God, that they which commit such things are worthy of death, not only do the same, but have pleasure in them that do them.

Satyricon is a "novel" that reveals the depravity of the indulgent in Rome during the first century. It depicts a society where the primary pursuit is pleasure through food, drunken parties, and sexual pleasure. Most of the "relationships" that take place are between mature men and boys, mature men and girls, mature women and boys, as well as mature women and girls. It contains several scenes where the party-goers are met upon arrival by the host and provided a young person of their choosing (male or female). It is a depressing account that reveals the debauchery of the society in which Paul ministered, and consistent with his description here (vv. 18-32).

In this chapter of Romans addressing those who reject God (the unrighteous, v. 18), three times Paul says "God gave them up" (or "over"; vv. 24, 26, 28). The literal translation is "God handed them over." In verse 26, He gives them over to the things they pursue—"vile affections" ("degrading passions" NASB). To explain further what he means, Paul says that "even the women have exchanged the natural sexual relations" to pursue "that which is unnatural" (author's translation). Likewise, the men have rejected "natural sexual relations with women, and passionately burned in their desire for one another—men with men" (v. 27, author's translation). Paul describes this as "unseemly" (literally, "shameful nakedness") and are receiving within "themselves the due penalty for their perversion" (v. 27 NIV). There are times we get what we want, but not what we expect.

Their rejection of God results in a "reprobate" (or "depraved," NIV) mind that is at enmity with God (v. 28). A person in such a state has ignored the promptings of the Spirit so many times that they have lost their spiritual sensitivity and are no longer aware of His drawing presence or the course they should follow. Thus, they are consumed "with every kind of wickedness, evil, greed and depravity" (v. 29 NIV), which leads to all the sins depicted in verses 29-31.

Paul makes it clear that these individuals know what God expects, yet they ignore it and persist in their deeds (v. 32). Thus,

---

not convenient (v. 28)—"not proper" (NASB)

implacable (v. 31)—"heartless" (NIV)

Talk About It:
1. What "vile affections" are described in verses 26 and 27?
2. What produces a mind that is "depraved" (v. 28 NIV) or "debased" (NKJV)?
3. What is the depraved mind "filled with" and "full of" (v. 29)?
4. What do "haters of God" invent (v. 30)?
5. What are these people "without" (v. 31)?
6. What wins "hearty approval" (v. 32 NASB) to those living in rebellion against God?

"My will was perverse and lust had grown from it, and when I gave into lust, habit was born; and when I did not resist the habit, it became a necessity. These were the links which together formed what I have called my chain, and it held me fast in the duress of servitude."
—**Augustine**

---

they have chosen the way of "death" (separation from God). Since sin loves company, they lure others into their lifestyle and encourage those who enter therein.

B. Abstain From Idolatry (Eph. 5:3-5)

3. But fornication, and all uncleanness, or covetousness, let it not be once named among you, as becometh saints;

4. Neither filthiness, nor foolish talking, nor jesting, which are not convenient: but rather giving of thanks.

5. For this ye know, that no whoremonger, nor unclean person, nor covetous man, who is an idolater, hath any inheritance in the kingdom of Christ and of God.

After reminding the Ephesians to be "imitators of God" (v. 1 NKJV) and live a life patterned after Jesus, the epitome of true and proper love (v. 2), Paul instructs to make sure three things are never "named among" them (v. 3). These characteristics should never be considered or hinted at, let alone embraced. The language is very forceful in communicating this.

First, "fornication" includes any extramarital, unnatural, or unlawful sexual activity, such as sex outside of marriage, adultery, prostitution, and unfaithfulness. Second, "uncleanness" refers to any action that is worthless, defiling, or immoral. It has reference to sexual immorality, but it is not limited to physical contact. It should be remembered that the Bible condemns "affairs of the heart" (see Matt. 5:28), as well as illicit physical relations. Third, "covetousness" (greed) is the desire to have more than one's share. It is as much an attitude as it is a desire upon which one acts. We are to present ourselves in public and private as is proper "for God's holy people" (Eph. 5:3 NIV). Our character is determined by who we are when no one is looking, but then God is always looking!

To further characterize the conduct becoming of a saint, Paul, in verse 4, instructs Christians to abstain from "filthiness" (literally "ugliness"), "foolish talking" (idle talk), and "jesting" (vulgar speech). These things are out of character and unfitting for a saint, and should be intentionally replaced with "thanksgiving"—an attitude of gratitude.

Paul gives the reason for emphatically reminding the saints to lead godly lives: "You may be certain of this, everyone who is sexually immoral, or impure, or desires what is improper—that is an idolater—has absolutely no inheritance in the kingdom of Christ and of God" (v. 5, author's translation). Paul repeats the same three sins from verse 3 and emphasizes that those who practice such things will have no part in God's kingdom (see 1 Cor. 5:11-13). To place our desires (illicit or otherwise) above God's will is the same as worshiping an idol. It is usurping God's rightful place on the throne of our hearts with an idol of our own making.

---

whoremonger (v. 5)—immoral person

Talk About It:
1. What should not be "once named" among Christians, and why not (v. 3)?
2. According to verse 4, what does and does not characterize a Christian?
3. What does God label as idolatry (v. 5)?

Consistent Stand
We are set apart unto God, in one sense of the term, the moment we receive Christ, for we are bought with the price of His blood. Some day we shall be set apart from sin forever, by being taken to glory with Christ. But [the Bible] speaks of our present responsibility. God wants us to take our stand against every form of known sin, and to maintain that stand consistently.
—**S. Maxwell Coder** (*God's Will for Your Life*)

Sexual Purity or Immorality?

III. OUR BODIES BELONG TO GOD (1 Cor. 6:12-20)
A. Freedom or Bondage? (vv. 12-17)

12. All things are lawful unto me, but all things are not expedient: all things are lawful for me, but I will not be brought under the power of any.

13. Meats for the belly, and the belly for meats: but God shall destroy both it and them. Now the body is not for fornication, but for the Lord; and the Lord for the body.

14. And God hath both raised up the Lord, and will also raise up us by his own power.

15. Know ye not that your bodies are the members of Christ? shall I then take the members of Christ, and make them the members of an harlot? God forbid.

16. What? know ye not that he which is joined to an harlot is one body? for two, saith he, shall be one flesh.

17. But he that is joined unto the Lord is one spirit.

Paul wrote this epistle to a church located within the city of Corinth, a place that could be called the ancient equivalent of Las Vegas, Los Angeles, and New York combined. It was a city of excess and pleasure. The letter seems to depict a church of extremes, whether in the operation of the gifts and spiritual realm of worship (1 Cor. 11:17-34; 12—14), the engagement of marital relations (ch. 7), freedom in dress and identity (11:1-16), "liberty" in lifestyle and conduct (ch. 5), or even theological beliefs (ch. 15). Chapter 6 indicates practices that should be considered extreme, but are experiencing a repackaging by some in the contemporary church.

As the apostle ministered in Ephesus, word came to him by at least three sources that there were serious problems brewing (or manifested) in the Corinthian congregation. A message from the house of Chloe was apparently delivered to him by servants from that household (1:11). Also, the congregation apparently wrote requesting guidance and information, and sent the delegation of Stephanas, Fortunatus, and Achaicus (16:17). This delegation also informed the apostle of some things that the congregation had not shared. First Corinthians is a response to those concerns.

As was his custom, Paul addresses the underlying theological issues first, then the behavior itself—an important step in addressing errors of conduct by those in the church. Apparently, some in the congregation were of the opinion that "everything is permissible for me" (6:12 NIV). Picking up on this unofficial creed, Paul asserts that "not everything is beneficial" ("expedient" or "profitable"). He repeats their slogan and replies, "But I will not be mastered by anything" (NIV). The Corinthians' view of liberty was a philosophy of life embraced by the Stoics (pleasure is the highest good, and whatever happens must have been ordained),

Talk About It:
1. What declaration did Paul make in verse 12?
2. What is the human body "not for," and what is it "for" (v. 13)?
3. Explain the teaching against prostitution (vv. 15-16).
4. What does it mean to be "joined unto the Lord" (v. 17)?

Cynics (nature, reason, self-sufficiency, and freedom from restraint are the guiding principles), and Gnostics (the body is evil matter, only the soul is of consequence). The idea was a dualism, which espoused that the body was to be indulged and what was done in the body was not significant anyway, since it was evil by nature and would return to dust. Only the soul matters and it is untouched by what the body does. The Libertines (pursuing liberty unrestrained by someone else's law) felt they could act as they pleased. Paul correctly points out that this is bondage, not liberty. We need to anticipate the consequences of our actions, not only for ourselves but others too. Is it really worth the damage it can inflict?

The argument of the Libertines was that "food [is] for the stomach and the stomach for food" (v. 13 NIV), and since we are sexual beings, they could indulge the body in sexual immorality, as that is what it was meant for, according to them. Paul counters sharply with a reminder that God has the power to destroy both food and stomach in the coming age, as they were intended primarily for this age (see Rom. 14:17). Paul asserts, however, that "the body is not meant for sexual immorality, but for the Lord, and the Lord for the body" (1 Cor. 6:13 NIV). This is further explained in the next verse with a reference to the Resurrection. What is done in the body does matter, since it will be raised in the resurrection and stand before God (Rom. 14:10). Since it belongs to the Lord, the things done by the body should honor Him.

Paul points out that our "bodies are . . . members of Christ" (1 Cor. 6:15) and asks if "members of Christ" should be joined with a prostitute. Paul exclaims, "Never!" (NIV), which is an extremely emphatic term indicating it is not even in the realm of being considered. It should not even be thought of (hence the "God forbid!" of the KJV), let alone considered as a possibility.

When two people are joined together physically, there is a spiritual union that takes place (v. 16). He quotes from Genesis 2:24 to illustrate this powerful biblical principle. This is the reason we are to remain pure until marriage and faithful after marriage. Illicit relationships bring third (or more) parties into the equation, with all the complications. These complications are not quickly dismissed by the stroke of a judge's pen or the breakup of the relationship. It is a binding union that must be reserved for God's intended purposes—it is for our own benefit and His glory. Likewise, when we are "joined to the Lord" (literally, "glued together"), we become "one spirit with Him" (1 Cor. 6:17 NKJV).

B. Flee Bondage (vv. 18-20)

18. Flee fornication. Every sin that a man doeth is without the body; but he that committeth fornication sinneth against his own body.

Decisive Resistance

One of our ministers several years ago was preaching a camp meeting. The phone in his motel room rang and a woman offered to come to his room. He replied, "Woman, you may not care about hell, but you're not taking me with you!" and hung up the phone. This is handling temptation decisively, firmly, and with finality. It is the only way to deal with it.

Sexual Purity or Immorality?

19. What? know ye not that your body is the temple of the Holy Ghost which is in you, which ye have of God, and ye are not your own?

20. For ye are bought with a price: therefore glorify God in your body, and in your spirit, which are God's.

To make his point crystal clear, Paul commands, "Flee sexual immorality!" (i.e., "take to flight" or "run from"; see Gen. 39:12). He has addressed why immorality is wrong from a theological standpoint. Now, as the apostle of the Lord, he commands the Corinthians to cease if it has been going on and to not start if they are contemplating doing so. The next part of verse 18 can be taken two ways: (1) They have argued that every sin does not affect the body; or, (2) Paul says that every sin, except sexual immorality, does not affect the body. Given the context, the former is preferred. It is a strong statement to say that "every sin," except sexual sin, does not affect the body. Either way, Paul's point is that immorality does affect the body. The "temple of the Holy Spirit" should remain holy for the gift we have received "from God" (v. 19 NIV). Therefore, we belong to Him, not ourselves. With the price that has been paid for our redemption, we can do no less than bring glory to God (v. 20).

Talk About It:
1. What is particularly damaging about sexual sin (v. 18)?
2. Explain the phrase "you are not your own" (v. 19 NKJV).
3. How are we to "glorify God" (v. 20)?

CONCLUSION

We live in a world of temptation—temptation that is flaunted in our faces through actions, songs, images, and the Enemy. In the midst of temptation is not the time to decide our actions. They must be decided long before temptation is knocking on our door. We must remember *who* we are and *whose* we are—and live every day with that in the forefront of our minds and actions. "That is not who I am" (with resolve) is an excellent reply to temptation's enticement.

GOLDEN TEXT CHALLENGE

"YE ARE BOUGHT WITH A PRICE: THEREFORE GLORIFY GOD IN YOUR BODY, AND IN YOUR SPIRIT, WHICH ARE GOD'S" (1 Cor. 6:20).

In Cleveland, Tennessee, there is a monument erected in memory of those brave men from Bradley County who died fighting for the Confederacy. On this memorial are inscribed these words: "Man is not born to himself alone, but to his country." In that same spirit, but respecting a much nobler and more urgent cause, Paul approached the Corinthian believers: "You are not your own; you were bought at a price. Therefore honor God with your body" (vv. 19-20 NIV).

The Corinthian church was predominantly Gentile; its constituents have been harvested for Christ out of the rankest paganism to be found anywhere in the first-century world. Formerly given

over to the grossest excesses in immorality, these Christians were enjoined to "be not deceived: neither fornicators, nor idolaters, nor adulterers, nor effeminate, nor abusers of themselves with mankind, nor thieves, nor covetous, nor drunkards, nor revilers, nor extortioners, shall inherit the kingdom of God" (vv. 9-10). With apparent insensitivity and detachment, Paul reminded them: "Such were some of you" (v. 11). But Paul's purpose was to contrast what they were in sin with what they had by grace become: "But ye are washed, but ye are sanctified, but ye are justified in the name of the Lord Jesus, and by the Spirit of our God" (v. 11).

Clearly, the apostle also intended for us to praise the Lord through the radical juxtaposition of sinful behavior and transformed lifestyle. A changed life is still the most effective witness to the world—more effective than the words we speak and the good works we produce. Glorifying God in body and in spirit is to be given wholly to Him and to the graces which He imparts. By appearance, decorum, and attitude, we reflect the praise of Him by whom we have been created anew.

Bought with a price! Peter advanced this Pauline motif by reflecting on our being "redeemed . . . with the precious blood of Christ" (1 Peter 1:18-19). Our only "reasonable service," therefore, is to "present [our] bodies a living sacrifice, holy, acceptable unto God" (Rom. 12:1), disallowing the world around us to "squeeze [us] into its own mold" (v. 2 Phillips). Only this kind of surrender glorifies the One whose purchased possession we are.

Sacred Institution or Social Option?

Genesis 2:18-25; Malachi 2:14-16;
Matthew 19:3-9; 1 Corinthians 7:1-5; Hebrews 13:4

INTRODUCTION

According to the U.S. Census Bureau and Americans for Divorce Reform, marriage is on the decline. In 2005, 2,230,000 marriages took place, down from 2,279,000 the previous year. The population increased 2.9 million during that time. Meanwhile, the divorce rate is declining. The rate has fallen from a high of 5.3 divorces per one thousand people in 1981 to 3.6 per one thousand people in 2005. These numbers, however, are some-what misleading.

In 1970, 72 percent of the U.S. population was married. In 2002, that number had dropped to 59 percent. It slipped 3 percent between 2000 and 2002 alone. Twenty-four percent have never been married and 10 percent of the U.S. population are divorced. Alarmingly, 43.7 percent of custodial mothers and 56.2 percent of custodial fathers are either separated or divorced. Of those marriages that end in divorce, the average lasts less than eight years. Second marriages do not last that long, on average.

There are 5.5 million couples living together without being married. That amounts to 8.1 percent of all couples, a number that keeps rising. The chance that a married couple will break up within five years of a first marriage is 20 percent. For unmarried couples the rate is 49 percent. After ten years, a first marriage has a 33 percent probability of failure. For those who cohabitate, it is 62 percent. Overall, unmarried couples living together are four times more likely to break up than married couples. Surveys also reveal that the quality of and satisfaction with the relationship is much lower for those who live together without marriage.

Only 63 percent of children grow up with both biological parents. Sixty-three percent of all youth suicides, 90 percent of all homeless/runaway children, 85 percent of children with behavioral problems, 71 percent of high school dropouts, 85 percent of incarcerated youth, and well over 50 percent of all unwed mothers come from fatherless homes.

There is a lack of commitment in today's society. This is reflected in the growing number of bankruptcies, foreclosures, and repossessions. Certainly some of these are due to circum-stances beyond the control of those involved; however, an ever-rising number are choosing to walk away from their pledges and allow someone else to clean up their mess. Likewise, marriage has become a social option for many, rather than a sacred institution to be actively engaged. A good marriage does not just happen. It requires work and dedication.

Unit Theme:
Bible Answers to Crucial Questions

Central Truth:
God established marriage between man and woman as the basic institution of human society.

Focus:
Acknowledge God's establishment of marriage and honor it as a sacred institution.

Context:
Selected passages teaching on the divine institution of marriage

Golden Text:
"Therefore shall a man leave his father and his mother, and shall cleave unto his wife: and they shall be one flesh" (Gen. 2:24).

Study Outline:
I. Origin of Marriage (Gen. 2:18-25)

II. Sanctity of Marriage (Mal. 2:14-16; Matt. 19:3-9)

III. Fulfillment in Marriage (1 Cor. 7:1-5; Heb. 13:4)

I. ORIGIN OF MARRIAGE (Gen. 2:18-25)

A. Need of a Helper (vv. 18-20)

18. And the Lord God said, It is not good that the man should be alone; I will make him an help meet for him.

19. And out of the ground the Lord God formed every beast of the field, and every fowl of the air; and brought them unto Adam to see what he would call them: and whatsoever Adam called every living creature, that was the name thereof.

20. And Adam gave names to all cattle, and to the fowl of the air, and to every beast of the field; but for Adam there was not found an help meet for him.

Moses, the author of Genesis, received and relayed revelation in a progressive manner, very much like the message of a sermon is revealed progressively through its parts (introduction, main points, illustrations for clarity, conclusion, and call to action). The Creation event is being revealed from humanity's perspective in this chapter, while it was revealed from God's perspective in chapter 1. This accounts for the interjection (vv. 19-20) that takes place in this section, though its placement is strategic, as well as the repetition from the previous chapter. God always has a point in what He communicates.

God saw it was not beneficial ("good") for Adam to "be alone" (v. 18). There is no discrepancy between this verse and 1:27, which indicates God made "male and female" on the sixth day. Another way of translating 2:18 is, "It is not good that man should become alone." *Alone* carries the idea of "being divided into parts" or "not whole," as well as the idea of "isolation." Thus, God saw what the future would be like for Adam without a wife and made provision for that need during Creation. All creation had a counterpart, and God wanted Adam to have a "helper suitable for him" (v. 18b NIV). *Helper* is "one who gives support"; it is the term used for military assistance, or even divine assistance to those in need. It is substantial and practical help given by the helper or assistant. The phrase "meet for him" is better understood when more literally translated "before him in a face-to-face position." It is often used in a covenantal context, as it is here. It denotes a corresponding relationship, based on mutual respect, and implies a relationship of equals.

One of the tasks that Adam was assigned was the naming of all the animals God created "from out of the ground," like He did humanity. Centuries after Creation, science has analyzed the components that make up animal and human bodies; we are a composite of minerals and elements found in the earth. Yet, Moses and readers of the Bible knew that we are "earthy" through revelation from God long before science. Adam's pre-Fall intellect must have been amazing (e.g., creativity, reason, speech, and

Sacred Institution or Social Option?

memory), as he was able to assign names to every creature created by God. To assign a name to something or someone is to place that thing or person under your authority (see 2 Kings 23:34). Some have speculated concerning the language Adam spoke and how the information was transmitted from generation to generation. Unfortunately, it is speculation that cannot be answered definitively, as Scripture is silent in this regard.

Notice that the "naming" section falls between the two references to a helper for Adam. This is not accidental. God is pointing out the following:

1. All creation had companions for procreation to fulfill God's command to fill the earth (see Gen. 1:28).

2. There is a natural order created by God, and to ignore that results in being unfulfilled.

3. None of the creatures around Adam could fulfill his spiritual, social, or ontological/existential needs (the core of who he was and how that is expressed; this includes sexuality, but is much more than that one aspect).

4. The creatures were not equal with Adam and could not share in his authority (authority in itself implies equality; e.g., the Trinity).

5. We are created in His Trinitarian image; therefore, we are by nature social beings that need fellowship and interaction with God, but also with other human beings.

It is God's design that we be completed through a godly partner. Certainly, allowances must be made for those whom God has called to celibacy (1 Cor. 7:7-9). This, however, is the exception, not the rule.

> "Happily married people live longer than do the unmarried or divorced, per insurance statistics. One essential reason is that they can talk over their inner tensions to each other, so their blood pressure goes down. Besides, they can relax more by realizing they have a helping hand to come to their rescue if they are sick, so they suffer less anxiety."
> —George Crane

B. Bone of My Bones (vv. 21-23)

21. And the Lord God caused a deep sleep to fall upon Adam, and he slept: and he took one of his ribs, and closed up the flesh instead thereof;

22. And the rib, which the Lord God had taken from man, made he a woman, and brought her unto the man.

23. And Adam said, This is now bone of my bones, and flesh of my flesh: she shall be called Woman, because she was taken out of Man.

Woman was created and existed in the image of God, not man (1:27), for it was God who made her, not man. They were created in equality in the image of God. The use of Adam's rib reveals she was created equally human and in unity with him. She completed Adam's nature and purpose. After her creation, God himself brought her to Adam (2:22).

Adam's proclamation in verse 23 (1) recognizes she is a gift from God; (2) asserts that she is equally human with him; (3) acknowledges the completeness of his life through his wife;

Talk About It:
How did God create the first woman, and why?

and (4) states, through naming her, that she has placed herself willingly, as an equal, under his protection, ability to provide, and authority. Subordination in a marital relationship requires equality and free will, as it does in the Trinity. In an interesting play on words that is reflected in English, Adam calls her "Wo-man" (*ishshah*), for "she was taken out of Man" (*ish*).

C. One Flesh (vv. 24-25)

24. Therefore shall a man leave his father and his mother, and shall cleave unto his wife: and they shall be one flesh.

25. And they were both naked, the man and his wife, and were not ashamed.

The nature of marriage is revealed in verse 24 through some interesting terms and concepts. It has been called the "leaving and cleaving" principle. When two people enter into the marriage covenant, they must "leave," or loose themselves from the safety, comfort, acceptance, and provision of their family and make their own home. Specifically, the verse is directed to the husband, but the implication is for both partners, as both must leave and cleave, or the marriage will not be fulfilling. It is not an abandonment of mother and father, but a subordinating of their interests and influence to the spouse and marriage covenant. In the covenant, there are three parties—man, woman, and God. God takes the husband and wife and "makes them to become one flesh" (v. 24, author's translation). It is a physical, emotional, spiritual, and ontological union. They are one in substance, origin, and the will/decree of God; therefore, they can "become" one in covenant and purpose. It is an all-for-all proposition—not a fifty-fifty proposition.

This same pattern of union is emphasized in the New Testament, being used by Paul to underscore the analogous relationship Christ has to His bride, the Church (Eph. 5:21-33). As the man and woman are bone of each other's bone, flesh of each other's flesh, they are indeed one. Likewise, the Church is in union with and one with Christ. This is the pattern God ordained and established for marriage. Thus, "What . . . God hath joined together, let not man put asunder" (Mark 10:9). What Adam declared in Genesis 2:23 was indeed the declaration of God himself concerning the character of marriage.

The strength of the union is revealed in that both the husband and wife were naked before each other (v. 25). There was no shame or embarrassment; therefore, the relationship was a holy relationship, that is, a relationship of equality and completeness. Neither is intimidated by the presence of the other. Thus, the sexuality that is part of the union of the two is the sexuality that is engaged in between equals.

Talk About It:
1. Describe the proper relationship between a husband and wife (v. 24).
2. Why were Adam and Eve "not ashamed" (v. 25)?

Wedding Gift
Bill Bennett tells the story of being invited to the wedding of a couple whose resolve to marriage was less than enthusiastic. They had changed the vows to reflect their view of marriage, including removal of the "until death do us part" commitment. After thinking about it, he gave the new couple a package of paper plates with an explanation that he figured the plates would last as long as the marriage.

II. SANCTITY OF MARRIAGE (Mal. 2:14-16; Matt. 19:3-9)
A. The Hatred of God (Mal. 2:14-16)

14. Yet ye say, Wherefore? Because the Lord hath been witness between thee and the wife of thy youth, against whom thou hast dealt treacherously: yet is she thy companion, and the wife of thy covenant.

15. And did not he make one? Yet had he the residue of the spirit. And wherefore one? That he might seek a godly seed. Therefore take heed to your spirit, and let none deal treacherously against the wife of his youth.

16. For the Lord, the God of Israel, saith that he hateth putting away: for one covereth violence with his garment, saith the Lord of hosts: therefore take heed to your spirit, that ye deal not treacherously.

putting away (v. 16)—divorce

The prophet Malachi was proclaiming "the word of the Lord" (1:1) to a land and people in need of a repentant heart. The priesthood was corrupt (v. 6); worship was perfunctory and mechanical, not motivated by love and passion for God (v. 13); concern for the less fortunate was less than enthusiastic (3:5); tithing was neglected (v. 8); grumbling against God was prevalent (v. 13); and divorce was rampant. It sounds a lot like our own society.

Malachi 2:13 is an introductory scripture to the issue of marriage and divorce as detailed by Malachi. It sets forth an extremely important principle that is at the heart of Malachi's treatise on divorce (and the other issues detailed above): worship and conduct in life are intimately intertwined in two ways. First, God receives glory and worship through lives that reflect His character and nature. Second, if our lives are not consistent with His character, He does not regard our worship, no matter how earnest it may be. What we profess with our mouths must be confessed through our actions.

"Wherefore?" or "Why?" (v. 14 NIV) is a reference back to verse 13 and God's rejection of their worship. "The Lord hath been [and still is] witness between thee and the wife of thy youth." This is the judicial language of a court. The witness is one who emphatically affirms and reaffirms his testimony (see Gen. 2:24; Mark 10:2-12). It is a true account. The wife whom God witnessed being joined to her husband was being treated unfaithfully. The union was a lifetime covenant, not a contract that could be negated at a whim.

The covenant concept is communicated in the Old Testament not only by "covenant" (*berith*), but also the Hebrew terms that convey "righteousness" (*tsedek*), "lovingkindness" (*hesed*), "uprightness" (*yasar*), "peace" (*shalom*), and "completeness" (*tom*). That is, those who are living in covenant are expected to live out the covenant in a way that exemplifies and exudes these qualities. Living in covenant brings about wholeness for both parties in the covenant. This is not what God was witnessing.

Talk About It:
1. Of what is the Lord a "witness" in verse 14?
2. What should a godly marriage produce (v. 15)?
3. What is God's opinion of divorce (v. 16)?

Verse 15 can be translated, "Did He not make them [husband and wife] one, with a portion ["a significant remnant" capable of blessing] of His Spirit in their union?" God was seeking godly children born from godly marriages. The implication is that He was still looking. Further, God reminds them through Malachi that they needed to guard ("take heed to") their spirits. Ungodly actions begin in the heart and spirit before they are manifested through actions (Prov. 4:23; 23:7). Guarding one's spirit will prevent unfaithfulness (Mal. 2:15).

God states emphatically that He "hates" divorce (v. 16). *Hate* is a very strong term that expresses the desire to have no contact or relationship with the object of the hatred. In this case it is divorce, *not* the divorced persons. God hates what it does to the individuals divorced, the children involved, and others who may be affected. He hates what it does to the marriage covenant, and He hates the complications that arise when two who have become one try to reverse that union. *Divorce* literally means "to put away" or "to send away," a graphic depiction of what happened to the wife who was divorced by her husband.

The imagery in verse 16 is that of one who divorces and treats it lightly by trying to hide it under a garment of violence. Again, they are admonished to protect the heart and remain faithful to the spouse and God. Incidentally, there is only one known reference to this verse in the multitude of rabbinic commentaries on Scripture. Most rabbinical leaders allowed men to divorce their wives, but the wife could only divorce her husband if the court instructed him to do so; thus, it was still the husband who granted the divorce.

Divorce Damages

Someone has described divorce as "the forever funeral." I can think of no more accurate description than this. It is the funeral that never ends.

I confess, I hate divorce. I hate what it does to people. I hate how it makes enemies of those who once declared undying love for one another. But I especially hate the damage it does to children.

—**Archibald Hart**
(*Helping Children Survive Divorce*)

B. Reestablishing the Ideal (Matt. 19:3-9)

3. The Pharisees also came unto him, tempting him, and saying unto him, Is it lawful for a man to put away his wife for every cause?

4. And he answered and said unto them, Have ye not read, that he which made them at the beginning made them male and female,

5. And said, For this cause shall a man leave father and mother, and shall cleave to his wife: and they twain shall be one flesh?

6. Wherefore they are no more twain, but one flesh. What therefore God hath joined together, let not man put asunder.

7. They say unto him, Why did Moses then command to give a writing of divorcement, and to put her away?

8. He saith unto them, Moses because of the hardness of your hearts suffered you to put away your wives: but from the beginning it was not so.

9. And I say unto you, Whosoever shall put away his wife, except it be for fornication, and shall marry another, committeth adultery: and whoso marrieth her which is put away doth commit adultery.

Some Pharisees approached Jesus with the intent of "tempting him" (v. 3). The term *tempt*, meaning "test" or "prove," usually is associated with hostile intent (see 4:1; 16:1), as it is here. "Is it permissible to divorce one's wife for any cause?" they asked (19:3, author's translation). They had little concern for His answer. Their intent was to create a situation in which He would offend the crowds through His stance on divorce. Divorce was allowed according to Jewish custom and the Law (Deut. 24:1-4). However, there were two primary schools of thought concerning divorce in the first century. First, Shammai viewed divorce as permissible only on the basis of adultery ("indecency," see v. 1 NASB) by the wife. Second, Hillel took the phrase concerning "indecency" to mean anything that displeased the husband, such as burning dinner. The Jewish teacher Akiba took the words of that verse ("find no favour in his eyes") to mean that if he found another woman whom he thought to be prettier than his wife, that was a legitimate cause (hence, "any cause") for divorce.

As Jesus was prone to do, He controlled the situation and redirected the focus back to the intent of God. In doing so, He utilized a rabbinic method of discussion, which gave greater weight to the more original or older teaching. Thus, Jesus points back to the Creation event and Genesis 1:27 and 2:24. He emphasizes, "For this reason [God's action in the union], they are no longer two, but one flesh" (Matt. 19:6, author's translation). Further, He points out that it is not humanity's prerogative to "separate" what "God has joined together" (NIV).

Not satisfied with His answer, which restricted divorce in a way they were not used to, they appealed to Moses and a certificate of divorce (v. 7). The rabbinic leaders drew up a certificate that a man who divorced his wife could give her. This certificate allowed her to remarry (The Mishnah said, "Lo, you are free to marry any man"). This made the divorce valid, according to their traditions.

Jesus corrects their faulty thinking: Moses did not "command" divorce, as the Pharisees said (v. 7), but "suffered" (allowed it) because of the "the hardness of your hearts" (v. 8). This was not God's intent. Jesus presents the correct view of divorce: there is only one reason in God's intent, and that is "marital unfaithfulness" (v. 9 NIV)—any premarital, extramarital, unlawful, or unnatural sexual activity. Further, anyone who divorces his wife apart from this exclusion commits adultery in the second marriage. This is the ideal that reflects God's perfect will for permanency in marriage.

It should be noted before leaving the subject of divorce that we must preach the Word with passion, authority, and love. We must proclaim the ideal, but deal with people where they are. Divorce is not the unpardonable sin. We must work to keep people in marriages and help them make those marriages godly.

Talk About It:
1. What is God's plan for marriage (vv. 3-6)?
2. What brought about divorce in Moses' day (v. 8)?
3. When is divorce acceptable (v. 9)?

"Divorce is an easy escape, many think. But in counseling many divorcees, I have discovered that the guilt and loneliness they experience can be even more tragic than living with their problem."
—Billy Graham

Where that is not possible, we must tend to their wounds and express God's love through our assistance, love, and compassion.

III. FULFILLMENT IN MARRIAGE (1 Cor. 7:1-5; Heb. 13:4)
A. Celibacy (1 Cor. 7:1-5)

1. Now concerning the things whereof ye wrote unto me: It is good for a man not to touch a woman.

2. Nevertheless, to avoid fornication, let every man have his own wife, and let every woman have her own husband.

3. Let the husband render unto the wife due benevolence: and likewise also the wife unto the husband.

4. The wife hath not power of her own body, but the husband: and likewise also the husband hath not power of his own body, but the wife.

5. Defraud ye not one the other, except it be with consent for a time, that ye may give yourselves to fasting and prayer; and come together again, that Satan tempt you not for your incontinency.

Verse 1 has been misunderstood by many readers of the New Testament. Paul, in response to questions from the congregation, is not saying that celibacy is ethically good and marriage is not. He certainly is not advocating celibacy within a marriage (see vv. 3, 5). He is saying that in one's service to God, it is less complicated ("good") if a person remains unmarried (see vv. 32-35).

Recognizing the propensities of the human nature and body ("since there is so much immorality," v. 2 NIV), Paul advises that each man should "have his own wife" and each woman "her own husband" in a committed and monogamous marriage. The marriage should be sexually fulfilling for both the husband and wife (v. 3). While intimacy should not be viewed as a duty to be fulfilled, it is a responsibility that each spouse has to the other. So serious is this responsibility that Paul says the husband is to willingly subordinate his body to his wife's needs, and likewise she to him (v. 4).

Some commentators believe that certain influences (false teachers and certain philosophical teachings) had entered the Corinthian congregation and affected them. One particular problem was celibacy in marriage. Paul has addressed this in the previous verses, but allows for the abstinence of sexual activity during a time of intense prayer and fasting. But even that is to be for a limited time, "so that Satan may not have the opportunity to tempt you in a time when self-control may not be the strongest" (v. 5, author's translation). We are not to "give place to the devil" (Eph. 4:27).

B. Honor and Judgment (Heb. 13:4)

4. Marriage is honourable in all, and the bed undefiled: but whoremongers and adulterers God will judge.

---

due benevolence (v. 3)—"his marital duty" (NIV), or "the affection due her" (NKJV)

defraud (v. 5)—deprive

incontinency (v. 5)—self-control

Talk About It:
1. What is "good," and why (v. 1)?
2. What is also good (v. 2)?
3. Explain the discussion of his/her "own body" (v. 4).

"After 20-plus years of counseling, I have come to the conclusion that the couples who enjoy the greatest sexual experience and most fulfilling intimacy are those who sanctify the bed with God-given love and an awareness of God's approval of the sexual experience in the context of marriage."
—Ray E. Hurt

whoremongers (v. 4)—"fornicators" (NASB)

Sacred Institution or Social Option?

In this verse, there is no verb in the first phrase of the Greek text. This is not unusual, as the verb is often supplied by the reader according to context. This allows for several different translations. First, it could be that the writer is saying, "Marriage is honorable among all and the (marriage) bed is to be undefiled." Second, it can be translated as a command: "Let marriage be held in honor, and let the (marriage) bed be undefiled." If this reading is correct, it could imply that there are certain practices that should not be part of the intimate life of a Christian. Third, the writer may be conveying, "Marriage brings honor to those involved, and the bed prevents one from being defiled."

Regardless of how it is understood, marriage is held in esteem by God. Those who ignore God's purposes for marriage, as discussed in this lesson, will face Him as Judge, who will pass sentence upon "the adulterer and all the sexually immoral" (NIV).

Talk About It:
What does God approve, and what does He condemn?

"There is no dishonor and no defilement, wrong, sin, shame, or any other negative appellation to be given to the God-ordained sexual intimacy between a husband and a wife."
—**Ray E. Hurt**

CONCLUSION

Marriage finds its source and fulfillment in God's plan and purposes for it. It is to be a sacred trust held in covenant between the husband, wife, and God himself. It can bring pleasure, satisfaction, and completeness. If it is not based on and motivated daily by the design and principles of God, it can be a source of great pain and turmoil. No gift of God should ever bring anything less than He designed.

GOLDEN TEXT CHALLENGE

"THEREFORE SHALL A MAN LEAVE HIS FATHER AND HIS MOTHER, AND SHALL CLEAVE UNTO HIS WIFE: AND THEY SHALL BE ONE FLESH" (Gen. 2:24).

God instituted the holy bonds of matrimony immediately after creating woman. As we study the Creation narrative, we find at least three biblical reasons the Lord God established the marital relationship between man and woman: (1) *companionship*—man was alone (v. 18a); (2) *complement*—the male member of the human species was incomplete and inadequate without a suitable mate (v. 18b); (3) *continuation*—God ordained that the human race be reproduced and perpetuated by male and female reproducing after their own kind (1:27, 28).

From the beginning, the divine mandate has been that a man and woman pledge themselves to one mate—monogamy.

Daily Devotions:
M. Comfort in Marriage
Genesis 24:61-67
T. A Husband's Love
Genesis 29:18-30
W. A Wife's Virtue
Proverbs 31:10-23
T. Be Committed to One Another
1 Corinthians 7:10-16
F. Submit to One Another
Ephesians 5:21-33
S. Consider One Another
1 Peter 3:1-9

Introduction to Spring Quarter

The theme for the first unit is "Ephesians: Understanding God's Eternal Purposes." These five lessons cover texts from every chapter in this important epistle.

The writer of this unit is the Reverend Dr. J. Ayodeji Adewuya (Ph.D., University of Manchester). Dr. Adewuya is an associate professor of New Testament at the Church of God Theological Seminary in Cleveland, Tennessee. Prior to joining the seminary, Dr. Adewuya served as a missionary in the Philippines for seventeen years. He is an active member of the Society for Biblical Literature, Wesleyan Theological Society, and the Society for Pentecostal Studies. He is the author of *Holiness and Community in 2 Corinthians 6:14–7:1*.

The second unit, "Commended by Christ," depicts interactions between various individuals and Jesus Christ as portrayed in the Synoptic Gospels. Needy children, a rich young ruler, a woman with a bleeding disorder, a believing centurion, Mary and Martha, the ten lepers, a blind beggar, and a generous widow are among the individuals studied.

These lessons were compiled by Lance Colkmire (see biographical information on page 16), as were lessons 5 (Easter) and 12 (Pentecost).

The Divine Purposes

Ephesians 1:3-23

INTRODUCTION

When Paul bade the Ephesian elders farewell, he was aware that he might never return to Ephesus (Acts 20:25). During his visit to Jerusalem he encountered great difficulty and was eventually sent to Rome as a prisoner. From Rome he wrote a number of letters, or epistles, which are now known as the Prison Epistles. The first of these letters was written to the Ephesians.

Paul's letter to the Ephesians is a joyful, victorious epistle. It is a letter about the nature of Christ's church. In the letter he described to the Ephesians what manner of church the Christian fellowship should be. God has taken diverse members from many walks of life and through Jesus Christ forged them into a fellowship of believers. The letter affirms that Christ is the foundation of the Church, believers in Christ are the brotherhood of the Church, and eternal life is the destiny of the Church. The epistle is a glorious statement of victory and promise. It does not indicate any degree of discouragement even though it was written from prison.

The first major section of chapter 1 (vv. 1-14) is Paul's praise to God for providing salvation to all humanity. Some have called it the "hymn of salvation." It is an expression of praise and blessing. It is Trinitarian in character, showing the work of the Father (vv. 3-6); the work of the Son (vv. 7-12); and the work of the Holy Spirit (vv. 13-14). The passage contains salvation truth, and each verse is filled with wonderful insights into God's mighty acts of salvation for all humanity. It is one long sentence in Greek, and Paul touches upon every aspect of saving experience. It is made up of two subsections: verses 3-10, where Paul enumerates the blessings of salvation, and verses 11-14, where Paul focuses particularly on the role of the Spirit in salvation.

The second major section is another long sentence that runs from verse 15 to 23. There we see Paul's thanksgiving and prayer for the Ephesians that culminates with a description of God's power.

Unit Theme:
Ephesians: Understanding God's Eternal Purposes

Central Truth:
God has made all spiritual blessings available to believers in Christ.

Focus:
Recognize and embrace God's purposes for His children.

Context:
Paul wrote his letter to the Ephesians from a Roman prison between AD 60 and 63.

Golden Text:
"Blessed be the God and Father of our Lord Jesus Christ, who hath blessed us with all spiritual blessings in heavenly places in Christ" (Eph. 1:3).

Study Outline:
I. Chosen by God (Eph. 1:3-10)
II. Sealed by the Holy Spirit (Eph. 1:11-14)
III. Empowered as Heirs (Eph. 1:15-23)

I. CHOSEN BY GOD (Eph. 1:3-10)

A. Blessed and Chosen (vv. 3-4)

3. Blessed be the God and Father of our Lord Jesus Christ, who hath blessed us with all spiritual blessings in heavenly places in Christ:

4. According as he hath chosen us in him before the foundation of the world, that we should be holy and without blame before him in love:

Talk About It:
1. Explain the two uses of the word *blessed* in verse 3.
2. What happened "before the creation of the world" (v. 4 NIV)?
3. What has God chosen us to be (v. 4)?

To be Holy + Without Fault

Paul's experience of God's goodness led him to praise God. So should it be with believers. Paul invites the Ephesian Christians to join him in praise for God's blessings. The Greek word for "blessing" in verse 3 is based on the verb *eulogeo*, which means "to speak well of." It is the word from which the English word *eulogy*, which we are used to hearing in the context of a funeral, is derived. But Paul uses it differently. God is to be eulogized, that is, we are to speak well of Him.

God is the source of all blessings and the originator of the plan of salvation. We bless Him because He has blessed us with "all spiritual blessings," or, as the literal translation of the Greek reads, "with every spiritual blessing." Every blessing—whether physical, material, or spiritual—is to be attributed to the Spirit of God. The "us" (v. 3), who are blessed by God, includes both Jews and Gentiles in the church at Ephesus and beyond.

Paul states that believers are blessed "in Christ" (v. 3.) and "in him" (v. 4)—important Pauline phrases that suggest the means by which believers are blessed and reveal the sphere of blessing and the intimate relationship between Christians and Christ. Believers are in union with Christ. It is God who chose us to be blameless before the creation of the world. God's plan of salvation was not an afterthought. It has been in place before the foundation of the world. The importance of the word *chosen* (v. 4) lies in God's initiative rather than a dislike for those who are not chosen. God did not select believers because He was obligated to do so or because they have any legal claim to God.

The word *holy* in verse 4 is more than a mere separation by God. It not only includes the idea of belonging to God, but also involves the inward moral state which prevails in the Christian as a result of God's operation in the heart. This observation is buttressed by the use of the word *amomos*, translated "without blame," or literally, "blameless." It has its background in the Old Testament sacrificial system, where it refers to the absence of defects in sacrificial animals (Lev. 1:3, 10). In the New Testament it is used of the offering of Christ (Heb. 9:14; 1 Pet. 1:19). Therefore, in the context of Ephesians, the combination of "holy" and "without blame" can be understood as referring to Christian living. Whereas the former refers to inner spiritual quality, the latter refers to the outer manifestation or conduct of that life. We are chosen not only for salvation, but also for holiness. Any understanding of

God's sovereign choosing that diminishes our personal responsibility for personal holiness and sanctification falls far short of the whole counsel of God.

B. Predestined and Accepted (vv. 5-6)

5. Having predestinated us unto the adoption of children by Jesus Christ to himself, according to the good pleasure of his will,

6. To the praise of the glory of his grace, wherein he hath made us accepted in the beloved.

Believers are "predestined . . . to be adopted as sons" (v. 5 NIV). Traditionally or historically, two views have been espoused: (1) God predestined individuals whom He would save, or (2) God chose or predestined the plan by which people would be saved. A right understanding of the passage shows that Paul's emphasis of predestination is on *what* rather than *who*. God took the initiative to predetermine the destiny of believers as adopted sons into the family of God. We are chosen to be holy and blameless.

Adoption as an important aspect of redemption is an idea which is peculiar to Paul (Rom. 8:15, 23; 9:4; Gal. 4:5). In its usage, Paul stresses the process by which believers become sons and daughters of God. It is a new relationship that is made possible through the work of God. The purpose of our adoption is the glory of God. Having been adopted by God, and having become His "beloved," we have the responsibility to live to the glory of our heavenly adoptive Father.

Adoption carries with it various benefits. First, it frees us from fear (Rom. 8:15). Second, it allows us an intimate relationship, even to cry, "Abba, Father" (v. 15). Third, it provides an inner assurance of relationship as God's Spirit bears witness with our own (v. 16). Fourth, we become coheirs with Christ (v. 17). Paul recognizes the significant part grace plays in our salvation.

Talk About It:
1. What is God's "pleasure and will" (v. 5 NIV)?
2. Who is "the beloved" (v. 6)?

C. Redemption and Revelation (vv. 7-10)

7. In whom we have redemption through his blood, the forgiveness of sins, according to the riches of his grace;

8. Wherein he hath abounded toward us in all wisdom and prudence;

9. Having made known unto us the mystery of his will, according to his good pleasure which he hath purposed in himself:

10. That in the dispensation of the fulness of times he might gather together in one all things in Christ, both which are in heaven, and which are on earth; even in him.

In verse 7, Paul moves on to accentuate the work of Christ in salvation. The key word is *redemption*, meaning "to release on ransom." It is deliverance at a cost. As Chrysostom says,

Talk About It:
1. What do believers receive through "the riches of [God's] grace" (vv. 7-8)?

2. What is the "mystery" God has revealed (vv. 9-10)?

"The wonder is not only that He gave His Son, but that He did so in this way, by sacrificing the One He loved. It is astonishing that He gave the Beloved for those who hated Him."

Sinners are in a spiritual bondage, sold under sin, and there is no freedom from this hopeless captivity apart from Christ. But praise God! We can sing and shout that "Jesus paid it all." Redemption is accompanied by the forgiveness of sins for all those who will put their trust in Christ and appropriate the blessing of salvation He provided through the shedding of His blood.

Not only has God given us redemption and forgiveness "according to the riches of his grace" (v. 7)—that is, in accordance with the wealth of His grace—He has done so in an extreme manner (v. 8). Grace is lavished upon us. Picture the Old Testament vision of anointing with oil that was done to the priests. When the oil was poured, it ran down the cheeks and through the beard until it flowed on the ground.

Paul concludes his description of God's salvation plan by referring to its revelation to humankind by God. Paul calls it "the mystery of his will" (v. 9). *Mystery* means something incomprehensible or unexplainable. It is something that was hidden but is now made known. For Paul, it is something that is known through faith and not human reason. Believers are given "wisdom and prudence" (v. 8) in order that their eyes may be open to God's purpose. Today many people still have problems with the idea of salvation. *How can a sinner become a saint? How does God transform lives? How are prayers answered? How do people get healed?* These are mysteries that need to be accepted by faith. They are intended by God's own good pleasure and purposed in Christ (v. 9), and put into effect when times reach their fulfillment; that is, when the time is right (v. 10). When the situation is right, God acts. God's timing itself is a mystery because we do not know why He acts at the time He acts.

> "Jesus whom I know as my Redeemer cannot be less than God!"
> —Athanasius

II. SEALED BY THE HOLY SPIRIT (Eph. 1:11-14)

11. In whom also we have obtained an inheritance, being predestinated according to the purpose of him who worketh all things after the counsel of his own will:

12. That we should be to the praise of his glory, who first trusted in Christ.

13. In whom ye also trusted, after that ye heard the word of truth, the gospel of your salvation: in whom also after that ye believed, ye were sealed with that holy Spirit of promise,

14. Which is the earnest of our inheritance until the redemption of the purchased possession, unto the praise of his glory.

earnest (v. 14)— "guarantee" (NKJV)

Paul makes a subtle distinction between the Jews ("we," v. 11), and Gentiles ("ye," v. 13). The thought here is that Israel was specially chosen by God, not due to her personal privilege but

for salvation purposes. The "we" group is defined as those who have "obtained an inheritance" and been "predestinated" (v. 11) according to God's purpose. God's choice of Israel was so she would live "to the praise of his glory" (v. 12).

Paul seeks to reemphasize what he has already said in verse 3 about God's initiative in the salvation plan for humanity. God had a design: believers are predestined according to His purpose. Further, Paul says in verse 11, God works out all things according to His will. Note that this is the second time Paul employs the word *will* (see v. 5). Believers are often engrossed with determining the will of God for each decision. As important as that may be, it is better that the Christian take a long and broad view of God's will in line with His purpose that is revealed in the Bible. We are chosen for "the praise of His glory" (v. 12). We do not have to wait until Christ comes or until the "sweet by and by" before we begin directing our praises to the heavenly Father. As a new people of God, believers are summoned to be a praise to God in the same manner that Israel was called as a nation to declare God's glory in their life, witness, and worship (Ex. 19:5, 6; Isa. 43:1, 21; Jer. 13:11). As we live a godly and productive life, people will see our good works and glorify God.

In verse 13 of the lesson text, Paul addresses the Gentiles and, in so doing, asserts the unity of the Jew and Gentile (non-Jew) in Christ. Paul, although a Jew, joins himself with his Gentile readers. The readers would no doubt have been struck by Paul's repetition of the phrase "in whom" (vv. 11, 13) and "in Christ" (v. 12). The ethnic and religious barriers between Jews and Gentiles are now broken down in Christ. The non-Jews have heard the word of truth, believed in Christ, and have been sealed with the Holy Spirit. As John Wesley suggests, the sealing of the believer implies "a full impression of the image of God on their souls." To be sealed with the Holy Spirit is a mark of ownership, which implies that the Christian is possessed entirely and unequivocally by the Holy Spirit.

III. EMPOWERED AS HEIRS (Eph. 1:15-23)
A. Reason to Give Thanks (vv. 15-16)

15. Wherefore I also, after I heard of your faith in the Lord Jesus, and love unto all the saints,

16. Cease not to give thanks for you, making mention of you in my prayers.

In this passage, Paul expresses his thankfulness to God on behalf of his readers. Thankfulness was an integral part of Paul's life, and he did not keep it to himself or express it sparingly.

Thankfulness is becoming an endangered species. It is easier to grumble than to give thanks. When we fail to express our thanks to those who deserve it, our fellowship ceases to edify and dies.

Talk About It:
1. What is meant for "the praise of [God's] glory" (vv. 11-12)?
2. How are believers "sealed" (vv. 13-14)?

"Life for the believer in this present age of adversity and suffering is blessed with the joy and peace of the Holy Spirit, but these blessings are only the first installment of the perfect joy and peace of heaven."

—French Arrington

Talk About It:
Describe Paul's ongoing ministry to the Ephesians.

Paul moves from praise to God to prayer. The combination of prayer and thanksgiving, and constancy in prayer, are characteristic of Paul (Rom. 1:8-10; Col. 1:3; 3:15-17; 4:2). Paul's reason for prayer in our text is based on the information he received concerning the faith of the Ephesians and their love for one another (vv. 15-16). He often mentions these qualities together, not only in prayers but also in other contexts (2 Cor. 8:7; Gal. 5:6; 2 Thess. 1:3; Phil. 4:5-7). The Ephesians have become participants in the blessings of God's saving plan. The integrity of the faith of an individual, local church, Christian organization, or denomination is evident in the way they live out their beliefs, and the Ephesians lived out their beliefs. However, today many believers, groups, churches, and denominations are known for the wrong reasons. They are no longer known by attributes such as love, faith, work, hope, and endurance, but of strife, politics, intolerance, hypocrisy, and so on. Sometimes the damage is so great that the "Christian" individual or organization becomes synonymous with hypocrisy, conflict, and prejudice.

> "Prayer moves the Hand which moves the world."
> —John Wallace

B. Ability to Know God (vv. 17-21)

17. That the God of our Lord Jesus Christ, the Father of glory, may give unto you the spirit of wisdom and revelation in the knowledge of him:

18. The eyes of your understanding being enlightened; that ye may know what is the hope of his calling, and what the riches of the glory of his inheritance in the saints,

19. And what is the exceeding greatness of his power to us-ward who believe, according to the working of his mighty power,

20. Which he wrought in Christ, when he raised him from the dead, and set him at his own right hand in the heavenly places,

21. Far above all principality, and power, and might, and dominion, and every name that is named, not only in this world, but also in that which is to come.

When Paul prays, he does so with confidence because he approaches "the God of our Lord Jesus Christ, the Father of glory" (v. 17). His requests are atypical of those we hear at prayer meetings. Paul's request has to do with "knowledge," or a full-grown understanding of spiritual things. He prays that God may give the Ephesians "the spirit of wisdom" so they may know Him better. For Paul, to know God is to be enlightened. Paul's prayer is not a request for a superficial religion, but a faith that cuts to the core of the individual and effects transformation (v. 18). The enlightenment for which Paul prayed would give his readers understanding of three things: (1) the hope of Christ's calling, (2) the riches of the glory of the inheritance in the saints, and (3) Christ's incomparable power for believers (vv. 18-19).

Talk About It:
1. Why do believers need "the spirit of wisdom and revelation" (v. 17)?
2. What is the hope of believers (v. 18)?
3. What is the power God wants to release in people (vv. 19-20)?
4. How does verse 21 describe Christ's power?

The Divine Purposes

God's revelation to us provides a source of anticipation by which we lead our lives.

Paul elaborates on the thought of God's power as revealed in Christ. He describes its ability and expression. First, it is manifested in the resurrection of Christ. The Resurrection is the chief demonstration of the power of God. As someone said, "If we keep silent about the Resurrection, we would not be speaking of God." Second, the surpassing and majestic power of God is manifested in the ascension and exaltation of Christ. He is above every created power—friendly and hostile, human and spiritual—that presently exercises authority in the world. He is in control.

Brooke Westcott wrote:

We can face the sorrows and sadness of personal and social history "in the hope of God's calling." We can rejoice in the possession of capacities and needs to which our present circumstances bring no satisfaction when we look to the "wealth of the glory of God's inheritance in the saints." We can overcome the discouragements of constant failures and weaknesses by the remembrance of the power of God shown in raising Christ.

C. Authority to Empower (vv. 22-23)

22. And hath put all things under his feet, and gave him to be the head over all things to the church,

23. Which is his body, the fullness of him that filleth all in all.

Jesus' authority is greater than the claims of all other leaders, earthly or otherwise. He is the head of all things, for God has placed all things under His feet. God has done this "for the church, which is his body" (NIV). Everything is under Christ's power for the benefit of His people.

Because earthly kings and rulers are subject to Christ's authority, their oft-repeated efforts to destroy the Church have failed. Because the angels in heaven are under divine command, they help to meet the needs of Christ's body (see Heb. 1:14). Because Satan and his forces must bow before Christ, "the gates of hell shall not prevail against [the Church]" (Matt. 16:18).

CONCLUSION

Paul not only clearly stated the nature of the Church, but also made clear the power that is available to the Church. The Church will only be what God intends her to be when she becomes more aware of and appropriates the power and privileges God has given to His people and the benefits of her relation to Christ who rules over the universe.

GOLDEN TEXT CHALLENGE

"BLESSED BE THE GOD AND FATHER OF OUR LORD JESUS CHRIST, WHO HATH BLESSED US WITH ALL

Prayer's Purpose
Prayer is not a way of making use of God; prayer is a way of offering ourselves to God in order that He should be able to make use of us. It may be that one of our great faults in prayer is that we talk too much and listen too little. When prayer is at its highest we wait in silence for God's voice to us; we linger in His presence for His peace and His power to flow over us and around us.
—**William Barclay,**
The Plain Man's Book of Prayers

Talk About It:
Describe Christ's relationship with the Church.

"In Scripture the Church is always represented as being an extension of Christ."
—**Charles W. Conn**

SPIRITUAL BLESSINGS IN HEAVENLY PLACES IN CHRIST" (Eph. 1:3).

Paul, writing from his prison confinement, was well aware of the pain, suffering, and disappointment in this world; but instead of focusing on those things, he gave more attention to the positive aspects of the peace and joy found in the spiritual realm of living in Christ.

After a believer enters the spiritual realm of a new life in Christ, he becomes a new person. His citizenship is now in heaven. He is only a pilgrim and sojourner in this world. His affections are on things above (see 2 Cor. 5:17; Col. 3:2; 1 Peter 2:11). Whereas, before, he was a stranger to God, now he is a child of God, as well as a joint heir with Jesus Christ. He is governed by the compelling power of Christ's love instead of his own lust.

New life in Christ provides a source of strength and satisfaction for today, as well as an assurance of an even richer life in the world to come.

Alive in Christ

INTRODUCTION

In last week's lesson, Paul gave the Ephesian believers a grand picture of their spiritual riches (ch. 1). These include not only the wonderful things they would see in heaven, but the wealth that was available to them for this life. This wealth had to be perceived and received—and it could only be done so by faith, and with spiritual senses. In 1:19 Paul prayed that the Ephesians might know the exceeding greatness of God's power toward those who believe. As a measure of it, he pointed to Christ's resurrection, ascension, and exaltation. Paul's purpose of referring to Christ's resurrection and ascension, as a proof of the power at work in us, now reappears. In 2:1-10, Paul declares that the salvation of all humanity, both Jew and Gentile, is part and parcel of the resurrection of Christ.

To further illustrate the mighty power of God and its impact on humanity, Paul contrasts the old life in sin (vv. 1-3) with the new life in Christ (vv. 4-10). Like Christ, the Ephesians once were dead, but in Christ they had been raised and enthroned.

In the second part of the chapter (vv. 11-22), Paul returned to the situation of his readers prior to their incorporation into the Christian community. He reminded them of their Christless, hopeless past and of their unity with the people of God now.

David Cooper writes:

> One of the greatest needs in our lives is the need for restoration. To *restore* means "to bring something back into existence or effect again; to bring back to a former or original condition; to put back in a former place or position; to reinstate; to return." We talk about restoring relationships, renovating antique furniture, reinstating a political leader, and returning something that was stolen or lost. These all demonstrate the idea of restoration.

> The essential meaning of salvation is restoration. To be saved means that we have experienced the miraculous restoring power of God to make all things new in our lives spiritually, psychologically, emotionally, and relationally.

Unit Theme:
Ephesians: Understanding God's Eternal Purposes

Central Truth:
Through His death and resurrection, Christ provides reconciliation and new life.

Focus:
Acknowledge that those who are apart from Christ are spiritually dead, and receive the gift of eternal life in Him.

Context:
Paul wrote his letter to the Ephesians from a Roman prison between AD 60 and 63.

Golden Text:
"And you hath he quickened, who were dead in trespasses and sins" (Eph. 2:1).

Study Outline:
I. Dead in Sin (Eph. 2:1-3)
II. Saved by Grace (Eph. 2:4-10)
III. One in Christ (Eph. 2:11-22)

I. DEAD IN SIN (Eph. 2:1-3)

A. Spiritually Dead (v. 1)

1. And you hath he quickened, who were dead in trespasses and sins.

The former manner of the life of the Ephesians is that of death, as a result of sins and trespasses. *Trespasses* (*paraptomata*) are lapses, while *sins* (*hamartiai*) are shortcomings. Such was their awful state, utterly beyond reach of human help. Paul's mention of "trespasses and sins" leads him to describe in fuller details the Ephesians' former way of life. They were utterly unable to meet the requirements of the divine law.

By using the word *dead*, Paul is not speaking about physical death nor only about the sinner's ultimate fate in the second death. Nor is the expression merely figurative. As sinners, the Ephesians had lived in a state of spiritual death.

In his book *Be Rich*, Warren Wiersbe said, "All lost sinners are dead, and the only difference between one sinner and another is the state of decay. The lost derelict on skid row may be more decayed outwardly than the unsaved society leader, but both are dead in sin—and one corpse cannot be more dead than another!"

B. Disobedient Children (v. 2)

2. Wherein in time past ye walked according to the course of this world, according to the prince of the power of the air, the spirit that now worketh in the children of disobedience.

The term rendered "walked" (v. 2) is prominent in Paul's writings. It recurs in this letter in 2:10; 4:1, 17; 5:2, 8, 15. The Ephesians' former walkabout, Paul says, was in accordance with the age (*aion*) of this world (*kosmos*). He combines two expressions that elsewhere he has used separately, emphasizing that anyone without Christ is a prisoner of the social and value systems of the present evil age, which radically oppose Christ.

"The prince of the power of the air," who rules the evil spiritual realm, is Satan, whom Jesus called "the prince of this world" (John 12:31). Paul called Satan "the god of this world" (2 Cor. 4:4). Unlike God, however, Satan cannot be everywhere at one time, and neither can he know everything. He is still a created being, and he must use evil tricks to influence people. He holds sway over unsaved humanity, and also seeks to sway believers. He longs for all people to live as "children of disobedience."

C. Children of Wrath (v. 3)

3. Among whom also we all had our conversation in times past in the lusts of our flesh, fulfilling the desires of the flesh and of the mind; and were by nature the children of wrath, even as others.

Alive in Christ

Human sinfulness is universal. The past life of Jewish Christians, like that of the Gentiles, was dominated by "the cravings of our sinful nature" (NIV). The "flesh" (*sarx*) is not merely the body but the whole person oriented away from God and toward its own selfish concerns. Because of this, the Jewish converts had once been in as much danger of judgment as anyone else. The phrase "children of wrath" denotes those who deserve God's punishment. Sin brings condemnation.

Talk About It:
Who are "the children of wrath"?

II. SAVED BY GRACE (Eph. 2:4-10)
A. Quickened With Christ (vv. 4-7)

4. But God, who is rich in mercy, for his great love wherewith he loved us,

5. Even when we were dead in sins, hath quickened us together with Christ, (by grace ye are saved;)

6. And hath raised us up together, and made us sit together in heavenly places in Christ Jesus:

7. That in the ages to come he might shew the exceeding riches of his grace in his kindness toward us through Christ Jesus.

The phrase "but God" (v. 4) shows the graciousness of God in stark contrast to lost and sinful humanity. Against human sinfulness and rude rejection of God, Paul sets God's gracious acceptance of humanity in Christ. Although God cannot approve of sin because He is righteous, He shows His mercy toward those He has created. He loves them and has made possible their reconciliation to Himself. "Mercy" (*eleos*) is God's compassion for the helpless, issuing in action for their relief. Had He decided to destroy His refractory children, He would have been entirely justified, and nothing could have averted the catastrophe. Instead, God's "rich mercy" and "great love" brought salvation to Paul and his readers.

Talk About It:
1. Explain the phrase "by grace you have been saved" (v. 5 NKJV).
2. What can believers anticipate (v. 7)?

Our being "dead in sins" (v. 5, a repetition of v. 1) is a vivid contrast with the foregoing description of God and His love. A close parallel is found in Romans 3:23, which says "all have sinned and fall short of the glory of God" (NKJV). Such use of contrast—especially contrast between past and present—is a favorite literary device of Paul.

In verse 5 of the text Paul moves to his main point in the opening paragraph of the chapter: God has made us alive with Christ. The Greek word rendered "quickened" (cf. Col. 2:13) is the first of the three verbs prefixed by *syn* ("with") that describe the participation of the believer in what God has done in Christ. The other two are in verse 6. When we were dead in sins, God gave us new life together with Christ. The life we now possess is an effect of Christ's resurrection. Christ's resurrection was by an act of God's power; the regeneration of believers is by an

act of God's grace. Being "made . . . alive" (v. 5 NIV) is a total reversal of all that is implied in the words "dead through our trespasses" (ASV). We were once, in consequence of our sins, a spiritual corpse given up to corruption utter and helpless, from which nothing could save us except the life-giving power of God. However, God has pardoned our sins and given to us the eternal life for which we were created.

In verse 6, Paul states that God has "raised us up together" (*synegeiren*; cf. Col. 2:12; 3:1) with Christ, a further proof of the act of God which raised Christ from the grave and brought Him back to the land of the living. And we are "seated . . . with him" (NIV; *synekathisen*) in the heavenly places, a phrase that provides further definiteness to the picture of Christ's exaltation in heaven, and declares that believers already share in its glorious environment. Not only do we anticipate resurrection and glorification at the end of the age, we also experience a present realization of the risen life in Christ and of participation with Him in His ascended majesty (see Col. 3:1-4).

God did everything in Christ with a single purpose in view. It was to demonstrate in successive ages "the exceeding riches of his grace" (Eph. 2:7).

B. Saved by Grace (vv. 8-9)

8. For by grace are ye saved through faith; and that not of yourselves: it is the gift of God:

9. Not of works, lest any man should boast.

Paul reminds his readers that they owe their salvation entirely to the undeserved favor of God. He says the means of salvation is faith, which is also its necessary condition. Such faith is simply a trustful response that is itself evoked by the Holy Spirit. Lest faith should be in any way misinterpreted as a person's contribution to his or her own salvation, Paul immediately adds a rider to explain that nothing is of our own doing but everything is in "the gift of God."

Talk About It:
1. Explain the role of faith in salvation (v. 8).
2. Explain the role of works in salvation (v. 9).

Paul firmly excludes every possibility of self-achieved salvation. As if it were insufficient that he should have insisted in verse 8 "and that not of yourselves," he adds "not of works" (v. 9). The apostle does not specify these "works" (*erga*) as related to the Law, since he is not thinking only of Jewish Christians. Any kind of human self-effort is comprehensively ruled out by this terse expression. The reason is immediately attached. It is to prevent the slightest self-congratulation. If salvation is by the sheer unmerited favor of God, boasting is altogether out of place.

C. God's Workmanship (v. 10)

10. For we are his workmanship, created in Christ Jesus unto good works, which God hath before ordained that we should walk in them.

Alive in Christ

Salvation produces good works that attest to its reality. We are God's "workmanship," His "poem" (*poiema*). The poem's purpose is to produce "good works." Works play no part in the cause of our salvation. But we must demonstrate the consequence of our salvation by works. Here Paul is in agreement with James (2:14-26).

Talk About It:
What have believers been "ordained" to do?

III. ONE IN CHRIST (Eph. 2:11-22)
A. In the Past (vv. 11-12)

11. Wherefore remember, that ye being in time past Gentiles in the flesh, who are called Uncircumcision by that which is called the Circumcision in the flesh made by hands;

12. That at that time ye were without Christ, being aliens from the commonwealth of Israel, and strangers from the covenants of promise, having no hope, and without God in the world.

In verses 1-10, Paul has considered the moral condition of the Gentiles before their conversion to Christianity. Now he reminds them of their previous deprivation in terms of their religious status as estimated from a Jewish point of view. They had been and indeed still were "the Gentiles." They were non-Jews or pagans, so far as their physical descent was concerned ("in the flesh," v. 11). The rest of the verse elaborates on the distinction by citing the contemptuous nickname attached to them by the Jews: "uncircumcised" (NIV). Paul does not himself use it in a derogatory manner; he simply reports its currency. As a Jew, however, he is quick to point out that Jews, who are "called the Circumcision in the flesh," have nothing to boast about, since an external man-made mark in itself holds no spiritual significance. The real circumcision is of the heart (Rom. 2:29; Gal. 5:6).

Talk About It:
Describe the former disadvantages of not being Jewish.

With four successive phrases, Paul describes the state of the Ephesians prior to their conversion (Eph. 2:12). First, they were "without [apart from] Christ." They had no expectation of a Messiah. Second, they had no rights of citizenship in God's kingdom because they were "aliens from the commonwealth of Israel." They were cut off from any such privilege by reason of their birth. Third, the Gentiles were not entitled to the benefits accruing to the covenantal community. They were in the position of "strangers" who could not claim the prerogatives of nationals. As a consequence, they lived in a world devoid of hope (1 Thess. 4:13). Lastly, they were "without God." They were not atheists, for they worshiped idols. They believed gods existed but did not know the true God. The moral and spiritual desolation of the Gentiles was complete.

"The word which God has written on the brow of every man is hope."
—**Victor Hugo**

B. Now in Christ (vv. 13-18)

13. But now in Christ Jesus ye who sometimes were far off are made nigh by the blood of Christ.

14. For he is our peace, who hath made both one, and hath broken down the middle wall of partition between us;

15. Having abolished in his flesh the enmity, even the law of commandments contained in ordinances; for to make in himself of twain one new man, so making peace;

16. And that he might reconcile both unto God in one body by the cross, having slain the enmity thereby:

17. And came and preached peace to you which were afar off, and to them that were nigh.

18. For through him we both have access by one Spirit unto the Father.

Talk About It:
1. What did Jesus Christ tear down (v. 14)?
2. How did Christ make peace (vv. 15-16)?
3. How does the Trinity work together in verse 18?

Paul quickly turns from the tragedy of the Gentiles' former desolation to the joy of their reconciliation in Christ. "But now" stands in sharp antithesis to verse 12. They are no longer "separate from Christ" (v. 12 NIV), "but now in Christ Jesus" (v. 13). He is the sphere of their new possibilities. Although previously far off, they are now brought near. This is possible "by the blood of Christ."

Paul moves from the change in relationship that the readers now had to the means of its accomplishment. "He himself is our peace" (v. 14 NIV) is emphatic (cf. v. 15, "in himself"). Christ alone has solved the problem of our relationships with God and others. He draws us to God and to each other in His own person. Christ is both peace and peacemaker.

Christ brought about the reconciliation of Jew and Gentile when He died on the cross. There He made two into one, removing the hostility that existed between Jews and Gentiles.

There had been a "barrier, [a] dividing wall" (v. 14 NIV) created by hatred. The first word means simply a "fence" or "railing." The second is much rarer and is literally a "middle wall" (KJV). This brings to mind the Berlin Wall that separated West and East Germany until it was torn down in November 1989. Unfortunately, people are still divided by many barriers today, ranging from race to socioeconomic status to educational attainments. And sadly, the Church has not been spared. It is time to read Ephesians 2 again.

The removal of the breach between the two great divisions of humanity results from the reconciliation of both Jew and Gentile to God "by the cross" (v. 16). The uniquely Pauline word for "reconcile" is *apokatallasso*, which means "to exchange." Here it means an exchange of relationships. As a result of Christ's work of reconciliation, believers are provided an access to God's presence. It is solely through Christ that both Jews and Gentiles now have their "access" to God the Father through the Holy Spirit (v. 18). Once again, Paul's Trinitarian view comes to the surface.

"The essence of the Christian religion consists therein: that the creation of the Father, destroyed by sin, is again restored in the death of the Son of God and recreated by the grace of the Holy Spirit to a kingdom of God."
—Herman Bavinck

C. The Temple of God (vv. 19-22)

19. Now therefore ye are no more strangers and foreigners, but fellowcitizens with the saints, and of the household of God;

20. And are built upon the foundation of the apostles and prophets, Jesus Christ himself being the chief corner stone;

21. In whom all the building fitly framed together groweth unto an holy temple in the Lord:

22. In whom ye also are builded together for an habitation of God through the Spirit.

Beginning with verse 19, Paul draws a conclusion from the previous paragraph (vv. 14-18) and goes on to expand what he has previously said in verse 13. He uses two terms that commonly denote inferiority of status and contrasts them with "fellow citizens." The first term, *strangers*, applies to "outsiders" in general, but in particular to short-term transients, something that is equivalent to tourists in our times. The second term, *foreigners*, were the resident "aliens" (NIV) who had settled in the country of their choice. These are like legal permanent residents (known in the USA as green-card holders) who enjoy all the privileges the government provides, but have no right to vote and can be subject to deportation. Such had been the position of the Gentiles in relation to the kingdom of God before the coming of Christ. But now they enjoy all the privileges of God's new people. They are united with the saints of the past (see 1:18) as well as with contemporary Christians. The Gentiles are "members of God's household" (2:19 NIV).

When the Ephesians became Christians, they were immediately placed on a firm foundation. In 1 Corinthians 3:11 we learn that this foundation is Christ himself, but here He is "the chief cornerstone" of the building, which literally means "at the tip of the angle." It refers to the capstone or binding stone that holds the whole structure together. Here the apostles are the foundation as being closely associated with Christ, the Revealer and Redeemer, in the establishment of the Church. They were the witnesses of His resurrection appearances and the first preachers of the good news. As one writer puts it, "The Church rests on the unique event of which Christ is the center, but in which the apostles and prophets, filled and guided by the Spirit, and doing their work in unique closeness to Christ, had an indispensable and untransmissible part."

In verse 21 of the text, Paul expounds the significance of the building. The function of the cornerstone is precisely defined by the verb "joined together" (NIV), used also in 4:16, where Paul describes the Church as a body. This term embraces the complicated process of stonework by which stones are "joined together harmoniously" on Christ (2:21 AB). Paul uses the word *naos* for temple instead of *hieron*. The former is the inner sanctuary where the presence of God, symbolized by the ark of the covenant, dwells, whereas the latter includes the entire precincts. Paul uses the image of the temple both to refer to the individual and the community. The true temple is the whole church.

Talk About It:
1. How does verse 19 describe the changed status of believers?
2. What does it mean to be "built upon the foundation of the apostles and prophets" (v. 20)?
3. What are God's people, and why (vv. 21-22)?

God's Building

In Christ both Jews and Gentiles meet, and constitute one church; and Christ supports the building by His strength. All believers, of whom it consists, being united to Christ by faith . . . grow unto a holy temple, become a sacred society, in which there is much communion between God and His people,

The emphasis on ongoing building is brought out by the present tense of "being built together" (v. 22 NIV). The goal is that the Church should become God's "habitation," or residence, a term that is frequently used in the Septuagint to denote the divine resting place either on earth or in heaven. Formerly, God's earthly abode was thought to be on Mount Zion and in the Temple at Jerusalem. Now He makes His abode in the Church. This is achieved only in the Holy Spirit, who is the means and the element.

CONCLUSION

The temptation to fall back on one's own resources and delude oneself that one can contribute something to one's standing before God is all too human. Believers must constantly recognize that it is "all of grace." Our new privileged position owes everything to Christ. He is the One who makes access to God possible, the Cornerstone of the structure, and the One who enables us to grow into what we are meant to be.

GOLDEN TEXT CHALLENGE

"AND YOU HATH HE QUICKENED, WHO WERE DEAD IN TRESPASSES AND SINS" (Eph. 2:1).

Paul in essence calls the Ephesians "the living dead." That sounds like the title of a horror movie, and in a spiritual sense, the Ephesians' lives before Christ had been horrible.

The Ephesians were physically mobile, but spiritually they had been taking "false steps" (the literal meaning of *trespasses*). They were carrying on with their daily affairs, but spiritually they were "off target" (the literal meaning of *sins*). They were alive on the outside, but inside they were lifeless.

Everything changed when they encountered Christ. He had breathed spiritual life into them, freeing them from their missteps and off-the-mark lifestyles. Rather than being dead in trespasses and sins, now they were empowered to take the right steps and lead lives focused on Jesus Christ.

Daily Devotions:
M. Consequences of Sin
Genesis 4:1-13
T. Noah Found Grace
Genesis 6:6-18
W. God Blesses His People
Psalm 84:1-12
T. Christ Gives Life
John 1:1-12
F. Alive in the Spirit
Romans 8:1-10
S. United in Christ
Galatians 3:22-29

Alive in Christ

The Mystery of the Church

Ephesians 3:1-21

INTRODUCTION

There has been a knowledge explosion in the last one hundred years. Many facts about the universe that were a mystery are now unraveling as space exploration continues to progress. The laws of thermodynamics have led to many inventions that have brought efficiency, luxury, and perhaps misery to our lives. Computer technology now makes it possible to store billions of information items that can be instantly recalled. However, the changes introduced into our world by science and technology in recent history are not as great and are incomparable to the change effected by Jesus' coming.

Christ's first advent made many things possible—one being the glorious truths of the Church. In His wisdom, God hid these wonderful truths from the previous ages and revealed them through His Son. Paul the apostle was chosen by God to reveal the mystery of the Church to his contemporaries and generations to come.

In Ephesians 2:11-22, Paul has discussed the union of Jewish and Gentile believers into one new humanity in Christ. He has declared the potential unity of humanity through God's work in Christ Jesus. Jews and Gentiles can become one people in the Christian church, the temple of God, through the Holy Spirit. In 3:1 he begins to offer a prayer on their behalf, but stops abruptly in the middle of the sentence and digresses to the subject of the mystery of Christ and the Church, something that he considers as his responsibility to proclaim. He later resumes his prayer in verse 14.

Today's lesson reminds us that the Church is immeasurably more than the physical buildings where believers gather to worship and fellowship. It is a spiritual organism which lives and breathes through Christ's Spirit and binds all believers together through His love.

Unit Theme:
Ephesians: Understanding God's Eternal Purposes

Central Truth:
The mystery of the Church is that God has chosen to save all people through faith in Christ.

Focus:
Appreciate the unity of all believers in Christ and be rooted in His love.

Context:
Paul wrote his letter to the Ephesians from a Roman prison between AD 60 and 63.

Golden Text:
"By revelation he [God] made known unto me the mystery; . . . That the Gentiles should be fellowheirs, and of the same body, and partakers of his promise in Christ by the gospel" (Eph. 3:3, 6).

Study Outline:
I. The Mystery Revealed (Eph. 3:1-7)
II. Purpose of the Mystery (Eph. 3:8-13)
III. Prayer for the Church (Eph. 3:14-21)

I. THE MYSTERY REVEALED (Ephesians 3:1-7)

A. Revealed to Paul (vv. 1-4)

1. For this cause I Paul, the prisoner of Jesus Christ for you Gentiles,

2. If ye have heard of the dispensation of the grace of God which is given me to you-ward:

3. How that by revelation he made known unto me the mystery; (as I wrote afore in few words.

4. Whereby, when ye read, ye may understand my knowledge in the mystery of Christ).

Talk About It:
1. Explain Paul's description of himself in verse 1.
2. What "grace" had God given Paul (vv. 2-3)?

Paul begins the paragraph by linking it with the discussion in 2:11-22, writing "For this cause," or "for this reason" (3:1). He reintroduces himself, but inserts a new element. He calls himself "the prisoner of Jesus Christ" (v. 1). There is neither a hint of self-pity nor any idea of victim mentality in the tone of his letter. His imprisonment was for a noble cause—Paul sees himself as a captive of Christ for the cause of the salvation of the Gentiles. As always, Paul sees his imprisonment and sufferings as marks of his apostleship.

He then elaborated on his commission as a preacher to the Gentiles. Paul refers to his commission as a *dispensation* (v. 2), or literally an "administration," of divine grace. The term is usually equivalent to "stewardship" or "task." The idea here is that of the coalescence of responsibility and grace. It is grace that enabled Paul to fulfill his calling as an apostle to the Gentiles (cf. vv. 7-8; 4:7-13).

Paul came to understand the truth of God's purpose concerning the universality of the Gospel early in his Christian life by "revelation" (3:3), an obvious reference to his Damascus-road encounter with Christ. The message he was commissioned to declare is *the mystery of Christ*. The "mystery" which was unknown was that Gentiles were to be incorporated into the one body of the Church (2:16) as equal partners with Israel (3:6). Christianity remains a mystery to many people today.

> "The strength and happiness of a man consists in finding out the way in which God is going, and going that way too."
> —**Henry Ward Beecher**

A young man from India, Sundar Singh, wrote that after hearing some missionaries preach he felt a great spiritual distress within himself. That night, unable to sleep, he prayed, "Oh God, if there is a God, reveal Yourself to me." Suddenly a bright light shone in the room where he lay. Expecting Buddha or Krishna to appear before him, instead, Jesus appeared. After this marvelous revelation, Sundar knew God was there and dedicated himself to Christ, becoming a great missionary among his people.

B. Revealed to Us (vv. 5-7)

5. Which in other ages was not made known unto the sons of men, as it is now revealed unto his holy apostles and prophets by the Spirit;

The Mystery of the Church

6. That the Gentiles should be fellowheirs, and of the same body, and partakers of his promise in Christ by the gospel:

7. Whereof I was made a minister, according to the gift of the grace of God given unto me by the effectual working of his power.

The Holy Spirit has now entrusted to us the same "mystery" (vv. 3-4) entrusted to Paul and "holy apostles and prophets" (v. 5). In verse 6 Paul states the content of the mystery in a summary fashion, using three Greek words that are each prefixed by *syn*, meaning "together with" or "co."

First is *co-heirs* ("fellowheirs," *synkleronoma*). In Romans 8:17, Paul speaks of believers being co-heirs with Christ. Here, as in Galatians 3:29 and 4:7, he stresses the fact that in Christ, Gentiles are co-inheritors of the Kingdom along with the Jews. All who belong to Christ are "Abraham's seed" (Gal. 3:29), thus heirs of the promise God gave him.

Second, they are *co-members* "of the same body" (*synsoma*), hence they enjoy a corporate relationship. Paul affirms the complete integration and equality of believing Gentiles with Jews.

Third, they are "partakers of his promise" (*synmetocha*)— that is, co-partners or "sharers together" (NIV). This term recurs in Ephesians 5:7 in a different context and stands in contrast with 2:12, which says Gentiles had once been "foreigners to the covenants of the promise" (NIV). Because of Christ, Gentiles are fellow partakers of the covenant promise made originally to the Jews.

This union of Jews and Gentiles in one body, which was so astonishing to all who saw it, is a logical consequence of the central doctrine of the Gospel—that God accepts all who believe. Paul "became" (a preferable translation to "I was made," 3:7) a servant of the Gospel, not through any ambition or qualification of his own but solely through the gift and calling of God (v. 2; cf. Col. 1:23, 25). Paul stresses the origin of his apostolic ministry—it came from God "by the effectual working of his power" (Eph. 3:7). He recognizes that the dramatic intervention that transformed him from an enemy into a friend of Christ was nothing less than an act of divine omnipotence. Now his apostleship reflects God's power at work in the Church (1:19-20).

II. PURPOSE OF THE MYSTERY (Ephesians 3:8-13)
A. God's Wisdom Revealed (vv. 8-10)

8. Unto me, who am less than the least of all saints, is this grace given, that I should preach among the Gentiles the unsearchable riches of Christ;

9. And to make all men see what is the fellowship of the mystery, which from the beginning of the world hath been hid in God, who created all things by Jesus Christ:

Talk About It:
1. To whom has the mystery been revealed?
2. What was the mystery?

"God is not saving the world; it is done. Our business is to get men and women to realize it."
—**Oswald Chambers**

10. To the intent that now unto the principalities and powers in heavenly places might be known by the church the manifold wisdom of God.

Talk About It:
1. Explain Paul's description of himself in verse 8.
2. What is God's intent for the Church (vv. 9-10)?

With all humility, Paul states that he who was formerly nobody has been made a somebody by God through God's power. As such, he is now able to proclaim among the Gentiles the "unsearchable," or untraceable, riches of Christ. Paul's commission is to announce the good news of Christ to the Gentiles. It is a continuation of Christ's own ministry (2:17). Paul was called to "make plain" (3:9 NIV), or to cast light upon, the outworking of God's mystery. It was not a new action on the part of God or a divergence from His original plans. It was "hid in God, who created all things" (v. 9), but is now available to all.

God's "intent" (v. 10) of creation and redemption is the demonstration of His wisdom. In particular, Paul's commission to proclaim the mystery is designed to promote this purpose as the Church becomes God's instrument. As one writer succinctly stated, "The Church becomes a mirror through which the bright ones of heaven see the glory of God. In order to show them this glory, God committed the Gospel to Paul."

In verses 9 and 10, with their talk of disclosure of the mystery to the principalities and authorities, the two main aspects of the discussion of the mystery—its theological and cosmic aspects—come together. The elaboration on Paul's apostleship supplies the context for integrating these two aspects, explicitly brought together earlier only in 1:21-23. What now becomes clear is that the Church provides hostile cosmic powers with a tangible reminder that their authority has been decisively broken and that all things are subject to Christ. The overcoming of the barriers between Jews and Gentiles, as they are united through Christ in the Church, is a pledge of the overcoming of all divisions when the universe will be restored to harmony in Christ (cf. 1:10). In this way, the Church as the focus of God's wise plan could give the readers an essential clue to the meaning of this world's history.

"The Church is the 'theater' for displaying God's wisdom."
—Jamieson, Fausset, and Brown Commentary

B. God's Purpose Accomplished (vv. 11-13)

11. According to the eternal purpose which he purposed in Christ Jesus our Lord:

12. In whom we have boldness and access with confidence by the faith of him.

13. Wherefore I desire that ye faint not at my tribulations for you, which is your glory.

Talk About It:
1. How should believers approach God (v. 12)?
2. What was the Ephesians' "glory" (v. 13)?

Paul continues his discussion by making again Christ the central point of the message. In Christ and through faith in Him "we have boldness and . . . confidence" to approach God (v. 12). Two significant truths must be noted. First, Paul says God's eternal purpose is "accomplished in Christ" (v. 11 NIV). Christ is central. There is no other means or hope of salvation outside of

Jesus. We cannot come to God through any merits of our own. Second, we must come to Him by faith. This is humankind's responsibility. Such faith is not mere mental assent to some expressed truths, but a willingness to embrace the fact of Christ's death for our sins and to trust fully in Him.

There are two expressions of favor enjoyed by all Christians who come to God through Christ: "boldness and access with confidence" (v. 12). Unlike the time of King Ahasuerus when Esther was afraid to enter the presence of the king, or today when we cannot see even church leaders except "by invitation only," we can boldly come to the King of kings anytime, anywhere, and on any day.

Paul concludes the section with an exhortation to his readers not to "faint" (v. 13)—or literally, "lose heart" or be discouraged—because of his tribulations or sufferings which he sustained in the fulfillment of his commission. He gives two reasons. First, his sufferings or tribulations were for the Ephesians' benefit, and second, his sufferings were their glory. What mattered to Paul was the welfare of his readers. If they rightly understood the reason and purpose of his sufferings, they could do nothing but rejoice with him even as he constantly did (Col. 1:24).

III. PRAYER FOR THE CHURCH (Ephesians 3:14-21)
A. Confidence Expressed (vv. 14-15)

14. For this cause I bow my knees unto the Father of our Lord Jesus Christ,

15. Of whom the whole family in heaven and earth is named.

Paul resumes his prayer that he broke off in verse 1. Because the Gentile Christians are now incorporated into the body of Christ, Paul prays that they may appropriate their spiritual privileges to the full.

He begins the prayer with an attitude of deep reverence and confidence. Paul says he kneels ("I bow my knees," v. 14). Standing was the normal posture among the Jews and the early Christians. *Unto*, or literally *before*, is a face-to-face preposition that suggests an intimate relationship. He addresses God as Father because, through the redemptive act of Christ, access is now made possible to the Father through the Spirit (2:18). The Father is the One after whom "the whole family" is named (3:15).

B. Requests Made (vv. 16-19)

16. That he would grant you, according to the riches of his glory, to be strengthened with might by his Spirit in the inner man.

17. That Christ may dwell in your hearts by faith; that ye, being rooted and grounded in love,

18. May be able to comprehend with all saints what is the breadth, and length, and depth, and height;

19. And to know the love of Christ, which passeth knowledge, that ye might be filled with all the fulness of God.

Talk About It:
1. How does God strengthen His children (v. 16)?
2. How are believers to be "rooted and grounded" (v. 17)?
3. What "surpasses knowledge" (v. 19 NIV)?

As in Ephesians 1:17-18, Paul's prayer is concerned with the appropriation of God's provision in Christ through the Spirit. Paul reminds himself and his readers that God's giving in response to supplication is in accord with the "riches of his glory" (3:16), or "His glorious riches" (NIV; cf. Rom. 9:23)—an inexhaustible wealth of His radiance and power active on behalf of humanity. Paul asks that God will endow his readers with spiritual blessings on an extravagant scale as a result of Christ taking up residence in their hearts. Paul is not praying for an experience unique to Christians in Ephesus, but something that is shared by all God's people. In a letter so concerned with the Church and its unity, we would not expect the corporate aspect of spiritual experience to be overlooked.

In the prayer, there are three major requests. The first is that the Ephesians will be strengthened through the Spirit in their inner persons, which need to be renewed constantly by the Spirit's energy (v. 16). The request is then spelled out in different terms as Paul asks that Christ might take up permanent residence ("dwell") in their hearts, at the center of their personalities, so that through a relationship of faith Christ's character and the pattern of His death and resurrection increasingly shape their values and their living (v. 17). Paul's desire is to see the Ephesian believers become vigorous Christians who are effective because of their quality of inner strength derived from the energizing of God's Spirit.

In his second request Paul prays that, as the Ephesians are strengthened, they will be enabled to "comprehend" or "grasp" (v. 18 NIV) in company with the whole Church the vast dimensions of the all-embracing love of Christ—that, despite its ultimate incomprehensibility and mystery, they might know this love of Christ personally and in a way that controls their lives. Paul desires to see Christians who understand their identity and security because they know the all-encompassing love of Christ and therefore sense His acceptance and affirmation. Such knowledge will result in their stability.

The love of Christ, exemplified in His magnanimity to the Gentiles, is too large to be confined by any geometrical measurements. It is wide enough to reach the whole world and beyond (see 1:9-10, 20). It is long enough to stretch from eternity to eternity (1:4-6, 18; 3:9). It is high enough to raise both Gentiles and Jews to heavenly places in Christ Jesus (1:13; 2:6). It is deep enough to rescue people from sin's degradation, and even from the grip of Satan himself (2:1-5; 6:11-12). The love of Christ is the love He has for the Church as a united body (5:25, 29-30)

and for those who trust in Him as individuals (3:17). Paul recognizes, however, that he is attempting to measure the immeasurable and so he paradoxically prays that the Ephesian Christians may come to know a love that is ultimately unknowable. It "surpasses knowledge" (v. 19 NIV).

Paul's final request is that the readers of the letter be "filled with all the fulness of God" (v. 19)—that they experience to their capacity the life and power of God himself. Paul wants to see Christians who, conscious of their significant role, have appropriated all the resources of the fullness of God. The fulfillment God intends for believers is the maturity that is reached through "the fulness of Christ" (4:13).

C. Praise Given (vv. 20-21)

20. Now unto him that is able to do exceeding abundantly above all that we ask or think, according to the power that worketh in us,

21. Unto him be glory in the church by Christ Jesus throughout all ages, world without end. Amen.

At the end of the prayer, Paul moves to doxology, expressing his conviction that he serves a great God. He ascribes glory to the God whose power infinitely transcends all human praying or imagining. This is no mere theoretical statement about the omnipotence of God as an attribute. It is an ascription of praise that springs from Paul's personal experience. For, as he says, this inexpressible power of God is the same power that believers know to be at work within them.

In the doxology he rehearses themes already touched on: the abundance of God's gift (1:18-19; 2:7; 3:19), the power made available to the Christian (1:19; 3:7, 16, 18), and the indissoluble link between Christ and the Church (1:22-23; 3:10).

The close combination of the Church and Christ in the doxology is striking, separating it from any Jewish counterpart. Glory is due to God in the Church and in Christ Jesus. It belongs to God in the Church as Christ's body, the one new community of Jew and Gentile, and it belongs to Him in Christ Jesus as the Head, the One through whom this community came into being and on whom it depends for its life. Both the Church and Christ will bring God glory "throughout all generations, for ever and ever!" (v. 21 NIV).

Talk About It:
1. What can God do (v. 20)?
2. What should happen "throughout all generations" (v. 21 NIV)?

CONCLUSION

One cannot but ask the question, "What made Paul tick?" Why did he never give up? Today's lesson provides two answers. First, he was the prisoner of Christ, and not that of Nero. Hence, there was no room for self-pity and resentment. Second, Paul counted it a privilege to participate in God's plan for the Church. He was not a reluctant preacher. He loved God and the Church.

Paul demonstrated his commitment to and love for the Church by his prayers. He knew that nothing short of a vision of the glory of God and nothing short of an experience of the greatness of the power of God at work within them could sustain the Ephesian believers in the task to which God had called them.

GOLDEN TEXT CHALLENGE

"BY REVELATION HE [GOD] MADE KNOWN UNTO ME THE MYSTERY; . . . THAT THE GENTILES SHOULD BE FELLOWHEIRS, AND OF THE SAME BODY, AND PARTAKERS OF HIS PROMISE IN CHRIST BY THE GOSPEL" (Eph. 3:3, 6).

The word *mystery*, "in the New Testament, does not denote the mysterious, but that which, being outside the range of unassisted natural apprehension, can be made known only by divine revelation, and is made known in a manner and at a time appointed by God, and to those only who are illumined by His Spirit. In the ordinary sense a 'mystery' implies knowledge withheld; its Scriptural significance is truth revealed" (W. E. Vines).

The mystery made known to Paul is that the Gentiles were chosen by God to receive the same spiritual blessings as the Jews through Jesus Christ. "The Gentiles are fellow heirs and fellow members of the body, and fellow partakers" (v. 6 NASB) of all the Gospel offers. Every person from every nation and race who puts his or her faith in Christ is an equal partner with every other believer in the inheritance afforded by Christ.

Daily Devotions:
M. Know the Lord's Ways
Psalm 25:4-14
T. Promise to Reveal Hidden Riches
Isaiah 45:1-7
W. Deep and Secret Things Revealed
Daniel 2:19-25
T. Jesus Reveals Truth in Parables
Matthew 13:31-35
F. The Mystery Revealed in Christ
Romans 16:24-27
S. The Spirit Reveals Hidden Wisdom
1 Corinthians 2:6-11

Fulfilling God's Purpose

Ephesians 4:1 through 6:9

INTRODUCTION

"Walk the talk" and "Be real" are common expressions that people understand as a call to authenticity. This is basically what Paul does in this section of his letter to the Ephesians. He emphasizes the importance of the believers living up to their new status as the people of God. Paul previously described the Ephesians as "aliens from the commonwealth of Israel, and strangers from the covenants of promise" (2:12). However, that has changed. He has now finished his discussion of the incorporation of Gentiles into the people of God.

The Ephesian believers' change in loyalty demands a change in lifestyle. Citizenship carries with it both privileges and obligations, and Christians are called to live according to the values, norms, and priorities of their heavenly commonwealth, not those of the dominant culture, wherever that may be. In short, Paul co-opts political language that was meaningful to his readers in order to reconstruct their identity and conduct. The tone for the rest of the letter is set in 4:1 as Paul challenges the Ephesians to "walk worthy" of their calling in Christ. The word *walk* figures prominently in chapters 4 and 5 as Paul gives practical guidelines to the Ephesians regarding Christian living (4:1, 17; 5:2, 8, 15). The outworking of the "worthy walk" is to be seen in various areas of the lives of the individuals and believing community.

Letter to Diognetus, which dates to the second century AD, describes early Christians:

> Christians are not differentiated from other people by country, language or custom. They live in both Greek and foreign cities, wherever chance has put them. They follow local customs in clothing, food, and the other aspects of life. But at the same time, they demonstrate to us the unusual form of their own citizenship. They live in their own native lands, but as aliens. . . . Every foreign country is to them as their native country, and every native land as a foreign country.

> They marry and have children just like everyone else, but they do not kill unwanted babies. They offer a shared table, but not a shared bed. They are passing their days on earth, but are citizens of heaven. They obey the appointed laws and go beyond the law in their own lives.

Unit Theme:
Ephesians: Understanding God's Eternal Purposes

Central Truth:
God empowers believers in Christ to live as followers of God.

Focus:
Explore and implement practical ways of fulfilling God's purpose in the Church.

Context:
Paul wrote his letter to the Ephesians from a Roman prison between AD 60 and 63.

Golden Text:
"Be ye therefore followers of God, as dear children; and walk in love, as Christ also hath loved us, and hath given himself for us an offering and a sacrifice to God for a sweet-smelling savour" (Eph. 5:1-2).

Study Outline:
I. Promote Unity (Eph. 4:1-6)
II. Live as Children of Light (Eph. 4:17-24; 5:1-2, 8-11)
III. Submit to One Another (Eph. 5:21-33; 6:1-9)

I. PROMOTE UNITY (Eph. 4:1-6)

A. Divine Calling (vv. 1-3)

1. I therefore, the prisoner of the Lord, beseech you that ye walk worthy of the vocation wherewith ye are called,

2. With all lowliness and meekness, with longsuffering, forbearing one another in love;

3. Endeavouring to keep the unity of the Spirit in the bond of peace.

"Beseech" (v. 1), or literally "appeal," is a gentle exhortation by the apostle to the Ephesians. Such an appeal, rather than a command, is appropriate, as Paul summarizes the Christian life by describing it as a "vocation." The Ephesians are to live worthy of their vocation. The word *vocation*, in its simplest sense, means "call." Although there are different calls to ministry—such as pastor, teacher, and missionary—the primary and fundamental call Paul has in mind here is the initial call to salvation and the ensuing Christian life. The believer must make every effort to walk worthy of that call.

The apostle specified four virtues that the Ephesians should maintain in their daily lives: lowliness, meekness, longsuffering, and love. The first two, lowliness and meekness, may be regarded as two ways of expressing the same quality. Jesus used the two terms together in Matthew 11:29 when He said, "I am meek and lowly in heart." Being "completely humble and gentle" (Eph. 4:2 NIV) are attitudes we as Christians show toward God, in which we recognize that before Him we are nothing, but through Him we become persons of worth. When we are lowly in heart and meek, we have a thankful sense of dependence on God; we are not proud or conceited; our emphasis is not on ourselves but on God.

To be longsuffering and forbearing is to reflect a proper attitude toward others. It is necessary to be patient, enduring the shortcomings of others because of love we have for them. When we manifest these graces we will not be short-tempered, impatient, and unfeeling toward people. These virtues must emanate from the Spirit within us and not from any virtue that is natural to us (see Gal. 5:22-23).

Christians have a responsibility to seek and keep unity among themselves. The word *endeavouring* (Eph. 4:3) means to "spare no effort toward keeping unity." Inner unity is the basis for interpersonal unity; the Spirit within us is the basis of individual unity; inner harmony makes unity with others a possibility. It is therefore necessary that we receive the Holy Spirit and cultivate His presence within us, because His fruit is peace, and peace creates unity.

B. Divine Oneness (vv. 4-6)

4. There is one body, and one Spirit, even as ye are called in one hope of your calling;

Talk About It:
1. Of what must believers "walk worthy" (v. 1)?
2. According to verse 2, how should Christians relate to each other?
3. Explain the term "bond of peace" (v. 3).

"Christians in community must again show the world . . . the bond of the love of Christ. Increasingly the ordered fellowship of the church becomes the sign of grace for the warring factions of a disordered world."
—Edmund Clowney

Fulfilling God's Purpose

5. One Lord, one faith, one baptism,
6. One God and Father of all, who is above all, and through all, and in you all.

Paul introduces a series of seven things that are one. These emphasize the fact that Christ cannot be divided, that His work in us constitutes a unity, and that He is "the same yesterday, and to day, and for ever" (Heb. 13:8).

The first three unities are *one body, one Spirit,* and *one hope.* "One body" refers to the Church, the body of Christ, which is referred to in Ephesians 1:22-23: "And [God] gave him [Christ] to be the head over all things to the church, which is his body, the fulness of him that filleth all in all." In Paul's day the emphasis was that the Church consisted of both Jew and Gentile, united as the spiritual body of Christ. Today the body of Christ has many members and many emphases, but it remains one spiritual body. The Church is one in the same way that the apostles were one (John 17:21-23).

The Holy Spirit is one. It is the Holy Spirit in the Church that gives it unity and makes it truly Christ's church. Furthermore, we come into the body of Christ by the drawing of the Holy Spirit. His regenerating and indwelling provide us the spiritual power to perform as Christ's body.

Believers in Christ are drawn together by a single hope—life in Jesus Christ. Hope in Christ is not wishful thinking, it is the active anticipation and pursuit of those promises that have been given by Him.

Three further unities in the Christian life are *one Lord, one faith, one baptism.* The "one Lord" is Christ. It is essential that we not only accept Christ as Savior from our sins but also as Lord of our lives, yielding to Him control, possession, and dominion over us. It is only when we receive Christ as Lord in this sense of ownership that we become fully integrated in Him (see Rom. 10:9; Acts 9:5-6).

Proceeding from "one Lord" is the virtue of "one faith." The reference is to faith in the lordship of Christ, which is the unifying foundation of the body of Christ. Those who do not accept the fundamental faith that He is Lord cannot be a part of His body. The "one faith" no doubt extends further to include "the faith which was once delivered unto the saints" (Jude 3).

The "one baptism" (Eph. 4:5) has reference to the new birth by which we are brought into the body of Christ and that is symbolized by the act of water baptism.

The ultimate unity is "*one God* and Father of all." It is interesting that "one Spirit" is mentioned in verse 4, "one Lord" in verse 5, and "one God and Father" in verse 6. This is seen as an unmistakable reference to the Trinity, moving forward from the third person, to the second person, to the first person—God the Father. That He is "above all" means He is absolute sovereign over all things. That He is "through all" means His

Talk About It:
1. Why does Paul repeatedly use the word *one* in verses 4-6?
2. How is God described in verse 6?

"God is in all things and in every place. . . . Just as birds, wherever they fly, always meet with the air, so we, wherever we go, or wherever we are, always find God present."
—**Francis de Sales**

presence penetrates and empowers the Church. That He is "in you all" means He abides in and with His people.

II. LIVE AS CHILDREN OF LIGHT (Eph. 4:17-24; 5:1-2, 8-11)

A. Not Like Others (4:17-24)

17. This I say therefore, and testify in the Lord, that ye henceforth walk not as other Gentiles walk, in the vanity of their mind,

18. Having the understanding darkened, being alienated from the life of God through the ignorance that is in them, because of the blindness of their heart:

19. Who being past feeling have given themselves over unto lasciviousness, to work all uncleanness with greediness.

20. But ye have not so learned Christ;

21. If so be that ye have heard him, and have been taught by him, as the truth is in Jesus:

22. That ye put off concerning the former conversation the old man, which is corrupt according to the deceitful lusts;

23. And be renewed in the spirit of your mind;

24. And that ye put on the new man, which after God is created in righteousness and true holiness.

Paul's personal and solemn appeal is precipitated by a strong conviction. His readers were to conduct themselves in such a way as to show the real difference that exists between them and their unbelieving neighbors. That would have been labeled a "holier-than-thou" attitude today. Not so with Paul. His readers were to dissociate completely from that former way of life which he goes on to describe. We sometimes wonder why what we would call a simple or basic truth of the Gospel remains incomprehensible to learned people. We feel that it is obvious enough for them to understand. Unfortunately it is not so, and Paul proffers some reasons. The Ephesians were previously like that. They walked in "the vanity of their mind"—that is, they were not able to recognize moral and spiritual truth. Their understanding was darkened and their minds were not illuminated by the Spirit of God. The Greeks, although cultured and refined in so many ways, were still guilty of callousness and lechery. Solon, the great lawgiver, made prostitution legal in Athens. They mixed religion and lust without blinking. It was in this moral atmosphere that Christianity grew and in which Paul's readers lived.

In verse 19, Paul continues his description of the vile, yet pitiable, condition of the Gentiles. They were so far removed from God, or any consciousness of Him, that they had lost all normal sense of right and wrong and had abandoned themselves to their sins. *Lasciviousness* means moral degeneracy, usually of a sexual nature, and *greediness* has to do with an inordinate desire for money. These two evils have ever plagued the world.

---

lasciviousness (v. 19)—"lewdness" (NKJV) IMPURE

greediness (v. 19)—"continual lust for more" (NIV)

conversation (v. 22)—"way of life" (NIV)

Talk About It:
1. According to verses 17 and 18, how must Christians "no longer live" (NIV)?
2. What does it mean to be "past feeling" (v. 19)?
3. Compare the "old man" with the "new man" (vv. 22-24).

Fulfilling God's Purpose

Against such a black backdrop of evil, the Ephesian Christians stood out in sharp relief, more notable because of the background from which they had come. They had "learned Christ" (v. 20), which means they had appropriated His grace and power to their lives and had followed His steps in their practices. The people had been "taught" by Jesus (v. 21), in the sense that He was the message that had been brought to them and His life was the lesson they had learned. The reference here is that of schooling, or learning, about Christ. Bear in mind that Jesus declared Himself to be "the way, the truth, and the life" (John 14:6), and that it was He who invited the people to "take my yoke upon you, and learn of me" (Matt. 11:29).

In verses 22-24 of the text, Paul asserts that the Ephesian Christians, and therefore all Christians, have had a total change in their lives. It is the putting off of past habits and attitudes, called "the old man," and the assuming of new attitudes and habits, called putting on "the new man." The *old man* and the *new man* are figures of speech to show how totally and dramatically a life is changed by Jesus Christ. The old man is pictured in verse 22 as being filled with corrupt and deceitful lusts. We also find references to the old man in Romans 6:6 and Colossians 3:9, both of which are references to the corrupt human nature that possesses all people before they come to Christ.

"God's work is not in buildings, but in transformed lives."
—Ruth Bell Graham

B. Followers of Christ (5:1-2, 8-11)
   1. Be ye therefore followers of God, as dear children;
   2. And walk in love, as Christ also hath loved us, and hath given himself for us an offering and a sacrifice to God for a sweetsmelling savour.
   8. For ye were sometimes darkness, but now are ye light in the Lord: walk as children of light:
   9. (For the fruit of the Spirit is in all goodness and righteousness and truth;)
   10. Proving what is acceptable unto the Lord.
   11. And have no fellowship with the unfruitful works of darkness, but rather reprove them.

sometimes (v. 8)—once

reprove (v. 11)—expose

Paul begins chapter 5 by appealing to the readers to be "followers of God." *Followers* is from the Greek word *mimetes*, which means "to imitate." Every occurrence of the word in the New Testament is in the context of moral living (*The Vocabulary of the Greek New Testament*, by Moulton and Milligan).

"As" indicates that what is to follow is the "characteristic quality" (*A Greek-English Lexicon of the New Testament*, by Bauer) of what it means to be a "follower of God." The primary trait of a follower of God is that he follows as a "dear child" would lovingly follow and obey his parents.

In verse 2, Paul extends his command to be followers of God with a command to "walk in love." The expanded translation of

Talk About It:
1. How will "followers of God" live (vv. 1-2)?
2. Why is Christ's death called "a sweet-smelling aroma" (v. 2 NKJV)?
3. What must believers "find out" (v. 10 NIV)?
4. What must believers avoid (v. 11)?

the opening phrase would be to "walk/conduct your lives in the sphere/realm of love." The Christian's life is to be lived within the boundaries of love.

The Christian's walk is to be conducted in comparison to the way in which Christ conducted Himself in the sphere of love. The action of Christ specified is the giving of Himself "for us an offering and a sacrifice to God for a sweetsmelling savour" (v. 2).

Paul's mention of being "darkness" or being "light" (v. 8) refers to the condition in which the believer once lived and should now live. *Darkness* refers to an immoral and obscure existence. *Light* was a term used by Paul and other religions of his day such as the gnostic cults. It referred to a lifestyle that receives the perception needed to master living. Existence in this sphere of living is marked by special insight into answers for the mysteries which often make life unbearable.

The phrase "in the Lord" is decisive to properly understanding what Paul means by "light." Unlike pagan sects which based their "light" on a variety of sources, Paul bases the "light" of the Christian "in the Lord." The Christian's light is within the power, authority, and origin of Christ. Being light is not a matter of theory but practice in living. This is why Paul exhorts at the end of verse 8, "Walk [live, conduct yourselves] as children of light."

The vast majority of ancient manuscripts of the New Testament translate the first part of verse 9, "fruit of the light." The word *for* indicates that what follows is the reason why the believer should "walk as children of light" (v. 8). They should do so because *the* Light, the Lord, exists in the midst of "all goodness, righteousness, and truth." There is no action in the midst of the Light that is not of these three characteristics. Therefore, Paul admonishes the believer to walk in a manner befitting the Lord, the Light.

Walking as children of light "[proves] what is acceptable unto the Lord" (v. 10). *Proving* means to receive something and then, by using it, find it to be of good quality. *Acceptable* indicates things that are of good pleasure to the Lord. When the Christian is obedient, he experiences ("proves") those things which are already of good pleasure to the Lord.

"And" at the beginning of verse 11 indicates that in addition to walking in the light (vv. 8-10), the believer is to reprove (expose) the works of darkness (vv. 11-13). These are coordinating activities that complement each other. Walking in the light indicates that the Christian must also reprove darkness, and reproving darkness must be accompanied by walking in the light.

Fellowship (v. 11) means "to be in common together with someone." In contrast to common association and bond with darkness, the believer is to "reprove" darkness. *Reprove* is from a Greek word which meant "to bring to light, to expose, to reveal hidden things, to convict or convince, to reprove, to correct, to punish, to discipline" (*Linguistic Key to the Greek New Testament*).

At the same time the Christian is walking in the light, that light exposes and passes judgment upon the works and character of darkness.

III. SUBMIT TO ONE ANOTHER (Eph. 5:21-33; 6:1-9)

A. A General Command (5:21)

21. Submitting yourselves one to another in the fear of God.

In an age of individualism, *submission* is not a well-received word. Yet, one of the far-reaching commands given by Paul is the need to submit to one another. The whole structure of society as ordered by God depends on the readiness of its members to recognize the importance of submission and practice it. The basic principle of Christian submissiveness that governs the community life of the church applies also to social relationships. Paul selects the most conspicuous of these relationships and shows how they are transformed when controlled by a prior obedience to Christ.

Talk About It:
Why should believers "submit to one another" (NIV)?

Paul begins the section with a general command, "Submit to one another out of reverence for Christ" (NIV). The key word *submit* (*hypotasso*) occurs twenty-three times in the Pauline corpus. It means to line oneself up under. Originally, it was used in a military sense of soldiers submitting to their superiors, or slaves submitting to their masters. The word conveys the idea of giving up one's own right or will; that is, to subordinate oneself to those considered worthy of respect, either because of their inherent qualities or the position they hold. Christians are to submit to civil authorities, church leaders, parents, and masters primarily out of "fear" for Christ (cf. v. 17). The word *fear* (*phobos*), as in the King James Version, does not mean a slavish fear. Rather, it connotes respect or reverence for someone. Moreover, within the fellowship of the church (and Paul has this more prominently in mind than the community at large), this submission to others is reciprocal. No one is to coerce another, for all voluntarily accept the discipline. Hence, any suggestions of superiority are banished.

Mutual or reciprocal submission is an important reality for the church if it is to function as it should. It is manifested in a variety of obedient expressions. Beginning in verse 22, Paul shifts to three specific social relationships and exhorts his readers to practice submission as an important aspect of Christianity. Paul focuses on relationships with spouses, children, and masters (or, more appropriately today, employers).

"Contemporary society . . . does not value personal submission. Rather, it teaches that the ideal, the highest position a human being can attain, is that of personal autonomy."
—**Stephen B. Clark**

B. Wives and Husbands (vv. 22-33)

22. Wives, submit yourselves unto your own husbands, as unto the Lord.

23. For the husband is the head of the wife, even as Christ is the head of the church: and he is the saviour of the body.

24. Therefore as the church is subject unto Christ, so let the wives be to their own husbands in every thing.

25. Husbands, love your wives, even as Christ also loved the church, and gave himself for it;

26. That he might sanctify and cleanse it with the washing of water by the word,

27. That he might present it to himself a glorious church, not having spot, or wrinkle, or any such thing; but that it should be holy and without blemish.

28. So ought men to love their wives as their own bodies. He that loveth his wife loveth himself.

29. For no man ever yet hated his own flesh; but nourisheth and cherisheth it, even as the Lord the church:

30. For we are members of his body, of his flesh, and of his bones.

31. For this cause shall a man leave his father and mother, and shall be joined unto his wife, and they two shall be one flesh.

32. This is a great mystery: but I speak concerning Christ and the church.

33. Nevertheless let every one of you in particular so love his wife even as himself; and the wife see that she reverence her husband.

Talk About It:
1. How are husbands compared with Christ (v. 23)?
2. Describe Christ's love for the Church (vv. 25-27).
3. How must husbands love their wives (vv. 28, 33)?
4. Describe the Church's relationship with the Lord (vv. 29-30).
5. What is the proper relationship between husband and wife (v. 31)?

Paul urges wives to submit to their own husbands "as unto the Lord" (v. 22). Two things are to be noted. First, Paul's exhortation is within the context of a Christian marriage. He does not suggest that women are inferior to men or that all women should be subject to all men. Second, the submission is voluntary, not forced. The Christian wife who submits does so because her vow is "as unto the Lord." Submission must never be confused with subjugation or subordination.

To strengthen his argument, Paul sets out the relationship between the husband and wife as being a reflection of the relationship between Christ and His church—Christ is the head of the Church as the husband is the head of the wife. The analogy raises marriage to a lofty level, something that we need to be reminded of today. Paul's primary concern was not to specify or go into details of what he meant by headship. Rather, the main issue here is that of "submission."

Paul then turns to the reciprocal duties of the husband. In Greco-Roman society, while it was recognized and accepted that wives had obligations to their husbands, there was none for the husband. In this, as in other areas, Christianity introduced

Fulfilling God's Purpose

a revolutionary approach to marriage that equalized the rights of wives and husbands, and established the institution on a firmer foundation than ever before. Although in context the word *submit* sums up the role of the wife (v. 22), and the word *love* (v. 25) does the same for the husband, the words are not to be understood as mutually exclusive; that is, that one operates or exists without the other.

In verse 25 Paul continues with his comparison between the marriage relationship and the relationship of Christ and the Church (cf. vv. 22-24). Christ gave Himself up for His bride. That was on the cross. The analogy is apt, since *ekklesia* (church) is feminine. The Lord's sacrificial death was "for her," that is, for the Church. Christ's atonement was "to make her holy" (v. 26 NIV) and "to present her to himself as a radiant church" (v. 27 NIV). To "sanctify" is not only to set apart, but also to make ethically holy. Christ's ultimate aim in giving Himself up for the Church was that at the end of the age He might be able to present her to Himself in unsullied splendor "as a bride adorned for her husband" (Rev. 21:2).

Christ loves the Church, not simply as if it *were* His body, but because it *is* His body. Husbands, therefore, are to "love their wives as their own bodies" (Eph. 5:28). So intimate is the relationship between man and wife that they are fused into a single entity. For a man to love his wife is to love himself. She is not to be treated as a piece of property, as was the custom in Paul's day. The wife is to be regarded as an extension of a husband's own personality and, so, part of himself. This is how Christ loves His body, the Church (v. 25). He cares for the Church because Christians are living parts of His body.

In verse 31, Paul introduces Genesis 2:24 to substantiate his argument from Scripture. The marriage tie takes precedence over every other human relationship and, for this reason, is to be regarded as inviolable. This divine ordinance is graciously designed for mutual satisfaction and delight. The word *joined* (literally, "will be glued") used in combination with *one flesh*, refers to sexual interaction, which is sanctioned by God within the marital context. It is because of this lofty view of marital relations that the Church has taken its stand on the indissolubility of the marital bond and the impermissibility of polygamy and adultery.

Paul concludes the section on a practical note. He addresses every husband individually (literally, "you each, one by one"). Every husband is to go on loving his wife as his very self (vv. 25, 28-29). The wife, for her part, is to give her husband the respect that is due him in the Lord (v. 22). As verse 21 has made plain, such respect is conditioned by and expressive of reverence for Christ. It also assumes that the husband will so love his wife as to be worthy of such deference.

"Marriage is never finished. The lesson is never learned. The effort is never at an end. Marriage, like life, is a matter of solving the little things. . . . It is a matter of surrendering small, personal preferences."
—Randolph Ray

C. Children and Parents (6:1-4)

1. Children, obey your parents in the Lord: for this is right.

2. Honour thy father and mother; which is the first commandment with promise;

3. That it may be well with thee, and thou mayest live long on the earth.

4. And, ye fathers, provoke not your children to wrath: but bring them up in the nurture and admonition of the Lord.

provoke . . . to wrath (v. 4)—exasperate

Talk About It:
1. What does it mean to obey one's parents "in the Lord" (v. 1)?
2. What does God promise obedient children (vv. 2-3)?
3. How are parents to rear their children (v. 4)?

The word *obey* (Greek, *hupakouo*) has in its background the idea of "listening" or "attending to," hence, obeying. It is a picture of a person submitting to the voice of authority. The phrase "in the Lord" defines the sphere of obedience and makes possible exception for children whose parents are not Christians and who sometimes are given commands that are in direct contradiction to God's words. Paul gives the reason why children are to obey their parents. It is right, and therefore it pleases the Lord (Col. 3:20). Children are also to "honor" their parents, says Paul. He clinches his argument by citing two quotations from the Old Testament (Ex. 20:12; Deut. 5:16)—the fifth commandment.

In Ephesians 6:4, Paul turns his attention to parents. In the Roman world, parents, particularly fathers, had absolute power over their children. But Paul places heavy responsibility on the parents. They must avoid exasperating their children by placing unnecessary or unreasonable demands on them. They must not arouse the bad passions of their children by severity, partiality, injustice, or inconsistency in their own lives. Parents are to bring children up in the "training and instruction of the Lord" (NIV) so they will fear Him.

D. Slaves and Masters (vv. 5-9)

5. Servants, be obedient to them that are your masters according to the flesh, with fear and trembling, in singleness of your heart, as unto Christ;

6. Not with eyeservice, as menpleasers; but as the servants of Christ, doing the will of God from the heart;

7. With good will doing service, as to the Lord, and not to men:

8. Knowing that whatsoever good thing any man doeth, the same shall he receive of the Lord, whether he be bond or free.

9. And, ye masters, do the same things unto them, forbearing threatening: knowing that your Master also is in heaven; neither is there respect of persons with him.

singleness (v. 5)—sincerity

Talk About It:
1. How should workers view their employers (v. 5)?
2. Why is "eyeservice" not acceptable (v. 6)?

Paul turns to one of the most serious social situations of his time. Paul lived in a world filled with slavery. Paul's injunction is neither a tacit approval of slavery nor a condemnation of the institution. It is based on the matter-of-fact recognition of the reality of the society in which Paul and the Christian communities

lived. Paul tells his readers that slaves are to obey their earthly masters. He uses the same word meaning "obey" that he used for children in the previous section. The obedience of the slave is to be expressed in three specific attitudes: deep respect, fear, and service with sincerity. Paul's exhortation gives us insight into how we should work for our employers and how our employers should treat their workers.

The Christian worker has a twofold responsibility as he or she obediently carries out an employer's expectations. First, we must work well at all times, regardless of whether we are being observed or not. Second, our service should be done wholeheartedly, as if serving the Lord. This may or may not result in promotion here on earth, but it will surely result in a reward from God.

Paul concludes the section with his appeal to masters to treat their slaves in the same way. He calls for reciprocity. The master is to treat his slaves as though he were serving the Lord. Slaves are not to be threatened. The Christian master must remember that God is both his Master and the Master of his slaves, and there is no partiality or favoritism with God.

In a day when productivity is valued above humanity, employers need to hear Paul speaking. No person is of such insignificance that he or she should be sacrificed by poor conditions, unfair practices, and low wages. The way Christian employers treat their workers should exemplify love for Christ.

3. Explain the promise in verses 7 and 8.
4. What instruction is given to bosses (v. 9)?

"When man loses the sacred significance of work and of himself as worker, he soon loses the sacred meaning of time and of life."
—Carl F. H. Henry

CONCLUSION

One saint of God remarked, "The true Christian life is not an isolated life. To always live alone, among divine and eternal things, is a false idea of moral and religious perfection." How true. Christianity is lived out in various settings and relationships. It is not enough to profess that we are Christians. We must live as Christians.

GOLDEN TEXT CHALLENGE

"BE YE THEREFORE FOLLOWERS OF GOD, AS DEAR CHILDREN; AND WALK IN LOVE, AS CHRIST ALSO HATH LOVED US, AND HATH GIVEN HIMSELF FOR US AN OFFERING AND A SACRIFICE TO GOD FOR A SWEET-SMELLING SAVOUR" (Eph. 5:1-2).

The word for *follow* means to "imitate" God—that is, "to act out in the same fashion." How do we mere mortals imitate God? We do so by learning of Christ and having Him live in our hearts by faith. This is the only time in the Bible that the phrase "followers of God" is used. But the Old Testament does refer to following the Lord. Markus Barth, in his commentary on Ephesians, writes, "The meaning of Ephesians 5:1 may be revealed by all those Old Testament passages that describe the Lord's holiness,

truth, righteousness, mercy, and that promise or command at the same time that holiness, faith, justice, charity are the proper response of God's covenant partner, the chosen people and each of its members" (*The Anchor Bible Series*, Vol. 34A).

This is why Ephesians 5:2 is so important. It shows exactly what it means to follow, or imitate, God. Christ is the only example. We are called to "walk in love, as Christ also hath loved us." The definition of Christian love leaves no room for guesswork. Christian love is concretely defined by the life of Jesus. His earthly ministry, recorded in the four Gospels, was the incarnate love of God.

His example is further illustrated in the fact that He "hath given himself for us an offering and a sacrifice to God." This clearly refers to His atoning death at Calvary. The two words *offering* and *sacrifice* are general terms referring to the practice of making sacrifices to God.

The reference to a "sweetsmelling savour" denotes the actual odor of the sacrifice entering into the presence of God. In the Old Testament sacrifices, the animal was consumed on the fire of the altar. It was totally given to God in accordance with His will and for His glory. The smell of this sacrifice permeated the air and was pleasing to God.

When we obey God and give gifts in His name, it is a form of contemporary sacrifice that rises to His nostrils and brings pleasure to Him.

Daily Devotions:
M. The Unity of God
   Deuteronomy 6:4-8
T. A Light to the
   Gentiles
   Isaiah 42:6-10
W. Christ's Kingdom
   of Light
   Isaiah 58:8-11
T. Jesus, Our
   Example of
   Submission
   Matthew 26:36-44
F. Submit to God
   James 4:7-10
S. Reign With God
   Forever
   Revelation 22:1-6

Experiencing the Resurrection (Easter)

Luke 24:13-35; John 20:1-18; 21:1-23

INTRODUCTION

The Gospel narratives are like a jigsaw puzzle with some pieces missing. Anyone who has tried to put such a jigsaw puzzle together knows that it cannot be done if one insists he has all the parts in his possession and is determined to make them fit. The procedure ends in total frustration. Once, however, the person admits that some parts are missing, he can fit the rest together successfully, even though there are gaps in the picture.

For reasons of His own, God has seen fit not to tell us everything that happened in the life of our Lord. If a person persists that he has all the parts within the four Gospels, and keeps on attempting to make a perfect and complete picture, he will surely become frustrated. If, however, he will face the fact that God has not given us all the parts, and will work from this assumption, he will be able to trace out the broad outlines and some details of Christ's life.

Henry Alford expressed the following conviction: "I believe much that is now dark might be explained were the facts themselves, in order of occurrence, before us. Till that is the case (and I am wiling to believe that it will be one of our delightful employments hereafter, to trace the true harmony of the Holy Gospels, under His teaching of whom they are the record), we must be content to walk by faith, and not by sight" (*The Greek Testament*).

Careful readers of the fourth Gospel are aware that John omits a great deal which the other three Gospels contain, and gives much which they omit. He does this in regard to the narrative of the Resurrection.

It would be a useful exercise each Easter for every Christian to read the complete account of the Resurrection in a harmony of the Gospels. Thus, we would all get all of the story which God has seen fit to leave us, in the sequence in which it occurred.

In today's lesson, drawing from accounts in Luke and John, we will see Mary Magdalene, Cleopas and his traveling companion, and Simon Peter have life-changing encounters with the risen Lord.

Unit Theme:
Easter

Central Truth:
Because Christ is alive, we can experience a personal relationship with the living Lord.

Focus:
Examine the effects of Christ's resurrection on those who witnessed it and experience its impact.

Context:
Three accounts of the resurrected Christ ministering to individuals

Golden Text:
"That I may know him [Christ], and the power of his resurrection, and the fellowship of his sufferings, being made conformable unto his death" (Phil. 3:10).

Study Outline:
I. Recognizing the Risen Christ (John 20:1, 11-18)
II. Relationship With the Risen Christ (Luke 24:13-18, 26-35)
III. Restored by the Risen Christ (John 21:1-2, 15-19)

I. RECOGNIZING THE RISEN CHRIST (John 20:1, 11-18)
A. Mary Magdalene's Discovery (v. 1)

1. The first day of the week cometh Mary Magdalene early, when it was yet dark, unto the sepulchre, and seeth the stone taken away from the sepulchre.

Talk About It:
Why did Mary come to the tomb so early?

The Synoptic Gospels (Matthew, Mark, and Luke) state that several women made an early Sunday morning visit to Christ's tomb for the purpose of anointing His body with spices (Matt. 28:1; Mark 16:1; Luke 24:1). John mentions only Mary Magdalene. However, as MacGregor says, "John, with his love of individualizing, mentions but one woman, but, as is hinted in the next verse ('we'), there may have been others with her" (*Moffatt's Commentary on John*).

The Jewish Sabbath ended at 6:00 p.m. on Saturday. Mary and her friends were at the tomb of Christ before daybreak. John says "early, when it was yet dark" (v. 1). The word refers to the last of the four watches into which the night was divided, the watch which lasted from 3:00 to 6:00 a.m.

The fact that the women went so early to the tomb is an indication of the way that love can conquer timidity and fear, and motivate one to action. Jenny Evelyn Mussey penetrated into the significance of this incident in the stanza, "Let me like Mary, through the gloom, come with a gift to Thee." It was not only gloom literally, but gloom also in Mary's soul, as of course in the souls of all the disciples. Her gloom was deepened when she found the tomb was empty. Without stopping to look inside the tomb with the other women (Mark 16:5-7; Luke 24:3-8), she at once turned and ran to tell Peter and John her own interpretation of what had happened: "They have taken away the Lord out of the sepulchre" (John 20:2).

> "With the stone in place, Mary would have had the problem of gaining access to the tomb; with the stone removed, she had a problem of another kind. To her mind, the situation had worsened."
> —*The Wycliffe Bible Commentary*

B. Mary's Sorrow (vv. 11-13)

11. But Mary stood without at the sepulchre weeping: and as she wept, she stooped down, and looked into the sepulchre,

12. And seeth two angels in white sitting, the one at the head, and the other at the feet, where the body of Jesus had lain.

13. And they say unto her, Woman, why weepest thou? She saith unto them, Because they have taken away my Lord, and I know not where they have laid him.

Talk About It:
Why was Mary crying?

John's record does not describe the reactions in Peter's mind to the staggering sight that confronted him in the tomb (vv. 6-7). Luke, however does so: "Then arose Peter, and ran unto the sepulchre; and stooping down, he beheld the linen clothes laid by themselves, and departed, wondering in himself at that which was come to pass" (Luke 24:12). His only reaction was wonder or amazement.

But let us now carefully notice the different reaction John had. Seeing, no doubt, the look of amazement on Peter's face, he also went into the tomb to see for himself, "and he saw, and believed" (John 20:8).

The question naturally arises, *Why was Mary not affected or influenced at all by the staggering discovery of Peter and John?* For this, it seems, was certainly the case. It may be that she was too full of her personal grief to understand what was happening. However, a simpler explanation, it seems, is that she was not present at the time. Mary had left the tomb on her first visit without seeing the "vision of angels" (Luke 24:23) which her women companions saw. She arrived back at the tomb only after Peter and John had left. And she was still ignorant of the truth. "She *continued standing* outside the sepulchre weeping" (John 20:11, Greek tense). The Greek word for *weeping* is a strong word implying audible crying—"sobbing, convulsed with tears."

It was her love for Christ that made Mary act like that, but it was love uninformed and unilluminated by the Truth. She was overwhelmed with her sense of personal loss. Jesus—though to her imagination, dead, stolen, vandalized—was still her "Lord," but she could not grasp that He was in the situation in which she imagined Him to be.

> "O for the touch of a vanished hand,
> And the sound of a voice that is still!"
> **—Alfred Lloyd Tennyson**

C. The Lord's Question (vv. 14-15)

14. And when she had thus said, she turned herself back, and saw Jesus standing, and knew not that it was Jesus.

15. Jesus saith unto her, Woman, why weepest thou? whom seekest thou? She, supposing him to be the gardener, saith unto him, Sir, if thou have borne him hence, tell me where thou hast laid him, and I will take him away.

The reason why Mary turned away from the angels is not obvious. There must have been a reason. After all, people do not see angels every day! But when she turned, she "saw Jesus standing, and knew not that it was Jesus" (v. 14). She was so dominated by the sense of personal loneliness and grief that though the Lord was present with her, and present in such a glorious manner, she failed to recognize Him.

Talk About It:
Why do you suppose Mary did not recognize Jesus?

Why did Mary suppose Jesus was the gardener? That was the obvious conclusion, for who else would be there that early? Oh, the suppositions that have been made by Christian people to account for happenings—both good and evil—in their lives, when all the time it was Jesus!

D. The Lord's Revelation (vv. 16-18)

16. Jesus saith unto her, Mary. She turned herself, and saith unto him, Rabboni; which is to say, Master.

17. Jesus saith unto her, Touch me not; for I am not yet ascended to my Father: but go to my brethren, and say

unto them, I ascend unto my Father, and your Father; and to my God, and your God.

18. Mary Magdalene came and told the disciples that she had seen the Lord, and that he had spoken these things unto her.

Talk About It:
1. What did Mary call Jesus, and why (v. 16)?
2. What message was Mary given to deliver (v. 17)?

MacGregor calls this "the greatest recognition scene in all literature. . . . The speaking of her own name by Jesus calls up memories and awakens recognition."

Cold print can never convey to us what the spoken word conveyed to Mary. But we can imagine it. If at any time we have waited long and anxiously for the return of a loved one, or for a message from that person, and suddenly, when the mind is heavy and the heart is sick, he or she arrives or calls, what a flood of relief and joy it brings! All that, and more, the familiar word spoken in a familiar way meant to Mary. And all recognition and all ecstasy were in her one-word reply, "Rabboni" (Master or Teacher)!

Christ's statement "Touch me not" (v. 17) is acknowledged by all commentators as difficult to understand, and there are several explanations. Jesus, a week or so later, invited Thomas to touch Him (v. 27). Even on the Resurrection Day, as Matthew records, the women "came and held him by the feet" (Matt. 28:9). It is said that clinging to the knees or feet was an ancient mode of worship. Why then was Mary forbidden to touch Him?

The forms of the Greek may hold the clue: it should be rendered, "Don't keep on holding Me or clinging to Me." Mary, in her relief and overwhelming gladness at seeing Jesus alive, and probably not even comprehending the nature of His resurrection, was attempting to cling to His body. She needed to learn that the Christ of resurrection life and glory was to be approached and contacted in a different way from the preresurrected Christ.

The form of the prohibition suggests that it is but temporary: "Touch me not; for I am not yet ascended to my Father" (John 20:17). When He has ascended, it would be possible to touch Him again! Nevertheless, it would not be a touching of His physical body but a touching through the Spirit.

"Enjoying God's immediate presence, face to face, is the Christian's anticipation."
—R. C. Sproul

Moreover, what Jesus said to Mary, He said on behalf of us all. We are to "walk by faith, not by sight [or by ear or by touch]" (2 Cor. 5:7). This is the nature of Christ's relationship to humanity and their relationship to Him in this age. What it will be in the glorified state is yet to be revealed.

II. RELATIONSHIP WITH THE RISEN CHRIST
(Luke 24:13-18, 26-35)
A. Two Men (vv. 13-16)

threescore furlongs (v. 13)—seven and a half miles

13. And, behold, two of them went that same day to a village called Emmaus, which was from Jerusalem about threescore furlongs.

14. And they talked together of all these things which had happened.

15. And it came to pass, that, while they communed together and reasoned, Jesus himself drew near, and went with them.

16. But their eyes were holden that they should not know him.

holden (v. 16)— "restrained" (NKJV)

Talk About It: What were the two travelers discussing (vv. 13-14)?

The two men featured in this passage were not from the eleven disciples, and not necessarily from the Seventy who had been sent forth. They were more likely from that wider circle of disciples who were now together at Jerusalem. The name of one of them is given, Cleopas (v. 18). The other remains unnamed, and speculation about who this person was has yielded no definite conclusion.

These men were from a village called Emmaus. It was located about six-and-a-half miles west/northwest from Jerusalem.

Walking along amid the beauties of nature is often a means of sorting out life's puzzles. But the experience of these two men illustrates that nature alone cannot possibly satisfy the heart that has lost its Christ. Into the sanctuary of creation, these wanderers take the recollection of the scenes they have witnessed and the reports they have heard about their Lord.

Apparently they discussed in great detail what had happened, what they had hoped for, and how this hope had slipped away from them. They reasoned together how things could be this way and what they could make of it. And as they were deep in conversation, the Lord, in the form of a common traveler, came up behind them and began to walk with them.

They did not recognize it was the Lord. They were still thinking of Him in terms of His death, so the reality of His resurrection had not dawned on them. Moreover, they had no thought that He would appear to them and join them in their journey. In this frame of mind, how could they recognize this traveler as the crucified One? It also appears that through some supernatural means they were not allowed to discover who He was. Brooke Westcott wrote: "It is vain to give any simply natural explanation of the failure of the disciples to recognize Christ. After the Resurrection He was known as He pleased, and not necessarily at once. . . . Till they who gazed upon Him were placed in something of spiritual harmony with the Lord, they could not recognize Him."

These two disciples show us what disciples love best to talk about when they are intimately together—their Lord. After all, the living Christ is always the third person in every Christian friendship. Another thought from this event is that Jesus is already near to us, even when we believe Him to be far away.

April 4, 2010

B. Jesus' Question (vv. 17-18)

17. And he said unto them, What manner of communications are these that ye have one to another, as ye walk, and are sad?

18. And the one of them, whose name was Cleopas, answering said unto him, Art thou only a stranger in Jerusalem, and hast not known the things which are come to pass there in these days?

Talk About It:
Why didn't Jesus reveal His identity at first (vv. 17-18)?

Jesus asked the two men what they were talking about and what had made them so sad. He desired to have them open up their heart to Him. What He already knew, He wished to hear from their own mouth. Then Jesus listened to them as they related what was on their heart. Cleopas sometimes spoke alone, at other times his companion spoke also, but together they told Him everything that lay so heavily upon the heart of both (vv. 19-24). What do you suppose were the emotions of Jesus as He listened to them? Perhaps He became silently displeased at their unbelief, but He must also have rejoiced at their love.

Apparently the two men thought Jesus a stranger who had been to Jerusalem to observe the Passover and was now headed home again (v. 18). They could not imagine that anyone could have been in Jerusalem for that purpose and not know what was going on. The news of the crucifixion of Jesus of Nazareth filled the whole capital as well as their own hearts, and how anyone could have missed it was beyond their comprehension.

If these two men could not imagine anyone not having knowledge of the events of the weekend, Jesus found it difficult to understand how they could be sad on such an occasion. This was not a day for sadness; it was a day for gladness. The greatest event in the history of the world had taken place, and these men did not comprehend its value and were therefore sad. Are we not guilty sometimes of forgetting the benefits God has made available to us? We sometimes carry burdens we should be letting Him carry. We sometimes dishonor Him through our lack of faith. We are not that different from these two men. Our Lord wants our full confidence, not for His sake but for ours.

> "There are no foolish questions and no man becomes a fool until he has stopped asking questions."
> —Charles Steinmetz

C. The Necessity (vv. 26-27)

26. Ought not Christ to have suffered these things, and to enter into his glory?

27. And beginning at Moses and all the prophets, he expounded unto them in all the scriptures the things concerning himself.

Talk About It:
What did Jesus explain?

Jesus would have the two disciples to understand that all these events were foretold. What they were offended by was inevitable. They would not have been in this state of confusion if they had given closer attention to what the prophets had said about the suffering Messiah. This suffering was necessary before the Lord should enter into His glory.

Experiencing the Resurrection

These men did not understand the connection between suffering and glory for Christ and the Christian. Suffering prepares the way for glory, suffering is transformed into glory, and suffering endured heightens the enjoyment and the worth of glory.

Verse 27 says Jesus began with Moses (the Pentateuch) and went on to the Prophets to explain what they had to say about His person and His work. We are not told what passages He used. However there are many expressions of Jesus and the apostles in reference to the prophecies of the Messiah contained in the New Testament. Rather than presenting isolated passages of Scripture, it is likely that Jesus gave an overview of the great whole of the Old Testament in its typical and symbolical character. After all, Christ is the central theme of the entire Bible. We have missed its main message if we fail to find Him in its pages.

The appearance before these disciples is one of the strongest proofs of the high value which the Lord Jesus places upon the prophetic scriptures, and upon the predictions of His suffering and of His glory. Whoever denies either the existence or the importance of these passages finds himself not only in conflict with the believing church of all centuries but also with the Lord himself.

D. Opened Eyes (vv. 28-32)

28. And they drew nigh unto the village, whither they went: and he made as though he would have gone further.

29. But they constrained him, saying, Abide with us: for it is toward evening, and the day is far spent. And he went in to tarry with them.

30. And it came to pass, as he sat at meat with them, he took bread, and blessed it, and brake, and gave to them.

31. And their eyes were opened, and they knew him; and he vanished out of their sight.

32. And they said one to another, Did not our heart burn within us, while he talked with us by the way, and while he opened to us the scriptures?

When Jesus and the two men arrived in Emmaus, He offered to continue on, but they insisted that He stay with them. Jesus probably offered the usual formula of benediction, but already they felt so close to Him that the thought of separation at this point was unendurable. They entreated Him with the utmost urgency; they invited Him in and reminded Him that the sun was about to set and that He could not possibly continue His journey in the night.

Jesus accepted their invitation and entered the house with them. When the meal was ready, they gathered at the table. Jesus took the bread, gave thanks to God before the meal, broke the bread, and gave it to the two men. It was not customary for the guests to break the bread and bless it, for this

Talk About It:
1. What caused the two men to recognize Jesus (vv. 30-31)?
2. Explain the phrase "burn within us" (v. 32).

was the responsibility of the head of the house. There was, however, purpose in what Jesus was doing.

Do you think there was something in the manner in which Jesus broke the bread and uttered the blessing that caused them to associate it with their earlier acquaintance with Him? Or did they now discover in His opened hands the marks of the wounds? Did He refer them back to a word He had uttered before His death? Whatever the reason, their eyes were now opened. Suddenly, they were fully persuaded that the identity of this person was Jesus of Nazareth. By the time they recognized Him, Jesus had miraculously disappeared from sight.

After Jesus' departure, the two men discussed how they had felt as He spoke to them along the way. They had experienced an extraordinary emotion of soul as they listened to Him. Even by that experience they should have recognized the Lord. It was now incomprehensible to them that their eyes were not opened sooner. It speaks well for their inner growth that after His departure, it was not the breaking of bread but the opening of Scripture which stood out in their minds.

> "To know the road ahead, ask those coming back."
> —*Chinese proverb*

E. Eager Witness (vv. 33-35)

33. And they rose up the same hour, and returned to Jerusalem, and found the eleven gathered together, and them that were with them,

34. Saying, The Lord is risen indeed, and hath appeared to Simon.

35. And they told what things were done in the way, and how he was known of them in breaking of bread.

Talk About It:
How did Christ's appearance affect the two men?

One of the arguments these men had used to persuade Jesus to stay at their house was that it was too late to travel. Well, it was later now than it was then. But this did not matter to these excited disciples. Even if it was midnight, they must return immediately to Jerusalem and announce the joyful message. What the women did at the express command of the angel, what Mary Magdalene did at the command of the Lord, these two disciples did at the impulse of their heart. Apparently they also left the meal untouched, and together they went to tell what had happened.

When they arrived at Jerusalem, they went to the place where the other disciples were staying. Even at this late hour, they were admitted to the company of believers. They were also greeted with some exciting news: "The Lord is risen indeed, and hath appeared to Simon." They answered this message with the narrative of what happened to them on the way and how the Lord had been recognized by them in the breaking of bread.

The attitude of these two men demonstrates that Christ is our life. How miserable life would be without Him, how rich and rewarding it can become through Him, and how yielded it must be to Him!

Experiencing the Resurrection

III. RESTORED BY THE RISEN CHRIST (John 21:1-2, 15-19)
A. Seaside Appearance (vv. 1-2)

1. After these things Jesus shewed himself again to the disciples at the sea of Tiberias; and on this wise shewed he himself.

2. There were together Simon Peter, and Thomas called Didymus, and Nathanael of Cana in Galilee, and the sons of Zebedee, and two other of his disciples.

Tiberias (v. 1)—another name for the Sea of Galilee

The phrase "after these things" (v. 1) usually marks off a distinct section in John's Gospel. It may or may not have any direct connection with what immediately precedes. The verb used here to describe Christ's appearance to the disciples is active in form and marks His appearance as depending on His own will. The manifestation took place somewhere near the Sea of Tiberias (or Sea of Galilee). The details of the revelation are recorded in the verses that follow. It is interesting that Matthew records only the appearances in Galilee; Luke and Mark, only those in Jerusalem; while John records some of both.

Talk About It:
What did Jesus do "again," and why?

At the familiar location on the shore of the Galilean lake, with its many memories, the risen Christ appeared to a group of seven disciples. Since *seven* seems to be the number of divine completeness, the revelation here may have special significance. Simon Peter is well known as the spokesman for the apostles. Thomas, the onetime skeptic but now a true believer, is given special mention. Nathanael was the guileless Israelite (John 1:47). The sons of Zebedee are, of course, James and John, perhaps left unnamed and placed in this order out of modesty on the part of the author. The "two other of his disciples" (v. 2) may have been Andrew and Philip, but more likely they were not of the apostles but were, rather, as G. Campbell Morgan says, "the representatives of the great anonymous crowd in the Christian church, which constitutes here real strength."

"Christians! Dry your
  flowing tears,
Chase those unbe-
  lieving fears;
Look on his deserted
  grave,
Doubt no more his
  power to save."
—**Collyer**

B. Probing Question (vv. 15-17)

15. So when they had dined, Jesus saith to Simon Peter, Simon, son of Jonas, lovest thou me more than these? He saith unto him, Yea, Lord; thou knowest that I love thee. He saith unto him, Feed my lambs.

16. He saith to him again the second time, Simon, son of Jonas, lovest thou me? He saith unto him, Yea, Lord; thou knowest that I love thee. He saith unto him, Feed my sheep.

17. He saith unto him the third time, Simon, son of Jonas, lovest thou me? Peter was grieved because he said unto him the third time, Lovest thou me? And he said unto him, Lord, thou knowest all things; thou knowest that I love thee. Jesus saith unto him, Feed my sheep.

Talk About It:
1. What "grieved" Peter (v. 17)?
2. What did Jesus tell Peter to do (vv. 15-17)?

After serving breakfast to the seven disciples, the Lord turned to the more serious business of probing Peter about his love for the Lord. Addressing him as "Simon, son of Jonas," Jesus recalled the examination given at their first meeting when the disciple had been addressed in like manner (Matt. 16:17-19).

The question "Lovest thou me more than these?" (John 21:15) has more than one possible meaning: (1) Do you love Me more than these other disciples love Me? (2) Do you love Me more than you love these things? or (3) Do you love Me more than you love these disciples? The first accords with Peter's previous boast of loyalty to Christ though all others would be offended (Matt. 26:33; John 13:37). It may then have been a painful reminder of his threefold denial, and provided the opportunity for a complete repentance and restoration by a threefold affirmation of love. By the word Jesus uses for *love* (*agape*), He questions Peter's loyalty and devotion. In response, Peter appeals to Jesus' knowledge and uses another word for *love* (*phileo*) meaning "personal and natural affection." He makes no claim here of any superior love, and offers no comparison of his loyalty with that of his fellow disciples.

Jesus' commission is correctly rendered, "Tend my lambs." This suggests the shepherd's responsibility for giving tender care and support to children and young Christians, and for providing spiritual food for them. Christ apparently accepted Peter's answer and renewed His commission.

In the second question Jesus omits the words "more than these" (v. 15), but makes use of the same word for *love* (v. 16), that is, "Do you very deeply love Me?" It is the love with understanding, and as required by the Law (Luke 10:27). Peter again responds with the word for personal and natural affection. His appeal to Jesus' knowledge indicates both humility and confidence united. Jesus again commands Peter to discharge his shepherd responsibility. He is called upon to shepherd the sheep. And this implies providing guidance and government as well as food. Peter would soon be doing this under the Chief Shepherd's direction.

For the third time Jesus probes Peter's love for Him. This time, however, the Lord condescends to use Peter's word for *love*. This is probably why Peter is "grieved" (John 21:17). Then, too, perhaps Peter would recall his threefold denial, an experience which would aggravate his grief still more. In his answer to the Lord, Peter casts himself entirely on the omniscience of Christ. He is certain that the Lord can read his heart and thus know even better than Peter himself the love in his heart.

The three verses just considered show that Peter used two different words in the original to express the knowledge of Christ. The two indicate supernatural intuition as well as to refer to

experience and discernment. Again, Jesus commands His apostle to feed or tend His sheep. Note that each time Jesus refers to these sheep as His own ("my sheep"), not Peter's. Thus, under-shepherds are the stewards of the Christians entrusted to them by the Chief Shepherd. No one is qualified as a spiritual shepherd who does not sincerely love the Lord Jesus Christ.

> "God created you for a reason; He has important work for you to do; and He's waiting patiently for you to do it. So why not begin today?"
> **—Woodrow Kroll**

C. Sobering Future (vv. 18-19)

18. Verily, verily, I say unto thee, When thou wast young, thou girdest thyself, and walkedst whither thou wouldest: but when thou shalt be old, thou shalt stretch forth thy hands, and another shall gird thee, and carry thee whither thou wouldest not.

19. This spake he, signifying by what death he should glorify God. And when he had spoken this, he saith unto him, Follow me.

In assigning to Peter his occupation as a shepherd of His sheep, Jesus made a prediction concerning the future. The apostle's love for the Lord and his responsibility as preacher and pastor would not exempt him from persecution in due time. The double *verily* introduces some solemn words. First, Jesus recalls for him his younger days, when he was alert, vigorous, independent, self-willed, and able to manage his own affairs. After meeting the Lord, however, Peter had learned dependence through some difficult experiences. As for the future, in later years, Peter would be compelled to stretch out his hands for help. Another would "gird" him (v. 18)—that is, bind him as a criminal and he would be taken against his will—not that he would be unwilling to die a martyr's death, but a violent execution as a criminal is what any man would naturally shrink from.

Talk About It:
1. What did Jesus prophesy about Peter (vv. 18-19)?
2. Why do you suppose Jesus said, "Follow me" (v. 19; also see Matt. 4:18-19)?

Since Peter's death would occur as a result of his obedience to the Lord, it was spoken of as glorifying God. Having predicted His apostle's persecution, Jesus exhorts him to "follow me" (v. 19). Although this exhortation might simply mean to follow Jesus on the seashore, its spiritual significance may be implied, especially in the light of its repetition in verse 22.

Jesus' personal examination of the apostle Peter, following the breakfast on the beach, served to restore him to full favor and fellowship with the Lord and to emphasize the motive and duty of Christian service. It is only those who truly love Christ that are fit to minister to His flock. After this important lesson, Christ exhorts Peter on the importance of personal responsibility on the part of a disciple—to follow Christ. To follow Christ is to have complete confidence in Him, to imitate Him as our example, to learn from Him whose yoke is easy and whose burden is light (Matt. 11:29-30), to obey His every command, and to suffer in fellowship with Him.

God's Purpose
God intends to use you in wonderful, unexpected ways *if* you let Him. But be prepared: finding God's purpose and following it will undoubtedly require work and sacrifice—which is perfectly okay with God (because He knows the marvelous blessings that He has in store for you *if* you give yourself to Him).
—Woodrow Kroll

CONCLUSION

Just as the risen Lord ministered to the believers in today's lesson in personalized ways, so He reaches out His scarred hands to each one of us at our point of need. Do we recognize Him? Do we have relationship with Him? Have we been restored by Him?

GOLDEN TEXT CHALLENGE

"THAT I MAY KNOW HIM [CHRIST], AND THE POWER OF HIS RESURRECTION, AND THE FELLOWSHIP OF HIS SUFFERINGS, BEING MADE CONFORMABLE UNTO HIS DEATH" (Phil. 3:10).

Suppose that fifteen years ago you deposited one thousand dollars in the bank. From that time you began withdrawing fifty dollars a month on that account, and are still doing so. But is such a thing possible? No, because you would have overdrawn the account years ago.

For this same reason, many Christians, spiritually speaking, are operating in the red. Years ago they received Christ into their heart. But all these years, they been drawing on a beginner's experience. Instead of reading the Bible each morning for a new deposit in their soul's resources, they hurriedly eat breakfast and rush off to work, utterly unprepared to face the problems of the day.

On the other hand, I read of a man whose motto was, "No Bible; no breakfast." Like that man we should spend time every day with the Word and in prayer with the Lord. This is essential if we are to know Christ experientially.

Paul gave three essentials of how we may know Christ experientially. First, we must know "the power of [Christ's] resurrection." Only when the believer makes a complete commitment of his life to the will of God can he know this miraculous power. Second, we must know "the fellowship of [Christ's] sufferings." Complete submission to Christ does not exclude suffering. But the suffering we know is as nothing when compared with our future glory in Christ. Third, we must be "made conformable unto [Christ's] death." To live victoriously requires a daily crucifixion of oneself with Christ.

Be Strong in the Lord

Ephesians 6:10-20

INTRODUCTION

In his book *Fuzzy Memories*, Jack Handey writes, "There used to be this bully who would demand my lunch money every day. Since I was smaller, I would give it to him. Then I decided to fight back. I started taking karate lessons, but the instructor wanted five dollars a lesson. That was a lot of money. I found that it was cheaper to pay the bully, so I gave up karate."

Does this sound familiar? Today, too many Christians believe it is easier to pay the bully—Satan—than learn how to defeat him.

Ephesians 6:10-20 is perhaps the clearest definition of spiritual warfare in the New Testament. It is a call to arms. Christians are in a battle against opponents that are far greater and stronger than themselves. This passage not only assures us that there is a spiritual war, but that, apart from utilizing the weapons God has provided for us, we are hopelessly underpowered. If we plan to win the battle, we must rely on provisions and resources beyond human capabilities. This passage tells us what our divine weapons are. Beyond this, these weapons imply the nature of the struggle we are in. The weapons God has provided for us repel the attacks of Satan, thus we can learn a great deal about the nature of Satan's opposition from simply considering each of the weapons at our disposal.

Ron Phillips writes:

Satan comes at us directly—through the world system in which we live and through our flesh. With God's armor we can fend off the attack of our Enemy:

- With our belt and breastplate we have integrity and identity in Christ. Satan cannot attack our character.
- With our shoes and shield we have balance and belief. Satan cannot penetrate our commitment.
- With our helmet we have assurance and anticipation of the good things of God. Satan cannot destroy our confidence.

James 4:7 tells us, "Resist the devil and he will flee from you." Defensive weapons can hold off Satan, but only offensive weapons can cause him to flee! God has supplied just such a weapon in the sword of the Spirit.

Unit Theme:
Ephesians: Understanding God's Eternal Purposes

Central Truth:
Christians are victorious in spiritual conflict when they pray and rely on God's power.

Focus:
Realize that strength in spiritual conflict comes through Christ and be strong in Him.

Context:
Paul wrote his letter to the Ephesians from a Roman prison between AD 60 and 63.

Golden Text:
"Be strong in the Lord, and in the power of his might" (Eph. 6:10).

Study Outline:
I. Know Your Enemy (Eph. 6:10-12)
II. Dress for Battle (Eph. 6:13-17)
III. Pray Without Ceasing (Eph. 6:18-20)

I. KNOW YOUR ENEMY (Eph. 6:10-12)

A. A Wily Enemy (vv. 10-11)

10. Finally, my brethren, be strong in the Lord, and in the power of his might.

11. Put on the whole armour of God, that ye may be able to stand against the wiles of the devil.

Talk About It:
1. Describe the Christian's strength (v. 10).
2. What is the purpose of "the devil's schemes" (v. 11 NIV)?

Proper preparation is key to prosecuting a successful war. One aspect of preparation is to know the Enemy's capabilities and limitations. Paul describes the devil as a wily enemy. The word *wiles* indicates trickery, cunning, and deception. The devil attacks believers at their most vulnerable point and often pretends that he is a friend, not the devil (2 Cor. 11:14).

To begin their spiritual battle, the Ephesians must recognize the need for strength beyond their own. An assured sense of victory must not be used as an excuse for inaction. One cannot speak of winning the victory where there is never a fight.

The phrase "power of his might" (Eph. 6:10) brings together again words for *power* previously used in 1:19 and 3:16-21. The Ephesians would have understood the implications. The same power that raised Jesus from the dead (1:20) and brought them to life when they were "dead in trespasses and sins" (2:1) is now available to them for spiritual warfare. There can be no doubt about its adequacy. Believers are to clothe themselves with the armor that only God provides. It is a complete outfit because the soldier must be fully protected.

"A person who accepts Christ as Lord is initiated into His victory. In this fierce and terrible ware, we are in the winning position."
—Ron Phillips

B. A Spiritual Struggle (v. 12)

12. For we wrestle not against flesh and blood, but against principalities, against powers, against the rulers of the darkness of this world, against spiritual wickedness in high places.

Talk About It:
Describe the battle-front of Christians.

Paul does not call the believer to enter into spiritual warfare. He simply announces it as a fact. The fact that our real battle is not against flesh and blood is lost on many Christians, who put all their efforts in that direction. Paul's idea here is much the same as in 2 Corinthians 10:3: "For though we walk in the flesh, we do not war according to the flesh" (NKJV). It is irrelevant if the particular opponent we face is a principality, a power, or a ruler of the darkness of this age. Collectively, they are all members of spiritual hosts of wickedness in the heavenly places. They are all part of a spiritual army that is organized and established into ranks under the headship of Satan, who comes against us with his wiles. These are not just "the world of axioms and principles of politics and religion, of economics and society, of morals and biology, of history and culture," as one scholar wrote. Such view is reflective of people in the Western hemisphere who downplay the existence of real evil forces that wreak havoc in the world. Paul believed in the personal character of the powers of evil in the universe.

The wording of verse 12 indicates a continuing struggle. To *wrestle* means to come into hand-to-hand conflict, usually extended over a period of time. There is never a time we can feel that the problem of spiritual warfare has been won once and for all.

II. DRESS FOR BATTLE (Eph. 6:13-17)
A. Take a Stand (vv. 13-14a)

13. Wherefore take unto you the whole armour of God, that ye may be able to withstand in the evil day, and having done all, to stand.

14a. Stand therefore.

Paul's use of "wherefore" (v. 13) is a way of catching up and applying what he has previously said. Christians must recognize the power of their enemies and, as a result, dress for battle. The exhortation to "stand" repeats the emphasis in verse 11 on the need for immovable steadfastness in the face of a ruthless foe. In verse 13, Paul talks about standing firm in the midst of battle. By keeping themselves strong in the Lord, that is, equipping themselves with God's armor, Christians can successfully win the fight against the forces of evil.

The command to "stand therefore . . ." (v. 14) teaches that the Christians are not to be dressed for battle and then sit at home cowering away from the conflict. We are not to spend our time preparing for battle—praying, worshiping, studying God's Word, and so on—and then be absent when the call to arms is sounded. Paul's command is a military charge to be about the work of a soldier.

B. Truth and Righteousness (v. 14b)

14b. Having your loins girt about with truth, and having on the breastplate of righteousness.

Paul lists several items of the soldier's armor in the order in which they would be put on. Together they comprise the *panoplia* worn before taking the field. With the free-flowing garments of the East, the first thing a soldier would do was to fasten the belt about the waist. The belt gathered in the tunic and helped steady the breastplate when the latter was fitted on. It not only provided uninhibited movement for the soldier but also provided support for the loins and abdominal region which endured great stress in marching and combat. In addition, the belt was a means of carrying a sword. From the belt hung the scabbard in which the sword was sheathed. The belt tied tightly around the waist indicated that the soldier was prepared for action. To slacken the belt was to go off duty.

The "breastplate" covered the body from the neck to the thighs. Polybius, an authority in war tactics who lived between 201 and 120 BC, tells us it was known as a heart-protector. Usually it was made of bronze, but the more affluent officers wore a coat of

"Spears, swords, bows, and battering rams may be adequate in a war of the flesh; but in a war of the spirit, when the foe is formidable, greater weapons must be found."
—David Griffis

Talk About It:
What is the individual's responsibility in spiritual warfare?

Talk About It:
1. How do we put on truth?
2. Where does righteousness come from?

Talk About It:
1. What is "the gospel of peace" (v. 15)?
2. What can faith accomplish (v. 16)?

chain mail. The front piece was strictly the breastplate, but a back piece was commonly worn as well. In Isaiah 59:17 we are told that the Lord himself puts on righteousness like a breastplate. The Christian's "breastplate of righteousness" stands for uprightness and integrity of character. This moral rectitude and reputation for fair dealing results directly from the appropriation of Christ's righteousness. The Christian's protection is not to be sought in any works of his own, but only in what Christ has done for him and in him.

C. The Good News and Faith (vv. 15-16)

15. And your feet shod with the preparation of the gospel of peace;

16. Above all, taking the shield of faith, wherewith ye shall be able to quench all the fiery darts of the wicked.

Once the breastplate has been fitted into position, the soldier puts on his strong army boots. Josephus, the Jewish historian, described them as "shoes thickly studded with sharp nails" so as to ensure a good grip. The military successes both of Alexander the Great and of Julius Caesar were due, in large measure, to their armies' being well shod, thus able to undertake long marches at incredible speed over rough terrain. The Christian soldier must have the protection and mobility that come with having their feet "fitted with the readiness that comes from the gospel of peace" (NIV). Paul is alluding to Isaiah 52:7: "How beautiful on the mountains are the feet of those who bring good news" (NIV). The good news Isaiah is talking about is the deliverance of Israel from exile. The good news we proclaim is the salvation message of Jesus Christ. Paul refers to the same passage in Romans 10:15. His point is that people of this world will never be changed from their sinful lives unless they hear the message.

"Above all," or "in addition to all this," the Christian soldier is to "take up the shield of faith" (NIV). The shield refers to the large oblong or oval *scutum* the Roman soldier held in front of him for protection. It consisted of two layers of wood glued together, covered with linen and hide, and bound with iron. Soldiers often fought side by side with a solid wall of shields. But even a single-handed combatant found himself sufficiently protected. For the Christian this protective shield is faith, both in action and in its objective content. With such a shield, the believer can extinguish all the incendiary devices flung by the devil. The Christian's shield effectively counteracts the danger of such diabolical missiles, not merely by arresting or deflecting them, but by actually quenching the flames to prevent them from spreading.

Just as the embracing of truth is the foundation of all our effectiveness for Christ, the beholding of faith is the primary requisite for our life in Him. This is that saving faith without which it is impossible to please God (Heb. 11:6). We must believe in

all circumstances that He is, and that He is a rewarder of those who diligently seek Him. A person of steadfast conviction will not be overwhelmed by any adversity that surrounds him. When we know who we are and for what we stand, and when we know that God is faithful and His Word is true, then we can withstand anything the devil may bring against us.

D. Salvation and the Word (v. 17)

17. And take the helmet of salvation, and the sword of the Spirit, which is the word of God.

Two more items of the panoply remain. The shield has to be fixed in place before the helmet, since the handle could not pass over it. The helmet was made of bronze with leather attachments. In 1 Thessalonians 5:8, the helmet is identified with the hope of full salvation. In Isaiah 59:17, Yahweh wears the "helmet of salvation" along with the breastplate of righteousness. The Christian shares the divine equipment. It is important to note that the word *take* means "receive" or "accept." The previous elements of the armor were laid out for the soldier to pick up. The helmet and sword would be handed to him by an attendant or by his armorbearer. As Joseph Beet notes, it is "a present deliverance from sin to be consummated in eternity by complete deliverance."

The final weapon is the sword, for there is no mention of the spear which was the regular offensive armament of the Roman foot soldier. Instead, Paul focuses on the short, two-edged, cut-and-thrust sword wielded by the heavily armed legionary. The Christian's only weapon of offense is "the sword of the Spirit." "The word of God" (*rhema Theou*) is the divine utterance or speech, and not the usual expression "word of God" (*ho logos tou Theou*). In Isaiah 11:4, the Messiah is portrayed as One who strikes the ruthless with the rod of His mouth, that is, by the authoritative impact of what He says. Elsewhere in Scripture, speech is compared to a sword. But what is this "word of God"? Many think it is "the gospel" (Eph. 6:15), which is "the power of God" (Rom. 1:16). Others regard it as words given by the Holy Spirit to meet the critical need of the moment, or as prayer in which the Spirit speaks through the Christian (Eph. 6:18). It is significant that, in Matthew's temptation narrative, Jesus himself (quoting Deut. 8:3) refers to "every word [*rhema*] that comes from the mouth of God" (Matt. 4:4 NIV) and employs relevant scriptures to defeat the devil's stratagems.

Talk About It:
Why is God's Word called "the sword of the Spirit" (also see Heb. 4:12)?

III. PRAY WITHOUT CEASING (Eph. 6:18-20)

A. Spiritual Prayer (v. 18)

18. Praying always with all prayer and supplication in the Spirit, and watching thereunto with all perseverance and supplication for all saints.

supplication (v. 18)— "petition" (NASB)

Prayer is not included among the weapons wielded by the Christian combatant. However, Paul is still concerned with the Christian's victory in struggle. So praying is connected with all the preceding commands. It has been said that "a prayerless Christian is a powerless Christian." Christians can stand firm and true, successfully resisting all enemies and spiritual foes, only as they remain in the spirit of prayer. Christians must pray "always," or "on all occasions," suggesting that Christians must pray in preparation for the battle as well as during the engagement itself.

Some people err in placing confines on prayer. Some reserve prayer only for times of trial and need. For others, prayer is an action to be observed in the worship service on Sunday and other appointed times. We must not allow prayer to slip away from us either because of adversity or prosperity. The adage is still relevant, "Whenever you find it hardest to pray, pray your hardest!" In 1 Thessalonians 5:17, Paul exhorts believers, "Pray without ceasing."

Christians must also "pray in the Spirit" (Eph. 6:18 NIV). The phrase "in the Spirit" could mean "in communion with the Spirit" or "in the power of the Spirit." Pentecostals also understand it as a reference to praying in unknown tongues. Every avenue of praying is to be thoroughly explored. We are to pray with all kinds of prayer. God is a God of variety. We must not limit the expression of prayer to a particular style or approach, but must always pray in agreement with God's Word. Praying must include watchfulness. Christians must be vigilant in prayer and not allow themselves to become listless.

"Prayer is the key of the morning and the bolt of the evening."
—**Matthew Henry**

B. Specific Prayer (vv. 19-20)

19. And for me, that utterance may be given unto me, that I may open my mouth boldly, to make known the mystery of the gospel,

20. For which I am an ambassador in bonds: that therein I may speak boldly, as I ought to speak.

Paul asked his readers to remember him in their prayers. Paul realized his dependency on the intercession of his friends for the furtherance and ability of ministry, despite his apostolic calling. Unlike many preachers and Christian leaders who talk, act, and think as if they are self-sufficient, Paul realized his weakness and potential for failure without the intercession of others. He acknowledged that he was counting on the prayers of the church so he might boldly proclaim "the mystery of the gospel." He knew it was only through what God himself supplied that he would be able to fulfill his role. If it was true for Paul, how much more so for us!

Verse 20 repeats Paul's request for boldness, but he introduces himself in an unusual manner. Paul was a prisoner because of his faithfulness in preaching the Gospel, so he calls himself

"an ambassador in chains" (NIV). What a paradox! Paul is an ambassador on behalf of Christ, yet he is in chains. Ambassadors normally enjoyed diplomatic immunity, but Paul would be compelled to appear in the imperial court as a prisoner. Instead of wearing a golden chain of office around his neck, he was probably shackled to his guard or a soldier in military custody (see Acts 28:20; 2 Tim. 1:16). Paul is not seeking sympathy. All he desires is the prayer of the saints in order to be able to speak boldly what he knows he ought to speak.

CONCLUSION

As Christians, we must never lose sight of the distinctive nature of our calling as members of the Church in the world. We are engaged in spiritual warfare, and we need to be courageous and prayerful as we face a formidable foe. Yet we can maintain a sense of security and confidence, because Christ's strength and God's full armor are ours to draw upon and use.

GOLDEN TEXT CHALLENGE

"BE STRONG IN THE LORD, AND IN THE POWER OF HIS MIGHT" (Eph. 6:10).

"Be strong" is from a Greek word which literally means "be equipped with strength." Paul is saying, "Be clothed in the strength of the Lord." The emphasis is on the Lord's sufficiency. The Lord is to dominate the Christian so the Christian is "in the Lord."

The word translated as "power" is from the Greek *kratos*, which is power that is effective rather than theoretical. It is power that is able to accomplish the goal. The goal here is overcoming Satan.

The source of the Christian's power is Christ. The believer can defeat the devil only through Christ's power.

> "Satan trembles when he sees The weakest saint upon his knees."
> —**Anonymous**

Daily Devotions:
M. God Is My Defense
   Psalm 62:1-12
T. Receiving Power From God
   Isaiah 40:28-31
W. Receiving Power From the Spirit
   John 7:37-40
T. Receiving Power From Christ
   John 14:11-18
F. More Than Conquerors
   Romans 8:31-39
S. Be Strong in Christ
   2 Timothy 2:1-7

A Receptive Heart

Mark 10:13-27; Luke 8:4-15

INTRODUCTION

W. E. Vine says "the heart, the chief organ of physical life . . . occupies the most important place in the human system. By an easy transition the word came to stand for man's entire mental and moral activity, both the rational and the emotional elements. In other words, the heart is used figuratively for the hidden springs of the personal life" (*Vine's Expository Dictionary of New Testament Words*).

"The Bible describes human depravity as in the 'heart,' because sin is a principle which has its seat in the center of man's inward life, and then will 'defile' the whole circuit of his action (Matt. 15:19-20). On the other hand, Scripture regards the heart as the sphere of divine influence (Rom. 2:15; Acts 15:9). . . . The heart, as lying deep within, contains 'the hidden man' (1 Peter 3:4), the real man. It represents the true character but conceals it" (*Hastings Bible Dictionary*).

This study of "A Receptive Heart" begins by declaring that small children have the kind of heart God is looking for. Jesus told His disciples, "Unless you change and become like little children, you will never enter the kingdom of heaven" (Matt. 18:3 NIV). "Entry into the kingdom requires recognizing one's childlike low estate and sensing one's helplessness. A person must acknowledge his sinful condition and his inability to save himself" (Roy Zuck, *Precious in His Sight*).

After the account of Jesus receiving the children and again saying they are the example adults must follow (Mark 10:13-16), the lesson focuses on a young man who wants to gain eternal life (vv. 17-27). The dilemma is whether or not he will put childlike faith in Christ instead of trusting in his own good works and clinging to his wealth.

Finally, in the parable of the soils, Jesus shows that various things can cause our hearts to be unreceptive, but individuals who will receive His Word will flourish (Luke 8:4-15).

I. THE KINGDOM RECEIVED (Mark 10:13-16)

A. Children Rejected (v. 13)

13. And they brought young children to him, that he should touch them: and his disciples rebuked those that brought them.

Matthew, Mark, and Luke all record this incident when children were brought to the Lord Jesus for His blessing. These were children too young to come to Jesus on their own, so "they"—presumably parents—brought their little boys and girls, including infants (Luke 18:15), to be blessed by the Messiah.

It was customary for Jewish parents to bring their young ones to rabbis to place their hands on them to pronounce God's blessing. "Even today Jewish children are taken to the rabbi, who places his hand on the heads of children in the synagogue on Friday nights and blesses them" (Zuck).

When the disciples saw what the parents intended on this occasion, they stood in the way. The Greek language indicates the parents "were bringing" and the disciples "were rebuking"—both ongoing processes. The disciples thought Jesus did not have time to spend on babies and small children; after all, what could they receive from Him or what could they offer the Lord?

This brings to mind the scene in Matthew 15:21-28, when the disciples did not feel Jesus should stop for a lowly Canaanite woman who refused to quit reaching out to Him for help. "Send her away, for she cries out after us," the disciples demanded (v. 23 NKJV). Similarly, there was a blind beggar who kept crying out for mercy even though the crowd tried to quiet him down (Luke 18:35-43).

In Jesus' day, some valued children as no more than "worthless" beggars or despised foreigners, but Jesus stopped and ministered to both the Canaanite woman and the blind man. He would do no less for the precious little children that were being brought to Him.

> **Talk About It:**
> Describe the disciples' actions.

> "As you ponder how to invest your personal resources of all types—time, money, experience, ability, facilities, expertise, and so on—keep in mind that there is no better investment than nurturing our youngsters for an eternal payback."
> **—George Barna**

B. Disciples Rebuked (vv. 14-15)

14. But when Jesus saw it, he was much displeased, and said unto them, Suffer the little children to come unto me, and forbid them not: for of such is the kingdom of God.

15. Verily I say unto you, Whosoever shall not receive the kingdom of God as a little child, he shall not enter therein.

The disciples had been quick to rebuke the parents, and Jesus was quick to do the same to the disciples because He was "indignant" (NIV). This is a "strong word of deep emotion" (Robertson), meaning "to feel a violent irritation, physically" (Vine). Jesus commanded the disciples to permit the little children to come to Him, and not to "forbid" (restrain or hinder) them. In other words, they must immediately stop what they had been doing.

> **Talk About It:**
> 1. Explain the phrase "of such is the kingdom of God" (v. 14).
> 2. What does it mean to receive God's kingdom "as a little child" (v. 15)?

It is amazing how quickly the disciples had forgotten the lesson in Mark 9, when they had been arguing about which of them should have the most prominent role in Christ's kingdom. The Lord had used a "little child" as an object lesson then, taking the boy in His arms and declaring, "Whoever welcomes one of these little children in my name welcomes me; and whoever welcomes me does not welcome me but the one who sent me" (v. 37 NIV). Jesus had gone on to warn the disciples about the dangerous folly of misleading a child (v. 42), but obviously His teaching had not yet sunk in. So now He takes it a step further, saying "of such is the kingdom of God" (10:14).

The disciples had a critical lesson to learn from children. In fact, if they did not learn this lesson, they could not go to heaven! Jesus declared, "Truly I say to you, whoever does not receive the kingdom of God like a child will not enter it at all" (v. 15 NASB).

Eternal life is something to be received, and it can only be received by those who realize they are helpless to gain it on their own. Just as small children naturally trust in parents for their physical survival, so we must trust solely on the Lord for our spiritual survival. Just as the little children had to be brought to Jesus to receive His touch, so we must be brought to Him through the convicting power of the Holy Spirit to receive salvation.

C. Children Blessed (v. 16)

16. And he took them up in his arms, put his hands upon them, and blessed them.

Talk About It:
Describe Jesus' actions.

With nothing to hinder them now, the children were brought to Jesus again. The Master did not condescendingly pat the children on the head. Instead, He took them in His arms, placed His hand on their head, and pronounced His favor on them.

Centuries earlier, Isaiah had prophesied that the Messiah would "feed His flock like a shepherd; He will gather the lambs with His arm, and carry them in His bosom" (40:11 NKJV).

Parents reading this passage might think, *How honored those families were to bring their babies to Jesus and see Him hold them and bless them.* Yet, it is still the responsibility and privilege of parents to bring their children to Jesus by having them dedicated to the Lord as infants; praying for them daily; teaching them the truths of Scripture; and taking them to church for corporate worship, learning, and fellowship. As did the disciples, Satan will try to hinder the parents' efforts, but Jesus Christ is waiting with open arms to bless the children.

II. THE KINGDOM REJECTED (Mark 10:17-27)
A. The Rich Young Ruler (v. 17)

17. And when he was gone forth into the way, there came one running, and kneeled to him, and asked him, Good Master, what shall I do that I may inherit eternal life?

A Receptive Heart

The rich young ruler (identified as "ruler" in Luke 18:18 and "young" in Matt. 19:20) is to be commended for the things he did as recorded in this verse. First, he came to Jesus. The most noble thing anyone can do is to come to Jesus.

Second, the rich young ruler came running to Jesus. If there is anything we need to get in a hurry about, it is our soul's salvation. How foolish it is to make careful plans and preparations for this life, and to neglect the future life.

Also, he kneeled before Jesus, even though he was the ruler and Jesus was the peasant. By all the standards of his day, Jesus should have been kneeling to him. Not only did he kneel to Jesus, but he did so in public. Unashamedly, so that everyone could see, he gives this allegiance to the Lord. By his action, he acknowledged that Jesus is Master.

Then the rich young ruler realized that salvation is a personal matter. He asked, "What must I do to inherit eternal life?" (NIV). He realized that he had to do something—that no one else could do it for him.

The rich young ruler was wrong in that he thought he could "inherit eternal life." Perhaps he thought he could use his money or his influence and thereby gain eternal life. But it cannot be so. Eternal life comes from God alone, and it comes in His way. Paul wrote: "For it is by grace you have been saved, through faith—and this not from yourselves, it is the gift of God—not by works, so that no one can boast. For we are God's workmanship, created in Christ Jesus to do good works, which God prepared in advance for us to do" (Eph. 2:8-10 NIV).

B. The Good Teacher (vv. 18-20)

18. And Jesus said unto him, Why callest thou me good? there is none good but one, that is, God.

19. Thou knowest the commandments, Do not commit adultery, Do not kill, Do not steal, Do not bear false witness, Defraud not, Honour thy father and mother.

20. And he answered and said unto him, Master, all these have I observed from my youth.

The rich young ruler referred to Jesus as a "good teacher." Immediately, Jesus asked him why he referred to Him as *good* when that attribute in its noblest sense can only be applied to God. Jesus was not denying that He was good, or that He was God. But He was putting the man's statement in proper perspective. He did not view Christ as God; he saw Him as a human teacher, yet he attributed goodness which belongs only to God. So Jesus was saying to him, "Let's get this matter straight. Don't call Me good unless you acknowledge that I am God. If you regard Me as God, then you can call Me good."

Talk About It:
How did this man approach Jesus?

"One might better sail the Atlantic in a paper boat than to get to heaven in good works."
—**Charles Spurgeon**

Talk About It:
1. Explain the phrase "none good" (v. 18).
2. What had this man done since childhood (vv. 19-20)?

Then, Jesus listed some of the Ten Commandments and reminded him that he must observe them. His reaction was, "All these I have kept since I was a boy" (v. 20 NIV). What a clear testimony that morality and good works will not bring eternal life. Apparently, this man had lived a respectable, honorable life. But these things will not save. Only faith in the shed blood of Jesus will redeem.

C. The Sad Conclusion (vv. 21-22)

21. Then Jesus beholding him loved him, and said unto him, One thing thou lackest: go thy way, sell whatsoever thou hast, and give to the poor, and thou shalt have treasure in heaven: and come, take up the cross, and follow me.

22. And he was sad at that saying, and went away grieved: for he had great possessions.

Jesus loved this rich young ruler. He knew the young man was sincere. Jesus told him that he must get rid of the things he was trusting in and then come to Him so that he might have life. He was trusting in his possessions; others are trusting in church membership, or water baptism, or tithing. Although every believer should be baptized, and should tithe, none of these things will save a person. For salvation, we must come to Christ, and Christ alone.

This story ends on a sad note. This rich young ruler walked away from all the promise there was for him in Christ. All the good things he had done—coming to Jesus, running to Jesus, kneeling to Jesus—were to no avail now. All that a person has to do to be lost is to turn away from Jesus.

The young man "went away grieved." There is no other way to walk away from Jesus. When a person turns his back on Christ, he is heading for sorrow, sadness, grief, heartache, and ultimately doom and despair. What a sad finish to an otherwise inspiring story.

Talk About It:
1. How did Jesus feel about this man?
2. How did Jesus challenge him?
3. How did he respond to Jesus?

D. The Eye of a Needle (vv. 23-27)

23. And Jesus looked round about, and saith unto his disciples, How hardly shall they that have riches enter into the kingdom of God!

24. And the disciples were astonished at his words. But Jesus answereth again, and saith unto them, Children, how hard is it for them that trust in riches to enter into the kingdom of God!

25. It is easier for a camel to go through the eye of a needle, than for a rich man to enter into the kingdom of God.

26. And they were astonished out of measure, saying among themselves, Who then can be saved?

27. And Jesus looking upon them saith, With men it is impossible, but not with God: for with God all things are possible.

A Receptive Heart

Jesus explained to the disciples that it is difficult for a rich person to enter the kingdom of God. They were astonished by that statement. This thought was the exact opposite of popular Jewish concepts about riches. They believed that prosperity was a sign of God's favor, and that therefore prosperity was evidence of a man's goodness. If a man was rich and prosperous, they believed God must have honored and blessed him. So, the disciples were shocked at the words of Jesus. To help them understand, Jesus repeated His statement but added, "It is difficult for those who trust in riches to enter the kingdom of God" (see v. 24).

Prosperity may indeed be the result of the blessing of God on an individual, but not necessarily so. There are many who have never named the name of Christ who are wealthy. Some of these have gained their riches through dishonest means. To believe that every believer is going to prosper just because he or she is a believer is to ignore the plight of the vast majority of believers, particularly many outside the United States. On the other hand, poverty is not necessarily a sign that one is devoid of the blessings of God. By earthly standards, Jesus was not wealthy. He can empathize with the poor. Are we going to say that He did not have the blessings of God on His life?

Jesus further explained what He meant about the difficulty of a rich man entering the kingdom of God by using an illustration. He said, "It is easier for a camel to go through the eye of a needle, than for a rich man to enter into the kingdom of God" (v. 25). Some commentators have concluded that Jesus was referring to a small gate in a city wall when He employed the phrase "the eye of the needle." The cities in those days were walled around to keep out bandits and hostile forces. There was always a big gate for the caravans to go through. At sunrise it would be opened, but at sundown that gate was closed. Beside the big gate was a small gate which might be called the pedestrian gate. Persons traveling on foot passed through this gate. Although small, this gate could accommodate a camel; but it would be a tight squeeze. It would appear that this gate was lower than the height of a camel and narrow. A camel could squeeze through if all his baggage was unloaded and he would get on his knees. Then he could squirm through the gate. Thus we have a picture of a rich man divesting himself of trust in his riches, and humbly coming to Christ for redemption.

Other biblical scholars conclude that Jesus liked to employ hyperbole in His teachings. He often used the most extreme examples to illustrate a truth—the building beam sticking out of a man's eye compared with a splinter; the camel trying to get through the eye of a needle, representing a rich man trying to get into heaven. The evil is not in riches themselves but in the trust that people put in these riches. Thus we understand the Lord's statement, "How hard is it for them that trust in riches to enter into the kingdom of God!" (v. 24).

Talk About It:
1. Why did Jesus make the same statement twice (vv. 23-24)?
2. How did Jesus' word picture (v. 25) affect His hearers (v. 26)?
3. What "impossible" thing was Jesus saying God could do (v. 27)?

The disciples conclude that if what Jesus is saying is true, then salvation is nearly impossible for anyone. Jesus confirms their fears by telling them that if salvation depended on a person's efforts, then no one would ever be saved. He explains that salvation is the gift of God with whom all things are possible. The man or woman who trusts in God will know the joy of eternal salvation.

III. A PARABLE OF RECEPTIVITY (Luke 8:4-15)
A. Teaching by Parables (v. 4)

4. And when much people were gathered together, and were come to him out of every city, he spake by a parable.

As Jesus traveled from village to village and from town to town, multitudes of people came out to hear Him preach. They had heard of His preaching and His miracles of healing and raising the dead, so they flocked to Him wherever He went.

Talk About It:
Why do you suppose Jesus taught with a parable?

The skill with which Jesus, the Master Teacher, was able to communicate is illustrated in this account from Luke's Gospel. By the use of parables, He spoke more indirectly to His hearers about spiritual things. Parables allowed Him to instruct them in spiritual truth by comparisons with familiar everyday things.

A parable has been defined as "an earthly story with a heavenly truth." A parable may serve one of three purposes: (1) It may illuminate a spiritual truth which the hearer might not otherwise understand. (2) It may help the hearer remember the truth longer or more accurately. (3) And strangely enough, it may conceal the truth. It may be difficult for outsiders to understand but be plain to disciples of the speaker. Surely all will agree with the one who said, "Whatever else is true of Jesus, it is certainly true that He was one of the world's supreme masters of the short story." This truth we will see as we study the parable of the sower.

B. Sowing Seed (vv. 5-8)

5. A sower went out to sow his seed: and as he sowed, some fell by the way side; and it was trodden down, and the fowls of the air devoured it.

6. And some fell upon a rock; and as soon as it was sprung up, it withered away, because it lacked moisture.

7. And some fell among thorns; and the thorns sprang up with it, and choked it.

8. And other fell on good ground, and sprang up, and bare fruit an hundredfold. And when he had said these things, he cried, He that hath ears to hear, let him hear.

Talk About It:
1. Why did the seeds experience various fates?
2. What did Jesus mean by "hearing" (v. 8)?

With one sentence Jesus introduced the central thought of this parable. He said a sower went out to sow his seed. He gave us a picture of a task begun and finished.

As the sower spread his seed, some of them fell on the hard, beaten paths which separated one farm from another and which

were used as paths for people to cross the fields. Without these paths, people would have to tramp across the grain to get to the other side. These paths, of course, were not plowed and were virtually impenetrable as the result of the feet, both of people and animals, that crossed them daily. The seeds, lacking fresh soil to receive them, could easily be sighted and devoured by the hungry birds which undoubtedly perched nearby expecting just this to happen.

Verse 6 reminds us that Palestine, being a mountainous country, has spots where the tilled land has underlying rock that crops out or comes close to the surface and has only a thin layer of soil. There is just enough soil to receive the seed. This shallow ground rapidly dries out after rain, so that the small plants that have come up in it while it was wet soon wither away. The seed that falls on these spots is unproductive.

Other spots in the field were infested with thorns which had become dormant. The sower tossed the grain in with them, and they shot up and sprouted again along with the good plants. Since these tougher thornbushes constantly took more of the vital nutrients from the soil, they choked out the weaker plants.

Verse 8 describes the ground on which the sower intended most of the seed to fall. It was porous and freshly plowed; rich and deep, without the stony subsurface; and clean of alien seeds. Thus, it was able to nourish the grain the sower tossed in.

Luke only mentioned the perfect yield of the good ground producing a hundredfold. He wanted to emphasize the abundance of fruit the right soil produces. But Matthew said the good parts of the land vary in fertility, so that one portion yields more fruit than others. "But other fell into good ground, and brought forth fruit, some an hundredfold, some sixtyfold, some thirtyfold" (Matt. 13:8).

Several times Jesus called on His hearers to use their ears and to listen to what He was saying. Such a call had the effect of impressing on their minds the words He was speaking. Thus they were stimulated to think further and meditate more deeply on the truths He was sharing with them. Also, His call implied His teaching about the seed had a hidden meaning and that if they applied their ears aright, they would discover that meaning.

Sometimes the discovery of truth is a painstaking process. But the more deeply we have to dig to uncover precious nuggets of truth, the more tenaciously do we cling to that truth.

> "In our own spiritual experience we find that when God gives us new truth He soon puts us into the test over it."
> —Lois LeBar

C. Questioning Jesus (vv. 9-10)

9. And his disciples asked him, saying, What might this parable be?

10. And he said, Unto you it is given to know the mysteries of the kingdom of God: but to others in parables; that seeing they might not see, and hearing they might not understand.

Talk About It:
What advantage did
Jesus' followers have?

One can almost visualize the consternation of the disciples as they listened to Jesus' parable. Apparently, as soon as He had concluded His teaching for the day, though we cannot be sure of the time, the disciples found the opportune moment to query Jesus for an explanation.

He informed them the parable was especially calculated to test the hearers' spiritual aptitude. If the listeners had very little concern for spiritual things, the truth would remain hidden and undiscovered. If, on the other hand, the hearers had an open mind and were eager to appropriate for themselves the truth—not only that which is heard with the ears but also that which is understood with the heart—the truth would be revealed.

Norval Geldenhuys observed: "Jesus excluded the multitudes from a deeper understanding of His teachings because they had up to that time willfully continued deaf and blind to the real significance of His preaching and conduct. They had remained worldly-minded and had refused to learn from Him. Accordingly He now proceeds as a judgment upon their stubborn blindness to speak mostly in parables for the short period that He will still be among them before His crucifixion."

"It is the peculiar ministry of the Holy Spirit to make the outer Word an inner experience."
—Lois LeBar

D. Explaining Three Soils (vv. 11-14)

11. Now the parable is this: The seed is the word of God.

12. Those by the way side are they that hear; then cometh the devil, and taketh away the word out of their hearts, lest they should believe and be saved.

13. They on the rock are they, which, when they hear, receive the word with joy; and these have no root, which for a while believe, and in time of temptation fall away.

14. And that which fell among thorns are they, which, when they have heard, go forth, and are choked with cares and riches and pleasures of this life, and bring no fruit to perfection.

The key to the whole parable is to understand that the seed represents the Word. The Word is the effective, creative power of God which can take root in the life of the receptive person and produce the fruits of the Kingdom. The Word is, as the writer of Hebrews says, "quick, and powerful, and sharper than any twoedged sword, piercing even to the dividing asunder of soul and spirit, and of the joints and marrow, and is a discerner of the thoughts and intents of the heart" (4:12).

The hearers represented by the roadside listen to the Word but do not give heed. Since they do not respond, the Word cannot reach the depths of their heart. Their heart is as hard as the beaten footpath that led through the field. Such willful hardness refuses to receive the Word.

Talk About It:
1. How is God's Word like a seed?
2. What can hinder the Scriptures from accomplishing their purpose (vv. 12-14)?

A Receptive Heart

When the Word is heard but not heeded, the devil snatches it from the heart in which it otherwise might have germinated. Luke pointed out that if the Word had been received and allowed to germinate, they would have been saved (8:12).

There are some people who, not counting the cost and taking little thought of the demands that will be made on their lives, happily receive the Word. In the lives of these people, represented by the rocky soil, the real test comes not in the manner in which they receive the Word but in the depth of their commitment to it. They receive the Word with emotional excitement and superficial enthusiasm, but when the struggle of life comes, they stumble.

How many people have you known who are like this? They follow the Lord by fits and starts. They leap into religion as the flying fish leaps into the air; they fall back again into their sins, as the same fish returns to its element.

We all have some rocks in our soil. That's why it can take so long for us to grow in the Christian life, to experience the power of Christ in our personalities, and to radiate the joy of Christ in our living. We are sometimes reluctant to surrender because we are afraid of what Christ might do with dimensions of our hidden selves.

It appears there is nothing basically wrong with the soil in verse 14; it is good, and the seed sinks deeply into its warm bed. Much is promised; much is hoped for. But also the seeds of thorns have been left in the ground; and as the good grain begins to grow, so do the thorns. They steal the needed nourishment and grow above the grain, taking away the needed light and heat. The grain continues to grow and produces in dwarf fashion a stalk and leaves, but there is no ear and no production of fruit.

Thus we see the dangers of the overcrowded life. It usually leads to a division of the heart and therefore to an inability to nurture the seed—the rule of God in all of life. The energy of the soul is used to sustain and replenish other things.

Jesus mentions three areas of concern: cares, riches, and pleasures of this life. Matthew Henry wrote, "The pleasures of this life are as dangerous and mischievous thorns to choke the good seed of the Word as any other. . . . The delights of the sense may ruin the soul, even lawful delights, indulged, and too much delighted in." Such pleasures demand so much of one's attention, absorbed so much of one's interest, and use up so much of one's time that very little remains for spiritual things. Thus, in a hurried and heartless fashion the most important things are pursued.

"The God-blessed churches in the world today have one common characteristic: an insistence upon an exposition of God's infallible Word."
—O. S. Hawkins

E. Examining the Good Soil (v. 15)

15. But that on the good ground are they, which in an honest and good heart, having heard the word, keep it, and bring forth fruit with patience.

Those represented by the good ground are described as having "an honest and good heart." The heart ought to be receptive to the Word, and the heart depicted here is. The Word thrives in a heart that is open to receive it. When the heart is soft and tender, it is stirred to its depths on the great things of God. It jealously guards itself against worldly entanglements. It receives the Word with the full intention of obeying it.

The good heart not only hears and receives the Word, it also keeps it. Jesus said, "If ye abide in me, and my words abide in you, ye shall ask what ye will, and it shall be done unto you" (John 15:7). By keeping the Word, the believer produces "much fruit" (v. 8).

What greater impact could the preaching and teaching of the Word have than to bear fruit of permanent character! When the Word, which is pure and powerful, reaches the right soil in the human heart, the results are a great harvest which transcends all human expectations. The believer continues to bear fruit; he or she perseveres in righteousness. It is not enough to begin to bring forth fruit, the believer must continue to be fruitful to the glory of God.

> "A readiness to believe every promise implicitly, to obey every command unhesitatingly, to stand perfect and complete in all the will of God, is the only true spirit of Bible study."
> —Andrew Murray

CONCLUSION

Jesus' parable of the soils places a great responsibility on the hearer. Buttrick wrote: "Hearing is an urgent business. We assume that because initiative is with the speaker a message controls the hearer. But the parts may be reversed: the hearer may control the message. An appeal, even the appeal of Jesus, may be frustrated by unreceptiveness."

GOLDEN TEXT CHALLENGE

"WHOSOEVER SHALL NOT RECEIVE THE KINGDOM OF GOD AS A LITTLE CHILD, HE SHALL NOT ENTER THEREIN" (Mark 10:15).

In most things, adults are to be the models for children to follow. But when it comes to the most important act of all—taking a faith step into the kingdom of God—adults are to emulate children.

As a nursing infant cries out to his or her mother for life-sustaining nourishment, so we must cry out to Jesus Christ for the "living water" that gives "everlasting life" (John 4:10, 14).

As a toddler must be led to the places he or she needs to go, so we must fully depend on Jesus as "the way" (14:6) and "the door" in order to "be saved" (10:9).

As a young child needs a nurturing parent to learn how to receive and give love, so we must realize we can love God only "because he first loved us" (1 John 4:19), and through this love "be called children of God" (3:1 NKJV).

Only those with childlike faith, humility, and dependence can receive the kingdom of God.

Daily Devotions:
M. Pharaoh's Hard Heart
Exodus 4:21-23
T. A Meek Heart Is Forever
Psalm 22:23-28
W. Saul's Changed Heart
1 Samuel 10:9-13
T. Solomon's Changed Heart
1 Kings 3:5-14
F. New Creature in Christ
2 Corinthians 5:17-21
S. Paul's Changed Heart
Galatians 1:10-16

A Receptive Heart

A Contrite Heart

Luke 7:36-50

INTRODUCTION

Before the times of the New Testament, the Pharisees (meaning "separatists") had come into being to preserve the holiness tenets of Judaism. They were an admirable people, without whose energies and dedication the Jewish faith may have disappeared from Israel. By the time Jesus was born, however, this sect was dominated by legalism and formality. They were particularly zealous in their insistence on tithing and the observance of purification rituals (see Matt. 23:23-26; Mark 7:1-13; Luke 11:37-42; 18:12). They had made holiness more a matter of law than of spirit. And these former champions of righteousness became Jesus' greatest adversaries.

In today's lesson, a Pharisee named Simon invites Jesus to eat with him in his house. Some suppose he is the same Simon who was healed from leprosy (see Matt. 26:6; Mark 14:3), but this is unlikely.

During the course of the meal, a woman who was probably a prostitute entered the house uninvited. No doubt the architecture of Simon's house was similar to that of a villa, with an open courtyard through which uninvited strangers might freely pass. At social functions such houses were generally left open.

Unusual as it was for sinners to enter the home of a Pharisee, this woman did so because of her contrition and repentance. The depth of her spiritual sorrow is seen in her profuse weeping that wet the feet of Jesus with her tears, apparently causing her to note that His feet had not been washed.

When a guest entered a home in Palestine, he was generally offered a basin of water to wash his feet which had become dirty as he walked along dirty roads in open sandals. Cleanliness was regarded as a virtue of highest order, especially among the Pharisees, yet Jesus' feet were still dirty.

In a greater need of cleansing, however, was the heart of Simon. He concluded that Jesus could be no prophet because supposedly He had not discerned the sinfulness of this woman. But Jesus proved a greater discernment than knowing her sins, by knowing even the thoughts of the Pharisee. So while the sinful woman with the contrite, believing heart received forgiveness, the religious man with the self-righteous, doubting heart remained unclean.

Unit Theme:
Commended by Christ

Central Truth:
God's love is extended to all who come to Him in humility and repentance.

Focus:
Contrast contrition and arrogance, and express our gratitude for God's love.

Context:
In AD 27 at the house of Simon the Pharisee, a sinful woman receives forgiveness.

Golden Text:
"The Lord is nigh unto them that are of a broken heart; and saveth such as be of a contrite spirit" (Ps. 34:18).

Study Outline:
I. An Act of Contrition (Luke 7:36-38)
II. An Attitude of Arrogance (Luke 7:39-46)
III. Power to Forgive (Luke 7:47-50)

I. AN ACT OF CONTRITION (Luke 7:36-38)

A. Jesus Invited (v. 36)

36. And one of the Pharisees desired him that he would eat with him. And he went into the Pharisee's house, and sat down to meat.

Talk About It:
Why would Jesus eat with this person?

When one remembers the hatred of most of the Pharisees for Jesus, one is inclined to ask what motivated this Pharisee to invite Jesus into his home. There are at least three probable answers. First, Jesus had become increasingly popular with the common people. Simon may have thought it would be to his advantage to openly befriend Jesus. This event seems to have occurred in the early part of our Lord's ministry before the Pharisees became His open enemies.

Second, the Pharisee had no doubt heard much about Jesus, and by inviting Him into his home he would have a better opportunity to more closely observe Jesus; then on the basis of this knowledge he could form his own conclusions. This would mean that he was sincere in his invitation.

Third, Simon may have been convinced that Jesus was an impostor and thought that by inviting Him into his home he would have an opportunity to gather some evidence against the Lord. His failing to extend to Jesus the common courtesies generally given by a host to a guest seems to lend support to this idea. Later the Pharisees did try to catch Jesus in something that they could use against Him (see Matt. 19:3; 22:35).

"Jesus clothes the Beatitudes with His own life."
—**Carl F. H. Henry**

B. Jesus Anointed (vv. 37-38)

37. And, behold, a woman in the city, which was a sinner, when she knew that Jesus sat at meat in the Pharisee's house, brought an alabaster box of ointment,

38. And stood at his feet behind him weeping, and began to wash his feet with tears, and did wipe them with the hairs of her head, and kissed his feet, and anointed them with the ointment.

Talk About It:
1. Why did this woman come to the Pharisee's house (v. 37)?
2. Choose two words that describe the woman's actions (v. 38).

In those days it was not uncommon for those who had not been invited to enter a home and speak with one of the guests. This woman with a bad reputation had heard that Jesus was in the home of Simon. She had no doubt heard Jesus preach before and had been led to deep sorrow and repentance. In Him she saw someone who could deliver even one as deeply involved in sin as she. It was a pure affection for Jesus, who had given her hope, that caused her to enter Simon's house and act as she did.

This woman stood behind Jesus, who, along with the other persons eating the meal, was reclining on His side with His feet behind Him. She was holding "an alabaster jar of perfume" (NIV), which she probably planned to use in anointing Jesus' head.

A Blotted Life
Ruskin was shown a costly handkerchief on which a blot of ink

A Contrite Heart

However, being in the presence of the holy Jesus caused this woman of unclean character to feel shame and sorrow for her past life. His very presence caused the tears to flow from her eyes and fall on His feet. She then wiped them with the hairs of her head. This act was not planned; but when the tears fell on Jesus' feet, she used the only thing she had available to dry them, even though it was indecent for a woman to let down her hair in public. Then, as an act of devotion and worship, she anointed His feet with the perfume.

II. AN ATTITUDE OF ARROGANCE (Luke 7:39-46)
A. Jesus Criticized (v. 39)

39. Now when the Pharisee which had bidden him saw it, he spake within himself, saying, This man, if he were a prophet, would have known who and what manner of woman this is that toucheth him: for she is a sinner.

Simon did not outwardly express his criticism of Jesus but rather spoke to himself. We will not only be condemned for our outward actions but also for the inner workings of the heart. "For God shall bring every work into judgment, with every secret thing, whether it be good, or whether it be evil" (Eccl. 12:14). Peter points out that God is concerned with the thoughts of our hearts: "Repent therefore of this thy wickedness, and pray God, if perhaps the thought of thine heart may be forgiven thee" (Acts 8:22).

The Pharisees adopted a "holier than thou" attitude (Isa. 65:5) and therefore could not understand how our Lord could associate with "sinners" and not be like them. Jesus never associated with sinners because He had anything in common with them but was always among them as a physician among the sick. He was there to bring a cure.

By his thoughts, Simon condemned Jesus of either the lack of spiritual knowledge concerning the character of this woman or of moral impurity by associating with her. In either case, in Simon's mind, He could not be a prophet. From this we learn the evil of judging by appearances only. Since we are not always aware of the inner motives of a person, we are to leave judgment to the Lord (see Rom. 8:33-34; 14:4, 12-13).

B. A Pharisee Questioned (vv. 40-43)

40. And Jesus answering said unto him, Simon, I have somewhat to say unto thee. And he saith, Master, say on.

41. There was a certain creditor which had two debtors: the one owed five hundred pence, and the other fifty.

42. And when they had nothing to pay, he frankly forgave them both. Tell me therefore, which of them will love him most?

had been made. "Nothing can be done with it now," said the owner. "It is absolutely worthless."

Ruskin made no reply but carried it away with him. After a time he sent it back, to the great surprise of his friend, who could scarcely believe his eyes. In a most skillful and artistic way Ruskin had made a design in India ink, using the ugly blot as a center for the design.

A blotted life is not necessarily a useless life. Jesus can make a life beautiful if it is yielded to Him.
—*Moody Monthly*

Talk About It:
What was the Pharisee's opinion of Jesus?

"Cynics are only happy in making the world as barren to others as they have made it for themselves."
—**George Meredith**

43. Simon answered and said, I suppose that he, to whom he forgave most. And he said unto him, Thou hast rightly judged.

The Lord did not leave Simon alone to his inevitable judgment but in mercy proceeded to reveal that He was aware of his thoughts. It is a mercy for the Lord to give such a revelation with its accompanying warning. We are not told what effect His knowledge had on Simon.

Jesus exposed Simon's thoughts by means of a parable and a question. The parable was simple: Two debtors owed debts they could not pay, yet their creditor forgave both of them, even though the debt of one was ten times more than the other. The question was pointed: *Which debtor would love the creditor more?* By getting Simon to answer this question as he did, the Lord used Simon's own words to give an answer that would both defend and justify this woman's actions and also vindicate our Lord in permitting her to express herself in the manner in which she did.

Not only does the Lord forgive the sinner when he or she repents, but also He will defend him or her against accusations. "We have an advocate [defender, lawyer, intercessor] . . . Jesus Christ the righteous" (1 John 2:1). As Simon would accuse this woman for her past, even so Satan would seek to have God condemn us for our past sins (Rev. 12:10). Yet, in spite of all our sins, if we repent, we shall "overcome him [Satan] by the blood of the Lamb [Jesus]" (see v. 11), and all of his accusations will come to nought, even though he accuses us "before our God day and night."

Through His parable, Jesus wanted Simon to understand that both he and this woman owed a debt of sin that they could not pay. Though the woman's sin may have seemed ten times worse, both she and this religious man needed forgiveness.

C. A Pharisee Condemned (vv. 44-46)

44. And he turned to the woman, and said unto Simon, Seest thou this woman? I entered into thine house, thou gavest me no water for my feet: but she hath washed my feet with tears, and wiped them with the hairs of her head.

45. Thou gavest me no kiss: but this woman since the time I came in hath not ceased to kiss my feet.

46. My head with oil thou didst not anoint: but this woman hath anointed my feet with ointment.

Simon condemned the woman for doing what he as the host should have done, but was prevented from doing because of pride. Notice the contrast between kissing the cheek and anointing the head, and the kissing of the feet and anointing of the feet. It was as if the woman said, "I am not worthy to anoint Your head, but I am humble myself and kiss and anoint Your feet."

Talk About It:
What connection does Jesus make between forgiveness (v. 41) and love (v. 42)?

"He that cannot forgive others breaks the bridge over which he himself must pass if he would ever reach heaven; for everyone has need to be forgiven."
—Lord Herbert

Talk About It:
Contrast Simon's actions with the woman's.

A Contrite Heart

Often there are those who will not do what they should do, and then they will condemn those who do. It seems that Simon considered himself superior to Jesus and therefore too good to show Him proper courtesy.

Our Lord, by making this comparison, was endeavoring to bring the Pharisee under conviction. We must first be convicted by the Spirit before we can come to the place of repentance.

III. POWER TO FORGIVE (Luke 7:47-50)

A. The Need for Forgiveness (v. 47)

47. Wherefore I say unto thee, Her sins, which are many, are forgiven; for she loved much: but to whom little is forgiven, the same loveth little.

We are not to understand that she was forgiven because she loved, but rather that her love was an evidence that she had been forgiven. Hence, we see that love is a sign of our forgiveness. It is possible to be correct in doctrine and yet not be right with God. The one fault the Lord had found with the Ephesian church was that they had "left [their] first love" (Rev. 2:4). May the truth that we have been forgiven never cease to break our heart and cause love to flow out in unselfish service.

This woman was known publicly for her sinful lifestyle, and she realized her need for forgiveness. Simon, on the other hand, like the Pharisees in general, saw himself as the spiritual elite who was justified by his religious acts. He did not realize his need to be forgiven for the sins of pride, hypocrisy, and unbelief.

B. The Assurance of Forgiveness (v. 48)

48. And he said unto her, Thy sins are forgiven.

There is no greater joy that can come to the heart of a sinner than God-given assurance of forgiveness. We can tell people of God's plan of salvation, but only the Holy Spirit can bring assurance to the heart of an individual that God has actually forgiven their sins. "The Spirit itself beareth witness with our spirit, that we are the children of God" (Rom. 8:16). The Holy Spirit lifts the sense of condemnation and guilt from the heart of the forgiven sinner, giving him or her the "full assurance of faith" (Heb. 10:22; Rom. 8:1).

C. The Source of Forgiveness (vv. 49-50)

49. And they that sat at meat with him began to say within themselves, Who is this that forgiveth sins also?

50. And he said to the woman, Thy faith hath saved thee; go in peace.

The guests of Simon looked upon this statement of Jesus as presumptive arrogance. This would be true if He had been only a man. Only God can forgive sins; and the Scriptures everywhere present Jesus as much more than a mere man, for He is "the great God and our Saviour Jesus Christ" (Titus 2:13). Forgiveness

---

"In true Christian worship the sincere believer is prostrating himself before the living God (though this may not involve a physical act) . . . so that he may offer the adoration, the praise, the thanksgiving, the exaltation of which God alone is entitled."
—**Robert Rayburn**

Talk About It:
Rephrase Jesus' statement.

"Let us, with a gladsome mind
Praise the Lord, for He is kind:
For His mercies aye endure,
Ever faithful, ever sure."
—**John Milton**

Talk About It:
What makes Jesus' four-word sentence so powerful?

Talk About It:
1. What question gripped the onlookers?
2. What had the woman been "saved" from, and how?

---

comes from the great heart of God. "For God so loved the world, that he gave his only begotten Son, that whosoever believeth in him should not perish, but have everlasting life" (John 3:16). Forgiveness is a gift of God's free grace.

Having sensed the negative sentiment of Simon and his guests as she poured out her devotion to Jesus, the woman now witnessed the guests' disapproval of Jesus himself. They did not just scorn His acceptance of her actions, but His authority to forgive her or anyone else's sins.

Jesus turned His full attention to the woman and reassured her that through her faith in Him, she had been saved from her sins. The skepticism of the religious professionals was irrelevant.

Though the source of forgiveness is to be sought in God himself, faith is the condition upon which God offers it to sinners. Faith is the disposition of the heart that accepts God's offer and trusts His faithfulness to keep His promise. It is simply taking God at His word.

> "[Jesus] offers the only way to eternal life, asking only that you admit your need, raise the empty hands of faith, and accept His gift."
> —Francis Schaeffer

CONCLUSION

Several great lessons have been brought to our attention in this study. First, we must guard against the danger of judging the actions of other people without a knowledge of their motives. Second, the forgiveness of sins is properly an act of God, and Jesus is our God and Savior; therefore "he is able also to save them to the uttermost that come unto God by him, seeing he ever liveth to make intercession for them" (Heb. 7:25). Third, we receive forgiveness when we come to Him with a contrite, believing heart.

GOLDEN TEXT CHALLENGE

"THE LORD IS NIGH UNTO THEM THAT ARE OF A BROKEN HEART; AND SAVETH SUCH AS BE OF A CONTRITE SPIRIT" (Ps. 34:18).

Daily Devotions:
M. Return to the Lord
  2 Chronicles
  30:7-9
T. Cry of Repentance
  Psalm 51:1-12
W. A Call to
  Repentance
  Hosea 6:1-11
T. Forgive and Be
  Forgiven
  Matthew 6:9-15
F. The Father's
  Response
  Luke 15:17-24
S. Forgive As Christ
  Forgives
  Colossians 3:12-17

Because the Lord is the omnipresent God, it seems strange to say He is "nigh" (near or close) to anything specific, since He is close to *every*thing. However, this verse is not focusing merely on the physical nearness of the Lord, but also on a relational closeness. He is ready to *hear* and *deliver* the "righteous" (v. 17).

Righteousness begins in the heart and spirit. A heart that is broken to pieces by sin or sorrow recognizes its need of a Savior and Healer, and is only a prayer away from receiving His help.

The second clause in the Golden Text echoes the first clause. A "contrite spirit" is one that is "crushed," "broken," or "beaten down" by sin or trouble. The Lord can save such a person because they realize they cannot be raised up through their own power.

"For this is what the high and lofty One says—he who lives forever, whose name is holy: 'I live in a high and holy place, but also with him who is contrite and lowly in spirit, to revive the spirit of the lowly and to revive the heart of the contrite'" (Isa. 57:15 NIV).

A Contrite Heart

Faith in Desperate Situations

Mark 5:25-34; Luke 7:1-10; 23:39-43

INTRODUCTION

The miracles of Jesus sometimes overlapped one another, and one sometimes occurred during the process of another. That is the case in the first event described in this lesson. Jesus had been appealed to by a man named Jairus and was accompanying him to his home to minister to his sick daughter when a suffering woman approached Him for her healing. Jesus stopped long enough to bring about the woman's healing and then continued on His way to Jairus' house.

About thirty-four miracles of Christ are recorded in the four Gospels, including the healing of the centurion's servant, which is the second account in today's lesson. This does not represent all of the miracles Jesus performed, for the Gospels do not purport to be exhaustive records of all Jesus did. We may safely assume that He performed many other miracles. Of the thirty-four recorded miracles, eighteen are physical healings, and some of these were healings of more than one person. Three of His miracles were raising the dead and four were casting out devils. It can be seen, then, that most of Jesus' work was relieving human suffering of various sorts.

The final account in today's lesson involves not a physical healing, but an amazing spiritual deliverance. As a criminal is dying alongside Christ on Calvary, Christ forgives him of his sins and promises him a home in heaven.

In each of these events, Christ performs miraculous deeds in response to individuals putting their faith in Him.

Unit Theme:
Commended by Christ

Central Truth:
Desperate situations serve as occasions for us to abandon self-reliance and trust God.

Focus:
Recognize difficult situations as opportunities for experiencing God's power and reach out to Christ.

Context:
Three New Testament accounts of individuals believing Christ to perform supernatural acts

Golden Text:
"God is our refuge and strength, a very present help in trouble" (Ps. 46:1).

Study Outline:
I. Pursue Christ's Help (Mark 5:25-34)
II. Respond to Christ's Authority (Luke 7:1-10)
III. Recognize Christ's Power to Save (Luke 23:39-43)

I. PURSUE CHRIST'S HELP (Mark 5:25-34)

A. Hopeless Condition (vv. 25-26)

an issue of blood (v. 25)—"subject to bleeding" (NIV)

25. And a certain woman, which had an issue of blood twelve years,

26. And had suffered many things of many physicians, and had spent all that she had, and was nothing bettered, but rather grew worse.

Talk About It:
Describe this woman's physical and economic condition.

This instance of divine healing concerns a woman who had suffered great affliction for twelve years. Her sickness of chronic and continual body hemorrhaging was so personal in its nature that even today it is spoken of with careful language. If we still speak of it with delicacy two thousand years later, it is easy to imagine the shame and humiliation it brought to the woman who had the affliction.

Leviticus 15:25-28 declares that such a woman was to be regarded as "unclean." The fact that this woman had suffered continual hemorrhaging for twelve years suggests she must by this time have suffered great psychological distress in addition to her physical affliction.

During the years of her sickness, the woman had desperately sought the assistance of physicians, spending everything she had in the search for healing. She had impoverished herself in her desire to be cured of her issue of blood. The primitive methods of physicians in that day were matched by a primitive understanding. She "suffered many things of [the] physicians," which means she alternated between hope and despair, between promise and futility.

"Never despair; but if you do, work on in despair."
—Edmund Burke

Not only was the woman not cured, but she gradually grew worse. In time her money was gone, her hope was gone, her self-confidence was gone, and likely the joy of living was gone. Her case appeared to be hopeless.

B. Desperate Effort (vv. 27-28)

press (v. 27)—crowd

27. When she had heard of Jesus, came in the press behind, and touched his garment.

28. For she said, If I may touch but his clothes, I shall be whole.

Talk About It:
What did this woman believe?

This woman had learned of Jesus' reputation as He performed miraculous cures in Galilee. As other afflicted persons, she wished that someday she might see Jesus so He could cure her. Hearing the tumult as Jesus proceeded with the throng to the house of Jairus, she knew that this might be her chance to be healed.

Ashamed as she was of her affliction, the woman did not dare to approach Jesus boldly. The uncleanness of her condition would have made her timid about even being seen in public. Discreetly she stooped and touched the hem of His flowing robe as He passed by. She did not intend for anyone to know what she had done or to pay her any attention.

Faith in Desperate Situations

The woman did not expect the Lord to lay hands on her, as Jairus had requested Jesus to do to his daughter (v. 23). As we see in later developments, she was an obedient follower of the Law, one who accepted the uncleanness of her condition. Being thus obedient to the Law, she would not have subjected Jesus to contamination by either touching His body or by asking Him to touch her. The alternative was to touch the clothing He wore. The desperation of her condition and her reverence for the Law combined to give birth to extraordinary faith.

This woman had waited for twelve years for a natural correction of her condition, which had not occurred; she had spent all her money on physicians that could not cure her; she dared not ask Jesus to lay hands upon her; she dared not expose herself publicly for fear of public humiliation; so she had to overcome her malady through faith alone.

> "The beginning of anxiety is the end of faith, and the beginning of true faith is the end of anxiety."
> —George Mueller

C. Miraculous Result (vv. 29-34)

29. And straightway the fountain of her blood was dried up; and she felt in her body that she was healed of that plague.

30. And Jesus, immediately knowing in himself that virtue had gone out of him, turned him about in the press, and said, Who touched my clothes?

31. And his disciples said unto him, Thou seest the multitude thronging thee, and sayest thou, Who touched me?

32. And he looked round about to see her that had done this thing.

33. But the woman fearing and trembling, knowing what was done in her, came and fell down before him, and told him all the truth.

34. And he said unto her, Daughter, thy faith hath made thee whole; go in peace, and be whole of thy plague.

The woman's desperation had driven her to a point of great faith, her faith had led her to a courageous act, and her act of faith resulted in healing. The malady was healed in an instant, and she felt the change in her body even as it happened. The willingness to act so boldly now gave her instant assurance that she was healed.

For twelve years a shameful timidity had been conditioned in her, so she withdrew without any outcry of gratitude or jubilation. Moreover, she dared not make a public outcry because the Law required any woman so afflicted to have seven days of purification even after being cured (Lev. 15:28). Even if her feeling of gratitude should match the great boldness of her faith, she dared not let the gratitude come forth in words of praise.

The Lord, however, would not leave so great an act of faith unnoticed and unacknowledged. He himself would bring it into

Talk About It:
1. What did the woman feel (v. 29)?
2. What did Jesus sense (v. 30)?
3. What seems strange about Jesus' question in verses 30 and 31?
4. Why was the woman "trembling with fear" (v. 33 NIV)?
5. How did Jesus comfort her (v. 34)?

the open. Just as the woman had felt healing occur in her body, so Jesus felt the healing virtue flow from Him to the healed woman. To make her act of faith public, He turned to the throng and asked, "Who touched my clothes?"

In the course of His walk through the streets of Capernaum, amid a great throng that surrounded Him, many people jostled against the Lord so that touching Him was a common thing. The disciples were therefore perplexed at this question of Christ.

Jesus had no intention of embarrassing the woman, but rather of pointing up the difference in the way that He might be touched. Many people touched Him daily and they were not healed. The difference was that the woman had touched Him in faith, and the touch merely gave outward expression to that inner faith.

Jesus looked searchingly at the throng of people about Him. Knowing all things, He knew who it was that had touched Him. However, it was necessary that He bring this woman's act of faith to light. He searched the crowd face by face until He found the woman that had been healed. Perhaps it would be more appropriate for us to say that He looked until the woman saw that He had fixed His eyes upon her. She had apparently endeavored to disappear in the crowd; but when she saw that His eyes were upon her, she could be quiet no longer.

In the presence of the great throng about Him, the woman told the story of how she had been afflicted in an embarrassing manner for twelve years. She told how she had heard of Him and believed that He would be able to heal her. She told how she had dared not openly approach Him and ask Him to lay hands on her for healing, but how she had instead approached Him discreetly and touched the border of His garment. This amounted to a public statement of faith, a testimony to the healing power of Christ.

The Lord immediately wiped away the woman's fears and apprehensions. With consoling words, He declared that her act of faith had made her whole. At His command, the woman was able at last to go in peace.

II. RESPOND TO CHRIST'S AUTHORITY (Luke 7:1-10)
A. The Centurion's Servant (vv. 1-2)

1. Now when he had ended all his sayings in the audience of the people, he entered into Capernaum.

2. And a certain centurion's servant, who was dear unto him, was sick, and ready to die.

After Jesus concluded His Sermon on the Mount (Luke 6:20-49), He returned to Capernaum, where His headquarters was. Before He could reach Simon Peter's house, where He was staying, He encountered a Roman centurion whose servant was sick.

> "Jesus Christ is the One by whom, for whom, through whom everything was made. Therefore, He knows what's wrong in your life and how to fix it."
> —**Anne Graham Lotz**

Talk About It:
What was the centurion's relationship with this dying man?

Faith in Desperate Situations

A Roman centurion was an officer of considerable authority and command. He supervised a battalion of 100 soldiers. The centurion was chosen from among the ranks, and worked his way to the top. Once he was selected to be a centurion, he was seldom promoted to a higher office. His promotions came through being given a more desirable position as a centurion. Sometimes that meant a better geographical location, and at other times it meant a better grade within the ranks. The centurions of the Bible seem to be men of high character.

By the request he made to Jesus, this centurion expressed confidence in the Lord's healing power and concern for his sick slave. The servant was lying at home paralyzed and in terrible distress. The centurion's attitude toward his servant marked him as a compassionate and considerate man.

B. The Centurion's Request (vv. 3-5)

3. And when he heard of Jesus, he sent unto him the elders of the Jews, beseeching him that he would come and heal his servant.

4. And when they came to Jesus, they besought him instantly, saying, That he was worthy for whom he should do this:

5. For he loveth our nation, and he hath built us a synagogue.

Since he was a Gentile and Jesus was a Jew, the centurion was not sure of the audience he would receive from Jesus. If He was like other Jews, He would have very little concern for the problems of a Gentile. For this reason, he approached the elders of the Jews about taking his request for help to Jesus.

The elders' approach to Jesus was instant and earnest. They contended that the centurion was worthy to be blessed on the basis of what he had done for the Jews. First, he loved their nation. This itself was a miracle. Here was one who belonged to the military profession and who was in Israel for the purpose of accustoming the Jews to endure the yoke of Roman tyranny. Yet he also submitted willingly to the God of Israel and yielded obedience to Him.

Second, the centurion built a synagogue in Capernaum for the Jews at his own expense. This action indicated the high regard he held for the Jews. Synagogues were places of worship and education. In them the young were trained in Jewish life and language, and worshipers gathered on the Sabbath to pray and read the Scripture.

Talk About It:
1. What did the centurion ask the elders to do (v. 3)?
2. How did the elders describe the centurion to Jesus (vv. 4-5)?

C. The Centurion's Understanding (vv. 6-8)

6. Then Jesus went with them. And when he was now not far from the house, the centurion sent friends to him, saying unto him, Lord, trouble not thyself: for I am not worthy that thou shouldest enter under my roof:

7. Wherefore neither thought I myself worthy to come unto thee: but say in a word, and my servant shall be healed.

8. For I also am a man set under authority, having under me soldiers, and I say unto one, Go, and he goeth; and to another, Come, and he cometh; and to my servant, Do this, and he doeth it.

Talk About It:
1. Describe the centurion's respect for and faith in Jesus (vv. 6-7).
2. What did the centurion understand about authority (v. 8)?

Jesus responded immediately to the request to help the centurion's servant. Jesus said, "I will come and heal him" (Matt. 8:7). It did not matter that Jesus had just had an exceptionally busy day and was inexpressibly weary in body. His compassion compelled Him to respond to this need.

Not prepared to speak face-to-face with Jesus, the centurion sent his friends to express his thoughts to Jesus as the Lord approached his house. The message was one of considerateness and modesty. The centurion did not feel worthy for Jesus to enter his house. For Jesus to enter his house would bring the scorn of the Jews down upon Him. The Jewish law stated that the dwelling places of Gentiles were unclean. The centurion would spare Him their scorn. Furthermore, he believed that if Jesus would just speak the word, his servant would be healed.

The centurion understood the nature of the authority of Jesus. He understood it because of his own situation. When he said he was "a man . . . under authority," he meant that his life was completely submitted to a central will. A Roman soldier was not permitted to say that he had a will of his own. His time was not his own; his dress was chosen for him; his food was chosen for him. By the law of Rome, no Roman soldier could hold any possessions. Perhaps he had never seen the emperor and would never see him, but to him the emperor was the center of life. Every march he took and every action he performed, he did under that authority.

He had somehow discovered that the Lord was living by exactly the same philosophy of life as he was. Jesus always acted and spoke conscious of the throne of God and of His relationship thereto (see John 8:26-29). Later on in His ministry, just before His ascension back to the Father, Jesus said, "All power is given unto me in heaven and in earth" (Matt. 28:18). This passage means He is now in the place of complete authority—over demons, over disease, over all the forces of nature. This centurion had discovered this truth, and he based his plea for the action of Jesus on that abiding fact.

D. The Centurion's Faith (vv. 9-10)

9. When Jesus heard these things, he marvelled at him, and turned him about, and said unto the people that followed him, I say unto you, I have not found so great faith, no, not in Israel.

"Humility is nothing else but the right judgment of ourselves."
—William Law

10. And they that were sent, returning to the house, found the servant whole that had been sick.

Jesus marveled at this man's faith. He said in effect, "I have not found such faith, no, not in a single instance in Israel." Jesus moved him to the head of the class. In faith, at least, he was higher even than the disciples.

Remember that the centurion was a Gentile and, as such, he had not been given an opportunity to develop faith. He had grown up under the influence of a polytheistic religion. He had not been born in a home where one God and one God only was honored. So, Jesus was astonished that this man who had so little had made so much of it. On the other hand, the Jews had so much and had made so little of it.

Jesus honored the faith of the centurion. In fact, He asserted that the measure of the man's faith determined the measure of the miracle. Matthew recorded that Jesus said to the centurion, "As thou hast believed, so be it done unto thee" (8:13). Jesus met faith measure for measure.

The centurion believed and acted on behalf of another. He could have desired the servant's healing and yet have done nothing about it. He added faith and action to his desire, and the servant was delivered.

III. RECOGNIZE CHRIST'S POWER TO SAVE (Luke 23:39-43)
A. Two Criminals (v. 39)

39. And one of the malefactors which were hanged railed on him, saying, If thou be Christ, save thyself and us.

Luke informs us that two "malefactors," or criminals, were led away to be crucified alongside of Jesus (v. 32). Who they were and for what crime they were to be executed is not stated. We do know, however, that this fact was a literal fulfillment of Isaiah's prophecy that the Suffering Servant was to be "numbered with the transgressors" (Isa. 53:12).

In Mark 15:32 we are informed that both criminals "heaped insults" on Jesus (NIV). This may have occurred earlier when both joined in the reproaches leveled against the Christ by almost all classes present. This one criminal, however, seems to have continually abused Christ with insulting and injurious language. He was obstinately impenitent.

B. One Criminal's Confession (vv. 40-41)

40. But the other answering rebuked him, saying, Dost not thou fear God, seeing thou art in the same condemnation?

41. And we indeed justly; for we receive the due reward of our deeds: but this man hath done nothing amiss.

Luke's account of the repentant criminal describes one of the most touching salvation scenes in all the New Testament. Horrified at the insults leveled at the Savior, and perhaps convicted by

Talk About It:
1. What caused Jesus to "marvel" (v. 9)?
2. How did the story end (v. 10)?

"Faith is the bird that sings while it is yet dark."
—Max Lucado

Talk About It:
Why did one of the criminals hurl insults at Jesus?

Talk About It:
How did the second criminal contrast himself with Jesus?

Christ's prayer of forgiveness for His executioners (v. 34), this dying criminal turned on his dying cohort with a severe rebuke. He rebuked him for not recognizing the reality and righteousness of God to whom he must some day give account.

This man confessed the innocence—yes, the sinlessness of Christ—after having confessed his own guilt and deserving of the penalty now inflicted. Here then is repentance that includes faith for salvation in the eleventh hour. But there is no record of the repentance of his comrade.

C. Forgiveness (vv. 42-43)

42. And he said unto Jesus, Lord, remember me when thou comest into thy kingdom.

43. And Jesus said unto him, Verily I say unto thee, To day shalt thou be with me in paradise.

Having expressed his personal repentance in his rebuke to his dying cohort, the one criminal now turns to the Savior at his side in faith. He addresses Jesus as "Lord," an essential expression of true faith (Rom. 10:9). He appeals for the Lord's recognition and mercy saying, "Remember me." He anticipates the kingdom of God and Jesus as its divine King.

In response to this prayer of faith, the Lord utters His second word from the cross with its promise of salvation. It is a word of divine mercy to a penitent sinner. It is a word of certainty, made with authority and assurance. It is a word of individuality: "I say to you, today you will . . ." (NKJV). It is a word of glory, for it promises paradise (see 2 Cor. 12:2-4). It is a word of immediacy: "today." It is a word of love: "Today you will be with Me" (NKJV).

CONCLUSION

A woman was exhausted from a dozen years of suffering, a Roman centurion was concerned about his gravely ill servant, and a condemned criminal was facing an eternity without God. When each one turned to Christ in desperate faith, each need was miraculously met.

If we will learn from these examples, we can expect Christ to graciously move in our lives.

GOLDEN TEXT CHALLENGE

"GOD IS OUR REFUGE AND STRENGTH, A VERY PRESENT HELP IN TROUBLE" (Ps. 46:1).

This psalm may have been composed on an occasion when Israel was facing an overwhelming military opponent. The Hebrew people were filled with fear and frustration because they thought their situation was hopeless. But God intervened on their behalf.

It is significant that Israel's boast on this occasion is in Jehovah, the living God. She could not boast in nor depend on her armies or fortresses.

Charles Spurgeon declared, "Others vaunt their impregnable castles placed on inaccessible rocks and secured with gates of iron, but God is a far better refuge from distress than all these; and when the time comes to carry the war into the enemy's territories, the Lord stands His people in better stead than all the valor of legions or the boasted strength of chariots and horses."

We must never forget that God is as much our refuge as He was when the psalmist penned these words. God alone is our all in all. All other refuges will ultimately fail. All other strength is really weakness. Power belongs to God alone. When He is our defense and strength, we are equal to all emergencies.

Daily Devotions:
M. Trusting God
   Despite the Odds
   Judges 7:1-8
T. A Daring Plan
   1 Samuel 14:6-15
W. Faith During a
   Drought
   1 Kings 17:8-16
T. A Leper
   Expresses Faith
   Mark 1:40-45
F. A Mother Believes
   Jesus
   Mark 7:25-30
S. A Father Trusts
   Jesus
   John 4:46-53

People Christ Commended

Matthew 16:13-19; Luke 10:38-42; 18:9-14

Unit Theme:
Commended by Christ

Central Truth:
Attitudes of the heart, such as faith, humility, and devotion, increase our openness to God.

Focus:
Acknowledge people Christ commended and emulate their example.

Context:
A parable and two real-life accounts of individuals whom Christ commended because of their response to Him.

Golden Text:
"The publican, standing afar off, would not lift up so much as his eyes unto heaven, but smote upon his breast, saying, God be merciful to me a sinner" (Luke 18:13).

Study Outline:
I. Commended for Faith
   (Matt. 16:13-19)
II. Commended for Humility
   (Luke 18:9-14)
III. Commended for Devotion
   (Luke 10:38-42)

INTRODUCTION

Today's lesson provides snapshot images of three individuals—one man, one woman, and a character in one of Christ's stories—who showed character traits we should emulate.

The man was Simon Peter. Until this point in his Gospel (16:13-19), here are four facts Matthew reveals about Peter: (1) He was a fisherman by trade (4:18); (2) Peter and his brother, Andrew, became disciples of Jesus (vv. 19-20); (3) Peter had boldly, though briefly, walked across stormy waves to Jesus (14:29-30); (4) Peter didn't mind asking Jesus questions (15:15).

Now when Jesus asks His disciples about His identity, it is Peter who unflinchingly states, "You are the Christ, the Son of the living God" (16:16 NKJV), and Jesus responds by calling him "blessed" (v. 17).

We, too, are blessed if we "believe" and "confess" that Jesus Christ is Lord (Rom. 10:9).

The woman in Luke 10:38-42 is Mary, the sister of Martha and Lazarus. She showed the discernment to choose between what is good and what is best. When Jesus and His disciples came to the home which she and her siblings apparently shared, Mary chose not to busy herself with preparations for the guests (which was the good thing Martha did), but instead opted to sit at Jesus' feet and learn from Him (the best option). Jesus said Mary had "chosen what is better, and it will not be taken away from her" (v. 42 NIV).

We, too, are wise when we prioritize actions that have eternal value over ones that only have earthly significance.

The person in the parable (18:9-14), called a publican, was "an agent or contract worker who collected taxes for the Roman government. . . . As a class, the tax collectors were despised by their fellow Jews. They were classified generally as 'sinners' (Matt. 9:10-11; Mark 2:15), probably because they were allowed to gather more than the government required and then to pocket the excess amount" (from *Nelson's Illustrated Bible Dictionary*).

In Christ's parable, the tax collector is commended when he humbly confesses his sins to God and begs for mercy. Emulating this man's attitude and actions—lowering ourselves before the Lord, repenting of our sins, and asking His forgiveness—will bring us into a position where God can elevate us (James 4:10).

I. COMMENDED FOR FAITH (Matt. 16:13-19)

A. A Vital Question (vv. 13-14)

13. When Jesus came into the coasts of Caesarea Philippi, he asked his disciples, saying, Whom do men say that I the Son of man am?

14. And they said, Some say that thou art John the Baptist: some, Elias; and others, Jeremias, or one of the prophets.

Elias . . . Jeremias (v. 14)—Elijah, Jeremiah

Talk About It:
1. Why do you suppose Jesus asked this question?
2. Was Jesus a prophet?

Mark indicates that this event took place while Jesus and His disciples were passing through "the villages of Caesarea Philippi" (8:27 NASB). Luke reveals that it happened while Jesus was praying and while no one was with Him but His disciples (Luke 9:18). Matthew is more indefinite about the time. John Calvin observes, "All the three unquestionably relate the same narrative; and it is possible that Christ may have stopped at a certain place during that journey to pray, and that afterwards He may have put the question to His disciples."

Jesus refers to Himself as the Son of Man. This title is found eighty-one times in the Gospels and only one time apart from the Gospels (Acts 7:56). George P. Gould offers three reasons why Jesus chose to refer to Himself frequently as the Son of Man: (1) It permitted the blending of the concept of the Suffering Servant with that of the Messianic King. (2) It was a title already associated with the glorious coming of One who should have everlasting rule over a world in which the powers of evil should no more have sway. (3) If the Son of Man, telling of descent from heaven, spoke of a closer association with God than did any other current Messianic title, so did it speak also of close association with humanity.

By the messages He preached, the miracles He performed, and the life He lived, Jesus had, for nearly three years, made known to His disciples that He was the Messiah, the predicted King, the Son of God. He now asks them two questions to determine how well they have learned from His teaching. The questions are also designed to probe their thinking.

Their answer to Jesus' question "Who do people say the Son of Man is?" (NIV) was very kind. They could have told Him that many regarded Him as a fanatic, an impostor, or even a glutton and a drunkard. Instead, they spoke of the great respect many had for Him. Some thought He was John the Baptist; others thought He was Elijah; still others considered Him to be Jeremiah or, at least, one of the prophets. The people were divided in their opinion of Jesus.

Perhaps the characteristic about John the Baptist that was most pronounced was his courage. It was reflected in the authority with which he spoke. It was seen in his bold denunciation of evil wherever he encountered it. It was revealed in his passionate

plea to prepare through repentance for the coming kingdom of God. And did not Jesus minister with the same courage, boldness, and authority?

What was there about Jesus that made some people believe He was Elijah? Perhaps it was because of His miracle-working power. Elijah was also noted for the many miracles that God wrought through him.

What was there about Jesus that made some people believe He was Jeremiah? Perhaps some thought they caught, in the cadences of His prayers and in His denunciations of the hypocritical religious leaders, the voice of the prophet Jeremiah. They must have seen in this Man of Sorrows reflections of the weeping prophet.

However lofty their notions about Jesus were, they were not high enough. He was far greater than the greatest man who ever lived before Him or after Him.

> "Among the Jews there suddenly turns up a man who goes about talking as He is God. . . . God, in their language, meant the Being outside the world who made it and was infinitely different from anything else."
> —C. S. Lewis

B. A Crucial Confession (vv. 15-16)

15. He saith unto them, But whom say ye that I am?

16. And Simon Peter answered and said, Thou art the Christ, the Son of the living God.

> **Talk About It:**
> What does "the Christ" mean?

Now Jesus asks His disciples the second question: "Who do you say I am?" (NIV). In other words, "Is your concept of Me on the same level with that of the people? Have My teachings revealed to you more than they have been able to grasp? How much of My teaching have you understood?"

The disciples were united in their opinion of Jesus. Peter expressed the sentiment of the group when he said, "You are the Christ, the Son of the living God" (v. 16 NKJV). His expression is that of a man who means what he says, who values the truth he speaks, and who attaches deep importance to it. He is definite in his answer. His words exalt and glorify Jesus.

Peter spoke not only for the disciples, but for believers in all ages. When he referred to Jesus as "the Christ" (the Anointed One), he meant the predicted Messiah, the Redeemer, the Savior of the world. His expression embraces all that is contained in our salvation. It includes both an everlasting Kingdom and an everlasting priesthood. The work of Christ is designed to reconcile us to God, to obtain for us a perfect righteousness, and to uphold and supply and enrich us with every description of blessings.

Peter also referred to Jesus as "the Son of the living God." He meant all those words could signify as contrasted with the prophets and saints of all ages. Christ is a unique Being to whom we can pray and in whose unseen presence we can trust. When the attribute *living* is ascribed to God, it is for the purpose of distinguishing between Him and dead idols who are nothing (see 1 Cor. 8:4).

> "Jesus Christ, the condescension of Divinity, and the exaltation of humanity."
> —Phillips Brooks

People Christ Commended

C. A Divine Revelation (v. 17)

17. And Jesus answered and said unto him, Blessed art thou, Simon Barjona: for flesh and blood hath not revealed it unto thee, but my Father which is in heaven.

A crude fisherman makes the greatest confession that a person can make and thereby declares God's greatest purpose for humanity. The religious leaders should have been aware of what was happening. Yet they were ignorant of what God was doing.

In those days, only those deeply learned in the Law were considered capable of leading God's chosen people. But Jesus gathered around Him a group of men who were without formal training but whose hearts were teachable. Upon these men, He placed His hopes for the winning of the world to Himself. God is still working through humble, honest, and faithful men and women today.

Peter's answer was a source of great joy to Jesus. He immediately assigned the source of Peter's knowledge to the heavenly Father. Likewise, everyone who has come to perceive this truth has had their eyes opened by God that they might see His glory in Christ.

Jesus' manner of making Himself known to His disciples was instructive. He did not tell them who He was, but He led them to make the discovery for themselves. Thus they were convinced in their own minds and were ready to share with others what they had learned. Someone has said that if a man is convinced against his will, he is unconvinced still. But when the glorious truth of the person and work of Christ shines upon the soul, one is ready to embrace it and share it. Peter had arrived at that point of faith.

Jesus also strengthened the disciples' faith by giving them an opportunity to confess it. Once they had admitted to one another what they believed, they were reinforced in that belief. They formed a bond of unity and shared a common faith. The same bond of unity should exist in each Bible-believing local church as well as in an entire denomination. We draw strength from the knowledge that others hold to our faith. No wonder the Lord told Peter that he was entitled to a great blessing—a type of joy higher than anything the world confers. Nothing the world has to offer can begin to compare with the riches of fellowship one finds in Christ Jesus.

D. A Divine Proclamation (vv. 18-19)

18. And I say also unto thee, That thou art Peter, and upon this rock I will build my church; and the gates of hell shall not prevail against it.

19. And I will give unto thee the keys of the kingdom of heaven: and whatsoever thou shalt bind on earth shall be bound in heaven: and whatsoever thou shalt loose on earth shall be loosed in heaven.

Barjona (v. 17)—son of Jonah

Talk About It:
What can natural understanding not accomplish (v. 17)?

Talk About It:
1. What is the Church built upon (v. 18)?
2. What does Christ reveal about hell (v. 18)?
3. What is meant by "bind" and "loose" (v. 19)?

Jesus says that He will build His church upon a rock. He means that the foundation on which He builds is sound, secure, stable, and impregnable. Many biblical references are made to God as a rock (cf. Ps. 18:1-2; 1 Cor. 10:3-4). But perhaps the most beautiful reference to Christ as a rock is made by Peter: "As you come to him, the living Stone—rejected by men but chosen by God and precious to him—you also, like living stones, are being built into a spiritual house to be a holy priesthood, offering spiritual sacrifices acceptable to God through Jesus Christ" (1 Peter 2:4-5 NIV).

Jesus says that Peter is a rock. By nature he was but a handful of sand, but Christ touched him and "petrified" him into a rock that neither earth nor hell could move. William Barclay comments: "[Peter] is not the rock on which the Church is founded; that rock is God. He is the first initial foundation stone of the whole Church. Peter [made] the leap of faith which saw in Jesus Christ the Son of the living God. . . . And in ages to come, everyone who makes the same discovery as Peter is another and another stone added into the edifice of the Church of Christ." Paul says that the Church is "built on the foundation of the apostles and prophets, with Christ Jesus himself as the chief cornerstone" (Eph. 2:20 NIV).

When Jesus gave "the keys of the kingdom" to Peter, He was sharing with him both opportunity and responsibility. Peter was to use those keys to open the door of the Kingdom to others. He used them on the Day of Pentecost (Acts 2:41); he used the keys again in the house of Cornelius, opening to him and his household dimensions of spiritual insight and reality they had never known before (10:44).

When Jesus gave Peter the keys of the Kingdom, He charged him to make decisions that would affect all believers. What an awesome responsibility! His decision about the life and practice of believers would have far-reaching consequences. Peter's activity and argument before the Council at Jerusalem (Acts 15:7-11) indicates how seriously he accepted the responsibility Christ gave him. The keys to the Kingdom were not given to Peter alone. Every believer has the opportunity to help open the doors of the Kingdom to others.

"These things are required of all church members: repentance from sin and faith in Jesus Christ."
—*Cambridge Declaration*

II. COMMENDED FOR HUMILITY (Luke 18:9-14)
A. Parable for the Self-righteous (vv. 9-10)
9. And he spake this parable unto certain which trusted in themselves that they were righteous, and despised others:
10. Two men went up into the temple to pray; the one a Pharisee, and the other a publican.

Making use of the effective teaching tool known as the parable, Jesus aimed His words at the self-righteous persons "which trusted in themselves." These were "self-made" individuals who had become prosperous in material things and felt superior to others who had not accumulated the status symbols of that day.

One of the worst spiritual conditions is having such conceit that one has contempt toward all others, looking down upon them with a holier-than-thou attitude (Isa. 65:5). If one trusts in his or her own righteousness, then that person gives up access to the righteousness of Christ and the power of His resurrection.

In verse 10, Jesus set the situation for His story—two men who are opposites with a pending conflict. In one short sentence, Jesus created suspense for His story.

It is good for people to come to church to pray, and it is good for churches to be open as much as possible for people to enter and pray. The Temple at Jerusalem had regular hours for prayer in the middle of the morning and in the middle of the afternoon, and at these times large crowds would gather. However, the motive for being in the Temple at the time of prayer was different for the Pharisee than it was for the tax collector ("publican"). The tax collector really came to pray, while the Pharisee came because it was a public place where he could show off his prominence. It is good to question our own motives today for going to church, for some still go mainly to show off, to be entertained, to maintain a front, to keep up social connections—all of which are unacceptable reasons before God for being present at the place of worship.

Talk About It:
1. For whom did Jesus teach this parable?
2. What did the Pharisee and the publican have in common?

"I wouldn't say he's conceited, but he's absolutely convinced that if he hadn't been born, people would want to know why not."
—*Quotable Quotations*

B. Prideful Pharisee (vv. 11-12)

11. The Pharisee stood and prayed thus with himself, God, I thank thee, that I am not as other men are, extortioners, unjust, adulterers, or even as this publican.

12. I fast twice in the week, I give tithes of all that I possess.

To compare one's own spirituality with that of another person is unwise. One should always compare himself with Christ, and he or she will always be humble.

An air of superiority makes a person inferior in God's eyes. Although the Pharisee undoubtedly was honest in that he had not done the crimes he mentioned, he had no right to consider himself better than anyone else in Jerusalem.

It is significant that the Pharisee's prayer was not heard—he was "praying this to himself" (NASB). Seldom was anyone more religious but less spiritual than this man! He tried to speak to God as an equal, selling himself on the basis of all his imagined qualities, trying to convince God of his worthiness and holiness. He was fooling only himself.

Talk About It:
1. Was the Pharisee correct in saying, "I am not like other men" (v. 11 NIV)?
2. How did the Pharisee justify himself (v. 12)?

The Pharisee did have two good qualities—fasting and tithing. We wish we had more people who would practice these disciplines today, but these commendable acts are canceled out by impure motives, especially pride.

C. Humble Tax Collector (vv. 13-14)

13. And the publican, standing afar off, would not lift up so much as his eyes unto heaven, but smote upon his breast, saying, God be merciful to me a sinner.

14. I tell you, this man went down to his house justified rather than the other: for every one that exalteth himself shall be abased; and he that humbleth himself shall be exalted.

Talk About It:
1. Describe the tax collector's attitude and actions (v. 13).
2. Who will experience humility (v. 14)?

The usual posture in prayer of the ancient Jews was to stand, with arms stretched upward, hands open to receive God's blessings, and eyes open toward heaven. The Pharisee prayed in this manner, undoubtedly in a prominent place where he could be seen of many in the Temple; but the tax collector sought a secluded spot. He was too ashamed of his sins to even open his eyes toward heaven. In his grief, the tax collector beat his chest, repeating the words, "God be merciful to me a sinner." He was pleading for God's forgiveness, recognizing that he did not deserve it.

The tax collector's prayer was answered because he acknowledged the true state of his heart and condition of his life before God and threw himself on the Lord's mercy. The Pharisee asked not for mercy but for justice, and that he received—what he deserved.

Jesus announced another foundational spiritual law here: "Everyone who exalts himself will be humbled, and he who humbles himself will be exalted" (v. 14 NKJV).

The Pharisee felt self-sufficient; the publican felt his dependence on God. If anyone will honestly confess his or her dependence on God, genuine humility will result naturally from this attitude. God will recognize it, grant mercy, and answer prayers.

Do we realize that we are dependent entirely on God for life's blessings? Do we give Him all the credit for anything we are able to accomplish? That is the starting point of humility, yet humility is nothing to be boastful about. If it is there, God will know it, and so will others. If it is not there, God and others easily recognize the fact. The tax collector's prayer is a proper prayer for anyone who realizes that they have been sinful in allowing pride to grow in their hearts.

"The higher a man is in grace, the lower he will be in his own self-esteem."
—Charles Spurgeon

III. COMMENDED FOR DEVOTION (Luke 10:38-42)
A. A Preoccupied Life (vv. 38, 40-41)

38. Now it came to pass, as they went, that he entered into a certain village: and a certain woman named Martha received him into her house.

40. But Martha was cumbered about much serving, and came to him, and said, Lord, dost thou not care that my sister hath left me to serve alone? bid her therefore that she help me.

41. And Jesus answered and said unto her, Martha, Martha, thou art careful and troubled about many things.

We know from John 12 that the "certain village" was Bethany. This village was about two miles from Jerusalem. Jesus and the Twelve had been traveling from Galilee back toward Jerusalem when they reached Bethany (Luke 9:51). It was the home of two sisters, Martha and Mary, and their brother, Lazarus.

There are no earlier references in Luke to this family. It is likely this was one of the first meetings between Jesus and the family; it is clear the entire family developed a close relationship with Him and were perhaps His most intimate friends outside the circle of the Twelve.

It is likely that Jesus and the Twelve are to be served a meal. If Lazarus is present (he is not mentioned in the text), that would make at least sixteen people to serve.

The word translated "cumbered" (10:40) in the King James Version is used only here in the New Testament. It has the sense of "distracted, quite busy, overburdened." Martha's busyness concerned "much serving." The Greek for "serving" is *diakonia*, a word that carries the sense of waiting on tables. Her attitude and action stands in contrast to earlier words of Jesus, "Seek ye first the kingdom of God, and his righteousness" (Matt. 6:33).

Jesus perceived that Martha's spirit was "careful and troubled" (Luke 10:41). *Careful* has the sense of "anxiety, worry." There are several New Testament passages that speak to this: Matthew 6:25; Philippians 4:6; 1 Peter 5:7. The word for *troubled* has the sense of "distracted, in disorder." We can take the meaning to be that Martha had her priorities in a wrong order. Because of this, her spirit was troubled and distraction was the order of her life.

Perhaps Jesus revealed her area of temptation: the control of the routine. This may be the greatest area of temptation facing many of us. We have learned to "flee from evil" when it presents itself as a clearly perceived moral problem. Yet, many of us are dominated by the god of preoccupation. This god is deceptive, but his tactics accomplish the same objectives of keeping us from hearing and obeying God's voice.

B. A Receptive Heart (vv. 39, 42)

39. And she had a sister called Mary, which also sat at Jesus' feet, and heard his word.

42. But one thing is needful: and Mary hath chosen that good part, which shall not be taken away from her.

cumbered about (v. 40)—"distracted by" (NIV)

careful (v. 41)— "worried" (NKJV)

Talk About It:
1. What did Martha request (v. 40)?
2. How did Jesus describe Martha (v. 41)?

"How rare it is to find a soul quiet enough to hear God speak." —Francois Fenelon

Talk About It:
1. Describe Mary's actions (v. 39).
2. How did Jesus describe Mary's choice (v. 42)?

Mary is presented in the Gospels as a contemplative woman who had a deep commitment to the kingdom of God and Jesus. In John 11 we are given additional insight into how she dealt with difficulty. She is terribly stricken by grief at the death of her brother. Upon hearing that Jesus had arrived at the house, she went to Him and lamented that her brother would not have died if Jesus had been present. Jesus was deeply moved by her grief as well as the grief of others around.

While it would be a mistake to try and read too much into Mary's and Martha's respective personalities, it is clear that Jesus had a very special relationship with this family.

Only in Luke 10:39 in the New Testament is this particular verb form used for "sat." It carries the sense of "having taken her place at the Lord's feet" (Bauer). The verb tense for "heard" is imperfect and can be translated as "kept listening to His Word" (Bauer). The stress of the meaning is upon Mary's apparent insistence on remaining near the Lord in order to keep listening. No doubt she heard Martha's complaint (v. 40). Yet, she remained where she was and was not detracted in her listening. This is a marvelous attitude regarding our place before the Lord. She was being criticized yet she still listened to Christ. Her spirit is one of single purpose. It has been said that "purity of heart is to will one thing." This saying captures the beauty of Mary's life before the Lord.

Jesus' remark in verse 42 is reminiscent of His statement to the rich young ruler, "One thing thou lackest" (Mark 10:21). While the focus was negative in that passage, the focus is positive here. The "needful" has a sense of the "necessary." The "good part" refers to an allotment, or inheritance. The same word is used in Colossians 1:12, where Paul rejoices that God in Christ has enabled us to share in the inheritance of the saints of His riches in glory. Mary chose to be in submissive relationship to Jesus prior to anything else. In His presence, there was no need for pretense or human effort to please. He received from her the adoration and willingness to hear and obey.

"Whatever is your best time in the day, give that to communion with God."
—Hudson Taylor

Such an attitude creates riches in glory that cannot be touched by moths or rust. Mary committed herself to priorities that were eternal. By sitting at His feet, she did not indicate a lazy attitude toward life; rather, she reflected the knowledge of combining time and priority for His sake. Worrying over serving Jesus was not nearly as important as being in relationship with Him and listening.

CONCLUSION

Mary was commended for prioritizing her relationship with Jesus. Peter was commended for vocalizing his belief that Jesus is the Son of God. A tax collector was commended for humbling himself before the Lord.

What does Jesus Christ find to commend in our lives?

GOLDEN TEXT CHALLENGE

"THE PUBLICAN, STANDING AFAR OFF, WOULD NOT LIFT UP SO MUCH AS HIS EYES UNTO HEAVEN, BUT SMOTE UPON HIS BREAST, SAYING, GOD BE MERCIFUL TO ME A SINNER" (Luke 18:13).

Rather than seeking a prominent place in which to pray, the tax collector "stood at a distance" (NIV). This perhaps meant he refrained from entering the courtyard that was immediately next to the Temple proper; he may have stayed in the Court of the Gentiles.

Nonetheless, the Pharisee spotted the man and obviously despised him. Rather than perceiving that the tax collector's bowed head and beating on his chest represented sincere prayer to God, the Pharisee bragged that he was "not . . . like this tax collector" (v. 11 NIV).

The tax collector was so awed by the holiness of God and so overwhelmed by his own guilt and unworthiness that he did not dare to look up, while the Pharisee was so enamored with himself that he could not look down . . . except to briefly note the "sinner" who was "standing afar off."

The Pharisee returned home with the same thing he had carried to the Temple—self-approval. The tax collector went with divine forgiveness, with a right standing in the courts of heaven.

Daily Devotions:
M. Honored by a Divine Visit
Genesis 18:1-5, 17-21
T. Blessed for Obedience
Genesis 22:13-18
W. Intimacy With God Recognized
Exodus 33:8-11
T. Commended for Endurance
Revelation 2:1-3
F. Commended for Faithfulness
Revelation 2:8-11
S. Commended for Perseverance
Revelation 3:7-13

Gratitude for Deliverance

Luke 8:26-39; 17:11-19; 18:35-43

Unit Theme:
Commended by Christ

Central Truth:
In response to God's goodness, a Christian should live in an attitude of thanksgiving and worship.

Focus:
Review three grateful responses to healing and live in an attitude of thanksgiving and worship.

Context:
Three accounts of individuals whom Christ delivered from hopeless situations

Golden Text:
"Bless the Lord, O my soul: and all that is within me, bless his holy name. Bless the Lord, O my soul, and forget not all his benefits" (Ps. 103:1-2).

Study Outline:
I. Gratitude Produces Testimony
    (Luke 8:26-39)
II. Gratitude Produces Thanksgiving
    (Luke 17:11-19)
III. Gratitude Produces Worship
    (Luke 18:35-43)

INTRODUCTION

Thanksgiving is one area of Christian discipleship that has largely been neglected. Once a year, in November, we remind ourselves of our responsibility to show gratitude. Other than that, very little is said about the subject. Yet the Bible speaks frequently of praise and thanksgiving. The Psalms in particular are filled with exhortations to express gratitude. In Psalm 107 the psalmist burst forth four times with the cry, "Oh that men would praise the Lord for his goodness, and for his wonderful works to the children of men!" (vv. 8, 15, 21, 31).

The Lord's dealings with us make thanksgiving and praise the fitting reply. As we reflect on the wondrous goodness of God, we ought to pause and show gratitude to Him. At the same time, we should be appalled at the little thought and strength and time that people give to thanksgiving. This is true even of the average Christian. Oh, that we would stir ourselves to show our Lord our love and gratitude for Him!

The psalmist says it best: "It is good to give thanks to the Lord and to sing praises to Your name, O Most High; to declare Your lovingkindness in the morning and Your faithfulness by night. . . . For You, O Lord, have made me glad by what You have done, I will sing for joy at the works of Your hands" (92:1-2, 4 NASB).

Thanksgiving is more than a privilege; it is also a responsibility. To fail to thank the Lord for His blessings is just as distinct and definite disobedience to God's commands as to steal or to murder. To the Ephesians, Paul said, "Among you there must not be even a hint of sexual immorality, or of any kind of impurity, or of greed, because these are improper for God's holy people. Nor should there be obscenity, foolish talk or coarse joking, which are out of place, but rather thanksgiving" (Eph. 5:3-4 NIV).

Today's lesson speaks of three people who expressed gratitude to the Lord for His intervention in their lives. Their gratitude produced testimony, thanksgiving, and worship.

I. GRATITUDE PRODUCES TESTIMONY (Luke 8:26-39)

A. The Distressed Demoniac (vv. 26-29)

26. And they arrived at the country of the Gadarenes, which is over against Galilee.

27. And when he went forth to land, there met him out of the city a certain man, which had devils long time, and ware no clothes, neither abode in any house, but in the tombs.

28. When he saw Jesus, he cried out, and fell down before him, and with a loud voice said, What have I to do with thee, Jesus, thou Son of God most high? I beseech thee, torment me not.

29. (For he had commanded the unclean spirit to come out of the man. For oftentimes it had caught him: and he was kept bound with chains and in fetters; and he brake the bands, and was driven of the devil into the wilderness.)

> **country of the Gadarenes (v. 26)**— a region near the cities of Gadara and Gergesa

Immediately after the stilling of the tempest, the ship bearing Christ and His disciples arrived in the country of the Gadarenes. He had just exhibited His limitless power over nature, spoken peace to the winds and waves, and hushed the violently disturbed elements with a word (vv. 22-25). Here in Gadara, however, was something more fearful than a storm at sea—a man broken loose from all restraint and possessed by demons. He presented a fearsome appearance, wore no clothes, occupied no house, and sheltered himself in hillside tombs.

Dropping to his knees, the wild uncontrollable man addressed the Savior as "Son of God most high." It appears that his saner, better self caused him to run to Christ with a hope of rescue from the demons that possessed him, spoke with his voice, and forced him to utter their wishes, fears, and hatred of Christ. Be that as it may, he had come to the only place where there was hope and to the only Being on earth who could free him (Acts 4:12).

How accurately Luke 8:29 portrays the condition of sinners! Bound by the power of Satan, they do their master's bidding as a slave. They are in the "gall of bitterness and in the bond of iniquity" (Acts 8:23), "carnal [and] sold under sin" (Rom. 7:14), a servant of the devil, whom they obey (6:16). Thus bound by the power of the devil and driven deeper and deeper into sin, life for them becomes a wilderness of despair.

> **Talk About It:**
> 1. Describe the unnamed man's physical, emotional, and spiritual condition (vv. 27, 29).
> 2. Describe and explain the actions of the suffering man (v. 28).

> "Demons have personality and speed, seem to express the emotion of fear, promote uncleanness, torment, and create mental disorders. Yet, the glorious truth is that demons must obey the commands of Jesus Christ."
> —Ron Phillips

B. The Sympathetic Savior (vv. 30-33)

30. And Jesus asked him, saying, What is thy name? And he said, Legion: because many devils were entered into him.

31. And they besought him that he would not command them to go out into the deep.

32. And there was there an herd of many swine feeding on the mountain: and they besought him that he would suffer them to enter into them. And he suffered them.

> **the deep (v. 31)**—"the Abyss" (NIV) or "the bottomless pit" (TLB)

33. Then went the devils out of the man, and entered into the swine: and the herd ran violently down a steep place into the lake, and were choked.

Talk About It:
1. What is the significance of the name "Legion" (v. 30)?
2. What did Jesus allow the evil spirits to do, and what was the result (vv. 31-33)?

As in every other critical situation in Christ's ministry, He was calm when confronted with the fury of the demons. With unruffled kindness, He asked the man his name. His inquiry was answered by the demons who said their name was Legion, for they were many.

Isn't it strange that demons pleaded with Christ for mercy and consideration? One would hardly expect it, but they did. Nothing confirms limitless power and authority over all things and creatures than this servile request. In making it, they freely confess His sovereignty and power over them.

The language of degradation, terror, and alarm used by the demons further confirms Christ's power over them (vv. 31-32). They knew there was a divine will at work against them, and that the bottomless pit would receive them in the end. When they found there was no alternative but to leave the man, they begged Christ's permission to enter into a herd of swine not far away. Anything was better than perdition. Christ's reason for permitting them to enter the animals is obscure, but it may have been to show the people of Gadara what mischief the devil could do were he not restrained by a mightier power. Or it may have been necessary to the complete healing of the man and his future peace of mind, that he should have visible evidence and testimony that the awful powers which had held him captive had come out of him.

"Strong man that he is, Satan has been dispossessed by One stronger."
—Ron Phillips

The demons gained their wish; their request was granted, and with it they suffered further abasement. They went out of the man into the swine. Suddenly maddened by the entrance of the demons into them, the whole herd stampeded down the hillside and perished in the waters of the Sea of Galilee.

C. The Amazed Multitude (vv. 34-37)

34. When they that fed them saw what was done, they fled, and went and told it in the city and in the country.

35. Then they went out to see what was done; and came to Jesus, and found the man, out of whom the devils were departed, sitting at the feet of Jesus, clothed, and in his right mind: and they were afraid.

36. They also which saw it told them by what means he that was possessed of the devils was healed.

37. Then the whole multitude of the country of the Gadarenes round about besought him to depart from them; for they were taken with great fear: and he went up into the ship, and returned back again.

The men who fed the pigs knew that Christ gave the demons permission to enter them. The result was disastrous. Consequently, they fled from the scene, not so much because of the destruction of the swine but because the presence of Christ filled them with terror.

The townspeople were more interested in what happened to the swine than in what happened to their demoniac neighbor. In fact, it appears that they either had not heard that angle of the story or were wholly unconcerned about it. Perhaps they were even surprised to find the man, whom they had known as a maniac, quietly sitting at the feet of Christ wearing clothes like anybody else and in his right mind. While he was in the power of the demons, he was ready to fly in the face of Christ. Now he sits worshipfully near Him, a changed, normal man again. The dangerous demoniac has become a meek disciple, and thereby a potential blessing to the community.

Those who were present when Christ cast the demons out of the man now informed the people from the city how it was done. This only added to their fear of Christ. And what did they fear in Him, if not His power and authority over the unseen world? The man crouching at the feet of Christ, now plainly no longer possessed by demons, was living proof of that. Being unable to describe their feelings of awe and dread in His presence, they shrank from Him as though they feared He would do them harm. They asked Jesus to leave them, so He did.

D. The Grateful Witness (vv. 38-39)

38. Now the man out of whom the devils were departed besought him that he might be with him: but Jesus sent him away, saying,

39. Return to thine own house, and shew how great things God hath done unto thee. And he went his way, and published throughout the whole city how great things Jesus had done unto him.

As Jesus sent His disciples away that they might help Him to do His work (10:1-3), so He sent the healed man back to his family and friends. He told him, in effect, to go to those who knew him best, and to testify of all the fearful circumstances from which he had been saved. His first task was to tell the good news to his own household.

Prior to this, Christ had told those He healed to keep silent concerning it, but that was in the part of Judea where Christ's enemies dwelled, where He intended to continue working, and where the people were ready to make Him a leader and to rise against the Romans. In the country east of the lake, there were none of these reasons for secrecy as to Christ's miracles, and moreover, this healed man was the only agent for evangelizing the region.

Talk About It:
1. What did the pig-herders do (v. 34)?
2. Describe the condition of the man whom Jesus helped (v. 35).
3. Describe the response of the local people (vv. 36-37).

"There is a true, living, all-powerful God on His throne ruling in omnipotent majesty—that fact, and that alone, is enough to make demons tremble."
—David Griffis

Talk About It:
What was the result of this man's transformation?

The healed demoniac obeyed Jesus and did more than Jesus asked. Verse 39 says he "told all over town how much Jesus had done for him" (NIV). In Mark's account of this miracle, he says the man went all over Decapolis—the region east and southeast of the Sea of Galilee. His message was simple but glorious. He told "how great things Jesus had done for him," and he told it with such loving compassion that "all men did marvel" (5:20).

"Christianity is one beggar telling another beggar where to find food."
—D. T. Niles

II. GRATITUDE PRODUCES THANKSGIVING (Luke 17:11-19)
A. Cry for Mercy (vv. 11-13)

11. And it came to pass, as he went to Jerusalem, that he passed through the midst of Samaria and Galilee.

12. And as he entered into a certain village, there met him ten men that were lepers, which stood afar off:

13. And they lifted up their voices, and said, Jesus, Master, have mercy on us.

Every village in Christ's day had its leprous outcasts, who lived on the dung heaps, ostracized from society. There were no charitable institutions to take care of these unfortunate souls in their dire need. They were left to perish in their agony of body and soul, despised and rejected.

Talk About It:
1. Why did the lepers stand "afar off" (v. 12)?
2. What did they request (v. 13)?

Although the Jews had no dealings with the Samaritans, in this group of lepers there was at least one Samaritan. William Barclay observes: "Here is an example of one great law of life. A common misfortune had broken down the racial and the national barriers. In the common tragedy of their leprosy they had forgotten that they were Jews and Samaritans and remembered only that they were men in need. It is sad that if a flood surges over a piece of country, and the wild animals congregate on some little bit of higher ground, you will see standing together animals who are natural enemies and who, at any other time, would have done their best to kill each other. Surely one of the things which should draw all men together is their common need of God."

The ten lepers who met Jesus as He entered the village stood afar off. This they were required to do by the Law. "As for the leper who has the infection, his clothes shall be torn, and the hair of his head shall be uncovered, and he shall cover his mustache and cry, 'Unclean! Unclean!' He shall remain unclean all the days during which he has the infection; he is unclean. He shall live alone; his dwelling shall be outside the camp" (Lev. 13:45-46 NASB). The exact distance at which a leper should stand is not stated. At least one authority declared that when the wind was blowing from the leper to the healthy person, the leper should stand at least fifty yards away. What a vivid illustration of the utter isolation in which lepers lived!

Although these ten lepers were outcasts, their wisdom is seen in their turning to Jesus in their hour of need. They had heard through some means about His miracle-working power. Perhaps they had heard of other lepers whom He had cleansed. With their weak voices they cried, "Jesus, Master, have mercy on us."

In this heartrending plea for mercy we hear all humanity crying to God for deliverance from the ravages of sin. We, too, were outcasts in our state of sin. We, too, needed the cleansing power of Christ to make us whole and set us in right relation again with God and with our fellowmen. Our salvation did not depend on our knowledge or understanding of the doctrines of the church. We were saved by throwing ourselves completely and utterly on the love of God as revealed in Jesus Christ.

> "Yes, there is only one thing that will save us in this hour of desperation, and that is prayer."
> —**Stephen Olford**

B. Command to Go (v. 14)

14. And when he saw them, he said unto them, Go shew yourselves unto the priests. And it came to pass, that, as they went, they were cleansed.

Jesus required these ten lepers to perform an act of faith in Him. They had not yet begun to feel their foul blood cleansed. The horrible dryness of leprosy had not yielded to healthy perspiration. Yet they were to go where the priests lived to be examined by them and to be pronounced clean. They were to exhibit faith in Christ's power to heal them by going to show themselves healed.

Talk About It:
How did Jesus test the lepers' faith?

The lesson Jesus is teaching us in this story is that faith obeys Him. This does not mean that He requires everyone to declare their healing before there is evidence of it. That is what He required of the ten lepers, but it is not necessarily what He expects from others. Some of those who came to Him He healed instantly. Others He instructed to do certain things, such as wash in the Pool of Siloam. The important thing always is that the subject do what the Master asks. We should not come to Him with preconceived notions about how He is going to deal with us. He is sovereign.

C. The Grateful Samaritan (vv. 15-16)

15. And one of them, when he saw that he was healed, turned back, and with a loud voice glorified God,

16. And fell down on his face at his feet, giving him thanks: and he was a Samaritan.

The combination of faith and obedience brought healing to the ten lepers. Jesus told them to go and show themselves to the priests. As they were on their way, they were cleansed. Jesus could just as well have performed the miracle when they were in His presence, but He chose to test their faith. The amazing miracle took place as they obeyed Him.

Talk About It:
Describe the actions of the Samaritan.

When one of the lepers realized that he was healed, he came back to Jesus, praising God in a loud voice. The weak cry for help had been changed into a strong voice of praise.

Think of how this leper must have felt. His body had been marred and disfigured as the treacherous disease ate away at his bones and flesh. Now, instead of decaying, raw flesh, he had clean, new skin. There was no more pain, and the stench and filth with which he had continuously lived were gone forever.

Can you imagine the mental and spiritual anguish this leper had suffered? What could be worse than utter loneliness and desolation? He had been cut off completely from family and friends and social fellowship. But now he could again enter into the stream of life. He could be reunited with his family and friends. He would no longer bear the stigma, "unclean," which had cut him off from others. All barriers were gone, and he was free to go wherever he desired.

Is it surprising that we hear him praising the Lord with a loud voice? The joy and happiness which he felt must have known no bounds. How sweet are the sounds of praise!

"The worship most acceptable to God comes from a thankful and cheerful heart."
—*Plutarch*

D. The Ungrateful Nine (vv. 17-18)

17. And Jesus answering said, Were there not ten cleansed? but where are the nine?

18. There are not found that returned to give glory to God, save this stranger.

Talk About It:
1. What was Jesus' question (v. 17)?
2. Why did Jesus call this man a "stranger" (v. 18)?

Jesus inquires about the nine Jewish lepers who were cleansed but who did not return to offer thanks. As long as their plight was the same as that of the Samaritan, they associated with him. But as soon as they were cleansed, they seemed to have separated themselves from him. It was as if now that they were saved from being outcasts, they could no longer associate together. Are we not guilty of adopting the same attitude? We express love for a native in a foreign land, but neglect to minister to our neighbor.

Not only did the nine lepers disassociate themselves from the Samaritan, but they also put their religious observance above their gratitude. They were more interested in seeing the priest than in praising God for the miracle they had experienced. They were more concerned about being declared fit to return to society than they were in worshiping the God who made them fit. How quickly we forget. In many ways we are as guilty as were the nine lepers. Have we never been more interested in the gift than in the Giver? Have we never put more stock in the healing than in the Healer? We need to take a look at our priorities. We need to reevaluate the things that really matter to us. In short, we need to put God first in our lives.

Inasmuch as only one man—and he a foreigner—returned to give thanks to the Lord, perhaps we can learn something about true thanksgiving. Genuine praise is marked by individuality. The Samaritan did not take his cue from the other nine. He did not

wait until they turned back to praise before he did so. No, he acted on his own. He felt a personal need to express the gratitude of his heart. Gratitude is a very personal thing. Nobody else can express for me what I feel. Each believer has a personal responsibility to render thanks to the Lord.

E. The Pronouncement (v. 19)
19. And he said unto him, Arise, go thy way: thy faith hath made thee whole.

There was for the healed Samaritan a glad word of blessed assurance and promise. Jesus declared him whole. His faith had resulted not only in his physical well-being, but in complete wholeness. In His statement, Jesus called attention to the means of the cure, namely, faith in Himself. In so doing, He is nurturing that germ of new life into fuller trust in His divine person. He also indicates that the faith which first had secured the healing of the body and which was manifested in the man's return and his gratitude now secured for him the salvation of his soul.

III. GRATITUDE PRODUCES WORSHIP (Luke 18:35-43)
A. Pleading for Help (vv. 35-39)
35. And it came to pass, that as he was come nigh unto Jericho, a certain blind man sat by the way side begging:

36. And hearing the multitude pass by, he asked what it meant.

37. And they told him, that Jesus of Nazareth passeth by.

38. And he cried, saying, Jesus, thou son of David, have mercy on me.

39. And they which went before rebuked him, that he should hold his peace: but he cried so much the more, Thou son of David, have mercy on me.

Jericho was a very popular resort about 18 miles from Jerusalem. It was often called "the City of Palms" and "the City of Perfumes." It had become an important city of Herod the Great. Its palm groves and balsam gardens had been given to Cleopatra by Antony. These had been purchased from her by Herod. He designated Jericho as one of his royal cities. He constructed many stately buildings and spent much of his time in the city. In fact, it was here that he died.

There was quite a contrast between Herod the Great, who had owned the city, and blind Bartimaeus, who sat by the roadside, begging, the day Jesus came to town. Bartimaeus, as he is called in Mark 10:46, must have heard that Jesus was the One who could cause people to see, the One who could meet human needs. The name of Jesus had become a household word in many of the villages and towns of Judea. It was a welcome sound among those who were sick and afflicted. Now Jesus was approaching Jericho! A new expectancy took over as Bartimaeus heard more people call the name of Jesus.

"If gratitude is due from children to their earthly parents, how much more is the gratitude of the great family of men due to our Father in heaven?"
—Hosea Ballou

Talk About It:
Rephrase the statement, "Thy faith hath made thee whole."

Talk About It:
1. What did the blind man hear (vv. 35-36)?
2. Describe the blind man's persistence (vv. 38-39).

It can be understood from the words of the blind man that the Rabbi of Nazareth was beginning to be accepted by more people as the long-looked-for Deliverer. The title "Son of David" was definitely a messianic term.

It has been said that no matter how accustomed one becomes to being blind or how skillful one is in making his way with a cane, he yet walks in darkness. He is dead to the natural beauty around him, seeing neither the flowers that line his path nor the fleecy clouds that sail in the skies above him. He is in constant danger of wandering into a snare or pitfall, stumbling over some object, or finding himself in a position of great danger. Bartimaeus was in this condition. He was blind.

Even though it might seem presumptuous to some, he cried out without apology. There were those who tried to stop him, but he paid no attention. He was more concerned about his need and the power of Jesus to meet that need than he was about the opinion of the crowd. And when the people tried to prevent him, Luke said that "he shouted all the more, 'Son of David, have mercy on me!'" (v. 39 NIV).

B. Praising the Healer (vv. 40-43)

40. And Jesus stood, and commanded him to be brought unto him: and when he was come near, he asked him,

41. Saying, What wilt thou that I shall do unto thee? And he said, Lord, that I may receive my sight.

42. And Jesus said unto him, Receive thy sight: thy faith hath saved thee.

43. And immediately he received his sight, and followed him, glorifying God: and all the people, when they saw it, gave praise unto God.

The blind man was a beggar. He was at the very bottom rung of the social ladder. He was an obscure person. His influence was nonexistent. Yet when he prayed, he stopped the Son of God.

Jesus was on a mission. He was going through Jericho. There was a crowd of people, with the accompanying noise. But He heard the cry for help above the noise of the crowd. Note the words "And Jesus stood" (v. 40). Doesn't this event suggest that prayer has the power to direct God's attention to a single individual who needs and asks for His help? This is an amazing revelation from God.

The blind man had cried for mercy. Now Jesus inquired what mercy he desired. All the years of darkness rolled forth in the single request, "Lord, that I may receive my sight" (v. 41). The man knew what he needed. He knew what he wanted. He knew what to ask for. Prayer is so simple yet so profound.

The blind man's faith may have been weak. Perhaps it was not fully developed. But the faith he had motivated him to cry out

"Too many people pray like little boys who knock at doors, then run away."
—*War Cry*

Talk About It:
1. Why do you suppose Jesus asked the obvious (vv. 40-41)?
2. Describe the response to the healing (v. 43).

to Jesus and to keep on crying in spite of obstacles and rebukes. Because he came with faith, Jesus did not refuse him. The desire of his heart was granted.

J. C. Ryle states: "When the blind man was restored to sight, 'he followed [Jesus], glorifying God.' He felt deeply grateful. He resolved to show his gratitude by becoming one of our Lord's followers and disciples. Pharisees might cavil at our Lord. Sadducees might sneer at His teaching. It mattered nothing to this new disciple. He had the witness to himself that Christ was a Master worth following. He could say, 'I was blind, and now I see'" (*Expository Thoughts*).

> "Great acts of God should produce great praise to God."
> —**Lance Colkmire**

CONCLUSION

The only proper ending for this lesson on gratitude is to join with the delivered demoniac, the Samaritan leper, and blind Bartimaeus in expressing heartfelt praise to God. Our praise should begin with giving thanks to God and then move to telling others about His goodness to us.

GOLDEN TEXT CHALLENGE

"BLESS THE LORD, O MY SOUL: AND ALL THAT IS WITHIN ME, BLESS HIS HOLY NAME. BLESS THE LORD, O MY SOUL, AND FORGET NOT ALL HIS BENEFITS" (Ps. 103:1-2).

Genuine worship does not begin with our tongue, hands, or feet, but with our *soul*—our heart or mind. "All that is within" us—our emotions, will, and affections—must be engaged in order for us to "bless the Lord."

This takes effort. Just as the psalmist told his soul to worship the Lord's holy name, so we must discipline ourselves to become worshipers of God.

We should bless the Lord for who He is ("his holy name") and for what He does for us ("all his benefits").

Daily Devotions:
M. Offerings of Thanksgiving
   Genesis 8:13-22
T. Song of Deliverance
   Exodus 15:1-13
W. The Joy of Deliverance
   2 Chronicles 20:20-29
T. Gratitude Stimulates Witness
   Matthew 9:27-31
F. Rejoicing in Christ's Power
   Luke 10:17-20
S. Deliverance Produces Rejoicing
   Luke 13:10-17

Why the Holy Spirit Came (Pentecost)

John 14:15-26; 15:26-27; 16:7-14;
Acts 2:1-4; Romans 8:26-27

Unit Theme:
Pentecost

Central Truth:
The Holy Spirit enables us to live for Christ and make the Gospel known to the world.

Focus:
Understand God's purpose in sending the Holy Spirit and rely on the Spirit's help for Christian living and witness.

Context:
New Testament teachings about the ministry of the Holy Spirit

Golden Text:
"When the Comforter is come, whom I will send unto you from the Father, even the Spirit of truth, which proceedeth from the Father, he shall testify of me" (John 15:26).

Study Outline:
I. The Spirit Came at Pentecost (John 14:15-18; Acts 2:1-4)
II. The Spirit Helps Believers (John 14:26; 16:12-14; Rom. 8:26-27)
III. The Spirit Convinces the World (John 15:26-27; 16:7-11)

INTRODUCTION

The doctrine of the Holy Spirit is called *pneumatology* in theology. This term comes from the Greek word *pneuma*, which means "spirit, wind, or breath."

We get our information concerning the Holy Spirit from the Bible. From other sources we learn that Christianity is the only religion that teaches the person of the Holy Spirit. Other religions have their founders, their sacred books, and their ethics; but not one of them has anything resembling the person of the Holy Spirit as found in the New Testament. The Holy Spirit is the mediator who makes real to humanity the divine revelation given historically in Jesus Christ. This is unique in Christianity.

One of the early-church fathers emphasized that the grace of the Spirit brings the machinery of redemption into vital connection with the individual soul. Apart from the Spirit the Cross stands inert, a vast machine at rest, and about it lies the stones of the building. Until the rope of the Holy Spirit has been attached, the lifting of the individual life to the place prepared for it in God's church cannot proceed.

"The great intellectual and religious struggle of our day turns on this question, whether there is a Holy Ghost." These were the words of a notable scholar of many years ago. Another scholar, referring to this remark, said: "I will venture to define this statement more closely and say that the struggle turns upon our belief in a Holy Ghost sent in the name of Jesus Christ according to His own emphatic promise."

One cannot fail to be impressed with the frequency, variety, fullness, and prominence of the references to the Holy Spirit all through the New Testament. The New Testament does not stop with the story of the Resurrection; it goes further, to the person and work of the Holy Spirit. The Holy Spirit enables believers to live for Christ and make the Gospel known to the world.

I. THE SPIRIT CAME AT PENTECOST (John 14:15-18; Acts 2:1-4)

A. Loving Obedience Required (John 14:15)

15. If ye love me, keep my commandments.

Verse 15 is a direct practical exhortation. It says the way to prove love for Jesus is by doing His will. The commandments referred to by Jesus would include all of His moral teachings while on earth.

Talk About It: How do we show our love for God (v. 15)?

Jesus does not expect us to live an obedient life through our own ability. We are to depend on His Spirit, as the following verses reveal.

B. The Comforter Promised (vv. 16-18)

16. And I will pray the Father, and he shall give you another Comforter, that he may abide with you for ever;

17. Even the Spirit of truth; whom the world cannot receive, because it seeth him not, neither knoweth him: but ye know him; for he dwelleth with you, and shall be in you.

18. I will not leave you comfortless: I will come to you.

Four times in His farewell discourse Jesus referred to the Holy Spirit as the Comforter. The Greek word for "Comforter" is *parakletos*. It carries with it the idea of an advocate who stands by, not only as an intercessor but as a helper, comforter, and consoler.

Talk About It:
1. What did Jesus pray for (v. 16)?
2. What did Jesus reveal about the Holy Spirit (v. 17)?
3. What did Jesus promise in verse 18?

From its derivation we rightly conclude that *comforter* suggests the idea of "strengthening, empowering in weakness." Jesus himself declared, "I will not leave you comfortless" (v. 18). We also correctly infer that the thought of comfort in sorrow is also included in the meaning.

However, it is important to consider that the thought of sorrow was not prominent in the mind of Jesus as He used the word *Comforter* in His Upper Room discourse. Three times He identified the Comforter as the Spirit of truth, who was to lead the disciples into all truth (v. 17; 15:26; 16:13). Once His function is said to be that of rememberer of and witness to Christ (14:26). And once the Spirit is seen convicting the human heart of sin, righteousness, and judgment (16:8). As Jesus used the word *Comforter*, it becomes clear that the idea of consolation and comfort is distinctly secondary to that of strength and help.

The word *Spirit* (14:17) comes from the Latin word *spiritus*, which is synonymous with the Greek word *pneuma*. Both literally signify "breath" or "wind." The Holy Spirit is called the "breath of God" with reference to His mode of subsistence, proceeding from God as the breath from the mouth. Observe the characteristic action of Jesus in John 20:22.

The Holy Spirit is not called *Spirit* merely because of the spirituality of His essence, for this is likewise true of the Father and Son. Neither is He called *Holy* in reference to the exclusive holiness of His nature, for He is no more holy than either of the

other persons of the Trinity. But this term has reference to God's official character—He is the author of all holiness.

The Holy Spirit is called the "Spirit of truth." It is His special office to apply the truth to the hearts of Christians. He is to guide them into all truth and to sanctify them by the truth.

The Holy Spirit is said to be One whom the world cannot know and receive. His operations are foolishness to sinners. The inward feelings of conviction, repentance, faith, hope, fear, and love—which He always produces—are aspects of religion which the world cannot understand.

The Holy Spirit is said to dwell in believers. He is known of them. They know the feelings He creates and the fruit He produces. They may not be able to understand them or to perceive how God could be pleased to bless them in such ways, but they can know Him.

It was very appropriate that Jesus referred to the Holy Spirit as the Comforter. He knew the disciples would need this kind of assistance. He himself had been a Paraclete to them. They had leaned on Him in every perplexity and trial. Now He was going away, and these words concerning another Comforter would be welcome. They were not to be deserted, but another Paraclete—the Holy Spirit—was to come to them.

> "There was a promise! The coming of the Holy Spirit was based upon the promise of the Lord Jesus Christ."
> —Billy Graham

C. The Promise Fulfilled (Acts 2:1-4)

1. And when the day of Pentecost was fully come, they were all with one accord in one place.

2. And suddenly there came a sound from heaven as of a rushing mighty wind, and it filled all the house where they were sitting.

3. And there appeared unto them cloven tongues like as of fire, and it sat upon each of them.

4. And they were all filled with the Holy Ghost, and began to speak with other tongues, as the Spirit gave them utterance.

cloven (v. 3)— "divided" (NKJV)

The Day of Pentecost came fifty days after the Passover. It was one of three Jewish festivals to which every male Jew living within twenty miles of Jerusalem was legally bound to come— the Passover, Pentecost, and the Feast of Tabernacles. It commemorated the giving of the Law to Moses on Mount Sinai.

Talk About It:
1. Explain the two uses of the word "one" in verse 1.
2. What was the significance of the wind (v. 2) and the fire (v. 3)?
3. What did the Holy Spirit do for the believers (v. 4)?

As people gathered in Jerusalem from around the world, about 120 believers were gathered in the Upper Room awaiting the coming of the Holy Spirit. They spent time in prayer and personal preparation so they could receive the Spirit.

These followers of the Lord were assembled in one place for one purpose. They were in one accord, that is, the occasion was marked by unity. The expression indicates they were knit together with a bond stronger than death. This kind of unity is needed in the church today.

After ten days of waiting, the Spirit came suddenly upon the believers. When God acts, He often acts suddenly. This is true of the conversion experience. The very instant one repents and believes, he or she is saved.

Waiting in the Upper Room, the believers heard a sound as of the blowing of a violent wind. Living in that area, they had witnessed many storms at sea and they had heard the blowing of violent wind many times. What they heard was the same sound, but this sound came out of a clear sky. They were sure of one thing—it came from heaven. It was a symbol of the Spirit; it indicated His power—mighty, mysterious, and heavenly, but unseen. The suddenness and strength of the sound struck the believers with awe, and completed their preparation for the heavenly gift.

The followers of the Lord in the Upper Room not only heard a sound as of a rushing mighty wind; they also saw what appeared to be tongues of fire that separated and came to rest on each of them.

In the Word, fire is frequently used as a symbol of the divine presence. It also represents fervor and enthusiasm. Touched by fire from heaven, one cannot remain cold and indifferent. Fire is a beautiful symbol of the Spirit's burning energy that is abundantly available to the Church.

The Pentecostal fire came in the shape of tongues. The tongue is the instrument God uses to proclaim the Gospel. Witnessing for Christ is directly linked with the coming of the Spirit. Jesus said: "Ye shall be witnesses unto me" (Acts 1:8). A witness is one who tells what he knows. A Christian is one who keeps the faith but does not keep it to himself.

The tongues of fire came to rest upon each person present in the Upper Room. They did not come to the apostles alone, but to every believer present. This is encouraging to believers at all levels of life.

These believers received an inward experience: "they were all filled with the Holy Ghost" (2:4). To be filled with the Spirit is to be brought completely under His control. This is essentially what happened to these believers. The power of the Spirit flooded their souls. Thereafter He manifested Himself in their lives on numerous occasions.

These devoted disciples also received an outward manifestation: they spoke "with other tongues." It is clear that the speakers themselves did not understand what they were saying. Their words were completely beyond their conscious control. They spoke in a language of which they had no command in normal circumstances.

These Christians spoke in other tongues as the Spirit enabled them. Luke is careful to point out that the Spirit initiated their utterances.

"Tongues of fire sat upon them; hearts were aglow and tongues were aflame witnessing the wonderful works of God. Pentecost then became a personal experience."

—Ray H. Hughes Sr.

II. THE SPIRIT HELPS BELIEVERS (John 14:26; 16:12-14; Rom. 8:26-27)

A. The Spirit Teaches (John 14:26)

26. But the Comforter, which is the Holy Ghost, whom the Father will send in my name, he shall teach you all things, and bring all things to your remembrance, whatsoever I have said unto you.

Talk About It:
Describe the teaching role of the Holy Spirit.

The disciples did not have the power and wisdom to be proper witnesses without the Holy Spirit. Of course they remembered experiences from the life and ministry of Jesus. As eyewitnesses they could have painted word pictures of His death, His resurrection, and His ascension. They could have done this with conviction and enthusiasm. No one can doubt that the disciples were bound to one another in one fellowship through their love for Christ and His love for them. But Jesus knew that even these virtues would not be sufficient for the task ahead. Therefore, He promised them the power from on high—an infilling of God's wisdom, strength, courage, and vision. Their new Spirit baptism would serve to comfort, teach, and challenge them in their life and witness.

"The Holy Spirit is called 'the Spirit of truth' because He is the great revealer of truth. He takes the things of Christ and makes them known to believers."
—**French Arrington**

If we allow the Holy Spirit to bring the words of Jesus to our remembrance, we will understand that they are the only infallible text of real orthodoxy, the only unerring touchstone of truth, the only immaculate code of laws, the only faultless system of morals, and the only immutable ground of hope.

B. The Spirit Guides (16:12-14)

12. I have yet many things to say unto you, but ye cannot bear them now.

13. Howbeit when he, the Spirit of truth, is come, he will guide you into all truth: for he shall not speak of himself; but whatsoever he shall hear, that shall he speak: and he will shew you things to come.

14. He shall glorify me: for he shall receive of mine, and shall shew it unto you.

Talk About It:
1. Why didn't Jesus reveal certain things to the disciples (v. 12)?
2. List ministries of the Holy Spirit (vv. 13-14).

The disciples' need for the Holy Spirit is seen in the fact that they could not understand the many things Jesus had yet to say to them. But Jesus assured them the Holy Spirit would guide them into all truth concerning Himself and the doctrines He taught. The reference here is to spiritual truth.

The ministry of the Holy Spirit is Christ-centered. It is characteristic of Him not to speak of Himself but of Christ.

The statement "He will shew you things to come" undoubtedly refers to the finished New Testament—the establishing of the church to include both Gentiles and Jews and the proclaiming of the full-gospel message.

Why the Holy Spirit Came

Verse 14 reminds us that rivalry does not exist within the Godhead. Each person in the Trinity delights in serving the others. Christ's passion was to manifest and to glorify the excellence of the Father (John 8:54; 17:4-5).

The primary concern of the Holy Spirit is to glorify Christ and to see Him enthroned as Lord in the hearts of believers. He does not add anything to the personal glories of the ascended Christ but glorifies Christ in the believer's experience. The Spirit reveals and explains Christ. What light is to the earth, the Holy Spirit is to Christ.

C. The Spirit Intercedes (Rom. 8:26-27)

26. Likewise the Spirit also helpeth our infirmities: for we know not what we should pray for as we ought: but the Spirit itself maketh intercession for us with groanings which cannot be uttered.

27. And he that searcheth the hearts knoweth what is the mind of the Spirit, because he maketh intercession for the saints according to the will of God.

In this chapter, Paul deals with three kinds of groanings. First, he pictures the creation growing and travailing in pain (v. 22). Then, he says that believers groan inwardly, awaiting our full adoption as sons—the redemption of our bodies (v. 23). Now, he writes of the Spirit making intercession for us with groans that words cannot utter.

As God, through the Holy Spirit, will take care of the future needs represented by the groanings of creation and of believers, so He will take care of the present needs of believers. He comes to our aid in our weaknesses and understands our present limitations.

Talk About It:
What is the Holy Spirit's role in the Christian's prayer life?

We need the help of the Holy Spirit in prayer because we don't know how we ought to pray. We cannot foresee the future. God knows the past, the present, and the future. Our knowledge of the past and the present is limited, and our knowledge of the future is practically nil. But God knows it all. The help of the Spirit is, then, essential to effective and Christ-honoring prayer.

Also, we need the help of the Spirit in prayer because in any given situation we do not know what is best for us. We may think we do, but in reality only God knows best. So, the only really perfect prayer we can offer is the prayer Jesus prayed: "Not my will, but thine, be done" (Luke 22:42). We cannot go wrong with this prayer.

Then, we can bring to God an inarticulate sigh which the Spirit will translate to God for us. He will plead our case with inexpressible yearnings, with groans that are too deep for words. His assistance is invaluable.

John Phillips observed: "We have an Advocate with the Father in heaven in the Person of the Lord Jesus (1 John 2:1), and we have One within our hearts as well who can lay bare before the eyes of God the deepest needs of our souls."

God knows all about us. He searches our inmost being. The psalmist wrote: "O Lord, thou hast searched me, and known me. . . . Search me, O God, and know my heart . . . and see if there be any wicked way in me, and lead me in the way everlasting" (Ps. 139:1, 23-24). God searches our heart as no one else can. Nothing is hidden from Him. No one knows us so well or understands as completely as He does. His eye is ever upon us.

God, who knows the needs of the human heart, also understands what the Spirit's meaning is even though the expressions have been inarticulate. He knows the unspoken desire of the Spirit, who always puts our prayer in the context of God's constructive purpose for our life. As someone has said, "Here is the secret of victorious Christian living. Without the Spirit's help in all these areas, no human being would be wise or strong enough to succeed. With it there is no reason for failure."

The Spirit pleads our case before God and He always intercedes in a manner that is in harmony with God's will. As believers, we need to avail ourselves of this help from the Spirit of God. By leaning upon Him, we may be guided in the path of righteousness and may be given a clearer and stronger assurance of God's presence. He assists us in our prayers and places within us high and holy aspirations.

III. THE SPIRIT CONVINCES THE WORLD (John 15:26-27; 16:7-11)
A. The Spirit of Truth (15:26-27)

26. But when the Comforter is come, whom I will send unto you from the Father, even the Spirit of truth, which proceedeth from the Father, he shall testify of me:

27. And ye also shall bear witness, because ye have been with me from the beginning.

The context of these verses is set in verse 18 at the beginning of this section of teaching. Christ said the world hated Him and would also hate the disciples. In light of this hatred, Christ instructs them so that they will not "stumble" (16:1 NKJV). The grammar of "hate" in 15:18 indicates a permanent attitude of hate. The world hates Christians as a basic attitude. It is not an occasional spurt of emotion. The attitude of the world is permanently set against Christ as well. Christ goes further in verse 19. The reason that the world hates the Christian is Christ's choosing of the Christian for His purposes.

The climax of the description of hatred is found in verse 25 when Christ says the world hated Him "without a cause." Christians feel this attack as well and need a secure foundation to stand on.

Help in Prayer

The Christian is not alone when he prays. He has Jesus Christ as intercessor and advocate on his behalf at the right hand of God (Heb. 7:25; 1 John 2:1). Then, dwelling in his heart, the Christian has the Holy Spirit who makes intercession for him according to the will of God (Rom. 8:26-27).

—Daniel Black

Talk About It:
1. Describe the relationship between Jesus and the Holy Spirit (v. 26).
2. What would the disciples do (v. 27)?

Why the Holy Spirit Came

Christ introduces this foundation with the word *but* in verse 26, when He says that despite the unjustified and brutal attack of the world there is a foundation. In contrast to the attack of the world, the "Comforter"—the Holy Spirit—will be the Spirit of truth.

"Spirit of truth" describes a vital work of the Holy Spirit in establishing the believer when the world would attack him. When the cause of the Christian to stand for Christ is attacked unjustifiably, the Holy Spirit works to establish the Christian. Despite the false claims of the world against the Christian, still there is stability. The Holy Spirit establishes truth in the life of the Christian.

Christ locates the source and the authority of the work of truth by the Holy Spirit. The source is "the Father." The work of the Spirit in establishing truth in the life of the Christian is to "testify of [Christ]."

B. The Convincer (16:7-11)

7. Nevertheless I tell you the truth; It is expedient for you that I go away: for if I go not away, the Comforter will not come unto you; but if I depart, I will send him unto you.

8. And when he is come, he will reprove the world of sin, and of righteousness, and of judgment:

9. Of sin, because they believe not on me;

10. Of righteousness, because I go to my Father, and ye see me no more;

11. Of judgment, because the prince of this world is judged.

The disciples were "filled with grief" (v. 6 NIV) because Jesus had told them He would soon be leaving them. The departure of Jesus was a disappointment of their greatest hopes. They had placed all their Jewish hopes concerning the Messiah in Jesus. They had expected Jesus to restore the kingdom of Israel. His telling them that instead of sitting on the throne of His father David He was going to die brought to them a paralyzing fear.

Understanding the attitude of the disciples, Jesus reassured them by saying, "Unless I go away, the Counselor will not come to you; but if I go, I will send him to you" (v. 7 NIV). He went on to point out that the coming of the Holy Spirit would be a greater blessing to them than His personal presence had been.

From these words of Jesus it can be seen that under certain conditions absence is better than presence. For the disciples it was worthwhile to lose Jesus' physical presence if they might find for themselves the way into that spiritual world in which they had seen Him moving. Jesus wanted them to learn to walk in the Spirit—to walk by faith and not by sight.

To "reprove" (v. 8) is to convince one of error or sinfulness. This is the work of the Holy Spirit in relation to man's condition before God.

"In essence Jesus said, 'I'll not let you down. I'll not leave you without help. I will come to you. So don't give up . . . and don't lose heart. Help is on the way. I will send Him to you.'"
—**Ray H. Hughes Sr.**

Talk About It:
1. What was to the disciples' advantage, and why (v. 7)?
2. What did Jesus say the Holy Spirit would do (vv. 8-11)?

In his book *The Holy Spirit in the Gospels*, J. R. Smith says of the Holy Spirit, "He so presents the truth to men that they ought to believe. . . . The end sought in conviction is conversion. The Truth is made plain, not that men may be condemned, but that they might be saved."

Jesus said the Holy Spirit would "convict the world of sin, of righteousness, and of judgment" (v. 8 NKJV). Sin is the basis of all the world's ills; but apart from the work of the Holy Spirit, the world does not recognize this. The world is aware of the defects that exist in humanity. We say that a person is unjust, cruel, proud, sensuous, or covetous. Yet, these are simply surface manifestations of a greater fundamental evil in the character of humanity. It is this that the world does not understand.

The Holy Spirit, working in people's hearts as the Word of God is presented, convinces individuals of their sin and of their need for a Savior. The Holy Spirit also convinces the world of the righteousness that is found in Christ. Jesus Christ, the Son of God, took upon Himself human flesh and in the flesh condemned sin. His entire life exemplified righteousness. His every thought, word, deed, and action was right in the highest sense. He lived among the ordinary people of His time. He was exposed to the same temptations, corruption, and weaknesses, yet He did not sin. He was God manifest in a human body. He was the world's model of a perfectly holy life. This was what the world needed to see. But the world was not wiling to receive the heaven-sent Light that penetrated its darkness.

Instead of accepting Christ as the Son of God, some of the religious leaders banded together and agreed that Jesus was blaspheming God when He declared that He was life and the pattern of holiness. They condemned Him to death on this pretext. He was crucified, but He arose, ascended to the Father, and sent the Holy Spirit into the world to convince sinners that He was the Son of God. So it was actually "the prince of this world" (v. 11)—Satan—who was condemned through Christ's suffering. And it is still the Holy Spirit who is convincing all who will listen that Jesus is the Savior.

> "No clergyman however brilliant, no evangelist no matter how eloquent or compelling, can bring about the revival we need. Only the Holy Spirit can do this."
> —Billy Graham

CONCLUSION

In the person of the Holy Spirit, God himself has been empowering, teaching, guiding, interceding on behalf of, and comforting Christians for more than two thousand years. His Spirit will continue ministering in all those ways and more until the return of Jesus Christ.

GOLDEN TEXT CHALLENGE

"WHEN THE COMFORTER IS COME, WHOM I WILL SEND UNTO YOU FROM THE FATHER, EVEN THE SPIRIT OF TRUTH, WHICH PROCEEDETH FROM THE FATHER, HE SHALL TESTIFY OF ME" (John 15:26).

The Holy Spirit testifies to His relationship with Christ. In Matthew 1:20 we see that the Holy Spirit was related to Christ in Christ's conception. The Spirit was also related to Christ in the anointing for Christ's ministry (Acts 10:38).

Matthew states that the Spirit was active in the leadership of Jesus (4:1). As one theologian stated, "Jesus, as the servant of Jehovah, for which position He had emptied Himself of His sovereignty, took His own initiative in nothing, but always acted under orders, being directed in His movement by the Holy Spirit, to whom He was subject."

It is recorded in Luke 4:1 that Jesus was filled with the Spirit, who gave Jesus direction. There was nothing in the life of Jesus that was opposed to the Holy Spirit.

Luke also records that Jesus accomplished His ministry in the power of the Holy Spirit (vv. 14, 18-19). And according to the writer of Hebrews, Jesus sacrificially offered Himself in death through the Holy Spirit (9:14). In Romans 8:11, Paul wrote that "the Spirit . . . raised up Jesus from the dead."

The commandment Jesus gave to His apostles after His resurrection was given through the Holy Spirit (Acts 1:1-2). Jesus was not only resurrected by the Spirit, He also continued under the direction of the Holy Spirit in the work given Him by the Father until He resumed His place in complete exaltation with God.

The primary purpose of a telescope is not to reveal itself but to bring things into focus for those who look through it. The ministry of the Holy Spirit is not to magnify Himself but to give prominence to Christ. So efficient has He been in discharging His trust that His own existence has been questioned. But He is real! Any information we have of Christ comes to us through the Spirit's illumination of the Scriptures He has inspired. As the Spirit of Christ, He delights in unveiling His glories to believing hearts.

Daily Devotions:
M. Anointed by the Spirit
1 Samuel 16:10-13
T. Led by the Spirit
Ezekiel 3:10-14
W. Born of the Spirit
John 3:1-8
T. Ministry of the Spirit
John 16:5-15
F. Witness of the Spirit
Romans 8:12-17
S. Filled With the Spirit
Ephesians 5:15-21

Surprising Generosity

Luke 10:30-37; 21:1-4; Philippians 2:5-11

Unit Theme:
Commended by Christ

Central Truth:
Christians are to be generous.

Focus:
Examine and follow biblical examples of generosity.

Context:
Three New Testament passages regarding the believer's call to be generous

Golden Text:
"Let this mind be in you, which was also in Christ Jesus: . . . he humbled himself, and became obedient unto death, even the death of the cross" (Phil. 2:5, 8).

Study Outline:
I. Sacrificial Generosity (Luke 21:1-4)
II. Unselfish Generosity (Luke 10:30-37)
III. Christ's Generosity (Phil. 2:5-11)

INTRODUCTION

We sometimes think of stewardship only in terms of money. However, the subject is much broader than that.

Stewardship begins with the life we live. By our manner of life, we either attract people to Christ or repel them from Him. We are witnesses for Him. To draw people to Christ, we must live a consistent Christian life. Others need to know that our confidence is in God. They also need to see that we are growing and expanding in our relationship with Him.

Stewardship includes our time. The psalmist wrote, "So teach us to number our days, that we may apply our hearts unto wisdom" (90:12). Paul admonished the Ephesians to "[redeem] the time, because the days are evil" (Eph. 5:16). He urged the Colossian believers, "Walk in wisdom toward them that are without, redeeming the time" (Col. 4:5). The discreet use of our time is essential to our being an effective witness.

Possessions are part of our stewardship responsibilities. The believer needs to understand that all good things come from God. Therefore, when we tithe and give in an offering, what are we doing? We are returning to the Lord a portion of that which He has given to us. We should regard all our possessions as gifts from God.

Stewardship includes our influence. Paul indicated to the Romans that no one lives to himself and no one dies to himself (14:7). What we say and do has an impact upon others. Jesus is the model we should follow.

Even our personalities are covered under the broad scope of stewardship. Such things as personal hygiene, appropriate attire, and a positive attitude are important in bearing a witness for Christ. Emotional stability, boldness, and love that manifests itself in action are traits which believers must cultivate.

Through this study, we should discover that stewardship involves the generous use of resources for God's glory.

I. SACRIFICIAL GENEROSITY (Luke 21:1-4)

A. What the Rich Gave (v. 1)

1. And he looked up, and saw the rich men casting their gifts into the treasury.

The event described in this passage occurred immediately after a lengthy and unfriendly question-and-answer session with unbelieving Jews. Jesus responded to them with dignity and finality until they had no more questions for Him. Weary from the exchange, the Master sat with downcast eyes in one of the Temple courts.

Talk About It:
What did Jesus see?

The place where we find the Lord is known as the Court of the Women. It contained 13 offering chests which were marked with letters of the Hebrew alphabet. The chests were trumpet-shaped (wide at the top and narrow below).

As donors came to make their contribution, Jesus observed their activity. It is instructive that the Lord took note of those who gave and of the manner in which they gave. He is still doing that.

No one entered the Temple without contributing something. Jesus observed that the rich gave a sizable amount.

We shall see that Jesus made a distinction between those who gave out of self-righteousness and those who gave out of wholehearted devotion to God. His view concerning good deeds was infinitely different from that of people. From His perspective, those who give the most, give often the least; and those who give the least, give often the most.

"Most people apportion their giving to their earnings. If the process was reversed and the Giver of all was to apportion our earnings according to our giving, some of us would be very poor."
—**World Vision**

B. What the Poor Widow Gave (v. 2)

2. And he saw also a certain poor widow casting in thither two mites.

mites—"small copper coins" (NASB)

Jesus observed a poor widow among those who brought their contributions to the Temple treasury. She cast into the receptacle two of the smallest copper coins which circulated in that region. They were each worth about one-eighth of a cent. Her gift indicates the extent of her poverty. According to Jewish laws at that time, it was not permissible to cast in less than two gifts.

The poor widow had fixed her trust in God. She was not worried about what tomorrow might bring. In this she obeyed the words of Jesus: "Take therefore no thought for the morrow: for the morrow shall take thought for the things of itself. Sufficient unto the day is the evil thereof" (Matt. 6:34).

This event reminds us that the Lord's eyes are on all offerings. In view of this, we should give willingly. We should also be properly motivated in our giving. Supporting the Lord's cause is our responsibility. When we obey the biblical pattern of tithing and giving, the needs of the Kingdom will be met.

If every believer was willing to do what this poor widow did, the Church would have no financial problems. She was ready to give all that she could claim as her own to support the Lord's work. Where can we find such zeal in the Church today?

"If you are not generous with a meager income, you will never be generous with abundance."
—**Harold Nye**

C. The Lesson Jesus Gave (vv. 3-4)

3. And he said, Of a truth I say unto you, that this poor widow hath cast in more than they all:

4. For all these have of their abundance cast in unto the offerings of God: but she of her penury hath cast in all the living that she had.

penury (v. 4)—poverty

Talk About It:
How did the widow's giving count as "more"?

The disciples were probably awestruck by the significant contributions made by the wealthy. By comparison, the two almost-worthless coins given by the widow seemed meaningless. Jesus reminded them that her giving reflected her total commitment to God and her trust in Him.

People judge the heart according to the deeds, but the Lord judges the deed according to the heart. For this reason, the Lord notices when a cup of cold water is given to one of His followers just because he is a follower of the Lord (Matt. 10:42). Small acts of generosity have infinite worth in His eyes.

The story of the poor widow should teach us to be careful how we judge others. They may be doing more in God's sight than we realize. Furthermore, the judgment of others is not our business. Jesus said, "Judge not, that ye be not judged. For with what judgment ye judge, ye shall be judged: and with what measure ye mete, it shall be measured to you again" (7:1-2).

II. UNSELFISH GENEROSITY (Luke 10:30-37)

A. Religion Without Love (vv. 30-32)

30. And Jesus answering said, A certain man went down from Jerusalem to Jericho, and fell among thieves, which stripped him of his raiment, and wounded him, and departed, leaving him half dead.

31. And by chance there came down a certain priest that way: and when he saw him, he passed by on the other side.

32. And likewise a Levite, when he was at the place, came and looked on him, and passed by on the other side.

Talk About It:
1. Describe the victim's condition (v. 30).
2. How were the priest and Levite similar (vv. 31-32)?

When a legal scholar asked Jesus, "Who is my neighbor?" (see vv. 25-29), Jesus replied by telling the parable of the Good Samaritan. Mistakenly some people believe that a parable is always fictitious, but that is not true; a parable might be either hypothetical or the account of an actual occurrence.

The road from Jerusalem to Jericho was a winding road through barren wilderness. There were no towns along the way—a distance of twenty-one miles. A long stretch of the road passed through a narrow, rocky pass, well-suited for the purposes of thieves and robbers. Travelers generally made the journey in groups for protection, and a lone traveler almost invited robbery and violence. The traveler in this story—and we do not know if he was Jew or Gentile—was robbed, beaten, and left for dead.

A priest and a Levite passed along the road and saw the helpless wounded man. Jericho was a city of priests, and the road had considerable traffic by these religious leaders. Very likely both men knew the road well, and yet neither offered to help the suffering man.

These religious men should have had compassion on the man in distress. Religion that is exercised only in ceremony and ritual is meaningless. Love, as it was commanded in the Law, should have been translated into deeds of kindness. Both men were too busy with their own affairs to be troubled by the plight of the traveler. They were unwilling to become involved.

> "Just because people are religious it does not make them any more saintly."
> —**Josephine of Medstead**

B. Love in Action (vv. 33-35)

33. But a certain Samaritan, as he journeyed, came where he was: and when he saw him, he had compassion on him,

34. And went to him, and bound up his wounds, pouring in oil and wine, and set him on his own beast, and brought him to an inn, and took care of him.

35. And on the morrow when he departed, he took out two pence, and gave them to the host, and said unto him, Take care of him; and whatsoever thou spendest more, when I come again, I will repay thee.

A Samaritan passed by and had compassion on the injured man. The lawyer could not possibly escape Jesus' meaning when He contrasted a priest and Levite with a Samaritan. The former two were religious leaders, men held in great respect and esteem among the Jews, and the Samaritan was hated of the Jews and regarded as the lowest of humanity. A common insult among the Jews was, "You are a Samaritan; you have a devil."

Samaria was a province situated between Judea and Galilee. The Samaritans were a mixed people, half Jewish and half Assyrian. They were the descendants of the Jews who had been carried captive to Assyria, where they had intermarried with the Assyrian people.

The Samaritan attended the wounds of the man and carried him to an inn for recovery. There was only one inn between Jerusalem and Jericho, so this site is still today pointed out as the "Inn of the Good Samaritan." Jesus related, and Luke recorded, all the details of the Samaritan's treatment of the injured traveler. The Samaritan went far beyond anything that could be expected of one in his situation. Without knowing the traveler, he demonstrated in repeated deeds a compassion and love that has lifted the stigma from the name "Samaritan." Today many good and worthwhile things are named for this kind man, even though we do not know his name. We simply call him the Good Samaritan.

Talk About It:
1. What is "compassion" (v. 33)?
2. List the sacrifices made by the Samaritan (vv. 34-35).

> "The purpose of human life is to serve and to show compassion and the will to help others."
> —**Albert Schweitzer**

C. Example to Live By (vv. 36-37)

36. Which now of these three, thinkest thou, was neighbour unto him that fell among the thieves?

How does Jesus define *neighbor*?

Compassion
Did you ever take a *real* trip down inside the broken heart of a friend? To feel the sob of the soul—the raw, red crucible of emotional agony? To have this become almost as much yours as that of your soul-crushed neighbor? Then, to sit down with him—and silently weep? This is the beginning of compassion.
—**Jess Moody**

Talk About It:
Restate this verse in your own words.

"The primary virtue of all, which is the love of God and neighbor, originates in the light of humility."
—**Angela of Foligno**

Talk About It:
How was Jesus "equal with God"?

37. And he said, He that shewed mercy on him. Then said Jesus unto him, Go, and do thou likewise.

Having completed the parable, Jesus turned to the lawyer and asked him a question: "Which of the three men was neighbor to the injured man?" The lawyer was put on the spot. A wrong answer would reveal a deep-seated prejudice, and a correct answer would convict both him and many of the Jewish people.

Although the lawyer answered correctly, he did not speak the word *Samaritan*. Instead, he said, "He that showed mercy on him."

Jesus concluded the dialogue with the lawyer by admonishing him to show similar love to his fellow man. We must bear in mind that love is more than an abstract sentiment; it is a deep emotion that motivates an individual to act on behalf of the one loved. If what we feel is not translated into action at every opportunity, then what we feel very likely is mere sympathy. We are not *advised* to love; we are *commanded* to do so. It is the first Christian responsibility.

III. CHRIST'S GENEROSITY (Phil. 2:5-11)
A. The Mind of Christ (v. 5)
5. Let this mind be in you, which was also in Christ Jesus.

This entire passage (vv. 5-11) may have been sung by the early church as a hymn. It crystallized a major message of the Gospel into a few words, illustrating Christ's humility and selflessness as the supreme example to follow.

A literal rendering of Philippians 2:5 from the Greek might be as follows: "Keep thinking this attitude among you, which was also in Christ Jesus." Obviously, believers cannot duplicate the actions and mind-set of the incarnate Lord, but we can imitate them as our example.

Jesus himself exhorted His followers to imitate Him. In Matthew 20:27-28, He said, "Whoever wants to be first must be your slave—just as the Son of Man did not come to be served, but to serve, and to give his life as a ransom for many" (NIV). Similar appeals can be found in Matthew 11:29; Luke 22:27; John 13:14-15. After washing the feet of His disciples, Jesus told them, "I have set you an example that you should do as I have done for you" (John 13:15 NIV).

B. The Preincarnate Lord (v. 6)
6. Who, being in the form of God, thought it not robbery to be equal with God.

Two aspects of Christ's divine person before He became a man are seen in this verse: (1) He has always existed with God in heaven, and (2) He is equal to God in power, eminence, preexistence, and nature. The exact thoughts were also expressed by John in his Gospel: "In the beginning was the Word, and the Word was with God, and the Word was God. He was with God in the beginning" (1:1-2 NIV).

The phrase "form of God" suggests the idea that the nature of a person remains the same, though the way it is expressed varies. Thus, although Jesus took upon Himself full humanity and lived out a life as a man, He never ceased to have the eternal qualities of God.

C. The Incarnation (vv. 7-8)

7. But made himself of no reputation, and took upon him the form of a servant, and was made in the likeness of men:

8. And being found in fashion as a man, he humbled himself, and became obedient unto death, even the death of the cross.

While Jesus absolutely retained His essence as God when He became a man, He nevertheless made Himself of a lower status in order to live totally as a man so that He would be able to relate completely to humanity. "The *Incarnation* was the act of the preexistent Son of God voluntarily assuming a human body and human nature. Without ceasing to be God, he became a human being, the man called Jesus. He did not give up his deity to become human, but he set aside the right to his glory and power" (*Life Application Bible*).

Christ limited Himself as the rest of humanity is limited with regard to time, place, and physical body. What made His humanity unique was the fact that He was able to live without sin. He showed us as much of the character of God as can be demonstrated within the limitations of humanity. And then He died as the sinless sacrifice.

D. Christ's Exaltation (vv. 9-11)

9. Wherefore God also hath highly exalted him, and given him a name which is above every name:

10. That at the name of Jesus every knee should bow, of things in heaven, and things in earth, and things under the earth;

11. And that every tongue should confess that Jesus Christ is Lord, to the glory of God the Father.

Is it not true that the name *Jesus Christ* is the greatest, most powerful, and most exalted of all names? But the exaltation mentioned here was not in name only, nor solely of reputation, for Christ arose from the dead, triumphant over death; and now He sits at the right hand of the Father, from where He shall come to judge the quick and the dead.

It is not the sound of "the name" (v. 10) but the authority of the Person whom the name represents. His dominion is over all things—living and dead, animate and inanimate. No one can hide from Him or escape His power. How much better it is to bow before Him in loving subjection rather than having to bow in forced submission.

"The Godhead of Christ is that which stamps value upon His sufferings and renders the whole of His obedience, in life and in death, infinitely meritorious and effectual."
—**John Gill**

Talk About It:
1. What did God's Son become?
2. Explain the phrase "obedient unto death" (v. 8).

Talk About It:
1. Describe God's actions (v. 9).
2. Explain the double use of the word *every* (vv. 10-11).
3. What brings glory to God (v. 11)?

The Greek word for "Lord" (v. 11) is *Kurios* and has three ascending levels of meaning. On the lowest level it simply means "sir" or "mister." At the next level it refers to the slave-owner relationship. A slave regarded his master as one who owned him. Paul presented himself as a slave in the introductions to some of his letters; for example, "Paul, a servant of Jesus Christ (Rom. 1:1), or "Paul, a servant of God" (Titus 1:1). The word for *servant* is the same as the one for *slave*.

On the highest level, however, *Lord* refers back to the Old Testament word *Adonai*, which denotes someone who is "sovereign over the kings of the world" (Sprout). When David wrote, "The Lord says to my Lord: 'Sit at my right hand until I make your enemies a footstool for your feet'" (Ps. 110:1 NIV), he was saying that God was talking with Someone who was David's *Lord*. Our present text reveals that God has given a supreme title to Jesus, one equivalent to that of God himself.

> "He clothed Himself with our lowliness in order to invest us with His grandeur."
> —Richardson Wright

CONCLUSION

The spirit of generosity shown by the poor widow and the despised Samaritan is the same selfless attitude that Jesus Christ had as the God-man on earth. While the widow's financial sacrifice and the Samaritan's sacrifice of time and money place in comparison with Christ's sacrifice on the cross, they both had "the mind of Christ," which is what He expects.

If we will also pursue and adopt Christlike thinking, generous actions will follow.

GOLDEN TEXT CHALLENGE

"LET THIS MIND BE IN YOU, WHICH WAS ALSO IN CHRIST JESUS: . . . HE HUMBLED HIMSELF, AND BECAME OBEDIENT UNTO DEATH, EVEN THE DEATH OF THE CROSS" (Phil. 2:5, 8).

The *mind* of Christ in us means not that we may have the same intellect that He had, but that we might have the same attitude, or think His thoughts after Him through becoming thoroughly acquainted with Him and absorbing His teaching. And we must have the same purpose or motivation in living and in dealing with others. Having the *mind* of Christ means being dedicated to the same cause as He was.

As God, Christ humbled Himself to become man. As man, Christ humbled Himself to be a servant, led a poverty-stricken, almost nomadic life of searching out people to help. As servant, Christ "humbled Himself" to the ultimate extent in accepting the cross.

The humility of Christ is beyond compare, yet we are called to follow His example. The work of Christ in humbling Himself at the Cross is the starting point of our redemption. It is also the starting point for our discipleship.

Daily Devotions:
M. God's Generosity
Exodus 16:12-18
T. Israel's Generosity
Exodus 35:21-29
W. The Joy of Giving
1 Chronicles 29:1-9
T. Radical Generosity Displayed
Acts 4:32-37
F. Abound in Grace
2 Corinthians 8:1-8
S. God Loves a Cheerful Giver
2 Corinthians 9:5-11

Surprising Generosity

Introduction to Summer Quarter

"Books of Samuel" is the theme of the first unit, which consists of eight lessons. These studies of the lives of Samuel, Saul, and David present powerful truths concerning the sovereignty of God, the call of God, leadership principles, worship, and restoration.

Lessons 1-3 were written by the Reverend Dr. Jerald Daffe (see biographical information on page 141).

Lessons 4-8 were written by the Reverend Joshua F. Rice (see biographical information on page 16).

The second unit, "Sin and Holiness," begins with the story of Adam and Eve in Genesis, highlights passages from Romans, 1 John, and the Gospel of John, and touches on various other books.

The expositions were written by Dale Coulter, associate professor of Historical Theology at Regent University School of Divinity. He holds a D.Phil. from Oxford University, an M.Div. from Reformed Theological Seminary (Orlando, FL), and a B.A. from Lee College. Prior to joining the faculty at Regent in 2007, he taught for eight years at Lee University. He is the author of two books, including a work on holiness, and numerous articles with various academic journals. Desiring to maintain a connection between the church and the academy, he holds the rank of ordained bishop with the Church of God and continues to teach at his local church in Virginia Beach as well as speaking engagements in other churches.

Samuel: Prophet, Priest, and Judge

1 Samuel 1:1-28; 3:1-21; 7:1-17

Unit Theme:
Books of Samuel

Central Truth:
God uses for ministry those who obey Him.

Focus:
Observe that God can use an obedient person in various ministries and minister according to our callings.

Context:
Stories of Samuel from 1100 to 1050 BC

Golden Text:
"As every man hath received the gift, even so minister the same one to another, as good stewards of the manifold grace of God" (1 Peter 4:10).

Study Outline:
I. Samuel the Prophet (1 Sam. 1:19-20, 24-28; 3:1-4, 10, 19-21)
II. Samuel the Priest (1 Sam. 7:5-12)
III. Samuel the Judge (1 Sam. 7:13-17)

INTRODUCTION

Intricately woven into the Book of 1 Samuel are the lives of three very different individuals. At the beginning we are introduced to Samuel and his miraculous birth. He serves Israel in three separate offices of prophet, priest, and judge. Saul stands second in the narrative. He holds the distinct honor of being the first king of Israel. Third, we see David being anointed by Samuel as the next king but having a difficult relationship with King Saul, who becomes his father-in-law.

The extensive material of the various aspects of their lives enables us to have a better understanding and feel for their frustrations and failures. We also see their years of service to God fulfilling His Word and will. Each of their stories demonstrates how God selects specific individuals to serve at a particular place and time. He does have a plan for our life which brings internal joy and external benefit to others, if we follow in obedience.

This first lesson continues to reveal God's having a corporate plan for His people, Israel. He desires the best for them and knows how it can be attained. The sad aspect of this lesson is once again seeing how independent-minded these people insist on being. Their desires to be like other nations is a strong temptation.

Usually we think of "peer pressure" as influencing younger people. But in reality no age group can claim immunity from the pressure of wanting to have, to do, or to be like someone. So, before we judge other age groups too harshly, we should examine our own lives. Are we principle-motivated people? Or, are we drawn along by others?

Before looking at the specific text of this lesson, consider the titles which apply to Samuel. As a prophet he becomes the spokesperson for God. The role of priest causes him to be an intermediary between the people and God. His position as judge involves administrative duties as well as settling disputes among the people.

I. SAMUEL THE PROPHET (1 Sam. 1:19-20, 24-28; 3:1-4, 10, 19-21)

A. A Miraculous Birth (1:19-20)

19. And they rose up in the morning early, and worshipped before the Lord, and returned, and came to their house to Ramah: and Elkanah knew Hannah his wife; and the Lord remembered her.

20. Wherefore it came to pass, when the time was come about after Hannah had conceived, that she bare a son, and called his name Samuel, saying, Because I have asked him of the Lord.

Repeatedly in the Scriptures are the accounts of married women who are barren for many years. Finally, when conception occurs the child is destined for a special purpose. Sarah is ninety years old when nature is reversed, and she bears the promised son, Isaac. Rebekah and Isaac are married for twenty years until God enables her to conceive, and she gives birth to twins. Zacharias and Elizabeth are in their old age before conceiving a child, who is John the Baptist, forerunner of the promised Messiah.

Hannah is also a barren woman who desperately desires a child. Not only does she want to overcome the cultural assumption that sin is the reason for her barrenness, but there is the problem of this being a polygamous marriage. Elkanah is a loving husband who attempts to satisfy her and make her feel valued. It isn't sufficient, especially since Peninnah, the other wife, has children and appears to really "rub it in." In 1 Samuel 1:6 she is described as Hannah's "adversary," or "rival" (NIV).

Hannah's heavy burden becomes very evident at one of their yearly trips to sacrifice at the Tabernacle in Shiloh. Elkanah's giving her a "double portion" (v. 5 NIV) cannot alleviate her anguish. To make matters worse, the priest, Eli, accuses her of being drunk as she weeps and prays silently. During this prayer she makes a sacrificial vow: If the Lord gives her a male child, she will give him back. Plus, she commits him to the Nazarite vow (see Num. 6:1-8).

In spite of Eli's initial spiritual insensitivity, he eventually accepts Hannah's explanation and blesses her to go in peace, saying, "May the God of Israel grant you what you have asked of him" (1 Sam. 1:17 NIV). After having poured her heart out to the Lord and receiving Eli's blessing, she goes out in a positive manner. She worships, stops fasting, and then returns home.

After returning home, normal marital relations occur between Hannah and Elkanah. The Lord chooses to bless her and to grant her request. Hannah conceives and bears a son. In the society of this era, bearing a son brings honor to a woman. The common thought is that a woman determines the gender of a child. We know it to be the complete opposite.

Appropriately Hannah selects a name for this newborn son which reflects the setting. She asks of the Lord; He in turn hears

Elkanah (el-KAY-na)—(v. 19)— Hannah's husband; his name means "God has possessed."

Talk About It:
1. Explain the phrase "the Lord remembered her" (v. 19).
2. Why did Hannah choose the name *Samuel* (v. 20)?

and grants her desire. There are differences of opinion as to the exact meaning of Samuel's name. Some lean to "God hears." Others, on the basis of the last verse in this section of study, prefer the idea of "to ask." Either one is a correct indication of what took place.

Hannah's fervent prayer enables her to enjoy the privilege of birthing a son when prior to this time it had been impossible. It also provides an individual who will be a transition between a theocracy and monarchy.

B. A Vow Fulfilled (vv. 24-28)

24. And when she had weaned him, she took him up with her, with three bullocks, and one ephah of flour, and a bottle of wine, and brought him unto the house of the Lord in Shiloh: and the child was young.

25. And they slew a bullock, and brought the child to Eli.

26. And she said, Oh my lord, as thy soul liveth, my lord, I am the woman that stood by thee here, praying unto the Lord.

27. For this child I prayed; and the Lord hath given me my petition which I asked of him:

28. Therefore also I have lent him to the Lord; as long as he liveth he shall be lent to the Lord. And he worshipped the Lord there.

Hannah's vow could not be fulfilled without the consent of her husband. The authority male in a woman's life could disagree with a vow, and she would not be held to it before the Lord (Num. 30:10-15). Elkanah's agreeing with Hannah's vow is a great sacrifice on his part. He will be giving up the firstborn child, a son, of his favorite wife. This is another reflection of the positive relationship between Elkanah and Hannah.

Samuel will stay with his father and mother until he is weaned. This normally takes place between ages two and three. If a child lives this long in an era of high infant mortality, the weaning of a child is a time for celebration. However, in this case it will become the point for separation and fulfillment of Hannah's vow. (Note: The weaning of a child could be as late as age five, though not the normal procedure.)

Without hesitation or an attempt to renegotiate the vow, they bring Samuel to Shiloh, where the Tabernacle is located and the high priest, Eli, resides. She reminds Eli, "I am the woman who stood here beside you praying to the Lord" (1 Sam. 1:26 NIV). Then Hannah states the content of her prayer and how God has fulfilled it. Now she intends to complete her part of the vow.

In verse 28, the word *lent* is more accurately translated "given." Samuel is to be the Lord's for his entire lifetime. There will be no reconsidering of this arrangement nor delaying until he is older. It begins now and will end only with Samuel's death.

"Those blessings are sweetest that are won with prayers and worn with thanks."
—**Thomas Goodwin**

three bullocks (v. 24)—either three bulls or one three-year-old bull

ephah (EE-fa)—(v. 24)—a measure of grain equaling about one bushel

lent (v. 28)—"dedicated" (NASB)

Talk About It:
1. When was Samuel taken to the Tabernacle (v. 24)?
2. How did Hannah identify herself (v. 26)?
3. How did she introduce Samuel (v. 27)?

There is so much detail that one wishes were included. How does Eli initially respond to taking such a small child into his care? Who will provide the normal care, since Eli is advanced in years? Exactly how old is Samuel? Whatever the specifics, it doesn't change the story. A miraculous work of God enables Hannah to conceive a child so desperately desired. She fulfills her vow, giving him to the service of the Lord while still a small child. This sets the stage for Israel's last judge and first of the distinctive prophets.

C. A Divine Encounter (3:1-4, 10, 19-21)

1. And the child Samuel ministered unto the Lord before Eli. And the word of the Lord was precious in those days; there was no open vision.

2. And it came to pass at that time, when Eli was laid down in his place, and his eyes began to wax dim, that he could not see;

3. And ere the lamp of God went out in the temple of the Lord, where the ark of God was, and Samuel was laid down to sleep;

4. That the Lord called Samuel: and he answered, Here am I.

10. And the Lord came, and stood, and called as at other times, Samuel, Samuel. Then Samuel answered, Speak; for thy servant heareth.

19. And Samuel grew, and the Lord was with him, and did let none of his words fall to the ground.

20. And all Israel from Dan even to Beersheba knew that Samuel was established to be a prophet of the Lord.

21. And the Lord appeared again in Shiloh: for the Lord revealed himself to Samuel in Shiloh by the word of the Lord.

While still a boy living in Eli's household and working in the Tabernacle, Samuel experiences the personal call of God. This is especially remarkable because "the word of the Lord was precious [rare]" (v. 1) in this era of spiritual darkness. So the Lord chose to speak to a spiritually sensitive child.

In the early hours of the night, God calls Samuel by name in an audible voice. This happens three times. On each occasion he immediately goes to Eli, assuming the elderly priest has called. Only on the third time does Eli realize it is God calling Samuel. Eli might have sooner realized what was happening if his spiritual eyesight had not diminished along with his physical vision (v. 2).

When God calls again, Samuel responds exactly as he had been instructed: "Speak, for your servant is listening" (v. 10 NIV). God then delivers a message of judgment which will come upon Eli and his sons. Though previously warned, Eli has allowed the sins of his sons to continue. In the morning, at the urging of Eli,

"A full night's sleep, time to oneself, the freedom to come and go as one pleases— all this must be given up. . . . Huge chunks of life are laid down at the behest of infants. And then, later, parents must let go."
—Elizabeth Dreyer

no open vision (v. 1)—"no widespread revelation" (NKJV) or "not many visions" (NIV)

Talk About It:
1. How did Eli's physical condition (v. 2) mirror Israel's spiritual condition (v. 1)?
2. How did Samuel respond to the Lord's call (v. 10)?
3. Explain the phrase "let none of his words fall to the ground" (v. 19).
4. What did "all Israel" know (v. 20)?

Samuel gives the specific message of the Lord. Eli responds, "He is the Lord; let him do what is good in his eyes" (v. 18 NIV).

This first encounter is just one of many other times when the Lord will appear to Samuel at Shiloh (v. 21). Samuel's life, marked by obedience to God's words (v. 19), confirms the rise of a prophet in Israel (v. 20).

II. SAMUEL THE PRIEST (1 Sam. 7:5-12)
A. A Spiritual Return (vv. 5-6)

5. And Samuel said, Gather all Israel to Mizpeh, and I will pray for you unto the Lord.

6. And they gathered together to Mizpeh, and drew water, and poured it out before the Lord, and fasted on that day, and said there, We have sinned against the Lord. And Samuel judged the children of Israel in Mizpeh.

Mizpeh (MIZ-pah)—(v. 5)—a town in the territory of Benjamin with a high elevation

The latter era of Eli's serving as the high priest results in marked spiritual decline strongly influenced by the sinfulness of his sons, Hophni and Phinehas. Their taking the ark of the covenant into battle results in its capture by the Philistines (4:1-11). When God inflicts judgment on the Philistines, the ark is sent back to Israel and eventually is stored in Abinadab's house (5:1—7:1).

In time the Israelites mourn their situation and begin to seek the Lord. Samuel admonishes them of the need to demonstrate their sincerity by getting rid of all foreign gods. Only then can they expect to receive God's deliverance from the Philistines. Samuel's role as their spiritual leader spans twenty years at this point. Finally, he begins to see some tangible results (7:2-4).

Talk About It:
1. What did Samuel do for Israel (v. 5)?
2. Explain the pouring out of water (v. 6).

In verse 5, Samuel calls for an assembly at Mizpeh in the territory of Benjamin. This gathering will have both spiritual and military implications. On the spiritual side, this is a solemn assembly to show God their repentant hearts and desire to serve Him. The pouring out of water (v. 6) is symbolic of what is occurring. In the same way in which the water is poured out, so are the Israelites pouring out their hearts to God. They are releasing their ties to the pagan gods and opening themselves to God. They are publicly acknowledging and confessing their sins.

The transparency of an entire nation confessing their sins as a whole is not popular. People are hesitant to acknowledge sin. For example, it has been more than 50 years since a United States president has made a proclamation calling for the nation to repent of its sins.

B. A Military Victory (vv. 7-12)

7. And when the Philistines heard that the children of Israel were gathered together to Mizpeh, the lords of the Philistines went up against Israel. And when the children of Israel heard it, they were afraid of the Philistines.

8. And the children of Israel said to Samuel, Cease not to cry unto the Lord our God for us, that he will save us out of the hand of the Philistines.

9. And Samuel took a sucking lamb, and offered it for a burnt offering wholly unto the Lord: and Samuel cried unto the Lord for Israel; and the Lord heard him.

10. And as Samuel was offering up the burnt offering, the Philistines drew near to battle against Israel: but the Lord thundered with a great thunder on that day upon the Philistines, and discomfited them; and they were smitten before Israel.

11. And the men of Israel went out of Mizpeh, and pursued the Philistines, and smote them, until they came under Bethcar.

12. Then Samuel took a stone, and set it between Mizpeh and Shen, and called the name of it Ebenezer, saying, Hitherto hath the Lord helped us.

Ebenezer (EB-un-NEE-zur)—(v. 12)—"stone of help"

Talk About It:
1. What did Israel ask of Samuel (vv. 7-8)?
2. How did Samuel respond (v. 9)?
3. How did Israel defeat the Philistines (vv. 10-11)?
4. Explain the monument Samuel erected (v. 12).

Israel's assembling is interpreted by the Philistines in a negative manner. Apparently they see it as a sign of rebellion which must be crushed. As the Philistine army gathers, the fear of the Israelites becomes apparent. They ask Samuel to intercede on their behalf. It is their only hope. He responds by verbally seeking God's help and by offering a burnt offering. This second action reminds us of Samuel's position and right as a priest of the Lord.

As Samuel presents the burnt offering, the Philistine military lines are nearing the assembled group. Before any attempt at resistance can be mounted, the Lord comes to their rescue. The loud thundering described in verse 10 panics the advancing troops. Also, Josephus, the Jewish historian of the first century, records an earthquake accompanying the storm and further creating havoc within the Philistines' military.

Seeing the enemy in flight, the Israelites pursue them and further the defeat. Although we do not know what type of weapons the Israelites had, we do know that in the early years of Saul's reign there were major limitations as to military weapons. All blacksmithing needs among the Israelites were done by going to the Philistine areas (13:19-22). Regardless of the availability of weapons, Israel pursues and furthers the routing of the enemy.

The exact location of Bethcar (7:11) is not known. But it is here that a stone is set up to commemorate the intervention of God on Israel's behalf. Samuel names this place *Ebenezer*—which means "stone of help"—saying, "Thus far has the Lord helped us" (v. 12 NIV). This is reminiscent of the memorial built when the Israelites crossed the Jordan River into the promised land of Canaan (Josh. 4). Twelve stones were taken out of the river bed and set up on the west bank. Together they represented the miraculous crossing and served as a teaching opportunity when future generations asked concerning the meaning of these stones.

"Knowing that I am not the one in control gives great encouragement. Knowing the One who is in control is everything."
—Alexander Michael

III. SAMUEL THE JUDGE (1 Sam. 7:13-17)

A. A Subdued Enemy (vv. 13-14)

13. So the Philistines were subdued, and they came no more into the coast of Israel: and the hand of the Lord was against the Philistines all the days of Samuel.

14. And the cities which the Philistines had taken from Israel were restored to Israel, from Ekron even unto Gath; and the coasts thereof did Israel deliver out of the hands of the Philistines. And there was peace between Israel and the Amorites.

Talk About It:
Describe Israel's life under Samuel's leadership.

Unlike most of the other judges, Samuel does not lead his nation in any military encounter with their enemies. Although there could be some incidents that are not recorded, the previous verses reveal God's dramatic intervention on behalf of the Israelites. This sound defeat of the Philistines seemingly robbed them of military strength or incentive to again confront Israel.

The last half of verse 13 tells of God's continuing oppression of the Philistines, not allowing them to retain their previous strength and domination of surrounding neighbors. His chosen means of keeping them in subjection is not given.

An aspect of the Philistines' subjection is the return of cities to Israel which had been captured. Instead of listing the names of the cities, an area designation indicates the extent. It was along the southern coastal plain of Israel. "The Israelites received back their cities up to the very borders of the Philistines, measuring these borders from Ekron to Gath" (*Keil and Delitzsch Commentary*). Meanwhile, the other Canaanite peoples ("the Amorites"), seeing how Israel had trumped the Philistines, lived at peace with Israel.

> "Leadership is a matter of having people look at you and gain confidence, seeing how you react."
> **—Tom Landry**

B. A Yearly Circuit (vv. 15-17)

15. And Samuel judged Israel all the days of his life.

16. And he went from year to year in circuit to Bethel, and Gilgal, and Mizpeh, and judged Israel in all those places.

17. And his return was to Ramah; for there was his house; and there he judged Israel; and there he built an altar unto the Lord.

Talk About It:
Describe Samuel's service to Israel.

Samuel's role in Israel's national life includes two dimensions. The first is when he stands out as the chief authority prior to the selection of Saul as the first king. This probably lasts for about twenty years.

During Samuel's years as judge, his influence is primarily within the southern portion of the nation. All four of the cities mentioned in verses 16 and 17 are in the territory of the tribe of Benjamin. This leaves the northern tribes and the Transjordan tribes with less influence from his godly leadership.

Samuel's second dimension of national life occurs during the reign of Saul. His influential actions continue though the nation is led by a king. On certain occasions Samuel boldly steps to the

Samuel: Prophet, Priest, and Judge

forefront. He chastises Saul for his sinful actions. Samuel also kills Agag, king of the Amalekites, who apparently has been brought back as a trophy of war in spite of God's direct command to completely destroy all the people (ch. 15).

Because of this last sin of the king, Samuel never sees Saul again. He will mourn the tragic path of this God-anointed king. However, Samuel is privileged to anoint David as the future king of Israel. Samuel will not live to see David take the throne some fifteen years later.

During his years as judge, the utilization of a home city, Ramah, and three circuit cities enables Samuel to have a greater impact by virtue of his accessibility. The people of the region didn't have to travel to a single location for spiritual advice and settlement of disputes.

CONCLUSION

Samuel's ministry stands distinctly above anyone (except Christ) in terms of his fulfilling the three offices of priest, prophet, and judge. By birthright as a son in the lineage of Levi, he could stand before the altar and offer sacrifice. By virtue of God's calling and commissioning, he ministered as both a prophet and priest. During a difficult time of transition furthered by the spiritual decline of Israel's first king, Samuel presented truth and righteousness to the nation. He boldly spoke against sin and mourned the path of the sinner.

GOLDEN TEXT CHALLENGE

"AS EVERY MAN HATH RECEIVED THE GIFT, EVEN SO MINISTER THE SAME ONE TO ANOTHER, AS GOOD STEWARDS OF THE MANIFOLD GRACE OF GOD" (1 Peter 4:10).

Just as God gifted Samuel for dynamic leadership, so He now gives every believer some endowment which he or she is to use in ministry to others. We are called upon to be "good trustees of God's many-sided grace [faithful stewards of the extremely diverse powers and gifts granted to Christians by unmerited favor]" (Amp.).

God has distributed among the membership of every believing community all the gifts necessary for their spiritual growth and activity. We are to be faithful stewards of these gifts. A steward owned no part of that over which he exercised control. He was fully accountable to his master for the way in which he carried out his task. Likewise, the gifts we have came from God, and we will answer to Him as to what we do with them.

"Christian leaders should be certain that their goal is to serve God and others, not to receive the title or honor that comes with leadership."
—**Millard Erickson**

Daily Devotions:
M. God Established the Prophets Deuteronomy 18:15-22
T. God Raised Up the Judges Judges 2:11-18
W. God Chose the Priests 1 Samuel 2:27-36
T. Exercise Wise Judgment Matthew 7:15-23
F. The Purpose of Prophesying 1 Corinthians 14:1-9
S. The Priesthood of Believers 1 Peter 2:9-12

God Gives Israel a King

1 Samuel 8:1-22; 9:1 through 10:27

Unit Theme:
Books of Samuel

Central Truth:
Selfish choices eventually bring trouble.

Focus:
Realize that sometimes what we desire is not best for us and guard against making unwise choices.

Context:
Around 1020 BC, Saul becomes the first king of Israel.

Golden Text:
"He [God] gave them their request; but sent leanness into their soul" (Psalm 106:15).

Study Outline:
I. Israel Demands a King
   (1 Sam. 8:4-7, 19-22)
II. God Chooses the King
   (1 Sam. 9:1-2, 15-19, 27; 10:1, 9-11)
III. Saul Is Made King
   (1 Sam. 10:17-27)

INTRODUCTION

Have you heard the statement "Be careful what you ask for because you might get it"? Selfish desires may have long-term results never even considered. This is due to shortsightedness and selfishness—looking for current fulfillment with little or no consideration for the future.

Usually we think of selfish desires and the resulting choices in relationship to an individual or a small group of people. Today's lesson expands far beyond such a limited circle. It reflects the wishes of an entire nation. The sad part rests on their being warned of the impact of a selfish choice, yet they persist. So God gives them what they want, knowing it isn't in their best interests.

The account of Israel's demand for a king provides an excellent opportunity for us to do both personal and corporate evaluation. It allows us to reflect on our personal wishes and how they measure up to God's choices for our lives. What price are we willing to pay to have it "our way"?

Let's also consider the power of peer pressure, which appears in different forms as we move through the various decades of life. In earlier years it usually concentrates more on clothes and personal appearance. As we mature, it moves to colleges, friends, and entertainment. Later inclusions are the pressures associated with what others have in terms of homes, cars, and personal earnings. Without realizing it, a person can be shaped by peer pressure throughout most of their life. To overcome this temptation, it is necessary to be inner-directed rather than other-directed. Values need to take precedence over wants and possessions.

I. ISRAEL DEMANDS A KING (1 Sam. 8:4-7, 19-22)

A. A Governmental Change (vv. 4-7)

4. Then all the elders of Israel gathered themselves together, and came to Samuel unto Ramah.

5. And said unto him, Behold, thou art old, and thy sons walk not in thy ways: now make us a king to judge us like all the nations.

6. But the thing displeased Samuel, when they said, Give us a king to judge us. And Samuel prayed unto the Lord.

7. And the Lord said unto Samuel, Hearken unto the voice of the people in all that they say unto thee: for they have not rejected thee, but they have rejected me, that I should not reign over them.

The first three verses of this chapter provide a brief background for what will take place. As Samuel ages, he passes some of the reins of responsibility to his two sons, Joel and Abiah. However, unlike their father, they do not prove to be men of integrity. Dishonesty, perversion of justice, and taking bribes create major problems. It is sad to see how Samuel's sons are like those of Eli (2:12-17). Neither man had sons worthy of their fathers.

These conditions are a major factor in the elders coming to Samuel with their request. Samuel's age and the actions of his sons are projected first in their request for a king. These issues cannot be discounted. However, we also know that in human requests and/or disagreements, what comes out first usually is not the major issue. Look specifically at the wording in 8:5. They ask for a human king to lead them. God's leadership and the peaceful conditions apparently does not suffice. They want a king "such as all the other nations have" (NIV). How ironic!

Samuel's initial reaction is one of displeasure, yet he prays before responding. Far too often we have a tendency to speak immediately rather than pray and reflect on the total situation. If we were to pray first, wiser words surely would follow. Also, our inner emotions would remain much calmer.

The Lord instructs Samuel to listen to them (v. 7). In other words, give them what they want. He repeats this instruction in verse 9. The Lord clarifies the picture so that Samuel doesn't see this request as a personal act against himself. Their actions stand as a rejection of God. In the following verses, God indicates this to be nothing unusual. It continues the pattern demonstrated from the beginning of the Exodus. Though separated by generations and approximately 400 years, the people still act the same.

B. A Stubborn Position (vv. 19-22)

19. Nevertheless the people refused to obey the voice of Samuel; and they said, Nay; but we will have a king over us;

Talk About It:
1. What was the elders' complaint against Samuel (vv. 1-5)?
2. What did the Lord explain to Samuel (vv. 6-7)?

"The picture of fallen man as given in Scripture is that he knows God but does not want to recognize Him as God."
—Cornelius Van Til

20. That we also may be like all the nations; and that our king may judge us, and go out before us, and fight our battles.

21. And Samuel heard all the words of the people, and rehearsed them in the ears of the Lord.

22. And the Lord said to Samuel, Hearken unto their voice, and make them a king. And Samuel said unto the men of Israel, Go ye every man unto his city.

Talk About It:
1. Why did the elders demand a king (vv. 19-20)?
2. Why do you suppose God replied as He did (v. 22)?

Following the Lord's directive, Samuel warns the delegation what will happen if they have a king (vv. 10-13). They are asking for a burden unlike any they have experienced before as a nation. Their sons will be drafted into military service. Others will be conscripted to serve in the king's fields and make instruments of war. Their daughters will be conscripted to serve the king as well.

Some in Israel will see their land, vineyards, and olive groves taken due to the king's wanting the best for himself (vv. 14, 16). All will be paying a 10 percent tax on their various crops and flocks for the support of the royal court (vv. 15, 17). Verse 18 indicates there will come a time when the burden placed by a king will become so great they will plead for the Lord's intervention on their behalf.

None of the conditions stated by Samuel changes the people's desire and decision. They want a king! The desire to be like other nations predominates. They want someone wearing a crown to make judgments and lead in times of war. One wonders what some of these same people may have thought as the Israelites under Saul's leadership would sit idly by while Goliath daily challenged them for forty days (17:8-11, 16). No leadership appears here until David, the shepherd boy, arrives.

"Don't think you're on the right road just because it's a well-beaten path."
—Author unknown

Samuel again seeks the Lord, repeating everything the people have said (8:21). The Lord's simple answer is a repetition of what was stated previously, "Listen to them" (v. 9 NIV). In this manner Samuel is instructed to give them what they desire. The delegation is dismissed, knowing their desire will be granted.

II. GOD CHOOSES THE KING (1 Sam. 9:1-2, 15-19, 27; 10:1, 9 -11)
A. The Right Person (9:1-2)

1. Now there was a man of Benjamin, whose name was Kish, the son of Abiel, the son of Zeror, the son of Bechorath, the son of Aphiah, a Benjamite, a mighty man of power.

2. And he had a son, whose name was Saul, a choice young man, and a goodly: and there was not among the children of Israel a goodlier person than he: from his shoulders and upward he was higher than any of the people.

goodly (v. 2)— handsome

Talk About It:
1. Describe Kish, the father of Saul (v. 1).
2. What made Saul stand out (v. 2)?

The Israelites' desire for a king doesn't include their wanting to select the person who will lead them. They entrust Samuel to work out the specifics. Since Israel is God's people, He will choose the person and reveal it to and through Samuel.

At this point Saul comes into the narrative. As would be expected in the patriarchal culture, his genealogical background precedes any personal description. Saul's father, Kish, is spoken of as "a mighty man of power," or "a man of standing" (v. 1 NIV). Both descriptions reflect his being a man of influence within the tribe of Benjamin.

Verse 2 provides an interesting description of Saul. It appears he follows the example of his father, being impressive in his conduct. Physically, he is eight to ten inches taller than the average Israelite. He was probably well over six feet tall.

God makes a selection of a man who will be accepted rather than rejected. First, he is respected within his own community. Second, being from the small tribe of Benjamin eliminates possible jealousies between larger tribes. Besides, the tribe of Benjamin is respected for their fighting men. Third, he is thirty years old, the age of maturity and service. Fourth, Saul demonstrates a heart of humility rather than pride and arrogance. Fifth, his height will automatically provide a sense of leadership credibility.

"The true measure of a man is the height of his ideals, the breadth of his sympathy, the depth of his convictions, and the length of his patience."
—Christians Quoting

B. The Future Revealed (vv. 15-19, 27)

15. Now the Lord had told Samuel in his ear a day before Saul came, saying,

16. To morrow about this time I will send thee a man out of the land of Benjamin, and thou shalt anoint him to be captain over my people Israel, that he may save my people out of the hand of the Philistines: for I have looked upon my people, because their cry is come unto me.

17. And when Samuel saw Saul, the Lord said unto him, Behold the man whom I spake to thee of! this same shall reign over my people.

18. Then Saul drew near to Samuel in the gate, and said, Tell me, I pray thee, where the seer's house is.

19. And Samuel answered Saul, and said, I am the seer: go up before me unto the high place; for ye shall eat with me to day, and to morrow I will let thee go, and will tell thee all that is in thine heart.

27. And as they were going down to the end of the city, Samuel said to Saul, Bid the servant pass on before us, (and he passed on,) but stand thou still a while, that I may shew thee the word of God.

No sense of time span between the Israelites' request and Saul's coming to Samuel is reflected in Scripture. We assume it is a relatively short time of weeks or even days. Of greater interest is the means of revealing God's choice for Israel's first king. He doesn't send Samuel to a particular household and then indicate the reason, as will be the case in selecting the second king. Instead, God uses what would seem to be a common circumstance to bring Saul to Samuel. Animals stray and the owners go looking for them.

Talk About It:
1. What had the Lord told Samuel (vv. 15-16)?
2. What brought Saul and Samuel together (vv. 17-18)?

In this case, Kish's donkeys have strayed and their whereabouts is unknown. No one has found them or informed Kish of their location. He instructs Saul to take one servant and begin to look for them (v. 3). Several days of an extensive search produce no sign of the lost animals. Concerned Kish would begin worrying more about the searchers than the donkeys, Saul decides to return home. His servant suggests going to the nearby city where the man of God resides. Maybe he will be of assistance. Saul agrees, but his immediate concern is having nothing to offer for the prophet's services. Once again the servant fills the void, indicating he has a small amount of silver which can be given (vv. 4-8).

A day earlier, prior to their decision to seek help, God informs Samuel of what will transpire. The one to be anointed will come to him. Only his tribe is revealed (vv. 15-16). However, the next day as Saul comes near, God indicates he is the man. God always knows what information we need and when we need it.

In response to Saul's inquiry concerning the location of the seer's house, Samuel reveals a number of items. After identifying himself as the seer, he indicates Saul is to eat with him and spend the night (v. 19). He adds that the lost donkeys are found. Then comes the unbelievable when Samuel states Saul's position among the Israelites (v. 20). Instead of accepting this pronouncement, Saul points out that his tribe is the smallest and his family is of least significance within it. Then he asks Samuel, "Why do you say such a thing to me?" (v. 21 NIV). One has to appreciate Saul's not immediately accepting the honor without considering his current status.

A special event takes place at the meal, at which some thirty invited guests attend. Not only is Saul given the place of honor, but also a special piece of meat. The shoulder of the sacrificial animal which was waved before the Lord and then given to the presiding priest is now placed before Saul. This action by Samuel is another indication of the honor being bestowed on Saul (vv. 22-24).

After staying the night, Saul prepares to leave for his home. As Samuel escorts him to the city gate, he requests Saul to wait while sending his servants ahead. This is so Samuel can privately offer a word from the Lord (v. 27).

"God reserves the right to interrupt our plans with His calling."
—David Cooper

C. The Prophetic Confirmation (10:1, 9-11)

1. Then Samuel took a vial of oil, and poured it upon his head, and kissed him, and said, Is it not because the Lord hath anointed thee to be captain over his inheritance?

9. And it was so, that when he had turned his back to go from Samuel, God gave him another heart: and all those signs came to pass that day.

God Gives Israel a King

10. And when they came thither to the hill, behold, a company of prophets met him; and the Spirit of God came upon him, and he prophesied among them.

11. And it came to pass, when all that knew him before-time saw that, behold, he prophesied among the prophets, then the people said one to another, What is this that is come unto the son of Kish? Is Saul also among the prophets?

Samuel presides in a solemn ceremony of consecration by anointing Saul with oil. The oil, which came in drops from a narrow-necked bottle, is probably the same oil used in the consecration of priests. Samuel's kissing Saul is an Oriental symbol of subjection. Saul now stands as the captain of the Lord's people with the sacred responsibility of their well-being.

Saul is informed of further confirmation which will be given to him (vv. 2-7). Three signs will occur. First, he will meet two men who inform him his donkeys are found and his father is worried about him more than the lost animals. Second, he will meet three men with young goats, bread, and a bottle of wine. They will give him two loaves of bread. Third, he will meet a company of prophets prophesying. The Spirit of the Lord will come on him, and he will prophesy; he will become a new person, with a changed heart. This doesn't mean a change from sinner to saint. Rather, this transformation will give him the ability to fulfill God's destiny. However, this is not automatic. Right choices will still be required.

All three signs are fulfilled on that very day. When people see Saul prophesying, they ask, "What is this that has happened to the son of Kish?" (v. 11 NIV).

III. SAUL IS MADE KING (1 Sam. 10:17-27)
A. The Meeting (vv. 17-19)

17. And Samuel called the people together unto the Lord to Mizpeh;

18. And said unto the children of Israel, Thus saith the Lord God of Israel, I brought up Israel out of Egypt, and delivered you out of the hand of the Egyptians, and out of the hand of all kingdoms, and of them that oppressed you:

19. And ye have this day rejected your God, who himself saved you out of all your adversities and your tribulations; and ye have said unto him, Nay, but set a king over us. Now therefore present yourselves before the Lord by your tribes, and by your thousands.

The private ceremony of Saul's anointing is followed with a public ceremony in front of the people of Israel. Samuel calls for them to gather at Mizpeh. This city, located in the territory of Benjamin, is also one of the cities which is served by Samuel in his circuit route as a judge (7:16). It stands as a logical location for this historical event due to its being within Saul's own tribal area.

Talk About It:
1. What did Samuel reveal to Saul (v. 1)?
2. Explain the phrase "another heart" (v. 9).
3. What did the people ask about Saul, and why (vv. 10-11)?

Talk About It:
1. Of what did Samuel remind the Israelites, and why (vv. 17-18)?
2. What charge was brought against Israel (v. 19)?

Von Ewald observed, "The secret meetings of the seer with Saul was not sufficient to secure a complete and satisfactory recognition of him as king; it was also necessary that the Spirit of Jehovah should single him out publicly in a solemn assembly of the nation, and point him out as the man of Jehovah."

Samuel's word from the Lord sets the stage for the public selection of their king. This is not just an expression of Samuel's personal feelings. God himself wants the people to understand His displeasure with their desire for a king which, in fact, means they have rejected their God. Their desire flies in the face of what they as a nation have experienced because of His working for them.

Verse 18 provides a summary of God's deliverance on their behalf. The events in Egypt were miraculous and culminated in their becoming a nation at Mount Sinai. The ten plagues on Egypt, the miraculous crossing of the Red Sea, and the marvelous provision of food and water must not be forgotten. Though weaker than their enemies, Israel defeated the powerful cities and alliances in Canaan as they took over their promised land.

Later, when sin resulted in God's allowing other nations to oppress them, God heard their repentance and sent deliverers. Through divine intervention, the nation was delivered from a wide variety of surrounding enemies. It begs the question as to why they now want a human leader to replace divine leadership.

> "There is no one so great or mighty that he can avoid the misery that will rise up against him when he resists and strives against God."
> —John Calvin

The bottom line is simply one of rejecting the very God who, for centuries, saved them from the bondage and oppression of other nations. Having made the reality of their rejection clear, Samuel tells them to present themselves tribe by tribe so the divine selection of their king can be made known.

B. The Selection (vv. 20-22)

20. And when Samuel had caused all the tribes of Israel to come near, the tribe of Benjamin was taken.

21. When he had caused the tribe of Benjamin to come near by their families, the family of Matri was taken, and Saul the son of Kish was taken: and when they sought him, he could not be found.

22. Therefore they enquired of the Lord further, if the man should yet come thither. And the Lord answered, Behold, he hath hid himself among the stuff.

Talk About It:
1. Why did Samuel go through the process in verses 20 and 21 instead of simply presenting Saul as God's choice?
2. Where was Saul, and why (v. 22)?

The selection process is very public, even though the exact method is not recorded. The choice probably occurs by drawing lots. Once the tribe of Benjamin stands as the chosen one, the process repeats first with the family names and then the males within the chosen one.

Samuel knows in advance what the result will be. Once the selection process indicates Saul to be the chosen man, Samuel's

God Gives Israel a King

next step will be to physically present God's man to all of Israel. But there is a problem. No one knows where Saul is. Inquiring of the Lord, it is revealed Saul hides within the baggage storage area. One can only speculate on the reason for his being there. Usually the characteristics of humility and modesty are suggested. If this is true, regretfully they do not last very long into Saul's reign.

C. The Response (vv. 23-27)

23. And they ran and fetched him thence: and when he stood among the people, he was higher than any of the people from his shoulders and upward.

24. And Samuel said to all the people, See ye him whom the Lord hath chosen, that there is none like him among all the people? And all the people shouted, and said, God save the king.

25. Then Samuel told the people the manner of the kingdom, and wrote it in a book, and laid it up before the Lord. And Samuel sent all the people away, every man to his house.

26. And Saul also went home to Gibeah; and there went with him a band of men, whose hearts God had touched.

27. But the children of Belial said, How shall this man save us? And they despised him, and brought him no presents. But he held his peace.

Once Saul stands before the people as God's chosen king, his physical stature is evident. He towers some twelve inches taller than the average Israelite. When Samuel presents Saul as their king, the people show their expression of homage and loyalty. However, verse 27 indicates a group of rebels ("children of Belial") who despise Saul and question his ability to lead. Unlike the others who present gifts honoring their king, these men withhold any action of support. Saul knows of their words, but wisely chooses to be deaf to their comments. In contrast to these men are a group who commit to Saul and act as a royal bodyguard.

An important detail in verse 25 is Samuel's stating the constitutional plan for the kingdom and then writing it in a book. Though the specifics are not given, we assume these are the guidelines given by God to govern the actions of the new monarch.

Talk About It:
1. How did the people respond to Saul (vv. 23-24)?
2. What did Samuel write in a book, and what did he do with it (v. 25)?
3. What did the Lord do for Saul (v. 26)?
4. What trait did Saul show in verse 27?

Greatest Discovery
In 1847 Sir James Simpson, a doctor in Edinburgh, discovered the use of chloroform as anaesthetic in surgery. Many years later, when lecturing at the university, he was asked, "What do you consider to be your most valuable discovery?" His reply was "When I discovered myself a sinner and that Jesus Christ was my Savior."

CONCLUSION

Israel makes a selfish choice in desiring a king and rejecting God's plan and provision for them. God grants their wish and provides a qualified individual for their first king. However, He also warns them through Samuel as to what will be in their future.

GOLDEN TEXT CHALLENGE

"HE [GOD] GAVE THEM THEIR REQUEST; BUT SENT LEANNESS INTO THEIR SOUL" (Ps. 106:15).

The context of this verse is the early stages of Israel's journey through the wilderness. God was providing His people with manna to eat, but they were not satisfied. Even though the Lord was miraculously feeding His people with this nutritious and delicious food six days per week, they were complaining.

Being ungrateful for what God had already done and was continually doing for them, the Israelites "gave in to their craving . . . [and] put God to the test" (v. 14 NIV). God gave them what they demanded, sending large quantities of quail into the camp. But even as the Israelites caught the birds and ate them, "the wrath of the Lord was aroused against the people, and the Lord struck the people with a very great plague" (Num. 11:33 NKJV). The place was named *Kibroth-Hattaavah* (v. 34), meaning "the graves of greed."

Greed is still digging graves in our day. Rather than testing God by being unhappy with His provision, we should be grateful, worshipful people who find our satisfaction in Him. Otherwise, we will experience "leanness [of] soul," greedily asking for things that will not satisfy, and putting our lives in harm's way.

Saul, a Failed Leader

1 Samuel 13:1-14; 15:1-35

INTRODUCTION

No one is exempt from failure regardless of his or her ability and insight. It comes to all of us. This isn't a fatalistic concept but a reality. Some experience it more frequently or to a greater degree than others.

Personal failure may be caused by many factors. Laziness sets the stage for a broad variety of lapses and eventually failure. Circumstances at times are beyond a person's control, regardless of how much planning is done and effort is put forth. Unexpected economic downturns result in job losses and other traumas, regardless of one's best efforts. Sometimes impetuousness creates settings for an unnecessarily high percentage of potential failure. Good ideas are pursued without sufficient preparation. Rushing ahead without considering the timing easily results in minimal success at best, which is a short distance from failure.

Some leaders become enamored with their positions and fall into the trap of entitlement. Assuming they deserve certain benefits may lead to unrealistic demands of those working for them, using money of others for personal use, or assuming authority beyond the job description. Though not initially reflecting these characteristics, the pressure of the office expectations and the pride of ego bring about major changes in behavior.

As indicated in the previous lesson, Saul appears to be the ideal first king of Israel. He appears as the "whole package." He is a mature man, possesses an above-average stature, and demonstrates a humble heart. But then we read of a man who seems so different. Within just a few years his actions and attitudes are no longer the same. He becomes a man of rebellion rather than obedience. As we explore the specific details of Saul's downfall, the Golden Text for this lesson needs to be pondered: "What doth the Lord require of thee, but to do justly, and to love mercy, and to walk humbly with thy God?" (Mic. 6:8).

Unit Theme:
Books of Samuel

Central Truth:
Rebellion against God leads to ruin.

Focus:
Consider carefully that rebellion against God can lead only to ruin and walk humbly with God.

Context:
Around 1015 BC, Samuel confronts Saul for disobeying the Lord.

Golden Text:
"What doth the Lord require of thee, but to do justly, and to love mercy, and to walk humbly with thy God?" (Mic. 6:8).

Study Outline:
I. Saul's Presumptuous Sin (1 Sam. 13:1-14)
II. Saul's Second Chance (1 Sam. 15:1-9)
III. Saul's Rebellion and Punishment (1 Sam. 15:10-23, 34-35)

I. SAUL'S PRESUMPTUOUS SIN (1 Sam. 13:1-14)

A. The Conflict (vv. 1-7)

1. Saul reigned one year; and when he had reigned two years over Israel,

2. Saul chose him three thousand men of Israel; whereof two thousand were with Saul in Michmash and in mount Bethel, and a thousand were with Jonathan in Gibeah of Benjamin: and the rest of the people he sent every man to his tent.

3. And Jonathan smote the garrison of the Philistines that was in Geba, and the Philistines heard of it. And Saul blew the trumpet throughout all the land, saying, Let the Hebrews hear.

4. And all Israel heard say that Saul had smitten a garrison of the Philistines, and that Israel also was had in abomination with the Philistines. And the people were called together after Saul to Gilgal.

5. And the Philistines gathered themselves together to fight with Israel, thirty thousand chariots, and six thousand horsemen, and people as the sand which is on the sea shore in multitude: and they came up, and pitched in Michmash, eastward from Bethaven.

6. When the men of Israel saw that they were in a strait, (for the people were distressed,) then the people did hide themselves in caves, and in thickets, and in rocks, and in high places, and in pits.

7. And some of the Hebrews went over Jordan to the land of Gad and Gilead. As for Saul, he was yet in Gilgal, and all the people followed him trembling.

Talk about overwhelming odds! Saul and his son, Jonathan, begin with a total of three thousand foot soldiers. Jonathan leads one thousand of those men in a successful assault against a garrison of Philistines. In response the Philistines mount an almost unbelievable force with which to attack Israel. In this type of military encounter, their having three thousand (see NIV) chariots would be like a modern force having the same number of tanks going against infantry. Also, they have a tremendous number of soldiers whose number isn't given. The description of their being "as numerous as the sand on the seashore" (v. 5 NIV) provides a sufficient picture.

It's no wonder the small force of Israelites begin to defect. They see a hopeless situation. Most of them try hiding from the enemy anywhere they can—in caves, thickets, dry wells, pits, and among the rocks. Approximately 80 percent of the army leaves (see v. 15). Those remaining are trembling in fear (v. 7). The best that can be said for them is they stay with Saul while others run for their lives.

Michmash (MIK-mash)—v. 2—a place in Benjamin about eight miles northeast of Jerusalem

Geba (GHEE-buh)—v. 3—a town in Benjamin where the Philistines had stationed troops

Talk About It:
1. What did Saul do two years into his reign (vv. 1-2)?
2. What riled up the Philistines (vv. 3-4)?
3. What did the Israelite soldiers do (vv. 6-7), and why (v. 5)?

"To one who is afraid, everything rustles."
—**Sophocles**

Saul, a Failed Leader

B. The Decision (vv. 8-9)

8. And he tarried seven days, according to the set time that Samuel had appointed: but Samuel came not to Gilgal; and the people were scattered from him.

9. And Saul said, Bring hither a burnt offering to me, and peace offerings. And he offered the burnt offering.

The military situation is hopeless. Only a miracle can change it. To make matters worse, Samuel doesn't arrive at the agreed time. He represents God in all three roles of priest, prophet, and previous judge of Israel. In desperation, Saul makes a totally unacceptable choice. We can label this as situational ethics. Even though he is not a priest and has no right to offer a sacrifice, Saul apparently assumes the situation allows him to break God's law.

It is always a fateful decision when a human chooses to place himself or herself above the directive of God. Though Scripture doesn't provide a detailed account of Saul's thinking and how long it took for him to come to the decision, it doesn't seem to have been one of great anguish. This seems to be brought out more clearly as he offers excuses for his actions.

Talk About It:
Describe and explain Saul's actions.

C. The Excuses (vv. 10-14)

10. And it came to pass, that as soon as he had made an end of offering the burnt offering, behold, Samuel came; and Saul went out to meet him, that he might salute him.

11. And Samuel said, What hast thou done? And Saul said, Because I saw that the people were scattered from me, and that thou camest not within the days appointed, and that the Philistines gathered themselves together at Michmash;

12. Therefore said I, The Philistines will come down now upon me to Gilgal, and I have not made supplication unto the Lord: I forced myself therefore, and offered a burnt offering.

13. And Samuel said to Saul, Thou hast done foolishly: thou hast not kept the commandment of the Lord thy God, which he commanded thee: for now would the Lord have established thy kingdom upon Israel for ever.

14. But now thy kingdom shall not continue: the Lord hath sought him a man after his own heart, and the Lord hath commanded him to be captain over his people, because thou hast not kept that which the Lord commanded thee.

What a change came over this God-chosen king of Israel! It was relatively early in his kingship. Instead of humility, we see a man who "passes the buck" and readily offers excuses for his sinful actions. When confronted by Samuel about his decision, Saul readily offers four reasons: (1) His troops were scattered. (2) Samuel was late for the agreed time of arrival. (3) The Philistines were gathered nearby for an imminent attack. (4) He had not sought the Lord's favor prior to this crisis. In light of these circumstances, he felt compelled to offer the sacrifice.

Talk About It:
1. When did Samuel arrive on the scene (v. 10)?
2. How did Saul defend his actions (vv. 11-12)?
3. What did Saul's actions reveal about him (vv. 13-14)?

Amalek (AM-a-lek)—v. 2—a nomadic tribe of people who made an unprovoked attack against Israel at the beginning of their wilderness journey (Ex. 17:8-13)

Telaim (tuh-LAY-im)—v. 4—the place where Saul gathered his fighting men

Talk About It:
1. What reminder did Samuel give to Saul (v. 1)?
2. Why was Amalek to be judged (v. 2)?
3. How explicit were the instructions given to Saul (v. 3)?

No circumstances ever provide sufficient reason for breaking God's laws. This becomes immediately clear as Samuel pronounces the consequences. Unlike God's initial intentions, Saul's dynasty will not continue. His replacement will be a man whose heart follows God. In the future this man will successfully lead Israel. Though this event is still some years in the future, it does not lessen the reality of God's judgment in stripping the throne from Saul's descendants.

II. SAUL'S SECOND CHANCE (1 Sam. 15:1-9)
A. The Mission (vv. 1-4)

1. Samuel also said unto Saul, The Lord sent me to anoint thee to be king over his people, over Israel: now therefore hearken thou unto the voice of the words of the Lord.

2. Thus saith the Lord of hosts, I remember that which Amalek did to Israel, how he laid wait for him in the way, when he came up from Egypt.

3. Now go and smite Amalek, and utterly destroy all that they have, and spare them not; but slay both man and woman, infant and suckling, ox and sheep, camel and ass.

4. And Saul gathered the people together, and numbered them in Telaim, two hundred thousand footmen, and ten thousand men of Judah.

There is no guarantee any person who fails will necessarily be given a second chance, though God in His mercy may provide such an occasion. When this takes place, the person needs to seriously consider every facet of the opportunity. Fortunately for Saul, God chooses to allow him a second chance to demonstrate the ability to follow divine directives.

Samuel comes to Saul as the messenger of the Lord. He begins with a brief reminder. It is the Lord who made the choice of Saul to be the first king. Samuel served as the instrument then, and is once again coming with a word from the Lord. For these reasons, it is important for King Saul to carefully listen to the words which will be spoken.

Though some four hundred years have passed since the Amalekites attacked the Israelites on their journey to the Promised Land (Ex. 17:8-13), God now chooses to punish them for this action. Though Israel had not acted aggressively toward these people, the Amalekites may have seen Israel's coming as an attempt to take over their territory. God intervened supernaturally, enabling Israel to defeat them in the first of many encounters with the Amalekites. Afterward, the Lord indicated He would be at war with the Amalekites in future generations (v. 16), yet the time would come when He would "completely blot out the memory of Amalek from under heaven" (v. 14 NIV).

The Lord's directions to Saul are very specific. He is to attack and destroy *everything*. So there will be no mistake or misunderstanding, people of both gender and all ages are listed. Various livestock are also listed. This precludes sparing animals to use for sacrifice.

Immediately Saul acts to fulfill the words of the Lord. He amasses a force of 210,000 soldiers. It is of interest how the number of men from Judah is listed separately. This will be seen throughout the next century. It seems to reflect the eventual division of the tribes.

B. The Attack (vv. 5-9)

5. And Saul came to a city of Amalek, and laid wait in the valley.

6. And Saul said unto the Kenites, Go, depart, get you down from among the Amalekites, lest I destroy you with them: for ye shewed kindness to all the children of Israel, when they came up out of Egypt. So the Kenites departed from among the Amalekites.

7. And Saul smote the Amalekites from Havilah until thou comest to Shur, that is over against Egypt.

8. And he took Agag the king of the Amalekites alive, and utterly destroyed all the people with the edge of the sword.

9. But Saul and the people spared Agag, and the best of the sheep, and of the oxen, and of the fatlings, and the lambs, and all that was good, and would not utterly destroy them: but every thing that was vile and refuse, that they destroyed utterly.

Saul's military skill is seen here as he sets an ambush as the tactic against the Amalekites. So no innocent people are harmed, he instructs the Kenites in the area to leave. This group of people are the descendants of Hobab, Moses' brother-in-law. Their residing in Canaan is the result of Moses' inviting his family member to come with them and be a pathfinder (Num. 10:29-32).

Swiftly Saul's forces attack the entire area populated by the Amalekites. The whole population, except for King Agag, is destroyed by the sword. Though not stated, the king may have been spared to have him as a trophy of war. Sometimes a captured king would be incapacitated by the cutting off of his thumbs and big toes, making him a human symbol of triumph.

In Israel's attack against Amalek, the diseased and weak livestock are destroyed; however, the very best are kept, just as King Agag is spared. So, Saul's actions are incomplete. Total obedience does not occur.

III. SAUL'S REBELLION AND PUNISHMENT
(1 Sam. 15:10-23, 34-35)
A. The Lie (vv. 10-15)
10. Then came the word of the Lord unto Samuel, saying,

"I was not born to be free. I was born to adore and to obey."
—C. S. Lewis

Kenites (KEE-nites)—v. 6—a tribe of nomadic metalsmiths who were kind to Israel at the beginning of their wilderness journey

Agag (AA-gag)—v. 8—probably a title like "Pharaoh" of Egypt

Talk About It:
In what ways did Saul disobey the Lord's commands?

"Two things are infinite: the universe and human stupidity; and I'm not sure about the universe."
—**Albert Einstein**

**It repententh me
(v. 11)**—"I am grieved"
(NIV) or "I greatly
regret" (NKJV)

11. It repenteth me that I have set up Saul to be king: for he is turned back from following me, and hath not performed my commandments. And it grieved Samuel; and he cried unto the Lord all night.

12. And when Samuel rose early to meet Saul in the morning, it was told Samuel, saying, Saul came to Carmel, and, behold, he set him up a place, and is gone about, and passed on, and gone down to Gilgal.

13. And Samuel came to Saul: and Saul said unto him, Blessed be thou of the Lord: I have performed the commandment of the Lord.

14. And Samuel said, What meaneth then this bleating of the sheep in mine ears, and the lowing of the oxen which I hear?

15. And Saul said, They have brought them from the Amalekites: for the people spared the best of the sheep and of the oxen, to sacrifice unto the Lord thy God; and the rest we have utterly destroyed.

Talk About It:
1. What do verses 10 and 11 reveal about Samuel's relationship with God?
2. What do Saul's actions in verse 12 reveal about himself?
3. How did Saul justify his disobedience (v. 15)?

We are reminded of God's omniscience. He knows everything that is or is not being done according to His word. We cannot hide our blatant disobedience or slight deviations. Also known to Him is the condition or attitude of our heart. Though our motivations may be hidden from those about us, He sees clearly the reason behind our actions.

Before Saul and the army return from their encounter, the Lord comes to Samuel with grievous words. The Lord grieves over His decision of making Saul king of Israel. The word *repenteth* (v. 11) does not mean God sinned or is just now realizing the type of man Saul could become. Instead, it reveals the grief our God experiences when His children choose the path of disobedience rather than obediently doing His will.

The words of verse 11 point to Saul's disobedience as being far more than a matter of poor judgment or a simple mistake. This is a heart issue. He is rejecting God's sovereignty over his life and choosing to be the leader of his own path. This news devastates Samuel. He too experiences deep grief and spends the night crying out to the Lord. The content of this night of prayer can only be surmised.

It becomes Samuel's spiritual obligation to confront Saul for his sin and deliver the message of the Lord. Instead of waiting for the king to eventually come to him at some later date, Samuel rises early and goes to meet Saul. Having been told the whereabouts of Saul, this isn't a hunt-and-find mission. Samuel is even told of Saul's setting up a monument in honor of his successful attack on the Amalekites.

When Samuel reaches Saul, the statements of the king appear as though he has thought through what he will report about the battle. He begins with a blessing on Samuel and states his obediently having carried out the Lord's directive. One gets the feeling of his attempting to establish a truth which, in reality, is only a half-truth.

Samuel's response is calculated to press Saul to explain the environment. He doesn't just come out and call him a liar. Instead, he asks for an explanation of why he hears the sounds of sheep and cattle. This would not be occurring if everything had been destroyed according to the Lord's directive.

Saul immediately places the blame on the soldiers, yet he places them in a positive light. They kept only the best, and it is for a positive purpose—to make sacrifices to the Lord. In passing the blame, Saul misses the point. He is the commander of these men. He bears the responsibility for their actions, especially when being aware of what they are doing. Attempting to defend himself, he essentially incriminates himself.

> "God is not a power or principle or law, but He is a living, creating, communicating person—a mind who thinks, a heart who feels, a will who acts, whose best name is Father."
> —Robert Hamill

B. The Reality (vv. 16-23)

16. Then Samuel said unto Saul, Stay, and I will tell thee what the Lord hath said to me this night. And he said unto him, Say on.

17. And Samuel said, When thou wast little in thine own sight, wast thou not made the head of the tribes of Israel, and the Lord anointed thee king over Israel?

18. And the Lord sent thee on a journey, and said, Go and utterly destroy the sinners the Amalekites, and fight against them until they be consumed.

19. Wherefore then didst thou not obey the voice of the Lord, but didst fly upon the spoil, and didst evil in the sight of the Lord?

20. And Saul said unto Samuel, Yea, I have obeyed the voice of the Lord, and have gone the way which the Lord sent me, and have brought Agag the king of Amalek, and have utterly destroyed the Amalekites.

21. But the people took of the spoil, sheep and oxen, the chief of the things which should have been utterly destroyed, to sacrifice unto the Lord thy God in Gilgal.

22. And Samuel said, Hath the Lord as great delight in burnt offerings and sacrifices, as in obeying the voice of the Lord? Behold, to obey is better than sacrifice, and to hearken than the fat of rams.

23. For rebellion is as the sin of witchcraft, and stubbornness is as iniquity and idolatry. Because thou hast rejected the word of the Lord, he hath also rejected thee from being king.

Talk About It:
1. How does verse 17 describe Saul at the beginning of his reign?
2. What did Saul claim in verse 20?
3. What is "better" (v. 22), and why?
4. How does Samuel characterize "stubbornness" and "rebellion" (v. 23)?

Not wanting to allow this charade to continue, Samuel tells Saul to stop. Now he will reveal what the Lord told him during the night. The only positive response in the whole dialogue is Saul's statement, "Say on" (v. 16).

The root of Saul's disobedience is revealed. It is pride, which Saul has allowed to take up residence within his heart. This is the same man who hid himself in the baggage when Israel gathered for the announcement of their first king (10:22). When reminded of his mission and questioned as to the reasons for his not complying, Saul does not admit his guilt. Instead, he argues for his innocence and obedience.

It is both sad and interesting how Saul defends himself. He does not say why he brought back King Agag alive, but again says it was the soldiers who selected and brought back the best animals "in order to sacrifice them to the Lord your God" (15:21 NIV).

In response, Samuel states a principle which continues today. Simply stated, obedience to God's directive is more important than acts of worship. Genuine worship occurs only when it comes from a pure heart in proper relationship with God.

Verse 23 is often overlooked in the emphasis on verse 22. It graphically expresses the seriousness of rebellion. Furthering the seriousness of Saul's actions is his position as the leader of God's chosen people. Saul's participating in divination and idolatry would be of no greater sin than his rebellion and continued arrogance. Following this description comes the final verdict. This second action of disobedience solidifies his fate of being rejected as Israel's king.

"In sacrifices a man offers only the strange flesh of irrational animals, whereas in obedience he offers his own will, which is our rational or spiritual worship."
—*The Berleburg Bible*

In verse 24 we see how Saul indicates his sin to Samuel but never confesses to God. He suggests fear of the people being the reason for his actions. Then he wants Samuel to accompany him to a place of worship. He desires the honor of people above God's favor (see v. 30). As Samuel turns to go, Saul grasps the hem of his robe, causing it to tear (v. 27). This action becomes the symbol of God's taking the kingdom from Saul and giving it to another (v. 28).

C. The Separation (vv. 34-35)

34. Then Samuel went to Ramah; and Saul went up to his house to Gibeah of Saul.

35. And Samuel came no more to see Saul until the day of his death: nevertheless Samuel mourned for Saul: and the Lord repented that he had made Saul king over Israel.

Saul's failure as a leader results in the fatal separation from God and the personal separation from his spiritual leader, Samuel. The king's persistence in doing his own thing and vigorously defending his disobedience guarantees the kingdom's being taken from him.

After killing Agag to fulfill the complete directive of the Lord (v. 33), Samuel returns to his home. Never again will Samuel and Saul meet. The king's persistent rebellion against God's directives and failure to repent results in a complete break of communication from the spiritual leader whom the Lord previously used. Now Saul is on his own.

This final phrase of verse 35 reflects an emotional dimension of our God: "The Lord was grieved that he had made Saul king" (NIV). Although God places people in positions to produce and to fulfill His will, the choices are still up to the individual.

CONCLUSION

Saul's failure as the first king of Israel stems not just from wrong choices without sufficient knowledge, but from rebellious, self-serving decisions which are directly in opposition to God's revealed will.

GOLDEN TEXT CHALLENGE

"WHAT DOTH THE LORD REQUIRE OF THEE, BUT TO DO JUSTLY, AND TO LOVE MERCY, AND TO WALK HUMBLY WITH THY GOD?" (Mic. 6:8).

This is one of the most powerful and all-embracing statements in the Old Testament. It is Micah's summary of religion. In succinct terms he gives us the minimum of what God requires from us. What He demands is the penitent heart of the individual—toward Him and one's neighbor.

The good that He requires is the doing of His will. *To do justly* is to act toward God and people according to the divine standard of righteousness revealed in His law. *To love mercy*, or kindness, is to show a compassionate warmheartedness toward others. *To walk humbly before God* is to recognize the absolute holiness and righteousness of God and to walk in humble and submissive obedience to His will.

> "Hope is the best possession. None are completely wretched but those who are without hope, and few are reduced so low as that."
> —**William Hazlitt**

Daily Devotions:
M. A Rebellious People
   Deuteronomy 9:7-14
T. Consequences of Rebellion
   2 Chronicles 36:11-20
W. A Teacher of Rebellion Judged
   Jeremiah 28:12-17
T. Jesus Teaches Humility
   Matthew 18:1-4; 23:11-12
F. Christ's Humility and Exaltation
   Philippians 2:5-11
S. The Humble Are Given Grace
   James 4:6-10

God Chooses a New Leader

1 Samuel 16:1-13; 19:1 through 20:42; 22:1-2; 27:1-4

Unit Theme:
Books of Samuel

Central Truth:
God chooses people through whom He accomplishes His purposes.

Focus:
Acknowledge that God chooses whom He will to serve Him, and affirm that God has chosen us in Christ.

Context:
Between 1015 and 1010 BC, the Lord prepares David to become Israel's king.

Golden Text:
"God is the judge: he putteth down one, and setteth up another" (Ps. 75:7).

Study Outline:
  I. David Anointed to Become King
     (1 Sam. 16:1-13)
 II. David Hated by Saul
     (1 Sam. 19:1-24;
     20:1-42)
III. David Gains a Following
     (1 Sam. 22:1-2;
     27:1-4)

INTRODUCTION

Throughout the modern world, as representative government continues to spread to nations on every continent, it is easy to look back at biblical times with little appreciation for the selection of political leaders. After all, we know that monarchies ruled the day, since this was thousands of years before democratic government was even conceived. The story of Israel begins with her liberation from the monarchy of Pharaoh, and she is constantly in danger from foreign monarchs long before Saul is anointed as the first official head of the Jewish state. In the books of Samuel, we get not only an inside look at Israel's shaky start at monarchical government, but a remarkable perspective on the controversy surrounding the entire transition.

Up to this point, Moses was recognized as the greatest leader in the nation's history, although he acted more as priest than king. The period of the judges foreshadowed the coming monarchy, since a series of individuals were raised up to lead Israel in military campaigns, but in most cases these leaders settled into average lives outside of these campaigns. They did not live in palaces, forcefully draft their armies, or tax the population. It was only with the coming of Samuel, and perhaps his failure as a parent, that monarchy fell on Israel.

This tension in the Book of 1 Samuel displays the remarkable diversity of perspectives in the Bible, as the two heroes—Samuel and David—successfully carry out their roles even as Samuel consistently castigates the concept of a king in Israel. In Samuel's view, monarchy is an exceptionally terrible idea in Israel, even though Deuteronomy 17:14-20 appears to presuppose its acceptance after the conquest of the Promised Land. He certainly has his reasons: High taxes, conscripted armies, and an expensive centralized government all typically tend toward excess. David will be guilty of all of these at different points in his reign, but he will also remain faithful to God's heart despite such lapses.

So is God anti-monarchy? It is a difficult question to definitively answer, since Scripture has multiple voices on this subject. All in all, the teachings of both Testaments are infused with enough flexibility to be equally applicable to all political situations, and this is a gift to God's people both then and now.

I. DAVID ANOINTED TO BECOME KING (1 Sam. 16:1-13)

It is notable that these books bear the name of 1 and 2 Samuel, not 1 and 2 David. Not only is the bulk of the material devoted to David, but the previous stories have a way of fore-shadowing, or leading up to, David—from the conception of Samuel in Hannah's womb, to the calling of the prophet as a boy, to the failure of King Saul. The consistent connection of all the characters back to Samuel says something about the way power was meant to operate among God's people: it begins with God, not with the ruler's sword.

A. The Confused (but Obedient) Prophet (vv. 1-10)
(1 Samuel 16:4-5, 8-10 is not included in the printed text.)

1. And the Lord said unto Samuel, How long wilt thou mourn for Saul, seeing I have rejected him from reigning over Israel? fill thine horn with oil, and go, I will send thee to Jesse the Bethlehemite: for I have provided me a king among his sons.

2. And Samuel said, How can I go? if Saul hear it, he will kill me. And the Lord said, Take an heifer with thee, and say, I am come to sacrifice to the Lord.

3. And call Jesse to the sacrifice, and I will shew thee what thou shalt do: and thou shalt anoint unto me him whom I name unto thee.

6. And it came to pass, when they were come, that he looked on Eliab, and said, Surely the Lord's anointed is before him.

7. But the Lord said unto Samuel, Look not on his countenance, or on the height of his stature; because I have refused him: for the Lord seeth not as man seeth; for man looketh on the outward appearance, but the Lord looketh on the heart.

Chapter 16 follows one of the saddest passages of the Old Testament. Saul committed a critical error of judgment and perhaps hubris when he kept plunder for himself and his army that Samuel had commanded him to sacrifice to God. When he is confronted, he immediately begs Samuel's forgiveness, but it is too late. In 15:29, the prophet declares that God does not change His mind, using the Hebrew word for "repent," *nacham*. The narrator, however, laments that God had somberly repented of making Saul king, employing the same word. It is a fascinating example of the tension between Samuel and the Lord that spills into the passage at hand. Samuel is still grieving over Saul's failure after God has moved on.

Here it is helpful to remember that Samuel plays a unique role during this period of Israel. Indeed, there is really no one else like him in all of the nation's vast history. There is a sense

Talk About It:
1. What new direction did God give to Samuel (v. 1)?
2. Explain the elders' response to Samuel's arrival (v. 4).
3. What misconception did God correct (vv. 6-7)?
4. What message did God speak concerning each of Jesse's first seven sons (v. 10)?

in which he exists for the chief purpose of finding David, which makes grasping his character of ultimate importance. He is a priest, of course, but functions both as a powerful political leader and as a prophet. Later, Elijah and Elisha will model much of their leadership after the office of Samuel. The Hebrew custom of the coronation of the king by the ceremony of oil anointing was akin to the medieval crowning ceremony. The power lies, of course, not in the recipient of the crown as much as the giver of the crown. To take a literal example, Pope Leo III's crowning of Charlemagne as Holy Roman Emperor in AD 800 was symbolic in its day not so much of the power of Charlemagne as it was of the power of Pope Leo. Samuel wields similar power in the monarchies of Saul and David. As God's prophet, only he can properly transfer political power.

God's commandment to Samuel to anoint a new king causes a quite reasonable fear. Samuel is well aware that following this word is nothing short of treason against the king, punishable by death and dishonor. Samuel's assumption is all the more realistic as the narrative continues, since Saul becomes mentally ill and even murderous. God does not chide Samuel in response, but instead gives him a covert operation. He is to travel to Jesse's town for the purpose of sacrifice, which will not arouse suspicion, and there God will indicate who the new king will be.

The veneration of Samuel in the land is apparent in 16:4, when Bethlehem's elders fear that trouble has been stirred up. Might they have recognized the rival monarch could come from their community? This is highly doubtful, as the point of the narrative is the invisibility of David's greatness. Instead, just the appearance of the prophet Samuel brings a holy fear. Samuel, of course, has not come for judgment, but for sacrifice, and he enlists the town elders in this feast, which required ritual consecration.

One by one, Samuel calls for Jesse's sons to pass before him. There is no indication that Jesse, his sons, or any of the town elders are conscious of Samuel's intentions. Perhaps they assume he is enlisting choice young men for service in the Tabernacle, which undoubtedly would bring great honor to the family and the community. Meanwhile, Samuel is having a conversation with God, and God is communicating truth so radical to him that it takes the entire story for the prophet to "get it." The linchpin of God's logic is verse 7, which is reflective of a vital center to Israel's theology—appearances simply don't matter. As Christians, we take this for granted, but it was quite revolutionary in its time. This teaching emanates from God's prohibition in the Ten Commandments against creating divine images, which perhaps set Israel apart more than any other external marker. Studying the cultures that lived around Israel, one encounters a remarkable industry of impressive image production. The pharaohs, for

"Anyone can count the number of seeds in an apple, but only God can count the number of apples in a seed."
—Robert Schuller

God Chooses a New Leader

instance, were renowned for building massive idols and pyramids that awed the populace with the government's power. Israel was not to be like this, because their God was not concerned with such externals. Instead, Yahweh sets apart a nation, a Sabbath, and most of all, the human heart.

B. God's Unlikely Choice (vv. 11-13)
   11. And Samuel said unto Jesse, Are here all thy children? And he said, There remaineth yet the youngest, and, behold, he keepeth the sheep. And Samuel said unto Jesse, Send and fetch him: for we will not sit down till he come hither.
   12. And he sent, and brought him in. Now he was ruddy, and withal of a beautiful countenance, and goodly to look to. And the Lord said, Arise, anoint him: for this is he.
   13. Then Samuel took the horn of oil, and anointed him in the midst of his brethren: and the Spirit of the Lord came upon David from that day forward. So Samuel rose up, and went to Ramah.

Jesse did not consider his youngest son significant enough to be invited to the sacrifice. His responsibilities with the sheep were more important to his father. Perhaps, with David as the family runt, Jesse did not see the need for his inclusion. Whatever the case, Samuel is learning to follow the unpredictability of Yahweh, so he takes the initiative to solve the problem created in verses 6-10. When he learns Jesse has one more son, Samuel says, "Send for him; we will not sit down until he arrives" (v. 11 NIV).

One can only imagine the tension that builds in the community as no one is allowed to eat until the young shepherd makes it to the sacrifice. He likely arrives with fear and trembling, not accustomed to such attention. When he arrives, he does not carry the physical bulk of Saul, but certainly looks presentable, perhaps more impressive than Samuel expected. Suddenly God whispers to the old prophet, "That's the one."

This is the grand entrance of King David, the one who would subdue nations, who would conquer armies; the one so famous that his name would echo into the very coming of Jesus of Nazareth. As one biblical scholar has observed: "The new king was so versatile that it is difficult to decide which of his qualities deserves most admiration. It would be just as difficult to find as gifted and rounded a personality within the last few centuries of our own times. Where is the man who could claim equal fame as soldier, statesman, poet and musician?" (Werner Keller, *The Bible as History*).

Yet the remarkable part of this narrative is the unlikelihood of this shepherd boy rising to such promise. Here in chapter 16, David is neither a soldier nor a statesman, just a sheepherder with a love for music. All of those skills would be cultivated later.

withal of a beautiful countenance (v. 12)—"with bright eyes" (NKJV)

Talk About It:
1. Describe David (vv. 11-12).
2. How did David's life change forever (v. 13)?

Unlikely Leader
   Antonio Villaraigosa, the mayor of Los Angeles, California, is a most unlikely success story. Early on, he showed almost no promise. Expelled from one high school only to then drop out of a second, he became involved in

gangs. But a teacher, Herman Katz, took the time to mentor him, helping him get into college. Reflecting on Villaraigosa's success, Katz remarked, "He just needed somebody at that particular time to say you could be something and do something in life."

God often chooses and uses the most unlikely people to raise up as leaders.

Right now he stands before the prophet Samuel and the community of Bethlehem as a ruddy-faced boy without the slightest credential to lead. After the disaster of Saul, this is precisely what God was looking for.

In the presence of his older brothers, David is anointed as a special leader. This was scandalous in any Jewish family. It was the custom for the oldest to be preferred. Note that Samuel does not make any public announcement of David's future kingship. As far as the attendees of this feast are concerned, David is being anointed for some sort of undefined service to Samuel and to God. Just as in the days of Samson and the judges, God confirms His choice by the powerful work of the Spirit in David's life (v. 13), perhaps the power by which he kills a lion and a bear with his own hands (17:34-36). After this ceremony, Saul unwittingly calls to David to live in his court (16:17-19), setting the process in motion for a new ruler in Israel.

II. DAVID HATED BY SAUL (1 Sam. 19:1-24; 20:1-42)
Immediately following the dramatic selection of David, Samuel drops off the scene. In fact, his next place of prominence in the narrative is at his death in chapter 25, which even there is not described in detail. This may point to the trustworthiness of David's developing leadership. During Saul's rule, Samuel is intricately involved, guiding and correcting the new leader. Saul even conjures Samuel up from the dead (ch. 28)! Apparently, David has no such need for Samuel to hold his hand.

A. Jonathan's Friendship (19:1-10)
(1 Samuel 19:3-8 is not included in the printed text.)
1. And Saul spake to Jonathan his son, and to all his servants, that they should kill David.
2. But Jonathan Saul's son delighted much in David: and Jonathan told David, saying, Saul my father seeketh to kill thee: now therefore, I pray thee, take heed to thyself until the morning, and abide in a secret place, and hide thyself.
9. And the evil spirit from the Lord was upon Saul, as he sat in his house with his javelin in his hand: and David played with his hand.
10. And Saul sought to smite David even to the wall with the javelin: but he slipped away out of Saul's presence, and he smote the javelin into the wall: and David fled, and escaped that night.

Talk About It:
1. Explain Saul's changing emotions toward David (vv. 1, 6, 8-10).
2. Describe Jonathan's defense of David (vv. 4-5).

The tragedy of Saul's reign is compounded by David's close relationships with the king's family members (see ch. 18). He wins Saul's daughter for his wife, and enjoys a nourishing friendship with Saul's son, Jonathan. This gives David an insider in the royal court who watches his back. Without Jonathan, David would not have survived.

Saul's demeanor has become so murderous that Jonathan must take every precaution. He loves David and desires to protect him. Therefore, he applauds David's faithful service to Saul. In his instability, Saul swears an oath on the name of Yahweh himself that he will spare David (19:3-6). This lasts only until David wins yet another military victory against the Philistines, causing the king to hurl a spear at the new hero of Israel. The writer describes Saul's condition as an "evil [injurious] spirit" from God (v. 9). The Hebrew adjective for this spirit is *raah*, which can mean "bad, sad, or displeasing." David is consumed by the Spirit of Yahweh, while Saul bears the mark of evil impulses. As a result, David is forced to flee.

> "Jealous people poison their own banquet and then eat it."
> —**Unknown**

B. Samuel's Help (vv. 11-24)

(1 Samuel 19:11-17, 21-24 is not included in the printed text.)

18. So David fled, and escaped, and came to Samuel to Ramah, and told him all that Saul had done to him. And he and Samuel went and dwelt in Naioth.

19. And it was told Saul, saying, Behold, David is at Naioth in Ramah.

20. And Saul sent messengers to take David: and when they saw the company of the prophets prophesying, and Samuel standing as appointed over them, the Spirit of God was upon the messengers of Saul, and they also prophesied.

Naioth (NAY-oth)— v. 18—a place in Ramah where the prophets lived together

Talk About It:
1. How did Michal save David's life (vv. 11-16)?
2. To whom did David flee, and why (vv. 18-19)?
3. Explain the unusual thing that happened to Saul and his servants (vv. 20-23).

The tragedy of Saul deepens as his own daughter makes a fool of him in front of his professional death squad, who fails to murder David in his own home (vv. 11-17). David's next defense is none other than the prophet Samuel, whose transcendent spiritual power confounds every lynch mob that Saul sends to find David. Here is a murderous troop on a deadly mission who cannot get past Samuel and his simple band of prophets. Finally, Saul himself makes the journey, only to also be overcome by God's Spirit (vv. 22-24).

The message is clear: God has chosen David, and neither Saul nor anyone else can thwart His plan. God has placed a hedge of protection around His anointed one.

> "Where God is, a spider web is like a wall. Where God is not, a wall is like a spider's web."
> —**Frederick Nolan**

C. Escape Plan (20:1-42)

(1 Samuel 20:3-29, 34-42 is not included in the printed text.)

1. And David fled from Naioth in Ramah, and came and said before Jonathan, What have I done? what is mine iniquity? and what is my sin before thy father, that he seeketh my life?

2. And he said unto him, God forbid; thou shalt not die: behold, my father will do nothing either great or small, but that he will shew it me: and why should my father hide this thing from me? it is not so.

30. Then Saul's anger was kindled against Jonathan, and he said unto him, Thou son of the perverse rebellious woman, do not I know that thou hast chosen the son of Jesse to thine own confusion, and unto the confusion of thy mother's nakedness?

31. For as long as the son of Jesse liveth upon the ground, thou shalt not be established, nor thy kingdom. Wherefore now send and fetch him unto me, for he shall surely die.

32. And Jonathan answered Saul his father, and said unto him, Wherefore shall he be slain? what hath he done?

33. And Saul cast a javelin at him to smite him: whereby Jonathan knew that it was determined of his father to slay David.

Chapter 20 inaugurates a new epoch in the life of Saul. He has now become a figure like Jonah, angrily charging against God no matter the consequence. Although caught up in the Spirit of God, he won't stop his pursuit of God's anointed one. As a result, Jonathan and David devise an escape plan. They realize that the conflict has reached a pivotal juncture.

By this point, David has figured out that the main threat of Saul is in his emotional instability and his virulent temper. Therefore, he devises a plan to test Saul's state of mind so he can convince Jonathan of just how serious the threat is. David recognizes that his life is in Jonathan's hands. Providentially, David and Jonathan enjoy a deep friendship that is confirmed through the creation of a covenant between them and their households (v. 16). The words of verse 17 should echo in the ears of any Christian, for they foreshadow the teaching of Jesus on the greatest commandments. The Hebrew verb for making a covenant is actually "to cut a covenant," and denotes the way in which David and Jonathan would make a small incision in their wrists, then place ash on the surface of each cut. They would then face one another and clasp hands until their blood mingled and the ash formed a mark in the scar that would last forever, thus reminding them of their covenant throughout their lives. As we will see, their survival will depend on it.

Jonathan carries out the plan and Saul reacts with the kind of extremism that we have come to expect from the downtrodden king. He berates Jonathan and demands that David be brought to him. Verse 33 is comedic in its irony. Saul has gone so crazy that now he attempts to kill his own son.

Recognizing that this could be their last time together, Jonathan and David weep at their parting (v. 41). Remarkably, this chaos does not tear their households apart, but binds them together (v. 42). David will not attack the court or family of Saul for his own gain. He will let God be his vindication.

Talk About It:
1. What was David convinced of (vv. 1, 3)?
2. What did Jonathan promise David (v. 4)?
3. According to Saul, how had Jonathan brought "shame" (v. 30 NKJV) to the royal family?
4. Describe David and Jonathan's covenant with each other (v. 42).

"The friendship that can cease has never been real."
—Jerome of Stridonium

III. DAVID GAINS A FOLLOWING (1 Sam. 22:1-2; 27:1-4)

The moment David and Jonathan break away from one another, the chase is on. David flees immediately to Nob (21:1). The priest Ahimelech's decision to aid David's men with food (v. 6) will have dire consequences in chapter 22, and David is smart enough to not stay there too long. He flees to Gath, the hub Philistine city; and through a bit of improvisational acting before King Achish, he protects his own life yet again (21:10-15). He also makes a connection that will pay off in the not so distant future.

A. A Ragtag Militia (22:1-2)

1. David therefore departed thence, and escaped to the cave Adullam: and when his brethren and all his father's house heard it, they went down thither to him.

2. And every one that was in distress, and every one that was in debt, and every one that was discontented, gathered themselves unto him; and he became a captain over them: and there were with him about four hundred men.

Word about David spreads wherever he goes. Fleeing to Adullam in Judah, a town that means "sealed-off place," David can still not escape publicity. Although his band remains small, his family hears about his whereabouts and seeks him out. But incredibly, Adullam becomes the place of David's salvation. It is not a notable place in Israel's history, certainly not a recruiting station for Israel's best warriors. Nonetheless, a ragtag group of four hundred men gather around David. These are not from the higher echelons of society. Many of them are also on the run, hiding from creditors and other henchmen. But after being trained in military skill and learning to submit to leadership, they will become the mighty men of David. The rise of this band of outcasts also reflects Jesus' selection of twelve disciples, none of whom were men of high standing in their society. It should be no surprise that since David himself was an unlikely choice, so should his followers be.

B. Back to Gath (27:1-4)

Chapters 22-26 recount the tumultuous journey of David as he barely eludes the hand of Saul. It seems that each time Saul makes peace with David, something else ignites his famous fury. In response, David decides to flee Saul's kingdom of Israel altogether.

1. And David said in his heart, I shall now perish one day by the hand of Saul: there is nothing better for me than that I should speedily escape into the land of the Philistines; and Saul shall despair of me, to seek me any more in any coast of Israel: so shall I escape out of his hand.

2. And David arose, and he passed over with the six hundred men that were with him unto Achish, the son of Maoch, king of Gath.

Adullam (a-DULL-um)—v. 1—caverns located near the city of Adullam

Talk About It:
1. Why do you suppose David's brothers "went down there to him" (v. 1 NASB)?
2. Describe the 400 other men who joined David.

3. And David dwelt with Achish at Gath, he and his men, every man with his household, even David with his two wives, Ahinoam the Jezreelitess, and Abigail the Carmelitess, Nabal's wife.

4. And it was told Saul that David was fled to Gath: and he sought no more again for him.

Talk About It:
1. Where did David go, and why (vv. 1-2)?
2. How well did David's plan work (v. 4)?

David chooses to withdraw from his own nation and wait for God to act. But where should he go? After all, David is renowned for his conquests throughout Philistia. However, he has cultivated a powerful ally there. So there in the region of Gath, David and his men will actually settle down, which must have been refreshing after being on the run for so long. They bring their families, and Achish offers them protection and solace. Why would a pagan king extend such an olive branch? Perhaps Achish too sees the "writing on the wall" and looks to forge an alliance with David for the protection of his own city in the future. The situation definitely works out in the king's favor, for David's raids on neighboring peoples strengthen Gath's powerful military position. David also profits from these raids and the needed break from Saul's tyranny. In Gath, David enjoys over one year of peace. In fact, he will never have to confront Saul again.

"It brings great comfort to have companions in whatever happens."
—**John Chrysostom**

The Book of 1 Samuel does not downplay the vital role of Samuel, Saul, and David in forming their own destinies. None of them are chess pieces unwillingly moved around history by Divine Providence. But the impression is duly given that God is fully in control, even when David flees the land he will one day rule.

CONCLUSION

Throughout Scripture, God chooses the most unlikely heroes. David is no exception to this rule. The youngest son of a run-of-the-mill Jewish family, he is found doing menial labor with sheep out in the hills. After Samuel anoints him as the future king, he spends the developing years of his adulthood dodging the murderous Saul and running for his life. His army consists of unskilled laborers and the dregs of society. Amid these challenges, through David's rule God will set up the greatest period in Israel's history.

Daily Devotions:
M. God Chose Abraham
Genesis 12:1-8
T. God Chose Moses
Exodus 3:1-10
W. God Chose Israel
Deuteronomy 7:6-11
T. The Twelve Chosen
Luke 6:12-16; John 15:16
F. Matthias Chosen
Acts 1:15-26
S. Barnabas and Saul Chosen
Acts 13:1-5

GOLDEN TEXT CHALLENGE

"GOD IS THE JUDGE: HE PUTTETH DOWN ONE, AND SETTETH UP ANOTHER" (Ps. 75:7).

Samuel, Saul, and David could all testify to the truth that it is God who "brings one down [and] exalts another" (NIV). God raised up Samuel from the womb of a barren woman; He exalted Saul from the smallest tribe of Israel; He lifted up David from a shepherd's field.

The previous verse declares that such promotion does not come horizontally—from the east, west, or south—but vertically, from the all-knowing and all-powerful Judge.

David Becomes King

2 Samuel 2:1-11; 3:1; 5:1-12; 6:1-23

INTRODUCTION

The significance of the leadership role is advertised in every culture in the world, especially Western nations whose worldview has largely been shaped by Scripture, for the Bible is filled with the real-life stories of leaders, great and small. Walk into any bookstore in these places and you are sure to find dozens of titles on every facet of leadership.

"Everything rises and falls on leadership" has become a popular mantra in marketplace and ministry circles. This principle is certainly borne out in both Testaments of Scripture. Perhaps the major theme of the Old Testament is God's calling on the nation of Israel, but this calling always comes through a specific leader. In fact, it begins with the calling of Abraham, moves to the enlistment of Moses, and culminates in the anointing of David. The New Testament, of course, begins with the call of Jesus, moves to the choice of His disciples, then finishes in the installment of dozens of everyday local church leaders. We should not be surprised, then, that traits appropriate to leadership mark the spiritual gift lists of 1 Corinthians 12 and Ephesians 4. Yahweh is a God who calls leaders!

The people God calls are not usually the smartest, richest, strongest, most skilled, most prominent, or most holy. The history of David's leadership alone proves this fact. Over and over again, the Bible refuses to present a cartoon caricature of the "perfect" leader, and instead depicts its heroes in vivid flesh-and-bone reality. Their successes are celebrated, of course, but their failures and shortcomings are not brushed under the rug.

This biblical portrait of a new kind of leader finds culmination in the leadership of Christ, who ended His ministry in what looked like the complete failure of His entire mission. The Resurrection, however, was the vindication of godly leadership, which is characterized by humility and trust, not power and coercion. As Paul writes about himself in 2 Corinthians 12: "Therefore I will boast all the more gladly about my weaknesses, so that Christ's power may rest on me. That is why, for Christ's sake, I delight in weaknesses, in insults, in hardships, in persecutions, in difficulties. For when I am weak, then I am strong" (vv. 9-10 NIV).

King David, too, experienced weakness, insults, hardships, persecutions, and difficulties. Yet he flourished as a leader by finding strength in God.

Unit Theme:
Books of Samuel

Central Truth:
God establishes and enables effective spiritual leaders.

Focus:
Recognize that God establishes and enables spiritual leaders and depend on Him for effective leadership.

Context:
Between 1010 and 1000 BC, David becomes the leader of Israel.

Golden Text:
"David perceived that the Lord had established him king over Israel, and that he had exalted his kingdom for his people Israel's sake" (2 Sam. 5:12).

Study Outline:
I. David, King of Judah (2 Sam. 2:1-11; 3:1)
II. David, King of Israel (2 Sam. 5:1-12)
III. David, a Spiritual Leader (2 Sam. 6:1-23)

I. DAVID, KING OF JUDAH (2 Sam. 2:1-11; 3:1)

David's rise to leadership over Judah captures the biblical mind-set all the way through the Book of Revelation. Indeed, Revelation 5:5 draws a direct parallel between the reign of David over Judah and the power and character of the resurrected Jesus. In this vision of John, the heavens are searched for someone who is worthy to inaugurate God's dramatic conclusion of world history. Finally, He is discovered: "Then one of the elders said to me, 'Do not weep! See, the Lion of the tribe of Judah, the Root of David, has triumphed. He is able to open the scroll . . .'" (NIV). This remarkable description of Jesus, the "Root of David," stems from David's peaceful rise to power over Judah.

A. Installation at Hebron (2:1-7)

Hebron (HEE-brun)—v. 1—Located 19 miles southwest of Jerusalem, it was David's capital city for the first seven years of his reign.

Ahinoam (a-HEN-oh-am)—v. 2—"The woman from Jezreel whom David married after Saul gave Michal to another husband" (*International Standard Bible Encyclopedia*)

Abigail (v. 2)—David married her after her harsh husband, Nabal, died from shock (1 Sam. 25:37-39).

1. And it came to pass after this, that David enquired of the Lord, saying, Shall I go up into any of the cities of Judah? And the Lord said unto him, Go up. And David said, Whither shall I go up? And he said, Unto Hebron.

2. So David went up thither, and his two wives also, Ahinoam the Jezreelitess, and Abigail Nabal's wife the Carmelite.

3. And his men that were with him did David bring up, every man with his household: and they dwelt in the cities of Hebron.

4. And the men of Judah came, and there they anointed David king over the house of Judah. And they told David, saying, That the men of Jabeshgilead were they that buried Saul.

5. And David sent messengers unto the men of Jabeshgilead, and said unto them, Blessed be ye of the Lord, that ye have shewed this kindness unto your lord, even unto Saul, and have buried him.

6. And now the Lord shew kindness and truth unto you: and I also will requite you this kindness, because ye have done this thing.

7. Therefore now let your hands be strengthened, and be ye valiant: for your master Saul is dead, and also the house of Judah have anointed me king over them.

Talk About It:
1. What does verse 1 reveal about David's relationship with the Lord?
2. What do you learn about David's character in verses 4-7?

Much has transpired at this part of the narrative, namely the deaths of Saul and Jonathan. One would naturally assume this was a cause for David's jubilation, but nothing could be further from the truth. Finally, his rival, the one who had been mercilessly pursuing him for so long, is gone. But David does not act quickly to seize power. Instead, he pays homage to the household of Saul by writing a lament poem (1:17-27), before asking Yahweh what he should do (2:1).

David Becomes King

We can only guess at what form this conversation between David and God took. The ancients did not have the modern concept of a "personal relationship" with God, so this exchange likely took place in a formal worship setting, complete with sacrifices.

We encounter the initiative of David in his inquiry to God. Although he does not rush to power, he also does not sit idly doing nothing to advance his cause. Unlike impulsive Saul, he requests specific guidance from the Lord. Not satisfied with the broad commandment to rule over Judah, he asks God to indicate a specific town. Hebron is God's choice, so David packs up his family and leads his mighty men to this new region. It was a logical place for David to set up his rule—a major city about twenty miles south of Jerusalem. In fact, archaeologists believe it was inhabited perhaps a thousand years before David, probably since it was a well-watered area and thus suitable for farming. It was a good land with a solid economy.

Hebron is not the only city involved in recognizing David. Men from all over the kingdom of Judah show up for his coronation. What a dramatic moment this must have been, so different from David's initial anointing by Samuel. Back then, David was unrecognized and unproven. Now an entire region unites to celebrate his leadership. In response, David once again proves his mettle by blessing the men of Jabesh Gilead who had shown kindness to Saul by burying him properly. He assures them that he will amply reward them as their new leader. They need not be afraid. What grace David showed to those he governed! He could have intimidated the land with the might of his militia, but instead he comforts the people.

B. A Divided Nation (2:8-11; 3:1)

2:8. But Abner the son of Ner, captain of Saul's host, took Ishbosheth the son of Saul, and brought him over to Mahanaim;

9. And made him king over Gilead, and over the Ashurites, and over Jezreel, and over Ephraim, and over Benjamin, and over all Israel.

10. Ishbosheth Saul's son was forty years old when he began to reign over Israel, and reigned two years. But the house of Judah followed David.

11. And the time that David was king in Hebron over the house of Judah was seven years and six months.

3:1. Now there was long war between the house of Saul and the house of David: but David waxed stronger and stronger, and the house of Saul waxed weaker and weaker.

To grasp Israel's tumultuous history, one has to understand the division of the nation between north and south. The southern kingdom is referred to as Judah, and the northern as Israel. During

Ishbosheth (ish-BO-sheth)—v. 8—A son of Saul whom Abner proclaimed as king over Israel after Saul's death

Mahanaim (may-huh-NAY-im)—v. 8—The place where Ishbosheth's throne was established and where he was later murdered (4:5-8)

Talk About It:
What contrasts are drawn between David and Ishbosheth in this passage?

the infrequent times when these kingdoms were united, such as under David's later rule and his son Solomon's, the whole is referred to as Israel. However, for large stretches of Israel's history, they lived divided.

This begins with a military decision by Abner, Saul's commander. Recognizing that Saul has died, and thus Abner's own prominent position is in jeopardy, he quickly installs Saul's son Ishbosheth as leader over the northern kingdom of Israel.

Even though there were skirmishes between the southern and northern kingdoms, David's leadership over Judah was not seriously challenged. Ishbosheth was little more than a thorn in David's side, carrying no operational threat. Saul's household, though still holding onto a measure of power, was simply no match for David's leadership.

During the seven and a half years David ruled from Hebron, he was blessed personally with the birth of six sons (3:2-5). In the northern kingdom, after Abner defected to David, Ishbosheth was quickly murdered in his own palace (ch. 4). His reign lasted only two years.

II. DAVID, KING OF ISRAEL (2 Sam. 5:1-12)

We have received numerous hints along the course of this narrative that David's rule will not be confined to the southern kingdom of Judah. His character is too strong and his military prowess too sharp to be relegated only to part of the nation. His rise to power in the north is not only a boon to his legacy, but also a dramatic unification of what was until then a broken and fragmented country. The incompetent government of Saul finally found its antidote in the excellence of David's leadership.

A. A United Kingdom (vv. 1-5)

1. Then came all the tribes of Israel to David unto Hebron, and spake, saying, Behold, we are thy bone and thy flesh.

2. Also in time past, when Saul was king over us, thou wast he that leddest out and broughtest in Israel: and the Lord said to thee, Thou shalt feed my people Israel, and thou shalt be a captain over Israel.

3. So all the elders of Israel came to the king to Hebron; and king David made a league with them in Hebron before the Lord: and they anointed David king over Israel.

4. David was thirty years old when he began to reign, and he reigned forty years.

5. In Hebron he reigned over Judah seven years and six months: and in Jerusalem he reigned thirty and three years over all Israel and Judah.

The kingdom of Israel, divided between Saul and David for too long, finally unites to anoint David as its sole leader. It is the

Talk About It:
1. What did "all the tribes of Israel" declare about David (v. 1)?
2. What did they recall about David (v. 2)?
3. Explain the events in verse 3.

David Becomes King

northern kingdom's elders who take the initiative, making the arduous journey to Hebron in order to strike an advantageous deal with David. These are the same elders who had been following Ishbosheth. They had no way of knowing what David's reaction would be in advance, and probably realized they were taking their own lives into their hands in approaching him. But David makes a formal treaty of peace with them, guaranteeing a peaceful and strategic alliance. Another anointing ceremony takes place, and the nation is finally united again.

It is common in the Old Testament narratives of Israel's kings to summarize their reigns as done in verses 4 and 5. The stunning part about David's reign is its remarkable length. In the accounts of 1 Kings, it is rare to find a king in Judah or Israel that lasts more than a few years. With life spans so short, perhaps an average of 40 years old for men, and much younger for women, a 33-year reign was tremendous. Sadly, the unity of Israel will only last through the reign of David's son Solomon before it is ripped apart again. And even in David's time, his son Absalom will threaten the peace. But overall, the unifying of the nation is especially significant in the light of Jesus' identity as the "Root of David." Part of the messianic program would be the re-unification of the nation of Israel back to the peaceful time of David. This is the peace which Jesus' teaching offered the Jewish people.

> Lives of great men
> all remind us
> We can make our
> lives sublime,
> And, departing, leave
> behind us
> Footprints on the
> sand of time.
> **—Longfellow**

B. The Holy City (vv. 6-12)

6. And the king and his men went to Jerusalem unto the Jebusites, the inhabitants of the land: which spake unto David, saying, Except thou take away the blind and the lame, thou shalt not come in hither: thinking, David cannot come in hither.

7. Nevertheless David took the strong hold of Zion: the same is the city of David.

8. And David said on that day, Whosoever getteth up to the gutter, and smiteth the Jebusites, and the lame and the blind, that are hated of David's soul, he shall be chief and captain. Wherefore they said, The blind and the lame shall not come into the house.

gutter (v. 8)—water shaft

9. So David dwelt in the fort, and called it the city of David. And David built round about from Millo and inward.

Millo (v. 9)—probably an earth-filled tower or an embankment

10. And David went on, and grew great, and the Lord God of hosts was with him.

11. And Hiram king of Tyre sent messengers to David, and cedar trees, and carpenters, and masons: and they built David an house.

12. And David perceived that the Lord had established him king over Israel, and that he had exalted his kingdom for his people Israel's sake.

Talk About It:
1. What miscalculation did the Jebusites make (vv. 6-7)?
2. What did David realize (vv. 10, 12)?

We do not know what provoked David to attack the Jebusites in Jerusalem, but judging from their arrogant and foolhardy retort to his peace proposal, there was obviously some venom between the parties. In ancient and medieval warfare, it was typical for the army commanders to meet between ranks in the center of the battlefield, or just outside the given city, in order to discuss peace arrangements. Apparently David expected a unilateral surrender, given his military fame, but was certainly prepared to take the city by force. The Jebusite leaders deride and humiliate him, saying, "Even the blind and the lame can ward you off" (v. 6 NIV), but David turns their insult into a motivator for his armies (v. 8). They scale the walls of the city to destroy the armies of the Jebusites. Their remnants will become Solomon's slaves (1 Kings 9:20-21).

We do not know if David originally intended to set up residence there in Jerusalem. However, since the stubborn Jebusites had lived there for centuries, even surviving the attack from the men of Judah in Judges 1:8, they had probably constructed formidable edifices for defense, commerce, and residence. The chief advantage to David was the strength and security of the city's fortress, which he bulwarked with further construction. This was yet another external sign of his growing power, perhaps the first suggestion that a formal kingship had begun. In ancient cities, the strength of a city's or palace's walls paralleled the strength of its governor, and now David enlists skilled laborers to build his official palace. Jerusalem is heretofore known as the "city of David," central to Jewish and Christian faith still today.

"Why rely upon yourself and fall? Cast yourself upon [God's] arm. Be not afraid. He will not let you slip. Cast yourself in confidence."
—Augustine

III. DAVID, A SPIRITUAL LEADER (2 Sam. 6:1-23)

From the beginning of David's leadership, he is known principally as a worshiper. It was for his musical ability that Saul drafted him into the royal court to begin with. The vast majority of the Psalms—the Hebrew hymnbook—bear David's name as the author. We might consider him as an ancient "Renaissance man," adept not only at warfare and administration, but also in the musical and literary arts. These, however, were not simply frivolous hobbies. They defined who David was as a spiritual leader.

A. David's Bold Worship (vv. 1-15)

(2 Samuel 6:1-11 is not included in the printed text.)

12. And it was told king David, saying, The Lord hath blessed the house of Obededom, and all that pertaineth unto him, because of the ark of God. So David went and brought up the ark of God from the house of Obededom into the city of David with gladness.

13. And it was so, that when they that bare the ark of the Lord had gone six paces, he sacrificed oxen and fatlings.

14. And David danced before the Lord with all his might; and David was girded with a linen ephod.

Obededom (OH-bed-EE-dum)—v. 12—Either a Levite or a Philistine from Gath who served David, his household was greatly blessed during the three months he kept the ark.

15. So David and all the house of Israel brought up the ark of the Lord with shouting, and with the sound of the trumpet.

The primary symbol of David's rule over the united kingdom of Israel from Jerusalem takes place with the arrival of the ark of the covenant. We have heard nothing of the ark since the first chapters of 1 Samuel, where its power terrorizes both Philistines and Israelites. The last thing we are told is that it is set in Abinadab's house in 7:1, where he consecrates his son as its guardian. Now at long last, David leads a delegation in bringing the ark from Abinadab's house with great celebration, including a traveling parade complete with a symphony (2 Sam. 6:1-5). However, when Uzzah irreverently grasps the ark, he is killed and the party dies out. In David's fear of God, he sends it to Obed-Edom's house. Unlike Saul, David is not casual with God's power. He admits his own unworthiness to stand in the presence of Yahweh. He is only convinced of the Lord's good intentions when Obed-Edom's house is blessed in unprecedented ways. This is a sure sign that the ark needs to be brought to Jerusalem.

In this ceremony, David has decided that music is not enough, so he stages an array of sacrifices. Each six steps, perhaps symbolizing the six days of Creation, requires a double sacrifice of a valuable bull and calf. Yet, not even this jubilant display of worship satisfies David's desire to praise the Lord.

The scene in verses 14 and 15 has been etched in the minds of Jewish and Christian believers for thousands of years. Here is the most powerful man in the ancient Near East forgetting his prestigious position and disrobing himself. The rituals of sacrifice are not enough for the dancing king; he whirls, leaps, and jumps about, overwhelmed with gratitude toward God. In response, the Israelites shout and blow trumpets in an outrageous celebration both of David and of the Lord. As author Frederick Buechner puts it, "How they cut loose together, David and Yahweh, whirling around before the ark in such a passion that they caught fire from each other and blazed up in a single flame of such magnificence that not even the dressing-down David got from Michal afterward could dim the glory of it" (*Beyond Words: Daily Readings in the ABC's of Faith*).

It is a moment that echoes with followers of God still today anytime sincere worship is practiced. But Saul's family would attempt to soil even this glorious day.

B. David's Generous Spirit (vv. 16-19)

16. And as the ark of the Lord came into the city of David, Michal Saul's daughter looked through a window, and saw king David leaping and dancing before the Lord; and she despised him in her heart.

Talk About It:
1. What was the significance of the ark of the covenant (v. 2)?
2. Describe the change of mood from verse 5 to verse 7.
3. Explain David's quandary (v. 10).
4. How was the ark handled differently this time (v. 13)?
5. Describe the worship of David and Israel (vv. 14-15).

"Let us learn from Uzzah, who touched the ark of God and died. We must be careful not to touch anything that is of God, because something will die in us spiritually if we try to stop what God is doing."
—Bob Sorge

17. And they brought in the ark of the Lord, and set it in his place, in the midst of the tabernacle that David had pitched for it: and David offered burnt offerings and peace offerings before the Lord.

18. And as soon as David had made an end of offering burnt offerings and peace offerings, he blessed the people in the name of the Lord of hosts.

19. And he dealt among all the people, even among the whole multitude of Israel, as well to the women as men, to every one a cake of bread, and a good piece of flesh, and a flagon of wine. So all the people departed every one to his house.

flagon of wine (v. 19)—"cake of raisins" (NKJV)

Talk About It:
1. Explain Michal's attitude (v. 16).
2. How did David minister to the Lord (v. 17) and to His people (vv. 18-19)?

Although we expect this remarkable day to end in perfection, verse 16 gives us a hint otherwise. There was a single Israelite who despised what David was doing—David's own wife. Yet David is unaware of her hatred, and he wouldn't have stopped on account of her anyway. He continues the celebration with a massive sacrificial feast for the city.

As if the earlier sacrifices of the day were not enough, David goes above and beyond average worship. Like the woman who breaks a year's worth of wages upon the feet of Jesus, David spends untold sums of the wealth of his herds in service to the Lord. Such a ceremony must have been awe-inspiring, and certainly validated David's divine appointment as king. But he would not use this appointment to harshly rule over the people.

"David danced before the Lord with all his might because it was the only way he could give full expression to his heart. . . . The Lord is delighted when we praise Him with everything that we are—spirit, soul, and body."
—Bob Sorge

Pulling out one of his poetic invocations, perhaps a psalm, David blesses the nation by the very name of God (v. 18). This is not David's day, it is Yahweh's day, and David ensures that God gets the glory. He also acts as a benefactor for the people. He gives gifts to everyone present, even the women, which was quite radical in his day. Everyone except David's wife left the celebration moved by this exuberant and generous king.

C. David's Commitment to Worship (vv. 20-23)

20. Then David returned to bless his household. And Michal the daughter of Saul came out to meet David, and said, How glorious was the king of Israel to day, who uncovered himself to day in the eyes of the handmaids of his servants, as one of the vain fellows shamelessly uncovereth himself!

play (v. 21)—celebrate

21. And David said unto Michal, It was before the Lord, which chose me before thy father, and before all his house, to appoint me ruler over the people of the Lord, over Israel: therefore will I play before the Lord.

vile (v. 22)—undignified

22. And I will yet be more vile than thus, and will be base in mine own sight: and of the maidservants which thou hast spoken of, of them shall I be had in honour.

23. Therefore Michal the daughter of Saul had no child unto the day of her death.

The exchange between Saul's daughter and David should be seen from several different angles. First, she is symbolic of the status quo expectations of the monarchy. What gives the story its impact is the simple fact that kings aren't supposed to do these kinds of things, especially in front of their subjects. Kings are to act dignified and in control, so that the people might revere them. King David royally broke this rule, which is why Michal specifically refers to his dishonor in front of the city's slaves. Even the lowest on the social ladder got to witness David's "humiliation"!

This leads to the second angle of the Michal story. Through such undignified worship, David has put his own honor at risk, as his wife correctly asserts. This may seem trivial in the modern world, where public servants are frequently humiliated on cable news channels, but the ancient consciousness was completely centered on honor. Honor alone was worth living and dying for. As biblical scholar Philip Esler explains:

> Honor is the pivotal social value in [ancient] society. Honor means the perception someone has of his or her own worth and an appreciation of how he or she is rated by a relevant social group. It is a claim to worth and a social acknowledgment of worth. Like all goods in [ancient] society it is thought to exist in limited amounts. It is either ascribed, that is obtained passively, simply by being who one is (typically, a member of a noble family) or by being granted by someone in a powerful and honorable position, or acquired, that is gained actively, through various forms of social interaction (*Social-Scientific Approaches to New Testament Interpretation*).

This is why David does not dispute with Michal on other grounds. Indeed, he retorts that he has gained honor, not dishonor, in front of the slaves and everyone else in the city by his actions. In contrast, the fact that Michal bears no children from this day forward brings about her dishonor in the eyes of the population. Her accusation completely backfires!

The third angle of the Michal story draws yet another line of differentiation between the reigns of David and Saul. Even though Michal continues to be loyal to David and not to the house of her father, she still represents the family of the royal king—a previous epoch in Israel's history. Saul lacked the confidence to act as boldly as David does before his subjects. Saul stood for a cold and ruthless kind of leader, one concerned with his own advantage. David, on the other hand, stoops to the level of his subjects, and is concerned with the glory of Yahweh, not his own aggrandizement.

What is more, the story points to the vital fact that the reign of David, not Saul, will set the precedent for godly leadership in Israel. Future righteous kings such as Solomon, Hezekiah, and Josiah will look to David for their model of leadership. And when the Messiah himself rides into Jerusalem to fulfill His mission as the greatest leader to ever live, it is no wonder that He is hailed as the "son of David" (Matt. 21:9).

Talk About It:
1. Describe Michal's sarcasm (v. 20).
2. How did David explain his actions (vv. 21-22)?
3. How was Michal judged (v. 23)?

Gracious Leadership

His grandfather was a poor sharecropper, and his father had only a sixth-grade education. Born in Atlanta in 1929, racism and segregation threatened to steal his future—a picture that did not change when he was rejected by multiple seminaries due to the color of his skin. Preferring the pastorate to a prestigious university position, he spoke out against racism, resulting in death threats and the bombing of his house. Even though his life was cut short, Martin Luther King will always be remembered for a different kind of leadership—a reign of nonviolence, forgiveness, and grace.

CONCLUSION

The life and reign of David form a template for leadership that is still inspirational and practical. David is a person of honor who respects authority, even when that authority is clearly in the wrong, and thus receives recompense for his kindness toward Saul and Saul's household. David does not divide people for his own advantage, but is a force for unity, bringing the northern and southern cultures back together to form one Israel. And David does all this out of joyful praise to God, giving glory away rather than keeping it for himself. Truly the Bible would be incomplete without this shepherd turned king.

GOLDEN TEXT CHALLENGE

"DAVID PERCEIVED THAT THE LORD HAD ESTABLISHED HIM KING OVER ISRAEL, AND THAT HE HAD EXALTED HIS KINGDOM FOR HIS PEOPLE ISRAEL'S SAKE" (2 Sam. 5:12).

The assurance David exhibited here with regard to his kingship and to God's part in it gives us an indication of the type of assurance each of us should have with regard to life and to God's place in it. It makes no difference whether we are a minister or a mechanic, an evangelist or an engineer, a missionary or a housewife—we should be able to take stock of ourselves, and say with positiveness, "This is God's will for my life. He has put me where I am." If we cannot say this, we are, to be sure, living beneath our spiritual potential.

David at Worship

2 Samuel 7:1-29

INTRODUCTION

If we could point to a singular practice that unites the diverse people of God throughout the Scriptural record and into our contemporary period, we would probably choose worship. Although various groups of believers have had different perspectives on numerous theological positions, the followers of God have always agreed that He is worthy of worship. This agreement goes well beyond a formal doctrinal statement. Instead, worship exists as a natural tendency for those who encounter the God of Scripture.

Theologian Millard J. Erickson writes: "Worship, the praise and exaltation of God, was a common Old Testament practice, as can be seen particularly in the Book of Psalms. And in the pictures of heaven in the Book of Revelation and elsewhere, the people of God are represented as recognizing and declaring His greatness" (*Christian Theology, Second Edition*).

In the Old Testament, there is an emphasis on the rituals and forms of Jewish worship, which centered first on the Tabernacle and later on the Temple. Yet just getting the ceremonial aspects of worship correct never satisfies the biblical writers. Instead, their worship goes well beyond ritual, exploding into diverse expressions of dancing, singing, and the use of musical instruments. The significance of King David is the way in which he uniquely expresses each of these. He was a musician, a singer, a songwriter, a poet, a fanatical dancer, even a preacher! He was not content to remain a stately governor in a remote palace. He authentically worshiped God in every corner of his kingdom. Perhaps this is why his leadership continues to resonate with people of faith today.

It is also notable that the great movements of faith throughout history have always been accompanied by new worship music. Perhaps David himself began this trend, proving himself not only a capable politician but also a skilled artist. Similarly, Martin Luther, the originator of Protestantism, wrote in 1538 that "next to the Word of God, the noble art of music is the greatest treasure in the world. . . . This precious gift has been given to man alone that he might thereby remind himself that God has created man for the express purpose of praising and extolling God." As believers, we have a history and a heritage of expressive worship.

Unit Theme:
Books of Samuel

Central Truth:
God is worthy of our worship.

Focus:
Perceive that God is always worthy of our praise and thanksgiving, and worship Him in all circumstances.

Context:
Around 1000 BC, the Lord gives David astonishing promises about his reign.

Golden Text:
"Give unto the Lord the glory due unto his name; worship the Lord in the beauty of holiness" (Ps. 29:2).

Study Outline:
I. God Defers David's Intention
   (2 Sam. 7:1-11)
II. God Makes a Promise
   (2 Sam. 7:12-17)
III. David Responds With Worship
   (2 Sam. 7:18-29)

I. GOD DEFERS DAVID'S INTENTION (2 Sam. 7:1-11)

The story of David defines him as a radical worshiper in 2 Samuel 6. There he becomes known as a ruler who brazenly chooses a public character of expressive worship rather than the common regal virtues of modesty and moderation. Chapter 7, then, displays the results of such an intense relationship David carries on toward Yahweh. It is one of the pivotal chapters of the Old Testament, paving the way for the coming of Christ himself.

A. David's Discontent (vv. 1-3)

1. And it came to pass, when the king sat in his house, and the Lord had given him rest round about from all his enemies;

2. That the king said unto Nathan the prophet, See now, I dwell in an house of cedar, but the ark of God dwelleth within curtains.

3. And Nathan said to the king, Go, do all that is in thine heart; for the Lord is with thee.

Talk About It:
1. Describe David's situation (v. 1).
2. What was David's desire (vv. 2-3)?

The opening of chapter 7 is in stark contrast to the closing of chapter 6. The Hebrew Bible was not originally written with chapters and verses, so we can sometimes lose the effects of how the chapters function together. We have just been told that Michal, who represents the household of Saul, must live the rest of her life in dishonor because she criticized the worship of David. David's lot in life, however, is just the opposite.

Finally, Israel is established as a firm nation. No longer do they wander about, searching for land. They can now boast of a king and a central government. What is more, invading armies no longer harass them. The tumultuous days of Joshua's conquest are a distant memory. Their military might has triumphed, and they can enjoy their status as a powerful nation for the purpose of living in peace. But there is more to verse 1 than might initially meet the eye. The language here directly reflects on Deuteronomy 12, where Moses instructed the people to look forward to a time of rest in which God would set up a particular city for His dwelling place: "But you will cross the Jordan and settle in the land the Lord your God is giving you as an inheritance, and he will give you rest from all your enemies around you so that you will live in safety" (v. 10 NIV).

Second Samuel 7:1, then, is nothing short of the definitive fulfillment of Moses' words in Deuteronomy, words that frequently rang in the ears of these ancient Jews. At long last, after hundreds of years of slavery and warfare, they have reached their land of rest. The only thing left for God's great dream of a people to be completed is the establishment of His dwelling place.

Once again, we get a remarkable insight into David's character. He is experiencing the most peaceful and prosperous period of

his life. He lives in a secure palace and enjoys the favor of the entire nation. Yet for him, something is terribly wrong. David simply cannot get around the inequity of the situation. Each week, or possibly even each day, he sacrifices and worships before the ark of God, then journeys back to his palace. He should feel joy at coming into the presence of the Lord, but instead he feels overwhelmed by guilt. While living in the opulence of a national palace, he cannot bear the fact that God's ark sits under a simple tent. This insight not only lets us in on David's intense passion for Yahweh, but also into his bent toward leading proactively. It is not the priests who raise such questions about the ark, even though they serve before it each day. Instead, it is the king, who happens to also be Israel's chief worshiper. What is more, he does not keep his thoughts private. He consults his top spiritual adviser, Nathan, who now makes his entrance into the life story of David.

Nathan is wise enough to discern David's heart and situation. He encourages the king not to hesitate to serve the Lord in any way he sees fit. His rationale is simple, and probably too hurried—God is obviously with David. The entire nation can see that David has been magnificently blessed, and Nathan doesn't hesitate in spurring him on. The prophet will soon learn, however, that God has a completely different plan in mind.

> "Oh, the fullness, pleasure, sheer excitement of knowing God on earth! I care not if I ever raise my voice again for Him, if only I may love Him, please Him!"
> —**Jim Elliot**

B. God Turns the Tables (vv. 4-11)

4. And it came to pass that night, that the word of the Lord came unto Nathan, saying,

5. Go and tell my servant David, Thus saith the Lord, Shalt thou build me an house for me to dwell in?

6. Whereas I have not dwelt in any house since the time that I brought up the children of Israel out of Egypt, even to this day, but have walked in a tent and in a tabernacle.

7. In all the places wherein I have walked with all the children of Israel spake I a word with any of the tribes of Israel, whom I commanded to feed my people Israel, saying, Why build ye not me an house of cedar?

8. Now therefore so shalt thou say unto my servant David, Thus saith the Lord of hosts, I took thee from the sheepcote, from following the sheep, to be ruler over my people, over Israel:

9. And I was with thee whithersoever thou wentest, and have cut off all thine enemies out of thy sight, and have made thee a great name, like unto the name of the great men that are in the earth.

10. Moreover I will appoint a place for my people Israel, and will plant them, that they may dwell in a place of their own, and move no more; neither shall the children of wickedness afflict them any more, as beforetime,

Talk About It:
1. Explain the Lord's phrase "have walked in a tent and in a tabernacle" (v. 6).
2. What had the Lord not done (v. 7)?
3. Describe the Lord's blessings on David (vv. 8-9).
4. Describe the Lord's blessings on Israel (vv. 10-11).

11. And as since the time that I commanded judges to be over my people Israel, and have caused thee to rest from all thine enemies. Also the Lord telleth thee that he will make thee an house.

The prophet Nathan has already given David the green light to get started on a new worship space for the ark, but he has bypassed seeking the direction of God. Nathan, too, is only a man, so God corrects his impulsiveness. Israel has never had a temple for Yahweh. What leads Nathan or David to determine that they suddenly need one now? God reminds David that the tent has adequately served the people for several centuries, and God has not commanded any of the nation's rulers to build Him a house of cedar. God does not think like humans. He does not require material goods to puff Himself up. Indeed, this is the impact of verses 5-7: God is not like the idols of other nations who are propped up in a single place. By nature, God moves around to wherever the needs of His people are.

Nonetheless, God honors the heart of David with a phenomenal edict filled with divine passion. While David had it in his heart to build a house for Yahweh, Yahweh promises that He will be the One to build a house both for Israel and for David! In this way God graciously turns the tables on David's intention to build God a house. It is a transcendent illustration of God's covenant love, as He lavishes promises on His people and their leader. Verses 8-11 read like a regal declaration—something that might be announced from the palace balcony by the prophet Nathan (at some point Nathan's vision obviously took written form). Yet this declaration is only the beginning of God's pact with David.

II. GOD MAKES A PROMISE (2 Sam. 7:12-17)

Until now, God's declaration to David has been fairly general, couched in the traditional Old Testament language of God's blessing. David and the people will continue to enjoy rest from their enemies as they become more settled in the Promised Land. Nathan's proclamation even leads us to believe that God is rejecting the construction of a Temple, but now we find out that this is not the case. However, it is certain that the Temple will be built on God's terms, not David's.

A. The Future Greatness of Solomon (vv. 12-14)

12. And when thy days be fulfilled, and thou shalt sleep with thy fathers, I will set up thy seed after thee, which shall proceed out of thy bowels, and I will establish his kingdom.

13. He shall build an house for my name, and I will stablish the throne of his kingdom for ever.

14. I will be his father, and he shall be my son. If he commit iniquity, I will chasten him with the rod of men, and with the stripes of the children of men.

David is first promised that he will be buried with his ancestors, a consistent Old Testament blessing for the righteous. His body will not be cast aside, but will be laid to rest with honor. Not only this, but God will bless David's successor with even more splendor than David himself will ever see.

To the kings of Israel, their greatest source of honor was the continuation of their lineage. Time and time again in the Old Testament we see the honor that comes from birthing sons at all levels of society, especially in the king's court. This was a day in which history mattered—in which the significance of long periods of time was frequently considered. Therefore, David was not content to only have peace and security during his reign. If no son succeeded him, he would be forgotten. Yahweh goes on to assure David that in establishing his house, He will secure the throne for a very special son.

The worthy dream that David has of housing God's ark in magnificence will be bequeathed to the next generation (v. 13). While some commentators see this as a prophecy of Christ, its immediate application is to the rule of Solomon. We know this from verse 14, where God hints that Solomon will struggle with imperfections and will require discipline. He will be headstrong and aggressive, and God will restrain him when necessary. But despite his shortcomings, God will walk with him as his father, and his reign will be even more secure and prosperous than David's. This was probably unimaginable to those who enjoyed the prosperous security of David, but the later narratives of Solomon confirm its accuracy. Archaeology has also shown that the period of Solomon was one of unprecedented economic growth for Israel. But the emphasis here is not only on material blessings, but also on God's commitment to Solomon's, and thus David's, household.

B. An Unconditional Covenant (vv. 15-17)

15. But my mercy shall not depart away from him, as I took it from Saul, whom I put away before thee.

16. And thine house and thy kingdom shall be established for ever before thee: thy throne shall be established for ever.

17. According to all these words, and according to all this vision, so did Nathan speak unto David.

The larger backdrop to the triumphant success of the royal court of David is the miserable and public failure of the reign of Saul. This contrast has a dual purpose in the narratives. First, the reader is reminded that God is the One who preserves for Himself the choice of ruler over Israel. In verse 15, God contrasts the future kingdom of Solomon with that of Saul. The Lord reminds David that it was not his military prowess or his popularity that unseated Saul from power; it was the hand of God alone. Second, the consistent reiteration of Saul's demise serves to illuminate

Talk About It:
1. What would David's son do (v. 13)?
2. Describe the relationship the Lord would have with David's heir (v. 14).

"We serve a gracious Master who knows how to overrule even our mistakes to His glory and to our own advantage."
—John Newton

Talk About It:
1. How would God deal differently with Solomon than He did with Saul (v. 15)?
2. What did the Lord promise regarding David's kingdom (vv. 16-17)?

the brightness of David's rule and character. In the same way that a diamond is often set against a black backdrop to fully display its brilliance, David always looks that much better compared to Saul, even when he acts immorally.

The amazing thing about the close of Nathan's edict from the Lord is that it espouses a dramatic shift in God's covenant with the nation. Up until now, the Torah law, expressed most simply in the Book of Deuteronomy, governs every Jew. And the Torah is an "if . . . then" proposition. It is not that God's love or commitment to Israel is conditional, but that the people do have specific requirements if they are to remain in an advantageous position both with God and with neighboring peoples. For example, in Deuteronomy 28, Moses summarizes Israel's responsibilities: "If you fully obey the Lord your God and carefully follow all his commands I give you today, the Lord your God will set you high above all the nations on earth. All these blessings will come upon you and accompany you if you obey the Lord your God" (vv. 1-2 NIV).

With the declaration of 2 Samuel 7, however, God's protection over David's house is proclaimed unconditionally. We get the impression that this means David's descendants will continue to literally rule in succession, as if Israel would never again experience foreign invasion. We know now, and so did the original readers of 2 Samuel, that this is not the case. Yet we also have a New Testament vantage point to this promise—that through the exaltation of Christ, the righteous rule of David continues among the people of faith today. This was not a promise only for the peoples of the ancient Near East. It reverberates even now around the entire world where communities of faith are gathered. The shift toward understanding God's unconditional love takes a leap forward in the rule of David.

> "God governs in the affairs of men. And if a sparrow cannot fall to the ground without His notice, is it probable that an empire can rise without His aid?"
> —**Benjamin Franklin**

III. DAVID RESPONDS WITH WORSHIP (2 Sam. 7:18-29)

Nathan's edict is short in length but eternal in scope. He has just proclaimed a word for David which any ruler would relish, and which no other ruler until Christ will ever receive again. So quickly we have traveled from the catastrophe of Saul to the hope of this new ruler! The only thing appropriate in the face of such promise is unfettered praise back to God, which David is already famous for.

A. Humble Response (vv. 18-21)

18. Then went king David in, and sat before the Lord, and he said, Who am I, O Lord God? and what is my house, that thou hast brought me hitherto?

19. And this was yet a small thing in thy sight, O Lord God; but thou hast spoken also of thy servant's house for a great while to come. And is this the manner of man, O Lord God?

David at Worship

20. And what can David say more unto thee? for thou, Lord God, knowest thy servant.

21. For thy word's sake, and according to thine own heart, hast thou done all these great things, to make thy servant know them.

David has just received the blessed news that God will uphold his power forever. A typical human response might be to swell with selfish pride under the reality of such a blessing. After all, God has proclaimed an unconditional covenant that He will uphold. David, however, will not take such a holy declaration for granted. Instead, he sits in awe before God's grace.

David fully recognizes that although he has worked arduously to develop his skills as a warrior, a governor, and a worshiper, it is not his own skills that have carried the day. Instead, he remembers his humble beginnings. He is not of royal blood, but from an insignificant family. He is the last in line of many brothers. No one would have logically chosen him for such power . . . except Yahweh.

Peace and prosperity in David's lifetime would certainly have been blessing enough, but the king is also astonished by the prophetic announcement of his future. David is fully conscious of the new quality of this word from God. Yahweh is not known for dealing with people in this way. Yes, He has always been loving, merciful, and just, but this measure of grace toward David's house is extraordinary. Yet David cannot challenge God's sovereignty, so he briefly renders himself speechless, asking, "What more can David say to you?" (v. 20 NIV).

David looks inside his heart and finds it hard to believe such goodness could be bestowed upon him. He knows he is a flawed human being. But he also knows that God knows him better than he can know himself, so he again defers to God's sovereignty. David does not even begin to try to understand God's motivation, but humbly trusts His judgment.

It is not simply the content of God's will that amazes David. The fact that God would choose to reveal it to him is also remarkable (v. 21). God could have brought these things to pass without David's knowledge, but He lets the king in on the secret, so that he can share in God's joy.

B. David's Characteristic Worship (vv. 22-24)

22. Wherefore thou art great, O Lord God: for there is none like thee, neither is there any God beside thee, according to all that we have heard with our ears.

23. And what one nation in the earth is like thy people, even like Israel, whom God went to redeem for a people to himself, and to make him a name, and to do for you great things and terrible, for thy land, before thy people, which thou redeemedst to thee from Egypt, from the nations and their gods?

Talk About It:
1. What amazed David (vv. 18-19)?
2. What did David conclude about "these great things" (vv. 20-21)?

Worthy Worship

Although it is common to talk today of "worship wars" in the church, reflecting the divide in music styles between traditional and contemporary, there is nothing new to such debate. Indeed, great heroes of Christianity including Martin Luther, John Calvin, and John Wesley were all criticized for their innovative approaches to worship. The key to healthily approaching this subject is to look at its focus. If worship is about us, we are out of line. If it is about God, it can take many forms and be pleasing to Him.

24. For thou hast confirmed to thyself thy people Israel to be a people unto thee for ever: and thou, Lord, art become their God.

Talk About It:
1. How did David describe the Lord (v. 22)?
2. How did David describe Israel (vv. 23-24)?

Now that David has viscerally responded to God's blessing with his own sense of inadequacy, he launches into a worship poem typical of his psalms. He takes references to himself completely out of the equation as his heart leaps in praise to Yahweh.

So David first praises the Lord's greatness and uniqueness. The Lord's unpredictable blessing on David reiterates God's originality and His sole claim to power over the universe. David again repeats God's title as "sovereign" (v. 22 NIV)—the One in complete control over these upcoming events.

David understands that this blessing is not directed primarily to him, but to the people of Israel (vv. 23-24). David has been handed a holy responsibility to remember their history, and thus to point them back to Yahweh in every aspect of his life and leadership. In no way does Israel belong to David. God established His own rule over the nation by redeeming them from Egypt. God established Israel as a nation under Moses. And now God has chosen Israel's line of rulers.

C. David Deflects the Glory (vv. 25-29)
(2 Samuel 7:26-29 is not included in the printed text.)
25. And now, O Lord God, the word that thou hast spoken concerning thy servant, and concerning his house, establish it for ever, and do as thou hast said.

Talk About It:
1. What did David request, and why (vv. 25-26)?
2. What gave David the "courage" (v. 27 NIV) to pray like this?

Because David understands that it is God in His sovereignty who will bring these things to pass, he closes his prayer of exaltation by further deflecting the glory of his blessed house back toward the Lord. Note that David does not lament his own unworthiness and so dishonor God's sacred decision. Instead, he openly affirms his acceptance of this blessing, but will absolutely not accept the glory that will come from it. The purpose of David's exhortation back to God is that God's great name might travel throughout the earth (v. 26). David desires that people come to know the God of Israel through his human reign of righteousness.

The poetic prayer closes with more affirmation of God's blessings mixed with considerable thanksgiving. The words of thanks overlap throughout the prayer. He concludes by declaring, "O Sovereign Lord, [You] have spoken, and with your blessing the house of your servant will be blessed forever" (v. 29 NIV).

In summary, 2 Samuel 7 represents perhaps the highest point in the life of David—a fascinating conclusion given that David is not even on center stage. His actions in the chapter are limited to a basic proposal regarding the construction of a proper dwelling place for the ark of God. Yet this is why God's eternal blessing on David's house here is so poignant! It does not come after

David wins a military victory or is blessed by the population. It comes in private, when David is simply at the mercy of God's grace. This grace will carry David through his ups and downs, even through his intense personal failures.

CONCLUSION

The expression that God is worthy of our worship is much more than a trite phrase repeated at worship gatherings. Indeed, it has weighty theological content. The life of David illustrates this expression well, in that even among the blessings on the king's house he consistently gives glory to God and so takes the spotlight off of himself. In this way he illustrates godly priorities, as David is a devout follower of what Jesus Christ will later deem to be the greatest commandment. Worship stems from a heart of love for God, and David loves passionately. Because of this, the Lord eternally blesses him, and we continue to reap the benefits of this unconditional covenant of love.

GOLDEN TEXT CHALLENGE

"GIVE UNTO THE LORD THE GLORY DUE UNTO HIS NAME; WORSHIP THE LORD IN THE BEAUTY OF HOLINESS" (Ps. 29:2).

The setting for this psalm is a powerful thunderstorm which "breaks the cedars . . . strikes with flashes of lightning . . . shakes the desert . . . twists the oaks" (vv. 5, 7-9 NIV). Yet this psalm "does not limit itself to the external phenomenon. It exalts the God of redemptive history, for behind all the glory of the invisible and natural things there is the God who is concerned about the world of humankind.

"The crashing thunderstorm which awakens fear in the ordinary mind, inquiry in the scientific mind, and imagination in the poetic mind, awakens trust and confidence in the child of God. The devout person realizes that the God who quells the storms is able to quell the tumults of the mind and give peace. Such a One merits the praises of His people in the beauty of holiness" (*Pulpit Commentary*).

Daily Devotions:
M. Worship of God Renewed
   Genesis 35:1-7
T. Worship Only God
   Exodus 20:1-7
W. False Worship Rebuked
   Isaiah 29:13-16
T. True Worship Described
   John 4:19-24
F. Worshiping God Ignorantly
   Acts 17:22-31
S. Worshiping the Creator
   Revelation 4:1-11

David Sins and Repents

2 Samuel 11:1 through 12:23

Unit Theme:
Books of Samuel

Central Truth:
God desires us to avoid sin and its consequences.

Focus:
Assess how severe the consequences of sin can be and overcome temptation and live in holiness by God's grace.

Context:
Between 995 and 985 BC, David sins terribly and is judged by the Lord.

Golden Text:
"He that covereth his sins shall not prosper: but whoso confesseth and forsaketh them shall have mercy" (Prov. 28:13).

Study Outline:
I. David's Terrible Sins (2 Sam. 11:1-27)
II. God Calls David to Account (2 Sam. 12:1-9)
III. David's Repentance and Punishment (2 Sam. 12:10-23)

INTRODUCTION

In 2003, world-renowned publisher Oxford University Press developed a line of books examining the seven deadly sins listed in Proverbs 6:16-19, and how they remain relevant today. With an unpopular perspective that cut to the heart of society's current ills, the series' authors argued that the seven deadly sins are not only matters of faith, but are important to a society's moral and psychological health. This conclusion resonated with biblical scholars, who have long recognized that the Bible's preoccupation with sin is usefully focused on society's well-being.

Perhaps better than any other preacher, Billy Graham has awakened nations to this reality of sin that is profoundly personal to each of us. In a 2006 national interview, with Graham well into retirement, the evangelist's message had not swayed at all: "I don't see much improvement in man's heart. The whole thing is in man's heart: his desire, his greed, his lust, his pride, his ego. All of these things meshed together bring about sometimes a world war and sometimes a small war, but wars are going on everywhere, even in families. It's a personal thing with each of us" (*Newsweek*, March 20, 2006). Sin is not some abstract force "out there" in the cosmos, but an individual reality that every human being must deal with.

The biblical heroes were not exempt from this rule. In fact, two atrocious acts of sin are central to the life and reign of King David. What is more, the Old Testament pulls no punches in telling the *whole* story with all of its grievous details. Yes, the Bible does celebrate David more than any other Old Testament figure. But it will not idealize or idolize him. He is still a man, subject to his own fleshly nature and in need of God's grace.

Although David's fall results in disastrous consequences for the rest of his life, God will not allow the king to remain a slave to his breach in ethics. Indeed, the story also highlights the sincerity and authenticity of David's repentance, an act of great faith in God's justice and mercy. It foreshadows the coming epoch in salvation history in which Christ will preach repentance to all—the opportunity for a fresh start not only for Israel but for the whole world. "Repent, for the kingdom of heaven is near!" will become the rallying cry of the Messiah. Yet this truth is also found hundreds of years before in the story of David.

I. DAVID'S TERRIBLE SINS (2 Sam. 11:1-27)

At this point in the life of David, the narrative has brought us to the pinnacle of the king's successes. After receiving the eternal promise of divine favor in chapter 7, he goes on to show mercy to the house of Saul in chapter 9, then to win a massive military victory against the Ammonites and the Syrians in chapter 10. He has every reason to swell with pride and live in the comfort of royalty, which is precisely the trap into which he falls.

A. A Scandal in the Making (vv. 1-5)

1. And it came to pass, after the year was expired, at the time when kings go forth to battle, that David sent Joab, and his servants with him, and all Israel; and they destroyed the children of Ammon, and besieged Rabbah. But David tarried still at Jerusalem.

2. And it came to pass in an eveningtide, that David arose from off his bed, and walked upon the roof of the king's house: and from the roof he saw a woman washing herself; and the woman was very beautiful to look upon.

3. And David sent and enquired after the woman. And one said, Is not this Bathsheba, the daughter of Eliam, the wife of Uriah the Hittite?

4. And David sent messengers, and took her; and she came in unto him, and he lay with her; for she was purified from her uncleanness: and she returned unto her house.

5. And the woman conceived, and sent and told David, and said, I am with child.

The story picks up with an introduction that cues the reader to expect something out of place. It is diplomatic season, the time when kings go off to negotiate and defend their territories with one another. David's unmatchable power would no doubt give him the upper hand in such diplomacy, but instead he delegates this kingly task to Joab and remains in Jerusalem. But this shirking of responsibility will have dire consequences.

Verse 2 finds David getting up from a mid-afternoon nap, which was a common practice in that time and place. As he walks around the flat-topped roof of his palace, his eyes catch a glimpse of another man's wife bathing in the uncovered court of a neighboring house. David immediately breaks the tenth commandment prohibiting coveting. But this is the king of Israel who can certainly have anything he wants, so he allows his impulses to lead him!

When David sends a messenger to find out about this woman, he is given the chance to turn away from this evil. The lowly messenger suggestively tells David that this is no loose woman. Her father is well known in the community, and she is married to a Gentile who is faithful to their cause. We do not yet know that Uriah is an Israelite warrior, a bit of irony that heightens the

Rabbah (RAB-uh)—v. 1—the chief city of the Ammonites

Uriah (you-RYE-uh)—v. 3—a foreigner who became a worshiper of the Lord God and one of David's mighty men

Talk About It:
1. Where was David, and where should he have been (v. 1)?
2. How do verses 2 and 3 describe Bathsheba?
3. What was the result of David's adulterous act (v. 5)?

impact of the story in verses 6 and 7. But David has made up his mind, and he sends more men to retrieve Bathsheba, who willingly comes. After David has sexual relations with her, she returns home.

Remember that government at this time is monarchical, functioning much differently than the modern Western world. For one thing, in the ancient world the king was considered a divinely appointed, religious figure. For this reason, the line between God and man was often blurred when it came to the king. So David's adulterous act would not raise many eyebrows in a world that considered the king's subjects to be his property. But this is not God's way of government.

David realizes that this egregious act will not go away quietly when he receives the dreadful message that Bathsheba is pregnant. One wonders if David has not feared such reprisal all along. He has now broken two of God's sacred commandments, one against coveting and the other against adultery. Will he come clean and receive punishment, or is a conspiracy in the making?

B. A Soldier of Honor (vv. 6-13)

(2 Samuel 11:6-13 is not included in the printed text.)

David sends a nondescript order for Uriah to be sent to him, and the cover-up has begun. If David can convince Uriah to sleep with his wife, no one will suspect anything, so David pulls out all the stops. He personally invites Uriah into his presence, then sends a gift back to his home. His commandment to Uriah to "wash [your] feet" (v. 8) is a common Hebrew euphemism, or metaphor, for sexual relations. Incredibly, Uriah is so committed to the Israelite cause that he will allow himself no such pleasure. He remains at the palace court, ready at any moment to serve his king.

When David is told that Uriah slept at the palace entrance, the king scales it up a notch. First he is convicted once more about his sin when Uriah humbly declines the king's commandment to enjoy a night of pleasure. Righteous Uriah loves God's ark and God's armies way too much to break from his command post. He will immediately head back to the battle lines. We can only speculate as to the demeanor of David in this exchange. Would he break under the guilt of being schooled by this faithful soldier? We quickly find out that David has no such intention, whether or not he wrestles with his better judgment. At this point, he is too neck-deep in a potential public scandal to change course.

Convincing Uriah to remain in Jerusalem another day, the king invites him to a royal feast. He pumps Uriah full of the choicest food and wine, hoping to impair his judgment so that he will return home. Again, the plan crashes. Uriah sleeps on the ground outside, rather than with his wife at home. Therefore, a more sinister strategy is necessary.

"If a man has no opportunity of living with another man's wife, but if it is obvious for some reason that he would like to do so, and would do so if he could, he is no less guilty than if he was caught in the act."
—Augustine

Talk About It:
1. How did David try to deceive Uriah (vv. 6-7)?
2. What do verses 8-11 reveal about Uriah's character?
3. How did David's second plot fail (vv. 12-13)?

"He has honor if he holds himself to an ideal of conduct though it is inconvenient, unprofitable, or dangerous to do so."
—Walter Lippmann

C. A Calculated Evil (vv. 14-27)
(2 Samuel 11:18-24 is not included in the printed text.)

14. And it came to pass in the morning, that David wrote a letter to Joab, and sent it by the hand of Uriah.

15. And he wrote in the letter, saying, Set ye Uriah in the forefront of the hottest battle, and retire ye from him, that he may be smitten, and die.

16. And it came to pass, when Joab observed the city, that he assigned Uriah unto a place where he knew that valiant men were.

17. And the men of the city went out, and fought with Joab: and there fell some of the people of the servants of David; and Uriah the Hittite died also.

25. Then David said unto the messenger, Thus shalt thou say unto Joab, Let not this thing displease thee, for the sword devoureth one as well as another: make thy battle more strong against the city, and overthrow it: and encourage thou him.

26. And when the wife of Uriah heard that Uriah her husband was dead, she mourned for her husband.

27. And when the mourning was past, David sent and fetched her to his house, and she became his wife, and bare him a son. But the thing that David had done displeased the Lord.

David had two days to confess his sin to Uriah, but his cover-up plan fails. He has one more choice to wash his hands of the matter in secret—the power to simply order Uriah's death. The irony of David's commandment is that he knows Uriah is so trustworthy that he will not read his own death letter. Uriah has no idea that he faithfully carries the message of his own demise from his king to his general. Even sadder, he will not be the only loss on this pitiful day.

The relocation of Uriah's platoon to a well-defended segment of the city results in many deaths. The move is such a blatant tactical error that Joab has to send a coded account of the battle back to David (vv. 18-21). David doesn't even flinch at the terrible news about his army. He now has what he wants.

At least David allows Bathsheba the ceremonial time of mourning before he usurps her as his wife. Surprisingly, their union is blessed with a son. Could this be a sign that David is somehow above God's law, that God will be with David regardless of his actions? Not at all. The story ends with God's pronounced displeasure at David's wicked choices. He has added the sin of murder to his account.

II. GOD CALLS DAVID TO ACCOUNT (2 Sam. 12:1-9)
We do not know how much time passes between the assassination of Uriah and the scene of chapter 12. Periods of mourning typically lasted from seven to thirty days, but beyond this the

Talk About It:
1. How much did David trust Uriah (v. 14)?
2. What was the result of David's new scheme (vv. 15-17)?
3. What is ominous about verse 27?

"Sin is a sum of addition which accumulates its weight to the condemnation of the sinner."
—Robert G. Lee

passage gives us no time markers. Apparently enough time has passed that David has grown calloused to his actions, whether this is a month or a year.

A. An Incisive Parable (vv. 1-4)

1. And the Lord sent Nathan unto David. And he came unto him, and said unto him, There were two men in one city; the one rich, and the other poor.

2. The rich man had exceeding many flocks and herds:

3. But the poor man had nothing, save one little ewe lamb, which he had bought and nourished up: and it grew up together with him, and with his children; it did eat of his own meat, and drank of his own cup, and lay in his bosom, and was unto him as a daughter.

4. And there came a traveller unto the rich man, and he spared to take of his own flock and of his own herd, to dress for the wayfaring man that was come unto him; but took the poor man's lamb, and dressed it for the man that was come to him.

Talk About It:
1. Compare the rich man with the poor man (vv. 1-3).
2. Describe the rich man's actions (v. 4).

Nathan takes his life into his hands by approaching the king with a parable that squarely calls him on the carpet. As a moral leader in the royal court, Nathan will not allow David's evil actions to move forward unchecked. Nathan will not sell out his prophetic calling for political advantage.

Nathan's story is an excellent illustration of the Jewish tradition of storytelling which stretches back well before the time of Jesus. Stories, of course, reel the listener in and allow him or her to engage God's truth in an exceptional way. Indeed, Nathan's story resembles the parables of Jesus in many ways. It incorporates vivid agricultural imagery, a stark distinction between two stock characters, and a shocking twist at the end. David, however, does not initially realize that his own court prophet is telling an illustrative story, which makes for one of the greatest confrontations in biblical history.

B. A Dramatic Confrontation (vv. 5-9)

5. And David's anger was greatly kindled against the man; and he said to Nathan, As the Lord liveth, the man that hath done this thing shall surely die:

6. And he shall restore the lamb fourfold, because he did this thing, and because he had no pity.

7. And Nathan said to David, Thou art the man. Thus saith the Lord God of Israel, I anointed thee king over Israel, and I delivered thee out of the hand of Saul;

8. And I gave thee thy master's house, and thy master's wives into thy bosom, and gave thee the house of Israel and of Judah; and if that had been too little, I would moreover have given unto thee such and such things.

David Sins and Repents

9. Wherefore hast thou despised the commandment of the Lord, to do evil in his sight? thou hast killed Uriah the Hittite with the sword, and hast taken his wife to be thy wife, and hast slain him with the sword of the children of Ammon.

In one of the greatest ironies in the Old Testament, David rushes to the fictional poor man's defense. Filled with righteous indignation, the king is prepared to pronounce a sentence of death against the rich offender on that very day. Such injustice will not be allowed in his kingdom, he retorts! Nathan's message, of course, is that David has committed a far worse evil.

We can only guess at Nathan's demeanor as he tells David, "You are the man!" (v. 7 NIV). Perhaps he trembles at such a harsh word, for he is taking his life into his hands before the king. Whatever the case, he boldly pronounces God's judgment. He is no weak prophet, no religious minion at the king's whim. He is charged to deliver the very word of Yahweh, so he points his finger straight into the face of David and declares him a lying murderer. Nathan goes on to rehearse a history of David's rise to power. Not only had God delivered him from Saul, God had given him the entire kingdom.

In verse 9 Nathan says the Ammonites will not get the blame for Uriah's death. Even though David was miles away from the battlefield, he alone bears the responsibility. His accomplices, Joab and his messengers, are not even mentioned. As the director of the plot, David must pay the price.

III. DAVID'S REPENTANCE AND PUNISHMENT
(2 Sam. 12:10-23)
A. Public Judgment (vv. 10-12)

10. Now therefore the sword shall never depart from thine house; because thou hast despised me, and hast taken the wife of Uriah the Hittite to be thy wife.

11. Thus saith the Lord, Behold, I will raise up evil against thee out of thine own house, and I will take thy wives before thine eyes, and give them unto thy neighbour, and he shall lie with thy wives in the sight of this sun.

12. For thou didst it secretly: but I will do this thing before all Israel, and before the sun.

Nathan has directly confronted the king with God's revelation of his brutal crime. He has held nothing back, and he continues the tirade. The judgment becomes specific, carrying dire consequences for David's enduring reign.

Just five chapters earlier, the eternal blessing of God was declared on David's house. It is not and cannot be taken away here, because God's promises are irrevocable. However, these promises will be fulfilled alongside unparalleled violence. Because David ransacked the home of Uriah the Hittite, his own house will experience agony to an even worse degree. David may have

Talk About It:
1. What was David's judgment against the rich man (vv. 5-6)?
2. What had the Lord done for David (vv. 7-8)?
3. What had David done to the Lord (v. 9)?

"Greed is the inventor of injustice as well as the current enforcer."
—Julian Casablancas

Talk About It:
1. How would God judge David (vv. 10-11)?
2. How would God carry out this judgment, and why (v. 12)?

presumed that his sin was only against Uriah, but Yahweh makes it clear that He takes David's act personally. It was as if David had stolen Yahweh's wife, not Uriah's. Because of this, God will not act in secrecy. David will reap public consequences for what he originally believed was a private sin. Indeed, the story proves that no sin can remain secret, no matter how well planned.

Nathan's pronouncement leaves us on the edge of our seats, waiting for the great king's response. David has the power to order Nathan's execution right then and there, but his heart is characteristically broken by the word of God. Although he buried it for a time, he has not lost his sense of God's justice.

B. Sincere Repentance (vv. 13-14)

13. And David said unto Nathan, I have sinned against the Lord. And Nathan said unto David, The Lord also hath put away thy sin; thou shalt not die.

14. Howbeit, because by this deed thou hast given great occasion to the enemies of the Lord to blaspheme, the child also that is born unto thee shall surely die.

Finally, David gives an outright confession. Not only has he terrorized the house of Uriah, but he has brazenly affronted the God of Israel. Without this acknowledgment, we can only guess how the story of David might have turned out. Thankfully, he comes completely clean. Even though David repents, he still must pay the price for his sin.

David's sins could have been his death sentence, but God is both just and merciful. Because of this, the fruit of his sins will be taken from him. God's word makes it clear that because David's acts had public consequences, so will the corresponding divine punishment. David had allowed the Ammonites to decimate a troop of God's armies, causing the name of God to be disdained by an enemy nation. And this sin could even embolden the Ammonites to invade Israel's territory. Such an act cannot be overlooked. Therefore, Nathan announces that David's innocent new son will die.

Talk About It:
1. How did David respond to Nathan's message (v. 13)?
2. What would the Lord do for David (v. 13)?
3. How else would David be punished, and why (v. 14)?

C. A Child's Death (vv. 15-23)

(2 Samuel 12:17-21 is not included in the printed text.)

15. And Nathan departed unto his house. And the Lord struck the child that Uriah's wife bare unto David, and it was very sick.

16. David therefore besought God for the child; and David fasted, and went in, and lay all night upon the earth.

22. And he said, While the child was yet alive, I fasted and wept: for I said, Who can tell whether God will be gracious to me, that the child may live?

23. But now he is dead, wherefore should I fast? can I bring him back again? I shall go to him, but he shall not return to me.

David Sins and Repents

David does not initially accept this word of judgment. Although Bathsheba's son immediately becomes deathly ill, David holds onto hope, fasting and praying many nights for the salvation of the child. We can only imagine the guilt David experienced, knowing that the punishment for his own actions had been laid upon the innocent. His court is in a panic, desperately trying to resuscitate the spirits of the king. The government slows to a halt as David awaits God's answer. But nothing can be done to deter God's wrath.

After a torturous week, the nameless son dies, and David's attendants are terrified to inform the king (v. 18). After such ardent prayer, they fear that his spirits will be crushed. Apparently though, King David has expected the worst all along. With great dignity, he rises from his place of mourning to enter the house of the Lord for a time of worship, before finally taking a meal (v. 20). His servants are understandably dumbstruck. Normally the grieving process takes place *after* a death, but David has gone about things in reverse. The king explains that he was falling back on the character of God. He knows that Yahweh is a God of great mercy, and he hoped beyond hope that the divine plan could be changed. He accepts it in its finality, however, recognizing that God has been just toward him.

The story ends on a note of hope, as David comforts his wife Bathsheba, again taking responsibility for his wicked actions. As a result, God gives them not just a new son, Solomon, but the very heir to the throne (v. 24). Leave it to Yahweh to redeem this dreadful situation with the birth of new hope. He fulfills the promise of 2 Samuel 7 so the world may know of His providence.

The overarching story of David's fall, then, reflects this journey of faith from oppressive bondage to exhilarating freedom, a journey reserved for any child of God. It illustrates not only the character of David, but the character of God. In the divine catalog, justice and mercy overlap and intermingle. They are both awesome in scope. The great Russian novelist Fyodor Dostoevsky captured this connection in his assertion that "the love of God is a harsh and dangerous love." God is no gentle uncle. His judgments are real and terrible. But they are never the final word, as His covenant love continually breaks through the darkness.

David's attempt to save his dying son also reflects a great movement of faith. He does not allow his error to move him away from God, but instead runs to God for salvation. In this movement, he finds the freedom to worship God even in the face of punishment. As theologian Karl Barth writes, "What happens in the event of faith is that the Word of God frees one man among many for faith itself. This is the motivation of faith; something is 'moved,' and something 'takes' place. By God's Word, together with the life-giving power and the unique sovereignty of the Spirit, one man among many is permitted to exist continually as a free man" (*Evangelical Theology: An Introduction*).

Talk About It:
1. What was David's servants' concern (v. 18)?
2. What is the significance of David's actions in verse 20?
3. How did David explain his actions (vv. 21-23)?

Our Salvation
In C. S. Lewis's famous allegory of the Christian story, *Chronicles of Narnia*, the evil white witch claims that the central human character, Edmund, belongs solely to her. However, the great lion Aslan gives up his life, thus saving Edmund and the land from her

power. Sin, like the white witch, also threatens to destroy us, but Christ has shed His blood for our salvation.

David finds freedom in faith, even in this horrific story. Even his servants are amazed, perhaps appalled, at his steadfast trust in the God who has smitten his house. This allows David to properly bear responsibility for his actions by comforting Bathsheba and by not giving up on his future. He knows that the same God who cut him down will graciously raise him up again.

CONCLUSION

In the Bible, calculated sin is nothing to be scoffed at, whether one is a peasant or a king. The story of David and Bathsheba illustrates the restraint that God expected from Israel's leadership. Even the most powerful man in the land was completely subject to God's laws. In this sense, Israel was not meant to be a monarchy, but a unique theocracy, with a rigorous commitment to the rule of divine law. Should a ruler try to usurp God's law for his own purposes, God would intervene for the good of society, and for the glory of His name.

Daily Devotions:
M. Consequences
   of Sin
   Genesis 4:8-16
T. Judgment and
   Mercy
   1 Kings 11:9-13
W. Sin Brings
   Suffering
   2 Chronicles 26:3-
   5, 16-21
T. Repent or Perish
   Luke 13:1-5
F. A Fatal Sin
   Acts 5:1-10
S. Abstain From Sin
   Romans 6:1-12

GOLDEN TEXT CHALLENGE

"HE THAT COVERETH HIS SINS SHALL NOT PROSPER: BUT WHOSO CONFESSETH AND FORSAKETH THEM SHALL HAVE MERCY" (Prov. 28:13).

This scripture presents two ways we can deal with our sin. First, we can try to conceal it, pretending it never happened. This is as foolish as the person who learns he has a cancerous tumor but pretends it is not there. The effects of the cancer might not be seen right away, just as the judgment for sin might not be experienced immediately, but trouble will come. We will not be blessed.

The second way to deal with our sin is to confess it and renounce it. Simply confessing our sin is not enough if we intend to return to it. We must both admit our sin and turn from it if we want to receive mercy from the Lord.

The Last Words of David

2 Samuel 22:1 through 23:5

INTRODUCTION

The final words of a dying person are sacred in any culture, and the biblical landscape is no exception to this rule. Its major characters such as Joseph, Moses, and Joshua are given space in the narratives for their last sayings. Indeed, the entire book of Deuteronomy is set up as a single speech—Moses' final charge to the nation of Israel before he climbs Mount Nebo to breathe his last. The Gospel writers also give plenty of attention to the Last Supper, where Jesus speaks His final commandments to His disciples. It is no surprise, then, that these lengthy records of the life and reign of David include and institutionalize last words.

The end of David's life is both similar and different from his initial rise to power. Although rival kingdoms from the outside no longer seriously threaten him, much of this conflict has danger-ously shifted to internal dissension. In fact, the rebellions of Absalom, Sheba, and Adonijah are the fulfillment of Nathan's prophecy that David's sin toward Uriah would result in continual family violence. How tragic that David's unparalleled power protects Israel from invading enemies, but not from his own family members! This is the grave consequence of David's sin.

David's ups and downs continue into the twilight of his reign. As usual, his military victories are second to none. But in an act of irrational pride, he orders Joab to count the number of soldiers in the armies of Israel and Judah, as if the nation's military might depended on men, not God (2 Sam. 24:1-9). As a result, a devastating plague strikes the land. This is King David in all his humanity: passionate, impulsive, imperfect, but still the one that Luke will call "after [God's] own heart" (Acts 13:22).

We should also view the end of David's life as a vital transi-tional period in the life of Israel. Nathan's prophecy about David's future son has already set the reader up to expect a great heir. As war engulfs his court, however, we are left to wonder about which son will emerge victorious. At the end of 2 Samuel this has yet to be cleared up, until the last days of David are recorded in 1 Kings. There, David himself installs young Solomon to take his place, one who will rule a very different, but equally significant, period of Israel's history. Nonetheless, the fact that we know David's lineage will continue is significant in 2 Samuel. This is no fly-by-night ruler. His legacy will live on forever.

Unit Theme:
Books of Samuel

Central Truth:
Living in the Spirit is a worshipful lifestyle.

Focus:
Realize that God inspires a worshipful lifestyle and be respon-sive to His Spirit in daily living.

Context:
Around 975 BC, King David writes his last inspired song of praise.

Golden Text:
"I will bless the Lord at all times: his praise shall continually be in my mouth" (Ps. 34:1).

Study Outline:
I. David Continually Praised God (2 Sam. 22:1-28)
II. David Had Confidence in God (2 Sam. 22:29-51)
III. David Was Inspired by God (2 Sam. 23:1-5)

I. DAVID CONTINUALLY PRAISED GOD (2 Samuel 22:1-28)

David is famous for his composition of psalms—poetic hymns set to music for the life of the nation—and here we find one typical of his pen. Indeed, it is identical to Psalm 18. This is an interesting double occurrence of the same passage in Scripture. It is not difficult to see why it captured the ancient imagination. It is beautiful in its verse but also muscular in its scope.

A. David in Need (vv. 1-7)

(2 Samuel 22:4-7 is not included in the printed text.)

1. And David spake unto the Lord the words of this song in the day that the Lord had delivered him out of the hand of all his enemies, and out of the hand of Saul:

2. And he said, The Lord is my rock, and my fortress, and my deliverer;

3. The God of my rock; in him will I trust: he is my shield, and the horn of my salvation, my high tower, and my refuge, my saviour; thou savest me from violence.

Talk About It:
1. What inspired David to sing this song (v. 1)?
2. What is similar about the names David ascribes to the Lord (vv. 2-3)?
3. Describe David's dilemma (vv. 5-7).

The psalm is introduced similarly to Deuteronomy 32, where Moses also charges the nation with a final poetic oracle. David sang to the Lord the words of this song when the Lord delivered him from the hand of all his enemies and from the hand of Saul (2 Sam. 22:1). The introduction in verse 1 is also found at the front of Psalm 18, but neither helps us accurately locate the poem within the life of David. At first glance, it even seems inserted into an awkward place in the narrative, sandwiched between further accounts of David's military machine. Perhaps this is the editor's rationale for the psalm's placement—it serves to deflect attention from David's victories back to their divine source. At the height of his power, we find David singing a majestic song to God, giving glory where it belongs. This song does not highlight David's greatness, but his neediness.

David begins by announcing not only the rock-solid character of Yahweh, but also his own need to be saved. The king is an expert on "violent men" (2 Sam. 22:3 NIV), and though he has overcome so many of them, beginning with the menacing Saul, he knows that this did not come from his own sword. Indeed, verses 5 and 6 depict just how near to death David has been time and time again. He has survived "waves . . . floods . . . sorrows . . . [and] snares."

The reference to "temple" in verse 7 is especially curious, given that no temple exists during David's reign. He knows explicitly that it will not be established until Solomon takes his place. It must refer, then, to a heavenly temple, which serves as a potent lead-in to the next section.

"Storms make oaks take deeper roots."
—George Herbert

B. The Awesome Entrance of Yahweh (vv. 8-20)
(2 Samuel 22:8-16 is not included in the printed text.)

17. He sent from above, he took me; he drew me out of many waters;

18. He delivered me from my strong enemy, and from them that hated me: for they were too strong for me.

19. They prevented me in the day of my calamity: but the Lord was my stay.

20. He brought me forth also into a large place: he delivered me, because he delighted in me.

Suddenly God arises from His heavenly temple to come to David's aid on the earth. Verses 8-16 describe this in typical Jewish fashion, with vivid and terrifying imagery regarding the quaking of heaven and earth, and the appearance of Yahweh in smoke, fire, thunder, and lightning. The verses reflect God's supremacy over and separation from the creation. The elements of the earth are not mistaken for God, but are affected and controlled by His awesome power. Still, this majestic God is not too great for dealings with humanity.

In the next verses, David moves from depicting the majesty of Yahweh as One who comes down to the earth, to personalizing the Lord's work in his life. "Deep waters" (v. 17 NIV) symbolized primordial chaos to the ancient Jews, a chaos which is no match for God's all-seeing eye.

In verse 18 David pulls no punches in admitting his own weakness. If God did not intervene, David's enemies would have overtaken him long ago. This is no surprise given David's first experience in battle, triumphing over a giant champion against all odds (1 Sam. 17). With this history, David knows firsthand the support of Yahweh. Without it, he would have been slain long ago.

David closes the words of salvation with God's rationale for the rescue operation: "He brought me out into a spacious place; he rescued me because he delighted in me" (2 Sam. 22:20 NIV). David can come up with no other explanation. God selected him, not because of David's goodness, but precisely because of his nothingness. God loved David unconditionally, and therefore blessed him with rule over a spacious land.

C. David's Righteousness (vv. 21-28)
(2 Samuel 22:23-28 is not included in the printed text.)

21. The Lord rewarded me according to my righteousness: according to the cleanness of my hands hath he recompensed me.

22. For I have kept the ways of the Lord, and have not wickedly departed from my God.

The next section of the hymn recognizes that although Yahweh has selected David for His own purposes, this does not leave

Talk About It:
1. How was nature affected by God's intervention (vv. 8-16)?
2. How does David describe his rescue (vv. 17-20)?

"Four things let us ever keep in mind: God hears prayer, God heeds prayer, God answers prayer, and God delivers by prayer."
—E. M. Bounds

Talk About It:
1. Why did the Lord bless David (vv. 21-25)?

2. How does the Lord deal with individuals (vv. 26-27)?
3. What can "the haughty" expect (v. 28)?

David without responsibility. Indeed, David doesn't hesitate in expressing his righteousness. This can be jarring to modern readers. It sounds like self-aggrandizement and seems arrogant. Remember, however, that David would be the first to admit his imperfections. They were advertised to the entire nation. But in the end, God would deal with him according to his better instincts and his heart of love for God's righteous law.

As verse 28 shows, David's humility has made himself usable to God. It is part of the scriptural consciousness that both evil and good be easily recognized. Therefore, for a leader like David to announce his own righteousness is not an act of arrogance, but an act of praise. The fact that God's laws can successfully be followed is a reason for celebration, not pride, and here David revels in his commitment to the commandments.

II. DAVID HAD CONFIDENCE IN GOD (2 Samuel 22:29-51)

Jewish psalms have a rolling cadence to them. They certainly have a forged structure, but this structure is flexible, allowing for overlap and repetition, as central themes flow over and back onto one another like the waves of the ocean. This is especially the case in David's song of praise in 2 Samuel 22. He constantly switches between extolling God for His greatness and describing the work of God in his own life—a vital shift for authentic worship. The second half of the poem particularly emphasizes Yahweh as David's chief source of military strength and personal greatness.

A. The Source of David's Strength (vv. 29-43)

(2 Samuel 22:38-43 is not included in the printed text.)

29. For thou art my lamp, O Lord: and the Lord will lighten my darkness.

30. For by thee I have run through a troop: by my God have I leaped over a wall.

31. As for God, his way is perfect; the word of the Lord is tried: he is a buckler to all them that trust in him.

32. For who is God, save the Lord? and who is a rock, save our God?

33. God is my strength and power: and he maketh my way perfect.

hinds' feet (v. 34)— "the feet of deer" (NKJV)

34. He maketh my feet like hinds' feet: and setteth me upon my high places.

35. He teacheth my hands to war; so that a bow of steel is broken by mine arms.

36. Thou hast also given me the shield of thy salvation: and thy gentleness hath made me great.

37. Thou hast enlarged my steps under me; so that my feet did not slip.

In a time well before electricity, light was the source of life. It is for a reason that God initiated the creation of the cosmos in Genesis 1 with the entrance of light. In David's era, darkness was feared as the unknown, but light brought by lamps dispelled such fear. Through faith in God, David was secure in the unknown.

This truth was especially important in military battles, where the momentum could swing at a moment's notice and thousands of lives could be lost. There was always some uncertainty in battles, so David was accustomed to the stress of losing men. However, David knew that with God in the equation such uncertainty was not a proper occasion for fear.

David's battle language (v. 30) is decidedly offensive. David is not describing his army defending their own territory, but conquering on the wide-open fields of battle. A troop consisted of several thousand soldiers marching in unison as a single battalion. David claims that God's help allows him to charge such an intimidating armored force. What is more, massive walls were erected for the protection of every city, even minor ones. When God helps David, however, these concrete structures are not an obstacle. God gives him the strength to stand on their heights and to topple them.

Even in his military might, David recognizes his own fallibility. With all of his public mistakes, he would be crazy to try to hide them now! God, however, makes no such mistakes. "His way is perfect," and His flawless word can be ultimately and completely trusted (v. 31). This provides a secure place of safety for those who choose God as their shield. The reality of this truth causes David to burst into rhetorical questions (v. 32). Can any other god rival Yahweh? Is any neighboring god so rock-solid? These questions expect the customary negative answer. God's uniqueness is a hallmark of this ancient Jewish poetry.

In verse 33, David transitions back to the militaristic images of his partnership with God, who is altogether the source of David's strength. The king is not known as a mighty warrior because of his own skill, but because of Yahweh's greatness. Therefore, in the following verses David ascribes to himself superhuman strength at the hand of God. He can run with the speed of a deer, bend a bow of metal, and fight without risk of injury—all this solely a result of God's empowerment. Armed with God on his side, David recounts his victories, how he crushed armies beneath his feet with utter finality (vv. 38-39).

For the modern reader, the violence of verses 38-43 can be troubling. However, we must keep in mind the historical context of these scriptures. David lived in a violent age, and his job as king also made him the automatic commander in chief of the army. Nation-state boundaries were not definite yet, so it was normal for invading armies to terrorize Israelite towns and villages in order to gain extra land for themselves. In this context, warfare was a matter not just of national security, but of national survival. These

Talk About It:
1. How is God like a lamp (v. 29)?
2. How should God's "way" (v. 31) affect our "way" (v. 33)?
3. Explain the statement, "Your gentleness has made me great" (v. 36 NKJV).
4. Why were David's enemies defeated (v. 42)?

passages should not be taken as God's de facto sanctioning of violence, nor should they be relegated to the sidelines as insignificant for nations today. The teachings of Jesus regarding violence have the final word on these matters.

B. The Source of David's Greatness (vv. 44-51)

(2 Samuel 22:44-49 is not included in the printed text.)

50. Therefore I will give thanks unto thee, O Lord, among the heathen, and I will sing praises unto thy name.

51. He is the tower of salvation for his king: and sheweth mercy to his anointed, unto David, and to his seed for evermore.

We know from the narratives that David's military victories brought him great fame, not only in Israel but throughout the ancient Near East. The final section of this song of praise describes this greatness from the perspective of foreign relations (vv. 44-51). Though David only sought peace and security for Israel, he has been blessed by the obedience of neighboring peoples. The Philistines, the Ammonites, and others have risen up against him only to be decimated. As a result, David concludes the poem with another strong round of praise to God.

The conjunction "therefore" (v. 50) should be taken in connection to all that has preceded this verse. As a result of all that David has described, God is worthy of exuberant praise. What is more, this praise should spill out beyond Israel's boundaries to engulf other nations as well, so that the name of Yahweh might be revealed to the entire world. Although many maintain the impression that Jewish faith was intended to be limited to their own nation, this is simply not the case. The apostle Paul quoted verse 50 in Romans 15:9 to underscore "that the Gentiles might glorify God for His mercy" (NKJV).

Yes, the Lord "shows unfailing kindness to . . . David and his descendants forever" (2 Sam. 22:51 NIV), and it is through David's ancestry that the Messiah, who offers divine mercy to all nations, would come.

III. DAVID WAS INSPIRED BY GOD (2 Samuel 23:1-5)

We are left to guess at the placement of chapter 22 in the king's life, but the song of chapter 23 is explicitly located as the king's final declaration. Charles Swindoll vividly describes this context:

> The long shadows of age and pressure are beginning to fall across David's face. He has lived a full life and experienced both the heights and the depths. He has entered what we might call his twilight years. David often had to trust God in impossible circumstances, but it seems as though recently things have occurred that have kept him on his knees. Long before he was a king, David was a singer of songs, and here we find what I am convinced is the last song he ever sang (*David: A Man of Passion and Destiny*).

So much is at stake in David's final song, as he seeks to summarize everything that is most important to him. Unsurprisingly, Yahweh again takes center stage. We would expect nothing else from the anointed warrior-poet.

A. The Righteous Ruler (vv. 1-4)

1. Now these be the last words of David. David the son of Jesse said, and the man who was raised up on high, the anointed of the God of Jacob, and the sweet psalmist of Israel, said,

2. The Spirit of the Lord spake by me, and his word was in my tongue.

3. The God of Israel said, the Rock of Israel spake to me, He that ruleth over men must be just, ruling in the fear of God.

4. And he shall be as the light of the morning, when the sun riseth, even a morning without clouds; as the tender grass springing out of the earth by clear shining after rain.

The introduction to David's final poem signifies its significance in the historical annals of Israel. This formal declaration has the feel of a regal declaration, not unlike Nathan's prophecy in chapter 7. We can only speculate as to its use, but perhaps it was central to David's funeral rites, or was marked in stone as an inscription on his tomb. The passage contains several important characteristics that give us insight into David's heart and meaning.

First, the passage is considered an oracle, which is something akin to a prophecy. That is, what David will say has vast implications for the future. It should not be relegated to the distant past as ancient history. Second, David was exalted by God himself, which reduces him to the secondary category. Third, Jacob's God, not just Samuel, anointed David to be king. This formulates David in the long line of Jewish leaders stretching back to Genesis and the patriarchs. Fourth, David will be known as Israel's chief worship leader—the joyful, wild, singing king—into perpetuity.

It is fascinating that David's final song says nothing of his military victories or his political greatness. Instead, it focuses completely on God. The opening formula (v. 2) is similar to the initiation of Jesus' public ministry in Nazareth, where Jesus quotes from Isaiah 61 to claim the Spirit of Yahweh's empowerment of His life and speech (Luke 4:18). David was installed as king to be God's instrument and mouthpiece. His final words will not glorify himself, but will speak of God.

In 2 Samuel 23:3-4, David reveals a specific word from the Lord. Who knows how long he has kept it to himself? This divine word has been the driving force of his leadership for decades. In typical poetic fashion, David describes the ideal ruler of God's people. He likely spoke this to communicate a path for Israel's

Talk About It:
1. How does verse 1 describe David?
2. In verse 2, for what did David credit God?
3. What did the Lord tell David regarding those who rule (vv. 3-4)?

Talk About It:
What made David confident?

future kings to follow, not the least being his son Solomon. This path of leadership is not based on strength, might, or military power, but on righteousness, which results from walking reverently before God. When such a king learns how to govern according to God's laws, his kingdom will be vibrant with brightness and hope. The darkness and secrecy of scandal and power-grabbing will have no place in such a holy kingdom.

B. God's Eternal Covenant With David (v. 5)

5. Although my house be not so with God; yet he hath made with me an everlasting covenant, ordered in all things, and sure: for this is all my salvation, and all my desire, although he make it not to grow.

David has not been a perfect ruler, but he has walked intimately with a perfect God. Throughout all of his failures, his ups and downs, he has understood the priority of this relationship. When things in national office have gotten out of hand, he has returned to this relationship countless times. At the close of his days he has one thing in mind—the righteousness of his household before Yahweh. As a result, he knows that he can die in peace and security.

Not only has David achieved, or received, such righteousness, but he is also the recipient of an eternal covenant with God that has resulted in his salvation and the fulfillment of his desires. Again, this covenant occurs in chapter 7. By "salvation," David does not refer to the afterlife, which is not a part of these final words. This sounds strange to our ears, but the Old Testament mostly concerns life on earth. What matters here, then, is the literal continuation of David's household in actual history. It will bear the fruit of salvation for generations to come, which is David's chief desire.

So what do we make of this eternal covenant with David? Although his son Solomon will rule with unprecedented wisdom over a time of extraordinary prosperity, this national security will not last long. The northern and southern kingdoms will split once again, inaugurating the tumultuous epoch of the kings, most of who do not follow the word of God. David's lineage will get lost in the shuffle, so clearly this covenant goes beyond the mechanics of monarchy. The answer comes with the advent of Jesus Christ, the One whose genealogy connects right back to the famed son of Jesse. It is no surprise then, that Jesus is constantly addressed as the "Son of David," a direct reference to the Messiah who would restore the grandeur of Israel to the former days of old. Christ did this, but in a way very few expected. He did not provide a militaristic freedom, but the inner freedom with God that David himself experienced and foresaw.

CONCLUSION

The life of David is one of the most gut-wrenching and inspiring epochs in Scripture. At times, it seems as if his reign will fall apart, but God always brings him back to rule righteously. His fame was known in the fields of military strategy, governmental policy, and the musical and literary arts. For this reason, he became the pattern and archetype for godly rule in Israel. Through the books of 1 and 2 Samuel, his life continues to guide believers today.

GOLDEN TEXT CHALLENGE

"I WILL BLESS THE LORD AT ALL TIMES: HIS PRAISE SHALL CONTINUALLY BE IN MY MOUTH" (Ps. 34:1).

The word *bless* comes from a root word which includes "to kneel in acknowledgment, to praise, and to worship." It implies our declaring the worth of God. *Worship* is "my response to God declaring His worth as He has revealed Himself to me."

Worship isn't to be limited to a particular time or place. It is not to be confined to the times of service held in the sanctuary.

God's presence isn't limited to our church buildings. He is omnipresent. We need to recognize this and offer our worship throughout the day regardless of the location. It may be brief moments where we quietly say, "Lord, I worship You." It may be meditating on Him while performing household chores. Anytime and anyplace is a good time to worship our great God!

Worship stems from our relationship with God and our knowledge of Him. It should never be dependent on a particular musical background or emotional atmosphere. Worship begins from within and then proceeds outwardly to be evidenced by our words and actions. There's no doubt it is easy to worship as we are surrounded by other worshipers and hear beautiful music extolling the greatness of God. Yet, it is equally easy to worship when we begin to meditate on His greatness and goodness in our own lives.

When David states "I will," he indicates that worship is a personal choice. We decide *if* and *when* we are going to worship. That's why some individuals leave a service with the praise of God on their lips while others leave having done nothing more than fulfill a ritual. All heard and saw the same stimuli. But each made a different choice. This is a truth that worship leaders need to understand. All that can be done is offer an opportunity.

Daily Devotions:
M. Celebrate God's Supremacy
Exodus 15:1-7, 20-21
T. Honor God in Adversity
Job 1:1, 13-22
W. Praise the Lord
Psalm 150:1-6
T. Acknowledge God's Faithfulness
Luke 1:67-75
F. Honor God by Your Living
Ephesians 5:1-10
S. Rejoice in the Lord
Philippians 4:4-9

Origin and Nature of Sin

Genesis 2:16-17; 3:9-12; Mark 7:20-23;
Romans 1:21-32; 5:12, 19; 7:18-21; 8:5-8

Unit Theme:
Sin and Holiness

Central Truth:
Sin, manifested in unbelief and disobedience to God, separates us from Him.

Focus:
Identify the sources and essential character of sin and refuse to engage in sinful thoughts and actions.

Context:
Various scriptural texts concerning the sinful nature of humans

Golden Text:
"As by one man's disobedience many were made sinners, so by the obedience of one shall many be made righteous" (Rom. 5:19).

Study Outline:
I. Disobedience to God
   (Gen. 2:16-17; 3:9-12; Rom. 5:12, 19)
II. Rejection of God
   (Rom. 1:21-27; 8:5-8)
III. Obedience to the Sinful Nature
   (Mark 7:20-23; Rom. 1:28-32; 7:18-21)

INTRODUCTION

The Christian understanding of sin powerfully describes the destructive side of human behavior. In this lesson on the origin and nature of sin, we will discover what the Scripture means by sin as a condition of human nature, a condition that humans have from birth. We cannot begin to understand why holiness leads to wholeness unless we first see how the disease of sin destroys us at the core of who we are by dividing us from ourselves, so that we no longer have control, even over our own bodies. In short, sin not only separates us from God but also from ourselves.

As an internal condition that plagues humanity, sin remains bound up with the psychology of human desire. Everyone experiences times when their desires and emotions explode outwardly, carrying them along like an irresistible tidal wave. The problem is not with the presence of desire or emotion, but the fact that human desire and emotion are fundamentally disordered in two ways. First, it is the sense of being misdirected toward the wrong objects. Second is the sense of being out of order or control within the person. The result is that humans find themselves led by their own desire and emotions into behaviors that are ultimately self-destructive.

Since all humans are plagued with the "desiring disease," all humans experience sin as an internal condition—all humans are sinners. Sin is "natural" to humans not because God created humans as sinners, but because they are now born with an innate disease. Scriptural writers use different metaphors to convey how all humans are born with a sinful condition, yet this condition is not what God had intended for them. Understanding sin as a disease from which humans must be delivered helps to balance the fact that this condition is part of human life while also affirming that it is really alien to human life.

I. DISOBEDIENCE TO GOD (Gen. 2:16-17; 3:9-12; Rom. 5:12, 19)

A. The Commandment and Its Purpose (Gen. 2:16-17)

16. And the Lord God commanded the man, saying, Of every tree of the garden thou mayest freely eat:

17. But of the tree of the knowledge of good and evil, thou shalt not eat of it: for in the day that thou eatest thereof thou shalt surely die.

To understand the commandment given to Adam and Eve and its purpose, we need to get a sense of what the original humans were like. First, it is clear that God created them fundamentally good, which means they were free from sin because they were innocent. This innocence does not imply that they were complete or that they could not grow and develop. To conceive of Adam and Eve as perfect, having already obtained all that God had for them, is to misunderstand a crucial part of the story. God wanted Adam and Eve to grow in their relationship with Him, which suggests that the prohibition against eating of the tree was not an arbitrary commandment, but the means by which they were to mature. This way of understanding the story corresponds to Jesus, the Second Adam, who, the writer of Hebrews declares, "learned obedience from what he suffered," so that he could be "made perfect" (5:8-9 NIV). If Jesus was perfected through a process of learning obedience, then it seems that God intended the same for Adam and Eve. Consequently, obedience to the divine commandment was designed to propel a process of growth and development that culminated in eternal life.

Another dimension to the story is the nature of the Tree of Knowledge of Good and Evil. Once we understand the purpose of the commandment as involving moral growth, we can see that the tree symbolized the wrong way to pursue knowledge of good and evil. In an important sense, the original humans already possessed knowledge of good and evil. They knew that to obey God's commandment was goodness and life, and disobeying the commandment was evil and death. The purpose of the tree was not to give knowledge that Adam and Eve did not possess at all, but it did offer a way of obtaining knowledge that was unacceptable to God. God did not want the original humans to come to know evil by experiencing its effects, in the same way that parents would prefer that their children not know the evil of addiction by ingesting a narcotic.

We can now bring together these two lines of thought to complete our picture of the commandment and its purpose. The beauty of holiness is what emerges from a process of learning obedience, even for the original humans, just as it did for Jesus, who was "in all points tempted like as we are, yet without sin" (Heb. 4:15). This is why God placed the Tree of Knowledge of

Talk About It:
1. What freedom was Adam given (v. 16)?
2. What restriction was given to him, and why (v. 17)?

Good and Evil in Eden at the outset. God knew that Adam and Eve needed to grow into perfection through a process of obedience. Like any good parent, God wanted to keep them from having to suffer in order to understand what was good and what was evil. To eat of the Tree of Knowledge of Good and Evil was to die and thus to understand through experience that evil brings death.

B. Awakening to Sin (3:9-12)

9. And the Lord God called unto Adam, and said unto him, Where art thou?

10. And he said, I heard thy voice in the garden, and I was afraid, because I was naked; and I hid myself.

11. And he said, Who told thee that thou wast naked? Hast thou eaten of the tree, whereof I commanded thee that thou shouldest not eat?

12. And the man said, The woman whom thou gavest to be with me, she gave me of the tree, and I did eat.

As a result of the transgression, Adam and Eve became experientially aware of themselves as sinners. This awareness was connected to their awakening to their sexual identities, and the sense of shame they attached to this awareness. This part of the story provides a clue as to how sin emerges as a condition of human existence. Sin gains a foothold through desires, especially those connected to the body. The serpent appealed to Eve's drive to eat by highlighting the pleasant appearance of the fruit and implying that it would taste good as well. Eve is faced with a choice between a desire for the fruit and a desire to obey God's will, but the desire for the fruit is connected to her bodily appetites. Likewise, when she and Adam "awaken" to their bodies, it may be because they were beginning to experience their own sexual desires in a way that they could not control.

We see here how the original humans became fallen creatures. By surrendering to their own bodily desires, they actually lost control of those desires. This is the death that they experienced. Death is about disintegration physically and spiritually. The beginning of that disintegration is when our bodies no longer work with us, but against us. Once Adam and Eve severed the relationship with God, they also severed the natural relationship with their own bodies. They experienced sexual desires and other kinds of desires uncontrollably. They no longer owned themselves, but they became slaves of these disordered desires.

C. The Reign of Sin (Rom. 5:12, 19)

12. Wherefore, as by one man sin entered into the world, and death by sin; and so death passed upon all men, for that all have sinned.

Talk About It:
1. Why did God ask the question in verse 9?
2. What emotions was Adam experiencing (v. 10)?
3. How truthful was Adam's response in verse 12?

Origin and Nature of Sin

19. For as by one man's disobedience many were made sinners, so by the obedience of one shall many be made righteous.

When Paul describes how sin enters the world, he is not referring to sinful actions, but to a condition that emerges within humanity from the disobedience of the original humans. God designed the original humans as a unified whole, consisting of souls in bodies united to God through His own breath (the Spirit). Given that the basic meaning of *integrity* is "wholeness," we can see that the original humans had a kind of integrity. They functioned as unified wholes with body and soul working together in the Spirit. When they disobeyed God, they lost their integrity in that they were no longer unified wholes.

For Paul, death is a power that now grips all human beings. He goes on to say, "sin exercised dominion in death" (Rom. 5:21 NRSV). Humans now experience life in a state of disintegration and decay because they are in the grips of death. Their bodily desires and passions now work against them. This is what it means to possess a sinful nature or to experience sin as a condition. Every human being has experienced desires and emotions that pull them down self-destructive paths. We might consider what happens when we place ourselves on a diet to lose weight. There are moments, like when we see a sumptuous piece of chocolate, where our internal desires work against us. If we add emotions to these desires, like feeling depressed over a situation, then the desire for chocolate can turn into an intense craving where we not only want to taste the sweetness but to bring emotional comfort. In that moment, we are divided against ourselves with our desire to eat chocolate in competition with our desire to lose weight. This competition results from the disintegration of our lives; we are in the grips of death's decaying power. Humans were made sinners in the sense that they lost their fundamental integrity and became slaves of sin and death as a result.

Our only hope comes "through the obedience of the One" (v. 19 NASB)—Jesus Christ—who lived a sinless life and can therefore make us "righteous."

II. REJECTION OF GOD (Rom. 1:21-27; 8:5-8)
A. The Cascading Effect of Sin (1:21-27)
   (Romans 1:22-23, 25-27 is not included in the printed text.)
   21. Because that, when they knew God, they glorified him not as God, neither were thankful; but became vain in their imaginations, and their foolish heart was darkened.
   24. Wherefore God also gave them up to uncleanness through the lusts of their own hearts, to dishonour their own bodies between themselves.

Talk About It:
1. Can we rightly blame "one man" for our sin predicament (v. 12)?
2. Describe the grace we can receive (v. 19).

"Does discovering who you are awaken a kind of inner unrest? . . . If you started accusing yourself of all that is in you, would your nights and days be long enough?"
—Brother Roger of Taize

Talk About It:
1. What is the danger of thanklessness (v. 21)?
2. Explain the two foolish "exchanges" in verse 25.
3. Explain the two uses of the phrase "God gave them over" (vv. 24, 26 NIV).
4. How do verses 26 and 27 describe homosexuality?

> "Satan does not here fill us with hatred of God, but with forgetfulness of God."
> —Dietrich Bonhoeffer

Talk About It:
1. What does it mean to "mind the things of the flesh" (v. 5)?
2. Contrast the spiritually minded person with the carnally minded (v. 6).
3. Who "cannot please God" (v. 8)?

In the opening chapter of Romans, Paul provides his own twist to the Genesis narrative. For Paul, sin as a condition emerges from the initial turn away from God. In the words of Pauline scholar James Dunn, misdirected religion produces sinful existence (*Theology of Paul the Apostle*). The fundamental failure of human beings is really twofold: (1) They do not really understand that they are creatures, and (2) they do not understand their need for God as creatures. Failure to honor God is really a failure to recognize one's status as a creature. Because they are created, humans cannot sustain their own existence: they cannot make themselves impervious to life's forces, and they certainly cannot escape the transitory nature of life on Planet Earth. To become "vain" (v. 21)—"futile" or "empty"—in one's thinking is to turn toward the rest of creation to handle life. This is fundamentally what idolatry is: thinking that some aspect of the created order (which will ultimately pass away) can enable one to overcome all of life's demands. How can anything that passes away help one to deal with life in its complexities?

This kind of wisdom—which claims humans need to build a better society in order to conquer life's forces, or that humans need to discover a fountain of youth, or that any dimension of creation can stabilize human life and make it meaningful—is "foolish" (v. 22). It is to exchange the stability from the infinite God for the instability of the creature.

What is the effect of turning away from God? In verses 24-27, Paul indicates that God "gives over" human beings to their own "lusts." The term *lust* denotes a strong desire or craving. God turns humans over to their own bodily cravings to be led about by those desires wherever they might lead. The judgment is that they lead to self-destruction.

B. Life in the Flesh (8:5-8)

5. For they that are after the flesh do mind the things of the flesh; but they that are after the Spirit the things of the Spirit.

6. For to be carnally minded is death; but to be spiritually minded is life and peace.

7. Because the carnal mind is enmity against God: for it is not subject to the law of God, neither indeed can be.

8. So then they that are in the flesh cannot please God.

Paul's use of the term *flesh* to describe the sinful condition of humanity is, at times, difficult to understand. It is clear that Paul is not denigrating the human body. The problem of sin is not reducible to possessing a body so that if we simply got rid of our bodies we would no longer be sinful. The human body is good because God originally gave humans bodies and because God plans to resurrect human bodies.

Origin and Nature of Sin

The term *flesh* is Paul's way of capturing the close connection between sinful existence and disordered desires and emotions. A disordered desire is one that is not directed toward the right object or that is out of control. When humans fail to direct their desires to the right object, or when they fail to bring order to their desires, then those desires become self-destructive forces.

Walking "according to the flesh" (vv. 4-5 NKJV) is about following the path of sinful desires. These desires alter human thinking so that the mind is in a position of hostility toward God. By "enmity" (v. 7), Paul does not necessarily mean direct hostility toward God, but the way in which human desire is always directed away from God toward some aspect of creation as the solution to life's problems. The thinking that emerges from bodily desires controlling human behavior leads to death because it takes the person down dead-end roads that ultimately disintegrate and destroy the person.

> "You'll never be able to speak against sin if you're entertained by it."
> —**John Muncee**

III. OBEDIENCE TO THE SINFUL NATURE (Mark 7:20-23; Rom. 1:28-32; 7:18-21)

A. The Source of Sinful Behavior (Mark 7:20-23)

20. And he said, That which cometh out of the man, that defileth the man.

21. For from within, out of the heart of men, proceed evil thoughts, adulteries, fornications, murders,

22. Thefts, covetousness, wickedness, deceit, lasciviousness, an evil eye, blasphemy, pride, foolishness:

23. All these evil things come from within, and defile the man.

In the course of a lengthy discussion of ceremonial cleanness, Jesus gets to the "heart" of the matter. The problem does not reside in regulating one's diet or in abiding by restrictions so as to avoid ceremonial uncleanness, but in the human heart. As Jesus proclaimed, food does not alter the behavior of a person (vv. 19-20). It is the heart, not the stomach, that determines human behavior.

In Jewish thinking, the term *heart* became a metaphor for the central part of human person where thinking and desire come together and are mutually shaped by one another. It is important to note that "evil thoughts" (alternatively "designs" or "schemes") is the overarching description so that adulteries, fornications, and so on, are simply these schemes in practice or drives connected to these schemes. Jesus indicates that evil emerges at the intersection of thoughts, desires, and emotions, that is, from within the "heart" of the individual.

Talk About It:
1. What makes a person spiritually unclean (v. 20)?
2. How are all the evils in verses 21-22 similar (v. 23)?

> "O miserable man, what a deformed monster sin has made you! God made you 'little lower than the angels' (Ps. 8:5); sin has made you little better than the devils."
> —**Joseph Alleine**

B. Debased Thinking (Rom. 1:28-32)

28. And even as they did not like to retain God in their knowledge, God gave them over to a reprobate mind, to do those things which are not convenient;

not convenient (v. 28)—"improper conduct" (RSV)

29. Being filled with all unrighteousness, fornication, wickedness, covetousness, maliciousness; full of envy, murder, debate, deceit, malignity; whisperers,

30. Backbiters, haters of God, despiteful, proud, boasters, inventors of evil things, disobedient to parents,

31. Without understanding, covenantbreakers, without natural affection, implacable, unmerciful:

32. Who knowing the judgment of God, that they which commit such things are worthy of death, not only do the same, but have pleasure in them that do them.

Some people wonder how we can reconcile God's love with God's wrath, especially given that Paul seems to be able to hold the two in tension. What does it mean to be under God's wrath when God is "not willing that any should perish" (2 Peter 3:9) precisely because "God so loved the world" (John 3:16)?

At the end of the opening chapter of Romans, Paul provides a clue when he claims that God "gave them up," or "handed them over" (see vv. 24, 26, 28). It is an act of divine judgment to be "handed over" by God to the powers of sin and death. Notice the play on words in verse 28. Because humans did not acknowledge God with their minds, God "gave them over" to the kind of debased thinking they did acknowledge. This debased thinking is closely connected to God giving humans up to the "lusts of their . . . hearts" (v. 24) and their "degrading passions" (v. 26 NASB), which Paul then provides a concrete list of in verses 29-31.

Divine wrath is expressed in God's surrendering humans to the slavery of their own sinful passions. These sinful desires distort human thinking and lead it down destructive paths. Consequently, while God deeply loves humanity and is unwilling that any should perish, God also judges by turning people over to what they really want even if, at the end of the day, what they want brings death. It is God's way of saying, "If this is what you really want, then I'm going to let you have it along with all of its consequences."

C. The Desiring Disease (7:18-21)

18. For I know that in me (that is, in my flesh,) dwelleth no good thing: for to will is present with me; but how to perform that which is good I find not.

19. For the good that I would I do not: but the evil which I would not, that I do.

20. Now if I do that I would not, it is no more I that do it, but sin that dwelleth in me.

21. I find then a law, that, when I would do good, evil is present with me.

When we think about original sin as an inherited condition, we need to consider it as a defect or a disease that prevents human beings from functioning as God intended. It is no mistake that, in Romans 7:7-12, Paul picks "You shall not covet" as his example

---

Talk About It:
1. What is a "reprobate mind" (v. 28)?
2. How did the knowledge of these sinful people affect their actions (v. 32)?

"The deadliest sin is the consciousness of no sin."
—Thomas Carlyle

Talk About It:
What dilemma did Paul face?

Origin and Nature of Sin

from the Ten Commandments. *Covetousness* refers to excessive desire, or desire that is out of control and thus disordered. Sinful existence is the desiring disease in which humans are enslaved to their own self-destructive cravings and emotions.

For Paul, it is disordered desire that carries people away and prevents them from obeying God's law. These disordered or sinful desires bring with them a kind of captivity because they compel people to engage in behavior they later regret.

There is usually a moment in the life of every person when they look at themselves in the mirror and wonder why they behaved in a particular way. What accompanies this glance are thoughts of how foolish or destructive the behavior was, but generally there is a sense of disbelief: "Why did I do that?" The sense of disbelief stems from the surprise that people have when they realize their desires and emotions have caused them to engage in a behavior that they normally would not do. This surprise is expressed in a form similar to, "I did not intend to spend $150 for that outfit, but I just got carried away." How many times do we find another law at work in our members, sweeping us up in its wake and compelling us to do something we later regret?

> "Brethren, it is easier to declaim against a thousand sins of others, than to mortify one sin in ourselves."
> —John Flavel

CONCLUSION

The sin of the original humans was the misdirecting of their own bodily desires away from God and toward the fruit that brought an experiential awareness of good and evil. From that moment, humans became divided from themselves and entered into a process of disintegration. They lost their integrity so that they no longer functioned as whole individuals.

This loss of integrity is on display by the way in which humans are now captives to their own disordered desires and emotions. When they turned their back on God, God "gave them up" to these desires and passions that ultimately culminate in death. The lie of the Enemy is that by "going it alone" humans could take control of their lives. Precisely the opposite is the case. When humans disobey God, they find that their own desires and emotions no longer obey them. They lose control rather than gain it.

GOLDEN TEXT CHALLENGE

"AS BY ONE MAN'S DISOBEDIENCE MANY WERE MADE SINNERS, SO BY THE OBEDIENCE OF ONE SHALL MANY BE MADE RIGHTEOUS" (Rom. 5:19).

Sin, in the course of the ages since Adam, has multiplied, abounded, exceeded, and overflowed. There are many instances of this in the history of man. The abundance of sin occasioned the Flood. The exceeding sinfulness of Sodom brought the overthrow of the cities of the plain. The sins of Israel brought the captivity of God's people.

As for the Gentile world, Paul, in the beginning of his epistle to the Romans, defined the crimes, vices, and horrible sins of the nations in such an appalling manner that we do not wonder at his denunciation of such practices as he told of the wrath of God against those who do such things.

Humanity's sin culminated when it brought the Lord Jesus Christ to the cross. The crucifixion of Christ shows the exceeding sinfulness of sin. The greatness of the ransom paid proved the terrible nature of the captivity from which men could only at such a price be delivered.

Origin and Nature of Sin

Consequences of Sin

Genesis 3:8-24; Ecclesiastes 12:13-14; Matthew 25:31-46;
Luke 16:22-25; Romans 6:23; 8:20-23; Ephesians 2:1-12; 4:18-19;
Revelation 20:11 through 21:8

INTRODUCTION

By their sin, the original humans unleashed a flurry of forces into the creation that produce slavery and ultimately lead to destruction. Humans experience this slavery whenever their desires and emotions lead them down self-destructive paths. They also experience this slavery when cultural and familial forces infect them through coercive influence with dysfunctional behaviors. Whoever said sin is "fun" lied, because it is never fun to deal with the way our own behaviors keep us from experiencing the fullness of life.

Behind these forces stands the devil, the serpent who participated in the overthrow of Adam and Eve, and who still seeks to destroy humanity. It is for the devil and all of the forces aligned with him that final destruction is intended. God has never desired, nor does He now desire, to send anyone to final destruction. Instead, God's purpose for humanity remains the same: to enable people to share in His own life and thus experience eternal life. It is only those who reject His offer of life that God "turns over" to final judgment.

By realizing that hell was never prepared for humanity, we can see that the severity of divine judgment stems from the depths of divine love, not divine wrath. God's warnings are the warnings of a parent who wants the best for his or her children. They are meant to keep us from destruction, not to send us there. In addition, they are grounded in the recognition that even now people experience the dominion of destruction that ends with eternal death. While God will honor the choices we make, He wants to alert us that deadly choices can be defeated. The "threats" of divine judgment are God's "early warning" signals to awaken us to the forces arrayed against us and turn us to the deliverance He offers.

Unit Theme:
Sin and Holiness

Central Truth:
Sin brings terrible consequences.

Focus:
Realize the fearful consequences of sin and commit to a life of holiness by faith in Jesus Christ.

Context:
Scripture passages warning about the consequences of sin

Golden Text:
"The wages of sin is death; but the gift of God is eternal life through Jesus Christ our Lord" (Rom. 6:23).

Study Outline:
I. Alienation From God (Gen. 3:8, 22-24; Eph. 2:1-3, 12; 4:18-19)
II. Suffering and Death (Gen. 3:16-19; Rom. 6:23; 8:20-23)
III. Retribution in the Afterlife (Eccl. 12:13-14; Luke 16:22-25; Matt. 25:31-32, 34, 41, 46; Rev. 21:8)

I. ALIENATION FROM GOD (Gen. 3:8, 22-24; Eph. 2:1-3, 12; 4:18-19)

A. Exiled From God's Presence (Gen. 3:8, 22-24)

8. And they heard the voice of the Lord God walking in the garden in the cool of the day: and Adam and his wife hid themselves from the presence of the Lord God amongst the trees of the garden.

22. And the Lord God said, Behold, the man is become as one of us, to know good and evil: and now, lest he put forth his hand, and take also of the tree of life, and eat, and live for ever:

23. Therefore the Lord God sent him forth from the garden of Eden, to till the ground from whence he was taken.

24. So he drove out the man; and he placed at the east of the garden of Eden Cherubims, and a flaming sword which turned every way, to keep the way of the tree of life.

Talk About It:
1. What is ridiculous about this scene (v. 8)?
2. Explain the phrase "is become as one of us" (v. 22).
3. How was God's judgment also an act of grace (vv. 22-24)?

Adam and Eve hid themselves from God for two reasons: (1) a newfound awareness of their sexual identities and (2) an awareness that they had violated the divine commandment. God's immediate response to Adam's realization of his nakedness was to inquire as to how Adam had come to this new knowledge (vv. 10-11). Adam's answer was to play the victim who had been led astray by his wife. Eve, in turn, claimed that she was victimized by the serpent (v. 13). The fact that God cursed the serpent (vv. 14-15) indicates He acknowledged the partial legitimacy of their claims. They were victims of a deception by the serpent, yet, this did not absolve them of complicity in the act of disobedience.

A second dimension of this story is God's acknowledgment that Adam and Eve had indeed gained a kind of knowledge. They had "become as one of us" (v. 22). This statement suggests that obtaining knowledge of good and evil was not the real issue, but the way Adam and Eve had acquired it. It is like a parent saying to a child, "You now know what addiction is like because you've become a drug user." Instead of trying to keep knowledge from humanity, God was trying to keep them from obtaining knowledge in a way that brought about their own destruction.

Through their disobedience Adam and Eve had exiled themselves from God who, in turn, exiled them from the Garden of Eden. Sin creates barriers by separating people from themselves, one another, and their God. Exile is the Old Testament way to signal how deep these divisions run.

God's judgment to exile Adam and Eve from the Garden was the culmination of what had already occurred. This exile was not punishment in the strict sense, but God's effort to restore them ultimately. Centuries later, when Israel's failure to abide by the covenant led God to exile them, His intention was to restore them

"The first chapters of the Bible tell us of the sin of man. The guilt of that sin had rested upon every single one of us, its guilt and

to covenantal relationship (Amos 9:14-15). God longed for Israel to return to Him, and He was willing to cut them off temporarily so they might see their situation more clearly and repent. It is the same with Adam and Eve. No wonder we find the Tree of Life again at the end of Revelation as part of the restoration of all things (22:2). Exile is more a form of discipline than a punishment because its ultimate purpose is to renew the covenant.

B. Exiled in Death (Eph. 2:1-3, 12)

1. And you hath he quickened, who were dead in trespasses and sins:

2. Wherein in time past ye walked according to the course of this world, according to the prince of the power of the air, the spirit that now worketh in the children of disobedience:

3. Among whom also we all had our conversation in times past in the lusts of our flesh, fulfilling the desires of the flesh and of the mind; and were by nature the children of wrath, even as others.

12. That at that time ye were without Christ, being aliens from the commonwealth of Israel, and strangers from the covenants of promise, having no hope, and without God in the world.

Paul uses a number of images to describe what life without Christ is like. He first notes that the Ephesians were "dead in trespasses" (v. 1). The term *death* highlights not only their separation from God, but also the self-destructive and disintegrating nature of this condition. To be dead is to be involved in an unsustainable way of living.

Second, Paul indicates that this death embodies a lifestyle characteristic of the devil, who is the spirit that stands behind the kingdom of darkness. The term *world* can also be translated as *age* (v. 2). It refers to the present evil age, which is shorthand for the kind of life that emerges in separation from God. The devil stands behind this other kingdom in the sense of being its initiator or the captain who propagates it. To say that this "spirit" is at work "in the children of disobedience" is a way of saying the Ephesians formerly belonged to the kingdom of darkness and were guided by its enslaving forces. This does not mean the devil is directly at work in every unbeliever, but that he stands behind all sinful behavior as the one who has orchestrated this life apart from God.

A third aspect of this lifestyle of death is walking in the "desires of the flesh," or following the impulses and imaginations of the flesh (v. 3). This verse characterizes death as being carried out by desires and impulses that fuel imaginative thoughts. Slavery to sin occurs through the intersection of the imagination and desires or impulses.

terrible results. . . . But [the Bible] tells us of something greater still; it tells us of the grace of the offended God."
—J. Gresham Machen

had our conversation (v. 3)—"once conducted ourselves" (NKJV)

Talk About It:
1. Explain the connection between "the course," "the prince," and "the spirit" in verse 2.
2. Explain the phrase "children of wrath" (v. 3).
3. How does verse 12 describe the status of unbelievers?

Our imagination can actually strengthen desires by idealizing activities. Consider how recalling a good meal can make you hunger for it. Sometimes the images are so vivid we can almost "taste" the meal. It heightens our awareness and makes us long to eat some of "Momma's cookin'." For Paul, sinful desires and impulses fuel the imagination, which in turn strengthens those desires. It is how we deceive ourselves into thinking that something will be good for us that is ultimately self-destructive.

In verse 12 Paul describes sin in terms of exile from one another. Gentiles were exiled off from Jews and thus "aliens from the commonwealth." While God had designed the Law for good, it had become a source of division because the Jews were using it as an identity marker that set them off from Gentiles. Gentiles were being called "the Uncircumcision" (v. 11), with the implication that the Law made the Jews better. It is no different than when Americans use the U.S. flag as an identity marker that sets them off from Christians in other countries or when Southerners brag about their heritage as though it makes them better than Northerners. Being American or Southern is not the problem, just like being Jewish was not the problem. The problem stems from the way in which sin can take identity markers and use them to create divisions among people.

> "I am a fallen, lost creature."
> —Samuel Coleridge

C. Exiled to Blindness (4:18-19)

18. Having the understanding darkened, being alienated from the life of God through the ignorance that is in them, because of the blindness of their heart:

19. Who being past feeling have given themselves over unto lasciviousness, to work all uncleanness with greediness.

lasciviousness (v. 19)—"sensuality" (NIV)

Talk About It:
1. Describe the "darkness" of verse 18.
2. What does it mean to be "past feeling" (v. 19)?

Two significant facts are here set forth with respect to the general pattern of sinners' conduct. First, Paul declares that their "understanding" is "darkened." By "understanding," Paul refers to moral insight or perception. The word in the original includes emotions as well as intellect. Elsewhere Paul attributes this moral darkening or blindness to the work of Satan (2 Cor. 4:4); here, he makes people themselves responsible in large measure for their moral blindness.

In the second place, says Paul, sinners walk in darkness because they are "alienated from the life of God." Paul traces humanity's condition back to the Fall. Prior to the Fall, man was a partaker of the light and life of God; as a result of the Fall, it is his nature to walk in darkness, which eventually leads to death. Two other words sum up the results of this alienation: "ignorance," not knowing, literally, agnosticism or wilful ignorance; and "blindness," or hardening of the heart, that is, the faculties of the soul. The latter is a medical term which was used even as early as Hippocrates (born about 400 BC), for callous hardening of the tissues. The word denotes a general loss of sensation.

Consequences of Sin

People of this class have lost all moral sensitivity; they are "past feeling" (v. 19), that is to say, they no longer feel pain by reason of their depravity. Their conscience is seared as with a hot iron (1 Tim. 4:2). They have become shameless and confirmed, as it were, in iniquity, the ultimate result of a long process of hardening. They have become bold and reckless in their wickedness. They have, as Romans 1:21-24 bears out, resigned themselves to unbridled lust, even to unnatural practices. They major in moral uncleanness.

II. SUFFERING AND DEATH (Gen. 3:16-19; Rom. 6:23; 8:20-23)
A. The Breakdown of God's Shalom (Gen. 3:16-19)

16. Unto the woman he said, I will greatly multiply thy sorrow and thy conception; in sorrow thou shalt bring forth children; and thy desire shall be to thy husband, and he shall rule over thee.

17. And unto Adam he said, Because thou hast hearkened unto the voice of thy wife, and hast eaten of the tree, of which I commanded thee, saying, Thou shalt not eat of it: cursed is the ground for thy sake; in sorrow shalt thou eat of it all the days of thy life;

18. Thorns also and thistles shall it bring forth to thee; and thou shalt eat the herb of the field;

19. In the sweat of thy face shalt thou eat bread, till thou return unto the ground; for out of it wast thou taken: for dust thou art, and unto dust shalt thou return.

To understand the point of God's judgment, we need to see the Genesis story from another angle. The role of the serpent illustrates the social context of sin. One cannot understand the complex way sin infiltrates human existence without recognizing how it trades on the relational dimension of life and breaks it down. God had designed humans for relationship with Himself by making them in His image (1:26-27), and for relationship with one another by making Eve part of Adam and thus Adam part of Eve (2:21-24). The serpent's deception traded partly on the relational connection as a point of influence and a kind of peer pressure. People rarely sin in a vacuum, and Adam and Eve are no exception. The serpent used the relationship Adam and Eve had with one another and with the animals in his favor.

Because the serpent successfully abused the relational dimension of human existence, God directed His judgment against this aspect of human life. Sin gains power from the relational connection, not to foster it but to break it down. As Cornelius Plantinga puts it, sin is vandalism of God's shalom (*Not the Way It's Supposed to Be: A Breviary of Sin*). When one examines Genesis 1 and 2, it is clear that God has created a world in harmony. In the first chapter, God arranges everything to create a kind of harmony and

Talk About It:
1. Describe the curse placed on woman (v. 16).
2. Describe the curse on man (vv. 17-19).

SHALOM
PEACE

symmetry. This purpose continues with the creation of humankind in which Adam and Eve are designed to live in relational harmony with themselves and their environment. This is what *shalom* is. It is peace in the sense of wholeness, integrity, and harmony. It is not simply the absence of war, but life in its fullness—a harmonious existence with God, humanity, and the environment. God's judgment was simply an extension of the way the acts of disobedience had violated His shalom.

When God cursed the ground and the serpent, one can see how this curse embodied the divisions that had already opened up between Adam and Eve, and between both of them and the serpent. If shalom is harmony—the result of God bringing order out of chaos—then sin involves the fundamental breakdown of that harmony and the return to chaos. Adam and Eve blaming one another was the first manifestation of the breakdown in relational harmony. God's judgment was that marital harmony would now be governed by the husband dominating the wife rather than mutual submission and love, which Christ would later restore (cf. Eph. 5:21-33). Likewise, God's judgment on Adam and the serpent both represent the breakdown in the fundamental harmony between humans and creation as a whole. The earth will no longer work in harmony with Adam, and enmity will exist between various parts of God's creation.

When Isaiah envisions a restored creation, he sees a world in which wolves and lambs lie down together with children guiding them (Isa. 11:6). This is the restoration of God's shalom—a relational harmony in which humans, animals, the natural world, and God all live together at peace. If this is what life should be like, we can begin to see what is wrong. Sin ultimately breaks apart relationships so that the horizontal and vertical dimensions of human existence are severed.

Sin Pollutes

To pollute or contaminate the environment, a foreign element must be introduced into the environment that harms it and keeps it from operating the way it should. Sin pollutes, causing us to contaminate others. Ultimately, it is a pollution that brings death and stems from the original polluter: the devil himself. While this pollution breaks down God's shalom, one day God will judge it with fire so that its destructive force will never again violate His creation.

Talk About It:
1. Contrast "the wages" we've earned with "the gift" we're offered (6:23).
2. How has creation been harmed by sin (8:20-21)?
3. Explain the groans mentioned in verses 22 and 23.
4. What are "the first-fruits of the Spirit" (v. 23)?

B. Death Results From Violating Shalom (Rom. 6:23; 8:20-23)
(Romans 8:20-23 is not included in the printed text.)

6:23. For the wages of sin is death; but the gift of God is eternal life through Jesus Christ our Lord.

While Paul described sin as death in Ephesians 2, in Romans he indicates that sin culminates in death. This is simply another way of describing the outcome of a sinful way of living, which is the disintegration of the self. Eventually bodies that are buried disintegrate and return to dust. What happens with physical death provides a window into what happens in spiritual death. Sin's wages are the disintegration of society, the human person, and creation as a whole. Sin divides individuals from themselves so that they are double-minded and therefore unstable (James 1:8), divides persons from one another so that they destroy rather than build up (see 4:1), and causes people to destroy the creation.

Consequences of Sin

Humans are incapable of holding their lives together. God's gift of eternal life not only means living forever, but living abundantly. Eternal life is a condition of happiness and stability. This is why all of creation is frustrated and groans for the complete liberty of the sons and daughters of God (Rom. 8:20-23). God's deliverance is a new birth freeing believers from all the corrupting, enslaving forces that lead to death. Evidence of God's redemption is seen in the Spirit-filled lives of His children, who long for the redemption of their bodies.

> "The Christian notion of the possibility of redemption is incomprehensible to the computer."
> —Vance Packard

III. RETRIBUTION IN THE AFTERLIFE (Eccl. 12:13-14; Luke 16:22-25; Matt. 25:31-32, 34, 41, 46; Rev. 21:8)

A. Fear of Judgment (Eccl. 12:13-14)

13. Let us hear the conclusion of the whole matter: Fear God, and keep his commandments: for this is the whole duty of man.

14. For God shall bring every work into judgment, with every secret thing, whether it be good, or whether it be evil.

Prior to writing the conclusion to this book, the author of Ecclesiastes summarized how he had put this literary work together. In an orderly fashion, with the right words, the truth was protected. This emphasizes how his style did not compromise the message. With this brief statement on methodology, he shared his conclusion.

Talk About It:
1. What is the connection between "fear" and "keep" (v. 13)?
2. What is certain about the future (v. 14)?

Living for God includes keeping His commandments. No one can truly fear God and not be actively fulfilling His directives. For the Jews of that day the commandments were not only the Ten Commandments but also all the other commandments in the Book of the Law.

The duty of every person who wants a growing, loving relationship with the heavenly Father is to daily keep His commandments. This concept continues in the New Testament: "For this is the love of God, that we keep his commandments; and his commandments are not grievous" (1 John 5:3).

Living for God means, of necessity, keeping His commandments. Neglect of them or only an occasional observance reflects that a person has not made a true commitment to be a follower.

"Judgment" (Eccl. 12:14) initially needs to be understood as an evaluation. Then, on the basis of the evaluation, reward or punishment is merited. This is how God deals with every person. The actions of each of us will be reviewed on the basis of our total work, even those things which have been kept hidden from everyone. God takes into consideration all our works, all our attitudes, and all our thoughts. For that very reason, our daily lifestyle should carefully reflect what we believe and the relationship we claim with God.

Talk About It:
1. Describe the beggar's new existence (vv. 22, 25).
2. Describe the rich man's new existence (vv. 23-24).

A life of wisdom expects that God will evaluate all we do. Wisdom causes us to live each day carefully and to be pleasing to the God we love and serve.

B. A Reversal of Roles (Luke 16:22-25)
(Luke 16:24-25 is not included in the printed text.)
22. And it came to pass, that the beggar died, and was carried by the angels into Abraham's bosom: the rich man also died, and was buried;
23. And in hell he lift up his eyes, being in torments, and seeth Abraham afar off, and Lazarus in his bosom.

The story of the rich man and Lazarus is most likely a parable. There are several pieces of evidence to support this interpretation. First, Jesus' dominant method of teaching was through the use of parables. Second, in the context immediately preceding the story, Jesus gives four parables: (1) the lost sheep (Luke 15:1-7); (2) the lost coin (vv. 8-10); (3) the lost son (vv. 11-32); (4) the unjust steward (16:1-13). Jesus is already utilizing parables to teach in this setting. Finally, Luke describes the Pharisees, who deride Jesus' teaching, as "covetous" (v. 14), or "lovers of money." The reason for the parable is to warn the covetous that there will be a reversal of fortunes between the poor and the wealthy in the afterlife.

In verse 22, the phrase "Abraham's bosom" most likely refers to the gathering of God's people and not a specific location. The term *bosom* literally means "lap," which suggests the intimate association between Abraham and God's people as a whole. After a life of oppressing the poor and living luxuriously, the rich man finds himself experiencing the pain of judgment. Lazarus, conversely, has been gathered to God's people. Jesus is warning the Pharisees that their love of money will cause them to share in the fate of the rich man if they remain unrepentant.

In this parable, the word "hell" (*hades*) referred to the unseen place beyond the grave. However, when Jesus talked about hell, He usually used the term *gehenna* (see Matt. 5:29-30; 10:28; 23:15, 33). Gehenna referred to the trash heap outside of Jerusalem that continually burned. With its continuous fire and rotten foods being consumed by worms, it presented a vivid portrait of hell as the waste dump of the universe.

In Luke 12:5, Jesus teaches that genuine fear should be felt toward the One who has the authority to send persons to this eternal wasteland. Yet, in verses 6 and 7 Jesus juxtaposes fear of God with trust in God to reinforce the point that God values humans more than sparrows and therefore this fear should not be the primary motive in serving God. While those who "waste" their lives will find themselves having to endure what they have created, this is not God's final desire for anyone.

C. Recipients of Everlasting Fire (Matt. 25:31-32, 34, 41, 46)
(Matthew 25:31-32, 46 is not included in the printed text.)

34. Then shall the King say unto them on his right hand, Come, ye blessed of my Father, inherit the kingdom prepared for you from the foundation of the world.

41. Then shall he say also unto them on the left hand, Depart from me, ye cursed, into everlasting fire, prepared for the devil and his angels.

What was implicit in Luke 16 now becomes explicit in Matthew 25. It has never been the purpose of God to destroy humanity. The ultimate purpose of eternal fire is punishment for those angels who fell from heaven and their leader, Lucifer. This speaks loudly against any view of double predestination that would claim God has predestined a portion of the human race for destruction. Before turning to Jesus' warning, it is important to see that this warning must be viewed in light of God's larger purpose, which is that all would receive eternal life. Those human beings who share the fate of the devil and his angelic horde do so because of their own choices.

The warning that God will judge those from the nations that fail to engage in acts of charity is real. This warning focuses on acts of charity in the same way that Luke 16 focuses on exploitation of the poor by the rich. Jesus' teaching here is similar to the two ways Yahweh presents to Israel in Deuteronomy 30:11-20. The sheep represent the way that leads to life, whereas the goats represent the way that leads to destruction. Jesus' final statement is essentially His appeal to choose life (Matt. 25:46).

D. The Second Death (Rev. 21:8)

8. But the fearful, and unbelieving, and the abominable, and murderers, and whoremongers, and sorcerers, and idolaters, and all liars, shall have their part in the lake which burneth with fire and brimstone: which is the second death.

The phrase "second death" is unique to Revelation. It is found in several places as a way to describe final judgment (2:11; 20:6, 14; 21:8). John indicates that the devil, the Beast, and the False Prophet will all be cast into the lake of fire (20:10). In addition, death and hades will be uprooted and cast into the same lake (v. 14). This is John's way of indicating the complete victory over death as the final enemy of God. As a power that grips humanity, death no longer has any sting (1 Cor. 15:26, 54-55). John makes it clear that the second death is for the enemies of God—all of the life-denying forces associated with the devil and his minions. However, he also warns that those who share the characteristics of the devil will also share his fate. To leave no doubt in his readers' minds, John lists the type of people who will face the second death: "The cowardly, the unbelieving, the vile, the murderers, the sexually immoral, those who practice magic arts, the idolaters and all liars" (Rev. 21:8 NIV).

Talk About It:
1. Describe the division in verses 31 and 32.
2. What was done "from the foundation of the world" (v. 34)?
3. What do verses 41 and 46 reveal about hell?

"Nations, like individuals, are subjected to punishments and chastisements in this world."
—**Abraham Lincoln**

Talk About It:
What is "the second death"?

"What more impiety can he avow whose heart rebelleth at God's judgment dread?"
—**Dante (*The Divine Comedy*)**

CONCLUSION

God's purpose for humanity has always remained the same: to give us eternal life. Eternal life is not simply a length of time, but a quality of life. It is a life of wholeness, integrity, and harmony. This is God's desire for the entire created order.

Final judgment is ultimately not for humanity, but the enemies of both God and humanity. God has prepared final judgment for sin, death, the devil, and his angels. However, God will turn over to this judgment all those who choose it over the life that He offers. He says today what He said to Israel: "See, I have set before you today life and good, death and evil. . . . therefore choose life" (Deut. 30:15, 19 NKJV).

GOLDEN TEXT CHALLENGE

"THE WAGES OF SIN IS DEATH; BUT THE GIFT OF GOD IS ETERNAL LIFE THROUGH JESUS CHRIST OUR LORD" (Rom. 6:23).

This verse contrasts the end result of humanity's activity apart from God with the end result of God's activity toward humanity. Apart from God, human activity earns the "wages" of sin. The eventual outcome of those wages is death.

God's desire for all people is the opposite of death; it is eternal life. Eternal life is a "gift" from God. The fuller translation of "gift" could be "grace gift." The concept of grace and gift is of a "favor given to someone undeserving." In light of the undeserving, sinful existence of humanity, God's grace is to those undeserving. The sin of men and women prompts God's grace and gift of eternal life.

Benefits of Salvation From Sin

Romans 5:1 through 6:23

INTRODUCTION

Romans is a rich and dense book that is difficult to understand at times. It is Paul's *magnum opus* in which he attempts to set forth in a systematic way his own views on Christianity and what it is that God has achieved in Christ and the Spirit. As difficult as understanding Paul's inspired thought might be at times, the payoff is worth the effort.

In this lesson, we will especially focus on the doctrine of justification by faith. Justification is God's way of setting a world right that had gone very wrong. This is part of what salvation entails. It presupposes that something has happened to humanity from which it must be delivered. The doctrine of justification is one way Paul attempts to articulate that deliverance.

To understand what Paul does and does not mean by *justification,* we need to move beyond the idea that it is purely a declarative act in which God "counts" believers as righteous by attributing the righteousness of Christ to them. This does not mean there is no declarative dimension to justification. On the contrary, part of setting right what went wrong involves the forgiveness of sins that brings reconciliation and makes people members of God's covenant family. God declares that all those who are in Christ Jesus are His sons and daughters.

We cannot grasp the full benefits of salvation until we understand *how* God sets things right. This setting right, or rectification, concerns the liberation of individuals from sin and death through the power of the Spirit who extends the life of Christ to all those who believe. As believers participate in Christ's death, they receive His life—a new life that makes them overcomers. This life does not merely secure a place in heaven, but it brings about abundant living even now because it frees believers from the law of sin and death.

Unit Theme:
Sin and Holiness

Central Truth:
The redemptive work of Christ saves from sin and provides many benefits.

Focus:
Consider the benefits of salvation and rejoice in Christ's provision.

Context:
Probably written in AD 58, Paul's letter to the Romans was sent from Corinth.

Golden Text:
"But now being made free from sin, and become servants to God, ye have your fruit unto holiness, and the end everlasting life" (Rom. 6:22).

Study Outline:
I. Peace With God (Rom. 5:1-11)
II. Life Through Christ (Rom. 5:12-21)
III. Freedom From Sin (Rom. 6:1-7, 11-13, 22-23)

I. PEACE WITH GOD (Rom. 5:1-11)

A. When God Sets Things Right (vv. 1-6)

(Romans 5:2-5 is not included in the printed text.)

1. Therefore being justified by faith, we have peace with God through our Lord Jesus Christ.

6. For when we were yet without strength, in due time Christ died for the ungodly.

Paul begins Romans 5 with a summary of what he had discussed in the previous two chapters. The phrase "being justified by faith" signals a key term in Paul's argument—justification—that has been the subject of much controversy in the history of Christianity. One of the issues is over translation because the Greek verb is the same as the noun translated as "righteousness." It is better to translate "to justify" either as "to set right" or "to rectify," both of which have been suggested by modern commentators (Robert Jewett, *Romans*; J. Louis Martyn, *Theological Issues in the Letters of Paul*). Believers are set right by faith.

With this translation, Paul's argument in the opening chapters of Romans comes into focus. The Gospel message of which Paul is "not ashamed" is that God's power is at work to bring salvation precisely because God's own righteousness has set things right (1:16-17). God's righteousness or uprightness is expressed in His covenant faithfulness. As Paul notes in 3:22, God reveals His righteousness through the "faithfulness of Jesus for all who believe" (author's translation). John Nelson Darby's translation refers to the "righteousness of God by faith of Jesus Christ towards all, and upon all those who believe: for there is no difference." Paul's point is that the faithfulness of Jesus manifests the righteousness of God because it is the expression of God's covenant faithfulness.

God's response to the unfaithfulness and sinfulness of humanity that Paul outlines in Romans 1:18—3:20 is to set things right through the faithfulness of Jesus. In 3:24-25 Paul spells out how this occurs, which can be translated, "Being set right undeservedly as a result of His grace through redemption in Christ Jesus, whom God put forward as an atoning sacrifice through [Jesus'] faithfulness by His blood to prove His righteousness." The term *redemption* points back toward God's liberation of Israel from Egypt in the Exodus. Paul is signaling that a new exodus has occurred in and through Christ. Part of this new exodus involves removing the guilt that keeps humans from relationship with God, which is why Paul uses the term "atoning sacrifice" ("propitiation," v. 25). The proof that God has set things right is in Jesus' own faithfulness to liberate humanity from sin, death, and the devil through His sacrifice on the cross. As Romans 5:6 declares, "At just the right time, when we were still powerless, Christ died for the ungodly" (NIV).

Talk About It:
1. What does it mean to be "justified" (v. 1)?
2. What access does faith give us (v. 2)?
3. Why can we "rejoice in our sufferings" (vv. 3-4 NIV)?
4. What will "not disappoint us" (v. 5 NIV)?

Near-Death Experience

Those who have a near-death experience feel like they have been given a new lease on life. Sometimes it takes a close encounter with death to realize how precious a gift our biological life really is. Usually, the person begins to see the

---

Benefits of Salvation From Sin

Personal trust in what God is doing in Christ is required for anyone to participate in God's setting things right. "We have access by faith into this grace" (v. 2) by which we stand in the liberating power of God's Spirit in which our sins are forgiven and the grip of the sinful nature is broken.

When we experience suffering we can rejoice because we are trusting in the providence of the God who sets things right. "We know that suffering produces perseverance; perseverance, character; and character, hope" (vv. 3-4 NIV). This hope "does not disappoint, because the love of God has been poured out within our hearts through the Holy Spirit who was given to us" (v. 5 NASB). The Spirit is the liberating power of love saturating the heart of believers to break the power of sin. Our hope is grounded in the liberating activities of Christ and the Spirit, through whom the power of God sets things right.

B. Reconciliation With God (vv. 7-11)

7. For scarcely for a righteous man will one die: yet peradventure for a good man some would even dare to die.

8. But God commendeth his love toward us, in that, while we were yet sinners, Christ died for us.

9. Much more then, being now justified by his blood, we shall be saved from wrath through him.

10. For if, when we were enemies, we were reconciled to God by the death of his Son, much more, being reconciled, we shall be saved by his life.

11. And not only so, but we also joy in God through our Lord Jesus Christ, by whom we have now received the atonement.

The point that Paul sets forth in verse 1, of having peace with God, is elaborated on by the concept of reconciliation. *Reconciliation* implies an enmity with God, indeed, an outright rebellion which needs to be overcome. The intensity of God's love revealed itself when Jesus died to liberate rebellious humanity from slavery to sin and death. Humans were hostile to God, which makes the loving grace displayed through Christ's death all the more amazing. It is a love that refuses to allow humans to die in sin, even when they seem to want to do just that.

Those who exercise faith in Christ are reconciled to God. This is part of the way God sets things right. He restores broken relationships. The covenant faithfulness of God is His acting rightly or keeping the faith in the midst of human unfaithfulness. By their faith in God's actions, which comes about as the Spirit enables individuals to see the depths of God's love for them, they are forgiven of their sins and reconciled. In short, they have peace with God.

world in a different way and changes their behavior accordingly. Paul wants believers to understand how precious the gift of new life in Christ really is. It is an utterly gracious new lease on life that God gives to us by liberating us from the forces of sin and death. Indeed, if we walk by God's Spirit, we will experience life in all of its abundance.

Talk About It:
1. What "scarcely" happens (v. 7)?
2. What is the greatest evidence of God's love (v. 8)?
3. What does it mean to be "saved from wrath" (v. 9)?
4. What is "the atonement" (v. 11)?

The cause for rejoicing (v. 11) is connected not simply to the reconciliation received, but also the ongoing salvation through the life of Jesus (v. 10). The verb is future tense: "we shall be saved by his life." Setting things right involves the ongoing participation in the power of the life of the risen Lord. God is sharing His life with believers to liberate them from sin and death. Romans 8:11 connects the power of this life to the Spirit. God gives life to "mortal bodies" through the same Spirit who gave life to Jesus' crucified body. It is the quickening power of God's own life poured out on the cross and into believers through Christ and the Spirit that will save as we continuously receive this life by faith.

II. LIFE THROUGH CHRIST (Rom. 5:12-21)
A. The Reign of Death (vv. 12-16)
(Romans 5:13-14, 16 is not included in the printed text.)
12. Wherefore, as by one man sin entered into the world, and death by sin; and so death passed upon all men, for that all have sinned.

15. But not as the offence, so also is the free gift. For if through the offence of one many be dead, much more the grace of God, and the gift by grace, which is by one man, Jesus Christ, hath abounded unto many.

Paul contrasts the faithfulness of Jesus, which brings about liberation, with the unfaithfulness of Adam. This allows Paul to discuss in greater detail both the problem and the solution to the plight of humanity. Adam's transgression or act of disobedience unleashed a flurry of negative forces on the human race. However, Paul notes that "death reigned from Adam to Moses, even over those who had not sinned according to the likeness of the transgression of Adam" (v. 14 NKJV). This passage highlights the difference between sin and death as cosmic forces unleashed upon humanity, on the one hand, and transgression as a personal act contrary to God's law, on the other hand. Even those who do not commit the exact sinful act that Adam did still experience the reality of life under the dominion of sin and death.

The world produced by the disobedience of Adam is a world caught in the grip of sin and death. Paul seems to understand death in terms of the disintegrating effects of sinful existence. Sin exercises its reign through the disintegration of the fundamental integrity of humanity. After Adam's disobedience, humans were no longer psychological wholes. Instead, their desires and emotions worked against them, which Paul gives a vivid depiction of in Romans 7. The term *flesh* is Paul's way of identifying what results from the disintegration of the individual. Humans can no longer control their desires and emotions, but are now controlled by them. Paul draws the conclusion that humans, under the sway of death, will sin.

Benefits of Salvation From Sin

B. The Defeat of Death (vv. 17-21)

17. For if by one man's offence death reigned by one; much more they which receive abundance of grace and of the gift of righteousness shall reign in life by one, Jesus Christ.

18. Therefore as by the offence of one judgment came upon all men to condemnation; even so by the righteousness of one the free gift came upon all men unto justification of life.

19. For as by one man's disobedience many were made sinners, so by the obedience of one shall many be made righteous.

20. Moreover the law entered, that the offence might abound. But where sin abounded, grace did much more abound:

21. That as sin hath reigned unto death, even so might grace reign through righteousness unto eternal life by Jesus Christ our Lord.

The contrast between Adam's unfaithfulness and Christ's faithfulness continues to illustrate from another angle the nature of salvation. Paul uses the term *life* three times in this passage (vv. 17-18, 21). Those who participate in the work of Christ by faith receive an uprightness that will "reign in life" (v. 17), receive the rightness that brings life (v. 18), and are now under the dominion of grace through an uprightness that leads to eternal life (v. 21).

The first designation refers to how believers will exercise a victorious reign even now over the powers of sin and death. Through Christ Jesus, God empowers humans to take control of their lives so they are no longer dominated by sinful drives and desires. The phrase translated "justification of life" (v. 18) may be also rendered "rightness that brings life." It refers to how God brings humans into a condition of righteousness that not only gives them life now, but also brings eternal life. This idea connects to the final use of the term in verse 21.

In his translation of these verses, Eugene Peterson summarizes Paul's thought nicely:

> If death got the upper hand through one man's wrongdoing, can you imagine the breathtaking recovery life makes, sovereign life, in those who grasp with both hands this wildly extravagant life-gift, this grand setting-everything-right, that the one man Jesus Christ provides? Here it is in a nutshell: Just as one person did it wrong and got us in all this trouble with sin and death, another person did it right and got us out of it. But more than just getting us out of trouble, he got us into life! (Rom. 5:17-18 TM).

III. FREEDOM FROM SIN (Rom. 6:1-7, 11-13, 22-23)
A. Buried With Him in Death (vv. 1-7)

1. What shall we say then? Shall we continue in sin, that grace may abound?

Talk About It:
1. Why do we need "abundance of grace" (vv. 17, 20)?
2. Contrast the two "reigns" mentioned in verse 21.

"My memory is nearly gone, but I remember two things—that I am a great sinner, and that Christ is a great Savior."
—John Newton

2. God forbid. How shall we, that are dead to sin, live any longer therein?

3. Know ye not, that so many of us as were baptized into Jesus Christ were baptized into his death?

4. Therefore we are buried with him by baptism into death: that like as Christ was raised up from the dead by the glory of the Father, even so we also should walk in newness of life.

5. For if we have been planted together in the likeness of his death, we shall be also in the likeness of his resurrection:

6. Knowing this, that our old man is crucified with him, that the body of sin might be destroyed, that henceforth we should not serve sin.

7. For he that is dead is freed from sin.

Talk About It:
1. What does "God forbid" (vv. 1-2)?
2. What deaths are symbolized by baptism (vv. 3-7)?

The graciousness of God's liberating action in Christ and the Spirit should not be an inducement to sin freely. Paul's emphatic, "God forbid" (v. 2), is his way of exclaiming, "Why would you want to return to Egypt?" It seems strange that someone who has finally achieved freedom and victory would choose to go back into slavery and bondage.

In verse 3, Paul says water baptism is a participation in the death of Christ. The passage highlights an important part of Paul's understanding of salvation. Strictly speaking, Christ does not substitute Himself for the believer. Instead, as Morna Hooker suggests, there is an "interchange" in which the believer and Christ share each other's death and life (*From Adam to Christ: Essays on Paul*). Christ's crucifixion causes Him to share the believer's life under the dominion of sin. As Paul elsewhere writes, "For our sake he made him to be sin who knew no sin, so that in him we might become the righteousness of God" (2 Cor. 5:21 ESV). Christ experiences the full fury of sin and death as hostile forces. His faithfulness causes Him to share even the darkness side of human existence.

The corollary of Christ's participation in sin and death is that those who die with Him and share His death also share His life. For Paul, one's baptism in water most vividly represents this participation in the death of Jesus. In Romans 6:4, Paul uses a compound verb to underscore that in baptism believers are "co-buried" with Christ. It is by participation in the death of Jesus that the grip of sin and death on the believer is broken. This is because sharing Jesus' death also involves sharing His powerful life.

To claim that the "old self" (v. 6 NIV) is crucified with Christ is to claim that the bondage of sin and death was broken decisively in the life of the believer. "For one who has died, has been set free from sin" (v. 7 ESV). All of the forces that gave rise to self-destructive behavior have been stripped of their power. This does not mean they are gone, but that believers are no longer subject to them. All believers have traded their slavery to sin for slavery to Christ.

"I believe I am not mistaken in saying that Christianity is a demanding and serious religion. When it is delivered as easy and amusing, it is another kind of religion altogether."
—Neil Postman

B. Sin No Longer Reigns (vv. 11-13)

11. Likewise reckon ye also yourselves to be dead indeed unto sin, but alive unto God through Jesus Christ our Lord.

12. Let not sin therefore reign in your mortal body, that ye should obey it in the lusts thereof.

13. Neither yield ye your members as instruments of unrighteousness unto sin: but yield yourselves unto God, as those that are alive from the dead, and your members as instruments of righteousness unto God.

If the enslaving power of sin and death have been decisively broken by participation in Christ's death, then Paul can exhort believers not to allow sin to reign anymore. This is Paul's call to live out in one's actions what has occurred. Paul seems to recognize that there are gaps between the experience of the liberating power of the Gospel in an individual's life and his or her lifestyle.

The Roman believers had to once again become convinced of what Christ had done for them. They really had the victory. They really could resist sin. They really could consider sin a dead issue for themselves. However, they had to focus on that victory in their minds. Otherwise their minds would wander where the carnal mind always wanders—back to the slavery of sin. They needed to constantly remind themselves that sin was behind them, the Cross was before them, and the living Christ was beside them. In Romans 8, Paul will spell out how the Spirit, who is the power of the new life of Christ, enables believers to continue to overcome sin in their lives.

Talk About It:
1. What must Christians not let happen (v. 12)?
2. How can we overcome sin (v. 13)?

C. Living as God's Servants (vv. 22-23)

22. But now being made free from sin, and become servants to God, ye have your fruit unto holiness, and the end everlasting life.

23. For the wages of sin is death; but the gift of God is eternal life through Jesus Christ our Lord.

Christians are slaves who have changed masters. They were formerly slaves of sin; now they are set free from sin, but bound in the service of righteousness. The apostle is declaring that Christians in their entirety are bondslaves to righteousness. He illustrates this absolute subjection by reference to the former status under sin, for that, too, was a total bondage.

Paul knows that this parallel has only a limited validity and that it falls short in some respects. To begin with, the difference between the two forms of bond service spoken of is as wide as the heavens. The service of sin is an actual bondage, but the service of righteousness and of God is an actual freedom. Christians live their life on the border between two worlds. They live "in Christ," but they still feel the drag of the flesh. Because of the weakness of the flesh, there is need for such advice that Paul gives.

Talk About It:
1. How are believers both free and in slavery at the same time (v. 22)?
2. Rephrase verse 23 in your own words.

All or Nothing
Christ is a most precious commodity; He is better than rubies or the most costly pearls; and we

must part with our old gold, with our shining gold, our old sins, our most shining sins, or we must perish forever. Christ is to be sought and bought with any pains, at any price; we cannot buy this gold too dear. He is a jewel worth more than a thousand worlds, as we all know who have Him. Get Him, and get all; miss Him and miss all.
—Thomas Brooks

Paul said "the wages of sin is death" (v. 23). The ages have proved the truth of Paul's words. It was death when Adam and Eve were driven from Eden and the mark of mortality was placed on their foreheads. It was death when the floodwaters of God's wrath deluged the earth, destroying every living, breathing thing outside the ark.

The wages of sin is death in our time. It is physical death, mental death, moral death, spiritual death, the second death. However, God's gift of eternal life is available through Jesus Christ our Lord. That means there is a way of escape from the curse, from the condemnation, from the doom, form the damnation of sin. It is a God-promised, a Jesus-provided, a Holy Spirit-proffered way. It is the Bible way, the Gospel way, the way of the Cross, the way of the Blood, the way of Calvary. It cost God all that He was and all that He had, but He offers it freely to all people.

CONCLUSION

Paul construes salvation from sin as God's setting right what went wrong. God sets things right because God remains faithful to His covenant, even in the face of human unfaithfulness and hostility toward Him. God's righteousness is His covenant faithfulness. This faithfulness is expressed in the faithfulness of Jesus, whose life, death, and resurrection sets things right by offering liberation from sin, the flesh, and death to the entire world.

Humans begin to share the liberating power of Christ's own life through the act of faith in which they place their destiny into His hands. As a result of this faith, humans are reconciled to God because their sinful actions are forgiven and the power of sin and death is broken in their lives. They are now reckoned as "right" before God; that is, they are made members of God's covenant family.

Not only do they receive forgiveness and reconciliation with God, but the Holy Spirit pours out God's love into their hearts that increasingly liberates them if they "walk by the Spirit." The Spirit restores a wholeness in which desires and emotions are no longer destructive forces that further disintegrate individuals. Instead, desires and emotions are tamed by the fruit the Spirit produces so believers regain their lives and live as God's servants.

GOLDEN TEXT CHALLENGE

"BUT NOW BEING MADE FREE FROM SIN, AND BECOME SERVANTS TO GOD, YE HAVE YOUR FRUIT UNTO HOLINESS, AND THE END EVERLASTING LIFE" (Rom. 6:22).

Holiness is a fruit, not a root. In other words, the Christian does not become holy in order to receive grace. Rather, because grace is present, holiness is a natural outcome. The root that bears holiness is the presence of grace and the absence of sin.

Holiness is not at the beginning of the Christian life; it is the result of the Christian life. At the beginning, the root of sin is replaced with grace. Sin has died on the cross and grace is in its place. Grace then—through the process of death to sin, something already accomplished on the cross (vv. 1-5)—feeds the believer and produces the "fruit" (v. 22) of holiness.

Daily Devotions:
M. Forgiveness
   Psalm 32:1-11
T. Regeneration
   John 3:1-8
W. Righteousness
   Romans 14:8-17
T. Adoption
   Ephesians 1:2-12
F. Reconciliation
   Colossians
   1:12-23
S. Sanctification
   Hebrews 9:8-14

Living a Sanctified Life

1 John 1:5 through 2:17

Unit Theme:
Sin and Holiness

Central Truth:
With Christ as Savior and Advocate, Christians can live victorious over sin.

Focus:
Discover dimensions of sanctification and live Christlike.

Context:
Around AD 90, the apostle John writes about holy living in a sinful world.

Golden Text:
"If we walk in the light, as he is in the light, we have fellowship one with another, and the blood of Jesus Christ his Son cleanseth us from all sin" (1 John 1:7).

Study Outline:
I. Walking in the Light (1 John 1:5-10)
II. Depending on the Advocate (1 John 2:1-6)
III. Living in Love (1 John 2:7-17)

INTRODUCTION

For many individuals, sanctification and holiness conjure up images of rules and regulations that restrict their freedom. These false perceptions stem partly from the bad theology of the past in which holiness was conceived primarily as lists of behaviors to be avoided and imitated. They also arise from false notions of freedom as though to be free is to be able to do anything one wants to do. In this lesson, the apostle John deals with both misconceptions and, instead, portrays holiness as a life of genuine freedom that enables individuals to achieve their complete potential as human beings.

The freedom that 1 John offers involves living in the truth about God, oneself, and the world. In contradiction to the idea that freedom is all about increasing choices, 1 John suggests that freedom is about making wise choices that lead to life. Some choices enslave, so merely increasing the number of choices people have does not increase their freedom. Wise choices emerge from abiding in the truth rather than in deception. Without knowing the truth about our lives and what is really good, we cannot achieve genuine freedom.

The entrance to the path of freedom is God's faithfulness to forgive. Once believers understand the depths of God's love, they can have the boldness to face their lives with honesty and candor. To those who recognize the truth of their own sinful behavior, God's word of forgiveness is that this behavior will not consume them, but can be overcome.

As individuals begin the journey of holiness, they will discover a freedom to love deeply because their love will not be grounded in deceptions about who they are, but in the love of God. This love not only embraces them, but heals them by rightly directing their desires and therefore teaching them how to love as God loves. God wants His people to refrain from disordered expressions of love, because that kind of love destroys life by enslaving individuals to others and to objects that can never fulfill or complete them. Holy living frees individuals to love because it enables them to love "in the truth."

I. WALKING IN THE LIGHT (1 John 1:5-10)

A. Holiness as Deepening Fellowship (vv. 5-7)

5. This then is the message which we have heard of him, and declare unto you, that God is light, and in him is no darkness at all.

6. If we say that we have fellowship with him, and walk in darkness, we lie, and do not the truth.

7. But if we walk in the light, as he is in the light, we have fellowship one with another, and the blood of Jesus Christ his Son cleanseth us from all sin.

Two important terms in the opening chapter of 1 John are *fellowship* and *light*. *Fellowship* (*koinonia*) occurs four times (vv. 3, 6-7). The Christian community is said to have fellowship with the Father, the Son, and one another. A believer's participation in the life of the Father and the Son enables his or her participation in the life of the community. In fact, the latter cannot be severed from the former. John portrays the Christian life as a community-centered endeavor in which participation in God's life leads to participation in the lives of one another.

Participation in God's life and in the life of the community is a dynamic rather than a static enterprise. It is an active process in and through which fellowship deepens. Fellowship with God involves "walking in the light" because this is where God exists. The point is that sharing God's own life involves acting like God acts, which is a summary definition of *holiness*.

A favorite verb in the Gospel of John and 1 John that helps convey this kind of dynamic process is "to remain" or "to abide." To love one's brother is "to abide" in the light (1 John 2:10). In other words, love must be active to abide. The way the believer abides in God's light or has fellowship with God is by the continuous activity of loving his or her brothers and sisters.

The basis for fellowship with God—that is, how one abides in God—is by receiving an anointing from Him. John links this anointing to the Holy Spirit by stating, "The *anointing* which you received from Him *abides* in you, and you have no need for anyone to teach you; but as *His anointing* teaches you about all things, and is true and is not a lie, and just as it has taught you, *you abide* in Him" (2:27 NASB). In the Gospel of John, Jesus indicates that the Holy Spirit will guide believers into the truth and teach them all things (14:26; 15:26-27; 16:5-15). It is clear that the anointing is the presence of the Holy Spirit guiding the believer and the community as a whole.

The second key term in 1 John 1 is *light*. John uses the term in a metaphorical sense to refer to the truth and insight into the truth. The basic message of "God is light" (v. 5) underscores that God is the source of all truth and knowledge. This is connected to the claim in the prologue of the Gospel of John that Jesus, the Incarnate Word, is the light that shines in the darkness (1:1-18).

Talk About It:
1. Explain the "darkness" in verses 5 and 6.
2. What are the benefits of living "in the light" (v. 7)?

There is a close connection between light and life so that the "Word of life" is enlightening (1 John 1:1-2). To really live is to live in the truth: the truth about God, the truth about ourselves, and the truth about the world. Thus, walking in the darkness involves deception of ourselves and others (v. 6). Those who do not walk in God's life-giving truth cannot share God's life precisely because God's life is truth. The darkness of deception and the light of truth cannot dwell together. They are like magnets with opposite polarities in which each repels the other.

We can now bring together these different lines of thought to complete the message in these opening verses. To share God's life is to live in the truth about God, ourselves, and the world. Ultimately, holy living is truthful living, which is one reason why it is a qualitatively better way of living. At the center of this lifestyle is the Holy Spirit, who guides believers into a deeper knowledge of the Son and thus the Father. This is how deeper fellowship with God occurs, which helps to deepen our fellowship with the community of Christ.

B. Living in the Truth (vv. 8-10)

8. If we say that we have no sin, we deceive ourselves, and the truth is not in us.

9. If we confess our sins, he is faithful and just to forgive us our sins, and to cleanse us from all unrighteousness.

10. If we say that we have not sinned, we make him a liar, and his word is not in us.

John now offers three conditional statements ("If we . . .") to emphasize how fellowship with God and with the community can and cannot be maintained. Part of knowing the truth involves knowing that we are sinners. The failure to acknowledge this facet of human existence involves self-deception, especially for the Christian. What verse 8 means by *sin* is sinful acts rather than a sinful nature or condition. Some in the community were making the claim that they did not commit any sinful acts after their initial acceptance of Jesus. Closely connected to this is the idea of guilt for sins committed. Awakening to one's sins involves realizing that one is guilty before God.

"The truth is not in us" (v. 8) indicates a refusal to acknowledge sinful behavior and thereby to live in deception. This deception breaks down relationships so that it destroys fellowship within the community, dividing Christians against themselves. The person who remains in such deception does not live in the truth.

It is important to see that verse 8 is directed against the claim to be free from all sinful actions. It does not mean that a Christian who fails to acknowledge one particular action as being sinful is devoid of the truth and therefore out of fellowship with God. What we must see is that, to the extent that any of us practice self-deception by rationalizing our sinful behavior, we fail to live in the truth with respect to that behavior.

Talk About It:
1. How can we deceive ourselves (vv. 8, 10)?
2. How are Christ's faithfulness and justice critical to us?

Self-Destructive Behavior
Many of us know individuals who were deceived about the

Living a Sanctified Life

By stating that confession does not lead to rejection but forgiveness, verse 9 supplies the confidence to face any behavior and ask, *What is the truth about it?* The primary issue here is ongoing sinful actions in the life of the believer. God's response to an honest desire to know the truth about one's behavior and so deepen one's walk with Him is to forgive rather than to reject the individual. This closely connects with verse 7, so that to forgive is to deal with the guilt incurred by sinful actions. This is how God "purifies us from all sin" (NIV).

Forgiveness is the portal to truthful and whole living. The verb translated "to forgive" (v. 9) literally means "to release" or "to let go." By forgiving individuals, God is saying, "Your past behavior will no longer dictate your identity." Consequently, forgiveness is the first step on the path to freedom; as Jesus declared, "He whom the Son sets free is free indeed" (see John 8:36). This is a freedom to live in the truth.

II. DEPENDING ON THE ADVOCATE (1 John 2:1-6)
A. The Form of Jesus' Advocacy (vv. 1-2)

1. My little children, these things write I unto you, that ye sin not. And if any man sin, we have an advocate with the Father, Jesus Christ the righteous:

2. And he is the propitiation for our sins: and not for ours only, but also for the sins of the whole world.

The second chapter opens with a brief statement ("sin not") that signals the writer's intention. Confession of sin should lead to removal of sin from the lives of believers. Living fully in the truth about God, oneself, and the world is 1 John's way of endorsing Paul's statement, "What shall we say then? Shall we continue in sin that grace may abound? Certainly not!" (Romans 6:1-2 NKJV). God's faithfulness to forgive is about freeing the person from the grips of sinful actions, not encouraging such actions.

Having addressed a possible misconception, John returns to God's faithfulness. In this passage, he grounds that faithfulness in the advocacy of Jesus. The Greek term is *parakletos*, which is the same term Jesus used of the Holy Spirit (John 14:16-17), whom He called "another Comforter [Advocate]." It can also mean "counselor" or "helper," but the best translation remains *advocate* because it encompasses all of the previous meanings. The advocacy of the Spirit is in convicting the world of sin and guiding the community into truth (14:26; 16:6-9, 13). In other words, the Spirit serves as the ongoing advocate of believers in their quest to proclaim the truthfulness of the message of Jesus Christ. Jesus' advocacy, on the contrary, resides in His ongoing mediatorial role between God and humanity. Jesus is the One who "always lives to make intercession" (Heb. 7:25 NASB).

destructive nature of their behavior. Consider for a moment a person whom you were trying to convince how destructive their behavior was. You might have repeatedly said something like "Don't you see that this is killing you?", to which their response might have been a look of puzzlement. They refuse, on some level, to see the truth about themselves.

propitiation (v. 2)— "atoning sacrifice" (NIV)

Talk About It:
1. How is Christ our "advocate" (v. 1)?
2. How is "the whole world" blessed (v. 2)?

The two bases on which Jesus' advocacy depends are His relationship to God as "the Righteous One" (1 John 2:1 NIV) and His being "the atoning sacrifice for our sins" (v. 2 NIV). There is a debate as to the precise meaning of the Greek term that the KJV translates *propitiation*. The word can suggest that Jesus' death atones for sin by appeasing God's wrath as well as removing guilt, or it can also simply mean that Jesus' death cleanses from sin by removing guilt. The debate is not over whether Jesus' death cleanses from sin, but if it also removes divine anger.

In his commentary on 1 John, John Christopher Thomas notes that the apostle describes the work of the Son as "cleansing from sin" (see 1:7, 9). In addition, the Gospel of John does not present God as being angry with individuals, but as loving the world (John 3:16-17). This is made clear in 1 John 4:10: "In this is love, not that we loved God but that he loved us and sent his Son to be the atoning sacrifice for our sins" (NRSV). Jesus' death is God's love in action for believers, not an appeasement of divine wrath.

"God is on one side and all the people on the other side, and Christ Jesus, himself man, is between them to bring them together, by giving his life for all mankind" (1 Tim. 2:5-6 TLB).

B. How to Know God (vv. 3-6)

3. And hereby we do know that we know him, if we keep his commandments.

4. He that saith, I know him, and keepeth not his commandments, is a liar, and the truth is not in him.

5. But whoso keepeth his word, in him verily is the love of God perfected: hereby know we that we are in him.

6. He that saith he abideth in him ought himself also so to walk, even as he walked.

Knowledge about God cannot be separated from keeping His commandments because God's commandments reflect His character. To "know him" (v. 3) is to fellowship with and abide in God. By keeping God's commandments, believers have an increasing intimacy with God. Holiness is deeply relational because it binds believers more closely to God by reproducing His life in them.

Talk About It:
1. How do we "know that we know him" (v. 3)?
2. How must Christians "walk" (v. 6)?

The person who claims to know God but does not keep His commandments is described as a liar (v. 4). This deception is a chronic condition. Liars exist in an alternative reality of their own making. It is not the real world, but the imaginary world of their own deception.

Keeping God's commandments is also described as keeping God's Word. By doing so, the love of God is brought to completion in the believer (v. 5). There is some ambiguity surrounding the phrase "love of God" in this verse. It can mean "God's love" or "love for God." Both possibilities are supported elsewhere in 1 John, so a choice between one or the other may be unnecessary (4:8-12, 16-21). God's love in the believer, which is expressed by the believer as love for God and others, comes to completion through keeping the commandments.

Keeping the commandments does not merit God's love, for the sending of the Son prior to any activity by believers is the full expression of this love. Instead, keeping the commands propels a process of conforming one's belief to love; indeed, of learning how to love. The verb *perfected* in this passage means "brought to completion." Holiness is the path to wholeness of relations because it is the way to achieve the completion of who we are in God.

III. LIVING IN LOVE (1 John 2:7-17)
A. An Old but New Commandment (vv. 7-11)

7. Brethren, I write no new commandment unto you, but an old commandment which ye had from the beginning. The old commandment is the word which ye have heard from the beginning.

8. Again, a new commandment I write unto you, which thing is true in him and in you: because the darkness is past, and the true light now shineth.

9. He that saith he is in the light, and hateth his brother, is in darkness even until now.

10. He that loveth his brother abideth in the light, and there is none occasion of stumbling in him.

11. But he that hateth his brother is in darkness, and walketh in darkness, and knoweth not whither he goeth, because that darkness hath blinded his eyes.

The writer describes the commandment that he is giving to the community as both old and new. It is old because the community to which he is writing has received this commandment, which was given to them at their conversion. They should be fully aware of this commandment because it has been part of their community life from the beginning. Yet, this commandment is new in the sense that it is part of the new revelation in Jesus Christ. It is connected to Jesus' statement in John 13:34: "A new command I give you: Love one another" (NIV).

The new commandment of love is at the center of Jesus' activity in the world. He is demonstrating God's love so people can come to embody and express this love. To accomplish this goal, it is necessary that people be cleansed of sin and depart from the realm of darkness. The light of God's truth is now shining in Jesus, which means the darkness is already being conquered. However, the believers in this community are in a battle between light and darkness: Do they abide in the truth and come to reflect God's love, or do they abide in deception and come to reflect the world's hatred?

The one who hates his or her brother or sister falsifies their claim to live in the light of God's truth (1 John 2:9, 11). Instead, abiding in the truth involves loving one's neighbor. This is understood to mean not becoming a stumbling block for one's brother or sister by virtue of one's behavior.

"Our example can be our most persuasive influence for Christ. Do others imitate us because we model Him?"
—*Christians Quoting*

Talk About It:
1. What is "new" about the "old commandment" (vv. 7-8)?
2. Describe the blindness some people live in (vv. 9-11).

"Satan separates; God unites; love binds us together."
—**D. L. Moody**

B. Do Not Return to Darkness (vv. 12-17)

(1 John 2:12-14 is not included in the printed text.)

15. Love not the world, neither the things that are in the world. If any man love the world, the love of the Father is not in him.

16. For all that is in the world, the lust of the flesh, and the lust of the eyes, and the pride of life, is not of the Father, but is of the world.

17. And the world passeth away, and the lust thereof: but he that doeth the will of God abideth for ever.

The writer begins a new section first by addressing the community as a whole with his most common designation: "my little children" (vv. 1, 12). Second, he divides the community into two groups: young believers and more mature believers (vv. 13-14). This sets the stage for statements that are made to each group before the writer turns to address the community as a whole again.

John exhorts believers not to love the world (v. 15). While the term *world* can have the positive meaning of "creation," here it is understood negatively as referring to all that life outside of God has created. Since it involves a way of life created apart from God, the world is the realm of the darkness, an alternative reality that denies God's truth. To love the world is to be enslaved or dominated by "lust" (v. 16), which means "disordered desires" or "unchecked cravings." These come through sensory stimuli—"the cravings of sinful man, the lust of his eyes" (NIV). John connects the sinful condition to internal desires that remain disordered and out of control. Love of the world, consequently, is a destructive force that gives birth to a slavery to things that are transitory and impermanent.

Talk About It:
1. What does Christ do "for his name's sake" (v. 12)?
2. What is John's affirming word for fathers (vv. 13-14)?
3. What is John's affirming word for young men (vv. 13-14)?
4. What does it mean to love the world (vv. 15-16)?
5. Who "lives forever" (v. 17 NIV)?

"The Christian must be consumed with the infinite beauty of holiness and the infinite damnability of sin."
—Thomas Carlyle

CONCLUSION

Sanctification and holiness are not paths that restrict freedom, but paths that open up freedom's possibilities: the possibility of living a life in the truth rather than deception; the possibility of living a life in which love liberates rather than ensnares; the possibility of living a life of intimacy with the Father, Son, and Holy Spirit, who created all things from nothing and who can forge a new destiny for each individual. These are just a few of the possibilities of genuine freedom.

GOLDEN TEXT CHALLENGE

"IF WE WALK IN THE LIGHT, AS HE IS IN THE LIGHT, WE HAVE FELLOWSHIP ONE WITH ANOTHER, AND THE BLOOD OF JESUS CHRIST HIS SON CLEANSETH US FROM ALL SIN" (1 John 1:7).

If is a huge word in this powerful scripture. It tells us that God allows us to choose the way we will conduct our lives. In providing us the opportunity to "walk in the light," the benefits of that choice are set before us.

First, God is inviting us to walk with Him. Not only is He "in the light," but He himself *is* the Light (v. 5). The One who is "the Way" (John 14:6) wants to live within us and enlighten us from day to day.

Second, He wants us to live in kinship with all of His children. There is no family like the family of God—it is everlasting and provides a spiritual bond that goes deeper than physical ties.

Third, the blood of Jesus Christ, which has covered our past sins that we have confessed, will continue to purify us of our sins. Walking in the light will expose our sins, which He will forgive when we confess (1 John 1:9).

By rephrasing the Golden Text in negative terms, we see the only other choice we have. And it's not an attractive one: "If we do not walk in the light, we will live apart from Christ in darkness, for He is the light, and we will not have close relationships with other Christians, and the blood of Christ will not cover our sins."

Daily Devotions:
M. Sanctification Commanded
Exodus 19:14-25
T. Sanctification Is Preparation
Joshua 3:1-6
W. Sanctification Precedes Service
2 Chronicles 29:1-5, 10-11
T. Sanctification by God's Word
John 17:14-19
F. Sanctification Through Obedience
2 Corinthians 6:14 through 7:1
S. Sanctification Pleases God
2 Peter 3:9-14

Holiness Is Christlike Living

John 15:1-17; 17:15-23; 1 John 4:10-21

Unit Theme:
Sin and Holiness

Central Truth:
Genuine identification with Christ produces holy living.

Focus:
Equate holiness with Christlikeness and reflect Christ in our living.

Context:
Words from Christ and from John's first epistle concerning life in Christ

Golden Text:
"I am the vine, ye are the branches: He that abideth in me, and I in him, the same bringeth forth much fruit: for without me ye can do nothing" (John 15:5).

Study Outline:
I. Spiritual Fruitfulness (John 15:1-17)
II. Spiritual Union With Christ (John 17:15-23)
III. Love for One Another (1 John 4:10-21)

INTRODUCTION

The call to holiness is a call to a relational intimacy with God that may be summarized by the term *friendship*. God calls humans to be His friends. Friends share their lives, and this is what God has done in sending the Son and the Spirit into the world. God's triune life is a perfect fellowship between the Father, Son, and Holy Spirit in which each member of the Trinity gives and receives love. There is perfect harmony, symmetry, and beauty within the Trinity.

By desiring to enter into friendship with humanity, God is calling humans to rediscover themselves as the image of God. Good friends make us better people. How does God make us better? The Father sends His Son who sacrifices Himself for His friends, shares the truth with them, and demands that they behave in ways that are truly loving. The Father also sends the Holy Spirit as an advocate for His friends. The Spirit is also the anointing that teaches believers and guides them into a more intimate knowledge of the Father and the Son. The Spirit provides the ground for God's fellowship with believers by abiding within them so that they can change and become conformed to Jesus. In all of this, God is initiating a friendship with His people that will make them stronger and give them more joy, more love, and more peace. This friendship, transcending even the best of human friendships, will make Jesus' disciples better human beings.

As we persevere in bearing the fruit of friendship with God, we will discover that we will be set apart from worldliness. Sanctification is the natural fruit of a genuine relationship with God. As God's friends, Christians can be engaged in loving the people of the world while continuing to reflect the character of God and so be different from the world. Rather than a stale form of behavior, holiness is a call to be God's friend and to receive all that friendship entails "so that whatever you ask of the Father in My name He may give to you" (John 15:16 NASB).

I. SPIRITUAL FRUITFULNESS (John 15:1-17)

A. The Life-Giving Vine (vv. 1-6)

1. I am the true vine, and my Father is the husbandman.

2. Every branch in me that beareth not fruit he taketh away: and every branch that beareth fruit, he purgeth it, that it may bring forth more fruit.

3. Now ye are clean through the word which I have spoken unto you.

4. Abide in me, and I in you. As the branch cannot bear fruit of itself, except it abide in the vine; no more can ye, except ye abide in me.

5. I am the vine, ye are the branches: He that abideth in me, and I in him, the same bringeth forth much fruit: for without me ye can do nothing.

6. If a man abide not in me, he is cast forth as a branch, and is withered; and men gather them, and cast them into the fire, and they are burned.

The Gospel of John incorporates a teaching of Jesus that has no clear parallel in the other Gospels. Jesus borrows the image of the vine used in the Old Testament for Israel and applies it to Himself and His followers (see Ps. 80:8-16; Isa. 5:1-7; Jer. 2:21). For Jesus to claim that He is the genuine vine is to describe Himself as the source of the new people of God, who "abide" in Him. Holiness is not an isolated form of activity, but the lifestyle of the people of God whose source resides in Christ.

Jesus portrays the Father as the gardener who prunes and cleans. This is a disciplinary action intended to produce growth. The English term *catharsis* is taken from the Greek term being used here for "purgeth" (John 15:2). A cathartic experience is an emotional event that purges the individual of deep-seated feelings. John has in mind a cleansing or purging that the Father will do. In verse 3, Jesus indicates to the disciples that they have been "cleansed" by the word He has spoken, which means that, unlike others who have left Jesus and thus been cut off, they have heard and obeyed His word. The Father's purging occurs every time the Word goes forth because it challenges individuals to leave behind old beliefs and patterns of behavior to embrace new ones.

One purpose of Jesus' use of the vine imagery is to convey the need to be fruit-bearing. Based on what Jesus will say in the subsequent verses, the type of fruit He has is mind is moral behavior. Consequently, John's use of this symbol resonates with Paul's notion of the fruit of the Spirit. For Paul, the indwelling Spirit of God makes an individual fruit-bearing (Gal. 5:22-25), whereas John 15 connects fruit-bearing to dwelling in relationship to the Son, who Himself is in relationship with the Father.

Related to the call to be fruit-bearing is the call to persevere. While the verb *abide* (v. 4) implies "dwelling within," it also has the meaning of "remaining connected to." The warning about

Talk About It:
1. As "the gardener" (v. 1 NIV), what does the heavenly Father do (v. 2)?
2. Describe Christ's plan for the Christian (vv. 3-5).
3. Who can expect disaster (v. 6)?

barrenness is a call to remain connected to the life-giving source. What becomes clear from verse 10 is that remaining connected to Jesus requires the action of keeping His commandments. Unlike vines and branches that share a natural, organic union, the relational union with Jesus requires a level of commitment manifested concretely in actions. If one's actions "wither" (see v. 6), it suggests there is no longer any serious commitment to persevere, which results in being thrown away.

B. Bringing Glory to God (vv. 7-8)

7. If ye abide in me, and my words abide in you, ye shall ask what ye will, and it shall be done unto you.

8. Herein is my Father glorified, that ye bear much fruit; so shall ye be my disciples.

Verse 7 is an amazing promise, but we must remember "the flaming sword which guards the way, 'If ye abide in me.' . . . If you abide in Me, and My words abide in you, utter your demands, whatever you are inclined to. It shall be done, and the word means 'generated, caused to be'; creative power shall operate" (G. C. Morgan).

There are many people who quote this scripture not really knowing what it means and not really being in union with Christ. Such people ask for things out of God's will and cause confusion. It stands to reason that a person who abides in Christ will ask nothing that is contrary to Christ's will, for he or she will always ask in the spirit of "not my will, but Thine be done," and in complete harmony with all that Christ has revealed concerning Himself. Hence, it is not hard to understand that a person will receive whatever he or she asks.

Verse 8 notes two things "about the good disciple. First, he enriches his own life. His contact makes him a fruitful branch. Second, he brings glory to God. The sight of his life turns men's thoughts to the God who made him live that way. God is glorified, as Jesus put it, when we bear much fruit and when we show ourselves to be disciples of Jesus. Surely the greatest glory of the Christian life is that we, by our life and conduct, can bring glory to God" (Barclay).

C. Friendship With Jesus (vv. 9-17)

(John 15:9-14 is not included in the printed text.)

15. Henceforth I call you not servants; for the servant knoweth not what his lord doeth: but I have called you friends; for all things that I have heard of my Father I have made known unto you.

16. Ye have not chosen me, but I have chosen you, and ordained you, that ye should go and bring forth fruit, and that your fruit should remain: that whatsoever ye shall ask of the Father in my name, he may give it you.

17. These things I command you, that ye love one another.

The broader context of Jesus' pronouncement that He chose His disciples (rather than them choosing Him first) is friendship (v. 16). Within verses 9-17, love and friendship function as twin themes that mutually reinforce and interpret one another.

First, Jesus' striking announcement that His disciples are not simply servants but friends underscores the importance of friendship for living the Christian life (v. 15). An important dimension of friendship is reciprocity—each party gives to the other. Jesus' disciples are not outsiders, but receive the benefit of intimate knowledge born of genuine friendship. In short, friends share vital knowledge with each other for mutual benefit. Jesus says, "Everything that I learned from my Father I have made known to you" (v. 15 NIV). He supports His friends with the knowledge of eternal life.

Second, friends sacrifice for the good of each other. In an allusion to His own death, Jesus shows how love and genuine friendship give rise to self-sacrifice (v. 13). Love is not a mere emotional connection with another human being, but a strong commitment that gives rise to sacrificial behavior. It is a covenant, which is why marriage is one of the deepest forms of friendship two human beings can share with one another. For Jesus, genuine love is always outgoing. The action or lack thereof reveals the depth of commitment.

Third, friends rejoice with one another. This is part of what it means to share one's life with another human being. It means to laugh, weep, and love. Jesus' understanding of friendship embodies all of these dimensions. He wept with Mary and Martha over Lazarus (11:33-35), and in chapter 15 He shares His joy (v. 11). Good friends have the capacity to communicate joy by giving of their own life and resources. Think of how friends are capable of cheering us up simply by being in their presence. There is a comfort and serenity that we receive when we are near good friends, and we crave their presence during times of hardship. From the wellspring of His own identity, Jesus invites His disciples to participate fully in His joy. Indeed, in His presence there is "joy inexpressible" (1 Peter 1:8 NASB).

Fourth, friends make demands of other friends. This is why we must choose our friends wisely. We give friends the authority to speak into our lives and tell us what we should do because genuine friendship requires it. Friendship with Jesus involves following His advice about our lives. The difference is that Jesus' advice is the wisdom of the incarnate God.

The best kinds of friends are those who make us better. We recognize that we have become a qualitatively better kind of person because of our relationship with them. When we think about it, the best friends make us more human by giving what we don't have, challenging us to grow in healthy and whole ways,

Talk About It:
1. How does Christ describe His love for us (v. 9)?
2. What example did Christ leave for us (v. 10)?
3. Describe the joy Christ gives (v. 11).
4. Who are Christ's friends (vv. 14-15)?
5. Summarize Christ's statements on loving others (vv. 12-13, 17).

Best Friend
Think of one of your best friends. It may be a spouse or a close companion. Consider how being in relationship with that person has made you better

and enabling us to achieve a destiny we could not have achieved otherwise. Occasionally, we hear someone acknowledge, "I would not be here if it were not for. . . ." These are the kinds of friends we hunger for, but they are difficult to find.

When Jesus tells His disciples, "I have chosen you," He is not referring to a choice made in an eternity past that now determines their individual destinies, but to His choosing them to be His friends (see John 1:35-51). Jesus chose to be friends with His disciples, not the other way around. This is John's way of pointing to God's grace. God has decided to be our friend when we were unworthy of His friendship because "God so loved" (3:16).

Picking up on the previous theme, Jesus notes that His choice involves the larger purpose of being a fruit-bearer, which at minimum means entering into loving friendship with others (v. 17). The call to love others is one of the ways in which friendship with Jesus makes one a better person. If holiness is friendship with Jesus, then we must see that Jesus loves us to wholeness by refusing to allow us to remain in the same patterns of behavior that lead down dead-end roads.

II. SPIRITUAL UNION WITH CHRIST (John 17:15-23)
A. The World (vv. 15-16)

15. I pray not that thou shouldest take them out of the world, but that thou shouldest keep them from the evil.

16. They are not of the world, even as I am not of the world.

In John 17, Jesus offers what scholars have called the "High Priestly Prayer." He prays specifically that the disciples remain in the world, even as God preserves them from "the evil one" (v. 15 NASB). The term *world* can mean the created world as it does in John 1:10 and 3:16-17. However, as one progresses through the Gospel of John the term takes on the negative sense of life without God. In Jesus' prayer, it is closely connected to what is meant by *culture*. An entire culture with its own values and behaviors has emerged from those beings that have consciously separated themselves from God. At the center of this culture is the "evil one," which is probably a reference to the devil (see 1 John 2:13; 3:12). Those who belong to this culture hate Jesus' disciples because they hated Him (John 15:18-19). Neither Jesus nor His followers belong to this world.

B. Sanctified by the Truth (vv. 17-19)

17. Sanctify them through thy truth: thy word is truth.

18. As thou hast sent me into the world, even so have I also sent them into the world.

19. And for their sakes I sanctify myself, that they also might be sanctified through the truth.

When Jesus prays that His disciples be set apart from the world by the truth, He is making a subtle allusion to Himself. In the prologue of the Gospel, it is God's Word that has become flesh and is identified with Jesus of Nazareth (1:1-3, 14). When Jesus claims, "Your word is truth," He is alluding to Himself as Truth incarnate. The prologue indicates that Jesus is the light that shown in the darkness and was not recognized (vv. 4-5). Jesus' mission was to love the world, but because His own creation had developed a different way of living (culture), it did not recognize Him (v. 10).

Jesus' mission immediately set Him apart from the culture that had grown up without God. It is to this culture that He speaks and brings God's love. This mission means that Jesus continues to set Himself apart from the world. His prayer is that the disciples might continue to grasp the truth so that they will continue to be sanctified, or set apart. Because Jesus is "the truth" (14:6), the prayer is that the disciples might grasp His identity and mission more deeply.

Talk About It:
1. How does Christ sanctify believers (vv. 17, 19)?
2. Where does Christ send His followers, and why (v. 18)?

"Jesus' disciples were no longer to live in the world, ruled by its passions. Instead, they were to live in the realm of God's truth, ruled by the governing principles unveiled in God's Word."
—**Larry Richards**

C. One in God (vv. 20-23)

20. Neither pray I for these alone, but for them also which shall believe on me through their word;

21. That they all may be one; as thou, Father, art in me, and I in thee, that they also may be one in us: that the world may believe that thou hast sent me.

22. And the glory which thou gavest me I have given them; that they may be one, even as we are one:

23. I in them, and thou in me, that they may be made perfect in one; and that the world may know that thou hast sent me, and hast loved them, as thou hast loved me.

The counter to being set apart from the world is to be made one in fellowship with the Father and the Son. One of the clearest testimonies to those whose lives remain shaped by the culture of death that exists apart from God is the fellowship that believers have with one another and with God.

Talk About It:
1. What does Christ want His people to do (v. 20)?
2. What is Christ's plan for believers (v. 21)?

This part of Christ's prayer forms the counterpart to Jesus' commandment to love one another. It is a challenge to Christians to overcome their divisions and exist as one visible body of Christ on earth in anticipation of the day when they will rejoice as one body around the throne.

III. LOVE FOR ONE ANOTHER (1 John 4:10-21)
A. The Pattern and Practice (vv. 10-14)

10. Herein is love, not that we loved God, but that he loved us, and sent his Son to be the propitiation for our sins.

11. Beloved, if God so loved us, we ought also to love one another.

12. No man hath seen God at any time. If we love one another, God dwelleth in us, and his love is perfected in us.

13. Hereby know we that we dwell in him, and he in us, because he hath given us of his Spirit.

14. And we have seen and do testify that the Father sent the Son to be the Saviour of the world.

First John locates the greatest expression of God's love, and consequently its pattern or shape, in the sending of Jesus as an atoning sacrifice. John states, "This is love: not that we loved God, but that he loved us and sent his Son as an atoning sacrifice for our sins" (v. 10 NIV). The contrast ("not that . . . but that") communicates clearly that the pattern of love is not to be found in its human expressions, but in the divine action of sending the Son. This unpacks what verse 8 means by "God is love." God's love is always in action, a dynamic movement in history of God's compassionate care toward humanity.

Although 1 John does not make the connection explicit, the fellowship between the Father and the Son is to be replicated in the fellowship between believers as they pattern their lives after God's love. Even within God's own being, love is always in action from Father to Son to Spirit and back again. The divine fellowship exists as the Father's love eternally moves out in the begetting of the Son, and inviting the Son to join with Him in the breathing forth of the Spirit. The procession or breathing forth of the Spirit eternally binds the Father, Son, and Spirit together and thus brings the entire Trinity to completion. When the Father sends the Son and the Spirit into the world, it is not the beginning of love's movement, but the redirection of that movement toward the good of humankind.

"No one has seen God" (v. 12 NASB)—no one has had a direct vision of God—but God is present through the presence of mutual love. As the writer states, "If we love one another, God abides in us and His love is brought to completion in us" (v. 12, author's translation). In verse 13 the Spirit is identified as assurance that God abides in the community; it is "of his Spirit" that a mutual indwelling or fellowship exists between God and believers. Consequently, the Spirit brings about the mutual love within believers, and when they love one another, they can rest assured that God is at work in them. Holiness is communal.

B. Abiding in Love (vv. 15-18)

15. Whosoever shall confess that Jesus is the Son of God, God dwelleth in him, and he in God.

16. And we have known and believed the love that God hath to us. God is love; and he that dwelleth in love dwelleth in God, and God in him.

17. Herein is our love made perfect, that we may have boldness in the day of judgment: because as he is, so are we in this world.

Talk About It:
1. What is love's greatest act (v. 10)?
2. Why must we "love one another" (v. 11)?
3. How do we know God lives in us (vv. 12-13)?

Flood of Love
I took up that word *love*, and I do not know how many weeks I spent in studying the passages in which it occurs, till at last I could not help loving people. I had been feeding on love so long that I was anxious to do everybody good I came in contact with. I got full of it. It ran out my fingers. You take up the subject of love in the Bible! You will get so full of it that all you have to do is open your lips, and a flood of the love of God flows out.
—D. L. Moody

Holiness Is Christlike Living

18. There is no fear in love; but perfect love casteth out fear: because fear hath torment. He that feareth is not made perfect in love.

Another activity of the Holy Spirit is given in verse 15, where abiding in love and abiding in God are connected to confession. This is because the Spirit is the "anointing" that will guide the community into all truth (2:27). Knowledge and love go together because seeing the truth that "God so loved the world" creates a love for God that, in turn, fuels the drive to know Him more.

The Spirit is at the center of the love that creates fellowship with God and therefore "drives out fear" (4:18 NIV). In this relationship love is "made complete" (v. 17 NIV) so that believers will have assurance when standing before God on Judgment Day because we will be like Him in character.

C. Love's Standard (vv. 19-21)

19. We love him, because he first loved us.

20. If a man say, I love God, and hateth his brother, he is a liar: for he that loveth not his brother whom he hath seen, how can he love God whom he hath not seen?

21. And this commandment have we from him, That he who loveth God love his brother also.

John reminds his readers of the source of genuine love (v. 19). At the same time he holds up the standard by which perfect love is to be measured—it must be of the same character and purity as His.

John could never stay in the realm of the abstract nor polemical without coming back to the practical. This perfect love must be manifested by brother for brother. Words about love for God could be voiced entirely by acts without love toward a brother. How could a person choose to love God whom he has never seen and really practice that love, if he could not choose to love his brother and practice love toward him whom he has seen?

In verse 21, John is not issuing a new commandment, but simply repeating that which was basic to the teaching of Christ. Believers love God and each other.

Talk About It:
1. What can we "know and rely on" (v. 16 NIV)?
2. What does "love made perfect" do for the believer (v. 17)?
3. How does love drive away fear (v. 18)?

Talk About It:
1. What did God do first (v. 19)?
2. Who is a liar (v. 20)?

"If you haven't love in your heart, you should throw your hope to the four winds, and go and get a better one."
—D. L. Moody

CONCLUSION

Christlike living involves and evolves from friendship with Christ. Friendship is another way of describing the fellowship that stands at the center of God's triune life and that God wishes to replicate in the world. Holiness stems from the kind of friendship that makes us better human beings by loving us to wholeness and demanding better from us. It is only through friendship with Jesus that we can escape the culture of death that is the world and, in turn, love deeply those caught up in that culture so that they can share in the wholeness of Christ we have received.

GOLDEN TEXT CHALLENGE

"I AM THE VINE, YE ARE THE BRANCHES: HE THAT ABIDETH IN ME, AND I IN HIM, THE SAME BRINGETH FORTH MUCH FRUIT: FOR WITHOUT ME YE CAN DO NOTHING" (John 15:5).

During His final discourse with the disciples on the night before the Crucifixion, Jesus used the metaphor of the vine to teach and encourage the Twelve. Calvary would not sever their relationship with Christ; rather, Calvary would change the nature of that relationship and make it permanent through His indwelling presence.

As a branch must maintain organic union with the vine as its source of life and fruitfulness, a disciple must continue to maintain a close and fixed union with Christ in order to be spiritually productive. To abide in Christ is not an intermittent association, but a continuous fellowship and communion with Him. Jeremiah was aware of humanity's weakness when he said that it wasn't in a person to direct his own steps (10:23). Jesus confirmed this truth when in the text He said, "Apart from Me you can do nothing" (NASB).

Since the branches bear the fruit, Jesus, as the Vine, has made His followers the instruments for evangelizing the world. To succeed in this mission, one should learn Paul's secret—"I live; yet not I, but Christ liveth in me" (Gal. 2:20)—and follow the Master's admonition, "Abide in me, and I in you" (John 15:4). Anything short of this is doomed to failure.

Holiness Is Christlike Living